AMIRI BARAKA

JERRY GAFIO WATTS

AMIRI BARAKA

The Politics and Art of a Black Intellectual

New York University Press • *New York and London*

For Traci Cassandra West

"life companion"

NEW YORK UNIVERSITY PRESS
New York and London

Grateful acknowledgment is made to Amiri Baraka and to the
Sterling Lord Agency for permission to reprint excerpts from Baraka's
works. The New York Public Library is acknowledged for permission
to use the LeRoy McLucas photograph of Baraka on the cover.

Library of Congress Cataloging-in-Publication Data
Watts, Jerry Gafio.
Amiri Baraka : the politics and art of a Black intellectual / Jerry
Gafio Watts.
p.   cm.
Includes bibliographical references and index.
ISBN 0-8147-9373-8
1. Baraka, Imamu Amiri, 1934– —Political and social views.
2. Politics and literature—United States—History—20th century.
3. Baraka, Imamu Amiri, 1934– —Criticism and interpretation.
4. African Americans—Politics and government. 5. African
Americans—Intellectual life. 6. Blacks—Politics and government.
7. African Americans in literature. 8. Blacks—Intellectual life.
9. Blacks in literature.   I. Title.
PS3552.A583 Z93 2001
818'.5409—dc21   2001002006

New York University Press books are printed on acid-free paper,
and their binding materials are chosen for strength and durability.

Manufactured in the United States of America

10   9   8   7   6   5   4   3   2   1

Contents

Acknowledgments

Like my first book, this volume has its origins in my dissertation. I had the great fortune to study political science at Yale University during the late 1970s and early 1980s. The political science department gave me the freedom to engage my humanist sensibilities, an act of intellectual toleration that went against the prevailing tendencies in the discipline. I want to thank my committee of Robert Lane, Juan Linz, and particularly David Apter, the chairman, for helping guide a confused graduate student through the bureaucracy of academia and doing so in a way that provided the space for me to follow my curiosity. In addition, I benefited from the intellectual generosity of Douglas Rae, James Scott, Stanley Greenberg, and the late Philip White.

While writing this work, I received encouragement and intellectual support from many friends and acquaintances, including associates from my Yale days: Horace Porter, Carla Carr, Frank Gonzales, Randall Kennedy, Adolph Reed, Eileen Hormel, Angelo Messore, Rabbi Arnold Wolfe, Marcus Bruce, Eugene Rivers, Henry Louis Gates, Norris Sakwe-Mante, Isabelle Gunning, Mary Davis, Deborah King, and the late Carl Price. I also benefited from my association with Kathy Rees, Larry Jackson, Helura Lyle, Tanya Green, Paul Kumar, Kris Graves, Eric Greene, Ethan Flad, Eve Goldberg, Fred Montas, Natalie Difloff, Joy Anderson, Nina Karnovsky, Steve Vacarro, Lisa Freeman, Alford Young, Carla O'Connor, Amy Randall, Beau Dunning, Josh Freely, "L.T.," Maureen Kay, Tanya Jones, Denise Burgher, the Whitters family, and former Wesleyan colleagues: Robert O'Meally, Peter Marx, Georgie Leone, Barbara Craig, Steven Gregory, Michael Harris, Ollie Holmes, Clarence Walker, Marshall Hyatt, Nat and Erness Brody, Alex Dupuy, Richard Williams, Robert Wood, and Mary Ann Clawson. Lee Siegel's unsolicited close reading of a very early version of this manuscript was a true gift. Dan Clawson and Gerald Gill have been two constant sources of encouragement and sanity. To Pop Kantor in Norfolk, I owe a special thanks for supplying me with good bourbon and good books. For almost three decades David Evans has helped me stay grounded. To Martin Kilson I owe a debt of immense gratitude for the time, energy, and spirit he has invested in me for a quarter century. Jackie Lindsay was there at the beginning. Melvin Fowler, E. J. Davis, and Melvin Maddox were inexhaustible suppliers of good conversation. Emma Ketteringham and Amy Randall remain foundational, though my behavior doesn't show it. Ashley Hammarth, Erin Blakeley, Roberta Gold, Jill Kantor, Stephanie Mandell, and Sandy Sydlo persist as soulmates. Although I can do without Mandell's terrible jokes, I do miss her. During the writing of this book, Lisa and Steve, Al and Carla, Kris and Fred and Joy have added new members to the American intellectual community. Congrats!

I want to thank supportive Trinity colleagues: Vijay Prashad, Raymond Baker, Joan Hendrick, Susan Pennybacker, Berel Lang, Steve Valocchi, Carol Clark, Renny Fulco, Laurie Waite, Noreen Channels, Hugh Ogden, Clinton Bailey, Dave Winer, Jack Chatfield, Stephanie Chambers, Peter Burns, Wally Swist, Maryam Elahi, Cheryl Greenberg, Ronald Spencer, Dianne Zannoni, and, gone but not forgotten, Lynn Tallit, Naomi Amos, Jeffrey Melnick, Van Gosse, Maurice Jackson, Jack Waggett, Hank Lewis, and Salim Washington. Different as "night and day," Johnny Williams and Margo Perkins have added humor, vitality, and a healthy dose of skepticism to my life at Trinity. Judy Moran is the only known spirit-replenishing mathematician. Barbara Sicherman and Dina Anselmi have been two of Trinity's gifts to my life. Dear and special friends, Barbara and Dina have tried to keep me whole through their humor, generosity, and critical introspection. Both have taught me a great deal about the expansiveness and intimacy of friendship. Whereas Barbara has a knack for expecting answers to endless questions about things of great and minor significance, Dina is the only person that I know who enjoys, more than I do, baiting people into arguments over minutia. Barb, I can't remember! Dina, you win! With love, I celebrate the deviance of both women. Manijeh Zavareei, a kind, decent, and thoughtful colleague who died far too prematurely, will always be remembered for, among other things, trying to teach me how to write my name in Farsi.

My immediate and extended families have always supported my intellectual ambitions. I want to thank Maria and James Watts, my mother and father, for the love they have always given me. I also give them credit for my various neuroses. I have been blessed to have my brothers James and Robert; my sister Brenda, and my nephews Jim, Gregory, and Michael. I also want to thank my in-laws—Bil Wright, Jean Powell Watts, Beckett Logan, Robynne West, Richard Perkins, Karen Amore and Estelle Amore, my "main man" Kyle, and Ravae, my favorite and very special niece. My late Uncle James and Aunt Sally were always among my most avid supporters—as is my Aunt Julia. Paula West's spiritedness will never be forgotten.

Cornel West, Werner Sollors, Traci C. West, Gerald Hudson, Michelle Wallace, Martin Luther Kilson, Farah Griffin, and James A. Miller have significantly informed my view of Baraka. Miller, a former Trinity College colleague, will probably reject most of the findings and arguments in this book. Because of that as well as his friendship with Baraka, I threatened to write here: "Jim Miller has been singularly responsible for shaping all the assessments contained within." Jokes aside, I could not have written this book without the writings of Werner Sollors, Kim Benston, Henry Lacey, Houston Baker, William J. Harris, David Smith, Lloyd Brown, Harold Cruse, Theodore Hudson, and Komozi Woodard.

While this book is highly critical of Amiri Baraka, it should be clear that I think that his intellectual journey was one of the pathbreaking models for my generation. I thank him for giving us a corpus of works worthy of serious engagement. More important, I salute him for living a life full of risks and the resultant bruises, regrets, and bumps.

The staff at the Moorland-Spingarn Collection of Howard University deserve special thanks, particularly Joellen El-Bashir. Similar thanks go to the prints and photographs division of the Schomburg Library. I also am grateful to Eric Zinner and Despina Papazoglou Gimbel at New York University Press. Werner Sollors has once again shown phenomenal generosity toward me.

This book is dedicated to Traci Cassandra West, a true companion, advocate for justice, and partner in crimes of political opposition. Traci was present when this project began as a thesis prospectus. From its very inception she steadfastly insisted that I grapple with issues of feminism not only in my life but in my work. In sharing her life with me, she inspired and reinforced whatever ethical impulses I now have. Most important, she helped me recognize that the goal of writing is not to hit flies with sledgehammers. In helping me control my abundantly endowed demons, particularly crude ambition, an unbridled desire for acclaim, and a resilient will to compare myself with others, I have become far more capable of accepting the limits and unpredictability of life. No means exist to adequately convey my gratitude to her for steadfastly contesting my sense of life as a burden.

Preface

In the best of worlds, it would be unwise to call out the name Amiri Baraka in a crowded hall of black intellectuals. To bring up Baraka in a symposium on art and politics is to bring a conversation to a standstill. One of the most controversial Afro-American intellectuals of the last forty years, Baraka is admired, hated, feared, dismissed, adored, and despised. During the height of the Black Power era, many black intellectuals believed that the validity of an argument could be enhanced merely by its association with his name: "Imamu Baraka has stated . . ." Others used his name as a device of rhetorical dismissal that allowed the arguer to proclaim a heightened rationality. In such instances one might have heard, "Unlike Baraka, I believe that . . ." In still other instances, invocations of his name functioned as a backdrop that allowed conversationalists to define themselves rhetorically. One frequently heard, "Certainly Baraka overstates the point but . . ." or "Most major black intellectuals, except perhaps Baraka, believe . . ." or "but how does your argument account for a figure like LeRoi Jones?" Whether celebrated or venerated, the singularity of Baraka's example was ubiquitous.

I cannot recall when I first became aware LeRoi Jones's existence. His name was neither prominently mentioned in my Northeast Washington, D.C., home, nor was he read in my high school. Of course, I could have read his writing on my own initiative, but I was too caught up in world politics and American political history. Several days before graduating from DeMatha Catholic High School in 1971, I received from Mrs. Hallie Ward, a family friend, a graduation present consisting of paperback copies of *Blues People* and *Black Magic Poetry*. Mrs. Ward gave me the books and asked: "You do know who he is, don't you?" I muttered some weak response and dishonestly nodded my head yes. I had heard of LeRoi Jones, but I did not know who he was or what he did. As a proud graduate of West Virginia State, a traditional black college, Mrs. Ward was thrilled by the "race advancement" embodied in my admission to Harvard. Unknown to me, she was intent on fortifying me with a recognition of my intellectual forebears.

The year was 1971. I eagerly awaited leaving home for Harvard College. During the summer before my matriculation, I received a welcoming packet from A.F.R.O., Harvard's black student organization. The packet included the requisite welcomes and declarations describing Harvard as racially alien to the interests of emancipation-minded black people. But the packet also contained a booklet written by Imamu Amiri Baraka in which he spelled out the seven principles of the Nguzu Saba, a black nationalist philosophy of life (code of conduct) created by Maulana Ron Karenga.

I was baffled by the packet, particularly Baraka's essay. Why did they send it to me? I did not immediately understand the relevance of Baraka's essay to my enrollment at Harvard. Shortly after arriving in Cambridge, I began spending time with a first-year Radcliffe student who sprinkled quotations from Baraka and Sonia Sanchez into her everyday conversation. For reasons that had little to do with intellectual curiosity, I decided that I had better learn more about these two writers.

I soon discovered that Baraka was a celebrated figure among many of the "politicized" black students at Harvard and other colleges in the Boston area. A photograph of his enraged face and bandaged head taken after his police beating during the Newark riots became a popular poster on dorm room walls. Moreover, his writings appeared regularly in *The Black Scholar* and *Black World*, the two journals most important to my exposure to contemporary black intellectual life during my undergraduate days.

At the time, I was too deeply committed to a rather unspecified pragmatic liberalism to give Baraka's views honest consideration. Although I viewed Nixon as a racist, I believed that some mainstream liberals were working toward an interracial democratic society. I was quite enamored of Edward Brooke, the black liberal Republican senator from Massachusetts. Not surprisingly, I disliked black nationalism and viewed black separatism as an absurdity. Yet I continued to read Baraka's political writings, for he played the role of the antagonist who legitimized my establishmentarian liberal sensibilities. Using a faulty logic, weaknesses in his arguments helped me sustain the belief that my political views were more rigorous. Consequently, Baraka's earliest importance to me was as a political foil. Perhaps none of this would have changed had there not been a war in Vietnam and an establishmentarian American liberalism that could not oppose it on principle. Increasingly enticed by the New Left currents floating around Harvard, I finally realized that my liberalism was as naive as Baraka's nationalism. For a while, I continued to advocate pragmatic liberalism out of a mind-set akin to "bad faith." I no longer truly believed but chose to act as if I did in order not to have to reconsider my political ambitions. Too much was at stake to live honestly. My decision to act contrary to my beliefs taught me not only a lot about myself but encouraged me to

entertain contradictions when trying to assess the political beliefs and actions of others.

This book is neither a biography of Baraka nor strictly intellectual history.
Rather, it should be read as a commentary on the idea of Amiri Baraka as
constructed by his contemporaries, his descendants, and, of course, himself. My interests are both scholarly and polemical. I have chosen to interrogate the idea of Amiri Baraka because I believe that it can illuminate some of the crucial political situations confronting twentieth-century
Afro-American intellectuals. Besides having a distinctive approach to political engagement, Baraka was a defining figure of a crucial moment in
Afro-American intellectual life. Baraka exemplified those traditional black
intellectuals who were trying to navigate the promise of the civil rights
movement, the despair that resulted from the popular recognition of its
limitations, and the enraged assertiveness that arose among those trying to
transcend that movement and its anguish. Baraka's example is instructive
because so many of the dilemmas confronting his generation of black intellectuals can be understood and charted by using as the focal points his life
and the accompanying idea of his life.

Baraka's involvement in politics is significant to me personally not
only because it has embellished the canvas on which my intellectual life has
been sketched but also because the choices he made influenced the choices
I did and did not make. In particular, I want to understand the interaction
between an intellectual's political involvement and the commitment to his
or her artistic/intellectual craft. How does one remain involved in communal activities and yet preserve one's "space" to function as a creative artist
or critical intellectual?

I claim no intimate knowledge of Amiri Baraka the man. At no time have
I tried to interview him or any of his closest former associates. As a student of
American politics, I am under no delusion that the public persona of a political actor reflects his or her interior life. Yet one's public persona is crucial to
determining one's political significance. For this reason I am primarily interested in the idea of Amiri Baraka, as opposed to the reality of Baraka the man.
Having said this, I also want to retreat from its Manichaean implications.
After all, the reality of the historical man Baraka and the idea of Baraka are
interdependent.

Most of us who have been influenced by Baraka have never had access
to his interior life. We must recognize, therefore, that his intentions in writing a certain poem or essay may have been different from its reception by
his reading audience. Nonetheless, I assume throughout this study that Ba-

raka's intentions are crucial to determining the meaning of his written and spoken words. When known, I comment on them. When unknown, I sometimes make educated inferences. In any case, I do not adhere to fashionable claims about the irrelevance of an author's intentions. In any study of this nature, the author runs the risk of being entrapped in Geertz's web of culture. I may mistake an involuntary blink of the eyelid for a wink. You, the reader, must be the ultimate judge of my efforts.

I remember my first fifteen-minute conversation with Baraka. It was not a particularly memorable occasion, but it remains fixed in my mind. At the time that we met, I was tinkering with the possibility of discussing him in my dissertation. But what immediately struck me about my first face-to-face encounter with Baraka was his political affect. The setting was the Yale University campus on a fall day during the late 1970s or early 1980s. Baraka, a visiting professor, was strolling past Sterling Library dressed in a Mao cap. The Yale University dining hall workers were on strike. Baraka and I were standing near a picket line outside Berkeley College when an older white man slowly walked past us. I remember Baraka stopping midsentence and derisively proclaiming, "That's the old fascist Robert Penn Warren." I was a little surprised by this characterization of the old man, for on several occasions I had engaged in informal chats with him. Our favorite topic of conversation was southern white politicians—usually Earl and Huey Long, Ben Tillman, and, of course, Jimmy Carter. Knowing little about Penn Warren's past, I decided not to acknowledge Baraka's statement.

What took place next inspired me to write about the former LeRoi Jones. From inside a small duffel bag drooped over his shoulders, he took out a pack of xeroxed leaflets that he distributed to the workers on the picket line. I cannot remember all of its exact words, but I do remember the leaflet's strident tone and rhetorical style. To the best of my recollection, the leaflet read: SUPPORT the YALE DINING HALL WORKERS! FAIR WAGES for the WORKING CLASS! CALL for GENERAL STRIKE! SMASH the CAPITALIST STATE! VICTORY to OPPRESSED PEOPLE EVERYWHERE! Underneath these declarations were listed Baraka's name and party affiliation (Revolutionary something or another). He also listed his phone and office numbers at Yale's Afro-American studies department as the local headquarters for this party.

After distributing these leaflets, he walked away. Our conversation was over. I stood there looking at the leaflet alongside some black women strikers. One of them shrieked "A communist!" and dropped the paper as if it had been infected with the plague. I stood there fascinated by Baraka's actions—fascinated because they were so politically inept. If he really wanted to help the workers, his actions did not convey it. I wondered if he had done this just to assuage his conscience, for he was teaching at the very institution that was op-pressing these workers, many of whom were black. When later walking away, I laughed not only at the language that always seemed to appear on these sec-tarian leftist leaflets and posters (as if they were all manufactured by the same sign company) but also because I suspected that Professors Charles Davis and my buddies Skip Gates and John Blassingame would have been shocked to know that their departmental offices housed the local offices of an effort to smash the capitalist state. I couldn't stop laughing at the prospect that a gen-eral strike would emanate from the strike at Yale.

I did not doubt that Baraka was on the right side of this labor conflict. Nor did I question the sincerity of his beliefs in the righteousness of the work-ers' cause. I did momentarily wonder whether Baraka was as tactically igno-rant as his actions indicated. I concluded that his actions conveyed a complete indifference to the political context, including the workers' unfamiliarity with him and his unfamiliarity with them. This further led me to wonder whether he was more interested in being seen as on the right side politically than in ac-tually involving himself in their struggle. What does it mean to be self-pro-fessed revolutionary if one is so divorced from concerns about political effi-cacy? I knew then that I would have to include him in my dissertation.

Baraka is a complex figure who can easily be misunderstood and misin-terpreted. My book is but one person's necessarily flawed, critical commen-tary on another's life and work. It does not claim to be definitive. Nor do I think that it will finally put to rest the controversies that it describes. Yet I be-lieve that my discussion will raise questions that cannot be ignored when dis-cussing Baraka. I'm even sufficiently confident to believe that I have answered some of these important questions.

Introduction

A CLASSIC TEXT in Afro-American studies, Harold Cruse's *The Crisis of the Negro Intellectual* remains one of the most provocative and suggestive treatments of the political behavior and beliefs of twentieth-century Afro-American intellectuals.[1] Cruse's importance lay in his ability to discuss and situate historically some of the major political and aesthetic controversies of the twentieth century's Afro-American intellectual enterprise. Published in 1967, *The Crisis of the Negro Intellectual* became the spark for intellectual exchanges in the Afro-American intelligentsia. Many of these debates centered on questions about the black intellectual's responsibilities. The very qualities that made *The Crisis of the Negro Intellectual* such a controversial text are, however, the same qualities that made it deeply flawed and time bound. It is an ideological tract, a political manifesto of sorts. Though informative, its importance did not and could not rest on its scholarly merits. Cruse interpreted the history of twentieth-century Afro-American intellectuals through the lens of a dogmatic ideology. In his quest to valorize a version of black nationalism as the "correct" ideology of the black intellectual, Cruse offered highly skewed interpretations of the intellectuals and their artistic projects. Non–black nationalist, Afro-American intellectuals, particularly anti–black nationalist, Afro-American intellectuals like those affiliated with the Communist Party, suffered the brunt of Cruse's tendentious analysis. *The Crisis of the Negro Intellectual* should be seen as a polemical call to arms for black intellectuals. As such, the book captivated a generation of engaged black intellectuals, although it remains unclear whether it actually influenced their beliefs and behavior or legitimated their political involvements ideologically.

The political and racial climate in the United States that greeted the publication of *The Crisis of the Negro Intellectual* only intensified the sense of political urgency in the black intellectual community. After years of optimism, by 1967 the Civil Rights movement was in decline for reasons having to do as much with its policy successes (e.g., the 1964 Civil Rights Act, 1965 Voting Rights Act) as with the failure of its policy outreach to address the economic needs of impoverished blacks.

By 1967, the year of the book's publication, black "urban riots" had broken out in large urban areas throughout the nation. Harlem "exploded" in 1964 and was followed one year later by a far larger and more lethal riot in the Watts section of Los Angeles. These riots were important as national public indicators of a rupture in the southern-generated, church-administered, civil rights vision of a peaceful black march to racial egalitarianism. As a result of the urban riots, the image of black political activists and, ultimately, black people was fundamentally altered in the national political discourse. The image of the black civil rights activist as a victim of "un-American" southern racist brutality was replaced by the image of the match- and brick-wielding, anti-American, black militant violator of law and order.[2] The former image had generated guilt in the eyes of a significant portion of the white American populace, whereas the latter image generated whites' fear and resentment. The political and public policy responses prompted by these different moral depictions of blacks were quite different. The Johnson administration's interventions on behalf of black civil rights and economic impoverishment (the War on Poverty), however flawed, were replaced by the law-and-order, economically callous presidency of Richard Nixon. Vice-President's Hubert Humphrey's racial liberalism was replaced by Spiro T. Agnew's spiteful venom.

After the initial wave of urban riots in the 1960s, significant remnants of the black Civil Rights movement intelligentsia remained intact and tried to recoup and develop new strategies for reaching out to nonsouthern black communities.[3] However, the deepening involvement of the United States in the war in Vietnam replaced civil rights as the dominant liberal and state concern of the day. The 1963 March on Washington was the last time that a major, organized, peaceful demonstration explicitly related to black civil rights took place in the nation's capital during the 1960s. From the mid-1960s through the early 1970s, most of the protest demonstrations in Washington centered on the involvement of the United States in the Vietnam War.

Black civil rights–oriented intellectuals, whom I term the *civil rights intelligentsia*,[4] generally viewed the urban riots as an indication of mass despair in American cities. They argued that the civil rights era and particularly the state's response had not gone far enough toward addressing the needs of those blacks who lived in urban ghettos without the possibility of economic mobility. In many respects, their explanations for those riots were reminiscent of Langston Hughes's poetic reflections on a dream deferred. Moreover, the civil rights intelligentsia tended to see the riots as politically dysfunctional acts of desperation. Many in the civil rights–oriented black intellectual circles still believed that the United States had the potential to become an egalitarian, multiracial society. Those who did not believe that the United States was irretrievably headed toward becoming a multiracial democracy may at least have believed that such a social vision was the only morally viable one for Americans, white and black.

The Black Power / black nationalist wing of the black intelligentsia tended to view the black urban riots as political rebellions or even revolts. Besides Amiri Baraka, the people in this wing included Dan Watts and the circles around *Liberator* magazine, Hoyt Fuller and the circles around *Negro Digest/Black World*, Stokely Carmichael, Julius Lester, H. Rap Brown, Maulana Karenga, and Nikki Giovanni. Because the anger and aggression of many of the rioters appeared to be directed against property and the protectors of property (i.e., police, national guard, army), some viewed these rebellions as protorevolutionary. According to this line of reasoning, black rioters were seen as rejecters of the "American dream" instead of frustrated aspirants to the bourgeois life. The idea of rejecting American socioeconomic inclusion in favor of a nebulously defined black separatist future gained a great deal of rhetorical currency in this sector of the black intelligentsia.

It is not clear how much a behavioral component figured in these various black separatist ideologies. Some members of this black separatist wing of the intelligentsia did physically relocate to Africa.[5] Nevertheless, one of the ways that the black nationalist / black separatist vision became prominent among the black intelligentsia was through various attempts to develop separate black intellectual and artistic infrastructures. These efforts ranged from the attempt by Amiri Baraka to develop a Black Arts repertory theater school in Harlem to the creation of various black mini-organizations and caucuses, usually located in larger, predominantly white academic organizations. For instance, black political scientists, sociologists, and psychologists established such organizations.[6] Another important feature of the black intellectual infrastructure during this time was the creation of Afro-American studies programs and departments throughout American academia.[7]

The most extensive effort by twentieth-century black intellectuals and artists to develop a black artistic infrastructure was undertaken by black nationalist intellectuals during the late 1960s. The result was the Black Arts movement, which gave rise to numerous black journals, cultural centers, and writers' collectives. Perhaps the most significant infrastructural component of the Black Arts movement was the massive explosion of black community theaters and theater companies. As a major champion of black artistic outreach into local communities, Baraka legitimized the movement for blacks in the theater. Because he had already succeeded "off Broadway," he could not be dismissed as an inferior artist seeking to sidestep the rigors of the white theater world. Indeed, his success in the "white" art world paved the way for his leadership role in the Black Arts movement.

The black nationalist resurgence of the late 1960s and early 1970s went far beyond the establishment of intellectual infrastructures. The black nationalist mood was crucial to confronting the psychologically debilitating aspects of life lived as a subjugated black person in a racist society, as it attempted to de-stigmatize blackness for blacks and concerned whites. The valorization of Africa was a large part of this effort.

Although he did not go so far as to advocate revolution, Cruse argued that the political and aesthetic orientations of black intellectuals needed to become more racially separatist. He discounted as naive or self-defeating those political orientations that diverged from black nationalism. Because of this narrow interpretation, Cruse could write as though most black intellectuals had been detrimental or irrelevant to the political struggles of twentieth-century black Americans. For Cruse, the political cul-de-sac of black intellectuals stemmed from their misreading of American history. He contended that black intellectuals were pursuing a vision of an integrated America when in fact American cultural norms were deeply embedded in ethnic pluralism.

Black intellectuals have a long history of participating in Afro-American activist politics. W. E. B. Du Bois, one of the founders of the NAACP, remains a model of political engagement. Ida Wells-Barnett and Monroe Trotter, intellectuals disguised as militant journalists, tried to raise the political consciousness of dormant and dominated black populations. Legal theorist Charles Houston used his Harvard Law School education and his deanship at the Howard University School of Law to train black lawyers in those techniques and strategies that would one day be used to confront and overturn *Plessy v. Ferguson*. Mamie and Kenneth Clark, two pioneer black psychologists, used their research skills to help strengthen the NAACP's case in pursuit of the *Brown v. Board of Education* ruling. And Pauli Murray, a poet, lawyer, and pioneer Episcopal priest, helped create a black presence in the feminist movement that began during the 1960s.

"Nonactivist" black intellectuals have played a crucial part in Afro-American politics as thinkers, ideologues, and conveyers of knowledge. Historian Carter G. Woodson's impact on black social and political life was immense, given that he spent his life rescuing the complexity of black history and cultural identity from the simplifications of the dominant American racist depictions of blacks, blackness, and Africa. In some ways, the example of Woodson raises questions about the appropriateness of an engaged-versus-disengaged dichotomy for Afro-American intellectual life. Reclusive and secluded scholars who were engaged in serious antiracist research were inadvertently engaged.

Even the more technical sector of the black intelligentsia has served the needs of the broader black community. When one thinks of those black intellectuals who did not participate in public-sphere politics but who, for instance, were competent teachers at various black colleges or segregated high schools, one realizes that many black intellectuals, broadly defined, were indeed part of the struggles and social uplift mission of the broader black community. In many respects, Cruse's "crisis" was a sectarian ploy. He wanted to frame the issues of black intellectual life and politics along a linear axis between black nationalism and integrationism. Needless to say, he endorsed the former as the only authentic emancipatory outlook for creative black intellectuals. Instead of analyzing the ongoing "crisis" in black intellectual life, Cruse was actually laying the intellectual groundwork for the emergence of a dominant black nationalist wing of intellectuals.

Ironically, the events of the late 1960s that set the stage for the emergence of *The Crisis of the Negro Intellectual* as a linchpin of black intellectual activity also became the first test case for the Cruse thesis. With the benefit of a thirty-year hindsight, it is clear that the Cruse thesis did not, in fact, work. This black nationalist moment quickly became mired in black parochialism, ethnic cathartic/therapeutic cheerleading, and sectarianism. It produced little of lasting intellectual and artistic value relative to its overblown, insipid claims. One need only read what Baraka wrote during the Black Arts movement to see the decline in his artistry once black nationalist politics became his primary stage. The journey from *Dutchman* to the banal agitprop black nationalist plays of the late 1960s and early 1970s is so long that one could legitimately wonder whether they were created by the same writer. Even the prose nonfiction that Baraka wrote during the late 1960s became insipid. As opposed to *Home*, there is little in his 1971 essay collection *Raise Race Rays Raze* that demands rereading.[8]

A decline in black artistic ambitions and performances was not the only problem in the black nationalist, Black Arts movement. Not surprisingly, the black nationalist intellectual movement, like all intellectual movements, was saturated with opportunism. Cruse thoroughly underestimated the degree to which the most vehement black nationalist intellectual was fundamentally American. These intellectuals were often as committed to material acquisition and status attainment as anyone in the academy. That is, many of the black intellectuals who embraced black nationalism had little authentic commitment to black nationalism as an oppositional form of politics. Instead, they appropriated nationalism because they thought that it was a rhetoric and ideology that could bring substantive benefits from academia or the state. The willingness of many black intellectuals to join the black nationalist bandwagon often stemmed from their desire to legitimate themselves in the broader black activist community and subsequently to gain access to the mobility that the political system offered to black nationalist intellectuals in response to the maintenance of black quietude in urban areas. Despite its militant-sounding rhetoric, black nationalism became a ideology of economic and status mobility for bourgeois intellectuals. Martin Kilson detected the self-interest of the black nationalist identity for many black intellectuals:

> Some professionals are adopting a Black Power ideological format not with the intent of preparing themselves for service to self-governing urban black communities but to make themselves more visible to the white establishment, which is not at all adverse to offering such persons good jobs as alternatives to Black Power. The more viable Negro businessmen are also simulating the Black Power advocates who have virtually no control over this use of their political style by the professional and business black bourgeoisie, which means the Black Power advocates will eventually lose the payoff potential of nationalist politics. If so . . . the Negro lower classes, whose riots legitimize Black Power will be joined by the Black Power advocates in holding the bag—with nothing in it save a lot of therapeutic miscellany.[9]

Kilson's predictions do not accurately describe Baraka's specific actions and beliefs. Baraka believed in a utopian vision of a black nationalist America free from white racist domination. Once he realized that many of his black nationalist confreres were quite bourgeois in their open solicitation of the American dream and its material largess, he not only felt disgust but gradually began to withdraw from the black nationalist ranks.

Once black nationalism ceased to be able to provide legitimacy and job mobility for bourgeois intellectuals, it began to recede in black intellectual ranks. Whether for pragmatic or opportunistic reasons, black intellectuals altered their ideologies. Cruse took insufficient account of the social class of traditional black intellectuals and their requisite material aspirations. He accepted their nationalist rhetoric at face value, as if black intellectuals were simply disaffiliated vessels carrying around enslaving or emancipatory ideas. How else, for instance, could he have assumed that the espousal of black nationalism by traditional black intellectuals meant that they were concerned about the broader black community? Cruse also failed to incorporate a sociology of knowledge into his discussion. For instance, if Cruse wanted to place the blame for black integrationist-minded intellectuals on their Jewish intellectual bosses, he should have situated the interactions between these black and Jewish intellectuals in a material social context. What was it that these black intellectuals and artists supposedly received as payoffs for opposing black nationalism? This is a question that Cruse should have but did not answer. Instead, his analysis of nationalism gets bogged down in his own naive nationalistic framework. Like all nationalisms, black nationalism is predicated on a reified consciousness. In this instance, all blacks are thought to share a collective interest as a result of their blackness. Cruse added to this belief the assumption that blacks shared a culture and a cultural heritage that needed to be intellectually mined by black intellectuals and artists.

The black nationalist movement of the late 1960s and early 1970s temporarily succeeded in establishing black nationalism as a hegemonic ideology in the Afro-American intelligentsia. For a brief moment, Afro-American intellectuals who were not black nationalists were scrutinized and even labeled ethnically traitorous. Writing in 1969 as a doyen of the black nationalist moment in Afro-American arts and letters, Baraka displayed his intolerance of non–black nationalist, black intellectuals and artists.

> The Negro artist who is not a nationalist at this late date is a white artist, even without knowing it. He is creating death snacks, for and out of dead stuff. What he does will not matter because it is in the shadow, connected with the shadow and will die when the shadow dies.[10]

The Cruse text and the equally didactic aesthetic formulations of Baraka and other Black Aesthetic ideologues became central to discussions of Afro-American intellectual life. Usually such discussions centered on the feasibility of a Black Aesthetic.[11] In the process, the tradition of sophisticated debates about the linkages between artistic creativity and political engagement was scuttled in favor of one-dimensional diatribes about the "correct" ideology for black intellectuals. Lost in these pedestrian discussions was a central question for black intellectuals and artists: How is it possible for black American intellectuals and artists to sustain artistically viable creative angsts and disciplines in the face of the sometimes overwhelming debilitations and influences of racial subjugation? To what extent does the political situation shape the ability of Afro-American intellectuals to realize their creativity?

TOWARD A POLITICAL SOCIOLOGY OF BLACK INTELLECTUALS

Despite the flowering of Afro-American literary studies and intellectual history in recent decades, the sociological study of black intellectuals has lagged.

It is my intention to begin to address this lacuna in Afro-American cultural studies. Using a sociological approach to the study of black intellectuals, I situate them in various political formations and social contexts.

The tradition of sociological studies of intellectuals tends to treat intellectuals as a semi-self-conscious social stratum, a knowledge elite.[12] Because of intellectuals' language-, analytical-, and information-processing skills, they play particular key roles in the social order. The sociology of the intelligentsia thus seeks to understand intellectuals' various and traditional roles (i.e., as legitimators of power, as critics of power) and to link these roles to their various occupations (i.e., journalists, teachers, and propagandists). The diversity of these intellectuals' roles ultimately helps determine their political behavior as a group.

SOCIAL MARGINALITY

A fundamental assumption of this study is that traditional Afro-American intellectuals, like all traditional intellectuals, have as one of their priorities the reproduction of themselves as intellectuals. That is, black writers want to write, and black painters want to paint. Whatever provides the time and space to write or paint becomes a priority for intellectuals. One of the greatest tensions of twentieth-century traditional Afro-American intellectual life is that the attempts of black intellectuals to flourish were severely hindered by the viciousness of white American racism. For most of the twentieth century, black American intellectuals did not have ready access to grants, fellowships, research positions at elite universities, or even membership on the editorial boards of prominent American intellectual journals. At the same time, these black intellectuals also had to confront the inability of their ethnic group to sustain ambitious, traditional artistic and intellectual activity. For most of the twentieth century, the broader black community had neither the resources nor the desire to give a high priority to the funding of traditional intellectual and artistic activities. Blacks did not create a sufficiently large and diverse intellectual infrastructure of journals, theaters, record production companies, and the like to fill the void left by racist white intellectuals. Consequently, black intellectuals and artists were frozen in status and caught in an economic limbo. Black audiences often were incapable of functioning as a critical audience for black artistic and intellectual works. An example is the case of a black opera singer in the 1930s who was denied access to the Metropolitan Opera and other major opera companies in the United States. The black community could not provide her with a qualitatively similar opera network. Indeed, the low economic and educational attainment of most blacks during the 1930s restricted their exposure to this and numerous other non–Afro-American folk art forms. Consequently, black Americans could provide neither a critical listening audience nor the necessary financial backing to support such highly trained artists.

The condition of being denied access to the mainstream (i.e., white-controlled) intellectual resources and critical audiences while belonging to an ethnic group that did not have the resources and/or educational attainment sufficient to sustain serious traditional intellectual activity placed traditional black intellectuals in a unique vice. I refer to this precarious betwixt-and-between social status as *social marginality*. For most of the twentieth century, traditional black intellectuals have been socially marginal to the white and black communities.

SOCIAL MARGINALITY FACILITATORS

To resolve this problematic social situation, black intellectuals developed strategies for creating functional intellectual/artistic spaces. I call the strategies employed by black intellectuals to navigate black artistic social marginality *social marginality facilitators*. Regardless of form, social marginality facilitators have ultimately one purpose, to increase the individual's artistic and intellectual "space."

Among others, Richard Wright used his membership in the U.S. Communist Party as a social marginality facilitator. Although Wright was attracted to Marxism, he was more attracted to the idea of becoming a writer. Where else but the John Reed clubs of the Communist Party could a southern black high school dropout have his writing examined seriously by published writers? The Communist Party provided Wright with the material necessities of a young intellectual life. Early in his writing career, Ralph Ellison also used the Communist Party as a social marginality facilitator. He did so to a lesser extent than Wright, for Ellison had already spent three years in college. Ellison was less dependent on the communists for an intellectual education.

Social marginality facilitators have many guises. Expatriation has been a major social marginality facilitator for some twentieth-century black intellectuals. Black writers have become expatriates in order to obtain access to an environment that affirms their racial and artistic identities. Other black artists such as Shakespearean actors and opera singers have become expatriates when they were not allowed to practice their craft in the United States. Bohemia has been another frequently used social marginality facilitator for black intellectuals. Those needing a supportive, stimulating, and nurturing environment often journeyed to bohemia, a place culturally distant from black and white mainstream societies. Jean Toomer, Claude McKay, Bob Kaufman, and LeRoi Jones, among others, used this social marginality facilitator.

LURES OF VICTIM STATUS

The problems confronting the black intellectual in twentieth-century America were not solely material. Blacks were also ensconced in American ideological discourses that rationalized their subjugated status. One of the most common ideological vices imprisoning black intellectuals centered on the way in which America has morally navigated the "race question." Except for racism itself, no ideological discourse has been more problematic to black intellectuals than the *victim status.*[13]

Victim status is a metaphor describing an ideological discourse that mediates the conflict for mutual recognition lying at the heart of the oppressed-oppressor interrelationship. As an ideological discourse, the victim status established moral guidelines for this relationship. Victim status hinges on the desire of the victimized to obtain from the victimizer recognition of his or her victimized status and the willingness of the victimizer both to accept the victimized as his or her creation and to grant to the victimized the desired recognition. In the process, the humanity of the victimized is supposedly affirmed, but the superiority of the victimizer is not challenged. The humanity and goodness of the victimizer also are affirmed, for the victimized cannot rationally appeal to an amoral or immoral victimizer. By helping the victim, the victimizer appears to act in a moral manner precisely because his actions are not perceived as self-interested. Orlando Patterson wrote:

> Why should the man who has enslaved and exploited you respond to your cry unless, far from being an immoral tyrant, he has more than a spark of magnanimity? Indeed, the greater the appeal or demand for redress from the oppressor, the greater the implied concession of the moral superiority of the oppressor. For the latter has nothing to gain and everything to lose by releasing his constraints on the ability of those he has oppressed to compete with him equally.[14]

For the victim status to emerge, the victimizer must experience guilt and/or shame (but sometimes fear) for his treatment of the victimized.[15] Although the victim-status demands of the victimizer more than simple acknowledgment of responsibility for the plight of the victimized, it does not demand a desire to relinquish control over the victimized. The victim status is thus an inherently unequal relationship, one premised on the fact that the victimized is necessary for the existence of the victimizer. The victimizer is able to enjoy the life he lives in part because of his exploitation of the victimized. As a result, the best moral posture that one can expect for a victimizer locked into a victim-status relationship with the victimized is *paternalism*. Through paternalism, the victimized can often receive material benefits and economic improvement, but paternalism cannot emancipate the subjugated.

Insofar as the victim status is a metaphor for an ideological discourse, it is not an empirical description of the machinations of an exploitative material relationship. The presence of the victim status does not tell us anything about the quality of the existent oppression. In a late capitalist society like the United States, the victim status is but one component of the hegemonic discourses that legitimate racial inequality (as well as class and gender inequalities) and ultimately shape and stymie the oppositional discourses. More precisely, the victim status may be a primary hegemonic discourse for obtaining the voluntary acceptance of inequality by oppressed groups. Such groups are encouraged through material inducements to enter into a victim-status relationship. Such material benefits, which might improve the living conditions of the oppressed, are offered in lieu of authentic political equality or self-determination. Because the victim status is an ideological discourse, we can readily see that not all those subjugated in the United States necessarily occupy a victim status. As stated earlier, the victim status is created only when the victimized seeks recognition of his victimization from the victimizer and the victimizer grants the victimized such recognition. But not all victimized persons seek such recognition, nor are all who seek such recognition granted it.

The victim status sacrifices moral autonomy for social acceptance and material gain. In appealing to the oppressor's justice and morality, the oppressed often participate in the legitimation of their own oppression. Guilt might result in more benefits given to blacks, but it cannot generate equality. By its very definition, it presupposes dependency.

The dialectical relationship between victim and victimizer has been explored in the writings of Frantz Fanon, Albert Memmi, Jean-Paul Sartre, and Paulo Freire, among others.[16] By revising the seminal arguments of Hegel and Nietzsche, these individuals have developed an ideal type of the victim as one locked in a struggle with the victimizer for recognition. In this struggle, the victims often desires to be like the victimizer. More precisely, the victimizer is viewed by the victim as a "free person." As a result, freedom becomes associated with the dominance of other human beings.

The victim is actually torn between hatred and envy of the victimizer. In desiring to be like the victimizer, the victim internalizes values that are antithetical to his freedom. In effect, he valorizes the victimizer for denying his own freedom. In this sense, the victim is torn between hatred and envy of the victimizer. The state of being torn is one in which the victim simultaneously adheres to his own values (the desire to be free and the values that support that desire) and the victimizer's values (the desire to deny him freedom and the values that rationalize this domination). This state of being torn I call the *victim-status syndrome* and consider it to be the principal component of the twentieth-century Afro-American ethnic identity.

When trapped in the victim status, black intellectuals become incapable of realizing their authentic creativity. Overly concerned about white recognition, they shy away from a self-affirmation of their creative products unless these have already been certified or praised by the "proper" or authoritative white gatekeepers. For instance, Richard Wright's early protest fiction was locked in a victim-status syndrome precisely because it was intended as a white guilt-inducing mechanism. Because Wright was intent on generating white guilt and, later, white fear, he sacrificed a complex discussion of black life.[17] Black victim-status intellectuals often use criteria for validating their people's existence that are not only derived from the victimizer but also further rationalize their own inferior status. For example, the widely practiced attempt to predicate black American pride on a knowledge of the great kings and kingdoms in African history is a victim-status appeal. This argument assumes that the greatness of a people lies in their ability to conquer and rule others, which, after all, simply validates the greatness of the Western world that dominated the black world. Instead of proudly proclaiming that we, too, have tyrants, black intellectuals might want to help delegitimize empires as the basis of human pride. To do so, however, would necessitate stepping outside the oppressor's values, an act of freedom that might sever the victim from the victimizer's umbilical cord.

For some black intellectuals, one of the enticements of the victim status is that its occupants are granted greater moral authority. In a Judeo-Christian culture, the victim is morally superior, a valued cultural status. Not surprisingly, groups fight over access to the victim status in "who-has-suffered-more" contests. James Baldwin was a quintessential black victim-status intellectual. A moralist, Baldwin cultivated a moral posture on the basis of his and his people's suffering. The intellectual problem with the victim status is that it is a parasitic status, dependent on recognition from whites. All one's energy is invested in obtaining this recognition, as opposed to perfecting one's craft or pursuing one's ideas, regardless of where they lead.

ESCAPING THE VICTIM STATUS

The black intellectual who tries to step outside the logic of the victim-status syndrome in whatever form it has assumed in her art world or intellectual field during her historical moment is called *ethnically marginal*.[18] Such individuals are pursuing greater artistic freedom and human agency than that typically allowed under the hegemonic victim-status ideology. I use the term *ethnically marginal* to highlight their deviancy in their ethnic group. Likewise, an *ethnic marginality facilitator* is an ideology or way of thinking that gives the black intellectual access to a creative space free or freer of the dictates of the prevailing victim status. Jean Toomer, for instance, used the ideas of the Russian mystic-philosopher Gurdjieff to enter an artistic/intellectual space in which the society's prevailing racial definitions took on secondary importance. As such, he was able, at least in his own mind, to relocate himself outside the prevailing ideological confines of black art dominant during his creative life.[19]

Many black intellectuals have used Marxism to redefine their identity vis-à-vis an Afro-American victim status. Marxism undermined claims for the special victim status of blacks and instead made the black situation part of a broader class assault on the capitalist domination. Marxism allowed intellectuals to struggle for the emancipation of black Americans without becoming mired in pleas to the "master" for recognition. It redefined the relationship between the oppressed and the oppressor so that the dependency of the oppressed was no longer an issue. It is important to note that an adherence to Marxism as an ethnic marginality facilitator sometimes overlapped with an adherence to the Communist Party as a social marginality facilitator. This did not need to be the case, though, for some black intellectuals were attracted to Marxism but did not want to divorce themselves from the black community to the extent that membership in the Communist Party signified. One such figure was the sociologist Oliver Cox.[20]

As was the case with social marginality facilitators, numerous ethnic marginality facilitators have repeatedly been used by twentieth-century black intellectuals. My study of Baraka uses both types of marginality facilitators as heuristic devices for locating and charting various rationales that have given order to Baraka's life. Yet Baraka remains a special case. When coupled with his desire to be politically engaged, his feelings of alienation from everyday black people generated tremendous conflict in his political and artistic life.

ESTRANGEMENT

Baraka usually utilized those particular social and ethnic marginality facilitators that helped resolve his ambivalence toward black America. Baraka used marginality facilitators to address contradictory impulses in order (1) to attain a greater rootedness in black community and (2) to mask the fact that he did not feel at home with ordinary blacks. It is my contention throughout this study that we cannot understand the various journeys of LeRoi Jones / Amiri Baraka without taking into account his lifelong feelings of estrangement from black America.

Most students of Jones/Baraka comment on his estrangement from mainstream white America and interpret his forays into the world of Beat bohemia as an attempt to create a life outside the prevailing mores of a money-driven, consumption-oriented, racist, parent society. They often forget that Jones was also simultaneously estranged from ordinary black communities. He routinely admitted feelings of distance from "bourgeois Negroes," but he rarely revealed his reticence toward poorer blacks.[21] During the height of his black nationalist days in Harlem, Jones behaved as if he had nothing to learn from the indigenous Harlemites. His hyper-Africanized, black cultural nationalism always contained an implicit patronizing condemnation of the ordinary cultures of black people. Jones, the "whitenized" bohemian, had come to Harlem to teach the indigenous folks how to be truly black.

Even though he celebrated the racial/ethnic authenticity of poor blacks in his writing, Jones was ill at ease with actual living poor blacks who supposedly embodied that racial authenticity. He could lead poor blacks and teach poor blacks, but he found it much more problematic, if not impossible, to work as an equal with poor blacks. Similarly, when Jones wrote for ordinary black audiences, he created his most banal work. It was as if he imagined that poorer black folks could grasp only the most rudimentary artistic depictions. No matter how hard he tried to mask his alienation from black people, Jones would never be a "man of the people." To his credit, Jones has remained a man "for the people."

ENGAGEMENT

Intellectuals from subjugated groups continually confront the literal and metaphorical option of dropping the pen and picking up the gun. Although most intellectuals who are confronted with this choice probably never entertain the possibility of picking up the gun, many have not only entertained this possibility but have acted on it. On the international scene, Ho Chi Minh, Fidel Castro, and Amilcar Cabral quickly come to mind. In the United States, where the viability of armed revolt appears at best remote, the most militant, self-professed revolutionary intellectuals like Amiri Baraka are usually found talking more about picking up the gun than actually doing so. The choice confronting Baraka and other intellectuals in the United States is not to put the pen down but whether or not to intensify the fire coming through it. The choice centers on the decision to be or not to be politically engaged.

The idea of the engaged writer was a favorite subject of discussion for Jean-Paul Sartre. In his essay "What Is Writing," Sartre wrote:

> The "engaged" writer knows that words are action. He knows that to reveal is to change and that one can only reveal by planning to change. He has given up the impossible dream of giving an impartial picture of society and the human condition. . . . He knows that words are . . . "loaded pistols."[22]

In his study of the historical development of the idea of political engagement, David Schalk centered his discussion on twentieth-century France. By analyzing the work of Emmanuel Mounier, Julien Benda, Paul Nizan, Robert Brasillach, and Jean-Paul Sartre, Schalk devised a composite thick-description of *engagé*:

> Whether or not intellectuals can exist apart from engagement, it is clear that to have engagement there must be intellectuals. . . . The most useful definition of engagement would disallow *témoignage* and *embrigadement*,[23] as well as "existential gambling," the violent commitment of the adventurer-intellectual. It is assumed that the individuals involved will have a clear awareness of their identity as intellectuals, and that in some fashion their actions will be group oriented. With these clarifications we may define engagement as the political or social action of an intellectual who has realized that abstention is a ruse, a commitment to the *status quo*, and who makes a conscious and willful choice to enter the arena, never abandoning his or her critical judgment.[24]

According to Schalk, the idea of *engagé* constituted more than commitment or mere activism by the intellectual. It also presumed a quality of philosophical purpose and rationality regarding political involvement and one's own behavior. Engagement demanded more than the expenditure of personal political energies. Given the rational presuppositions of the idea of engagement, it is not clear that Baraka, even at the height of his political involvement, could be considered engaged in the manner described by Schalk. Yet the intensity and diversity of Baraka's involvements and the rational hopes that they embodied allow us to consider Baraka as *engagé*. He was, at times, fanatical in his actions and rhetoric. But it would be unfair to call his political engagement that of a fanatic. One person's *embrigadement* is another person's strength of commitment.

Of the Afro-American (and American) artists/intellectuals who came to prominence during the 1960s, no single figure was more politically active than LeRoi Jones / Amiri Baraka. The literary scholar Werner Sollors could have been accused of understatement when he wrote, "More than any other American writer, white or black, Baraka is the committed artist *par excellence.*"[25] From the mid-1960s through the mid-1970s, Baraka devoted his artistic skills to the creation of art, particularly poetry and drama that affirmed the new assertive militancy of black people. He willingly sacrificed aesthetic complexity in order to write didactic plays and prose, intent on educating a black mass public. As founder of the Black Arts Repertory Theatre/School in Harlem and later Spirit House in Newark, New Jersey, Baraka established models for community-based art centers throughout the nation. In 1968, he helped organize a major Pan-Africanist congress in Atlanta. Afterward, he became the guiding light in the creation of a black nationalist political infrastructure, the Congress of Afrikan People (CAP). On the local front in Newark, Baraka was instrumental in the 1970 election of that city's first black mayor. From his leadership position in CAP, Baraka played a crucial role in organizing the largest demonstrations ever organized by black Americans in protest of American foreign policy. Though short lived, the African Liberation Support Committee and the celebrations of African Liberation Day were important challenges to a racist American foreign policy toward South Africa, Rhodesia, and Portugal (the brutal colonizer of Angola, Mozambique, and Guinea Bissau). In addition, Baraka was the motivating force and glue behind the National Black Political Convention, which was held in Gary, Indiana, in 1972. What is significant here is that Baraka, a poet and playwright, had become so prominent in black America that he was able to convince black Republicans, black nationalist activists, integrationists, and established black political figures (e.g., mayors and U.S. congresspersons) to pursue a unified black political agenda. While his understanding of racial unity was naive, he was momentarily successful at injecting black nationalism into the very center of Afro-American political discourses. Baraka's political activism also extended far beyond this. His everyday life was rooted in political struggle. One can understand how Addison Gayle, a celebrant of Baraka's artistic achievements, could write: "Though his contributions in the area of literature are remarkable, his contribution in the area of commitment is even greater."[26]

Baraka's political involvements have become legendary. His greatest legacy might have been to generate a new style of political engagement for Afro-American intellectuals/artists. Baraka's political engagement centered on a will to express black rage, to embrace the anger against white America that had long been repressed in black America. Concerning the rage of oppressed Africans that was beginning to be heard in France following World War II, Sartre wrote in his essay "Orphée noir,"

> When you removed the gag that was keeping these black mouths shut, what were you hoping for? That they would sing your praises? Did you think that when they raised themselves up again, you would read adoration in the eyes of these heads that our fathers had forced to bend down to the very ground? Here are black men standing, looking at us and I hope that you—like me—will feel the shock of being seen. For three thousand years, the white man has enjoyed the privilege of seeing without being seen. . . . Today, these black men are looking at us, and our gaze comes back to our own eyes.[27]

Published in 1948 as the introduction to a collection of Negritude poetry, "Orphée noir" (Black Orpheus) was an attempt to grant a measure of recognition to the justness of the cause of black French colonial subjects. Twenty years after the appearance of "Orphée noir," white American writers were faced with a similar choice. Black rage was ever present: rage at the historical legacy of white supremacy in America as well as rage at contemporary racism. But no American intellectual figure of Sartre's stature (nor any recognizable grouping of white intellectuals) saw fit to recognize the motivations for the explosion of black rage. White Americans (including white artists and intellectuals) were not yet ready—nor would they ever be—to view black anger as a rational response to the vicious history of American racist subjugation.

The American nexus for confronting the legacy of racist subjugation of blacks had always been to deflect black rage by declaring it irresponsible and even marginal to the prevailing sensibilities of black peoples. In this vein, America had been historically quite successful in regulating the responses of its oppressed or in channeling those responses through controlled venues. One tactic was to certify black leaders by declaring some "responsible" and others "irresponsible." Responsible black leaders were supported through media attention, tradeoffs, and patronage, all of which made their leadership appear effective. Conversely, "irresponsible" black leaders received little except repression from the powers that be.

Perhaps more than any other twentieth-century black leader, Booker T. Washington exemplified the success of white America at determining and certifying black leadership. But Washington's political significance would have been minor had there not been similar-thinking black leaders in cities, towns, and rural areas throughout the country. Such individuals were able to stifle black rage. By employing the argument that articulations of black rage would only intensify the racist repression, Washington and his kind were able to tap into the pragmatic Americanism of black Americans. It is testimony to the depth of the penetration of American hegemonic discourses in black everyday life that the white certification of black leadership did not lead to the illegitimation of such leaders by the black community. The white powers that be were aided in this endeavor by the deeply embedded pragmatic logics that saturated black American political sensibilities, a saturation that ultimately spoke to the Americanness of subjugated blacks.

In most important respects, the civil rights organizations that arose to protect and advance the rights of blacks were built on the idea that black rage hindered black advancement. In the NAACP, there was no tolerance of black outrage. When the practices of these organizations are coupled with the socialization afforded to those blacks who could attend school and those various Afro-American religious practices and beliefs that viewed indignation as sinful and hatred "of the devil," there is little wonder that the articulation of black rage was stifled in the black community.

Enter Malcolm X. Malcolm's emergence as a popular spokesperson testified to the quality of rage lurking beneath the veneer of black political acquiescence and respectability. Malcolm embodied black rage and, in the process, broke through those hegemonic discourses and practices that had channeled black oppositional affect toward respectability. Malcolm's emergence as the voice of black outrage could have occurred only outside the society's prevailing black socialization. In this sense, had there been no Nation of Islam, there would not have been a Malcolm.

White tolerance, American-style, could not acknowledge the deservedness of the enraged black gaze. Committed to projecting its mirrored image onto black Americans, American white tolerance would never acknowledge the reversed black gaze. As objects of white construction, blacks did not exist as subjects. On those occasions when whites granted blacks a degree of subjective agency, they certainly did not extend to them the power to make whites the objects of their gaze. Whites, as Sartre proclaims, were "seen" only by other whites.

LeRoi Jones was attracted by this new freedom to speak openly, and he credited Malcolm for showing him the way. Among prominent, traditional,

Afro-American intellectuals, Jones became the most vociferous articulator of black rage. Unlike Malcolm, his emergence as the spokesperson for black rage went through channels that traditionally had been controlled by the dictates of "white tolerance." Clearly, the norms of "white tolerance" in Beat bohemia were far more accepting of Jones as a black than were the subcultures of mainstream white intellectual circles (i.e., *Partisan Review, Dissent, The Nation*). Even in Beat bohemia, "white tolerance" did not extend to black rage. Instead of mimicking mainstream America by declaring it morally irresponsible or dysfunctional to the advancement of black people, Beat bohemia defined black rage as a disorder of the mind, akin to a stigmatized illness that should not be mentioned in public. This bohemian dismissal of his growing rage inspired Jones (1) to create enraged black dramatic characters and (2) to participate in furious rhetorical assaults on white people. All the while, Jones was living in Greenwich Village and married to a white woman.

Jones's embrace of black rage while living and working in predominantly white intellectual/artistic circles necessarily led to numerous ruptures in his personal life. He could not be an articulator of black rage and remain in Beat bohemia. Because his intellectual roots lay in predominantly white artistic/intellectual circles, Jones's black rage was quite disturbing to the American intellectual community: "If our Roi could turn into a hater of whites, who and what is next?" Though disturbing to many American intellectuals, Jones's embrace of black rage would normally have been ignored by the American powers that be. Unlike Malcolm X, he had no mass base of support. Unforeseen were the thousands of blacks who were embracing black rage at precisely the moment that Jones was undergoing this metamorphosis. Jones became one member, albeit a prominent one, of an entire generation of black Americans who had decided to follow Malcolm's lead. This generation gave rise to the Black Power movement that emerged on the heels of the Civil Rights movement.

It is perhaps easy to understand how Jones became attracted to articulating rage. It seemed like a new moment of black freedom—to be able to speak one's mind in public. Rage is a terribly difficult emotion to master, however, as it is easy to become seduced by it. Rage can become so enticing that one begins to live for it or off it. Many blacks, including Baraka, confused the Malcolm-inspired freedom to articulate rage with the idea that black freedom is to be enraged. Even Malcolm stumbled on this dilemma throughout his short political life. The false lure of rage is that one can become consumed by the catharsis that it stimulates. The catharsis of rage may purge one's psyche of guilt and other emotions linked to former acts of racial obsequiousness, but it can easily entrap the enraged in its therapeutic allure. As the catharsis of rage becomes more and more enticing, it becomes more and more difficult to sustain the desire to change the social order. Hurling invectives at whites for what they have done to blacks may be justifiable and "healthy," but it can easily function as a pressure release that allows one to endure a wretched status quo. Like religion, rage can be an opiate of the oppressed.

Similarly, rage is difficult to harness to the political tactics necessary for any oppositional struggle. At times, Baraka became so enamored of articulating rage that he was incapable of channeling it into a viable program of action. An emotionally repressive character to tactical thinking is at cross-purposes with the release of rage. One who is committed to rage can too easily view any concern with political tactics as a compromise.

The conundrum confronting Baraka was to develop a political and intellectual worldview that could simultaneously facilitate tactical political and social thinking, authorize but discipline the articulation of black rage, mediate his erratic feelings of estrangement from black America, and nurture the psychic space necessary for him to realize his creative, artistic talents. By exploring the idiosyncratic paths that Baraka took when navigating these pressures, we can obtain a sense of his Olympian project. Whether he succeeded more than he failed or vice versa, Baraka's intentions were nothing less than to redefine the role of the black intellectual.

1

Birth of an Intellectual Journey

AMIRI BARAKA, THE former LeRoi Jones, was born Everett LeRoy Jones in Newark, New Jersey, on October 7, 1934. The son of Coyette ("Coyt") LeRoy Jones, a postal supervisor, and Anna Lois Russ Jones, a social worker, LeRoy was raised in a stable lower-middle-class, upper-working-class black family.[1] Even though his family aspired to the bourgeoisie, Jones was fundamentally shaped throughout his early years by a rather typical American lower-middle-class socialization, with one qualification: He was born and raised black in a significantly racist society. In describing his religious upbringing, Jones provided a glimpse of the black, lower-middle-class world of his youth:

> My own church in Newark, New Jersey, a Baptist church, has almost no resemblance to the older more traditional Negro Christian churches. The music, for instance, is usually limited to the less emotional white church music, and the choir usually sings Bach or Handel during Christmas and Easter. In response to some of its older "country" members, the church, which was headed by a minister who is the most respected Negro in Newark, has to import gospel groups or singers having a more traditional "Negro" church sound.[2]

Despite the limited musical offerings of his status-conscious church, Jones was undoubtedly exposed to robust, "traditional Negro" secular music. The Newark of Jones's early years was a hub of black night life. In *Swing City,* author Barbara Kukla claims that between 1925 and 1950, Newark was a "thriving mecca of entertainment."[3] A center for jazz, musicians going into and out of New York City performed regularly in Newark. One testimony to this vibrant black musical culture was a black girl born in Newark in 1924 who performed in local night clubs before professionally emerging on the national scene as "the Divine One," Sarah Vaughan. Certainly, the young Jones must have been exposed to some aspects of this rich musical tradition. Perhaps his love of black music dated from these earliest encounters.

For much, if not most, of LeRoy's youth, the Jones family resided either in black neighborhoods located on the fringe of Italian American neighborhoods or in black enclaves in Italian American neighborhoods. Jones attended predominantly white public schools. When recalling his days at the McKinley and Barringer Schools, Baraka mentions that he was not prepared for the racism there, and he responded to being called nigger by learning curse words in Italian. His outsider status led to the development of a split life between the black playground worlds of his buddies and the hostile white surroundings of these schools. Concerning this dual existence, Baraka surmised, "It must be true, maybe obvious, that the schizophrenic tenor of some of my life gets fielded from these initial sources."[4]

After graduating from high school, Jones enrolled in the Newark branch of Rutgers University. He once again found himself in a predominantly white environment. In explaining his year-long stay at Rutgers, one biographer wrote, "The effort to prove himself in an 'essentially mediocre situation' and the experience of always being an outsider in any school social activities made him transfer to Howard University."[5]

Howard University proved critical to the development of Baraka's ethnically marginal identity, for at Howard he was exposed to the world of the Negro elite, the authentic "black bourgeoisie." Long considered the "capstone" of Negro education, Howard University was the national centerpiece for the education of the black bourgeoisie. Founded in 1866 by General Oliver Howard (head of the Freedman's Bureau) to educate the former slaves, Howard University was, and continues to be, the best-funded, predominantly black center of higher education because of its direct subsidies from the federal government. By the early twentieth century, Howard had become specifically endowed with the mission of educating the black professional class.[6] Through this university came a disproportionate share of the country's black lawyers, doctors, dentists, ministers, teachers, social workers, and scholars.

Except for the sporadic intellectual exchanges in classes taught by Sterling Brown, Nathan Scott, and E. Franklin Frazier, Jones strongly disliked Howard. He considered it anti-intellectual.[7] Howard students appeared to be more interested in acquiring the "proper" black bourgeois weltanschauung than in obtaining a serious education. Jones was disgusted by what he thought to be Howard's educational philosophy. "The Howard thing let me understand the Negro sickness. They teach you to pretend to be white."[8] Theodore Hudson, author of *From LeRoi Jones to Amiri Baraka*, mentions Jones's involvement in a "watermelon episode" that has almost become a legend. Though somewhat imaginary, the episode captured Jones's disenchantment with Howard and, more precisely, his disillusionment with the black middle class. As the story goes, Jones and a buddy bought a watermelon and sat down to eat it on a bench in front of one of the college halls. Shortly there-after, his buddy left to attend a class. Now sitting alone, Jones was approached by a university administrator, the dean of men, who asked Jones just what he thought he was doing sitting outside a campus building eating watermelon. Jones claims to have nonchalantly answered that he was simply eating the melon, whereupon the insulted dean ordered Jones to discard it. Rather mis-chievously, Jones replied that he could chuck only his half of the melon for the other half belonged to his friend. According to Jones, the agitated dean's re-sponse was shocking: "Do you realize that you're sitting right in front of the highway where white people can see you? Do you realize that this school is the capstone of Negro higher education? Do you realize that you are compromis-ing the Negro?"[9]

Jones's story may have been apocryphal, for as Hudson discovered, sev-eral key details were incorrect.[10] In any case, the story's facts are less impor-tant than its unstated premise. The story portrays Howard University as situ-ated in a victim-status ideology. Because the dean wanted black students to convey to whites an image of themselves that was deserving of white accept-ance, black students were not taught to innately value themselves. Instead, the properly socialized bourgeois Howard student should internalize this "white gaze" in his or her psyche. White persons did not have to be physically pres-ent. Jones realized that Howard's inability to redefine itself in a non–victim-status manner led to and reinforced a disrespect for the artistic expressions and cultural artifacts of black folk culture, particularly those art forms that had yet to acquire an acceptable status in white artistic and intellectual circles. More important, though, such attitudes embodied and/or reinforced a disre-spect for black people.

Jones recalled several other incidents at Howard that manifested the vic-tim-status syndrome. After a Howard student production of James Baldwin's play *The Amen Corner*, a professor of English stated that the production of this play about the lives of poor blacks in a storefront church had "set the speech department back ten years."[11] On another occasion, upon being in-formed that Sterling Brown and others wanted to sponsor a jazz concert, the dean of the music school told them that jazz would never be performed in the Music and Art Building.[12] Humorously, Baraka later noted, "When they fi-nally did let jazz in, it was Stan Kenton."[13]

Concerning the victim status and Howard University, Jones wrote:

> Howard University shocked me into realizing how desperately sick the Negro could be, how he could be led into self-destruction and how he would not realize that it was the society that had forced him into a great sickness.

... These are all examples of how American society convinces the Negro that he is inferior, and then he starts conducting his life that way.[14]

Jones flunked out of Howard in 1954. This was no surprise, insofar as Jones was never able to discipline himself academically. Not quite willing to embrace bourgeois black achievement norms yet sufficiently "Americanized" to value a college degree, Jones felt ambivalent during his Howard years. This sense of personal anomie was compounded once outside the imposed constraints of college life. Describing his lack of direction upon flunking out of college, Jones observed:

> I was completely unslung. Disconnected . . . Like how could I flunk out of school, who had never had any problems in school? I was supposed to be some kind of prodigy. . . . I came back home but didn't go out. I had to do something. I didn't think I could be walking Newark's streets when I was supposed to be in school and I couldn't even explain it.[15]

MILITARY LIFE: ESCAPING THE BOURGEOIS LOGIC

Baraka enlisted in the U.S. Air Force as a way of reimposing order in his life. The military, with its strong tradition of discipline, would provide Jones with the externally imposed volition that he could not generate on his own. Military service has historically functioned as an agent of discipline for many young men and women and, as such, has often been seen as a socializing mechanism for upward mobility. But Jones was not seeking upward mobility; he had entered the military after having failed at upward mobility. Evidently he perceived the disciplined life of the military as a negation of the undisciplined life of the black bourgeoisie. It was no accident that in later life when Jones attempted to fashion a revolutionary posture, he did so by adapting a highly ordered, paramilitary lifestyle.[16]

Jones claimed that he left Howard because he was repulsed by the anti-intellectual ethos of the black bourgeoisie. He referred to Howard as an "employment agency," implying that it was in the business of training people for the workforce, as opposed to educating them.[17] But Jones did not leave Howard radicalized. To what extent was he authentically alienated from bourgeois black life when he left Howard? It is hard to imagine a self-proclaimed radical student or an estranged college dropout seeking haven in the U.S. Air Force, unless the alienation stemmed less from opposition to the broader American social order than from not succeeding in it. Jones was obviously at odds with his bourgeois aspirations, but this rejection of bourgeois black society did not necessarily extend to bourgeois white America. Several years later, when he became disaffected from white "middle America" (as embodied in the military), it was not surprising that this alienation lacked an explicit political content. He emerged then as a Beat poet. However, when Jones entered military service after having flunked out of college, he was a young man experiencing the pangs of status dislocation.

Baraka has interpreted his days in the air force as his introduction to the sickness of white America.[18] Howard University, he claims, had exposed him only to the sickness of black America.

> When I went into the Army it shocked me into realizing the hysterical sickness of the oppressors and the suffering of my own people. When I went into the Army I saw how the oppressors suffered by virtue of their oppressions—by having to oppress, by having to make believe that the weird, hopeless fantasy that they had about the world was actually true. They actually do believe that. And this weight is something that deforms them and finally, makes them even more hopeless than lost black men.[19]

While in the air force, or "error farce" as he called it, Jones began to consider seriously the realm of ideas. No longer subjected to lists of disaffiliated required readings as he had been in the university, Jones for the first time in his adult life let his inquisitiveness dictate his reading matter. Although this inevitably made for eclectic reading, the variety of texts nourished his curiosity.

In his autobiography, Baraka describes a trip to Chicago while on weekend leave from the air force. While walking near the University of Chicago, he went into a bookstore and saw books there that grabbed his attention, including some that he had read before. He recognized *Portrait of the Artist as a Young Man* but was fascinated by the eccentric opening lines of Joyce's *Ulysses*, "Stately plump Buck Mulligan." Unsure at that moment just what was happening to him, he was aware, however, that he was in the midst of a cataclysmic occasion.

> I suddenly understood that I didn't know a hell of a lot about anything. What it was that seemed to me then was that learning was important. I'd never thought that before. The employment agency I'd last gone to college at, the employment agency approach of most schools I guess, does not emphasize the beauties, the absolute joy of learning. . . . I vowed, right then, to learn something new everyday. . . . That's what I would do. Not just as a

pastime, something to do in the service, but as a life commitment. . . . I needed to learn. I wanted to study. But I wanted to learn and study stuff I wanted to learn and study. Serious, uncommon, weird stuff! At that moment my life was changed.[20]

Once shielded from the "education-as-a-means-of-upward mobility" ethos and its powerful reinforcements in the broader social order and black subculture (i.e., careerism, economic self-sufficiency, church, family), Jones became freer to engage in "impractical" tasks such as reading poetry and writing essays. But Jones was not completely free to become an intellectual, for he still held to some of those social beliefs defining a successful life as the acquisition of economic and social status.

The influence of the military on Baraka's intellectual development cannot be overstated. Insofar as his military service seemingly placed him in a bounded social strata, suspended in time and divorced from the mores and mobility norms of mainstream society, it provided Jones with a necessary social space in which he could pursue intellectual interests without concern for their utility. That is, the military functioned as a social marginality facilitator for the young Baraka. Not seeking to make a career in the military, Baraka's enlistment in the air force as a lowly private after three years of college must be considered, according to middle-class norms, as a deliberate effort at downward mobility.[21] Jones's enlistment was the second indication that he was guided by norms different from those expected of him. His rejection of the bourgeois achievement norms that ultimately resulted in his forced departure from Howard was followed by a social marginality facilitator, military life, that shielded him from the logic of black bourgeois, social-status acquisition.

Like most black intellectuals, Jones could not write about an early childhood spent in intense study, as described in Sartre's *The Words* or as chronicled in Flaubert's letters. Most blacks have entered the intellectual life through emotionally uprooting acts of commitment undertaken at a mature age rather than through the seemingly natural progression of individuals nurtured from the crib on poetry, classical music, and belles lettres. This manifestation of personal dislocation as a result of the decision to become an artist/intellectual is not limited to blacks, for many working-class white intellectuals have also experienced similar degrees of dislocation/alienation on their journey to bourgeois intellectualism.[22]

Jones's decision to enter the world of ideas seems not to have been definitive, although we can now see that the young LeRoi constantly risked adversity to begin his intellectual journey. Not only did he have doubts about the utility and validity of the intellectual and artistic life, but he also could not necessarily rely on encouragement and understanding from those closest to him. For Jones and numerous other blacks, the decision to become an intellectual was a very lonely one. Like many black intellectuals, Jones began his intellectual journey burdened with guilt for betraying the crude economic mobility expectations of those who supported him and for "selfishly" participating in a bourgeois pursuit that seemed unrelated to improving the lives of those to whom he felt an attachment.

Baraka is acutely aware of those factors that led to his initial immersion in the life of the mind.

> Coming out of Howard and getting trapped in the Air Force had pulled me away from the "good job" path."[23] . . . the service was my graduate school or maybe it was undergraduate school . . . it was the pain and frustration of this enforced isolation that began to make me scrawl my suffering to seek some audience for my elusive self-pity. . . . Because now, so completely cut off, I read constantly, almost every waking hour. . . . The best-seller list became a kind of bible for me. I tried to read everything on it. . . . I wanted to become an intellectual.[24]

During this period, the moment of his intellectual birth, Jones often reflected on how he had misused his time at Howard. Whatever anxieties he experienced concerning his wasted Howard years was overshadowed by his relief at having avoided the crude "upward-mobility" trajectory. This realization was brought home to him on those occasions when he encountered graduates of Howard who were pursuing careers in the air force. Their careerism, which masked a weltanschauung hostile to a creative engagement with ideas, reinforced in Jones's mind the belief that he was, after all, on the right path.[25] Although military life provided him with relief from the resilient pressures of "being a credit to his race," the military could not sustain his desire to be a credit to himself intellectually. For that, Jones would have to look elsewhere.

ENTERING BOHEMIA: NURTURING THE INTELLECTUAL QUEST

In 1957 Jones left the military after being given an "undesirable discharge" on the erroneous grounds that he had been a communist. He was accused of having belonged to a communist front organization during his days at Howard and later hiding this information from the military when he enlisted.[26] A latter-day victim of the residual phobias of the McCarthy period, Jones was thrilled to leave the "error farce."[27] Paradoxically, his escape from the military coincided with an event that foreshadowed an intensifying dependence of blacks on the federal government for protection of their citizenship status. During the same year as his discharge, President Dwight Eisenhower reluctantly ordered federal troops into Little Rock, Arkansas, to guarantee the safety of nine black children who were integrating the formerly all-white Central High School. Eisenhower had decided in this instance to place the federal government behind the implementation of the *Brown* decision because a state official, Arkansas Governor Orval Faubus, openly challenged the authority of the federal government to issue and implement the ruling. Under the national spotlight, Central High School was integrated with the help of a federalized Arkansas National Guard and the 101st Airborne Division of the U.S. Army.

One can only wonder how the Little Rock crisis affected Jones's spirit.[28] Although all black Americans lived daily with the hypocrisy of America's contradictory commitments to democracy and white supremacy, the impact of this incongruity on a black person's psyche varied with the individual. What did it mean for Jones to be part of the Strategic Air Command, an organization whose mission was to protect a country (and to destroy the world, if need be), even though that country did not protect and value his existence? Did Eisenhower's actions give him a ray of hope, or did the necessity for the federal troops' intervention appear to doom the long-run prospects of a multiracial nation?

Upon his discharge from the air force, Jones moved to Greenwich Village. Just a short distance from his home town of Newark, the Village was nonetheless an abrupt departure from his past and expected future. Jones's parents helped him move into his first New York City apartment. In his autobiography, he recalls the dissonance and disappointment in his mother's face when she first saw his dark, empty, cold-water flat. This was not what she had envisioned for her son, the "child prodigy."[29]

Jones had visited the Village several times before moving there. A childhood friend who considered himself a writer was already living there. Jones had been fascinated by both his friend's intellectual self-definition as a writer and his circle of bohemian friends. The deviance of the bohemian scene with its romantic intellectual intensity was tempting, particularly to an aspiring writer escaping the regimentation of military life.[30] Jones's foray into the bohemian world of the Beat generation became crucial to his emergence as a significant American writer.

In his excellent study *Amiri Baraka / LeRoi Jones: The Quest for a "Populist Modernism,"* Werner Sollors explains much of the significance of bohemia to Jones's artistic development. Bohemia, Sollors remarked, is a response to bourgeois society. Borrowing from the writings of Helmut Kreuzer, Sollors argues that at the very center of the choice to become a bohemian is an emotional identification with the socially downtrodden, economically exploited, racially stigmatized, and persecuted. Bohemians typically extend their definition of the "oppressed" to anyone in conflict with the middle class.[31] The bohemian emphasis on aesthetic protest, however, is much more similar to bourgeois politics than most bohemians would like to admit.

> In their desire to be as anti-middle class as possible, Bohemians present no political alternatives to bourgeois rule, but merely invert images of bourgeois values. In their alternative aristocratic and plebeian masquerades, they reject the bourgeois obsession with money by acting as wasteful dandies or as penniless oppressed artists, by withdrawing to the ivory towers of the arts or by agitating for spontaneous violence in the streets.[32]

Sollors maintains that owing to bohemia's belief in the virtue of negation, bohemianism can easily appear more politically radical than any sustained project of political engagement. This bohemian fixation on being different can also just as easily lead to an identification with the extreme right or the extreme left. "Disgust for the political center makes the bohemian discard the conservative and the liberal and embrace the fascist and the communist."[33]

Jones considered his emergence in the bohemian subculture of the Beat community as a negation of the lifestyle of the black bourgeoisie to which he had been exposed at Howard and had always been expected to join. He followed a well-used path. Greenwich Village had long been a haven for blacks, particularly black artists seeking a less racially confining life. James Baldwin had lived off and on in the Village during the 1940s. His mentor, Buford Delaney, had been there since the early 1930s. By the mid-1950s, the Village had become a contact zone of cultural intermingling. According to Mary Pratt, contact zones are "social spaces where cultures meet, clash, and grapple with each other, often in contexts of highly asymmetrical relations of power."[34] The interracial exchanges and cross-fertilization between white and black artists that took place then have become part of Village lore. Perhaps the most explicit nexus for the cross-cultural fertilization was jazz, particularly bebop. By the early 1950s, Charlie Parker, Thelonius Monk, and Dizzy Gillespie had achieved heroic status in bohemia. Later they were joined by John Coltrane,

Horace Silver, Miles Davis, and Sonny Rollins, among others. Jazz clubs pro-liferated in the Village. In addition, there was a vibrant jazz subculture at-tached to Village lofts and coffee shops.

In the eyes of many of the disaffiliated whites drawn to the Village bo-hemian scene, jazz musicians were the quintessential alienated artists. Char-lie Parker was a revered figure not only because he was an outstanding musi-cian but also because his drug habit signaled his alienation from the mun-danities of bourgeois life in 1950s America. This infusion of Afro-American culture via jazz into the very core of bohemian Village life must have attracted the young LeRoi. When this respect, if not reverence, for jazz was situated in a subculture that apparently accepted interracial relationships, Jones could easily have viewed the Village as a haven of racial tolerance and equality.[35]

In choosing to flee the lifestyle of the black bourgeoisie, Jones did not re-treat to a Harlem or Roxbury. Instead he chose as his new home an environ-ment populated by the outcast sons and daughters of bourgeois white Amer-ica. But then, he regarded himself as an outcast "native son" of bourgeois black America! College had given Jones a glimpse of bourgeois black life, and he had realized that he did not really belong to the Negro bourgeoisie. His parents were neither high-status professionals nor high-income earners. It is probably more accurate to consider Jones a product of the stable upper-work-ing class, a black socioeconomic sector that often deferred to middle-class so-cializations (i.e., children should attend college). In black America, the Jones family would undoubtedly have been viewed as middle class.[36] This catego-rization speaks to the racially circumscribed socioeconomic world of black Americans, a world in which few black families were able to attain economic or status equality with their supposed peers in the white middle class. Even the so-called black upper class, small numbers of which could be found in any large urban area, was at best on a par economically with the lower rungs of the white upper middle class.[37]

By moving to the Village, Jones was not actually trying to escape a bour-geois world. Instead, it would be more accurate to say that Jones wanted to give up the bourgeois life as an ideal worthy of pursuit. He was renouncing a possibility, not an existing empirical actuality. Rejecting bourgeois aspira-tions was crucial to Jones precisely because when funneled through the status insecurities of the black upper working class, such ambitions often led to an obsessive attachment to middle-class styles and mores. As a black person in pre–civil rights era America, Jones's occupational possibilities were far differ-ent from those of his white bohemian peers. He could not defect from a soci-ety that had never included him. The affected and thus tenuous nature of

Jones's "rejection" of bourgeois black life may help explain why he would spend so much energy throughout his career demeaning the black middle class. By rhetorically assaulting the black middle class via retelling personal narratives (e.g., his stories about Howard University), Jones could solidify his vicarious entrance into its ranks, all the while intending to renounce it.[38] In so doing he would be perceived as a class renegade (i.e., a bohemian). To the extent that his simultaneous claim to black middle-class status and his rejection of a middle-class identity were partly figments of his psyche, Jones could never quite put them to rest. Bourgeois Negroes haunted him throughout his life. Ironically, once Jones attained a degree of prominence, he used his celebrated artistic status to sustain a peculiar noblesse oblige disdain for bourgeois blacks.

From the vantage point of the parent society, Jones's racial identity continually tested the boundaries of his bohemian identity. In the eyes of nonbourgeois blacks and whites, Jones's immersion in a predominantly white world could be interpreted as an example of successful racial integration. Because of the prevailing status and class encodings that many blacks projected onto whites, whiteness, and integration, Jones's journey to an impoverished life in the Village was tantamount to "moving on up." When attached to Jones's life in the predominantly white Village, the rhetorically hegemonic ideal of a racially integrated America may have suffocated his bohemian identity in the eyes of non-bohemian blacks (and even some whites). Bearded "white boys" in need of a shower could never become "niggers," even if they loved Charlie Parker! White women dressed in black skirts, black stockings, and sandals were still white and generated fears of miscegenation when seen in the company of black men.

In an article published in 1958, Norman Podhoretz, the editor of *Commentary* magazine, denounced the Beats as "Know-nothing bohemians."[39] Religiously possessed by the idea of "making it," Podhoretz surprised few in attacking a movement of writers and artists who were gaining prominence without having bowed to establishmentarian intellectual certification.[40] Podhoretz felt threatened by writers who thumbed their noses at what meant everything to him. Even though his critique of the Beats contained significant insights, the status-grasping editor may have written the article intending to appease more established but similarly unsympathetic critics of the Beats like Lionel Trilling, Alfred Kazin, Diana Trilling, and Irving Howe. The denial of intellectual validity to the Beats by the New York intellectual establishment only reinforced their raison d'être. Podhoretz had inadvertently legitimated the Beats by defining them as worthy of establishmentarian attack. Reflecting on Podhoretz's self-anointed role as the protector of cultural hierarchies, sociologist Daniel Bell, his friend and ideological confrere, wrote:

> Norman had always been told that he was going to be the spokesman for his generation. In the late fifties, he turned around and found a whole phenomenon called the Beats, who were far out, doing things that Norman never dreamed of—being on the road, taking hashish, screwing madly. Norman's reaction was to write "The Know-Nothing Bohemians."[41]

Despite disparaging the apolitical character of the Beats, Podhoretz found them lacking when compared with the Village bohemians of the 1920s and 1930s. According to Podhoretz, the bohemianism of the 1920s "represented a repudiation of the provinciality, philistinism, and moral hypocrisy of American life—a life, incidentally, which was still essentially small-town and rural in tone." He concluded that the bohemia of the 1920s was "created in the name of civilization,"[42] arguing that the idealized midwestern life captured in a Sinclair Lewis novel was a less civilized and less enlightened form of existence than life in New York City. He substantiated this claim by invoking Lewis, Pound, Hemingway, Fitzgerald, and Eliot as midwesterners who sought a more cosmopolitan existence in the bohemia of the 1920s. In making such claims, Podhoretz revealed an East Coast urban bias, which ill concealed the parochialness of his "universal" criteria for assessing degrees of civilization. As for the politically radical bohemia of the 1930s, Podhoretz noted that despite its political engagement, it was marked by "deep intellectual seriousness."[43] Not so for the Beat bohemia of the 1950s. Not seriously committed to cosmopolitanism, politics, or intellectualism, the Beats were "Knownothings." According to Podhoretz, Beat bohemia was

> hostile to civilization; it worships primitivism, instinct, energy, "blood." To the extent that it has intellectual interests at all, they run to mystical doctrines, irrationalist philosophies, and left-wing Reichianism. The only art the new Bohemians have any use for is jazz, mainly of the cool variety. Their predilection for bop language is a way of demonstrating solidarity with the primitive vitality and spontaneity they find in jazz and of expressing contempt for coherent, rational discourse which, being a product of the mind, is in their view a form of death. To be articulate is to admit that you have no feelings.[44]

In these astonishing statements, Podhoretz reveals his racist criteria for calibrating degrees of civilization. Apparently, the most injurious accusation that he could hurl at Beat bohemia was linking the Beats to the primitivism of jazz, a primitivism that was supposedly contemptuous of reason.

Had Podhoretz been better versed in American intellectual history, he would have known that the emergence of a politicized American bohemia could have been dated at least from the founding of *The Masses* in 1910.[45] Many early American bohemian intellectuals were de-politicized, including Jean Toomer's Gurdjieff circles.[46] Yet Podhoretz accurately captured the ethos of political disengagement among the Beat bohemians of the 1950s, in contrast to the religiously politicized bohemian circles of John Reed, Randolph Bourne, Floyd Dell, and Max Eastman.

Because of Beat bohemia's cultural ramifications, a broader conceptualization of "the political" might consider the Beats' retreat from middle-class society as significantly political and politically significant. Insofar as they developed a community and/or subculture with distinct norms and boundaries, the Beats provided a glimpse of an alternative America. Unfortunately, this glimpse did not escape the lure of an entrenched American sexism. Beat bohemia was conspicuously male centered, although it did contain qualities of enduring political significance in the Beats' tolerance of homosexuality and interracial relationships, less repressive sexual mores, and respect for black artistic expression, particularly jazz.[47] But such cultural possibilities may have been exaggerated, given the enfeebled cultural conformity of the Eisenhower years. The Beats did not, however, create a critical cultural alternative to mass society, for their social vision was not necessarily emancipatory. Given their attachment to anarchism, the Beats equivocated in their commitment to changing the parent society, particularly since the alternatives (e.g., socialism and communism) seemed equally committed to the oppressive concentration of state power. As often as not, the Beats propagated an ad hoc negation of bourgeois society, which led Hazel Barnes to refer to them as "negative rebels."[48] The radical stature of the Beats depended on the continued existence and viability of bourgeois America. Beat bohemia neither projected an indigenous utopian vision nor sustained hope for mass social change.

The Beats' dialectical dependency on the parent society was typical of most American oppositional movements. The Civil Rights movement and the ideals it projected existed in what Albert Murray called a state of "antagonistic cooperation" with the parent racist order.[49] The more pertinent issue, however, is the degree to which the Beats or any oppositional formation becomes trapped in a rejection of what they oppose. The Beats were sometimes but not universally knee-jerk, although factions in the Beats developed different orientations. The knee-jerk tendencies in Beat bohemia were clearly present wherever the beatnik style was adopted. As inventions of a consumer culture, the beatniks were commodified versions of the Beats, devoid of oppositional intent or character. In *The End of the American Avant Garde*, Stuart Hobbs commented on the attempt of American consumerism to co-opt the Beats:

> The absorption of the Beat "lifestyle" into postwar society was fraught with additional ironies. The writers for *Time, Life,* and other media presented the Beat vanguardists as silly and deplored their lack of moral values. At the same time, however, they popularized the superficial aspects of the vanguard rebellion among young people who felt alienated from the bourgeois conformity of the decade. In this way, the media controlled the rebellion. By discrediting the substance of the vanguard critique of America, the mass-media popularizers enabled a "safe" rebellion that did not undermine the consumer culture, but rather created a new consumption community.[50]

This mass-marketed image affected the actual lives of various Beats, leading some of them to act like reified embodiments of "themselves." Others rebelled against these consumerist images. During the late 1950s, Allen Ginsberg spent a lot of time trying to inform the public of the differences between Beats and beatniks. Ginsberg's biographer wrote,

> He took pains to show the difference between the Beat Generation with its philosophy of love and tenderness, and the beatniks, who were mostly weekend bohemians out for a good time, but the press generally blurred the distinction, and the public perception was that Allen was the progenitor of all the bearded young men who wandered around Greenwich Village in handmade leather sandals, carrying bongos and a bottle of Chianti.[51]

Jones's first published essay was a letter to the editor responding to Podhoretz's attack on the Beats.[52] Jones directed his response to Podhoretz's commentary about the romanticization of blacks in Beat life and literature. In arguing simultaneously that blacks en masse occupied the status of primitive in Beat circles and black bohemians were too "whitenized" to fill this niche in bohemia, Podhoretz had touched an exposed nerve in Jones. To support his argument, Podhoretz offered extensive quotations from an essay written by Jack Kerouac, a Beat mainstay. Kerouac described how when walking through the "colored" section of Denver, he had wished that he was a Negro, "feeling that the best the white world had offered was not enough ecstasy for me, not enough life, joy, kicks, darkness, music, not enough night." In true romantic imagery, Kerouac further stated: "I passed the dark porches of Mexican and

Negro homes; soft voices were there, occasionally the dusky knee of some mysterious sensuous gal; and dark faces of the men behind the rose arbors. Little children sat like sages in ancient rocking chairs."[53] Such ludicrous claims evoked a trenchant reaction from Podhoretz: "It will be news to the Negroes to learn that they are so happy and ecstatic; I doubt if an idyllic picture of Negro life has been painted since certain Southern ideologies tried to convince the world that things were just as fine as fine could be for the slaves on the old plantation."[54]

Podhoretz astutely perceived that Kerouac's supposed "love" for Negroes did not include a commitment to their social advancement. In Beat circles, Kerouac was well known as a zealous antiblack racist.[55] His celebration of "Negro ecstasy" was little more than a crude romanticization of the Afro-American as the embodiment of primitivism. But Podhoretz was not finished. He then claimed that the white bohemians' celebration of Negro rawness and primitive simplicity could not have been premised on knowledge of their Negro associates in the Beat scene. "The last place you would expect to find evidence of this is among bohemian Negroes. Bohemianism, after all, is for the Negro a means of entry into the world of the whites, and no Negro bohemian is going to cooperate in the attempt to identify him with Harlem or Dixieland."[56]

Jones's response to Podhoretz's comments reveals more by what he did not say. Taking issue with Podhoretz's implicit claim that Dixieland was a black art form as well as his contention that the black bohemian was using bohemia to assimilate into the white world, Jones observed,

> No Negro Bohemian is going to cooperate in an attempt to identify him with Harlem or Dixieland: Harlem is today the veritable capital city of the Black Bourgeoisie. The Negro Bohemian's flight from Harlem is not a flight from the world of color but the flight of any would-be Bohemian from what Mr. Podhoretz himself calls "the provinciality, philistinism and moral hypocrisy of American life." . . . Dixieland . . . is to traditional jazz what Rock and Roll is to Blues, or Rhythm and Blues—a cheap commercial imitation. The Negro intellectual certainly has no responsibility either for it or to it.[57]

Podhoretz had thrown down the gauntlet. First, he accused Jones and his kind of attempting to racially assimilate, an accusation young LeRoi found quite disturbing. Second, in pointing out Kerouac's racially parochial comments, Podhoretz cleverly raised implicit questions about the willingness of Jones and other black Beats to tolerate bohemian racism in order to find a home among whites.[58] Finally, and perhaps most threatening, were Podhoretz's comments that focused suspicion on the relevance of the black bohemian to the political, social, and economic plight of broader black America. To a young black intellectual, these were devastating insinuations. At the time of his exchange with Podhoretz, Jones had not yet developed an intellectual self-definition that could ethnically legitimize his life as a black bohemian intellectual without organic connections to a black community. He never did.

Jones's response to Podhoretz was contrived. He conspicuously chose not to comment on Podhoretz's characterization of Kerouac's writings (or if he did, it was not published). Nonetheless, we must consider whether Podhoretz caught Jones in a racially obsequious and/or uncritical posture vis-à-vis white bohemians.[59] Harlem in 1958 was not, as Jones claimed, the capital of the black bourgeoisie, and Podhoretz knew it. There is reason to doubt that Jones would have known this or much of anything substantive about Harlem, had it in fact been a bourgeois haven. He admitted as much in his autobiography, written more than twenty years after the exchange with Podhoretz. Reminiscing about his coterie of black Villagers who eventually left bohemia for Harlem, Jones noted that "most of us were from downtown and knew next to nothing about Harlem."[60] This point about Harlem need not be academic. Had Harlem been the capital of the black bourgeoisie, as Jones asserted, the sting of Podhoretz's insinuations would have remained, for the issue was not Harlem per se but Harlem as representative of black America in general. If Harlem remained in the grasp of the black bourgeoisie, why, then, didn't Jones move to Brownsville, Bedford-Stuyvesant, Roxbury, or any other nonbourgeois black community in America? Or was all of black America bourgeois?

What Jones evidently could not admit was that he had come to Greenwich Village to gain access to a community that could and would help him master his craft as a writer. Instead of defending his intellectual and personal freedom, he hid his artistic motivations behind the deceptive claim that his flight to the Village was an escape from the black bourgeoisie. If Jones had revealed his reasons for moving to the Village, Podhoretz and others might have regarded them as a confession of estrangement from the black community. And such an interpretation would not have been completely wrong. Living in Greenwich Village was Jones's way of distancing himself from a life governed by bourgeois mores. An aspiring writer, he could not have found respite in black, nonbourgeois communities, for they could neither materially nor culturally sustain his intellectual quest. Poor black communities were not necessarily the bearers of values different from those of the black bourgeoisie. Jones sought haven amid those who had rejected the bourgeois life, not amid those who desired it but had failed to achieve it.

Insofar as the bohemian Beat subculture may have been the only accessible intellectual community in which an unsponsored, novice black writer like Jones could have obtained an artistic apprenticeship, his move to Greenwich Village of the 1950s was fortuitous. Where else could Jones have gained access to a circle of peers and literary advisers as talented as Allen Ginsberg, Joel Oppenheimer, Robert Creeley, Frank O'Hara, Charles Olson, Ed Dorn, Gilbert Sorrentino, A. B. Spellman, Diane Di Prima, Gregory Corso, and even Jack Kerouac?[61] Podhoretz and the "New York intellectuals" had not been and never would be overly receptive to emerging black literary talents, particularly those who entertained avant-garde ambitions. Had Jones not entered bohemia, it cannot be assumed that he would have artistically surfaced elsewhere. Bohemia, in sum, was a social marginality facilitator for Jones.

In his exchange with Podhoretz, Jones was unable to admit that he had interests as a black intellectual that were not necessarily synonymous with the immediate interests of the broader black community. Jones was in Greenwich Village in order to write, a fact that he was simply unable to acknowledge. Insofar as Podhoretz arrogantly defined black inauthenticity for black bohemians, Jones timidly accepted Podhoretz's terms of debate. By Podhoretz's reasoning, the only way that a black bohemian or any black could be authentically "black" was by linking himself or herself to a Harlem. What this specifically demanded of the black bohemian is unclear. The generic claim is that the black bohemian wasn't "black" unless he was ethnic. Being ethnic meant being in Harlem, which meant not being bohemian. According to Podhoretz, a black bohemian's authentic identity was defined by his material relationship to his ethnic group, leading to an inescapable conclusion that the black bohemian was ethnically inauthentic.

Jones's reply indicated that he believed that he should have been in Harlem and implied that he would have been there if Harlem had been authentically "black." According to Jones, the black community—that is, the black community under the direction of the black bourgeoisie—wasn't "black," but he, bohemian LeRoi, was. Podhoretz deemed Harlem to be black and Jones to be an impostor.

Podhoretz realized that the black bohemian had not only distanced himself from the black community but had probably done so intentionally. But he erred in claiming that this was necessarily a bid for assimilation. Podhoretz failed to grasp that the black bohemian was in bohemia precisely because he viewed it as something other than the typical "white community." As a bohemian, Jones viewed himself as a member of a deviant subculture outside the tolerated boundaries of the dominant white society. For Jones, "white America" was an ethos, not simply a place where whites were found in large numbers. The Village scene, though primarily white, was far less culturally parochial than midtown Manhattan or the Upper East Side.[62]

Had Podhoretz recognized the possibility of a black ethnically marginal existence, he probably would have been more careful in characterizing black bohemians. In his eyes, blacks were authentic only when they were "black" and left being "white" to whites. "Black" blacks lived in Harlem, or at least wanted to. "White" blacks lived everywhere else. "White" whites, including Jews, could live anywhere, including, unfortunately, Beat bohemia. Herein lies a "catch-22" in Podhoretz's reasoning. Why would black bohemians who were supposedly interested in being white-like join a subculture in which the whites were supposedly interested in being black-like? Had Jones really wanted to be white-like, he would have tried literally and metaphorically to move next door to the Podhoretzs of the world, but then he would have discovered that authentic whites did not want to live near either authentic or inauthentic blacks. Podhoretz could not admit that even in his liberal vision, assimilated blacks were only figments of the printed page.

Nevertheless, if Jones did not want to publicly confess his racial inauthenticity, Podhoretz would acknowledge it for him. The irony is that the degree of cultural assimilation and artistic conformity demanded of Jones in bohemia was significantly less than what would have been demanded of him had he attempted to serve out his literary apprenticeship at the *Partisan Review* or any of the other major journals of the "New York intellectuals," including Podhoretz's *Commentary*. Podhoretz, ironically, became the prime reminder of the intellectual and moral costs of pursuing establishmentarian recognition.[63]

Jones was not the first black intellectual to use bohemia as a social marginality facilitator. Jean Toomer, Wallace Thurman, and Claude McKay, among others, spent a great deal of their intellectual youth in bohemian circles.[64] In fact, Jones was not the only black bohemian in the Village and/or Beat scene of the late 1950s and early 1960s to gain notoriety. According to Harold Cruse, who also was living in the Village when Jones arrived, "he [Jones] was just another addition to the black intellectual scene of Greenwich Village—and rather late at that."[65]

Ted Joans, a black painter and poet, candidly admitted how the Beat scene facilitated his emergence as a commercially viable artist.

> Well, I'm not really a poet except for Allen Ginsberg who grabbed me one November day in nineteen fifty eight and said he was bored with reading in the coffee shop and why didn't I do it because I was great. He insisted I go with him and try. I tell you I was scared silly at first but it all worked

out and now I'm making more money than I ever made from my painting
. . . as for all the showoff stunts well hell that's just part of the job and
making a living.[66]

If true, Joans's naked admission provides a glimpse of the material benefits available to the black bohemian who chose to live under the veil of a distinctly bohemian, racially motivated, reverse patronization often referred to
as "Crow-Jimism." "Crow-Jimism," a term attributed to Kenneth Rexroth, was
defined by Sollors as an "inversion of white segregationist society in the bohemian sub-culture."[67] Blacks were considered by the Beats as heroic precisely
because they were seen as the true antithesis to decadent bourgeois society.
This romanticization of the black lumpen ignored the possibility that their
tenuous socioeconomic situation might not have been a conscious rejection
of bourgeois society but vice versa.[68]

"Crow-Jimism" surfaced particularly around the issue of sexual norms.
As a reversal of or a contrast to the Jim Crow taboo on interracial relationships between black men and white women, Crow-Jimism valorized such
relationships.[69] "Crow-Jimism" (sometimes called "Crow-Janeism") constructed the white woman as the dominant player in interracial relationships.
Sollors describes "Crow-Jane" as a white bohemian woman who rejects bourgeois civilities,[70] often by having affairs with black lumpenproletarians, young
men that Baraka poetically referred to as "Young gigolos of the 3rd estate. /
Young ruffians / without homes."[71]

Because of "Crow-Jimism" (or "Crow-Janeism"), black bohemians were
sometimes viewed by white bohemians as intellectually or artistically unambitious. In negating the intellectual establishment's overly critical appraisals
of black intellectuals (most often to the point of ignoring them entirely), bohemia often uncritically celebrated black artists. Black bohemians who came
to the Village in search of artistic development were often accepted by white
bohemians who were not committed to supporting their artistic growth critically and honestly. This may explain why Jones and other previously unknown and unpublished black writers were easily accepted into the Village's
intellectual/artistic circles.

After having gained admission to bohemian circles, even if by means of
"Crow-Jimism," black artists soon realized that they had to step outside
"Crow-Jane" protocol if they were to expand artistically. Less serious and perhaps less talented black artists like Ted Joans opted for the upwardly mobile
benefits they acquired a result of remaining behind the "Crow-Jimism" veil.[72]
Jones, however, a black bohemian with significant artistic ambitions, remained constantly on the alert to "Crow-Jimism."

The presence of "Crow-Jimism" among the Beats was only one moment in a long tradition of "philo-Negroism" in American bohemia. In her fine study of an earlier generation of Greenwich Village bohemians, Leslie Fishbein described the racially parochial ideas of the editors of *The Masses*, a radical bohemian journal published between 1911 and 1917.

> If the Socialist party viewed blacks as workers to be organized and the NAACP viewed them as victims of American racism, the new radicals in Greenwich Village found in blacks a new cultural symbol. Villagers envied the paganism of blacks, and believed them to be free of the puritanical repression that plagued whites.[73]

According to Fishbein, Carl Van Vechten was the pivotal link between black Harlem and these white bohemians. While Van Vechten may have been a crucial white patron of the Harlem Renaissance artists, his motives in valorizing blacks appear to have been explicitly racist and divorced from any real engagement with the dominant issues of black life.

> Reveling in the sex and spontaneity of blacks, denied to whites by their puritanism, Van Vechten failed to question whether freedom and escapism should be equated, whether drunken revels could compensate for the deprivation and discrimination that blacks faced in their daily lives.[74]

Bohemia's embrace of the Negro as a "noble savage" and exotic primitive reasserted itself forty years later in Norman Mailer's abrasive but celebrated essay "The White Negro":

> Knowing in the cells of his existence that life was war, nothing but war, the Negro (all exceptions admitted) could rarely afford the sophisticated inhibitions of civilization and so he kept for his survival the art of the primitive, he lived in the enormous present, he subsisted for his Saturday night kicks, relinquishing the pleasures of the mind for the more obligatory pleasures of the body, and in his music he gave voice to the character and quality of his existence, to his rage and the infinite variations of joy, lust, languor, growl, cramp, pinch, scream and despair of his orgasm.[75]

Written shortly before Jones's emergence in the Village, Mailer's 1957 essay conveyed the depth of the "Crow-Jim" racist romanticism present in Beat bohemian and progressive intellectual circles. After reading this essay, James

Baldwin rhetorically asked its author, "Why malign the sorely menaced sexuality of Negroes in order to justify the white man's own sexual panic?"[76]

We should not conclude that the avant-garde art world was free of the "normal" contours of white American, antiblack racism. Mimicking the parent society, white avant-garde artists devalued the works of black artists when their work was deemed to be too obsessed with "black concerns." In a study of the avant-garde New York school of the early 1960s, Rosenberg and Fliegel interviewed prominent white painters who asserted that there were no important black American painters. Summarizing these interviews, Rosenberg and Fliegel wrote:

> Artists are convinced that an important part of the Negro's predicament lies in his inescapable preoccupation with himself as a Negro. They see that he is unable to separate his existence as a member of an oppressed group from his art. He is unable to transcend his immediate life and enter competently into artistic developments of broader, let alone universal, significance. . . . Surrounded by a brutal reality, it is virtually impossible for him to forget that he is a Negro. This reality is too much with him. . . . As long as the Negro is caught up in this vicious circle his art will suffer. As long as the Negro paints as a Negro he is doomed to disappointment. This is not a dilemma of the Negro's choosing, it is the consequence of his extreme social subordination.[77]

Similar "friendly" arguments have historically been used to devalue black writing. Indeed, when writing about black American life, black novelists and poets have often been accused of sacrificing "universal" concerns.

Even in white liberal circles during the late 1950s and early 1960s, the prevailing attitude toward black Beats and black cultural artifacts remained mired in images of the "uncultured others." The white writer Seymour Krim chose the racially parochial pages of the white liberal/left newspaper *The Village Voice* to issue an astounding racist commentary on black Beats and the valorization of blackness by white Beats. Krim argued that jazz was the music of black squalor and ignorance. Even though the music was breathtaking, its socioeconomic origins in black blight should have prevented white jazz lovers from identifying too strongly with it.

> What would you white jazz lovers say if you saw your own people, thousands of them, enslaved in the hocus pocus of various Father Divines—still operating by the carload in Harlem and Philadelphia—buying furniture and

especially the needed music boxes, phonograph or radio on time, time, time, the girls buying earrings and the men booze or sharp ties when the kids need medical help or the ex wife is forced to "go into the life" become a prostitute, "because my old man don't give a—— what happens to me" . . . every true, religious jazz-lover I have ever met who is white has degraded a part of himself to be something he can never be, nor would ever want (nor would his colored friends want him) to be if he looked at it calmly. Most ordinary Negroes, whose emotions are naturally put into jazz . . . would gladly have sacrificed the music to a white skin and a less brutal standard of living.[78]

The black bohemians' attempt to sidestep mass culture and crass, philistine elements in American society as well as forthright American racism led them into a community that valorized their social marginality. Once in Beat bohemia, these blacks were often celebrated for being precisely what mainstream society had made them, outcasts. Nonetheless, mainstream society had a difficult time viewing their entrance into bohemia as a deliberate rejection of the parent society, for the parent society had already stigmatized them as outcasts. By birthright, blacks were the quintessential American deviants, a fact that lay at the root of their valorization by white Beats. When black bohemians attempted to reject not only American cultural tastes but also Western artistic norms, they were accused of nothing less than a rejection of civilization itself (and blacks were most in need of Western acculturation).

Locked in racial parochialism, Podhoretz could view Jones's bohemian proclivities only as a pretense. "Who do these parvenu Negroes think they are fooling?" The absurdity of a Negro rejecting white America was too much for him to bear. As the quintessential parvenu Jew, Podhoretz was intent on proclaiming any cultural authority that he could muster, which wasn't much in the realm of the cultured highbrow. But when commenting on a black, he could embrace his whiteness. In so doing, Podhoretz, the parvenu Jew, could refuse to grant Jones, the parvenu black, the right to refuse—the very right that had been denied to Podhoretz by his status superiors.[79] Regardless of what Jones said or wrote, Podhoretz knew that he had gone to the Village in order to gain access to "white culture." The circle was not only complete but inescapable. In or out of bohemia, a black was always and only a black. Krim was more forthright. Blacks, including black bohemians, would cease being black if they could. Honest blacks would admit this but they, evidently, weren't talking.

Like Krim and Mailer, Podhoretz assumed the authority to explain black life to blacks and whites. Whether or not blacks agreed with his description and diagnosis was irrelevant. The white authoritative father had spoken and other white readers could testify to the validity and acuteness of his observations. Once again, black artists and intellectuals witnessed a discussion about themselves that they were barred from joining. They could, like Jones, enter the discussion uninvited, but they would still be viewed as interlopers. Into such a world, a self-conscious aspiring writer named LeRoi Jones emerged.

2

Bohemian Immersions

ON MONDAY, OCTOBER 13, 1958, Jones and Hettie Cohen were married in a Buddhist temple in New York City.[1] Jones's decision to marry a white woman was his clearest articulation of ethnic "outsiderness" and perhaps even social marginality. The marriage produced two daughters.

Raised in New York City, Hettie Cohen had come to Greenwich Village after attending Mary Washington College in Virginia. According to Theodore Hudson, she had gone south to get away from the ethnically parochial expectations of her family and milieu (i.e., to marry "a nice Jewish boy").[2] Like LeRoi, Hettie wanted to be ethnically cosmopolitan and had come to the Village in search of such a lifestyle. In her autobiography, the former Hettie Cohen, now Hettie Jones, provides a revealing excursion into the Greenwich Village bohemian life of the late 1950s and early 1960s. She discusses the manner in which her life as a woman and particularly as a bohemian wife and mother restricted her opportunities to edit, write, and otherwise engage her mind in ways available to her husband, LeRoi. Her autobiography is an important corrective to the prevailing view of Baraka's life in the Village in which she becomes the invisible backdrop to a "genius-at-work."[3]

Several months before their marriage, Hettie and LeRoi began editing and publishing *Yugen*, a literary journal.[4] The title was a Japanese word meaning "profound mystery."[5] Jones launched the journal as an outlet for the avant-garde writings that he found so interesting.[6] In producing the journal, an implicit division of labor developed between LeRoi and Hettie. Jones acted as the journal's primary literary editor while Cohen was in charge of production. Hettie's previous experiences as the subscription manager of the *Record Changer* and the business manager of the *Partisan Review* prepared her for this endeavor. Perpetually short of funding for the journal, Hettie functioned as a one-woman production unit. She typed the first issue on a rented IBM typewriter and laid it out on the kitchen table in the apartment she shared with Jones. The initial issue included contributions from Philip Whalen, Ed James, Judson Crews, Diane Di Prima, Jack Micheline, Allen Ginsberg, LeRoi Jones, and others. Hettie described the range of authors whose articles were published in *Yugen*:

From a quick first look at *Yugen 4* you'd say Beat, as the three Beat gurus—Kerouac, Corso, and Ginsberg—were represented. Except the "New consciousness in arts and letters" was more inclusive. Like Basil King, Joel Oppenheimer, and Fielding Dawson, the poets Robert Creeley, John Wieners, and Charles Olson were out of Black Mountain College, where Olson was the last rector. Frank O'Hara, like the painters he knew, was a poet of the "New York School." Gilbert Sorrentino lived in Brooklyn, Gary Snyder in Japan, Ray Bremser in a Trenton, New Jersey, prison.[7]

In hindsight, it is rather amazing that such youthful and relatively unpublished writers such as Hettie Cohen and LeRoi Jones would presume to edit a poetry magazine. Their presumption was facilitated by their membership in an art world outside the interests of established literary journals. The very novelty of the "new writing" gave Cohen and Jones an editorial entrée. Fortunately for them, Allen Ginsberg passed on the name of the journal to Beat writers and other potential contributors. In certifying their journal by attaching his imprimatur to it, Ginsberg aided the young editors in their quest to publish what they deemed to be the best of the new. *Yugen* published eight issues from 1958 to 1962. Concerning the journal, Beat poet Diane Di Prima wrote:

> The early issues were very rough, both in content and format: great things and real junk, side by side. I used to go over to his house on 20th Street and paste them up with his wife Hettie. The later issues became more professional looking, and also the writing was more professional. It had become a regular little magazine instead of something done out of somebody's living room.[8]

As publishers of an important "little magazine," LeRoi and Hettie gained access to the Village's inner circles and Beat literary communities and became friends and acquaintances with major Greenwich Village intellectual figures. Their apartment on West Twentieth Street became an unofficial artist salon. According to one student of the period,

> the Joneses' party guest included the habitués of the Cedar Bar, the painters who showed in the new storefront galleries that appeared on East Tenth Street, jazz musicians, and writers. Hettie cooked up spaghetti for a hundred and got kegs from A&M Beer Distributors, and the bashes became regular events. Ginsberg described them as "an Acme of good feelings. A lot of mixing, black white hip classic."[9]

Jones does not highlight these parties in his autobiography but does mention that he and Hettie regularly hosted groups of people in their apartment, particularly on weekends. Occasionally, they housed visitors who stayed for weeks at a time.

In addition to coediting *Yugen*, LeRoi Jones coedited with Diane Di Prima the first twenty-five issues of the thirty-seven-issue publication life of an underground literary magazine, *The Floating Bear*.[10] The impetus behind the creation of *The Floating Bear* lay in the need for a quick-turnover, up-to-date organ that would publish not only "Beat poetry" and the new writing but also reviews of books, plays, and dance performances; announcements of events; and correspondence.[11] Jones wrote a variety of short essays and poems for *The Floating Bear* as well as reviews of dance performances and opinion pieces. His writings appeared under his own name and several pen names: John King, Johannes Koenig, Miles Campion, and Duke Mantee.

Early in the morning of October 18, 1961, Jones was aroused from sleep and arrested by the U.S. Postal Service and the FBI on charges of mailing obscenity.[12] The practice of the editors of *The Floating Bear* was to mail the journal to anyone who seemed genuinely interested in the "new writing." One subscriber to the newsletter was incarcerated, and on one occasion, his mail was read by prison authorities. They found two contributions in *The Floating Bear* that they deemed obscene: Jones's play *From the System of Dante's Hell* (*The Eighth Ditch*), and William Burroughs's "Routine." Although the case never went to trial, Jones requested a grand jury hearing, at which he stayed on the stand for much of two days discussing the difficulties in distinguishing pornography from literature. At some point during the proceedings, the prosecuting attorney asked Jones to tell him the percentage of homosexuals on the *Bear*'s mailing list. Jones replied by asking the federal attorney to divulge the percentage of homosexuals in the district attorney's office.[13] After two days, the grand jury refused to issue an indictment. The cover of the twentieth issue of *The Floating Bear*, which reported on the outcome of its case, borrowed its victory slogan from former heavyweight boxing champion Joe Louis: "HELLO, MA! I GLAD I WIN! BEAR K.O.'S P.O IN TWO."

Jones also worked for Totem Press and Corinth Books, editing works by Jack Kerouac and Allen Ginsberg.[14] In 1961, Jones and Di Prima founded an experimental theatrical group. During the same year, Jones's first collection of poetry was released by Totem Press/Corinth Books, entitled *Preface to a Twenty Volume Suicide Note*. *Blues People*, his seminal study of the African and American character of black music, was published in 1963. Jones also edited and published a collection of the "new writing" in 1963, *The Moderns: An An-*

thology of New Writing in America, which included prose compositions by Jack Kerouac, William Burroughs, Diane Di Prima, John Rechy, Edward Dorn, Fielding Dawson, and others. For our purposes, what is significant about this edited volume is that except for himself, it included no Afro-American writers. In 1964, another collection of poems, *The Dead Lecturer,* was published, and in March of that year, Jones's play *Dutchman* began a year-long run at the Cherry Lane Theater in the Village; *The Eighth Ditch* premiered at the New Bowery Theater; and *The Baptism* opened at the Writer's Stage. *Dutchman* later won the Obie Award as the best Off-Broadway play of the year.

During this same period, Jones published numerous essays, some of which were later collected in *Home: Social Essays* (1966) and *Black Music* (1967); poems that were later collected and published in *Black Magic: Collected Poetry 1961–1967,* (1969); short stories that were later published in the collection *Tales* (1967); and a novel, *The System of Dante's Hell* (1965).

BOHEMIAN POET

Jones first and foremost aspired to be a poet. Although he later was acclaimed as a playwright, he was initially recognized as a poet. In 1961, his first collection of poetry, *Preface to a Twenty Volume Suicide Note,* was published, its dedication reading *This Book Is Hettie's.* Jones acquired from William Carlos Williams the authority to write poems in the manner of his speech and not according to formalistic rules. T. S. Eliot also had a major influence on Jones, first as a model and later as an antagonist to his poetic style and ambitions. Eliot represented the sterility of Anglophone poetry. Anglo-Eliotic poetry was the poetry of the American academy, an institution against which Jones railed because of its insular aesthetic values. Sollors, however, perceived in Jones's earliest poetry an attempt to navigate the tensions between the twin influences of Eliot and Williams.[15]

Charles Olson may have been the greatest single influence on the young poet. William Harris states that "from Olson in particular, Baraka absorbed his sense of the poem as open form, his sense of line, his sense of the poem as recorder of process and his conception of the poem as definition and exploration."[16] After talking with other Beat writers, Jones decided that autobiographical events were appropriate subjects for poetry. Even so, Jones had not developed an approach to his poetry that emphasized his racial identity. He did not hide his racial identity, but his poetry was not self-consciously black in the way that it became later. When asked during a 1960 interview if and how his identity as a Negro influenced his poetry, Jones replied:

> There are certain influences on me, as a Negro person, that certainly wouldn't apply to a poet like Allen Ginsberg. I couldn't have written that poem "Kaddish" for instance. And I am sure that he couldn't write certain things that have to deal with, say, Southern Baptist church rhythms. . . . I am fairly conscious all the time that I am an American Negro because it's part of my life. But I know also that if I want to say, "I see a bus full of people," I don't have to say, "I am a Negro seeing a bus full of people."[17]

Jones's early artistic influences show that he was located not only outside a black artistic/poetic community but also outside of a black poetic tradition. For the most part, Jones was not part of a black literary tradition. Rather, his early poetry reflected his bohemian sentiments. Less concerned with explicit social and political concerns, Jones's poetry instead highlighted the comical, absurd, and mundane aspects of everyday life. In the poem "For Hettie," Jones humorously describes the awkwardness of his wife's left-handedness:

> . . . *TAKE THAT DAMN*
> *PENCIL OUTTA THAT HAND. YOU'RE*
> *RITING BACKWARDS. $ SUCH. But*
> *to no avail. & it shows*
> *in her work. Left-handed coffee,*
> *Left-handed eggs; when she come*
> *in at night . . . it's her left hand*
> *offered for me to kiss. Damn*
> *& now her belly droops over the seat*
> *They say it's a child. But*
> *I ain't quite sure*[18]

Bohemian tendencies proliferate in *Preface*, particularly those endless introspections and explorations of the arbitrariness of personal histories, the inconsequentiality of life, and the meaninglessness of death. Comparing the intensity of Jones's introspection with that of other Beat poets, Kimberly Benston stated that "none of these poets . . . felt more poignantly or recorded as vigorously the pains and desires of his alienated soul than did Imamu Baraka."[19] Perhaps no single poem in the collection better captures this than "Look for You Yesterday, Here You Come Today":

It's so diffuse
being alive. Suddenly one is aware
   that nobody really gives a damn. . . .
   My wife is pregnant with her child.[20]

Lines conveying non-sequitur meanings and images are juxtaposed with the verse's flowing rhythms. This discordance creates a perception of boredom and monotony, both of which intensify the bleakness of his reflections on death.

. . . My life
seems over & done with.
Each morning I rise
like a sleep walker
& rot a little more.

All the lovely things I've known have disappeared
I have my pubic hair and am lonely
There is probably no such place as Battle Creek, Michigan![21]

Later in the poem, Jones engages in a moment of candor:

but this also
is part of my charm
A maudlin nostalgia
that comes on
like terrible thoughts about death
How dumb to be sentimental about anything
To call it love
& cry pathetically
into the long black handkerchief
of the years[22]

In "The Death of Nick Charles," Jones conveys his disgust at the inauthenticity of his life. Worse, he is angered at his peers for viewing his inauthentic identity as authentic.

Sad
long
motion of air
pushing in my face. Lies

weakness, hatred
of myself. Of you
for not understanding
this. Or not
despising me
for the right causes. I am
sick as, OH,
the night is. As
cold days are, when we must watch them
grow old
& dark.[23]

Jones's poetry also conveys his bohemian disdain for the plasticity of bourgeois life. In "Hymn for Lanie Poo," Jones caricatures a black woman (his sister) to reveal his distaste for the racial self-hatred of bourgeois blacks.[24] He ridicules the rabid fear of many lighter-skinned Negroes that overexposure to the sun might darken their skin. Likewise, he mocks the black female's dread of the heat of the sun, which, in causing her to perspire, could turn her hot-combed, white-like, straightened hair into a woolly kink.

Beware the evil sun . . .
turn you black
turn your hair
crawl your eyeballs
rot your teeth.[25]

He comments on his sister's bourgeois, aspirant-white, consumerist tastes:

my sister drives a green jaguar
my sister has her hair done twice a month
my sister is a school teacher
my sister took ballet lessons
my sister has a fine figure: never diets
my sister doesn't like to teach in Newark
because there are too many colored
in her classes
my sister hates loud shades
my sister's boy friend is a faggot music teacher
who digs Tchaikovsky
my sister digs Tchaikovsky also[26]

The green Jaguar, ballet lessons, hair straightening, fondness for Tchaikovsky, and dislike of teaching in Newark all are supposed to indicate his sister's assimilationist desires as well as her embrace of American consumerist values.

Although at this stage, Jones's racial identity is not a featured part of his poetry, he sporadically interrogates the intersection of his blackness and his bohemianism. In "Notes for a Speech," he writes,

> *African blues*
> *does not know me. Their steps, in sands*
> *of their own*
> *land. A country*
> *in black & white, newspapers*
> *blown down pavements*
> *of the world. Does*
> *not feel*
> *what I am*
>
> *. . . My color*
> *is not theirs. Lighter, white man*
> *talk. They shy away. My own*
> *dead souls, my, so called*
> *people. Africa*
> *is a foreign place. You are*
> *as any other sad man here*
> *american.*[27]

Jones describes his shattered relationship to Africa: Africans are only his "so called people," and African blues do not capture him. Even though he is lonely, Jones is neither a pariah nor homeless. Instead, he is "as any other sad man here american." This poem is a meditation on his dislocated racial identity, but it does not exhibit the political angst and anger that later characterize Jones's meditations on Africa and blackness. A bohemian, Jones was much more interested in the deviance of his personal identity and the psychic costs of that identity (i.e., loneliness).

"CUBA LIBRE"

Besides the "nudging" from the growing Civil Rights movement, Jones was also intensely affected by the political success of the Cuban revolution. In celebration of the revolution's victory over the Batista forces, Jones edited *Fidel Castro, January 1, 1959*, a small pamphlet of collected poetry by Kerouac, Ron Loewinsohn, Joel Oppenheimer, Gilbert Sorrentino, and Jones, among others. Less political than it might seem, the origins of the pamphlet lay in the Errol Flynn–like images through which Jones imagined Castro: "The Cuban thing seemed a case of classic Hollywood proportions."[28]

In July 1960, Jones, a delegation of black artists and scholars, and members of the Fair Play for Cuba Committee traveled to Cuba as guests of the Cuban government. Along with Jones, the black delegation included Julian Mayfield, Sarah Wright, Richard Gibson, Robert F. Williams, and John Henrik Clarke.[29] Harold Cruse also went along and recorded his memories of the trip in *The Crisis of the Negro Intellectual*. After the revolution, the new Cuban government wanted to increase its visibility among those sectors of the international community that might be sympathetic to the revolution's aims and spirit. Founded in April 1960, the Fair Play for Cuba Committee was a national organization designed to generate the American public's support for postrevolutionary Cuba.[30]

Jones had been asked to be a part of the delegation by Richard Gibson, a black American who was one of the committee's founders.[31] Apparently Jones was unaware that Gibson was a highly suspect and controversial figure.[32] While living in the black American expatriate community in Paris during the 1950s, Gibson had been accused by some of the Afro-American expatriates of having had a connection to U.S. intelligence agencies. He had falsely signed the names of black American expatriates Richard Wright and cartoonist Ollie Harrington to essays that he had secretly written condemning France for its colonial policies in Algeria.[33] These essays were then sent to newspapers and journals in the United States and published, intensifying the spread of paranoia in the black expatriate community, for they were, in effect, attempts to compromise the expatriate status of Wright and Harrington. The French government allowed black Americans to live as expatriates in Paris as long as they did not become active in internal French political affairs. In exchange for the freedom to criticize the racist practices of the United States during McCarthyism and the cold war, black American expatriates were to remain silent on French politics, particularly the Algerian question. Upon being caught, Gibson confessed to forgery and was deported. Only a few years later, Gibson was in the United States leading delegations to Cuba.

"Cuba Libre," Jones's chronicle of the trip, was first published in the *Evergreen Review* in 1960. It was his first sustained prose essay to be published. "Cuba Libre" reveals an artist who, although artistically supportive of emancipatory ideals, had yet to learn the difference between politically influenced

artistic expression and political acts. According to Sollors, "the Cuban experience . . . was one cause of Jones's transformation from aesthetic to political
protest, from a belief in the end of ideology to a new political awareness."[34]
Jones later called the Cuban trip a turning point in his life.[35] "Cuba Libre" is
written in the form of a travel journal. Jones comments on the conditions and
people that he met in Cuba and uses them and the foreign setting as back-
drops to probe the behavior and thoughts of his fellow travelers. Jones portrays his own political naïveté through the depiction of a discussion held on
a crowded train on which he, his entourage of visiting Americans, and thousands of Cubans were heading to the July 26 celebration in honor of the revolution. The other discussant, Senora Betancourt, a Mexican graduate student and delegate to the youth congress, repeatedly attacked Jones's political
beliefs and passivity, and Jones reportedly replied, "Look why jump on me? I
understand what you are saying, I'm in complete agreement with you. I'm a
poet . . . what can I do? I write, that's all, I'm not even interested in politics."[36]
Though not given to modesty, Jones's overstated depiction of his apoliticization stemmed from the realization that his interest in politics would have appeared as bourgeois intellectualism, if not outright frivolity, had he tried to
describe his meager political activities amid the euphoric ambience of the
Cuban revolutionary spirit.

After having been with intellectuals who had actively helped change
material living conditions, Jones returned from Cuba feeling empowered
and politically challenged. He would no longer be satisfied with merely
writing about the cultural mundaneness and moral dishonesty of mainstream America:

> The rebels among us have become merely people like myself who grow
> beards and will not participate in politics. Drugs, juvenile delinquency,
> complete isolation from the vapid mores of the country, a few current ways
> out. But name an alternative here. Something not inextricably bound up in
> a lie. Something not part of liberal stupidity or the actual filth of vested in-
> terest. There is none. It's much too late. We *are* an old people already. Even
> the vitality of our art is like bright flowers growing up through a rotting car-
> cass. . . . But the Cubans, and other *new* peoples (in Asia, Africa, South Amer-
> ica) don't need us and we had better stay out of their way.[37]

One major consequence of Jones's trip to Cuba was a moment of intense
ambivalence about his conspicuous cultivation of the social marginality that
bohemia fostered. The isolation from mainstream America that bohemia afforded him had cut him off from the political tensions and movements of the

black masses. Jones now saw bohemia's success at protecting the space for his artistic growth and expression as the source of his failure to act politically in a significant manner.

BOHEMIAN RACE MAN

Whereas bohemian LeRoi had long written about the cultural and artistic destructiveness of mainstream white liberal society, "Cuba Libre" can be regarded as Jones's opening salvo on the racial implications of white liberal politics. In the 1961 essay "Letter to Jules Feiffer," Jones continued his assault on white liberal racial arrogance.[38] Feiffer, a popular and politically liberal cartoonist for the *Village Voice,* had written a letter to the editor defending himself against Richard Gibson's attacks on Feiffer's "white liberalism." (Gibson was the fellow from the Fair Play for Cuba Committee who had invited Jones to visit Cuba.) Feiffer not only defended himself as a white liberal but also criticized the political program and writings of Robert Williams, even calling Williams's newsletter "a hate sheet." In addition, Feiffer ridiculed the growing black usage of the term "Afro-American" as ethnic nomenclature.

Jones defended the actions of Robert Williams, the North Carolina NAACP official turned self-defense advocate. But Jones did not dispute Feiffer's claim that Williams's newsletter was hateful. Instead, he stated that "Afro-Americans (Negroes, spades, shades, boots, woogies, etc.) in this country can afford, I believe, the luxury of hate. They certainly have enough to hate."[39] Most of Jones's letter to Feiffer is a condemnation of white liberalism, using Feiffer as a case study. Jones exposes the arrogance of Feiffer's views, attributing it to his whiteness. He argues that white liberals are little better than outright white racists: "You liberals are people with extremely heavy consciences and almost nonexistent courage. Too little is always enough. And it is always the symbol, the token that appeals to you most."[40] Jones's overkill of Feiffer prefigured much of his political writing during his Village days. He often reserved his harshest criticism for suspected white liberal "allies" of blacks, as if he had more at stake than merely unmasking their complicity as whites in the racial status quo. That is, the vociferousness of Jones's attacks on white liberals indicates that he is not merely stating a matter of fact. Instead, Jones wants both to expose and abuse white liberals, thereby exacting revenge against all whites. White racists were never imagined as mere individuals but, rather, as representatives of all white Americans.

In 1962, Jones extended his critique of white liberalism in an essay, "Tokenism: 300 Years for Five Cents." More systematic than his assault on Feiffer,

"Tokenism" exposes the crude hypocrisy in American life of viewing every minuscule improvement in the living standard of a black individual as a major indication of progress for all blacks. Jones was angered by the willingness of the *New York Times*, the NAACP, and other prominent liberal organizations to highlight token black advancements, as opposed to the stagnant plight of the overwhelming majority of blacks. Moreover, Jones warned white liberals not to confuse increased black consumption with improvements in black citizenship status. While white liberals may have celebrated the fact that more southern blacks were able to buy cars in 1960 than they were in 1940, Jones reminds whites that with or without cars, blacks in 1960, like blacks in 1940, were not allowed to vote in the South.

During the same year, Jones also promoted a rationality for black nationalist sensibilities. In his essay "'Black' Is a Country," Jones defined nationalism as "acting in one's own best interest,"[41] and for Jones, black nationalism was a metaphor for black ethnic consciousness.[42] As early as this 1962 essay, Jones had begun to equate freedom for blacks with black nationalist self-determination. He invokes self-determination as a wedge against the prevailing liberal assumption that black freedom necessarily mirrored white American freedom (which, according to Jones, was the freedom to consume goods and dominate others). This invocation of self-determination then led Jones to defend nationalism but not, yet, aspire to racial separatism.

> The struggle is for independence, no separation—or assimilation for that matter. Do what you want to with *your* life . . . when you can. *I want to be independent of black men just as much as I want independence from the white.* It is just that achieving the latter involves all black men, or at least those who have not already taken those available roads into the mainstream I mentioned earlier—subservience, cowardice and loss of manhood.[43] [my emphasis]

Although in a few years Jones became an ardent black nationalist, in 1962 he comprehended nationalism as a collective means toward an individual end. It was a necessary but strategic evil. Blacks should unify, but only to attain the benefits of liberal freedom or what Isaiah Berlin called "negative liberty," the freedom of the individual from unjustified external constraint.[44] Any racial unity that extended beyond the role of liberalism's midwife was a denial of freedom. Predictably, in 1962 LeRoi Jones was an individualist, for individual authenticity was the driving ambition of the bohemian life. At this point in time, Jones was somewhat Ellisonian in his understanding of America as a racially hybrid society. "America is as much a black country as a white one.

The lives and destinies of the white America are bound up inextricably with those of the black Americans."[45] Thoroughly American, blacks had a vested interest in expanding their freedom within the confines of this nation and its purportedly democratic ethos.

Despite the centrality of blacks to American life and the rich cultural interdependencies of racial groups, Jones did not conclude that the United States was therefore democratic. In the 1962 essay "City of Harlem," Jones used Harlem as the focal point for an eclectic commentary on the economic and political marginalization of black America. Whereas he had once considered Harlem a black bourgeois enclave, he now proclaimed it the "capital of Black America." For Jones, Harlem was simultaneously a myth and a material reality intersecting to produce an image of black Americans and black life full of contradictions. On the one hand, Harlem represented pleasure—a raucous, expressive black joie de vivre and a sensualistic release from inhibitions. On the other hand, Harlem also represented immorality and childlike blacks too lazy to take advantage of their opportunities.

Jones offers a very short history of the evolution of Harlem into a predominantly black neighborhood. He traces the momentary allure that Harlem held for hip white voyeurs during the Jazz Age of the 1920s. With the arrival of the Depression, however, the jazzy glitter of Harlem could no longer mask its actuality as a site of black subjugation.

> For many Negroes Harlem is a place one escapes from, and lives in shame about for the rest of his life. But this is one of the weirdest things about the American experience, that it can oppress a man, almost suck his life away, and then make him so shamed that he was among the oppressed, rather than the oppressors, that he will never offer any protest.[46]

Although Jones clearly meant to be sympathetic to the people inhabiting Harlem, his ignorance of their political history is somewhat demeaning. After all, black Harlemites had engaged in numerous protests throughout the twentieth century, including the two major race riots of 1935[47] and 1943. Harlem had given a platform to Rev. Adam Clayton Powell Jr., arguably the most significant black protest figure in American politics between the death of Ida Wells Barnett and the rise of Malcolm X and Martin Luther King Jr. An even greater testimony to the richness of Harlem's protest tradition was its receptivity to communism. Harlem had been the only major black community during the Depression to sustain an active presence by the Communist Party, even to the point of electing Benjamin Davis Jr., a black Communist Party official, to the New York City Council in 1943.[48]

In attempting to dissect myths about Harlem, Jones created his own. In his case, the new myth was that of a Harlem too subjugated to protest politically but too alive not to sustain eclectic articulations of Negro creative energy and nonconformity. Reminiscent of Norman Mailer's "White Negro," Jones wrote that "any black American, simply by virtue of his blackness, is weird, a nonconformist in this society."[49] Such a view indicates Jones's continued concern about the image of blacks in white eyes. Certainly, black Harlemites did not view one another as weird nonconformists. More important, in romanticizing the outsider identity of blacks, Jones placed a well-worn bohemian veneer over Harlemites. Jones was somewhat ambivalent about Harlem, an ambivalence that mirrored his attitudes toward black America. In the short essay "Cold, Hurt, and Sorrow (Streets of Despair)," Jones speaks of Harlemites as depressed and defeated, beaten down by years of neglect, humiliation, racist subjugation. This Harlem is a living mortuary. Yet in "Street Protest," another essay written in 1962, Jones describes the proliferation of political speakers on the sidewalks of Harlem. It is an essay that celebrates Harlem as a democratic public space, one in which black thinkers and charlatans are given the right to speak. This Harlem is quite different from that Harlem described in "City of Harlem." Jones was fixated on Harlem. The bohemian Race Man was trying to fashion a worldview that allowed him to grasp the wretchedness of black subjugation without denying black agency. He did not successfully merge these contradictory impulses until he adopted black cultural nationalism. For now, Harlem was a thorn in the side of his existence in the Village, a constant reminder that increased freedom for individual blacks, including black bohemians, had no impact on the unfreedom that governed the lives of most blacks.

One attempt by Jones to wade through the artistic labyrinth of the Afro-American victim status was his 1962 address "The Myth of a Negro Literature." Delivered before a gathering of black artists and intellectuals of the American Society for African Culture, Jones castigated black writers for creating fiction mainly to obtain white recognition. He claimed that black writers, particularly novelists, were guilty of copying white artistic mediocrity in their quest for whites' acceptance. Instead of being preoccupied with aesthetic issues, black writers were preoccupied with social/literary status. Jones cited Phyllis Wheatley and Charles Chesnutt as examples of early black writers who sought to obtain the status of the "exceptional Negro" (a Negro who wants to be seen by whites as being "unlike" the other Negroes). The "exceptional Negro" is a parasitic status because it is formed by appearing to be distant and different from other blacks, blacks who may be justly penalized for being the way that they are. The status of the "exceptional" black is a status rooted in the most explicit desire for white acceptance and hatred of one's own affinities with other blacks.

Jones could not persuasively claim, without substantiation, that Wheatley or Chesnutt were aspiring to an exceptional Negro status. The mere fact that they were Negroes who lived in a more affluent manner than most blacks of their time did not make them guilty of seeking exceptionalism. Jones implied that middle-class status alone indicated the presence of a quest for exceptionality, but he offered no proof. Wheatley was not middle class. She was a slave, a slave to a somewhat benevolent master, but a slave nonetheless. Jones writes about her as if she were vacationing in Oak Bluffs.

Jones viewed jazz and the blues as black Americans' greatest artistic statements, a result largely of the unwillingness of black musicians to defer to the assessments of jazz by white American music critics and the white American populace in general. Had Afro-American jazz, blues, and gospel musicians sought the bourgeois respectability that accompanied the recognition of whites, they would have killed the uniqueness of black music. Although it is a bit ludicrous to compare black music and black literature on some linear scale of creativity, Jones's point about the creative futility inherent in respectability-minded art was a sound critique of a well-used black victim-status aesthetic dating back to Du Bois and others.[50] Such an approach to literature did not allow black writers to investigate the "soul" of black people, a necessary step in creating serious black literature. Protest literature also was inadequate precisely because it, too, was primarily "other regarding."

Written four years before David Littlejohn's venerated commentary *Black on White: A Critical Survey of Writing by American Negroes*, Jones's "Myth of a Negro Literature" was similar in its harsh and sweeping denunciation of black literature:

> Only Jean Toomer, Richard Wright, Ralph Ellison, and James Baldwin have managed to bring off examples of writing . . . that could succeed in passing themselves off as "serious" writing, in the sense that say, the work of Somerset Maugham is "serious" writing. That is, serious, if one has never read Herman Melville or James Joyce. And it is part of the tragic naivete of the middle class (brow) writer that he has not.[51]

Divorced from the black community and a black literary tradition, the Village-based Jones tells black writers how to write good black fiction—this from the author of one small collection of poems. "The Myth of Negro Literature" is an apologia for his personal decision to distance himself from the

historical and contemporaneous black literary worlds. In a world that produced William Yeats and James Joyce, how could a writer with the ambitions
of Jones be inspired by Countee Cullen or John Oliver Killens? Jones's statements concerning Ellison and Toomer led the critic David Lionel Smith to
question whether Jones had read these authors before commenting on them:

> In this gospel according to Jones, black writers have failed. . . . Negro writ-
> ing, he argues, is inferior writing. Negro writers are not honest, and fur-
> thermore, they are ignorant. American racial discourse makes assertions
> of Negro ignorance inherently credible. Still, how could anyone read the
> first 10 pages of *Invisible Man* and claim that Ellison has not read Melville
> and Joyce?[52]

Smith perceives Jones as a participant in a long-standing racist discourse
about blacks, a racist discourse that leads Jones to patronize black writers,
some of whom may have been his artistic superiors. Smith continues:

> Jones's comments suggest that he probably had not read the work of these
> authors. In accusing them of ignorance, he reveals his own, but to be igno-
> rant of Negroes is no sin in our culture. After all, we assume Negroes to be
> unworthy of serious attention. Being black does not necessarily exempt us
> from the condescending modes of race thinking.[53]

Ironically, Jones's "Myth of Negro Literature" is actually a bid by a young
black writer for the status of exceptional Negro. He is a Negro writer but does
not want to be associated with a black literary tradition.

Another brazen but less conceptually developed critique of the black victim status appeared in the 1963 "Brief Reflections on Two Hot Shots," in
which Jones condemns two black writers, American James Baldwin and
South African Peter Abrahams. He implies that both men are less concerned
about writing about the struggles of their people than in proclaiming themselves men of refinement who have suffered dearly as a result of their plight.
In conveying their personal anguish, these men appear to write as if they want
their white oppressors to see them as individuals independent of their people,
who also were suffering. Jones states that if a writer has nothing to say but "'I
can feel' or 'I am intelligent' there is really no need saying it." That is, in their
quest for white recognition of their suffering, they do not take a stand. "A
writer must have a point of view . . . he must be standing somewhere in the
world, or else he is not one of us, and his commentary is of little value."[54]

Being unfamiliar with Peter Abrahams's writing, I cannot verify the validity of Jones's criticisms of him. At any rate, the Jones critique of Baldwin is misleading. At the very moment that this critique of Baldwin appeared in *Kulcher*, few in the American intellectual community would have claimed that James Baldwin's writings lacked a point of view. *Notes of a Native Son* (1955) and *Nobody Knows My Name* (1961) were neither noncommittal nor lacking a point of view. In 1963, the same year that Jones attacked Baldwin, Baldwin published *The Fire Next Time*. As a politicized essay writer, Baldwin, at his best, grasped a complexity in the Afro-American psyche and the American racial conundrum that forever eluded Jones (except perhaps in his play *Dutchman*).

More important, Baldwin did not merely whine about his treatment at the hands of whites. It is true that he wrote as a Christian-influenced moralist who believed in the redemptive nature of suffering. Nevertheless, Baldwin labeled as dehumanization his racist oppressors' urgency to subjugate black "others." In sum, he was not simply trying to invoke his specialness as a sufferer but to use suffering as cultural capital in his efforts to morally critique the world around him. Jones's misinterpretation of Baldwin may have been deliberate, as Baldwin's thought contained an element of the victim status that may have struck Jones as ethnically self-demeaning. Yet instead of concentrating on that one facet of Baldwin's writing, Jones attempted to sweep all of it under a rug of irrelevance. It was a clever polemical ploy but somewhat dishonest, and in overstating Baldwin's dependence on whites, Jones overstated his own posture:

> If Abrahams and Baldwin were turned white, for example, there would be no more noise from them. Not because they consciously desire that, but because then they could be sensitive in peace. Their color is the only obstruction I can see to this state they seek, and I see no reason they should be denied it for so paltry a thing as heavy pigmentation. Somebody turn them! And then perhaps the rest of us can get down to the work at hand. Cutting throats![55]

A dramatic but childish ending, Jones needed to explain why Baldwin's existence prevented him (and "the rest of us") from getting down to the work of cutting throats. As a foretaste of the pronouncements encouraging violence that emerged from Jones's pen during the Black Arts era, he invokes a disingenuous obstacle to explain why he cannot, just yet, actualize his threats.[56]

In the short 1963 essay "Black Writing," Jones extends his discussion of the plight of the Negro writer. He begins the essay focusing on the various debilitations faced by black writers as a result of the distorted and dishonest racist images that they must confront in their daily lives and work. Yet the racist devaluation of blacks offers black writers a unique vantage point for understanding America. Jones advises them to embrace their pariah identity and make use of their racial outsider status.

> I think though that there are now a great many young black writers in America who do realize that their customary isolation from the mainstream is a valuable way into any description they might make of an America. In fact, it is just this alienation that could serve to make a very powerful American literature.[57]

Jones was asserting that blacks had a dual social location and that this location might inspire enormous creativity.

> The vantage point is classically perfect—outside and inside—at the same time. Think of the great Irish writers— Wilde, Yeats, Shaw, Synge, Joyce, O'Casey and Beckett—and their clear and powerful understanding (social as well as aesthetic) of where they were and how best they could function inside and outside the imaginary English society, even going so far as teaching the mainstreamers their own language, and revitalizing it in the doing.[58]

At face value, this comparison of Irish writers and black American writers is enticing. This enticement no doubt stems from the enormous presence of these Irish writers in twentieth-century literature and the fact that they were members of a subjugated group that had been victimized by economic exploitation, colonization, and a vicious racism.[59] Nonetheless, the case of Irish writers is immensely different and probably incomparable to that of black American writers. The main shortcoming of the comparison lies in the colonial history of the Irish and the absence of such a history for blacks in the United States. Irish writers participated in numerous stages of anticolonial and postcolonial writing. Initially, anticolonial Irish writing of the twentieth century attempted to create a romantic historical memory of an Irish past before the arrival of the British. Some, like Yeats, yearned for an Irish romantic past before the time when "men gave their lives to Greece and Rome and Judea."[60] Irish anticolonialist writers were able to call on two distinct romantic pasts, one Celtic and the other Gaelic. But black Americans had no similarly indigenous black American, pre-American historical past. Since the antebellum period, black Americans' cultural outsider status in the United States has become more and more like a subcultural distinction. Afro-American cultural inventiveness has been part of American life for centuries.

Conversely, once Ireland became independent, writers like Joyce and, later, Beckett confronted Ireland's cultural dependence on England.

The significance of Jones's invocation of the Irish writers that he so admired is that even though these writers were members of a subjugated group, they won the acclaim of the broader European literary community. He now wanted blacks to take their place among the seminal literary artists of the Western world and to influence white minds. Ironically, blacks were already exerting such influence on the white world through their music.

In "What Does Nonviolence Mean?" an essay that was published in 1963 in the Jewish American journal *Midstream*, Jones offered his views on nonviolence as a strategy of black social change. Jones clearly perceived the victim-status syndrome inherent in Martin Luther King Jr.'s political project. Whereas black writers had mistakenly sought white acceptance, black nonviolent protesters were seeking to elicit white guilt. Jones mistakenly argued that nonviolence, as in nonviolent civil disobedience, was the strategy of the black bourgeoisie. In addition, he erred in claiming that nonviolent civil disobedience was acceptable in the eyes of the white powers that be. Ironically, King and the Southern Christian Leadership Conference (SCLC) had a larger base of support in the black working class than Baraka and other black nationalist militants would ever have. At the time, King's popularity among the black poor probably exceeded that of Malcolm X. Furthermore, it was not apparent that the black bourgeoisie viewed imprisonment in southern jails as a status-validating exercise. King, SCLC ministers, SNCC field organizers, and local NAACP activists were jailed repeatedly, and some were killed. Many were members of the black middle class. One such bourgeois fellow was the courageous, soft-spoken, college-educated Medgar Evers, head of the NAACP branch in Jackson, Mississippi. In universalizing his narrow exposure to the black bourgeois frivolity that he found at Howard University, Jones could not understand bourgeois blacks like Evers, King, Septima Clark, Ella Baker, Andrew Young, or Bob Moses.

Jones attributed too much significance to the celebration of King by northern white liberals like those who lived with him in the Village. Jones failed to view King and other black nonviolent activists through the eyes of the black community. Paradoxically, the "blacker" that Jones became, the more significance he attributed to white American perceptions of the Civil Rights movement. Jones's obsessive concern for the image of blacks in white minds endured throughout most of his political life.

Coincidentally, Martin Luther King Jr. shared Jones's concern with the image of blacks in white minds but did so from a diametrically different vantage point. King devised a leadership style that embodied bourgeois respectability, whereas Jones tried to tear it down. But King did not seek bourgeois respectability as an end in itself. Instead, his quest became a crucial ingredient of his strategy for social change. If blacks could project to whites an image of themselves as devout, well groomed, good mannered, property respecting, and sexually repressed, King believed that they might have a better chance of convincing whites that racist infringements on their rights were unjust. Jones's desire to flaunt bourgeois respectability was not linked to a strategy for social change, however, but was an end in itself, part of his deeply embedded bohemian tendencies.

Jones misunderstood the radical implications of King's bid for victim status. Hadn't it been the white South's claim that "our Negroes" were not unhappy with their plight? Jones was both angered and perplexed by black political leaders like King, who instructed black people to become objects of southern white brutality in order to obtain a victim status that could then give them the moral capital necessary to prick nonsouthern, white American popular concern. King believed that widespread white support would lead the federal government to act on behalf of subjugated southern blacks. In other words, King thought that he could use the victim status to undermine black political subjugation. Jones recognized that the problem with King's victim-status strategy (of reliving the Christ event) was that it does not and cannot lead to self-determination. King's strategy was so dependent on white moral gratuity that one may have wondered whether he was the tail that was wagged by the dog or the dog that wagged the tail.

In hindsight, it is clear that King miscalculated the nonsouthern black response to the white brutalization of southern black nonviolent civil disobedience. King's strategy relied on instigating white southern brutality against nonviolent, predominantly black demonstrators to generate nonsouthern white guilt toward southern blacks. This blueprint for inducing white guilt apparently overlooked those nonsouthern blacks who would not feel guilt but humiliation and rage as a result of this strategy. Consequently, many nonsouthern blacks became bent on revenge. However morally superior King and his followers may have appeared to whites in not fighting back, in the eyes of many nonsouthern blacks, black southern demonstrators seemed disgustingly weak. Like many northern blacks, Jones was outraged by the ways in which southern blacks were being brutalized by local law enforcement agencies.

After writing about racial tokenism, nonviolence, and other "black issues" in such a scathing manner, Jones edited and published an anthology in which all of the contributors, except for himself, were white Americans. *The*

Moderns: An Anthology of New Writing in America, was published by Corinth Books in 1963. As an additional rationale for his selections, Jones wrote:

> One characteristic that binds most of the writers in this volume together, at least as far as a common distinction which separates them immediately from the serious middlebrow establishment fiction of our era, is that for the most part they are interested in those personalities (and people) who exist outside the mainstream of the American social organism.[61]

I do not mean to imply that these writers were insufficiently innovative or dynamic but that Jones's criteria for selecting the creators of "the most interesting and exciting writing that has taken place in this country since the war"[62] evidently led him to dismiss all black writers but himself. Despite his protest against tokenism, Jones helped construct himself as a racial token. Once again, Jones was flirting with the status of "the exceptional Negro," the one who is not like the others.

A PLAYWRIGHT EMERGES

Jones never assumed the identity of a bohemian "who happened to be black," but he was able to construct a creative life in Beat bohemia despite the overwhelming whiteness of the Village scene. Jones's desire to become more explicitly politicized in his writings and actions initially gave rise to efforts to expand the boundaries of his bohemian art world. In contrast to the broader apoliticization of many of his closest bohemian confreres, Jones attempted to become increasingly politicized without abandoning his artistic community. He remained attracted to the idea that the artist's political sensibilities were best expressed aesthetically, but he now wanted to articulate his politics in more direct ways than could be sustained by the manipulation of poetic meter, metaphor, symbol, and rhythm. Although bohemian poetics were antagonistic to the broader society, their driving force was aesthetic innovation and protest (or implicit cultural critique). Jones's political desires led him to question the viability of avant-garde poetics. But these contradictory desires soon gave rise to unresolvable tensions that ultimately led Jones to reject bohemia. For now, however, these tensions fueled a momentous period of creativity.

In response to the growing Civil Rights movement, the Village theater scene became far more receptive to serious drama about black life. During the early 1960s, Langston Hughes's *Jericho Jim Crow*, James Baldwin's *Blues for*

Mister Charlie, and Martin Duberman's *In White America* opened in the Village. Despite this new interest in black theater, few theatergoers and critics were ready for the militancy introduced into the American theater by the relatively unknown playwright LeRoi Jones. Jones's entrance onto the American stage scared, angered, and inspired both blacks and whites. In addition to the content of his plays, Jones's emergence was magnified by the simultaneous opening of three of his plays in the Village during one week in March 1964. In his "Across the Footlights" column, *New York Post* drama critic Jerry Tallmer wrote: "This is LeRoi Jones week in the theater. A few days ago we had his *The Eighth Ditch* at the New Bowery, now shuttered by officialdom. Tonight we have his *Dutchman* at the Cherry Lane. And last night we had the premiere of his *The Baptism* at the Writers' Stage."[63]

FOUR PREREVOLUTIONARY BLACK PLAYS

The Baptism

The Baptism was first performed at the Writer's Stage Theater in New York City on March 23, 1964. It was part of a double bill with Frank O'Hara's *The General Returns from One Place to Another.*

The setting is the altar area of an affluent Baptist church. Minister is talking with Homosexual (the characters in the play are nameless). Although their dialogue is somewhat absurd, we learn that the homosexual is hip and celebrates sexuality while the finely tailored minister affects an air of piety. Homosexual knows that Minister is a fraud, and they informally but vulgarly needle each other. Interrupting their discussion, a young boy enters the church looking for the minister and expecting to be baptized. Boy is weeping as he begs the minister, whom he calls father, to pray for him. He admits to the minister that he needs absolution before he can be baptized.

Minister reassures crying Boy that there is nothing to fear from God, for God will not abandon him. As Minister talks to Boy, Old Woman rushes into the church shouting that the little boy is a wretched sinner, "an agent of the devil." Old Woman's accusations lead the minister to ask Boy just what he had done to make her angry. The boy denies knowing her or having seen her before now. The woman says that she saw him through her kitchen window as he was pretending to pray. The boy insists, "I was praying." But Old Woman cannot be sidetracked. Feeling divinely empowered to expose wrongdoings, the woman describes in detail how the boy appeared to pray but was really masturbating. Obviously aroused by the young boy's sexuality, Old Woman's gaze had been fixated on his penis. The passionate condemnations of the boy's soul are indications of the sexual excitement the woman felt. Old Woman describes his crime and then collapses as she tries to grab the young boy by the legs. Minister is also sexually attracted to Boy. As Old Woman elaborates her accusation, Minister is seen softly stroking Boy's head. Minister still believes that Boy can be saved, but he views Old Woman as having done a true Christian deed in reporting his masturbation. Boy admits that woman's charges were correct. He admits that "thinking of God always gives me a hard-on." Homosexual provides a running commentary. He tells Boy that he is not in need of saving. Instead, sex—like the devil—is a part of life and ultimately God's creation. For uttering such statements, Minister considers Homosexual to be blasphemous. Homosexual inquires and discovers that Boy has masturbated three times a day every day of that year. Homosexual comments, "That's one thousand ninety-five beatings. Not bad. Not bad."[64]

Six young women enter the church. They are the minister's "usherettes . . . holy young virgins." These women refer to the boy as the Christ child returned, the Son of God. While simultaneously moaning and kneeling in prayer, the women admit to the preacher that they have had sex with the Son of God, "our holy husband." The minister and the woman who accused the boy of masturbation throw themselves on their knees begging his forgiveness. They now believe that Boy is the returned Jesus. Instead, Boy beckons them to their feet while claiming, "I am not the Son of Man. I lied, I am not the Son of God."

At this point the minister and everyone present except Homosexual feels betrayed and angry at Boy. The women who had sex with Boy now proclaim that they have "fucked for nothing." In anger, Minister, Old Woman, and Women approach Boy, demanding that he be put to death as a sacrifice. Their motives are to cleanse themselves. Homosexual tries to protect the boy but is knocked out. Boy begs for forgiveness but sees that none is forthcoming. At that point the boy reveals his true identity as the Son of God and slashes all of them to death with a sword. Only Homosexual is spared.

After the Son of God kills the eight people, a messenger from God arrives on a motorcycle. He has been told by God to bring his son home, for he has "fucked up royally." The son asks God for another chance and begs him not to destroy the world. The son also refuses to return to Heaven. While resisting the order to return, he is clubbed unconscious by the messenger, who rides off with the son of man drooped over his motorcycle. The play ends when Homosexual awakens, extricates himself from beneath the pile of dead bodies, and decides to go to the bar before it closes. He knows nothing of the earth's impending doom.

The Baptism is a hilarious play criticizing the moral bankruptcy of the Christian Church, particularly the black church. The play reveals the dishonesty, phony love, and repressed sexuality that motivates the minister as well as the other believers. Sollors believes that *The Baptism*, Baraka's first attempt to explore the social implications of drama, does not quite succeed. The characters are underdeveloped, particularly the boy. The minister never earns a status worthy of murder; the women are too shallow and stereotypical; and Homosexual, who is depicted as a humorous if not ludicrous figure, remains the only character with any common sense. But Kimberly Benston considered *The Baptism* a "theatrical tour de force, a whirling succession of self-consciously struck poses, nonsense patter, surreal images and exposed perversions." According to Benston, Jones was influenced by the European theater of spectacle, particularly the works of Genet and Cocteau:

> Baraka unites images of the Sunday-morning commercialization of religious services, the garish bourgeois expression of wealth in religious edifices, and the sexual perversion latent in religious "ecstasy" and "worship" in one sweeping critique of the American Christian church and its cultural, moral and spiritual failures.[65]

Dutchman

In the estimation of most critics, *Dutchman* is Jones's best play. As his best-known single work, *Dutchman* launched Jones into prominence as an indignant and contentious voice of Afro-American literary protest. Reviewing the play in *The Nation* magazine, theater critic Harold Clurman wrote:

> *Dutchman* indicates the emergence of an outstanding dramatist—LeRoi Jones. His is a turbulent talent. While turbulence is not always a sign of power or of valuable meaning, I have a hunch that LeRoi Jones' fire will burn even higher and clearer if our theatre can furnish an adequate vessel to harbor his flame. We need it.[66]

The play begins with Clay, a black man, sitting alone in a speeding subway car. The train stops at a station where Clay's idle glance catches the gaze of an attractive red-headed white woman who is standing on the landing. They smile at each other. Lula enters the subway car from the rear door, carrying a bag and eating an apple. She walks to where Clay is sitting and flops down next to him. This act is conspicuous because empty seats are plentiful. Soon, staring directly at him, she accuses him of having stared at her "ass and legs" when she was standing at the station. Clay protests, whereupon the white woman informs him that she came close to the window so that he could get a better look at her body. Moreover, she boarded this train in order to see him, even though it is not going in her direction. Lula taunts Clay with sexual innuendoes. He perceives her as wanting to "pick him up." She succeeds in enticing Clay but speaks to him as if his response is utterly ludicrous. She says, "You think I want to pick you up, take me somewhere and screw me, huh?" He feigns ignorance. She begins to make educated guesses about him that are generally correct. She surmises that he is trying to grow a beard and that he lives in New Jersey with his parents. While not all this may be true, he is amazed that Lula knows about the beard and that he lives in Jersey. Baffled, he asks her if they have met before and quizzes her about potential mutual friends who must have told her about him. She attempts to further entice him, going as far as putting her hand on his knee and rubbing his thighs. She asks about his desire for her.

> LULA: Would you like to get involved with me, Mister Man?
> CLAY: Sure. Why not? A beautiful woman like you. Huh, I'd be a fool
> not to.[67]

Still intrigued by her knowledge about him, he once again asks about her source. Lula responds, "I told you that I don't know anything about you . . . you're a well-known type." She guesses correctly that he is on his way to a party and suggests to him that he ask her to come along. He agrees to do so but first asks her name. After a few games, she tells him her name is Lula. He tells her to guess his name. She mocks "colored" New Jersey names but is unsuccessful. When Clay gives her a choice of three last names from which to guess his, she does so correctly, "Williams." Clay then asks her to go to the party with him, but she replies that she doesn't know him. They exchange small talk, but Lula is annoyed.

> LULA: . . . What've you got that jacket and tie on in all this heat for?
> And why're you wearing a jacket and tie like that? Did your peo-
> ple ever burn witches or start revolutions over the price of tea?
> Boy, those narrow-shoulder clothes come from a tradition you
> ought to feel oppressed by. . . . What right do you have to be wear-
> ing a three-button suit and striped tie? Your grandfather was a
> slave, he didn't go to Harvard.
> CLAY: My grandfather was a night watchman.[68]

Not recognizing the theme of her taunts, Clay continues to converse with her. She snidely asks him just who it is that he thinks he was in college and is today. He informs her that in college he imagined himself as Baudelaire. Lula mockingly responds, "I bet you never once thought you were a black nigger." Their dialogue continues, and Lula informs him that her mother was a communist. Clay's mother, he claims, was a Republican. This first scene ends with Lula telling Clay that he is a murderer. Clay doesn't understand.

The second scene begins with Lula hugging Clay's arm. A few other people are now seated in the car. Clay's tie has been loosened, and he seems more relaxed. Lula fantasizes about what they will do at the party and later when they arrive at her apartment. Of course, the evening she describes culminates in sex. As she predicts these events, Clay is kissing her neck and fingers and appears excited about his forthcoming sexual escapade with Lula. Once again Lula "shifts gears" and begins a critique of Clay. The train begins to fill with people, all of whom are white. Clay expresses mild but meaningless surprise that they are no longer alone. He is more aware of the numerical presence of the people than their particular racial identities. Lula tells him that she knows those people even better than she knows him. She wonders whether he is now frightened. Astonished by the question, Clay indicates that he does not know why he would be scared.

CLAY: . . . Why should they frighten me?

LULA: 'Cause you are an escaped nigger.

CLAY: Yeah?

LULA: 'Cause you crawled through the wire and made tracks to my side.

CLAY: Wire?

LULA: Don't they have wire around plantations?

CLAY: You must be Jewish. All you think about is wire. Plantations didn't have any wire. Plantations were big open whitewashed places like heaven, and everybody on 'em was grooved to be there. Just strummin' and hummin' all day . . . and that's how the blues was born.[69]

Repeating Clay's refrain, "and that's how the blues was born," Lula dances up and down the subway aisle, bumping into people. Somewhat amused, Clay tries to mask his embarrassment by engaging her in humorous banter. Lula ups the ante by calling on Clay to dance with her. Lula taunts, "Come on, Clay, Let's rub bellies on the train. The nasty. The nasty. Do the gritty grind, like your ol' rag head mammy." Clay becomes increasingly angered by Lula and her public display of annoyance at his refusal to accede to her demands to dance. She calls him a middle-class black bastard, a liver-lipped white man. "You would-be Christian. You ain't no nigger, you're just a dirty white man." Following more racial invectives from Lula, Clay tries to grab her but fails. Lula continues to taunt him, calling him "Uncle Tom-Thomas Woolly-Head." Other whites seated on the train laugh at her comments. A drunk white man gets up from his seat and tries to dance with her. Now angered, Clay punches the drunk to the floor, grabs Lula, and slings her into her seat. Undaunted, she tells him that he fears white people. Clay slaps her twice very hard and then states:

> I could murder you now. Such a tiny ugly throat. I could squeeze it flat, and watch you turn blue, on a humble. For dull kicks. All these weak-faced ofays squatting around here, staring over their papers at me. Murder them too. . . . It takes no great effort. For what? To kill you soft idiots? You don't understand anything but luxury.[70]

In denying her accusation that he feared whites, Clay asserts that he has no need to fear whites, since he could, with ease, murder all the whites seated on the subway. But Clay does not explain that given the ease with which he could kill whites, why it is that he dances to the puppet strings held by whites. In what may be the most revealing lines in the play, Clay states,

> If I'm a middle-class fake white man . . . let me be. . . . Let me be who I feel like being. Uncle Tom. Thomas. Whoever. It's none of your business. You don't know anything except what's there for you to see. An act. Lies. Device. Not the pure heart, the pumping black heart. . . . I sit here, in this button-up suit, to keep myself from cutting all your throats.[71]

As if the audience would not find such dialogue sufficiently scandalous, Clay crudely questions Lula's pretensions of familiarity with blacks.

> You great liberated whore. You fuck some black man and right away you're an expert on black people. What a lotta shit that is. The only thing you know is that you come if he bangs you hard enough. . . . The belly rub? You don't even know how. . . . Belly rub is not Queens.[72]

He tells her that Charlie Parker wouldn't have played his sax had he just walked up to East Sixty-seventh Street and killed the first ten white people that he saw.

If Bessie Smith had killed some people she wouldn't have needed that music. She could have talked very straight and plain about the world. No metaphors. No grunts. . . . Crazy niggers turning their backs on sanity. When all it needs is that simple act. Murder. Just murder! Would make us all sane. Ahh Shit. But who needs it? I'd rather be a fool. Insane. Safe with my words, and no deaths, and clean, hard thoughts, urging me to new conquests.[73]

Lula informs Clay that she has heard enough. Clay begins to collect his briefcase and books in order to get off the train. Facetiously, he apologizes to Lula for short-circuiting their sexual plans for that night. When he bends down to retrieve his belongings, she plunges a knife into him. Clay dies. The train stops at a station. As if on cue, the other white passengers on the train pick up his body and, on Lula's orders, toss it off the train. Following her instructions, the whites get off the train at the next stop. The play ends as another solitary young black man enters the train and sits several seats behind Lula. She turns around and stares at him. A black conductor shuffles down the aisle, says hello to the black man, tips his hat at Lula, and continues through the door of the car.

Dutchman is primarily an absurdist play, with elements of realism. Jones did not create a coherent plot or maintain a realistic stage setting. The play contains themes that appear in Jones's work throughout the 1960s. First, Clay, the assimilated bourgeois Negro, is not only artificial but is also attracted to death (in the form of Lula's stupefying whiteness). It is his cultural assimilation that makes him vulnerable to Lula's evil intentions, for he is preoccupied with the belief that he is just "one of the crowd." Thus, there was nothing unusual about Lula's come-on to him. Clay does everything in his power to ignore the realization that this white woman sees him as a black other. She, of course, forces him to confront their racial difference. When he does so, he explodes. Through his repressed rage, we see the "real Clay," or what Jones has described elsewhere as "a renegade behind the mask. And even the mask, a renegade disguise."[74]

Although Clay carries himself as a respectable figure, he seems incapable of rejecting the overtures of a less than respectable white woman. Why is he so enticed by this crazed white woman? Do we see images of "Crow-Janeism" here? On another level, Lula may represent white America and its death-dealing enticements to all blacks who believe that they have entered the ranks of the racially "acceptable." The repressed rage of blacks is not unknown to whites. Whites merely demand that such anger remain repressed, for all that matters to them is how blacks navigate public space. When such rage is publicly articulated, whites will respond in a repressive manner, perhaps even with murder.

Symbolically, the play invokes images of Eden and the fallen woman. Lula enters the train eating an apple. The play moves from innocence and ignorance through knowledge to death. Yet, as Leslie Sanders notes, Lula is both serpent and an aspiring Eve. She is not quite Eve because she does not really seek or possess any "true" knowledge, even though her stereotypes of Clay are well grounded. She does know a great deal about Clay's repressed anger and its short fuse. It is obvious that the play concerns the sexual energies between a white woman and a black man, a taboo relationship that in the past led to the murder of many black males. For an audience aware of this historical backdrop, the anxieties and fears generated by the play become all the more intense because of the black male's naïveté and the white female's apparent sexual abandon and aggressiveness.

Harold Clurman perceived more in Jones's anger than a protest against white racism. Instead, he imagined Lula as "the absolute neurosis of American society."

> She is "hip": she has heard about everything, understands and feels nothing. She twitches, jangles, jitters with a thin but inexhaustible energy, propelled by the vibrations from millions of ads, television quiz programs, newspaper columns, intellectual jargon culled from countless digests, panel discussions. . . . She is the most "informed" person in the world and the most ignorant. . . . She is the bubbling, boiling garbage cauldron newly produced by our progress. She is a calculating machine gone berserk; she is the real killer. What she destroys is not men of a certain race but mankind.[75]

By removing the play's racial implications, Clurman certainly softens its message. In his eyes, *Dutchman* is less of an indictment of white America than an indictment of American civilization—which thankfully, for Clurman, has no racial specificity. Ironically, Clurman probably thinks that he is elevating the play's status by making its racial message of secondary importance.

Jones also, at times, softened the play's racial image. In an interview published in 1964, he added to the confusion surrounding the meaning of *Dutchman*. Jones argued that the play had no broader social message. When asked if Lula represented all of white America, he asked:

> But how can one white person be all white persons, unless all white persons are alike? . . . Similarly, it is equally stupid to think of the Negro boy as all Negroes, even though, as I've said, most white people do think of black men simply as Negroes and not as individual men. But I showed one white girl

and one Negro boy in that play, and the play is about one white girl and one Negro boy, just them, singularly, in what I hope was a revelation of private and shared anguish.

But I will say this, if the girl (or the boy) in that play has to "represent" anything, I mean if she must be symbolic in the way demented academicians use the term, she does not exist at all. She is not meant to be a symbol, but a real person, a real thing, in a real world. She does not represent any thing—she is one. And perhaps that thing is America, or at least its spirit. . . . *Dutchman* is about the difficulty of becoming a man in America. It is very difficult to be sure, if you are black, but I think it is now much harder to become one if you're white.[76]

What is striking about this particular "spin" on Jones's play is that it did not last long. In a very short time, he could be heard referring to *Dutchman* as a metaphor of black-white interactions in the United States.

Howard Taubman, theater critic for the *New York Times*, was overwhelmed by *Dutchman*:

Everything about LeRoi Jones's *Dutchman* is designed to shock—its basic idea, its language and its murderous rage. This half-hour long piece . . . is an explosion of hatred rather than a play. It puts into the mouth of its principal Negro character a scathing denunciation of all the white man's good works, pretensions and condescensions. . . . If this is the way the Negroes really feel about the white world around them, there's more rancor buried in the breasts of colored conformists than anyone can imagine. If this is the way even one Negro feels, there is ample cause for guilt as well as alarm and for a hastening of change.[77]

The power of *Dutchman* stemmed from its message and the shocking but intelligent manner in which it was conveyed. Ironically, the play's dramatic power became for some critics, particularly some perverse white critics, a sign of its dishonesty. After all, a Negro playwright who could write in such a powerful fashion and have his play produced could not really harbor such rage against whites and white racism. If white Americans had been as racist as Jones's play described them, how could we explain the existence of Jones, the writer? And how do we explain his marriage to a white woman?

Jones's *Dutchman* forced whites to confront their own wishful thinking concerning American racial dynamics. His willingness to express black disgust with whites was interpreted by many whites as hateful. Yet hidden beneath such assessments was the nagging reality that however much whites may have believed that blacks wanted to love them, they also knew that blacks had reason to hate them.

The play also comments on certain existential choices confronting black American intellectuals/artists who were using the written and spoken word as the primary means to assert their existence and/or protest their subjugation. In a moment of profound introspection, Clay states that instead of murdering white people, he would "rather be a fool. Insane. Safe with my words, and no deaths." Clay's statements imply that writing, at least for subjugated black Americans, is an act of weakness or cowardice insofar as it constitutes a decision to remain safely away from the repression that the state might unleash on political activists. The British critic C. W. E. Bigsby captured the dilemma confronting Jones (via Clay):

> His doubts about language extend to the work itself in which action tells a truth which the words would conceal. His doubts about his position as a writer, warning against the deceptions of language, pose questions which not only address the special circumstances of the committed artist but also acknowledge the unreliability of language itself. In other words the insecurities that he confronts go beyond simple acts of racial prejudice, just as the real betrayal that he addresses is the betrayal of the self rather than the other. Clay is condemned to death and Lula to her everlasting task because, like the Flying Dutchman, they have in a sense blasphemed against the natural order. They have betrayed themselves.[78]

The Toilet

The Toilet is a one-act play that takes place in a high school lavatory. The lavatory is dirty and reeks of urine. It is at the end of the school day, and several black male students casually enter the lavatory in anticipation of an impending fight. The would-be combatants are not yet present. Instead we are witness to the badgering among several of the black students. Most frightening is the gang bully, the pathologically violent Ora. The others don't joke with Ora in the same manner as they do with one another. Always one step away from ferocity, the tormented Ora does not know how to "play."

We learn from several characters that James Karolis, a white male student ("a paddy") is being chased on the third floor of the school by a group of black male students. Terrified, Karolis has been difficult to corner. But word comes to those waiting in the lavatory that Karolis is now locked in a third-floor closet and will soon be brought to the basement lavatory where he will be forced to fight. The black guy who is supposed to have the "beef" with Karolis is Ray Foots. Foots, the leader of the gang, has not yet entered the lavatory. He is in class, where he is a favorite student of the teacher. His studiousness clearly distinguishes him from the other gang members.

Wanting to see the fight, other black males soon enter the lavatory. One black student brings with him a white male student, Donald Farrell. Farrell does not know that he has been brought there by his black friend to watch a fight. Several of the black students present, including Ora, demand that Farrell leave. After much protest and banter, he is allowed to stay. Ora then informs Farrell that they all plan to "kick Karolis's ass," an assertion more indicative of Ora's desires than the collective ambitions of the other black fellows present. One black gang member says that he isn't going to fight Karolis ("Shit Karolis never bothered me"). When Farrell protests the impending gang assault of Karolis, Ora punches him in the stomach. Farrell is doubled over when a bloody-faced Karolis is dragged in by two gang members. Already beaten, Karolis is dropped on the floor. Ora goes over to the beaten lad and taunts him to suck his penis. Ignorant of the preceding events, Foots, the gang leader, enters the room joking, only to be startled when he sees Karolis's condition. He manages to mask his shock. It is made clear to the audience that Foots does not want to fight Karolis but that the other gang members are not aware of his ambivalence. Because of his rhetorical agility, Foots is almost able to avoid the fight on the pretense that Karolis has already been beaten. "Just poor water on the cat and let's get outta here." Upon hearing Foots's rationale for not going through with the arranged fight, Farrell, the other white guy, states, "I sure am glad somebody got's some sense here." In making this statement, Farrell unknowingly stigmatizes Foots as an "exception," more sensible than the other black fellows present, particularly Ora. Farrell thus has inadvertently undermined Foots's strategy for avoiding the fight, for he makes Foots look as if in not fighting, he is siding with the "white boy" against his black gang. Foots, recognizing the danger that Farrell presents, demands that he leave. Farrell won't, perhaps believing that his presence will prevent a gang attack on Karolis. He demands to know why Foots is going to fight Karolis. Foots remains adamant about making Farrell leave, but one of the gang members mentions out loud that the fight is over a letter that Karolis sent to Foots. Now aware of the reasons behind the imminent fight, Farrell responds as if he knows more about the Foots-Karolis relationship than the gang members do. After Farrell is forcibly thrown out of the lavatory, Foots is about to leave when Karolis speaks up, announcing a desire to fight him.[79]

KAROLIS: No. You have to fight me. I sent you that note, remember. That note saying I loved you. The note saying you were beautiful. You remember that note, Ray?

FOOTS: Goddamn it, if you're going to fight, fight you cocksucker.

KAROLIS: Yeh. That's what I'm going to do Ray. I'm going to fight you. We're here to fight. About that note, right? The one that said I wanted to take you in my mouth.

Did I call you Ray in that letter . . . or Foots? Foots! I'm going to break your fucking neck. That's right. That's the one I want to kill. Foots![80]

The fight begins. When it becomes clear to the gathered crowd that Karolis is getting the upper hand, the gang jumps in. Foots, who was being strangled by Karolis, crawls on his hands and knees away from the gang attack. Only Ora has the audacity to admit what they all know, that "good ole" Foots was beaten by Karolis. Some gang members help Foots to his feet. They all leave. Karolis's motionless body remains sprawled on the floor. A short time later, Foots returns to the lavatory, stares at the outstretched Karolis, and kneels before his limp body, weeping and cradling his bloodied head.

As Werner Sollors notes, the meaning of *The Toilet* is not apparent. Even Jones sometimes offered two contrasting interpretations of the play. In the "Introduction by the Playwright" that accompanied *The Toilet* when it was included in the collection *The Best Plays of 1964–65*, Jones described these competing interpretations:

> *The Toilet* is about the lives of black people. White people tell me it is not. They have no way of knowing, but they insist they do. They try to deny my version (and any black man's version) of American reality, on the stage, just as they do in the street. . . .
>
> *The Toilet* is also a play about love. And a boy's inability (because he is a victim) to explain that he is something stranger than the rest, even though the blood and soul of him is as theirs. It is a play about social order, and what it can mean, ie: the brutality its insistence will demand, if it is not an order which can admit of any man's beauty.[81]

Gerald Weales also found competing meanings in *The Toilet*:

Given Jones's obsessive concern with his own identity in his work, the struggle that he defines as a pull between whiteness and blackness, the play is ironic since its final effect is to suggest that Foots has lost by his choice. It is possible, however, to read the play in other than racial terms, as the story of a boy, lacking the courage to face his own individuality and its implications, who chooses the mindless, cheerful brutality of the group.[82]

According to Harold Clurman's review, *The Toilet* was fundamentally about hypocrisy.

> The two youths who beat each other nearly to death are secretly and shame-facedly in love with each other. That the love is between black and white as well as being homosexual is undoubtedly significant, but far less significant than that we are made to realize that its frustration must result in the most shameful and horrifying cruelty.[83]

In "That Boy LeRoi,"[84] a review of *The Toilet* that appeared in *New York Post*, Langston Hughes also read the play as being more concerned about un-requited homosexual love than about race. Hughes recommended that the play be racially double-cast "for the sake of sensitive Negroes and battered white liberals." He also proposed changing the performers' racial identities on alternating nights.

> Every other night, let all the present Negro characters be played by white ac-tors, and vice versa. Four times a week I would like to see *white* school boys in "The Toilet" beating up a *colored* boy and sticking his head into a urinal. . . . Black would then be white—and white, black—which alternatively would cancel out each other.[85]

Hughes's suggestion would thoroughly revise the meaning of the play, turn-ing it into a love story only, a story of two individuals. But to write as if the characters' racial identities were incidental would be to ignore the desperate-ness of black urban life that Jones depicted so well. Jones situated the homo-phobic violence in the cultural context of a high school, a location in which these black males had no agency. In beating Karolis, the cowardly black gang members were able to witness the triumph of their worldview over that of the school environment. The ending of the play in which Foots cradles Karolis seems contrived, as it is not earned by the preceding dialogue and actions and appears more shocking than tragic. The final scene can be read as a racial res-olution of sorts, a re-connectedness between the two interracial lovers (turned racial antagonists) that transcends racial conflict.

Jones has admitted to having compromised the meaning of the play in order to introduce the possibility of interracial harmony. In a 1978 interview, he stated,

> The ending is peculiar because I tacked it on. It actually invokes my own social situation at the time. . . . If you ever look at the manuscript you'll see that the manuscript stops at the end of the fight. But then I sat there for a while thinking, was that really the way it had to end? . . . Well the whole thing needed some kind of rapprochement—there was a question of wanting to offer that kind of friendship that existed across traditional social lines. At the time I was married to a white woman, and most of the friends I had were white, on the Lower East Side. I didn't go round thinking in my mind this is the case, but I think that is why that kind of ending seemed more appropriate to me at the time.[86]

The Slave

Often viewed as Baraka's most racially militant play, *The Slave* opened on December 16, 1964, at St. Mark's Playhouse, on a double bill with *The Toilet*. A prologue proceeds the main narrative of the play. Walker, the central character, appears as an old, white-haired field slave dressed in ragged clothing and grinning. His physical movements are reminiscent of Willie Best. Walker delivers a soliloquy worthy of an academic philosopher:

> Whatever the core of our lives. Whatever the deceit. We live where we are, and seek nothing but ourselves. We are liars, and we are murderers. We invent death for others. Stop their pulses publicly. Stone possible lovers with heavy worlds we think are ideas . . . and we know, even before these shapes are realized, that these worlds, these depths or heights we fly to smoothly, as in a dream, or slighter, when we stare dumbly into space, leaning our eyes just behind a last quick moving bird, then sometimes the place and twist of what we are will push and sting, and what the crust of our stance has become will ring in our ears and shatter that piece of our eyes that is never closed.

The prologue is a call to distrust habitual perceptions and long-held certitudes. The slave tries to unsettle all our preconceived notions:

> I am much older than I look . . . or maybe much younger. Whatever I am or seem . . . to you, then let that rest. But figure, still, that you might not be right. Figure, still, that you might be lying . . . to save yourself.[87]

While some students of Baraka's drama have offered an intricate analysis of the prologue's meaning, others have ignored it in favor of dissecting the meaning of the main narrative.

The main narrative of the play concerns a race war in the United States at some unspecified moment in the future. During a raging battle, Walker Vessels, the leader of the blacks, leaves the ranks of his fighting comrades and walks alone, behind enemy lines, to the house now occupied by his former wife, who has custody of their two daughters. Grace, his former wife, is white. She lives on the "white America" side of town with her two biracial daughters and second husband, Bradford Easley, a white man. Easley is Walker's former literature professor. Grace divorced Walker and took custody of their daughters in response to his intensifying allegiances to black nationalism and his growing hatred of whites. Walker is tortured by ambivalence. He is the revolutionary leader of blacks, and yet he remains sentimental about Grace. Nonetheless, Walker has not come here to pursue his former wife. Instead we are informed that he has come to Grace's house to take back his two "black" daughters with him to the side of "black America."

Most of the play takes place in the bourgeois intellectual ambience of the well-appointed house that Grace and Easley call home. Grace is beautiful and blond. Easley is stereotypically depicted as a wimpy white liberal professor. Easley is an expert on literature and friendly toward the Negroes but opposes their revolutionary intentions. He emphatically expresses disdain for the blacks who are shelling the city and destroying the country. Unknown to both Grace and Easley, Walker has broken into their home while they were out.

Upon entering the house with Grace, Easley removes the protective steel helmet that has become a necessity in the face of the race war. He is startled to find Walker Vessels standing in the living room holding a pistol. Annoyed and angered by Vessels's intrusion into his house, Easley tells Walker, "Look, you arrogant maniac, if you get drunk or fall out here, so help me, I'll call the soldiers . . . and turn you over to them. . . . If I get the slightest advantage, some cracker soldier will be bayoneting you before the night is finished." Annoyed with Easley's arrogance, Walker slaps him several times and pushes the gun barrel into Easley's stomach. He is knocked to the floor. Grace is angered and hysterically calls Walker a "nigger murderer." Humorously surprised, Walker asks Grace how long had she been harboring the desire to call him a nigger. Grace begs him to leave before he kills somebody, particularly another white person. Walker tells her that only she and Brad are white, that the two daughters upstairs are black. "You know circa 1800, one drop makes you whole."[88]

This argument continues, as does Walker's drinking. Intermittently, Walker speaks to Grace in a warm and tender manner as if he is still haunted by her departure from his life. Clearly, it is important to Walker that Grace understand him. Occasionally Walker exchanges comments with Easley concerning poetry he had written under Easley's tutelage. He even recites some of his badly written verse, which Easley wittily condemns. Easley chides Walker for not being with his troops, asking, "How can the black liberation movement spare its illustrious leader for such a long stretch?"

Walker becomes increasingly intoxicated but manages to announce to Grace's horror that he has come to take the two girls with him. She panics at the idea but cannot decide whether Walker really wants their daughters or is merely saying something that he thinks will terrify her. Ultimately she believes that he has come for the girls as if to rescue them from her and Brad in the same way that she had earlier rescued them from Walker's antiwhite hatred. Grace fears losing her daughters more than anything else.

> GRACE: . . . You're lying. You don't want those children. You just want to think you want them for the moment. . . . Today you want to feel like you want the girls. Just like you wanted to feel hurt and martyred by your misdirected cause, when you first drove us away.
>
> WALKER: Drove you away? You knew what I was in to. You could have stayed. You said you wanted to pay whatever thing it cost to stay.[89]

Walker continues to state that he wants to take his two daughters. Easley cannot understand how Walker can have so much love for two little girls but still manage to kill large numbers of people. Walker states that in spite of the people that he has killed and in spite of his responsibility for single-handedly starting the war between whites and blacks, he still loves those girls.

Walker then acknowledges the ultimate futility of his revolutionary activities. He admits that "this is at best a war that will only change the complexion of tyranny." He expresses his contempt for his fellow black officers by referring to them as "ignorant motherfuckers who have never read any book in their lives." He even goes as far as to admit that he would rather discuss politics and literature with Easley rather than his black officers.[90]

Grace, fearing that Walker will abduct the children, tries to persuade Easley to physically intervene. Walker is shocked at her naïveté. Evidently she does not really understand that he would, without hesitation, kill Easley if necessary. He then informs Grace that he thought she would have understood his need to condemn all white people. He thought that if any white person could understand his need, it would have been Grace. But even though they had been together a long time, she didn't understand.

> GRACE: Walker you were preaching the murder of all white people. Walker, I was, am, white. What do you think was going through my mind every time you were at some rally or meeting whose sole purpose was to bring about the destruction of white people?
> WALKER: Oh Goddam it, Grace, are you so stupid? You were my wife . . . I loved you. You mean because I loved you and was married to you . . . had children by you, I wasn't supposed to say the things I felt. I was crying out against three hundred years of oppression; not against individuals.[91]

Grace becomes more emotionally involved, even saddened by this nostalgic journey through their marital demise. Easley intervenes and asks Walker if he really thinks that blacks could run the society in a more just and equitable fashion. "Do you think Negroes are better people than whites . . . that they can govern a society better than whites? Do you think they'll make fewer mistakes."[92] Walker cannot bring himself to deem blacks morally superior to whites. Instead, he responds that whites have had their chance, now blacks can have theirs. Following this fatalistic message, we hear explosions getting closer to the house. The house lights go off. Using the sudden darkness, Easley gets out of his chair and creeps silently and deliberately toward the sitting Walker, who is drunk with his head drooping toward the floor. Act 1 ends.

Act 2 begins with the sounds of explosions in the background. The lights in the house flicker. The battle outside is raging and coming closer by the minute. Walker, still drunk, sits with his head down as if nodding. Easley continues to tiptoe toward him. As he carefully advances, Grace continues her chatter in hopes of maintaining an air of normality. A nearby explosion rocks the house, and the lights suddenly come on. Walker's head jerks up, whereupon he sees the advancing Easley. Frozen, the two men stare into each other's eyes for several seconds. Now confronted with the reality of Walker's intentions, Grace screams "Walker" as if to plead for Easley's life. Easley jumps on Walker, but during the ensuing scuffle, Walker shoots him in the chest. Fatally wounded, Easley tries to speak, but Walker taunts him into silence. Walker screams at Easley to shut up and die quietly. Grace runs to her dying husband, who is lying on the floor. Walker tells Easley that he will not allow him to utter anything dignified before he dies. He can either shut up or repeat the lines "I only regret that I have but one life to lose for my country." Grace, angered and crying, grabs for Walker, but he throws her to the floor.

While lying on the floor, Grace ponders her future. With Easley now dead and Walker threatening to take the children, she worries about being left alone. Walker, still emotionally attached to Grace, asks her what she thought would happen to him when she took the children and left him alone. "Did you ever think about that?" Grace concedes that after leaving Walker, she began to pity him. Walker confesses that he became enraged for he recognized the smugness of her belief that she and Easley were "good and compassionate." He was even more enraged by the thought that Easley would pity him. Looking at Grace, he states, "You and that closet queen, respected, weak-as-water intellectual, pitying me. God. God!"

Grace now wonders if Walker will kill her. But he tells her that he has no intention of killing her. Is he still going to take the girls? she asks. Walker now shakes his head no. Grace, thrilled by this answer, wants to make sure and repeats the question while getting to her feet. At the very moment that she stands, an explosion rocks the house, and Grace is knocked down by a falling beam. Her chest is crushed. She is hurt badly but still manages to call to Walker to look in on the children. "Walker, the children . . . the girls . . . see about the girls." Walker also seriously hurt, crawls to Grace but can't help her. Walker tries to calm her, but she continues to tell him to check on the girls. Walker now standing, starts to climb the stairs but then stops. He tells Grace: "They're dead, Grace. Catherine and Elizabeth are dead." Grace cannot believe Walker's words. She wonders how he knows that they are dead. Her frantic last words are "How do you know they're dead, Walker?" Tortured by the possibility that Walker has killed their two daughters, Grace dies. Walker screams, "They're dead, Grace, dead!" He then stumbles out of the door of the house. At this point Walker's character reverts back to the old man at the beginning of the play. After more explosions and a silence, a child is heard crying and then loudly screaming. The curtain falls. More explosions are heard.

Jones's portrayal of a racial Armageddon was performed during a moment in the life of this nation when white people of goodwill were supporting black Americans' attempts to attain full citizenship status. Perhaps at no other time in the history of this country and the colonies that preceded it did white Americans appear to be more concerned about the plight of blacks. Such popular concern was the result of a massive nonviolent civil rights struggle that used hegemonic rhetoric about American freedom to legitimate black and white civil disobedience. While liberal white Americans probably knew that the status of blacks would not in the near and/or distant future be elevated to anything resembling racial equality, white liberalism was in a mood of self-celebration as historical barriers to black equality were being struck down. Enter *The Slave*.

Though shocking, the play's characters are akin to the ideal types employed in sociological theory by Max Weber and Georg Simmel. As ideal types they are exaggerated depictions of real phenomena. Easley is an ideal type of a white liberal male professor. He has every stereotypical quality associated with that image, including a soft body. Because it has no complex characterizations, the dialogue in *The Slave* is stilted, and the plot is predictable. Who did not know that Walker would somehow murder Easley but not Grace? And the unresolved status of the children is more annoying than provocative. Why would Walker kill them, or why would he want Grace to think that he killed them? —And if he didn't kill them, why didn't he check on them after the explosion that killed Grace? It is one thing to view Walker as a morally flawed revolutionary, but Jones's ending makes him out to be a rather disgusting thug, whereupon the play loses any semblance of meaning. After commenting on the play's dramatic failure, Gerald Weales teases out its potential meanings:

> Jones calls his play a "fable." Presumably the moral is that whites and blacks must hate each other, and not even love (the marriage of Grace and Walker) or friendship (if that is what Walker and Brad had) or education (Brad as professor) or art (Walker as poet) or reason ("The way things are, being out of your mind is the only thing that qualifies you to stay alive," says Walker) can alter that "fact."[93]

Howard Clurman interpreted *The Slave* as being concerned with

> the futility of the white man's liberalism and the hysteria its failure causes in the souls of those who suffer most through that failure. . . . What is actually communicated is the sense that our incapacity to make true contact with one another must head our world to a hopeless shapeless shambles—destruction and annihilation with a "lesson."[94]

Unlike Weales, Clurman took Jones's bait and viewed *The Slave* as a political statement rather than a work of art about politics. He proclaimed the play important, not because it was good art, but because it conveyed a frightening idea. Commenting on the twin bill of *The Slave* and *The Toilet*, Clurman wrote, "I do not 'admire' these plays or call them 'good.' But despite their malformation and immaturity I believe them important. They are to be heeded. They say 'Beware.'"[95]

The Slave was undoubtedly intended to traumatize the whites in the audience. The failure of the play—and it was a great failure—lay in Jones's naive belief in dramatic shock therapy. By the time *The Slave* was produced, Jones had already published poems and nonfiction essays in which he used his talents to offend and abuse white readers in the name of articulating a just black rage. Even though his rage may have provided a tremendous source of creative energy, Jones was rarely able to harness it beyond a scream. Simply put, he had become more invested in offending and frightening whites than in writing good plays, poems, or essays. Ironically, the intention of this play is so overwhelming that it hides its few dramatic moments. White viewers of *The Slave* may have left the theater frightened, but they were neither intellectually nor emotionally engaged.

In a 1966 interview, Jones confronted the ambiguity of Walker Vessels and the underlying rationale for titling the play *The Slave*:

> Walker Vessels is still a slave in the sense that he's supposed to be leading this army, yet he's spending all his time talking to this white man . . . he has no business being there in the first place; he was supposed to be with his own people. . . . If he were really free, the only sound that professor would have heard is cannon-fire.[96]

Walker Vessels embodies the ambivalences felt by the play's author. After all, Jones was caught in a situation in which he felt increasingly pulled toward a more militant assertiveness of blackness and yet was still living in the predominantly white Village scene. He was married to a white woman and had two mixed-race daughters. Prophetically he described Walker's increasing nationalism as having caused his wife to leave him. In real life, Jones would soon leave Hettie and their two children. The close resemblances between some of the characters in the play and intimates in Jones's real life may have indicated an internal rage. Not only was it emotionally costly for his wife to be subjected to the personal disjunctures with her husband that were occurring as he became more assertive in projecting an insular blackness, but for Hettie to have seen this very personal crisis exposed on the stage must have been humiliating. By 1978, even Baraka was willing to admit that there was a certain cruelty in the choices he had made at that time.[97]

3

An Alien among Outsiders

SHORTLY AFTER RETURNING from Cuba, Jones became active in the Fair Play for Cuba Committee. During one Fair Play demonstration in July 1961, he was arrested.[1] Then in late 1961, Jones was elected president of the Fair Play for Cuba's New York chapter. Spurred on by his pro-Cuban activities, Jones tried to organize a political consciousness-raising group in the Village. Known as the Organization of Young Men (OYM), Jones's group contained black males only, a fact that he deemed significant because it testified to the growing uneasiness of many black Village-based intellectuals and artists who found themselves isolated from the Civil Rights movement. "We issued at least one statement but the sense of it was that we knew it was time to go on the offensive in the Civil Rights movement. We did not feel part of that movement."[2] It seems rather presumptuous that this group of relatively unknown figures would issue a political statement, as if their opinions, individually or collectively, had public significance. But perhaps recognizing the feebleness of public statements, the group decided that its political duty was to "work" in Harlem. Evidently this group work in Harlem never progressed beyond the planning stage. That in becoming politicized, Jones and his companions thought it necessary to go to Harlem indicated the peculiarity of the emerging racial consciousness of black Village-based intellectuals during the early 1960s. This need to be physically located in Harlem became apparent only a few years after Jones told Podhoretz that Harlem was a haven for the black bourgeoisie.

Shortly after its founding, OYM was merged into On Guard, a larger, more experienced, predominantly black group of Village intellectuals. Like the Organization of Young Men, On Guard also decided to be active in Harlem. An office was opened on 125th Street which, Jones notes, allowed them to participate in a "few struggles." Most of the members of both OYM and On Guard were black male intellectuals who had white wives or lovers. These black men decided that their white female companions could not accompany them to Harlem.[3] Their implicit admission of the possibility that they had done something ethnically illegitimate in crossing over the racial barrier in their choice of companions suggests that the journey to Harlem would be, in part, a petition for ethnic reconciliation. Despite being restricted to males, On Guard was an interracial organization. The peculiar taboos associated with interracial heterosexual/intimate relationships meant that white male members could accompany them to Harlem but white women had to stay away. Harold Cruse found it fascinating that in 1961, the LeRoi Jones of On Guard defended interracial political formations even when such defenses alienated black nationalists in Harlem. Cruse, a member of On Guard, claimed that at one of their meetings in Harlem, Jones not only stated that he did not understand why it was necessary to restrict whites from membership but expressed bewilderment as to why black Harlemites hated whites.[4] But Cruse never bothered to question the absence of black women (or white women) in On Guard, an omission that probably speaks to his complicity in the organization's gender dynamics.

Even though the members of On Guard had fewer ties to Harlem than to the Village, they believed that the only effective politicization on behalf of the black struggle was one that directly worked with black people.[5] In many instances, and certainly in the case of Jones, this belief implied that politics was being used to regain an ethnic legitimacy that had been threatened as a result of living in bohemia. Many of those who felt ethnically illegitimate because of their distance from the political struggles of black America as well as their romantic involvements with white partners soon become exceedingly ethnically identified. Extremism is the religion of recent converts.

Jones felt increasingly ambivalent about his bohemian life. The Village had provided him with a setting in which he could create, but he had never felt completely at home there. Even though the literary subculture of the Village was racially liberal, Jones was one of very few blacks to have gained access to its serious artistic circles.[6] This sense of racial isolation was accentuated by the increasing political activity taking place in black America during the late 1950s and early 1960s. Jones has consistently written of his distaste for Martin Luther King Jr. and the nonviolent politicization of blacks, but his lack of involvement in the Civil Rights movement or in any alternative movement concerned with bettering the plight of black Americans led him to question both the character of his ethnic identity and the utility of his artistic journey. This inability to resolve questions about the political utility of the black artist/writer troubled Jones throughout his career.

It is not surprising that Jones became alienated from the Beat bohemia subculture that valorized alienation. Self-conscious about their alienation, most Beat bohemians tended to trivialize substantive political distinctions and conflicts in the mainstream social order. In his discussion of Western avant-garde movements, Poggioli stated that avant-garde artists cannot sustain a relationship with political movements, be they revolutionary or reactionary. The avant-garde has as its raison d'être a quest to be contrary—to oppose any status quo. To the extent that a political movement, even a counter-hegemonic one, becomes organizationally rationalized and embedded in the realpolitik concessions and strategies necessary to increase its viability, it becomes tainted by the parent society. Poggioli further noted that Western avant-garde artistic communities tended to maintain only fleeting allegiances with political movements. He concluded that "the only omnipresent or recurring political ideology in the avant-garde is the least political or the most antipolitical of all: libertarianism and anarchism." Instead of political engagement, the avant-garde is committed to aesthetic protest.

> The artist is in a continual state of social protest, but it does not signify that he becomes, politically, a revolutionary. Analogously, the modern artist, even when driven to embrace a reactionary ideal (sometimes for purely aesthetic reasons), does not thereby necessarily become a conservative . . . his social protest shows itself principally on the level of form, and thus alienation from society becomes *alienation from tradition*. . . . Avant-garde art seems destined to oscillate perpetually among the various forms of alienation—psychological and social, economic and historical, aesthetic and stylistic. There is no doubt that all these forms are summed up in one other, namely in *ethical alienation*.[7] [italics in original]

As a black writer in a predominantly white artistic subculture, Jones was far more vulnerable than the typical white Beat writer to political pressures originating outside the subculture. After all, he was in bohemia not simply because he was alienated from the mainstream society but also because he was seeking a less racist art world in which to grow. Ethically and racially alienated from the parent society, Jones was continually made to recognize that an individual resolution to his problematic existence was in itself a mimicry of the mainstream.

Jones embraced his betwixt-between status in bohemia. The psychological demands of trying to navigate an outsider position among outsiders was quite demanding and often debilitating. Jones tried to negotiate this space through his art. Perhaps the clearest testimony to his artistic attempt to embrace his insider/outsider status in bohemia was his novel *The System of Dante's Hell*. The novel was a tortured effort, as Jones seemed to have even been ambivalent about using the novel as an artistic genre. Nonetheless, writing this novel helped nurture his emergence as a significant and distinct voice in American letters.

NOVELIST OF CULTURAL AMBIVALENCE

In 1965 Grove Press published *The System of Dante's Hell*, various sections of which had been written and/or published as early as 1959. Literary critic Theodore Hudson was perhaps correct to consider the novel a "thematically and stylistically controlled anthology."[8] Jones claimed that *The System of Dante's Hell* was an attempt to devise a writing style more in tune with his own being.

> I guess the pivotal work for me was a novel called *The System of Dante's Hell*. That's when I consciously stopped trying to write like people whose work I was around, people like Charles Olson and Allen Ginsberg. In *Dante*, even though I worked in a ready-made frame modeled upon Dante's *Inferno*, still I used that frame to develop, I think a different writing style, a more personal one anyway.[9]

Jones also described how he used Western forms to undermine the hegemony of Western forms in his own psyche:

> What I was doing was trying to break away from European influences and the strong influences of many white poets who had affected my work. . . . I did it consciously, but I didn't know that I was specifically breaking away from white forms at the time. I did know that the forms weren't mine. I was trying to find a voice, my own, and I needed to oppose myself to the European influence. Dante was an attempt to illuminate all the elements of myself to myself against the backdrop of European form.[10]

Although I do not know whether the novel actually played the crucial role in Jones's development that he claims, it is clear that it cannot be read as a major political statement. Rather, its aesthetic significance is far greater than its political significance.

The System is only loosely structured on Dante's *Inferno*, whose structure is an antagonistic-cooperative backdrop to a highly individualized exploration of the various states of mind of the protagonist, Roi. Roi is also known as Dante. Clearly, the novel is autobiographical, but it is not a factual rendition of events in Jones's own life. Instead, it could be read it as an excursion through the psychological torment that Jones experienced from the upward mobility–premised journey of his youth in Newark to his decision to embrace the downward mobility of a bohemian writer. The central agon of the text is representative of the struggle between the allure of a society intent on generating assimilationist tendencies among those blacks who sought mobility and the internal desire of the poet to remain true to his black cultural authenticity. In this sense, *The System* embodies the struggles of Clay in *Dutchman* and Walker Vessels in *The Slave*. The effort to remain authentic in the face of societal enticements either to culturally assimilate or pursue "racial exceptionality," as in the Negro who is "unlike the others," is so central to Jones's novel that he grants the lowest realms of hell to "heretics." "I put the Heretics in the deepest part of hell, though Dante had them spared on higher ground. . . . It is heresy, against one's own sources, running in terror from one's deepest responses and insights . . . the denial of feeling . . . that I see as basest evil."[11] As if to reinforce the condemnation of heretics, Jones explicitly rejects Dante's Christian notion of hell and instead defines it as the state of mind in which a black person endures a fractured and unresolved racial identity.

> Hell in the head. . . . The torture of being the unseen object, and, the constantly observed subject. . . .The flame of social dichotomy. Split open down the center, which is the early legacy of the black man unfocused on blackness. The dichotomy of what is seen and taught and desired opposed to what is felt.[12]

The first half of the novel is a collection of streams of consciousness that Jones termed "association complexes." These include vivid descriptions of scenes and incidents during Roi's youth. In particular, Roi is haunted by his growing alienation from his black "home boys." A thoroughly narcissistic novel, its central subject is the development of Jones as a person and writer as told through the eyes of the young Roi, who is a creation of the reminisces of the older LeRoi.

A few examples of the intense self-gazing found in the "association complexes" should suffice to convey the reader's difficulty in creating meaning out of the text. In the first chapter, entitled "Neutrals: The Vestibule," Jones describes the proper "Europeanized" black church that he attended as a child:

> Stone on stone. Hard cobblestones, oil lamps, green house of the native. Natives down the street. All dead. All walking slowly toward their lives. Already, each Sunday forever. The man was a minister. His wife was lightskinned with freckles. Their church was tall brown brick and sophisticated. Bach was colored and lived in the church with Handel. Beckett was funeral director with brown folding chairs.[13]

Without racial agency, the neutrals exist in a deadened world of mediocre respectability. Their lives reflect the "proper" social mores to a fault. Their houses are orderly; their marriages are stable, their grass is cut; and, worse, they own books that they will never read. Insular and anti-intellectual, the neutrals merely exist and then die, justly forgotten.

> Even inside the house linoleums were cold. Divided in their vagueness. Each man his woman. Their histories die in the world. My own . . . I point out forever their green grass. Brown unopened books. The smell of the world. . . . Each man his own place. Each flower in its place.[14]

In another chapter, an adult Roi reflects on the orthodox choices that he has made despite having aspired to live differently. For Roi, dishonesty is a sign of the inauthenticity of his life, an inauthenticity rooted in his adherence to convention.

> You've done everything you said you wdn't. Everything you said you despised. A fat mind, lying to itself. Unmoving like some lump in front of a window. Wife, child, house, city, clawing at your gentlest parts. Romance become just sad tiny lies. And your head full of them. What do you want anymore? Nothing. Not poetry or that purity of feeling you had.[15]

Despairing over his decision to become a writer, Roi ponders his downward mobility as a bohemian. Whereas his rejection of the materialistic life was supposed to fuel his artistic commitment, he now wonders whether his poverty has become an end in itself, divorced from any creative impulses.

> A dirty floor full of food particles and roaches. Lower middleclass poverty. In ten years merely to lose one's footing on a social scale. Everything else, that seriousness, past, passed. Almost forgotten.
>
> Another man walked through me like hours. Not even closeness of flesh. Not against this blue ugly air. Not against you or myself. Not against the others, their unclosing eyes. The fat breasted fashionable slut of letters. Her blonde companion in the sulking dugouts of stupidity. She clasped my face in her bones & kissed silence into my mouth.[16]

While these vignettes are imaginatively written and perhaps reveal insights into Roi's and thus Jones's character, they do not sustain the reader, as they are too brief and scattered to justify the intensity demanded of the reader by the form. In addition, Jones's references to scenes and individuals can be so thoroughly insular that they may not make sense to anyone but him or his alter egos. For example,

> Did John Holmes really jump off the Warren St. bridge? But his legs healed and he watched us hump the big italian bitch in Sweeney's cloakroom. . . . This is Orlando Davis, who with his curly hair & large ass, steps thru mists everywhere. They caught him stealing on his scooter. They, the cops(?), moralists dropped on him from the skies. The music: Rachmaninoff's 3rd piano glinting. Remarkable thick weather he moved thru. Not as a woman this time, a sultry male. He looked tired, or bewildered. And they mobbed him at the river's edge, yelling their faces at heaven.[17]

These snippets read as if Jones sporadically jotted down fleeting memories and then later tried to organize them into some type of thematic unity that he subsequently called chapters. Not only does he attempt to recall those interpretations of these events (and people) that he had at the time of their occurrence, but he also offers his current reflections on those historical events and peoples. In addition, he comments on his earlier interpretations. These "association complexes" read like contemporary journal entries written in response to a rereading of other journal entries that were written at the time of the occurrences. He appears to be using this process to give some type of meaning and thus closure to the various ruptures, fears, and joys that he experienced in his younger days, a sort of self-analysis. But given the narcissistic concerns and insular references of many of these "association complexes," why did Jones share them with a reading audience?[18]

Once past the vignettes comprising the first half of the book, the text becomes much more accessible. The major transition in the book occurs at its midpoint with the inclusion of the play *The Eighth Ditch*.

The Eighth Ditch takes place in 1947 in a black youth camp and centers on the rape/seduction of a middle-class Negro fellow, "46," by an older, more experienced and underprivileged black male, "64." The two young men are talking while sitting on their bunks. First, 46 speaks in the tone of a young alienated poet: "Brittle youth, they say, I am dead america. . . . Young, from sidewalks of wind."[19]

Commenting on the stilted and protected world of 46, 64 states: "Call me Herman. . . . Your earth is round & sits outside the world. You have millions of words to read. And you will read them." When 46 asks who he is, 64 replies: "The Street! Things around you. Even noises at night, or smells you are afraid of. I am a maelstrom of definitions. . . . But as you know, whatever, poorer than yrself."[20] The two men, 46 and 64, are from different sides of the tracks, and 46 makes disparaging remarks about people like 64. As they talk, 64 steadily moves closer to 46, who is reading while lying down. Soon 64 undresses both himself and 46. Even though 46 is initially somewhat hesitant, 64 enters him from behind. As 64 penetrates 46, he tells him about the experiences that he will empty into his body. Referring to these experiences as blues, 64 promises to teach 46 about many of them (e.g., Bigot Blues, adultery blues, Modern Jazz blues, Kafka blues). Soon Otis, another camper, appears and also expresses a desire to have sex with 46, but 64 chases him away. Later, two other campers stumble on the two young men once again having sex. When 64, atop 46, sees these two, he begins to make loud sexual sounds for their enjoyment. These two new onlookers ask 64 if they can "have some." He indicates that he will let them get some, too, as soon as he is finished. Otis, the first onlooker who had been chased away, returns and hears that 64 will allow the two new onlookers to have sex with 46. He becomes angry and begins a fight with the new onlookers. The play ends as 64 continues having anal intercourse with 46. And 46 asks, "What other blues do you have Herman?" At first, 64 tells him that he has many more blues. But with his mind completely focused on intercourse, 64 responds, "Oooh baby, just keep throwing it up like that." The chapter ends.

For our purposes, this chapter (play) has little political significance except as an indication of the depth of Jones's bohemian commitments at this time. The play is decidedly bohemian in its avoidance of a distinct social or political message. It uses social outcasts—black homosexuals—as key characters. Although the play is not well developed, it is clear that the tender sexual moments experienced by 46 and 64 become distorted once their actions become publicly known. Although 64 is willing to act like 46's lover in private, when others appear, he assumes the mask of "the man fucking 46." One could perhaps tease out of this a bohemian theme that societal life is fatal to authenticity. Jones's treatment of the proposed gang rape of 46 is disturbing. How did 64 obtain the authority to grant other men permission to have sex with 46? In the sexist and homophobic caverns of Jones's mind, 46 is considered female-like because he is being penetrated. As a metaphorical woman, he relies on the protection of his male lover against the advances of other males. His lover, like the others wanting to have sex with 46, consider themselves hyper-heterosexual. In popular urban sensibility, the only one who is "stigmatized" as effeminate or even gay is the man who is being penetrated.

Werner Sollors and Kimberly Benston interpreted *The Eighth Ditch* as a metaphorical excursion into Jones's split identities, seeing 46 and 64 are different sides of the same person.[21] If read in this manner, the play portrays 46 as the naive and bourgeois young intellectual, juxtaposed against the blacker, more experienced, less intellectual, but streetwise 64. In fucking 46, 64 impregnates him with knowledge and experience. But 64 betrays 46 in the presence of the others, thereby introducing 46 to the wretchedness and exploitation that also accompany experience.

In the chapter entitled "The Rape," Roi and five bourgeois friends are home for the summer from college. Local celebrities of sorts (as Negroes on the move upward), they enjoy attending various parties given by bourgeois Negro college students. As a member of this college set, Roi appears to enjoy the partying but somehow does not quite feel at ease in this setting. Nonetheless, he continues to frequent these social gatherings. The scene is one of these college parties in the integrated Newark suburb of East Orange.

> This one was the hippest for our time. East Orange, lightskinned girls, cars pulling in, smart clothers our fathers' masters wore. But this was the way. The movement. Our heads turned open for it. And light, pure warm light, flowed in.
>
> . . . I sat on a stoop. One of the white stoops of the rich (the Negro rich were lovely in their non-importance in the world). Still, I sat and thot why they moved past me, the ladies, or why questions seemed to ride me down. The world itself, so easy to solve . . . and get rid of. Why did they want it? What pulled them in, that passed me by. I cd have wept each night of my life.[22]

While the college Negroes are enjoying these rites of class affirmation, Jones feels excluded from their class pretensions and ambitions. He does not yet understand himself sufficiently to understand why he doesn't feel driven to join in their pursuit of the "American dream," but he knows that there is something about him that is rebelling at the thought of disappearing into mainstream America, even if it is mainstream black America. What should be his crowd, isn't. Nevertheless, he endures his alienation silently while acting in public as if all is right with his world. In private he is tortured.

Leaving the party, Jones and his friends pile into a car. They spot a drunken and disheveled black woman stumbling down the street. After she asks them to give her a ride into Newark, they seat her in the back seat of the car between Jones and one of the other fellows. With rape on their mind, Jones and the other fellows begin to explore her body with their hands without her consent. Jones even tries to place his hand inside her dirty underwear. Instead of generating aversion, the dirtiness of the woman allows these bourgeois black college students to think about sexually assaulting her. Her dirtiness signifies her lack of virtue. Though intoxicated, she recognizes their intent and cleverly foils their plans by casually mentioning that she has a venereal disease. Disgusted with her, they throw her out of the moving car, and she lands on the street near the curb. They scream with excitement as they drive away.

In the final chapter, "The Heretics," Jones describes an incident in his life during his days as a member of the U.S. Air Force. With a weekend pass, Roi and a friend leave the military base in pursuit of fun in the local town's black section, known as "the bottom." There Roi meets Peaches, a young semiliterate but thoroughly carnal seventeen-year-old black female prostitute. Peaches is captivated by Roi's foreignness, particularly his "white" way of talking. She leads him to several juke joints and bars where Jones, the transplanted northerner, immediately confronts an alien side of black life—the sensuality of gut-bucket country Negroes. He is perceived as "an imitation white boy." Jones writes: "And when I spoke someone wd turn and stare, or laugh, and point me out. The quick new jersey speech, full of italian idiom, and the invention of the jews. Quick to describe. Quicker to condemn." Roi later goes home with Peaches. Drunk, he is not sexually aroused. His hesitation and inability to sustain an erection are interpreted by Peaches as a lack of heterosexual desire. In response, she decides to teach him how "to fuck," as she regards him as a "bigeye faggot."[23] Unknowingly, Peaches has stumbled on an accurate perception of Roi's sexuality, for in the text are intermittent flashbacks to various homosexual encounters earlier in Roi's life. After forcing coffee down Roi's throat and telling him that she will have sex with him for free, Peaches does manage to stimulate two minor erections from Roi, each time telling him that she will teach him how to do it better.

Despite momentarily thinking of going AWOL and staying a while with Peaches, Roi knows that he is in alien territory. Yet her simplicity coupled with the immediacies that govern her life create in Roi's mind a comforting black pastoral vision of a noble savage. Though highly sexually experienced, Peaches is completely naive and innocent of the complexities of the world that Roi holds dear. Jones eventually escapes from Peaches and the "bottom," but on his return to the air force base, he is jumped by three black men who had seen him earlier at the clubs. They interpreted the weirdness of his foreign ways and northern accent as an attempt to declare himself superior to them. They viciously beat him.

In both chapters, Roi is confronted with alien black worlds. In "The Rape," the destitute and vulnerable status of the "street woman" makes her ripe for gang raping—a privilege bestowed on Roi and his boys not only because they were male but also because they were bourgeois college students.

They want to do it because they can get away with it. Despite her being their "home girl" from Newark, they feel no affinity with her. If anything, her de-based economic condition has turned her into a desired, exploitable object. But the women they really want are the light-skinned, bourgeois suburban ones like those in the party they just left. Even though the drunken woman's "street smarts" outmaneuver the better-educated college students, she is still forced to endure physical pain and psychological humiliation when they kick her out of their car.

Roi hides his complex sexuality in the group camaraderie of his male "crew," but then, he is hiding a great deal about himself from them. Even the camaraderie is not sufficient to conceal Roi's difference completely, for he, unlike the others, tries to lift the fallen woman back into the car, presumably for the ride to Newark. Unsuccessful in this effort, he submerges his unease in collective hell-raising screams as they pull away from her sprawled body.

In the encounter with Peaches, Roi, now alone, is less sexually empow-ered. In fact, he is frightened of her sexuality and can barely perform. Peaches smacks him in the face, pulls on his penis, and tells him repeatedly, "Goddam punk, you gonna fuck me tonight or I'm gonna pull your fuckin dick aloose." Roi wants to tell Peaches that the failure of his penis to harden does not di-minish his stature as a man. For Peaches, Roi's manhood lies in his erect penis. If he cannot get an erection, he must not be a man (i.e., heterosexual). Roi, however, tells her, "Please, you don't know me. Not what's in my head. I'm beautiful. Stephen Dedalus."[24] As soon as the words slip out of his mouth, Roi knows that Peaches cannot possibly understand what he is trying to say. The gulf between their worlds cannot be bridged with words. It is the world out-side words that Peaches symbolizes.

The System of Dante's Hell is very difficult to read. Whatever one may think of Jones's claims that the work represents his coming to terms with his own voice, the novel appears to be Jones's most self-consciously "arty" text. Its difficulty makes it inaccessible to many readers, including many, if not most, blacks.

The novel speaks to Jones's bicultural identity. Roi is too "white" to be ac-cepted by nonbourgeois blacks (the only authentic blacks) and yet not "white" enough to be attracted to black bourgeois life. Jones devises a self-ori-ented writing style and appropriates the form of a canonical Western text to facilitate this self-quest. In this regard, the novel should not be read as the artist's attempt to discard Western literary tradition but as an attempt to as-sert more racial agency in his appropriation of Western cultural forms. Jones announces that he will no longer be a passive receptacle. In his earliest Village writings, he had been guilty of racially disappearing. Thus *The System of*

Dante's Hell has significance for his developing art insofar as it is a radical break with his earliest, most parasitically bohemian approach to writing. We even could conclude that the same forces that led Jones to reevaluate his passive acceptance of Western literary canons and forms is the same spirit that ultimately led to the more definitive racial self-definition in his art and politics during the late 1960s.

POET OF ALIENATION

Various poems that Jones had written and/or published between 1961 and 1963 were later included as *Sabotage* in his 1969 poetry collection *Black Magic*. In trying to situate Jones's changing political sensibilities in their various historical moments, it seemed appropriate to place my discussion of these poems alongside the poems of *The Dead Lecturer*, which were written during the same period.

Sabotage

Concerning the continuity between *Sabotage* and his first two poetry collections, *Preface to a Twenty Volume Suicide Note* and *The Dead Lecturer*, Jones writes:

> You notice the preoccupation with death, suicide, in the early works. Always my own, caught up in the deathurge of this twisted society. The work a cloud of abstraction and disjointedness, that was just whiteness. European influence, etc., just as the concept of hopelessness and despair, from the dead minds the dying morality of Europe.
>
> There is a spirituality always trying to get through, to triumph, to walk across these dead bodies like stuntin for disciples, walking the water of dead bodies europeans call their minds.[25]

One of the poems included in *Sabotage* (and thus written between 1961 and 1963) was entitled "A Poem Some People Will Have to Understand" and addresses the tortured existence of a poet who is forced to faced his social irrelevancy.

> *What*
> *industry do I practice: A slick*

colored boy, 12 miles from his
home. I practice no industry.
I am no longer a credit
*   to my race. . . .*[26]

A poem of intense reflection, Jones once again questions his decision to become a writer. The existential leap required to violate his upward mobility–premised upbringing necessitates the creation of an entirely different value system on which he can try to legitimate his self-worth. Because he is not earning a large salary or employed in a high-status position, he knows that many blacks will view him as a failure. A poet without a real job ("I practice no industry"), Jones is no longer a credit to black people. The idea of being a credit to one's race is based on a bourgeois black notion of achievement, supposedly to elevate the status of blacks in the eyes of whites.

The conclusion of the poem is a testimony to the poet's loss of faith in social progress and the future. Instead of naively believing that "things are getting better" for the Negro, Jones argues that the time has now come for militant action in behalf of change.

We have awaited the coming of a natural
phenomenon. Mystics and romantics, knowledgeable
workers
of the land.
*   But none has come,*
*   (Repeat)*
but none has come.

Will the machinegunners please step forward?[27]

A jarring and frightful statement, the poem's advocacy of violence violates bohemian ethics.[28]

The poem "The Burning General" is also an expression of the dilemma confronting Jones as a black artist. As a member of an oppressed group, he believes that subjugation is a ripe subject for artistic engagement, but creating from a state of subjugation may be akin to "savoring one's oppression." Jones may have also been addressing the implicit romanticism of black subjugation that was rampant in Beat bohemia. Speaking to himself, Jones asks whether his sophistication and commitment to the world of ideas have mistakenly led him to believe that he could have a social impact.

Can we ask a man to savor the food of oppression? Even if it's rich and full of mysterious meaning. Can you establish (and that word must give my whole game away) any kind of equality?

Can there be such thing forced on the world? That is, that the poor and their owners appreciate light wherever they are, simply as light. Why are you so sophisticated? You used to piss and shit in your pants. Now you walk around *thinking* all the time, as if that sacred act would rewrite the world in bop talk, giving medals to every limping coon in creation.[29]

Some of Jones's poems consider the psychic costs to those blacks who seek to "get ahead in life." In "Letter to E. Franklin Frazier," Jones wrote:

Those days when it was all right
to be a criminal, or die, a postman's son,
Those days I rose through the smoke of chilling Saturdays
hiding my eyes from the shine boys, my mouth and my flesh
from their sisters. I walked quickly and always alone
watching the cheap city like I thought it would swell
and explode, and only my crooked breath could put it together
again

By the projects and small banks of my time. Counting my steps
on tar or new pavement, following the sun like a park. I imagined
a life, that was realer than speech
. . . Shuddering at dust, with a mile or so up the hill
to get home.
. . . The quick step, the watchful march march,
All were leading here, to this room.[30]

This poem reflects on his days walking around Newark as a boy. It is significant that even at this age he has begun to view himself as destined for something that most other Negroes could never attain. He cannot make eye contact with the "shine boys," nor would he stoop so low as to physically interact with their sisters. He walks past housing projects in fear. His fear of urban life and what could happen to him after dusk is indicative of his fear of these poor blacks and their ability to perceive his fear of them. As darkness approaches, he walks faster, wary of the enclosing blackness.

Many of the poems in *Sabotage* have bohemian themes. In "The People Burning: May-Day! May-Day!" Jones employs the typical Beat bohemian despair of mass consumption and uniformity to rage against cultural assimilation. The subtitle, "May-Day! May-Day!" is included to invoke images of an impending disaster. May-Day is the universal distress call, and Jones uses it to announce America's impending fall:

> The Dusty Hearts of Texas, whose most honest world
> is the long look into darkness, sensing the glittering
> affront of reason or faith or learning. Preferring
> fake tiger smells rubbed on the balls, and clothes
> the peasants of no country on earth would ever be
> vulgar enough to wear. The legacy of diseased mediocrity[31]

In behaving in such a manner, Americans have lost their creative agency by living vicariously through consumerism. This emphasis on false identities has also given rise to the blandness of an assimilated America.

> Become an Italian or a Jew. Forget the hatred of natural
> insolence. The teetering sense of right, as balance, each
> natural man must have. Become a Jew, and join the union,
> forget about Russia or any radicalism past a hooked grin.
> Become an Italian quietist in some thin veneer of reasonable
> gain. Lodi, Metuchen, Valley Stream, welcomes you into its
> leather ridiculousness.
>
> Now they ask me to be a jew or italian, and turn from the moment
> disappearing into the shaking clock of treasonable safety.[32]

A theme in much of Jones's pre–black nationalist writing is that white ethnic Americans have entered a Faustian pact with American cultural blandness. In order to attain upward mobility and acceptance, white ethnics have relinquished the richness of their cultural heritages for the homogenous mediocrity of American cultural respectability. Nothing better illustrates their escape from life than their willingness to forgo the dynamic life of New York City in order to live in pedestrian, homogenized, "brain-dead" suburban Jersey townships like Metuchen and Valley Stream.

In "After the Ball," Jones continues his commentary on the plasticity of contemporary life in the United States:

> The magic dance
> of the second ave ladies
>   in the artificial glare

> of the world, silver-green curls sparkle
> and the ladies' arms jingle
> with new Fall pesos, sewn on grim bracelets
> the poet's mother-in-law thinks are swell.
> So much for America, let it sweep in grand
> style up the avenues of its failure. Let it promenade smartly
> beneath the marquees of its despair.[33]

In the short essay included in *Sabotage*, "Gatsby's Theory of Aesthetics," Jones describes his aesthetic approach.

> I write poetry only to enlist the poetic consistently as apt description of my life. I write poetry only in order to feel, and that, finally, sensually, all the terms of my life. I write poetry to investigate my self, and my meaning and meanings.
>   . . . But it is possible to feel with any part of our consciousness. Whatever part of us does register; whatever. The head feels. The heart feels. The penis feels. . . . The point of life is that it is arbitrary, except in its bases forms. Arbitrariness, or self imposed meaning, is the only thing worth living for. It is the only thing that permits us to live.[34]

"Square Business" is a meditation of the values undergirding the social order. In particular, Jones views the profit motive and greed as the governing values of American society, in which everything is turned into a commodity.

> The faces of Americans
> sit open hating each
> other. The black ones
> hating, though they laugh
> and are controlled by
> laughter. The white ones
> blown up hot inside, their projects
> are so profitable . . . sixteen stories
> in a sultry town . . . wind bends them
> back
>
> These are boxes
> of money. With lids
> these winds wont lift.
>   Winds from foodless mouths.

Steel boxes floating in tears.
. . . They own each
other. They own
my mother. They own
and own, go on, what else
is theirs?
Time. Time is.
The pop of the clock, your head
on the block.
. . . They own
language. Churches. But not the strong ones
Four Five Six, they own. But not Beaulah
Bapt. or Drifting Image Church of Christ In
Dreams. Where the old ladies fan themselves
with God.[35]

In this society, ownership is an obsession. Everything has been commodified and thus distorted. Squares even "own each other." Time is another phenomenon governed by the logic of the profit motive. The time clock represents the commodification of labor: "the pops of the clock, your head on the bloc." Even Benny Goodman has made a profit by ripping off jazz and blues and then turning the art form into a money-making "whitenized" commodity. This argument is elaborated in *Blues People*.

THE DEAD LECTURER

Jones's sense of multiple alienation saturated the poetry he composed following his initial volume, *Preface to a Twenty Volume Suicide Note*. Much like the poems in *Sabotage*, Jones's 1964 collection, *The Dead Lecturer*, continues his obsession with alienation and death. The poems in this collection reflect his bohemian disdain for the mechanistic, profit-before-people ethos of the modern industrial social order. Yet unlike *Preface*, this new collection described far more explicitly the costs to black humanity of trying to integrate/assimilate into the cold, antihuman, rational world of the parent society.

Jones's intensifying political consciousness is evident in the poem "A contract (for the destruction and rebuilding of Paterson")).[36] Paterson, an industrial city in New Jersey, was the home of poet William Carlos Williams, the greatest influence on Jones's desire to write poetry in his own voice. First he describes the wretched physicality and inhumane ambience of a city governed by the profit motive.

> Flesh and cars, tar, dug holes beneath stone
> a rude hierarchy of money, band saws cross out
> music, feeling. Even speech, corrodes.
> I came here
> from where I sat boiling in my veins, cold fear
> at the death of men, the death of learning, in
> cold fear, at my own. Romantic vests of same death
> blank at the corner, blank when they raise their fingers.[37]

But amid the inhumanity of this society, blacks and Puerto Ricans seem far too compliant in their willingness to defer to the sick, racist social order.

> Criss the hearts, in dark flesh staggered so marvelous
> are their lies. So complete, their mastery, of these
> stupid niggers. Loud spics kill each other, and will not
> make the simple trip to Tiffany's. Will not smash their stainless
> heads, against the simpler effrontery of so callous a code as gain.[38]

Jones is angered by the futile antics of blacks and Puerto Ricans, wondering why they have not chosen to direct their energy toward struggling against the unjust urban social order, as opposed to killing each other. Why not steal from those with superfluous wealth (i.e., Tiffany's) instead of each other?

"Contract" is one of Jones's earliest poetic advocacies of the black robbery of white wealth. In this call for unlawful but justifiable agency against white-owned property, Jones prefigures themes in his Black Arts poetry. Now, the ease with which whites manipulate blacks into compliance creates a disdain in Jones that is nothing less than disgust.

> You are no brothers, dirty woogies, dying under dried rinds, in
> massa's
> droopy tuxedos. Cab Calloways of the soul, at the soul's juncture.[39]

Given the popular usage of the term *brother* in black urban, public greeting rituals, Jones's claim that "you are no brothers" expresses his aversion to them while appropriating their language.

> . . . *Killed in white fedora hats, they stand so mute*
>   *at what*
> *whiter slaves did to my fathers. They muster silence. They pray*
>   *at the*
> *steps of abstract prisons, to be kings, when all is silence, when all is stone.*[40]

Jones is using "whiteness" in this poem as a metaphor for evil and black self-hatred. Those blacks who can only "muster silence" are implicitly referred to as "white," albeit less "white" than those blacks who sold Afro-Americans ("my fathers") into slavery. Where, he wonders, is their rage?

In "An Agony. As Now," Jones continues his autobiographical reflections.

> *I am inside someone*
> *who hates me. I look*
>   *out from his eyes. Smell*
>   *what fouled tunes come in*
>   *to his breath. Love his*
>   *wretched women.*[41]

Some critics of Jones's poetry do not view the sentiments contained in the preceding verse as racially linked. But this stanza could be read as a statement of racial self-hatred as manifested in a pathological attraction to white women: "love his wretched women."[42] Buried in anguish, Jones conveys his tormented soul:

> *Cold air blown through narrow blind eyes. Flesh*
> *white hot metal. Glows as the day with its sun*
> *It is a human love, I live inside. A bony skeleton*
> *you recognize as words or simple feeling.*
>
> *But it has no feeling. As the metal, is hot, it is not,*
> *given to love.*
>
> *It burns the thing*
> *inside it. And that thing*
> *screams.*[43]

In "A Poem for Willie Best," Jones offers a meditation on Willie Best, the actor who played the role of Sleep 'n Eat. Much like his Hollywood counterpart, Step 'n Fetchit, Sleep 'n Eat was a stereotypical black buffoon.

Such figures were characterized by their dim-witted, word-slurring speech; shuffling; head scratching; and eye-ball rolling facial expressions of bafflement. Jones describes him as

Lazy
Frightened
Thieving
Very potent sexually]
Scars
Generally inferior
(but natural
rhythms.[44]

But Jones sees the birth of an oppositional subjectivity in Willie Best. Even though Best plays the role of Sleep 'n Eat, his inner consciousness increasingly views this role as a phony public posture, a public marketing device that hides his anger and rage at America. Jones considers the possibility that Willie Best is

A renegade
behind the mask. And even
the mask, a renegade
disguise. Black skin
and hanging lip.[45]

No longer willing to play the role of the obsequious black buffoon, Best is ready to act.

. . . He said, I'm tired
of losing.
"I got to cut 'cha."[46]

In a 1980 interview with literary scholar William Harris, Jones commented on "A Poem for Willie Best":

> The Willie Best poem is again the whole question of how does one relate realistically to one's environment if one feels estranged from one's environment and especially a black person in a white situation. And especially a person who is growing more and more political, and that politics is showing up his closest friends in a negative light but yet having to relate to those friends.

Willie Best presents the black as the minstrel—the black as the bizarre funny person, yet the black as victim, and this black minstrel victim having to come to grips with that, with his victimhood, with his minstrelsy in order to change that.[47]

In SHORT SPEECH TO MY FRIENDS, Jones further explores his outsider identity as a black and a writer in a predominantly white, culturally philistine society. Why, he wonders, should he enter a "burning house"? After all these years of trying to be like them, write like them, and, in fact, be them, Jones now sees through the charade of their false creativity.

> *The perversity*
> *of separation, isolation*
> *after so many years of trying to enter their kingdoms.*
> *now they suffer in tears, these others, saxophones whining*
> *through the wooden doors of their less than gracious homes.*
> *The poor have become our creators. The black. The thoroughly ignorant.*[48]

"The Politics of Rich Painters" offers Jones's impressions of the commercialization of a "bohemian hustle."

> *is something like the rest*
> *of our doubt, whatever slow thought*
> *comes to rest, beneath the silence*
> *of starving talk.*
> *   . . . You know the pity of*
> *democracy, that we must sit here*
> *and listen to how he makes his money.*
> *Tho the catalogue of his possible ignorance*
> *roars and extends through the room*
> *like fire . . .*
>
> *They are more ignorant than the poor*
> *tho they pride themselves with that accent. And*
> *move easily in fake robes of egalitarianism. Meaning,*
> *I will fuck you even if you don't like art. And are wounded*
> *that you call their italian memories petit bourgeois.*[49]

This poem expresses Jones's disdain for the monetary motivations of so-called radical artists who are actually quite bourgeois. Jones was friends with some commercially successful bohemian artists (e.g., William de Kooning), and perhaps this poem was written about them. Diane Di Prima believes, however, that it was more specifically targeted, that it "was one of many episodes in an endless quarrel between LeRoi and Larry Rivers."[50] By the late 1950s, Rivers had become an artist celebrity of sorts. He appeared on televised "game shows and in *Life* magazine. Even his marital problems and drug taking were well publicized."[51] In a 1955 edition of *Fortune* magazine, the editors noted that Rivers was one of the avant-garde painters whose work constituted a good speculative investment.[52] It thus would not have been out of character for Jones to offer an intrabohemian critique of the nonbohemian commercial practices of his confreres who claimed to be antibourgeois.

In "I Substitute for the Dead Lecturer," Jones invokes a common theme in his writing: anguish over his will to live a dissimilar life and torment over the possible uselessness/decadence of his unique intentions (including his decision to become a writer).[53] As a strategy to illuminate the solitary nature of his artistic journey, Jones accentuates other people's disapproval of his life. Often he describes his sense of estrangement as if it were all but invisible to others. But in "I Substitute for the Dead Lecturer," the others recognize Jones's deviance and reject him because of it.

> They have turned, and say that I am dying. That
> I have thrown
> my life away. They
> have left me alone, where
> there is no one, nothing
> save who I am. Not a note
> nor a word.[54]

In pursuing his aesthetic vision, Jones follows various paths that lead ultimately to an interrogation of his inner being. So intense is his self-examination that he wonders whether he will be consumed by it and thus fail as a writer.

> For all these wan roads
> I am pushed to follow, are
> my own conceit. A simple muttering
> elegance, slipped in my head
> pressed on my soul, is my heart's
> worth. And I am frightened
> that the flame of my sickness

> *will burn off my face. An leave*
> *the bones, my stewed black skull,*
> *an empty cage of failure.*[55]

Jones long associated honesty with craziness and lying with normality. In *Home*, he stated that he aspired to the craziness of all honest men. The poem "The Liar" is an unmerciful act of self-introspection in which he declares himself guilty of distorting the truth.

> *What I thought was love*
> *in me, I find a thousand instances*
> *as fear.*[56]

It is the fear of being known that causes Jones to lie. Is this fear that has been mistaken for love somehow directly linked to Jones's intimacies with whites? Although he publicly announces changes in his ideas and actions as if he knew all along what he was doing and where he was heading, this is not the case.

> *Though I am a man*
> *who is loud*
> *on the birth*
> *of his ways. Publicly redefining*
> *each change in my soul, as if I had predicted*
> *them,*
> *and profited, biblically, even tho*
> *their chanting weight,*
> *erased familiarity*
> *from my face.*[57]

Jones's dishonesty is so fundamental to his being that he wonders whether his true self, which was unknown in life, would ever be missed in death.

> *A question I think,*
> *an answer; whatever sits*
> *counting the minutes*
> *till you die*
> *When they say, "It is Roi*
> *who is dead?" I wonder*
> *who will they mean?*[58]

This quest for personal authenticity was a central theme of Baraka's poetry and speaks to the pervasive influence of bohemia on even his postbohemian self.

TARGET STUDY

The poems included in *Target Study* were composed between 1963 and 1965. Concerning his mind-set at that time, Jones later wrote: "*Target Study* is trying to really study, like bomber crews do the soon to be destroyed cities. Less passive now, less uselessly 'literary.' Trying to see, trying to understand . . . trying as Margaret Walker says, 'to fashion a way,' to clean up and move."[59] In "Ration," Jones provides one of the earliest examples of the militant didactic poetry that later became his trademark:

> *Banks must be robbed,*
> *the guards bound and gagged.*
>
> *The money must be taken*
> *and used to buy weapons*
>
> *Communications systems*
> *must be seized, or subverted.*
>
> *The machines must be turned*
> *off.*
>
> *Smoke plenty of bush*
> *before and after work,*
> *or during the holdup*
> *when the guards are iced.*[60]

Unlike his later invocations to militant action, Jones now registers a certain hesitance to engage in violent actions. The recommendation to "smoke plenty of bush" could be understood as a therapeutic necessity for those who are about to rob and kill. An entirely different reading of the mention of bush is that it is invoked as an act of comic relief, a juxtaposition with the seriousness of the acts about to be undertaken. In this instance, though, the drugs would still dilute the militancy of the message.

Justifiable killing in behalf of black emancipation should not be confused with murder. Murder is an immoral and unjustifiable killing. The United

States murders people, as it did in Vietnam. In "Word from the Right Wing," Jones writes,

President Johnson
is a mass murderer,
and his mother,
was a mass murderer
and his wife
is weird looking, a special breed
of hawkbill cracker

Johnson's mother, walked all night holding hands
with a nigger, and stroked that nigger's
hard. Blew him downtown Newark 1928. . . . I got proof.[61]

Ending the poem through the use of the "dozens" is a rather hilarious counterposition to the image of the almighty president of the United States. In "talking bad" about Johnson's mother, Jones was partaking of a black ritual of vicarious empowerment. In ridiculing the president's mother, the grandeur of the president is reduced to manageable proportions. Nothing could have been more scandalous than to accuse the president's mother of having performed fellatio on a "nigger."

Jones includes in the collection *Here He Comes Again* a poem that describes his highly cathartic verbal "shoot-outs" in the Village in which he often viciously attacked whites. Jones was angered at the attempts of whites, particularly Jews, to claim an equal or superior victim status to that of blacks.

. . . the black sealed in me flies to
the surface, and beneath it, more
of the same. Like a hard deep rock
I had to tell a hooknosed lady panting
at my fly, I didn't care whether she died
I had my own history of death and submission[62]

His disrespect for a Jewish woman who challenged his vicious message is reflected in his use of a pejorative term "hooknosed lady" to describe her. Worse, in claiming that she was "panting at his fly," Jones tries to reduce her disagreement with him to a repressed sexual desire for him. If anything, the poem speaks to Jones's embrace of traditional stereotypes of white women and black men.

Jones's dislocation from the Village scene and white people is more explicitly addressed in his poem "I don't love you."

> Whatever you've given me, whiteface glass
> to look through, to find another there, another . . .
>
> I don't love you. Who is to say what that will mean. I don't
> love you, expressed the train, moves, and uptown days later
> we look up and breathe much easier
>
> I don't love you.[63]

This is a poem of extreme vulnerability, even though Jones appears to imagine it as an act of assertive defiance. Yes, he is telling whites, including perhaps Hettie, that he does not love them. But the poem makes sense only if he believes that whites would care about the loss of his love. Otherwise there would be no reason to tell them. Announcing that you do not love someone that you never loved is rather mindless.

In "Return of the Native," Jones describes his return to Harlem and the mutual embrace between himself and the black people of the neighborhood.

> Harlem is vicious
> modernism. BangClash
> Vicious the way its made.
> Can you stand such beauty?
> So violent and transforming.
>
> The place, and place
> meant of
> black people. . . .
> We slide along in pain or too
> happy. So much love
> for us. All over, so much of
> what we need.[64]

The poem captures Jones's sense of himself as a prodigal son who, in leaving the Village for Harlem, had spiritually and physically returned home.

Another poem specifically condemns the life choices of the black middle class. Entitled "Black Bourgeoisie," probably in deference to E. Franklin Frazier's "The Black Bourgeoisie," the poem mocks the racial obsequiousness of the black middle class's obsessive concern with proper etiquette.

has a gold tooth, sits long hours
on a stool thinking about money
. . . works very had
grins politely in restaurants
has a good word to say
never says it
does not hate ofays
hates, instead, him self
him black self [65]

In "A Poem for Black Hearts," Jones offers a moving testimonial to the centrality of Malcolm X to emancipatory-minded black Americans. Malcolm's example was an inspiration but burdened Jones with the responsibility to carry on the fight for black freedom.

For Malcolm's eyes, when they broke
the face of some dumb white man, For
Malcolm's hands raised to bless us
all black and strong in his image
of ourselves, For Malcolm's words
fire darts, the victor's tireless
thrusts, words hung above the world
change as it may, he said it, and
for this he was killed, for saying,
and feeling, and being change, all
collected hot in his hear, For Malcolm's
heart, raising us above our filthy cities
for his stride, and his beat, and his address
to the grey monsters of the world, For Malcolm's
pleas for your dignity, black men, for your life,
black man, for the filling of your minds
with righteousness, For all of him dead and
gone and vanished from us, and all of him which
clings to our speech black god of our time.
for All of him, and all of yourself, look up,
black man, quit stuttering and shuffling, look up,
black man, quit whining and stooping, for all of him,
For Great Malcolm a prince of the earth. let nothing in us rest
until we avenge ourselves for his death, stupid animals
that killed him, let us never breathe a pure breath if

we fail, and white men call us faggots till the end
of the earth.[66]

"A Poem for Black Hearts" became one of Jones's more widely read poems in the Black Power era. A compelling lamentation of Malcolm's life, it was republished in Jones's later volume, *Eulogies*. In tune with the prevailing logic of Black Power, the poem celebrates black men as the source and defenders of the race's pride. Malcolm's assassination demands retribution from black men against white men. If black men fail to avenge Malcolm's murder, then white men are justified in calling black men faggots, which, by homophobic implication, is an unbearable fate.

Collectively, the poems of *Target Study* display an artistic sensibility less ambiguous and tortured than that of his earlier poetry. Jones is freer to be racially and politically offensive. It sometimes appears that he believes he is saying something far more strident than his actual verse conveys. But he is moving closer to the highly politicized, didactic poetry of the Black Arts movement. His poetic identity now has crossed the divide from Beat poet to black poet.

JAZZ CRITIC AS CULTURAL CRITIC

The Village scene facilitated Jones's growing attachment to black music, particularly jazz. The prevalence of jazz clubs and lofts in the Village ultimately helped ground Jones's identity. Jazz became his ethnic/racial lifeline in his predominantly white environment. Although many of the Beats recognized jazz as a sophisticated art form, mainstream white America relegated jazz to a status beneath that of the middlebrow schmaltz of Mitch Miller, Lawrence Welk, or Patti Page's "Tennessee Waltz."[67]

Some white bohemians were attracted to jazz for reasons having less to do with its integrity as an art form and more to do with their desires to acquire an outsider identity.[68] Blackness and jazz were mutually reinforcing metaphors for opposition to the prevailing mass culture. Nevertheless, those white bohemians who viewed jazz as a means of escaping blandness, when coupled with those who respected jazz as art, nurtured the Village's supportive environment for the music and the musicians. Although he was inspired and energized by the new music, Jones never made peace with those whites who viewed jazz as a vicarious lifeline to a dynamic existence.

Jones entered the Village as a lover of jazz, but he was not yet a serious student of it. Luck would have it that his first stable job after arriving in the

Village was as a clerk for a jazz magazine. The magazine, *The Record Changer*, was directed to an audience interested in pre–Louis Armstrong jazz. Jones spent numerous hours poring over the old jazz albums in the magazine's archives, an exploration that culminated in his writing his now-classic study, *Blues People.* His job at *The Record Changer* not only fed his growing curiosity about jazz but also introduced him to coworker and future wife, Hettie Cohen.

Jones became personal friends with some of the well-known black jazz musicians who lived in the Village and became acquainted with some of the leading lights of the jazz avant-garde scene. While Jones, the aspiring writer, may not have been raised in a black literary tradition, his fondness for Afro-American music grounded him in a black artistic tradition. A self-professed "schwartze bohemien," Jones dwelled in cultural ambivalence. As a Beat writer, he was immersed in a literary tradition and art world without significant Afro-American influences except jazz. In hindsight, Jones's attraction to avant-garde jazz seems all too predictable. Like Jones, black avant-garde jazz musicians were creative hybrids: blacks attempting to capture a creative space in a musical community adverse to dominant commercial influences yet forced to confront the money-making desires of the established, white-controlled music industry.

The history of black music in the United States exemplifies the white exploitation of black creativity. However skillful and innovative, black jazz artists often were barely able to make a decent living, whereas less talented white artists became popular and commercially successful by marketing a middlebrow, watered-down version of black music.

Jones had been exposed to a rich black musical heritage while growing up in Newark. Musically, Newark benefited from its close proximity to New York City. In addition, Jones mentioned that he deepened his exposure to black music through an informal seminar at Howard University taught by Professor Sterling Brown. Jones also used his time in the air force to broaden his exposure to jazz.

The Village was an excellent place to study jazz as an artistic tradition. Jazz was valorized in the Beat scene, although sometimes for reasons that had as much to do with the exotic nature of black music as with the hypermarginalized, destructive lives of black musicians who, owing to poverty and frequent drug dependence, were often romanticized by the Beats as black bohemians. More precisely, despite the Beat recognition of jazz as a valuable art form, little in the subculture could predict the depth of Jones's appreciation of it.

Jones's first writings on jazz were short reviews of jazz and blues albums as well as occasional reviews of jazz performances. From early 1959 through the mid-1960s, Jones published in *Jazz Review* six short reviews of albums by Sonny Rollins, the Cannibal Adderly Quintet, and blues singers Brownie McGhee and Snooks Eaglin. In 1961, Jones became a regular reviewer for *Metronome*. Beginning in March, his reviews appeared monthly, including those of albums by Jackie McLean, John Coltrane, Cecil Taylor, Muddy Waters, and Dizzy Gillespie. From 1962 through 1966, Jones wrote reviews for *Down Beat*, *Jazz*, and *Kulchur*.

One of Jones's earliest critical essays on jazz, "The Jazz Avant-Garde" (1961), describes the artistic legacies and cultural contexts of the avant-garde musicians. First, he wanted to show that the jazz avant-garde was a distinct creative impulse in modern music that could not be simply attributed to Stravinsky, Schoenberg, Bartok, and the like. According to Jones, the most energizing influences on the new jazz was the bebop movement of the late 1940s. Although some prominent jazz critics claimed that the vanguard of creative jazz could be found in the merging of the classical musical influences with jazz, Jones looked instead to those musicians who "have come to the beautiful and logical conclusion that BeBop was perhaps the most legitimately complex, emotionally rich music to come out of this country."[69]

The issue for Jones was not that black avant-garde musicians like Ornette Coleman could ignore contemporary European "art" music. Rather, he believed that black musicians would inevitably be influenced by European music because they were subject to many of the same social forces and ideas that gave rise to that music.

> Ornette Coleman has had to live with the attitudes responsible for Anton Webern's music whether he knows that music or not. They were handed to him along with the whole history of formal Western music, and the musics that have come to characterize the Negro in the United States came to exist as they do today only through the acculturation of this entire history.[70]

Such sensibilities had become ingrained into the psyches of Afro-American jazz musicians as Westernized Americans, albeit not fully equal. Jones was therefore not claiming that jazz needed to be viewed as distinctly uninformed by Western classical music (or other Western music, for that matter) but that it existed as a subcultural creative sphere in Western culture. As such, jazz should be defined by members of that subcultural group who created it. This is where he racially privileged his own voice as a jazz critic.

In disclosing the richness of jazz, Jones refuted those nonsensical arguments that have historically consigned jazz musicians to the status of "talented but technically limited." The elevation of technical virtuosity over mu-

sical content is a misunderstanding of the character of the music and undoubtedly a misplaced borrowing from the Western classical tradition: "To
my mind, *technique* is inseparable from what is finally played as content. A
bad solo, no matter how 'well' it is played is still *bad*."[71] The essay ends on one
of Jones's signature arguments. He contends that black jazz musicians continually explore new avenues for playing the music in response to the en-
croachments of white cultural appropriation and mass culture influences.

In 1963, Jones published "Jazz and the White Critic," which became
one of his best-known essays on jazz. In much the same way that Noam
Chomsky addressed the "responsibility of intellectuals,"[72] Jones could be
said to have addressed "the responsibilities of jazz critics." In so doing, the
essay became his personal announcement of his own commitment to the
craft of jazz criticism.

Jones confronted the paradox that most jazz critics have been white, even
though jazz is an Afro-American art form, most of whose greatest innovators
were black Americans. He believes that one of the reasons for the paucity of
black jazz critics lies in the bourgeois orientation of most educated blacks
who could have become critics. That is, this sector of black America was the
least respectful of an art form too closely associated with lower-class blacks
and too devalued by whites. Like the blues, jazz was considered a music of
"bad taste." While Jones offered no proof to support this assertion, it follows
from his general views about the assimilationist desires of black middle-class
Americans.

Jones was not critical of white jazz critics because they were white and the
music "black." As of 1963, he had not yet adopted his racial essentialist beliefs.
Instead, he argued that white critics often did not approach the music seriously as an art form but treated it as if it could be understood far more easily
than Western classical music. No serious critic of classical music would attempt to interpret Mozart without studying the social and cultural milieu that
produced him. Yet white critics of jazz routinely skipped this stage when judg-
ing jazz. Jazz, Jones contended, could not be understood without also understanding the sociology and philosophy of Negro culture that gave rise to the
music. "Negro music is essentially the expression of an attitude, or a collection of attitudes, about the world, and only secondarily an attitude about the
way music is made."[73] The least informative jazz criticism was based on a discussion of the musical score and notation.[74]

A printed musical example of an Armstrong solo, or of a Thelonius
Monk solo tells us almost nothing except the futility of formal musicol-
ogy when dealing with jazz. Not only are the various jazz effects almost

impossible to notate, but each note *means something* quite in adjunct to musical notation.[75]

Jones asserted that historically, the scarcity of intellectuals among the ranks of white jazz critics had led to major shortcomings in their jazz criticism. Not interested in the ideational aspects of jazz, most of them approached the music as if it was a hobby. Worse, their cultural orientation was middle class. According to Jones, jazz "in its most profound manifestations is completely antithetical to such standards, in fact, quite often is in direct reaction to them."[76] He cited a few examples of misguided criticism written by white critics but did not and perhaps could not document the assertion that white jazz critics tended to be nonintellectuals. Although he does not explicitly say so, a reader might think that those jazz critics who disliked bebop did so because they were white. Yet I suspect that many blacks did not immediately gravitate to Charlie Parker's "Billie's Bounce." Do blacks who dislike Parker's music want to be white-like?

While Jones was undoubtedly correct in claiming that the differences in the musical approaches of Paul Desmond and John Coltrane represented two very different attitudes toward life, he mistakenly generalized this claim to racial groups. Desmond and Coltrane cease to be individuals rooted in different life histories and contexts and instead become proxies for racial difference. By implication, all Negroes share a similar temperament and approach to life that is distinctly different from the temperament and approach to life of all whites. Jones's various claims about the intrinsic differences between jazz played by whites and jazz played by blacks dredges up memories of racialist arguments.

The belief in racially demarcated cultural essences conflicts with Jones's argument about the impact of class differences on black American psyches and attitudes toward black music. Jones confuses his readers because he repeatedly employs race language to describe class issues. According to his argument, the black middle class rejected the blues because they wanted to be white, not because they sought middle-class respectability as blacks. In fact, Jones is almost saying that being middle class is being white.

Racial and class differences probably did influence attitudes toward jazz, but in much more fluid ways than Jones would have us believe. After all, the poorest of the poor blacks never gravitated to Duke Ellington or Charlie Parker. And despite his affected "lower-class" vernacular, Miles Davis was the very bourgeois son of a dentist. Did Miles respect the blues tradition? Conversely, the novelist Richard Wright was raised in a poor black southern family. Yet according to his friend and fellow novelist, Ralph Ellison, Wright knew little about the blues and, in fact, was quite divorced from the world of jazz as well. To claim that the blues and jazz are Afro-American art forms does not mean that all Afro-Americans appreciate or even understand this music. Moreover, a black American who does not like the blues or jazz is not necessarily aspiring to assimilate. Simply put, some blacks may not like jazz. I, for one, am not a fan of the blues.

The contradictions in the argument of "Jazz and the White Critic" reappeared in *Blues People*. What remains striking about this essay is how similar the 1963 version of LeRoi Jones was to Ralph Ellison in his approach to Negro culture. Ellison could easily have written Jones's closing lines:

> Negro music, like the Negro himself, is strictly an American phenomenon, and we have to set up standards of judgment and aesthetic excellence that depend on our native knowledge and understanding of the underlying philosophies and local cultural references that produced blues and jazz in order to produce valid critical writing or commentary about it.[77]

BLUES PEOPLE

Jones's classic study *Blues People: Negro Music in White America* was published in 1963.[78] Combining the scholarly and the polemical, *Blues People* charts the historical development of black music and then uses that historical development as a metaphor for exploring the Americanization of the Negro. Beginning with a discussion of the cultures and musical sensibilities of the enslaved Africans, Jones chronicles the ways in which changes in black music reflected changes in the social status of blacks. Writing as a sociologist of music, Jones states:

> It seems possible to me that some kind of graph could be set up using samplings of Negro music proper to whatever moment of the Negro's social history was selected, and that in each groupings of songs a certain frequency of reference could pretty well determine his social, economic, and psychological states at that particular period.[79]

Using this "graph," *Blues People* focuses on certain moments of rupture/dislocation in the historical lives of black Americans: from Africans to Afro-Americans, from slaves to freedmen, from southerners to northerners, from rural to urban, and from working class to middle class.

Blues People begins as a meditation on the immensity of the cultural dislocation experienced by the Africans brought as slaves to America. African slaves were not only thrown into an alien culture, but they also were perceived, because of their foreignness, as less than full human beings. The unintelligibility of their various languages to their white masters only reinforced the perception of their "difference." Borrowing from the work of anthropologist Melville Herskovits, Jones argued for the existence of certain cultural continuities between Africans and Afro-Americans despite the gulf separating the first slaves who were Africans from those slaves who had been born and raised in the United States. Despite the stories and musical tales that informed the lives of the first Afro-American slaves, they were at a decided disadvantage in retaining their cultural continuity with Africa because they could not reflect on or remember a life lived in Africa.

Of all the slaves brought to the New World, the enslaved descendants of those Africans first brought to the United States were the most culturally assimilated. Behind the quick dissolution of African traits and cultures in the American colonies was the greater interaction experienced here between the slaves and their white masters. In the American colonies and later in the United States, small-scale farmers were able to buy slaves. Unlike the huge plantation systems in Brazil and Haiti, where individual slaves had little interaction with their masters, in the United States, the small-scale farmer in the United States had extensive contact with his slaves. The intensity of this interaction accelerated the cultural dislocation of the enslaved from their African past.

In proclaiming a uniqueness to Afro-American culture vis-à-vis African cultures, Jones is not participating in those narratives that view this cultural shift as a progressive movement toward civilization. Instead, his intent is to valorize African cultural roots while simultaneously granting cultural agency to the enslaved and their descendants.

> Blues is the parent of all legitimate jazz, and it is impossible to say exactly how old blues is—certainly no older than the presence of Negroes in the United States. It is a native American music, the product of the black man in this country or to put it more exactly the way I have come to think about it, blues could not exist if the African captives had not become American captives. . . . The immediate predecessors of blues were the Afro-American / American Negro work songs, which had their musical origins in West Africa.[80]

Blues People should not be read as scholarly historiography, although the book is historically informed. Instead, it is a historically astute, impressionistic, cultural studies polemic. Jones is not interested in merely telling the tale of black cultural development but of rhetorically righting historical wrongs. In particular, he wants to undermine the credibility of those scholars and the general populace who participated in the negative stigmatization of black people. By focusing on the creative products of these devalued peoples, Jones questions the criteria used to determine just who in America is and isn't "cultured."

When writing *Blues People*, Jones availed himself of the scholarship available at that time.[81] Several decades after its publication, he reflected on the work that went into that book:

> That took a *lot* of research. You know, I once read someone felt I just tossed it off the cuff—that it was something that flashed through my mind, in other words. Nothing could be farther from the truth. I had a fundamental knowledge about the subject and, to one degree or another, I have studied music, *devoured* music all my life. But *Blues People* was an education for me. Writing a book about the history of black music is a self-teaching job in terms of your own history, and that was tremendously beneficial to me.[82]

What was and remains pathbreaking about the text is Jones's neo-Marxist, cultural studies approach to the study of black music. Jones's novelty lay in his ability to describe and analyze black music as a site of black opposition and a historical repository of black struggle. Whereas Ellison viewed the blues primarily through the lens of the psychocultural humane intentions and meanings universally expressed through art, Jones saw black music as an ever changing response to the economic, social, and material alterations in black life. Both Ellison and Jones recognized the cultural affirmation present in the blues, although Ellison made this aspect central. Jones, on the other hand, wanted to highlight the concerted oppositional elements in black music. For Ellison, the blues and jazz were conspicuously American art forms. In Jones's mind, the blues and jazz were primarily African, albeit continually filtered through American culture. Ellison viewed the music as an indication of the Negro's fundamental American identity. Jones saw the music as an indication of the Negro's status as a cultural outsider in America.

One strength of *Blues People* is its historical reconstruction of various genres of the blues and jazz. At each stage in their development, Jones situates its black cultural creators in the context of their economic function in the American social order. For instance, the early "shouts" and "hollers" arose as accompaniment to the heavy physical labor of plantation slavery. As blacks in the postslavery era gravitated to tenant farming, their group-oriented work songs changed into more solitary music. In much the same way, Jones describes the urban influences on the music that arose after the "great migration" to northern industrial centers and how they differed from its rural, southern origins.

In chronicling the journey from Africa to Detroit via slavery, Jones's discussion continually invokes the idea of a changing but nevertheless resilient, black cultural particularity. Negro Americans, that is, authentic Negro Americans, are culturally different from white Americans. In Jones's mind, many Negroes have forsaken their authentic cultural identities in order to gain white people's acceptance and recognition. Such Negroes can be found disproportionately in the middle classes. It is not surprising, then, that the most polemical and tendentious chapter of the book is Jones's commentary on the black middle class and its relationship to black culture. Jones asserts that the black middle class rejected "gut-bucket" blues because they were trying to escape all links with Africa and their black "Africanized" lower-class ethnic peers. He claims that the black middle-class rejection of "primitive" black music was premised on a desire to be white.

> The black middle class, from its inception (possibly ten seconds after the first Africans were herded off the boat) has formed almost exclusively around the proposition that it is better not to be black in a country where being black is a liability . . . it was the stench of Africa these aspirant *Americans* wanted to erase.
>
> . . . It was the growing black middle class who believed that the best way to survive in America would be to *disappear* completely, leaving no trace at all that there had ever been an Africa, or a slavery, or even, finally a black man.[83]

Jones is only partially correct. While there were middle-class blacks who rejected the "primitive" black music out of a desire to "whitenize" themselves, there was a larger tradition in the black middle class that rejected such music because its sociocultural status was deemed to be beneath them. It is true that the reason for the black middle class's sense of the music as low status stemmed from their devaluation of the poorer blacks who created it. But the act of distancing themselves from the poor was not the same as trying to racially "disappear." It could be considered an act of racial disappearance only if poor black folks and their music had a complete monopoly on authentic black existences. Jones writes mistakenly as if the black middle class were engaged in a collective effort to racially "pass."[84]

In his formulaic denouncements of the black middle class, there is no room for the middle-class Negroes who were proud to be Negroes. Jones is forced to ignore the existence of the African Methodist Episcopal Church and the African Methodist Episcopal Zion Church, both of which were made up of nonpoor blacks and yet were explicitly identified as black. Likewise, some Congregational and Episcopalian churches were openly identified as black, albeit black middle class. Jones did not and would never understand those elements in the black middle class who took pride in being black and middle class. Yes, they may have had some disdain for poor blacks, but they were not trying to rid themselves of their racial identity. Such privileged blacks established social networks, recreation facilities, and schools, not with the hope of racially disappearing, but with the hope of reinforcing whatever privileged status they enjoyed.

Middle-class Negroes often did reject black folk culture music in favor of European music or even white popular culture. Jones, however, confused acculturation with assimilation. Privileged blacks were often trying to identify with "white culture" while maintaining their allegiances to racial uplift and the broader ethnic group. Aren't Alexander Crummell and W. E. B. Du Bois examples of this? Ironically, it is possible in America for a highly Europeanized black man like Du Bois to maintain strong ethnic/racial affinities for his non-Europeanized ethnic peers. Jones mistakenly posited cultural similarity as the core unifying element in ethnic consciousness when in fact, similar economic, political, and social conditions were far more determinative. If cultural similarity actually was the primary basis of group unity, then on what grounds did Jones, a Beat writer, escape accusations of racial apostasy?[85]

Jones has a peculiarly simplistic understanding of black cultural assimilation. As described earlier, Jones believed that assimilation and acculturation were identical and attributed moral weakness to those blacks who acculturate. He deemed this a moral failure because he saw it as the result of a decision to break away from the masses of black folks and a denial of black cultural authenticity. We need only remember that in *The System of Dante's Hell*, Jones placed heretics in the deepest part of hell. Contrary to Jones's assumptions, no moral quality is linked to assimilation or its rejection. Assimilationism is not a moral issue, even though it is common for ethnic groups to try to make their members believe it is in order to keep them in the ethnic fold.[86]

To create this false ontological aspect of assimilation, Jones was forced to make assimilation/acculturation a deliberate action. Historically, the process by which blacks became increasingly assimilated and acculturated was far more complex and nonlinear than he seems to understand. For instance, assume that the black slaves in the United States experienced what literary scholar Robert Stepto described as a will to literacy.[87] Slaves or even freedmen and women who were taught to read were far more assimilated than their illiterate brethren. They learned to read not in order to be "white" or unlike the other Negroes but because they viewed literacy as the embodiment of freedom and personal empowerment.

Blacks who adhered to certain social norms in hopes of gaining upward mobility may have acculturated in ways denied to those blacks who did not have similar opportunities. Those blacks who did not assimilate as readily as other blacks may not have done so intentionally. Rather, they may not have had many options. What does it mean to say that black sharecroppers in Mississippi were less assimilated and acculturated than Robert Abbott, owner of the *Pittsburgh Courier*? Such comparisons are not relevant, for the sharecropper and Abbott had different opportunities and pressures in the social structure. Isn't it possible that Abbott and/or the hyperacculturated W. E. B. Du Bois could have had a stronger ethnic consciousness than the impoverished black sharecropper? Once again, Jones's conceptual problems stem from his obsessive concern with a fictional "black authenticity."

Black cultural particularity attenuated in accordance with blacks' increased access to the socioeconomic mainstream of American society. Black cultural particularity was at its height during the antebellum period. If acculturation, the decline of Afro-American cultural particularity, is a function of increased black socioeconomic inclusion, then Jones has set up an analysis in which slaves were the most authentically black of all Afro-Americans. To the extent that he valorizes a black cultural purity, Jones places blacks in a no-win situation. If they become upwardly mobile, they will lose some of their cultural distinctivenesses. If they are able to maintain their cultural distinctivenesses, then they may not be able to advance economically. In order to protect black cultural authenticity, would Jones have opposed the emancipation of slaves, the abolition of Jim Crow, or the integration of Julliard? Here we see that Jones's neo-Marxism is compromised by an unwillingness to situate the culture of blacks in a dynamic Marxist framework. It is as if the nation's economic forces were constantly changing everything in society but the cultural core of black America. In Jones's mind, this core could be retained and shared by blacks, whether they were located in Biloxi, Mississippi, during the 1920s or South Philadelphia during the late 1950s.

If acculturation is both a cause and effect of economic inclusion, why did Jones write as if the black middle class took an immoral or unprincipled stance in divorcing itself from legacies of black cultural distinctiveness like the blues? He offers them a phony choice, for his analysis rests on the assumption that macrosociological processes fueled their acculturation. Jones's analysis implies that the only authentic blacks are poor blacks. He mistakenly reifies the impoverishment of blacks by treating poverty as if it were an ethnic black trait. In so doing, he creates an ethnic black identity that is far less adaptable than the ethnic identities of most whites. His analysis would have been richer if he had realized that the forces promoting the disappearance of black cultural peculiarities were also at work in the lives of white Americans. The amorphous cultural mainstream that Jones labels white helped coerce the peculiarity of white ethnic subcultures, whether Jewish American, Italian American, or Irish. Why, then, does Jones persistently refer to mass culture as "white culture"? Given the extent that blacks culturally inform American popular culture, can the cultural mainstream be accurately designated as "white culture"?

As simplistic as it sounds, Jones overlooks the fact that folk music is truly organic only to the folk. As some blacks gained a foothold in the mainstream American economy, their links to traditional black folk cultures became thoroughly attenuated. When Jones, the blues aficionado, listens to recordings of early blues musicians, he does so outside the folk culture that produced these musicians. He, too, is an interloper or, worse, a consumer of a cultural commodity. Yet Jones writes as if something in the core of black identity is not only timeless but makes these early blues musicians and their music *his* in a way that no white person could honestly claim. Today, the blues as an art form no longer generates the support it once did from black audiences. Part of the disappearance of a black audience is the broadening gulf between Afro-Americans and the folk culture that produced the music. Certainly blacks can enjoy the blues today, but they would have to be exposed to it in much the same way that whites are. Like whites, black audiences must be educated to enjoy the blues. Is this a sign of something wrong with black America? Are the white audiences that now fill blues clubs incapable of truly understanding or appreciating the music?

Jones seeks to isolate early periods of black cultural agency as the standard bearer of black cultural authenticity, and by doing so, he succumbs to a reification of black culture. Black culture (i.e., an affinity for black music) becomes a constantly changing but timeless object in the possession of different generations of black people. In commodifying black culture by freezing it into an ahistorical kernel of authenticity that can be either accepted or rejected, Jones is guilty of the very charge that he has leveled against Benny Goodman—*changing a verb to a noun*.[88] Had he taken his argument to its logical conclusion, black "culturing" would not have needed to be constrained by the existing black culture.[89]

While *Blues People* justifiably expresses outrage at the commercial exploitation of black music by white-owned record companies, white musicians of lesser talent, and generic white powers that be, it pays too little attention to those serious white jazz musicians who respected the tradition and fought against the encroachment of consumerism. Is jazz not also theirs?[90] Can't less-talented black jazz musicians and black record companies also exploit jazz?

One of the major problems in Jones's analysis is its overt emphasis on politics as a conscious, driving element in black music.[91] Jones is quite adept at extracting the cultural memory, hope, and opposition embedded in black music. He is far less persuasive when he argues that bebop was intentionally created as an act of political opposition.[92] The relationship of the music to politics was far more elusive. The creators of bebop were trying to develop a style of playing that deviated from the homogenizing tendencies of the market. They were seeking a new space for artistic freedom. But does this make them political revolutionaries who viewed their music as a weapon? I think not. After all, we should acknowledge that Dizzy Gillespie, one of the central figures in bebop, was also prominently featured on international tours sponsored by the U.S. Department of State. Worse, Gillespie and others consciously acted as tools of the American government's desire to show the world that black Americans were not subject to vicious oppression. In the face of international Soviet propaganda that highlighted America's racist treatment of blacks during the 1950s, Gillespie's willingness to champion the United States may have been a form of international "uncle toming."[93]

Bebop was quite radical, but mainly because of the way that it broke with and built on traditions of jazz. Even if bebop was stimulated by a desire to play something that "whites couldn't play," this fact alone cannot explain why bebop was created as bebop.[94] It just identifies the underlying angst that gave rise to an attempt to create something innovative and different.

In appropriating a macrosociological vantage point, Jones is unpersuasive when he tries to link a particular style of playing jazz with a sociohistorical environment and condition, because he biases his findings by focusing on the innovators. Although most of them were black, most black jazz musicians were not innovators. Certainly, many black jazz musicians who were contemporaries of Monk, Dizzy, and Bird chose not to embrace bebop (e.g., Louis Armstrong). Why, then, was bebop deemed more representative of the mood of the times than the "traditional" approach of the more numerous, less innovative black jazz musicians? The macrosociological vantage point of *Blues People* generates too broad a sweep to provide insightful commentary on all but the most generalized tendencies.

Herein lies the origins of another analytical shortcoming of the proto–cultural studies framework found in *Blues People*. For example, Charlie Parker was undoubtedly a virtuoso musician, a man with the talent to realize his unique vision of music. He attained the status of an "artist as revolutionary-genius." In the Beat bohemian community, he became a revered icon, for he seemed to embody the combination of artistic creativity and disaffiliation from the parent social order. Much of his romanticized image stemmed from his heroin addiction, which was posited as the embodiment of an outsider sensibility. Heroin solidified the image of Parker and other jazz musicians as outlaws.[95] Concerning the "outsider" identity of Parker and other bebop musicians, Jones wrote:

> The goatee, beret, and window-pane glasses were no accidents; they were, in the oblique significance that social history demands, as usefully symbolic as had been the Hebrew nomenclature of the spirituals. . . . Narcotics users, especially those addicted to heroin, isolate themselves and are an isolated group in society. They are also the most securely self-assured in-group extant in the society, with the possible exception of homosexuals. Heroin is the most popular addictive drug used by Negroes because, it seems to me, the drug itself transforms the Negro's normal separation from the mainstream of the society into an advantage. It is one-upmanship of the highest order.[96]

Contrary to Jones's clever but irresponsible claim that the use of heroin gives black addicts an "advantage," heroin addiction could more accurately be described as the physical embodiment of despair and defeat. As Sidran notes, heroin "suppressed aggressive feelings and allayed anxieties."[97] The use of heroin became a means by which Parker and others therapeutically acclimated to the broader racist society. Ultimately, the addiction undermined their ability to live a functional life. To valorize Charlie Parker as an oppositional figure is far too simplistic. In celebrating heroin addiction, Jones essentially admitted that he had abandoned all critical pretense when assessing the lives of bebop musicians.[98]

Finally, in Ralph Ellison's often quoted review of *Blues People*, he mentions that Jones did not pay enough attention to the degree to which white America was culturally changed by the music of black Americans.[99] Consequently, Ellison rejects Jones's Manichaean typology between a *changing-same* black culture and a static white culture.[100] Instead, he argues that both cultures were continually changing and being changed by each other.[101] Andrew Ross also perceived the nondialectical aspects of Jones's analyses of the interplay between black music and the mainstream society.

> In *Blues People*, Baraka focuses on the conflict between what he sees as autonomous "Afro-American" developments in jazz and their assimilated forms. But his account of the perpetual cut-and-thrust between pure and

impure, black and white, good and evil, always depends on his demonizing the cut-and-paste mainstream culture of musical meanings as a Gehenna of white appropriation and black Tomming. So while Baraka's polemical purism ensures his sensitivity to the changes wrought in black music, it leaves him little room to consider the actual changes wrought upon mainstream popular culture by black musical influences. As a result, black meanings, in whatever form, which reach "acceptance by the general public" can only be seen as evidence of "dilution," and testimony to a "loss of contact with the most honestly contemporary expression of the Negro soul."[102]

Despite its many limitations, Jones's *Blues People* provides a new road map for the emergence of cultural studies types of nonfiction works and attempts to generate a holistic thick description of the cultural plight of Afro-Americans. Given the scope of its ambitions, *Blues People* was bound to fail in many respects. But to the extent that its "failures" are the result of unanswered questions or ill-conceived formulations used to explain an as-yet-unexplainable phenomenon, the book succeeds even when it fails. Most important, it continues to inspire others to interrogate the rich theoretical and intellectual undercurrents of black American cultural projection, particularly black music. And in so doing, it brings the splendor of jazz and the blues to new generations of readers.

AMBIVALENT ANGER / INCUBATING RAGE

During 1964, Jones's aesthetic and political views became increasingly unsettled. The openings of *The Baptism* and *Dutchman* in March of that year, followed by *The Slave* and *The Toilet* in December, gave Jones a heretofore unknown celebrity status. As a successful black writer, he was forced to devise strategies to maintain his artistic and ethnic integrity. He wanted his works to be well known and acclaimed, but he had no intention of allowing himself to become a poster boy for Negro opportunity in America. Jones was decidedly ambivalent. In April 1964, *Newsweek* published a profile of him in which he distanced himself not only from political engagement but racial militancy as well. He described himself as "a literary person first of all, before anything. . . . I think of myself as a poet." When prodded to compare himself with the politicized Jimmy Baldwin, Jones refused to be made a spokesman for anything except art. He was quoted as saying:

Jimmy Baldwin. He's a friend of mine. I love much of his work. But we're
different persons, we each do what we have to do. I don't think that any artist
can divorce himself from ideas. His work has to have something to do with
the world. But a lot of my plays have nothing to do with the Negro Problem.
I try to make people out of my Negro characters, people on a stage, not
causes or social documents. Any man, black or white, has something to say,
but a black man these days will seem to have something to say. Othello is
profound, but not because he is a Negro.[103]

Not yet the Imamu, Jones is so adamant about declaring himself depoliticized on matters of race that he ends up distorting his work. For the playwright to deny that most of his plays were concerned with the Negro problem is ludicrous. Only a year earlier, Jones published the essay "Brief Reflections on Two Hot Shots" in which he claimed that Baldwin's writings
were spavined whines and pleas for the white recognition of his humanity.
But in *Newsweek* in April 1964, Jones juxtaposes himself against Baldwin,
the Negro-writer-as-race-spokesman, in order to proclaim an artistic space
for himself that was free of explicit political engagement. This posture was
short lived, however.

By mid-1964 Jones began to cultivate the image of the "angry young
black man." He regularly engaged in public rhetorical attacks on whites, often
ad hominem in character. Jones displayed his characteristic "black anger" at a
town hall meeting held in New York City on June 15, 1964. This symposium
was entitled "The Black Revolution and the White Backlash." The black panelists included novelists John Oliver Killens and Paule Marshall, actors Ossie
Davis and Ruby Dee, playwright Lorraine Hansberry, and Jones. The white
participants included the talk show host David Suskind; James Wechsler, editor of the liberal *New York Post*; and Charles Silberman, a journalist on the
staff of *Fortune* magazine. Predictably, Jones attacked the white liberals for
their weak commitment to racial justice. After attacking *Fortune* and the *New
York Post* for their editorial slant, Jones even declared that he "objected to sitting next to people I despise." Addressing his comments to the white panelists
as well as the whites in the audience, Jones stated:

When you say violence you usually mean violence to the white man and to
the economic and political power structures . . . the everyday violence
against black people is taken for granted like the weather . . . we want control over who we're going to fight, over where the tax money goes . . . you can
call it a stick-up.

Silberman responded that Jones had used the wrong metaphor: "It sounded to me like a mugging."[104]

While the Jones-Silberman exchange might have been entertaining for the audience, it does not suggest a serious dialogue. One of Jones's postures at the time was that dialogues between blacks and whites (particularly white liberals) were futile, for there was little to talk about anymore. Thus he refused to accept the fundamental premise of authentic dialogue and intellectual exchange: respect for the "opponent." Why was Jones on the panel if he was not committed to dialogue? Few discussants are more capable of irresponsible speech than those who claim that they see no reason to participate in a political discussion but do so anyway.

Could Jones be honestly faulted for distrusting the words of Silberman, a writer for *Fortune* magazine? In conveying his personal disgust for the white liberal panelists, Jones circuitously placed under scrutiny the personal lives of the white participants. Instead of treating them like disembodied bearers of liberal doctrine, Jones's ad hominem dismissal inadvertently opened their material lives to the audience. If Silberman was so liberal on matters of race, why was he working at *Fortune*? Did his racial liberalism inform his behavior there (e.g., *Fortune*'s editorial position)? Did he fight to integrate the magazine's staff and editorial board? And how integrated was the staff of Weschler's *New York Post*? Jones could not assume that self-proclamations of liberalism on the "Negro question" would translate into behavior.

Gatherings like the town hall meeting were really public theater, ritualistic performances that sustained a sense of community. In the presence of an audience, such a dialogue becomes a performance. Did his love of theater lead Jones to participate in a dialogue that he thought was fruitless? It was as if these public rhetorical assaults on whites allowed him to reverse momentarily the power hierarchy between whites and blacks. Throughout his political life, Jones was attracted to the catharsis of momentary symbolic "victories" over his opponents. In such outbursts Jones could also claim to have become a protégé of his fearless idol, Malcolm X.

In a revealing interview that appeared in the *San Francisco Chronicle* in August 1964, Jones tried to describe his anger: "People have said about me that I'm hateful and bitter.... Sure I'm bitter about a lot of things. I'm trying to work with complications of feelings, love and hate at the same time.... What I'm after is clarity; if it sounds like anger maybe that's good in a sense."[105] Jones explained to the interviewer that writing was the most important thing in his life, that it kept him from becoming violent or even self-destructive.

I have to write poetry. . . . I'd last about maybe a day if I didn't. I'd go crazy. Any artist has a lot of energy that won't respond to anything else. The reason I'm not a violent man—that what I'm trying to say in *Dutchman*— is that art is the most beautiful resolution of energies that in another context might be violent to myself or anyone else. . . . Neither sex, now whiskey, nor drugs would do it. People need something to do. If you really have something to do and really want to do it, you use up all that energy and violence in making sure you do it right.[106]

Although Jones was passionate about his political involvements and the political direction of his playwriting, he had not yet become the political activist that would rise to national prominence. In this interview, Jones was still capable of warmly invoking friendships with apolitical white artists in the Village who repeatedly advised him to stay out of politics.

In New York, I have a lot of friends—Larry Rivers, William de Kooning—people who say you shouldn't get involved in politics. People say, "Just stick to your poetry. . . ." "Why are you getting involved?" You have to be involved, whether you say you are or not. I'm black. I have to be involved. When I walk down the street, a man doesn't say, "There goes a cultured nigger." He says, "There's just another nigger." All the white friends I have, people I genuinely love, probably only one or two understand what I mean.[107]

Notably, at this pre–black nationalist stage, Jones could publicly admit to feelings of genuine love for his white friends. He even seems quite willing to tolerate the inability of some of them to understand his unique plight as a black writer. Nevertheless, in the same interview, Jones stated that the United States was on the verge of "blowing up" because most whites could not admit that "America is not a white middle-class country in toto." But despite the warped character of most American whites, Jones remained committed to his white bohemian buddies. Allen Ginsberg was the "only white man in New York I really trust. . . . I trust him and love him completely." Furthermore, it was the writings of "outlaws" like Ginsberg that he most valued. "I always associate with the people thought of as 'beats' . . . [because] they are outside the mainstream of American vulgarity."[108]

In December 1964, Jack Newfield published a short profile of Jones in the *Village Voice*. Written in the afterglow of the dramatic successes of *The Toilet*, *Dutchman*, and *The Slave*, Newfield was somewhat perplexed by the enigmatic playwright.

In the last year Jones has been swept into fashion on a wave of white masochism, curiosity about underground culture, and a gift that is more controlled than Baldwin, hipper than Killens and more direct in its hatred than anyone else. But Jones is a victim of a paradox. The wilder, more obscene, the more jugular his thrusts become, the more he draws acclaim instead of blood.[109]

Newfield's attitude toward Jones reflects the ambivalence that even white progressives felt when talking to the physically small, mild-mannered man whose plays appeared like hand grenades tossed into crowds of bourgeois white thrill seekers. Like many white critics, Newfield saw fit to compare one black writer only with another black writer. In this case, he inappropriately compared Jones with Killens, a writer known primarily for his novels. Claiming that Jones's plays were "obscene" was a rather meaningless comment, albeit one with negative implications. Evidently Newfield never considered the possibility that stunning theater need not be civil. Clay, a central figure in *Dutchman*, is not a representative of an "underground culture," whatever that is. Rather, the play rests on the assumption that Clay is an orthodox bourgeois black man seeking to forge an establishmentarian career in white-dominated America. Finally, neither *Dutchman* nor *The Slave* is a statement of race hatred. Both plays are, instead, articulations of repressed and not so repressed black rage. It was all too convenient for white Americans, progressives included, to experience black rage against white antiblack racist subjugation as black hatred for whites. In so doing, a lazy moral erasure occurs as the dominated become the moral equivalent of the dominating (i.e., "both people are hateful"). To the extent that Newfield's misreading of Jones's plays was probably widely shared, he is justifiably puzzled as to why whites appeared to be enthralled by the playwright.

Ironically, Newfield probably interpreted Jones's statements as substantiation of his claim that Jones was a creator of hateful dramas. By late 1964, Jones had begun to issue apocalyptic denunciations of the West. Besides believing that the West was morally bankrupt, he issued hopeful predictions of its ultimate destruction. He became increasingly obsessed by dreams of revenge. But even though they were frightening to many whites, Jones's apocalyptic fantasies were admissions of political impotence. Jones told Newfield,

My ideas revolve around the rotting and destruction of America, so I can't really expect anyone who is part of that to accept my ideas. But 90 percent of the world knows they are true. They know the West is done. . . . Guerrilla

warfare by blacks is inevitable in the North and the South. . . . Even SNCC
doesn't realize this because they are just a bunch of middle-class vigilantes
. . . every black is a potential revolutionary.[110]

The preposterousness of some of these statements testifies to Jones's inability
to divorce wishful thinking from critical analyses. They speak to his ignorance
of black America. Not only was guerrilla war not an inevitability, but if it had
been, Jones probably would not have known. What was the basis of his claim
that SNCC was mainly composed of middle-class students? Students, yes, but
what did Jones know about their class backgrounds? On what basis could they
be called vigilantes? Despite the distortions and hyperbole, what remains pertinent about Newfield's profile of Jones is that it indicates that the playwright
was no longer seeking to reform the United States. He now wanted to contribute to its destruction.

Jones's outsider status in the Village intellectual/art scene was further
captured in a profile published in the *New York Herald Tribune* in December 1964. Written by Isabel Eberstadt and entitled "King of the East Village," the article describes Jones as an integral part of the Village's avant-
garde artistic life. According to the article, Jones could be found at almost
every avant-garde Village event—dance performances, jazz concerts, films,
plays, or poetry readings in coffee houses. On many occasions he would
read his own poetry. Eberstadt noted that even though Jones was an important participant in this circle, "he always polarized this underground world
by the force of his personality and by his violation of the few conventions
which exist in it." Unlike most Village intellectuals, Jones was willing to engage in moral and artistic critiques of fellow Village writers and artists. His
rejection of total artistic permissiveness was viewed by many as unbo-
hemian-like. But Eberstadt informs us that most incongruous and startling
in the Village scene was Jones's "commitment to action, to violence if necessary, in the furtherance of what he considers right. This is the most foreign of all to the East Villagers, who espouse passivity and usually think of
using nothing sharper than satire against the society of manufacturers,
merchants, and advertisers from which they are so estranged."[111] The "King
of the East Village" was an outsider among outsiders.

In an essay published in the *Sunday Herald Tribune Magazine* in 1964,
Jones once again described his alienation from American society. Although
written for a broader and more mainstream audience than Jones usually
addressed, "LeRoi Jones Talking" is both a diatribe against the mundane
and vulgar governing values of American society and an autobiographical

statement in which the author uses his own experiences to comment on the generic plight of black writers. The essay begins:

> I write now full of trepidation because I know the death this society intends for me. I see Jimmy Baldwin almost unable to write about himself anymore. I've seen Du Bois, Wright, Chester Himes, driven away—Ellison silenced and fidgeting in some college. I think I almost feel the same forces massing against me, almost before I've begun. But let them understand that this is a fight without quarter, and I am very fast.[112]

Like many American writers, Jones believed that the American obsession with money and material gain had produced a society in which artistic creativity was thoroughly devalued. Upon attaining any type of artistic acclaim, a creative artist is deluged with financially lucrative offers to create the most facile and pedestrian art. All that matters is that it sells. Any writer must wrestle with the ways that American success hinders creativity. No sooner does an American writer begin to create serious art than he or she is lured by the artistic death hiding behind profitability.

Jones informs the reader that the designations "Negro writer" and "Negro literature" are used to categorize certain writing as second rate. Such assessments are made by cultural arbiters, often academics. But the judgments of these critics are suspect. As proof, Jones notes the superior status granted to Henry Wadsworth Longfellow over far greater poets like Emily Dickinson and Walt Whitman. Using warped value systems derived from their own culturally impoverished lives, these critics possessed the power to establish the American literary canon. This canonical celebration of artistic mediocrity is indicative of a debased moral character that ignores the realities of the Harlems of America when proclaiming American progress. In such a social context, Negro writers must appeal to their richest inner selves and try to convey that to their readers, knowing all the while that America cannot tolerate honesty. All honest artists, the only great ones, will suffer in such an environment. Such artists will be rightly accused of being crazy and naive. Jones openly admits that he aspires to "the craziness of all honest men."[113] He proudly proclaims himself a "raver" in the tradition of Blake, Rimbaud, and Allen Ginsberg.

Jones hypothesizes that the interests of Negroes would be advanced if they turned to craziness. He asserts that the entire nation would cease to function if Negroes "just stopped behaving, stopped being what Charles desires, and just flip, go raving in the streets, screaming in verse an honest history of America, walk off their jobs."[114] Despite their powerlessness, blacks are implicated in the corruption of this society if only because they appear to be quite at home with their subjugation by compliantly fulfilling their subservient roles.

He argues that the prevailing dishonesty of this society exists to mask the actions of the American economic elite. Only art that celebrates the capitalists, those to whom Jones refers as the "basest elements of the society," will be considered great.

> The Negro writer is in a peculiar position because if he is honest, most of what he has seen and experienced in America will not flatter it nor can that seeing and experiencing be translated honestly into art by euphemism. And while this is true of any good writer in America, black or white, it is a little weirder for the Negro, since if that Negro is writing about his own life and his own experience, that writing must be separated from what the owners and the estimators think of as reality, not only by the intellectual gulf that causes any serious man to be estranged from the mainstream of American life, but by the social and cultural estrangement from the mainstream that has characterized Negro life in America which his work will reflect.[115]

"LeRoi Jones Talking" ranks among the very best of Jones's efforts to discuss his plight as a black writer. What remains so fascinating about the essay is Jones's naïveté and inflated sense of self. If serious art is as thoroughly marginalized as Jones claims that it is in the United States, why would he, a serious writer, be threatening to that social order? In 1964, Jones also wrote the essay "The Last Days of the American Empire (Including Some Instructions for Black People." Except for "The Revolutionary Theater," "The Last Days of the American Empire" was probably the most racially assertive and politically militant statement that Jones wrote before he became a separatist black nationalist.

"The Last Days of the American Empire" is an explosion of rage with no consistent theme or argument. Jones harbored so many complaints about racist American society that he could not devise a style of writing that would allow him to do more than vent his frustrations. Early in the essay Jones rhetorically asks, "Is there anyone in the real world America who thinks Slavery Has Been Abolished?"[116] This question sets the stage for the sledgehammer effect of the writing. Over the twenty pages, we learn that the morally debased white America is destined for political decline, that the black middle class has closed ranks with whites, that it is silly and weak to let some racist sheriff beat your head, and that black people could change their situation if they only would unite and discard racist images of themselves.

While this essay contains little substantive analysis, it is significant because it was one of the first times that Jones openly endorsed black nationalism as the strategy for black people. Even though his understanding of it at this point is nothing more than black group unity, we can see now that he has shifted the vantage point from which he contemplates society. The vantage point has shifted from the idea of a decadent society run for the benefit of mindless consumerist capitalists to a decadent society that has been deliberately committed to domestic and international racism as a means of maximizing its economic profitability.

The essay is an early articulation of some of the themes that soon became standard Jones arguments. He tells us that the United States is destined to fall because it is immoral and out of touch with the needs and interests of most of the world's people. This is why he can title the essay "The Last Days of the American Empire." In issuing prophecies of white American destruction, Jones conceals his inability to conceive of an agent of social change. Instead of considering the possibility that American economic exploitation of the world could continue indefinitely (or, worse, permanently), Jones retreats to moral claims to substantiate assertions about America's demise. Having no agent of change (like Marx's working class), Jones retreats to the efficacy of moral condemnations. And for this, he criticizes black advocates of nonviolent social change!

In a raging didactic fashion, Jones instructs black people that whether or not they know it, they have stronger characters than whites do, for oppression breeds strength in the oppressed and weakness in the oppressor.

> The stupid arrogance, the ignorance, AND FEAR, in those cracker eyes, those firemen, state patrolmen, the dog holders, all that fear is in the bones of this society.... Look at those weak fag faces on those patrolmen arresting that beautiful chick, and finally there is something in her face which is stronger than anything in white eyes' life.[117]

A second lesson is to beware of any and all attempts of white America to divide blacks against one another. In particular, whites will try to split blacks into different classes, even though they know that the only division in America that matters is the one that labels someone white or black.

> I cannot repeat it too many times, nor can any of you black people repeat it too many times to one another. DO NOT ALLOW YOURSELF TO BE SEPARATED from your brothers and sisters, or your culture. This is what makes us think we are weak.[118]

A third lesson centers on Jones's attempt to convince his readers that the racist attacks on blacks in Birmingham, Alabama, are directly linked to the racist behavior of the United States (and other "white" countries) in Africa. He asserts that Patrice Lumumba and Medgar Evers were murdered by the same people. Finally, Jones wants blacks to know that the idea of a nonviolent social change is both demeaning to black people and a political scam.

In the essay's conclusion, Jones's argument implodes on the basis of his inability to construct a viable alternative plan of action.

> The hope is that young blacks will remember all of their lives what they are seeing, what they are witness to just by being alive and black in America, and that eventually they will use this knowledge scientifically, and erupt like Mt. Vesuvius to crush in hot lava these willful maniacs who call themselves white Americans.[119]

It is not clear just what Jones intended when he subtitled the essay "Including Some Instructions for Black People." If he meant to instruct black people, why do so in a book that would be read predominantly by whites? I suspect that these so-called instructions for blacks were actually directed at a white reading audience. Their purpose was to instill in whites the belief that Jones had tapped into an undercurrent of black popular sentiments. If successful, Jones's hypermilitant essay would have functioned as a fear-inducing plea/warning to white folks. Once again, we see the depth of Jones's entrapment in a black victim status.

BAD NIGGER IN THE VILLAGE

In contrast to his many artistic talents, Jones more frequently than not displayed a penchant for simplistic social views and the resultant dogmatic politics. During his latter days in the Village (1964–65), Jones and his friend jazz musician Archie Shepp engaged in bitter verbal attacks on whites at public forums.[120] In *The Crisis of the Negro Intellectual*, Harold Cruse describes a joint Jones-Shepp tirade at the Village Vanguard. During an exchange with the audience, artist Larry Rivers spoke from the floor. A friend of Jones, Rivers had created the sets for Jones's plays *The Toilet* and *The Slave*.[121] In the course of his remarks, Rivers reminded Jones and Shepp of the 6 million Jews who had perished in the Nazi Holocaust.[122] According to Cruse, Jones replied to Rivers, "You're like the others [whites], except for the cover story."[123] As if Jones were not provocative enough, Shepp went further, " I'm sick of you cats talking about the six million Jews. I'm talking about the five to eight million Africans killed in the Congo. King Leopold is his name."[124] Cruse then notes that a white woman in the audience argued that Jones and Shepp should appreciate the assistance that whites and, in particular, Jews had given to the cause of black civil rights. Once again Shepp replied in an inflammatory tone, "I give no civil service charity for going to Mississippi to assuage their consciences."[125]

Another public forum that turned into a LeRoi Jones tirade against white people took place at the Village Gate. Three decades after this event, Jones referred to it as "the public shootout that remains most clearly etched in my memory."[126] He recollected that a white woman, "in all earnestness"[127] asked him if whites couldn't be of some help to the black struggle. He remembers emphatically telling her that she and other whites could help by dying, for "you are a cancer." Another white audience member brought up the names of Andrew Goodman and Michael Schwerner, the two young Jewish American men who, with James Chaney, had been murdered in Mississippi. Jones answered that blacks had many of their own to mourn. "Those white boys were only seeking to assuage their own leaking consciences."[128]

When commenting on this episode in his autobiography, Jones finally admitted that the willingness of Goodman and Schwerner to commit their lives to the black civil rights struggle was not only heroic but constituted a degree of engagement that outstripped his own contribution to that movement.[129] Jones mentions that the anger in his responses was intensified because the very people (i.e., white people) who had invoked the memory of Goodman and Schwerner had not mentioned the name of their murdered black companion, James Chaney. Jones claimed that he was enraged by the silence of Chaney's murder and the corresponding implication that the value of white life superseded that of blacks. This response sounds contrived, however, for the audience may have mentioned the murdered white civil rights activists precisely because Jones and Shepp were attributing racism to all whites. Concerning these public tirades against whites, Jones wrote,

> There were questions from the audience; I now regularly put down "whitey."
> I had long done this in my writing. The torturous years the African and
> African American have spent as slaves and chumps for this white suprema-
> cist society obviously provided enough factual resources to support a tirade
> against whites. The Muslim example, particularly and most inspirationally
> the message of Malcolm X, supported my attack. But still I was married to a
> white woman, I still had many white friends.[130]

Even many years later, Jones still did not grasp the underlying vulnerability that may have led him to such fanatical and irresponsible articulations of rage. Jones cites his marriage to Hettie as if it canceled out his antiwhite tirades. On the surface, this certainly was the case. But it seems equally plausible that the necessity for cursing white liberals arose precisely because of his intimate relationships with white friends and a white wife, not in spite of them. One can easily imagine a self-assured black political activist who was situated in a black community speaking to the same Village audience without feeling the need to "act out" in such an immature manner. In denouncing whites, Jones was actually condemning himself for his lack of involvement in the black movement. The whites he vilified as "poseur-liberals who sashayed safely through the streets of Greenwich village, the behind-the-scenes bleeding hearts"[131] were essentially transferred and detested images of himself. Ironically, it was Jones and Shepp, not Goodman and Schwerner, who were trying to assuage leaking consciences.

Jones's depictions of his life, whether in his autobiography or in his numerous interviews, often assume a teleological narrative in which one action necessarily leads to another, which then necessarily leads to yet another action and so forth up to the present. The present incarnation of Jones is therefore posited as the culmination, negation, and moral erasure of all the previous ones. For example, Jones's autobiographical narrative assumes that the contradiction between having a white wife and publicly vilifying all whites could have been resolved only through his emergence as a militant black chauvinist. In actuality, the supposed contradiction between his private life and his public speech might just as well have been resolved by ceasing to engage in such cathartic diatribes. But since he did not choose this path, Jones writes as if such a course of action was never a viable option.

While he does reflect on his past, his reflections are usually constrained by a priori limits that ultimately reduce his responsibility for any previous actions, however wretched. Dreadfully irresponsible, Jones is unremittingly morally evasive. We, his audience, are supposed to restrict our judgments to his present configuration and thus participate in his moral amnesia. Jones's contemporary rationalization for his past attacks on Andrew Goodman and Michael Schwerner (i.e., the whites did not mention Chaney) is only one part of a larger project to obfuscate any obscene behavior in his past.

Jones's attempts to equate his diatribes against whites with Malcolm's rhetorical style was a gross distortion. Certainly Jones knew that Malcolm did not curse at white audiences on those numerous occasions when he spoke to them. Even though Malcolm was angry at whites, he did not use such occasions to exorcise his internal demons. Malcolm, unlike Jones, did not have to

engage in theatrical spectacles of conflict in order to create an image of opposing white racism. Instead, Malcolm's everyday life embodied that opposition. It was therefore not surprising that Malcolm praised the very Jewish civil
rights activists whom Jones condemned in the Village. Concerning the death
of Andrew Goodman and Michael Schwerner, Malcolm stated, "I've come to
the conclusion that anyone who will fight not *for* us but *with* us is my
brother."[132] During one 1964 speaking engagement at Wayne State University,
Malcolm deliberately confronted a black member of the audience who had
uttered a string of anti-Semitic denunciations. Malcolm stated, "I suspect that
our moderator today is Jewish and I won't put him in the position of silencing you. So I will. Shut up and sit down."[133] Had Malcolm been in the audience in the Village when Jones launched into his antiwhite, anti-Jewish
tirades, he might well have told Jones to sit down and shut up. Had he done
so, Afro-American politics and literature might have been spared some of the
infantile outbursts that became characteristic of Jones's political rhetoric during the next seven years. Unfortunately, Malcolm had been murdered by the
time that Jones exploded at these Village rap sessions. The legacy left by Malcolm was so open-ended that Jones and others could tease out of it whatever
they so chose. In need of dramatic performances to rhetorically create the
image of estrangement from whites that his life did not embody, Jones became a walking antiwhite, invective machine. Provided with an audience,
preferably white, and a microphone, Jones would hurl a crescendo of curses.
In pursuit of hurt white feelings and black applause, Jones would sacrifice
complexity and ambivalence. This aversion to ambivalence forever made
Jones politically a Manichaean dogmatist.

The Village attacks on white audiences were typical articulations of
Jones's mistaken belief that rhetorical assaults were analogous to radical
praxis. It was not therefore surprising when Jones wrote about this period in
his life, "I rejected Martin Luther King's philosophy. I was not nonviolent. I
had written a poem about this time that ended:

We have awaited the coming of a natural
phenomenon. Mystics and romantics, knowledgeable
workers
of the land.

But none has come
(Repeat)
But none has come.
Will the machinegunners please step forward?" [134]

Evidently, Jones thought that writing a poem about violent political activity was a negation of and thus, by extension, on a par with nonviolent political praxis. While Jones viewed himself—and desired to be viewed—as increasingly radicalized because of his willingness to engage in antiwhite verbal tirades and antiwhite, cathartic poetry, he continued to refrain from active political engagement. His actions were not only nonviolent but passive, whereas the nonviolent Martin Luther King Jr. was anything but passive.

It is not surprising that while living a politically passive life in the Village, Jones was willing to play the role of the "big, bad, violent nigger" for an audience of bohemian whites. Jones had clearly sought and acquired a black victim status in the Village scene. Unlike mainstream white society, which wanted its victim-status blacks to be cross-carrying messiahs like Martin Luther King Jr., Village whites evidently expected their victim-status blacks to tell them just how despicable they were as whites. Many of these whites were, as Tom Wolfe later announced, engaged in "radical chic."[135]

In an interview published in 1966, the avant-garde pianist Cecil Taylor might well have been speaking about Jones and Shepp:

> When you want to go in for politics you don't stay in New York. I've no great admiration for people—white or black—who take up positions here. The people I respect are the young blacks of Mississippi or Alabama who don't hesitate to get themselves clubbed by the police in order to win the case.[136]

At some point between 1964 and 1966, Jones became New York society's fashionable black-writer-who-hates-whites. In commenting on Jones's shrewd manipulation of white guilt and fear, Stephen Schneck noted:

> The more he attacked white society, the more white society patronized him. Who'd have suspected that there was so much money to be made from flagellation? Whitey seemed insatiable; the masochistic vein was a source of hitherto untapped appeal, big box office stuff, and LeRoi Jones was one of the very first to exploit it.[137]

Schneck concluded his article by claiming that Jones's willingness to leave the "white" New York art world was an indication that he was not merely engaged in an ethnic "hustle." What Schneck did not foresee at the time of his article was that Jones would reemerge "on the other side" as a prominent figure during the Black Power era. Schneck also did not understand that Jones—a man who had evaded the entire Civil Rights movement and who was not necessarily perceived as ethnically legitimate by those circles he hoped to join and ultimately lead—needed an ethnically legitimating admission ticket into black America. The ticket was purchased through his rejection of the "white world," including, supposedly, his Greenwich Village celebrity status. That is, Jones's willingness to walk away from white acclaim became a trademark of his commitment to black people. But Jones never abandoned his quest for public recognition. What he supposedly sacrificed in the Village became his mode of entry into Harlem.

Concerning his last days in the Village, Jones wrote:

> What we did, concretely, was polarize the people downtown. We talked a black militance and took the stance that most of the shit happening downtown was white bullshit and most of the people were too. The fact that we, ourselves, were down there was a contradiction we were not quite ready to act upon, though we discussed it endlessly.... For us it was *Harlem*, that was the proper capital of our world and we were not there.... So we settled for jumping on people, mostly verbally... we carried the fanaticism of the petty bourgeoisie.[138]

Harlem had not only relinquished its status as the haven for the black bourgeoisie but had become the "capital of our world."

4

Rejecting Bohemia

The Politicization of Ethnic Guilt

DISCARDING HETTIE

Only after Jones renounced the Village did his tormented identity as a black bohemian became subject to wider public scrutiny. Perhaps the most apparent indication of his identity conundrum was his decision in 1965 to leave his wife, Hettie, and their two daughters. The interracial marriage to Hettie had evidently been a source of joy and endurable anxieties until Jones began to feel the need to reconcile with the black community. In Jones's mind, such a reconciliation demanded his direct physical involvement in black political affairs, an involvement that simultaneously revealed an intensifying affinity to the black freedom struggle as well as nagging feelings of guilt about blacks. Hettie Cohen was not necessarily a liability to Jones's becoming politically active in order to improve the lives of black Americans. She, too, was committed to this end. Nevertheless, Hettie, "the white wife," was a liability for a young Afro-American male who felt ethnically illegitimate and who wanted now to be black, which tragically for Jones meant being seen as black by both blacks and whites.[1] Contrary to Jones's claims that he had become increasingly politicized—and thereby socially and politically distanced from his bohemian life and closer to a "deeper black" identity—Jones's obsessive desire to overcome his feelings of ethnic illegitimacy may have led to his political activity. Had other avenues been open to meet this psychoethnic need, he might well have never become so overtly politically engaged, at least not at this point in his life. The absence of a highly developed intellectual infrastructure in black America (e.g., journals, radio shows, organizations) to facilitate the political articulations of writers/intellectuals must be seen as partially responsible for Jones's emergence as a full-time black political activist. For the black artist seeking to apply his talents to the black freedom struggle, few opportunities were available that could both fulfill this desire and protect the necessary "space" to function as a creative intellectual.

Before the publication of his autobiography, Jones had been somewhat hesitant to discuss his marriage to Cohen publicly. Moreover, the discussion presented in the autobiography appears contrived.[2] Jones says that he stumbled into a marriage with a white woman in America during the 1950s. The implication is that while he knew that interracial relationships were generally seen as aberrant in the United States, his own decision to enter such a marriage never considered this. Despite the place and timing of his marriage to Hettie (in the United States during the 1950s), we are supposed to believe that he viewed the decision to marry interracially as insignificant. Later, as if to diminish his commitment to this interracial marriage, Jones described his relationship with Cohen as passionless.[3]

Jones attributes a racist self-hatred to many of his male black bohemian peers who were dating or married to white women, and he does not exclude himself from such allegations. But it was a politically and ethnically risky posture for him, at any time, to admit that he had ever been excessively attracted to a white woman. Although Jones later claimed that in rejecting Hettie, he rejected "the white woman," he could never admit to its obvious inverse: of having desired "the white woman" when desiring Hettie Cohen. Instead, Jones objectified white women in another manner. He says that he sexually pursued white women because it was a sign of a black bohemian identity. In describing his first sexual encounter with a white Soho woman, he wrote,

> I had never talked to a white woman before at such length or with such intentions. Because as we wound down toward her place I could see sleeping with her. It seemed to me part of the adventure of my new life in the Village. The black man with the white woman, I thought. Some kind of classic bohemian accoutrement.[4]

Given the previously described "Crow-Jim" cultural tendencies present in bohemia, Jones may well have been the overdetermined, objectified sexual object. In making the interracial sexual union a bohemian fixture, Jones tries to sidestep the question of his potential complicity in his own racist objectification, not to mention his objectification of the white woman.

In his autobiography, Jones is simply incapable of admitting that he consciously and willfully dated and loved Hettie. He could never admit that he had loved her, for, I suspect, his ultrareified approach to confronting the world would have regarded such a claim as an admission of love for "the white woman" and thus "white people" (over and above "the black woman" and "black people"). Jones sometimes claims that he had mistakenly thought he once loved Cohen but that the price of this inauthentic love was an authentic alienation from his black self. Assuming that LeRoi had various reasons for marrying Hettie, one motivation that cannot be ignored is that she was a desired sexual/gender commodity, a public and private style, much like his beard and dark sunglasses.[5] Jones provided a glimpse of his reified thinking about Cohen when he reflected on his decision years earlier to marry her:

> The running bohemians of the black-white hook-ups I knew didn't (I didn't think) get married. . . . Hey, but here I was going off into some normal US social shit. I could feel that contradiction in a funny way. The black-white thing wasn't no normal US shit, it was out. . . . I didn't come over to the Village for no regular middle class shit, yet here I was in it.[6]

Jones contemplated rejecting marriage for reasons that have everything to do with an approach to self-identity based on differentiating himself from others through his attachments to individually chosen, commodified images. Much like selecting a certain style of shoes, Jones chose a certain style of wife. He was the quintessentially reified individual. The same alienated self that produced the ad hoc distaste for "normal US shit" created a fondness for interracial marriages because "the black-white thing . . . was out." Such ad hoc negations of middle-class social norms, as Barnes and Sollors noted, attest to the bohemian's dependence on the parent society. At its worse, bohemia fostered a parasitic identity.

In addition to his dramatic excursions into the world of interracial sexual relationships (*Dutchman*, *The Toilet*, and *The Slave*) Jones wrote several essays on the topic. One, "American Sexual Reference: Black Male," was published around the time of his divorce from Hettie. Jones wrote that interracial marriages most often occur in the deviant sectors of the middle class (e.g., artists, bohemians). These sectors are somewhat more "liberated" to the extent that they are not as deeply embedded in traditional racial identities and beliefs.

> For the black man this would mean that he had grown, somehow, less black; for the white woman it means, at one point, that she has more liberal opinions, or at least likes to bask in the gorgeousness of being a hip, ok, sophisticated outcast. . . . For the black man, acquisition of a white woman always signified some special power the black man had managed to obtain (illicitly, therefore with a sweeter satisfaction) in white society. It was also a way of participating more directly in white society. One very heavy entrance into White America. (No matter if any of these directions said "Love.")[7]

Here Jones is plainly admitting that in marrying a white woman, a black man's ethnic identity becomes diluted. Although this is debatable, the significance of the assertion is worth pondering. Equally important is Jones's assumption that one's ethnic/racial identity is one's most inalienable and authentic identity.[8] Jones, the racial essentialist, posits "blackness" as if it were a phenomenon divorced from living black human beings. Unfortunately, being black is being authentically reified![9] Problematic as this is, what is pathetic about Jones's depiction is his unwillingness to admit that by marrying a black man, a white woman could become culturally less "white." While many, if not most, interracial relationships in America probably tilt toward the cultural world of one partner over and above that of the other, Jones denies the possibility that an interracial relationship could result in a culturally creolized union. Whatever her cultural origins, Hettie Cohen Jones became quite racially cosmopolitan. Interestingly, LeRoi and Hettie seem to have created a mulatto family culture. Hettie noted that "with me he hadn't abandoned but emphasized—and taught—his culture."[10] Because Cohen could neither change her racial designation in America nor step outside those historical discourses that created race as meaningful, she would always be a beneficiary of white privilege in ways denied to her black husband. Nonetheless, she had relinquished some of those privileges and comforts in marrying Jones.

Concerning the mutual racial objectification that can occur in the United States in interracial relationships, Eugene Victor Wolfenstein created a compelling but worse-case ideal type. Concerning the white female–black male relationship, he described the ways that the racial climate in the United States might distort the intimacy into a relationship of racial/gender types. And concerning an interracial relationship based on these distorting reifications, Wolfenstein wrote:

> The white woman wishes to be black, which means to overcome her inhibitions, release the sensuality repressed in her whitened-out character structure. She is mesmerized by images of black manhood, tantalized by violating a racial taboo. By violating the taboo she is being "bad"—a fallen and free woman. Her triumph over her repressive whiteness lies in her surrender to his phallic blackness.... The black man, by contrast, wants to be white, to have the power and prestige of the white man. The woman's sexual surrender serves to affirm his manhood and his whiteness. It is also his triumph over the white man—not only a violation of the white man's taboo but also a conquest of his woman.[11]

Wolfenstein's commentary poses the possibility that interracial relationships can occur between parochial whites and blacks who are comfortable with their racial identities but who wish to escape them. A black man who desires a white woman because she is white may be enacting a ritual that is hyper-Afro-American in its origins, despite what some may well view as indicating a desire to escape blackness. There are many reasons that white and black individuals choose to intermarry. Undoubtedly, some reasons are healthier than others. If Wolfenstein is correct in pointing out deeply embedded cultural race-scripts that can poison such a relationship, there may be something heroic about interracial unions of persons who are in love and yet aware of the social forces intent on making them view each other as racial types and symbols.

For the sake of argument, let's suppose that initially Jones did racially objectify Cohen in the way Wolfenstein described. If so, these initial objectifications might have changed as the two of them created a daily life as a couple. If LeRoi Jones could not adequately differentiate the individual Hettie Jones from her reified racial/gender type, "the white woman," we should not assume that Hettie had equal trouble recognizing his humanity and individuality.

When writing about his marriage to Cohen, Jones was unable to escape Wolfenstein's formulaic race/gender ideal-types. Jones's comments on this issue appear to have been borrowed from Franz Fanon's *Black Skins, White Masks*.[12] A sympathetic reader can imagine how easy it might be for both partners to reify the other, particularly during relational crises. LeRoi, however, describes his own participation in his marriage to Hettie as if he had been a distant observer of the interaction. Certainly, in numerous interracial relationships, the race roles become objectified in this manner.

Jones trivializes interracial romantic relationships as if a bond of love between two individuals of different races cannot create a union that can cross existing racial borders and remain healthy. Worse, Jones writes as if every action he took while married to Hettie had a racial significance. In order to maintain this depiction, Jones is forced to racially overdetermine his everyday life with Cohen. Despite the apparent ubiquity of race, there are many moments in the everyday life of an interracial couple when race is not an issue. After all, someone has to fix the leaking sink, wash the dirty clothes, and put the kids to bed. Jones appears incapable of admitting that he shared an "everyday life" with Cohen.

In the *Village Voice* in 1980, Jones returned to the theme of interracial marriage, continuing to speak of his marriage to Cohen in ultrareified terms:

For a Black intellectual, such as I was, to marry a white woman in the late
'50s was simply another sign that I had imbibed the Euro-American worldview, history, and aesthetic and was prepared to live by it. . . . It became clear
that I could only really "love" a white woman at the expense of giving up the
things in myself that I cared most about, the collective memory of Black
love. That love itself was not possible unless I loved my own image—and
what I committed myself to loving, in such a fearful land, was in reality what
I was committed to *being*. As these feelings welled up in me, a terrible sense
of estrangement began to pull me away from Hettie, until she became only,
"the white woman I am living with."[13]

Jones comes dangerously close to asserting here that in becoming an intellectual, he became "white" or, at least, "whiter." What he misinterprets is the estrangement that he, a traditional black intellectual, felt vis-à-vis the broader
"black community." More precisely, he felt socially marginalized from the
black community. This estrangement is not necessarily synonymous with
ceasing to be black (whatever that is), for many white artists have felt a similar estrangement from their own home communities. Jones wanted to be an
intellectual, an avant-garde intellectual no less, and yet he felt guilty about
its social and psychological costs. Soon he stopped celebrating the estrangement of Irish-Catholic writers (e.g., Joyce, Beckett) as the model for Afro-
American artistic marginality. In fairness to Jones, ethnic loneliness is not
easy. It is particularly difficult when one is a member of an oppressed ethnic
group, for at some point, willed ethnic distancing is seen as an act of significant moral consequence.

Jones's post-Village comments about his ex-wife were typical overstatements for the ethnic renegade who seeks readmission into the graces of the
ethnic group.[14] Reason is jettisoned and replaced by trite tautologies. Simply
put, Jones asserted that a black person, albeit an authentic one, could never
love a white person. So upon regaining his connection to that "blackness"
lurking in himself, he gradually stopped being able to love his wife, the white
woman with whom he was living. Again, the morality of Jones's decision to
divorce his first wife is not at issue here. But the reified notions of self-identification that lay at the center of Jones's discussion of his marriage to her are
critical to comprehending his marriage's role as a social marginality facilitator for him and his inability at a certain moment to exist as an authentic ethnically marginal individual.

In his autobiography, which, as stated earlier, was published almost a
quarter century after his marriage to Cohen, Jones described one aspect of
their marriage.

But there is a mutual mythology that gets built in those relationships and built by the people in them. Information about the other's world becomes one main topic of discussion. . . . The conflicting opinions that come with those lives are discussable as well as the dynamic that makes the meeting interesting. But white supremacy creates an inequality in those relationships that probably most of the people in them cannot identify by name but certainly they can by what emotions and ideas it produces.[15]

Jones is certainly correct to note that the pervasiveness of racism in American society continually threatens to infiltrate and distort an interracial relationship. Vigilance is necessary. He perceptively describes the ways that interracial relationships can appear to be intrinsically engaging intellectually as a result of cross-cultural fertilization. He implies, however, that this type of intellectual stimulation might be inauthentic. Why? Jones once again concludes that interracial unions between black and white Americans are doomed, particularly for those interested in racial egalitarianism.

Reading these quotations leads to a macabre conclusion. At one point in his life, a white wife had served his identity needs. But when deciding to assume a new identity, as he did on numerous occasions, his attachment to her became dysfunctional.[16] As if having been purged of evil during an exorcism, leaving his white Jewish wife became a rite of passage into a new state of "blackness."[17] Ironically, if we accept Jones's post-bohemia explanations of his life in bohemia, we could conclude that Podhoretz's original assertions concerning black bohemians were, by and large, correct. In claiming that his marriage to Cohen was only a manifestation of black intraracist self-hatred, Jones virtually validated Podhoretz's claim made years earlier that black bohemians were in bohemia essentially because they were running away from the black community and their black identity.

We must be skeptical of accepting at face value Jones's post-bohemian self-explanations of his Beat past. After leaving the Village Beat bohemian scene for black nationalist politics, he attempted to rewrite his past in order to minimize its significance. Such simplifications were necessary for his black nationalist political aspirations. In order to diminish the vulnerability he faced vis-à-vis other black nationalists who may have doubted his "black" authenticity for having been married to a white woman, Jones thought it beneficial to describe this previous life as if it had been a sick phase in his existence.[18] This "insanity plea" relieved Jones of the need to make explanations, particularly to the racially parochial audience of his new home.

The significance of the interracial marriage in Jones's life has too often been overlooked or misunderstood. Critics have frequently gauged Cohen's influence on Jones by analyzing her impact on his writing and dramatic styles. In *From LeRoi Jones to Amiri Baraka*, Theodore Hudson wrote, "He [Jones] claims that Hettie had no special influence on his art"[19] Whether Hettie influenced LeRoi's actual writing style is beyond my knowledge and concerns. But less than a decade after Hudson published this statement, Jones publicly claimed that during his Beat period, "two of the most important influences on me . . . were Allen Ginsberg, and my first wife Hettie Cohen."[20] Hudson may have been looking for her influence in the wrong place. Hettie was probably crucial at helping Jones arrive at a psychosocial space in which he could be creative. Indeed, it may have been that Hettie's ears were the first to hear the incomplete and finished products of Jones's novice efforts at writing. Hettie also probably functioned as the first line of defense to bolster the ebb and flow of his self-doubts.

It was his marriage to a white woman coupled with the rise in ethnic consciousness among blacks that probably led to the battery of antiwhite invectives from Jones during his black nationalist phase. This included a large dose of anti-Semitism which undoubtedly was aimed at the Jewish Cohen or at least at her exposed memory. Shortly after leaving the Village, the former bohemian Roi maliciously referred to Hettie in a poem as "a fat jew girl." Several lines later, in the same poem he wrote,

> *Smile, jew. Dance, jew. Tell me you love me, jew. I got*
> *something for you now though. I got something for you, like you dig,*
> *I got. I got this thing, goes pulsating through black everything*
> *universal meaning. I got the extermination blues, jewboys. I got*
> *the hitler syndrome figured.*
> *. . . So come for the rent, jewboys, or come ask me for a book, or*
> *sit in the courts handing down yr judgments, still I got something*
> *for you, gonna give it to my brothers, so they'll know what your whole*
> *story is, then one day, jewboys, we all, even my wig wearing mother*
> *gonna put it on you all at once.*[21]

The vulgarity of Jones's poem leaves me stunned even when I read these lines today. The sentiments are inexcusable, an indication of a twisted, deeply disturbed psyche. That he would use such imagery in order to wound and offend Jews, including his former wife and friends like Allen Ginsberg, indicates a vulnerability so potent that it precluded measured and reasoned responses. What caused these wounds? I hypothesize that unknown to his reading public and many of his friends and acquaintances, Jones may have been entangled in a psychological deference to Jews, and perhaps to whites in general, that must have bordered on a crass desire to be Jewish and/or white. At some point he discovered his complicity in his self-erasure, felt ashamed, and transferred his anger to Jews. Jews were culpable because they disproportionately comprised his closest friends and thus were complicit in accepting and validating his unreal, self-hating, black self. His rage toward them was a testimony to his reliance on their recognition. Irrational and ultimately ineffective, this anger led him to the absurdity of invoking Hitler, absurd not only because of the unimaginable crimes that Jones trivialized but absurd because Hitler also wanted to rid the world of blacks. To attach himself metaphorically to Hitler's final solution was to commit suicide. Irrational indeed, but Jones was speaking from an emotional anguish that had overwhelmed his powers of reason.

Sollors also noted that Jones's anti-Semitism was directed not only at his former wife but also at his Village literary milieu.[22] He attributes Jones's anti-Semitism to various influences, including the right-wing chauvinism that often inhabits modernism and bohemianism. Perhaps Sollors is correct, but if so, only partially. As a black American, Jones was well aware of the tortured paradoxes surrounding his own marginal racial identity in his bohemian circles. Simply put, he could never have felt so thoroughly "at home" in bohemia as to pretend to be able to appropriate all traditional bohemian cultural proclivities. Whether in Beat bohemia or American society at large, the appropriation of anti-Semitism did not and does not facilitate black acceptance into the white mainstream in the same way that the appropriation of antiblack racism facilitated the social inclusion of stigmatized European immigrants (and their descendants) by intensifying their claim to "whiteness." But this is beside the point, for Jones was not trying to use anti-Semitism as an entrée into American respectability.

The anti-Semitism of Jones and some of his black nationalist peers was as crude and vulgar as white racism. Sollors, I suspect, would not see a white bohemian writer's racism as stemming primarily from his bohemianism. Nevertheless, he was reluctant to recognize that blacks' provincialism toward Jews could be merely one articulation of the anti-Semitic notions that lay buried in the psyches of many Westerners, white or black. Sollors also participated in Jones's reification by calling these vulgar pronouncements Jones's "anti-Semitic phase." It is as if anti-Semitism could be explained away as merely something that one grew into and out of, like a pair of pants.[23]

In December 1980, the *Village Voice* printed on its cover page an essay by Jones entitled "Confessions of a Former Anti-Semite." Jones did admit that he had been anti-Semitic. What was so pathetic about his public confrontation with his anti-Semitic past was his inability to admit a moral error. We would not expect Jones to "ask for forgiveness." But instead, Jones tried to explain his anti-Semitism by referring to himself in the third person and describing the various "phases" that this person went through— phases that included a period of intense hatred of Jews. Jones argued that he was anti-Semitic because he went through a phase when he hated Jews, which was an unscientific thing to do, which was . . . ad infinitum. Jones thus reduced his anti-Semitism to an ideological error in the mind of a black petit-bourgeois intellectual who had yet to discover the correct ideology. Armed now with Marxist-Leninism, *the* correct ideology, anti-Semitism would no longer be useful to his political project.

The black attraction to anti-Semitism may be linked to the Negro's appropriation of dominant white—Gentile—behavior when formulating an image of "freedom." If so, it would be another perverse form of ressentiment and thus the victim status. Think of the obscene, cathartic image of empowerment that is particularly linked to killing the "slimy Jew," from Jones's poem "Black Art":

> We want poems
> like fists beating niggers out of Jocks
> or dagger poems in the slimy bellies
> of the owner-Jews. Black poems to
> smear on girdlemamma mulatto bitches
> whose brains are red jelly stuck
> between 'lizabeth taylor's toes. Stinking
> Whores! We want "poems that kill."
> Assassin poems, Poems that shoot
> guns. Poems that wrestle cops into alleys
> and take their weapons leaving them dead
> with tongues pulled out and sent to Ireland. Knockoff
> poems for dope selling wops or slick halfwhite
> politicians Airplane poems, rrrrrrrrrrrrrr
> rrrrrrrrrrrrrr . . . tuhtuhtuhtuht uhtuhtuhtuhthu
> . . . rrrrrrrrrrrrrrrrr . . . Setting fire and death to
> whities ass.[24]

Jones exhibits the extremism of the renegade who finds himself constantly forced to profess loyalty to his new allies. Proof of his love for black women becomes his professed hatred of white women, including most conspicuously his former wife. In a vein similar to Isaac Deutscher's discussion of the conscience of the ex-communist,[25] Jones described his mental state on arriving in Harlem after having rejected the Village and his Jewish wife:

I even stopped going downtown, and I'm sure certain aspects of the stances I took were based on my feeling of revulsion when my Greenwich Village days were focused on. . . . We hated white people so publicly, for one reason, because we had been so publicly tied up with them before.[26]

Although Jones wrote as if his marriage to a white woman hindered his identification with black people, it seems equally plausible that Jones married Cohen in part to legitimate not living in a Harlem. His marriage to Cohen was both a manifestation of his reified bohemian, deviant identity and a further justification for maintaining that identity. It was a signifier of willed "distance" and thus ethnic independence. The interracial marriage and children stood between him as a writer and any unproblematic organic connection to the black community, particularly its growing black nationalist sentiments. His marriage to Cohen cognitively facilitated his existence as an avant-garde writer. He had, after all, a wife and two children and, more important, a white wife and two racially mixed daughters who could not have lived with him in psychological comfort just anywhere.

What made leaving bohemia so difficult for Jones is that it clearly involved leaving his family. In his mind, one went with the other. Interracial marriages were bohemian statements. Furthermore, Jones clearly realized that many blacks regarded his interracial marriage as a violation of black ethnic boundaries. Even though becoming a bohemian had been a crucial social marginality facilitator, this behavior would probably have been seen by most blacks as an extension of ethnic boundaries. Consequently, when Jones wanted to leave bohemia for a more ethnically engaged life, we need not ask why he didn't ask his wife to accompany him. She, too, may have wanted to leave bohemia and to become active in the black freedom struggle.[27]

Jones left bohemia to reclaim a nostalgic, wholesome, reified ethnic home, a task his wife could only have hindered. Leaving his family, particularly his white wife, gave Jones an image of wholehearted dedication to the black struggle. Ironically, the significance that many black nationalists attributed to Jones's rejection of his white wife was in direct proportion to the immense value black nationalists placed on "the white woman." However crude his logic, Jones seems honest when he claimed in 1989 that leaving Hettie Cohen and his daughters was an agonizing decision.[28] Twenty years earlier, he had been incapable of such an honest, public admission.

Jones's admitted agony over the decision to leave Hettie and the children is troublesome precisely because of his claim that he had never been passionately attached to Cohen during their marriage. This assertion, if true, does not coincide with Jones's need to discard Cohen publicly and abusively when he decided to obtain what he considered an authentically black identity. If she was but a mere fixture around the house, he would not have felt the need to make his rejection of her his agent of racial baptism. Note the previous quotation in which he states, "We hated white people so publicly for one reason, because we had been so publicly tied up with them before." What Jones meant but could not allow himself to say is, "We hated white people so publicly for one reason, because we had so privately loved them before." In his warped logic, his marriage to a white woman could have been interpreted only as a public manifestation of ethnic self-hatred. Sufficiently guilty, he could never admit that he had once loved her.

The pathology of Jones's "acting out" his ethnic insecurity regarding the lives of his first wife and their two children cannot be ignored. However much his behavior can be attributed to feelings of ethnic insecurity and the resulting quest for a secure, essentialist racial identity, real lives were attacked and existences altered. What remains tragically astounding about Jones in this episode and elsewhere throughout his life is that his psychopolitical behavior has often been so mechanistic and predictable as to make him appear to be living a farce.

THE ASSASSINATION OF MALCOLM X

On February 21, 1965, Malcolm X was murdered in Harlem. The assassination of the only black leader that Jones regarded as politically credible heightened his disgust for the Village scene. He felt considerable guilt and shame at having only thought about becoming politically engaged while Malcolm was risking his life daily. Jones had been captivated by a man who excelled in apocalyptic, cathartic tirades against whites, and Jones soon adopted this rhetorical style. In explicitly directing his rage at white Americans, Malcolm violated the prevailing social norms of bourgeois civility to which most prominent black civil rights leaders adhered. Transgressing the accepted maxims of black public speech, Malcolm passionately voiced the anger of large numbers of blacks. Many blacks, particularly men, felt vicariously empowered by Malcolm's spoken words. His rhetoric held a special appeal for black males insofar as his emphasis on self-defense and combat readiness appealed to male sensibilities in a patriarchal society. Malcolm's sexism was legendary[29] and perhaps exceeded in the black popular leadership arena only by that of his mentor, Elijah Muhammad. Given Jones's rather deeply embedded homophobic concerns about the need for black male virility and assertiveness in the face of "faggy white boy" oppressors (e.g., Brad Easley in *The Slave*), Jones would not have found anything offensive in Ossie Davis's moving eulogy that declared that "Malcolm was our manhood." Fueled yet blinded by guilt at his bohemian complicity in the American dream of individualistic artistic productivity, Jones was simply unable to recognize that beneath the gallant rhetoric, Malcolm had no viable program for social change.

Following Malcolm's assassination, a *New York Times* editorial stated,

> He was a case history, as well as an extraordinary and twisted man, turning many true gifts to evil purpose. . . . Malcolm had the ingredients for leadership, but his ruthless and fanatical belief in violence not only set him apart from the responsible leaders of the Civil Rights movement and the overwhelming majority of Negroes, it also marked him for notoriety and a violent end. . . . Malcolm X's life was strangely and pitifully twisted. But this was because he did not seek to fit into the society or into the life of his people.[30]

Perhaps Jones read these patronizing and paternalistic comments on the life of Malcolm. We can speculate that the response of the *New York Times* was representative of the commentaries on Malcolm's life by liberal and not-so-liberal media throughout white America. Such attitudes must have made Jones livid. More important, such responses indicated the degree to which white America expressed its moral conceit by viewing itself as just. To claim that Malcolm did not "fit into the life of his people" was absurd.

It was extraordinarily narcissistic and naive for Jones to entertain the idea that Malcolm's death left a leadership vacuum that he alone could fill. That Jones believed he could fill Malcolm's shoes only indicated how far out of touch Jones was with the black community.[31] Regardless of the virulent invectives he hurled at white America, Jones could never have replaced Malcolm as the voice of the disenfranchised urban blacks. Harlem was foreign turf to Jones. He was, after all, a bohemian intellectual with little history of active involvement in black America's political affairs. Jones knew a great deal about Afro-American folk culture and art, as indicated by his brilliant analysis of black music in *Blues People*, but he did not intimately know these folks. Equally important, these folks did not know him. Feeling politically irrelevant and ethnically guilty, Jones moved to Harlem shortly after Malcolm's death to seek revolution. A bothersome question lingers. If Malcolm X was Jones's hero and guiding light, as Baraka now claims, why didn't Jones "follow and/or join" Malcolm X when Malcolm was alive?

The narrative of Malcolm's murder adopted by most black activists, including Jones, was that Malcolm was killed by agents of the state. The real possibility that Malcolm was killed by members of the Nation of Islam who either took direct (or indirect) orders from Elijah Muhammad or assumed responsibility for avenging Malcolm's departure from the Nation is usually given scant validity by those who want to claim that "white America" assassinated Malcolm. Black nationalists like Jones found it difficult to contemplate that other black nationalists might have murdered a seminal black freedom fighter. Entertaining the possibility that Malcolm's death was orchestrated and carried out by black men might have strained Jones's budding black nationalism beyond its breaking point. Even at this early stage, his devotion was quasi-religious and, as such, relied on incontrovertible moral categories of bad whites and better, if not good, Negroes. Even if Malcolm's murder had been arranged by hidden white powers that be, the blacks who actually emptied their bullets into Malcolm's chest should have problematized Jones's views of this incident.

In the immediate aftermath of the assassination, Jones and his confreres were in shock. The magnitude of their loss was so immense that they probably could not immediately consider its implications. Yet as time passed and the shock wore off, Jones still continued to evade the facts of the case. That is, Malcolm's death represented one early moment in the intellectual life of LeRoi Jones when he intentionally operated in "bad faith." Jones could not reconcile the known facts of Malcolm's murder with his desired depiction of it. In this instance, the desired idea was more serviceable and easier to accept, so Jones chose it rather than wrestle with the anxieties of indetermination, however honest. Any admission of uncertainty about the cause of Malcolm's death would have prevented Jones from claiming that Malcolm was killed because he was too dangerous to the powers that be. Even at that moment, it was quite plausible to contend that Malcolm had been killed by members of the Nation of Islam. Malcolm certainly feared them and thought they were capable of killing him.

One can rhetorically indict the entire United States in Malcolm's death. Such amorphous claims, however, often have at their root a failure of nerve to pursue the truth. Such intellectual laziness and fear saturated Jones's approach to Malcolm's very real murder. Isn't it surprising that a man who claimed to love Malcolm intensely and thoroughly could continue to celebrate Elijah Muhammad as a major figure in the black freedom struggle, even in the aftermath of Malcolm's murder? In dramatic form, Jones valorized Elijah Muhammad's frivolous fictional ontology of Yacub, the mad scientist who invented white people (i.e., devils).[32] It also is strange that Jones invited Louis Farrakhan, a man who openly called for Malcolm's murder, to speak at a 1968 Pan-African conference at a time when Farrakhan was continuing to speak of Malcolm as a traitor.[33] Unlike Jones, a true devotee of Malcolm could not have been all things to all people even in the black nationalist community. Certainly Malcolm understood this. Jones supposedly loved and adored Malcolm, but he did not want to criticize and alienate Elijah Muhammad or distance himself from Louis Farrakhan, a man who celebrated Malcolm's murder. Evidently, Jones was less interested in grasping Malcolm's legacy than in borrowing an idea of his to justify his own status ambitions as an oppositional figure. It is therefore not surprising that Jones would attempt to resuscitate the ethnically parochial Malcolm of his Nation of Islam days and not the later Malcolm who, though still a black nationalist, was moving in a progressive transracial trajectory. It was the early Malcolm that Jones appropriated and invoked as the model for effective black leadership. This version of Malcolm gave license to Jones's need to hurl invectives at whites. Lost in this charade was the fact that the real Malcolm had learned that his black nationalist public persona had reached a political dead end. Malcolm was too serious to be satisfied with rhetorical assaults and emotional highs and was searching for a viable political strategy when he was murdered. Even so, Jones overlooked this radical change in Malcolm's leadership portfolio.

The impression that Jones came to Harlem solely to engage in political activity is as unfounded as the claim that Jones went to bohemia only to escape bourgeois black society. Jones went to Harlem to "be black;" to "be seen as black;" and to lead blacks. Having decided to go to Harlem "to help raise the race," Jones described the cultural dissonance he had to overcome:

> The arrival uptown, Harlem, can only be summed up by the feelings jumping out of Cesaire's *Return to My Native Land* or Fanon's *The Wretched of the Earth* or Cabral's *Return to the Source*. The middle-class native intellectual, having out integrated the most integrated, now plunges headlong back into what he perceives as blackest, native-est. . . . If we had known what faced us, some would've copped out, some would've probably got down, to study, as we should've, instead of the nowhere shit so many of us were involved with.[34]

Jones's journey to Harlem has occasionally been portrayed as the return of the prodigal son.[35] This image has two problems: First, Jones could not return to a place where he had never before been, and second, when he did return, he never really went to Harlem but, rather, to its fringes.[36] Jones entered the black community as a self-anointed black leader who had come back home to lead his people to independence. Political engagement would be his vehicle for ethnic legitimation. No significant voice in that black community had sought his return, nor for that matter, was he greeted by a significant welcoming committee of its denizens. Unlike the prodigal son, few in Harlem knew that Jones was "missing." Under the pretense of leading "the race" after Malcolm's assassination, Jones actually came to Harlem seeking the comfort of a secure, guilt-free, ethnic identity. His desire to undo his bourgeois upbringing and bohemian past, however, colored his political activities in Harlem.

When he left the Village, Jones believed that he could best aid blacks' political struggle by harnessing his creative intellectual/artistic capacities to a black nationalist agenda. In Harlem, Jones conspicuously remained an intellectual. It was therefore not accidental that Jones devised mechanisms for exerting ethnic leadership that protected his creative artistic/intellectual "space." He had not migrated to Harlem in order to work on voter registration drives or to help unionize black workers.

BLACK ARTS REPERTORY THEATER

Shortly before arriving in Harlem, Jones and his cadre of black activists/intellectuals made plans and raised funds for the Harlem-based Black Arts Repertory Theater/School (BART). Even though Jones was an established playwright, poet, and essayist, his earnings were relatively meager when placed alongside the start-up costs of a theater/school. A large brownstone, suitable for the repertory theater/school, had been found on West 130th Street in Harlem. Initially, BART's activities were funded by the profits from two of Jones's plays which were then running at St. Mark's Theater in the Village before predominantly white audiences. Paradoxically, Jones's venture into anti-white artistic expression was first funded by those very liberal whites whom he had "rejected" in coming to Harlem.

In the summer of 1965, one summer after the Harlem riots, the Black Arts Repertory Theater/School applied for and received more than $200,000 from HARYOU (Harlem Youth Opportunities Unlimited), a New York City conduit for the federal government's Great Society funds.[37] As if the private white funding of black separatist theater hadn't been sufficiently contradictory, Jones and company appealed to the state itself to fund their "revolutionary" activity.

HARYOU was established by Kenneth Clark, a prominent black psychologist and Harlem native. In 1962, HARYOU received its original planning grant from the President's Committee on Juvenile Delinquency. After 1964, HARYOU became the recipient of funding from the newly created Office of Economic Opportunity (OEO), the mainstay of President Lyndon Johnson's "war on poverty." Clark resigned in mid-1964 when HARYOU came under the control of the autocratic Congressman Adam Clayton Powell Jr. Powell was afraid that the OEO goal of generating the "maximum feasible participation" of community groups might create in Harlem a new political base independent of his control. With a greater vested interest in controlling HARYOU than in helping it succeed, Powell engineered the appointment of one of his flunkies into the position of executive director of what became known as HARYOU-ACT. It was little surprise that Powell's appointee was an incompetent administrator. He squandered much of the money in Harlem as "poverty pimps" undermined the intentions of what some consider the most progressive effort ever made by the U.S. government to empower the poor politically. An equally compelling argument could be made that OEO was not radical but repressive in its desire to dispense federal funding in order to momentarily siphon off rebellious energies that might otherwise be expressed in a riot.[38] This argument appears most convincing once we realize that much of the OEO funding was stopgap money directly targeted to black urban areas during the middle and late 1960s.

In his oral history of the "war on poverty," historian Michael L. Gillette published candid interviews with the officials who planned and administered different poverty programs. A 1969 interview with William P. Kelly Jr. was particularly instructive. Kelly, formerly the assistant director for management at OEO (and later the acting director of the Community Action Program), made the following comments concerning HARYOU:

> HARYOU was a calculated risk in the summer of 1965. At that time it was our judgment that in funding HARYOU we were taking some risks in terms of the sophistication of HARYOU to operate its program. . . . HARYOU-ACT lost some money. To this day nobody has ever proven that anybody ever stole any money from HARYOU. They got a program off very rapidly. Harlem was cooled. The people in Harlem participated. There were no riots, no property burned. Nobody was hit in the head with rocks, . . . that was a very successful summer program.[39]

Though still marked by oppressive living conditions, Harlem in the summer of 1965 had been "cooled." For reasons having little to do with modesty, Jones and his confreres at the Black Arts Repertory Theater have never admitted how much they contributed to maintaining order. It would have been understandable and perhaps wise for Jones to have argued that the time was not right for a riot/rebellion in Harlem, for Harlem had rioted during the previous summer. But for Jones and others to write about the creation of BART as a radicalizing event without confronting its conservative political impact is to hide the theater's paradoxical reality. While Jones believed that his dramatic productions and jazz concerts were educational, it seems clear that the state viewed them as tranquillizing entertainment.

Jones pointed out that BART was able to bring roving outdoor art exhibitions to different neighborhoods in Harlem. Jazz concerts were performed impromptu in vacant lots, playgrounds, and parks. Through his personal contacts, Jones was able to persuade Cecil Taylor, Sun Ra, John Coltrane, Archie Shepp, and other major jazz artists to perform at these events. Plays were produced on Harlem streets and playgrounds. Jones noted, "Each night throughout that summer we flooded Harlem streets with new music, new poetry, new dance, new paintings, and the sweep of the Black Arts movement had recycled itself back to the people. We had huge audiences, really mass audiences." In addition, the Black Arts Repertory Theater offered classes in play writing, poetry, music, painting, and black history.[40]

In his autobiography, Jones conveys the exhilaration of the variety and intensity of the events of that summer.

> Bringing art to the people, black art to black people; and getting paid for doing it was sweet. Both the artists and the people were raised by that experience. . . . We knew next to nothing about bureaucratic games or the subtlety needed to preserve so fragile a program as we had erected. We had no funds of our own and no correct understanding of the economic self-reliance needed to push a program calling for black self-determination, even in the arts.[41]

The state funding of these Harlem activities was only one manifestation of "inauthentically autonomous," black nationalist activities during the 1960s. The inability and/or the unwillingness of black nationalists and the broader black community to support black nationalist activities eventually undermined much of the black nationalist agenda of the Black Power era. Of course, Jones and his colleagues always had the option of "living within their means." Although this would have resulted in a much smaller choice of artistic offerings, they would have been truer claimants to the mantle of authentic ethnic autonomy. Concerning the contradictions and paradoxes in the state funding of Jones's supposed revolutionary theater, Genevieve Fabre wrote,

> It seems illogical that Jones would seek financial support from the government for such a theatre; it is even more surprising that the government

would provide the money. Did the power structure consider the project inoffensive, or did it want to exert control over him? Jones's tactic, one commonly used by militants in the United States succeeded in getting some reparation for the cruelty inflicted on his people. One is tempted to see in American society's tolerance of such a radical enterprise proof of its confidence in the power it wields and in its capacity to absorb dissent, a major feature in cultural politics.[42]

News stories concerning the HARYOU's funding of the Black Arts Repertory Theater became a major source of embarrassment to OEO officials in Washington. Projects like the repertory theater threatened the congressional funding of OEO because they went beyond the legislative mandated goals of empowering poor people. Instead, they were perceived as attempts to politicize and indoctrinate poor people in an "anti-American" (i.e., antiwhite) manner.[43] Given the uneven congressional and popular support for federal intervention on behalf of the black urban poor, the vulnerability of Community Action Programs like HARYOU to "bad" publicity should have been evident to Jones. It wasn't. In a 1965 *U.S. News and World Report* article, "Tax Funds a 'Hate the Whites' Project," Jones offered his usual incendiary comments. "I don't see anything wrong with hating white people. Harlem must be taken from the beast and gain its sovereignty as a black nation."[44]

Jones conspicuously omits mention of such immature and unnecessary pronouncements in his autobiographical reflections on the problems between BART and HARYOU.[45] He writes as if the media's claims that the Black Arts Repertory Theater was producing racist, antiwhite plays were not only ludicrous but indicative of antiblack racism. The media did not have to invest a great deal of energy in distorting Jones's views of whites. Accurate quotations were sufficiently damaging. Simply put, all that was demanded of the media was that they grant Jones an interview or place a microphone in front of his face. As if on cue, he would make an asinine comment that later would be justifiably reported as racist.

The director of the Community Action Agency, Sargent Shriver, called the federal funding of BART one of the failures of the "war against poverty." Shriver described the offerings of the Black Arts Repertory Theater "as vile racist plays in vile gutter language unfit for youngsters in the audience."[46] As director of the federal government's poverty program, Shriver and other federal administrators went to New York to look at HARYOU's programs. But as if to parade his defiance of white people, including those whites who controlled the funding of BART, Jones refused to allow Shriver and his entourage to enter the Black Arts Repertory School building.[47] By insulting Shriver,

Jones once again revealed his political immaturity.[48] Soon thereafter, the funding was terminated.

When discussing the Black Arts Repertory Theater/School in his 1984 autobiography, Jones describes his frustrations at having had to work so closely with the many confused individuals who also worked at the theater/school. The absolutist commitment that lay at the root of the school's purpose was attractive not only to those committed to a black nationalist praxis but also to some black sociopsychological misfits who just wanted "to belong." Fringe movements, based on ascriptive traits (e.g., race) and demanding "greedy institution" allegiances, were vulnerable to those "lumpen" blacks who sought to instill order in their own lives.[49] Jones intuitively perceived this phenomenon but was constrained by an ideology that did not allow him to confront it. Because he simultaneously believed that "street niggers" with their rebellious attitudes toward social norms were the authentic black Americans and felt insecure about his own ethnic identity, he was unable to treat these people as a "problem":

> I felt that I had failed in New York. The last days at the Black Arts had thoroughly disgusted me . . . while we had made some real contributions we (I) had also gotten bogged down with non-productive nuts. Why? That was what plagued me. Why had all that happened? Probably it was something about me. The guilt I carried about my life in the Village always undermined the decisive actions I had to take to preserve any dynamic and productive development in the Black Arts.[50]

Disgusted after less than a year in Harlem, Jones left BART and New York City. The experiment, or more precisely, the dream of replacing Malcolm X, had not materialized. It failed because Jones had misunderstood Malcolm X. Malcolm recognized that his own self-discipline was not the norm for the black lower classes with whom he dealt daily. He understood that the "greedy institution" nature of the Nation of Islam was responsible for its success at restoring order in the lives of many of its members, including his own. Although Malcolm spoke for the lower classes and sometimes lived with them, he had long ceased to be one of them. As a convert to the Nation of Islam, the cost of his escape had included giving up his individual rationality.[51]

Despite Jones's personal feelings of failure, the Black Arts Repertory Theater and School had not been a complete loss. Although Jones could not have known it when he left Harlem, BART had been a test case and soon became a model for similar efforts in urban areas throughout the United States. The repertory theater was undoubtedly one of the key launching pads for the crystallization and emergence of the Black Arts movement, as it encouraged traditional black intellectuals and artists to begin to question the scope of their intended audiences. Indeed, the very success of the Black Arts Repertory Theater in attracting black street audiences proved that the rank-and-file black community was not opposed to theater or serious music, provided both were made physically accessible and economically affordable. This issue of artistic and/or intellectual accessibility might well have been the most important question raised by the example of the Black Arts Repertory Theater, as it recognized the need for a far more extensive black intellectual/artistic infrastructure. How could the arts be used to inform the masses of black people if they did not have access to them? If Jones was serious about reaching black people, he now knew that he could not use the established intellectual and artistic infrastructures.

In literally taking his plays "to the streets," Jones began to redefine his intellectual character and purpose. No longer would he be satisfied with creating art that was inaccessible to the masses of black people. But in his quest to reach larger black audiences, his art became increasingly facile and ultimately emerged as crude propaganda. How else can we explain the journey from *Dutchman* to *A Black Mass* to *Arm Yourself, or Harm Yourself?* We do not know whether the increasing simplemindedness of Jones's "black" art was a response to the realities of an impoverished black mass audience or the result of the demeaning projections of a bourgeois black artist concerning the aesthetic capabilities of a black mass audience. I suspect that both are partially true, and I address this issue in a later chapter.

After the collapse of BART, Jones returned to Newark, moving in with his parents. Next, Jones organized Spirit House, a brainchild of the Black Arts Repertory Theater/School. No longer on the alien soil of Harlem and much more aware of the need to maintain organizational discipline, Jones's Spirit House was more successful than the Black Arts Repertory Theater/School.

Whereas Jones and his Village-based black peers could have come to Harlem to discover what it meant to live as a black person in a black inner-city neighborhood, their strategy was to live among the black people of Harlem while teaching them what it meant to be authentically "black." Jones and his newly "blackenized" associates—who for the most part, had not been involved in the black struggle up to that moment and had distanced themselves from the black community in choosing to live in the Village—presumed that they were in a position to raise the racial consciousness of Harlemites. Jones's claim to a more authentic ethnic consciousness was little more than a kind of cultural capital marketed to black people in order to purchase the status of revolutionary artist and political leader.[52] That many black people bought his idea of how they could become "blacker" was perhaps a testimony to their dire needs in the face of internalized negative stigmas and structurally reinforced inabilities to prosper economically.

One essay from this period stands out as a transition piece. "Philistinism and the Negro Writer" was one of the first indications that Jones's deepening connectedness to black America was accompanied by a new and intensifying respect for the Afro-American literary tradition. Published in 1966 in Herbert Hill's edited collection *Anger, and Beyond*, Jones's essay was probably written in 1965. Its significance lies in Jones's attempt to repudiate the argument contained in his earlier essay, "The Myth of Negro Literature," and he does so without ever openly admitting that his views have changed.

> I once wrote an essay called "The Myth of Negro Literature," which was published in a rather weird form in the *Saturday Review*, and the point I tried to make there was that, until quite recently, most of what could be called the Negro's formal attempt at "high art" was found in his music, and one of the reasons I gave was that it was only in music that the Negro did not have to respect the tradition outside of his own feelings—that is, he could play what he felt and not try to make it seem like something alien to his feelings, something outside of his experience.[53]

At first glance, this appears to be a rather innocuous restatement of "The Myth of Negro Literature," but it actually twists the meaning of that earlier essay. In "The Myth of Negro Literature," Jones did not maintain that "it was only in music that the Negro did not have to respect the tradition." To the contrary, he did not endorse any claim for the necessity of adhering to an artistic tradition. Rather, in this earlier essay, Jones granted creative agency to all black artists. The problem of black writers had nothing to do with their forced confinement to certain traditions of writing. Instead, he speculated that some black artists working in the world of jazz were more ambitious and successful than those black artists who wrote prose fiction. In his mind, black jazz musicians used their agency for creativity, whereas black writers used their agency in pursuit of white recognition. To explain these different paths, Jones invoked the supposed middle-class orientations of black writers.

But now, instead of condemning Charles Chesnutt as an assimilationist-minded "exceptional Negro," as he had previously done in "The Myth of Negro Literature," Jones celebrates him: "Even so fine a writer as Charles W. Chesnutt, one of the earlier black writers, had to 'cop out,' as they say, by being a 'refined Afro-American.'"[54] We are left to ask who or what supposedly forced

Chesnutt to "cop out"? When and why, in Jones's estimation, had Chesnutt risen to the status of "so fine a writer"?

Whereas Jones's "Myth of Negro Literature" was a condemnation of black fiction writers as bourgeois cultural sellouts, "Philistinism and the Negro Writer" revises that image to one of bourgeois black writers forced by American racism to create mainstream art. The black writer who aspired to mainstream recognition had to forgo the artistic mining of his own culture. Financial success for the black writer was usually acquired at the expense of his artistic integrity. Inoffensiveness, cultural or political, was lucrative. But why does Jones now write sympathetically as if he understands the black writer's quest for mainstream acceptance? Interestingly, the Beat bohemian author of "The Myth of Negro Literature" assumed that great writing would not result in commercial success or popular acclaim.

The idea that the demands of mainstream society influenced black writers is undoubtedly accurate. But the implication that the mainstream dictated black writing styles and quality is not convincing, for black writers had the option of not seeking mainstream acceptance. In any case, Jones asserts that black writers who entertained serious artistic ambitions had to give up wanting to enter the mainstream. He concludes, "The Negro writer can only survive by refusing to become a white man." Most surprisingly, Jones now believes that black writers were quite successful as artists. Their quest for mainstream success, a quest dictated by white racism, had not hindered their artistic achievements.

> If you think of W. E. B. Du Bois, Richard Wright, Jean Toomer, Langston Hughes, Ellison, Baldwin, Chester Himes and all the others, if you think of these people you are forced to realized that they gave a top-level performance in the areas in which each functioned. The most meaningful book of social essays in the last decade is *Notes of a Native Son*, by Baldwin. The most finely constructed archetypal, mythological novel, utilizing perhaps a Kafkaesque sense of what the world really has become, is *Invisible Man*, by Ralph Ellison. The most completely valid social novels and social criticism of South and North, non-urban and urban Negro life, are Wright's *Black Boy* and *Native Son*.[55]

To read now that Langston Hughes, Wright, Ellison, Baldwin, and others gave "top-level" performances is startling. Only a few years earlier, Jones had written that these writers could be considered serious only in the sense that Somerset Maugham's work was serious, that is, "serious if one has never read Herman Melville or James Joyce."[56] Certainly, Jones's estimations of black writers has dramatically risen. Yet to call their performances "top-level in the areas in which each functioned" is a clever way to obscure the breadth of his praise. What does it really mean to say that Wright's *Black Boy* and *Native Son* are "the most completely valid social novels"? With how many other writers does Jones compare Wright? More important, even if Jones assumes that Wright may be as good as any other American writer in his arena (i.e., Theodore Dreiser, Nelson Algren, James Farrell), Jones still may not view any of these American writers as particularly outstanding.

On its own literary and intellectual merits, "Philistinism and the Negro Writer" is a minor essay. Not only does it offer minimal insight into the problematic situation of the black writer, but it reads like a spontaneous lecture—undisciplined, disjointed, and somewhat incomplete. But as a means of understanding Jones's changing intellectual perceptions as he became more politically engaged, the essay is essential. No longer condemning black writers for a lack of attention to craft, Jones now declares everyone a master. Disregarding former apprehensions about the parochialness of black writing, Jones now celebrates black writers who embrace their blackness. Whereas Jones once found black writers lacking when compared with Joyce, he now has stopped trying to assess black literature by "white" literary standards. "Philistinism and the Negro Writer" is a declaration of Jones's embrace of the ethnic artistic fold. No longer content to be an isolated, innovative avant-garde stylist, he now was attaching himself to a black literary tradition in the hope that it would also facilitate his growing political commitment to the black struggle.

ASPIRING PRODIGAL SON OF HARLEM

Hidden in Jones's proclamations of having returned "home to Harlem" is a distortion of immense proportions. Buried under rhetoric of black authenticity, it is difficult now to recognize that Jones's move to Harlem was grafted onto a foundation of utter disrespect for and paternalistic devaluation of the black people who lived there. It was commonplace during the 1960s to hear black militants claim that those blacks who were not truly black were not worthy of respect. But what did this really mean?

What did typical black residents of Harlem think about BART? Did they even know about it? I cannot imagine many Harlemites being intensely attuned to the plays and concerts of BART, given their daily struggle to endure an overbearing and oppressive situation. And on what grounds could the post-bohemian Roi and his followers tell the sisters in a Lexington Avenue beauty parlor that by straightening their hair, they had become instruments of white domination? While I have not surveyed the opinions and remembrances of black Harlemites concerning BART and Jones, I recognize as problematic the prevailing accounts of his political efforts in Harlem, since they rely almost exclusively on the impressions of those associated with BART. We cannot accept at face value Jones's claims that the black masses of Harlem were captivated by the offerings of BART.

When Jones entered black America, he did not come with democratic sensibilities. More specifically, nothing in BART's structure required Jones to take into account the thoughts and feelings of his supposed clientele, the people of Harlem. It thus is incorrect for him to claim that the "new music" that BART presented on Harlem street corners was the Black Arts recycling itself back to the people. If this new music was so closely related to black Americans, it would not have had to be recycled back into the black community. Rather, it was because this music was not organic to black urban culture that made it avant-garde and allowed Jones to attribute an insurgent political consciousness to it. Once again, we can perceive an ethnic dissidence in Jones's artistic/cultural agenda. Although he regarded the music of the black jazz avant-garde as politically dissident, we cannot assume that Harlemites similarly viewed the music of Shepp, Sun Ra, or Cecil Taylor when hearing it at neighborhood street corner concerts.

In capitalist America, including Harlem, black people needed jobs and decent housing. They wanted better schools and less police brutality. They did not need Jones to educate them about the impact of white racism on their lives. In fact, on this issue they probably could have taught him something. To the extent that BART brought a wider cultural life to Harlem, Jones was addressing a crucial human need. The problem was that Jones marketed BART as a political institution intent on black consciousness raising. Had he understood his role as a cultural one, he might have been able to create a more durable arts center. Instead, he erroneously imagined that he was intensifying Harlem's political radicalness.

Harvard University political scientist Martin Kilson was one of the very few writers at that time to comment on the status ambitions inherent in the black nationalist appeal and its sociopsychological attraction to many blacks:

> Some professionals are adopting a black power ideological format not with the intent of preparing themselves for service to self-governing urban black communities but to make themselves more visible to the white establishment, which is not at all adverse to offering such persons good jobs as alternatives to black power. The more viable Negro businessmen are also

simulating the black power advocates who have virtually no control over this use of their political style by the professional and business black bourgeoisie, which means the black power advocates will eventually lose the payoff potential of nationalist politics. . . . If so . . . the Negro lower classes, whose riots legitimize black power, will be joined by the black power advocates in holding the bag—with nothing in it save a lot of therapeutic miscellany.[57]

Kilson realized that various Black Power ideologies could be used to manipulate elements of the black professional and middle classes. He argued that the white establishment would rather satisfy the desires of the black middle class and its various spokespersons than grant the black masses substantive "Black Power." The black masses wanted their subsistence needs met as well as to gain political self-determination (i.e., authentic democratic participation), whereas large elements of the black bourgeoisie wanted greater access to consumer goods (e.g., more money). Segments of the black professional and middle classes ingeniously used "Black Power" rhetoric to market their particular interests as encompassing the interests of all black America. For instance, in response to mass-based black political unrest, the American public and private sectors created numerous civil rights compliance bureaucracies and departments that were virtually powerless but were staffed with mobility-minded Negroes. Under newly instituted affirmative action programs, government and private sectors awarded contracts on a noncompetitive basis to black businesses. At the same time, black middle-class children were given greater access to elite, predominantly white, colleges.

Was Jones a member of the professional sector that manipulated Black Power ideology, or was he one of those Black Power advocates who lost the political payoffs to the black bourgeoisie? To the extent that his various theater groups and cultural centers were the recipients of "poverty" funding, he functioned as one of those clever elements of the black bourgeoisie. To the extent that he later helped give militant racial legitimacy to nonmilitant blacks like Mayor Kenneth Gibson of Newark, he was used by them.

Jones always had a tenuous relationship with the black people that he intended to lead. He never acquired a large mass following in Harlem, yet the limited following that he did attract was probably as large as that of any other traditional black intellectual of his time. Despite his overblown ambition to replace Malcolm X, Jones finally recognized his blunder and adjusted the scope of his ambitions. Simply put, he realized that he was not organically connected to the black Harlem community but was an interloper from Jersey via the Village. Once in Harlem, Jones was only another black face among many. Consequently, Jones learned the crucial lesson that being and feeling black were insufficient credentials for leading black people. He also was forced to review his ideas concerning the political utility of black art. Most important, he departed for Newark finally understanding that artistic productions, however radical and black, could not effect change unless they were part of a broader political infrastructure or movement.

Jones's later decision to clothe himself in Kawaida, an ersatz African Afro-American nationalism, was a shrewd attempt to create an intraethnic, counterhegemonic ideology and organizational mechanism through which he could attack the established black leaders in hopes of replacing them. Jones, the bourgeois nationalist, sought to supplant the bourgeois integrationists who were not averse to hiding behind the rhetoric of black nationalism. He tried to do so by appropriating the mantle of the "blacker-than-thou" revolutionary. Because of those elements in the black bourgeoisie who clothed themselves in a supposedly radical black nationalism (i.e., Nathan Wright), Jones had to adopt a "hyper-blackenized" identity in order to corner a unique political market. The blacker" that bourgeois blacks became, at least in their rhetoric and dress codes, the more Jones was compelled to "outdo" them.

It is crucial that we recognize the peculiarity of Jones's nationalist tendencies. Even as early as his days at BART, Jones's nationalist vision was brought to Afro-Americans, not derived from them. His black nationalism was not grounded in indigenous Afro-American folk or urban cultures, and consequently he marketed as revolutionary a vision that was merely novel. The peculiarity of an ethnocentric nationalist vision not rooted in an indigenous ethnic culture was lost on those observers who linked Jones's nationalism to a unified black nationalist "tradition." It should also be apparent that Jones's black nationalism was not based on intraracial equality. Blacks like Jones were "in the know," whereas other blacks, the majority, had to be educated. Jones's elitist tendencies became even more pronounced when he became a devotee of Karenga and Kawaida and a self-anointed Imamu.

In his thought-provoking essay "Politics and Identity among Black Intellectuals," Martin Kilson correctly interprets Jones's embrace of a black nationalist ideology as an indication of his retreat from the anxiety-ridden identity of a Beat bohemian to the more secure confines of an ascriptive ethnic identity. Kilson believes that Jones was at his creative best when he lived as a Beat poet amid the apprehension and consternation of an ethnically ambivalent identity. He states that the art produced by Jones/Baraka during the

height of black cultural nationalism was "strongly ideological but of little lasting value":

> As a Beat poet and novelist Baraka/Jones displayed signs of viable creativity.
> He was somewhat apolitical, in regard to organizational ties, though not
> ideologically. His ethnic or racial ties in his Beat period identified him as a
> follower of what I call "the strategy of the Marginal Man"—independent of
> a priori ethnic and political obligations. He strengthened this identification
> by taking on the trapping of Marxist ideology and marrying a white woman.
> Later, Baraka discarded this strategy and defined himself in more totalistic
> political terms: he became a militant black separatist.[58]

Kilson's discussion, however, is riddled with questionable assertions. Most
problematic is his conceptualization of ethnic marginality. He seems to believe that ethnic marginality is intrinsically manifested in certain behaviors. For Kilson, the mere fact that at one moment Jones espoused Marxism
or married a white woman is, ipso facto, evidence of his "marginal man"
identity. It is not. Marxism, insofar as it is an intellectual self-definition
that allows one to transcend ethnic allegiances as primary, can function as
a marginality facilitator for those ethnically marginal individuals who
choose to use it in that fashion. Blacks have adopted Marxism for many
reasons, even to mask attempts to assimilate with whites. On what basis can
Kilson claim that an adherence to Marxism is inherently more "independent of a priori political obligations" than is an adherence to nationalistic
sentiments? Because Marxism involves a nonethnically constrained political vision and black nationalism does not, we cannot assume that one is
any less intellectually confining than the other. Kilson would have us believe that the only crucial constraint on a black intellectual's development
was that derived from his or her ethnic allegiances.[59]

Kilson implies—or, rather, hints at the implication—that works created
out of a black nationalistic framework are inherently more ideological than
works created out of an ethnically marginal framework and that ideologically
motivated artistic works are inherently less creative than nonideologically
motivated works. Certainly, Kilson cannot be condemned if he drew these
conclusions from an analysis of Jones's artistic life, for it could be argued that
Jones's best work was produced in the Village as a Beat bohemian before he
became overtly politicized. But what about sophisticated, ideologically motivated art like Ignazio Silone's *Bread and Wine* or the writing of Malraux,
Brecht, Cesaire, Dos Passos, Neruda, Forche, or even Alice Walker? Jones's failure to create a sophisticated, ideologically motivated art should not be gener-

alized to an entire genre. Finally, Kilson's argument raises the question of whether there is such an entity as a nonideological artistic expression or a nonideological motivated art in modern society.[60] His attempt to place Jones in predetermined, inviolate categories appears too restrictive to encompass the Janus-faced LeRoi.

More significant is Kilson's inability to recognize that a black intellectual can remain ethnically marginal and operate in a black nationalist framework. Depending on its content, black nationalism can function as a social marginality facilitator, particularly when the majority of the designated individuals with whom one is supposedly expressing solidarity (in this case, Afro-Americans) are neither receptive to nor governed by the designated nationalistic consciousness. It is incorrect to assume that nationalistic political beliefs are inherently ascriptive and/or affective beliefs. For instance, early-twentieth-century American Zionists tried to politicize issues of Jewish ethnicity and in so doing revealed traits of ethnic nationalism, although they often lived on the fringes of the mainstream Jewish American community. Consequently, by becoming ethnic nationalists, these early American Zionists were not necessarily "returning home" but were distancing themselves from their home community.[61]

Kilson errs in not perceiving distinctions in Afro-American nationalism.[62] Black nationalism has never been a monolithic force. In many, if not most, instances, a black nationalist identity probably coexists with an organic attachment to Afro-Americans and Afro-American culture or at least aspires to have such an organic connection. Such ethnic attachments can take many forms of expression. Kilson failed to realize that when Jones left the Village for Harlem, he was not retreating to the boundaries of the existing black community and black culture but to the fringes of the black community where he tried to market himself as more "black" than the "average" resident of Harlem.[63] His claim to have realized an ontologically black identity that was different from the "normal" black identity was an attempt to fashion a social marginality facilitator, albeit different from those most often appropriated by black intellectuals. Jones's appropriation of a novel black nationalism, particularly during his Kawaida days, masked the degree of his estrangement from the black community. Instead of contending that black American life was too limiting compared with European intellectual/artistic traditions, Jones postulated that black American life was too confining compared with the intellectual/artistic offerings of Africa and the African diaspora. The main reason that Jones's visit to the cultural fringe of black America is often interpreted as a trip to its very center is that for a short while, Jones and his ideological compatriots successfully challenged the established definers and definitions of black ethnicity and even replaced them in certain strategically located sectors of the black community (i.e., those of college students, intellectuals, and street activists).

A troubling question remains. Were Jones and his confreres at the BART, poverty pimps? Did they siphon off money for their own bourgeois concerns that could have been spent in ways much more beneficial to the poor of Harlem? Jones and his cronies had only recently arrived in Harlem when they were granted funding that was supposed to be used to support the political empowerment of indigenous Harlemites. Whatever great importance BART may have had for the growing Black Arts movement, its significance in the lives of the people of Harlem was minuscule. Indeed, on one occasion, Jones honestly described his relative insignificance in Harlem:

> We had been away in New York down in the Lower East Side and Greenwich Village theorizing about the black community and then even in Harlem, we were not a part of that community's development. Really most of the black intellectuals there, even though all of us lived in Harlem, were still not part of the whole organic, dynamics of the community. We were sort of, I think, superficial to the community even with the Black Arts.[64]

5

The Quest for a Blacker Art

THE BLACK ARTS MOVEMENT

The collapse of the Black Arts Repertory Theater provided the impetus for Jones to reflect on the peculiar needs of black cultural-nationalist institutions. BART's inception and demise became centerpieces of discussions in Afro-American intellectual circles similarly intent on establishing black cultural-nationalist institutions in other locations. At least for the moment, many traditionally educated black intellectuals and artists tried to incorporate the "commonplace" Afro-American individual into their artistic agendas. The "black masses," however imagined, became the ideal audience. This quest to increase accessibility to a broader black audience profoundly affected black artists' genres and styles. Once "ordinary" black people became the exemplary audience, black writers had to create poetry, novels, and plays especially for them. Because BART was frequently emulated throughout the nation as a model of innovative, politicized black public intellectual/artistic outreach, it must be considered a bedrock of the Black Arts movement. While we can remain skeptical about assigning to any single event or person the responsibility for launching a national arts movement, we must recognize that Baraka was a pioneer and leader in this endeavor.

Before going to Harlem, Jones delivered what now appears to have been a manifesto for the emerging Black Arts movement. In April 1965, he was on a panel that brought together black dramatists as well as black and white drama critics to talk about "What Black Dramatists Are Saying." According to Genevieve Fabre, he delivered a ferocious lecture that "brought an abrupt end to the hope of reconciliation between black artists and representatives of the dominant culture."[1] Later published as "The Revolutionary Theater" in the July 1965 edition of *Liberator*, a black cultural-intellectual journal,[2] this essay proclaimed that the new revolutionary black theater would expose the moral pretensions of white Americans not only in the theater world but also in everyday American life. Jones declared, "White men will cower before this theater because it hates them.... The Revolutionary Theater must teach them their deaths. It must crack their faces open to the mad cries of the poor. It must teach them about silence and the truths lodged there." Jones designated the revolutionary theater as the theater of victims, and as such, it must "accuse and attack." Its dramatic sensibilities would show the black public the wretchedness of their plight in the United States and do so in ways that shamed their political passivity and tolerance for subjugation.

> And what we show must cause the blood to rush, so that pre-revolutionary temperaments will be bathed in this blood, and it will cause their deepest souls to move, and they will find themselves tensed and clenched, even ready to die, at what the soul has been taught. . . . The force we want is of twenty million spooks storming America with furious cries and unstoppable weapons. We want actual explosions and actual brutality: AN EPIC IS CRUMBLING and we must give it the space and hugeness of its actual demise. The revolutionary theater, which is now peopled with victims, will soon begin to be peopled with new kinds of heroes—not the weak Hamlets debating whether or not they are ready to die for what's on their minds.[3]

An incendiary essay, "The Revolutionary Theater," is full of graphic and ridiculous images of white folks in various stages of depravity. Given the frequency of its citation, "The Revolutionary Theater" appears to have been one of the most widely read essays of the Black Arts era. But then, what black reader in tune with the consciousness of the time would not embrace the image of "twenty million spooks storming America"?

Jones believed that his essay forged a new direction for the black theater. He also claimed to have long subscribed to the ideas of "The Revolutionary Theater" insofar as the lead characters in his previously written plays— *Dutchman, The Slave,* and *The Toilet*—were black victims. But does the mere presence of victims as protagonists identify a drama as revolutionary? Dodging this issue, Jones's "Revolutionary Theater" uses wordplay to seduce the reader. Once enveloped in the essay, readers may imagine themselves seated before a rapidity of furious staged images that crescendo in ethnic catharsis. The dramatization of "the destruction of America"[4] was electrifying and emotionally explosive. But despite the allure of such drama to an audience of the racially downtrodden, the centrality that Jones grants to ethnic catharsis and other emotive responses might, in practice, obscure the difference between this so-called revolutionary theater and black group therapy.

Written during a moment of personal transition as Jones withdrew from the Village to Harlem, this "revolutionary" manifesto is entangled in contradictions. First, how could a revolutionary theater be a theater of victims? Unlike revolutionaries, victims are the objects, not the subjects, of history. Victims are locked in a struggle for the recognition of their plight by their victimizers. The protest orientation of Jones's revolutionary theater gives his drama a victim-status orientation, even though Jones uses the word *victim* as a metaphor for the "oppressed." First, a theater of the oppressed that is directed toward the conscience of the "oppressor" remains a theater of victims. Even if the victims succeed in obtaining recognition from their victimizers, such recognition is framed by the superior values and status of the victimizer. Second, because the essay was written before Jones's full-blown immersion in black nationalism, he clearly is confused about the intended audience for his revolutionary drama. Although the primary audience is, I suppose, black Americans, "The Revolutionary Theater" portrays the potential effect of this theater on whites. In describing this effect, Jones's dramatic ambitions do not appear to have escaped protest art, which, incidentally, is not revolutionary. Third, Jones's "Revolutionary Theater" seems to have been derived from Antonin Artaud's theater of cruelty. Jones's manifesto announces intentions similar to Artaud's. "Even as Artaud designed *The Conquest of Mexico*,[5] so we must design *the Conquest of White Eye*, and show the missionaries and wiggly Liberals dying under blasts of concrete. For sound effects, wild screams of joy, from all the people of the world."[6]

Concerning Artaud's notion of the theater, Daphne S. Reed noted,

> Artaud's basic approach to theater emphasized the mise-en-scène instead of the spoken language, alleging that the true function of theater is to impel man to see himself as he is, to recover that religious and mystic function of renewing a sense of life, in which a man makes himself master of what does not yet exist and evokes it into being. According to Artaud, "true theater" disturbs repose, frees the repressed unconscious, incites a kind of revolt, uncovers sources of conflicts, exteriorizes latent cruelty, and exemplifies true freedom which is always identified as sexual freedom.[7]

But according to drama critic Robert Brustein, Artaud's theater never advocated violence or sadism in daily life. Rather,

> what he proposes is that the theatre serve as a harmless "outlet for repressions" in much the same manner as the analyst's couch. . . . The theatre of cruelty, then, will evacuate those feelings which are usually expressed in more destructive ways: "I defy that spectator," Artaud asserts, "to give himself up, once outside the theatre, to ideas of war, riot, and blatant murder." . . . The world is rapidly moving toward suicide and destruction while continuing to mouth Christian ideals of peace and harmony. . . . Artaud wishes

to cut through these lies and deceptions, "for impelling me to see themselves as they are, it causes the mask to fall, reveals the lie, the slackness, baseness and hypocrisy of the world." Thus Artaud would purge the spectator of those bloody impulses he usually turns on others in the name of patriotism, religion, or love.[8]

Brustein views the Artaudian theater as a mechanism for purging fantasies. In exteriorizing the audience's desire for criminality and brutality, the theater acts as a catharsis, draining the audience of its violence. Artaud refers to the theater as a double, because it holds to the audience a mirror of their unconscious.[9]

It seems rather dubious that a theater premised on the ideas of Antonin Artaud could be considered politically a revolutionary theater, as opposed to an anarchic, libertarian, or even fascist theater with bohemian tendencies.[10] One can imagine the radical, if not revolutionary, aesthetic potential of an Artaudian-influenced theater in the United States. Yet Jones's idea of the revolutionary theater is based on a politicized aesthetic directed to the social and political worlds. He is not invoking revolutionary in the sense in which a dramatic production called for a radical aesthetic rupture in its own theater tradition. In trying to escape the politically disengaged world of Greenwich Village, Jones turned to a politicized theater, although his invocation of Artaud reveals his ambivalence about leaving the bohemian art world. Moreover, his mimicry of Artaud indicates that he had not yet rejected Western culture.[11]

"The Revolutionary Theater" is cleverly written, but it lacks substantive ideas. It does not adequately characterize a revolutionary theater aesthetic but instead describes this theater's ideal and intended impact on various audiences. Suppose, as intended, black theater audiences became angered and excited by Jones's revolutionary drama. Would such responses transform them into urban guerrillas? Would his theater intensify their oppositional sensibilities?

The significance of "The Revolutionary Theater" to the Black Arts movement was not in its conceptualization of aesthetics. Instead, Jones's essay functioned as a call to arms to black playwrights, writers, and scholars of all varieties. Jones implores them to stop hiding behind elusive symbolisms and complicated metaphors, for modernist Western aesthetics have no place in the black American struggle for freedom. To hell with T. S. Eliot, Robert Penn Warren, Joseph Conrad, Norman Mailer, and their white literary defenders who continued to celebrate them despite their racism! Embrace racial conflict!

Jones, the advocate of the revolutionary theater, refrained from writing plays that "evenhandedly" interrogate the internal complexities of American race relations. His call for a revolutionary theater was actually an announcement of a dramatic sensibility that ceased to view harmonious race relations as either a viable goal or a social ideal. This new, revolutionary black theater would not only embrace racial difference and divisiveness but dramatically intensify them so that no one present could escape its ramifications. It would be a theater of strife, struggle, discord, and disharmony.

Home, Jones's 1966 essay collection, concludes with the minuscule essay "state/meant" in which he reiterates his call for a new black artist. This essay (particularly its first sentence) also became one of the most frequently mentioned manifestos of the Black Arts movement.

> The Black Artist's role in America is to aid in the destruction of America as he knows it. His role is to report and reflect precisely the nature of the society, and of himself in that society, that other men will be moved by the exactness of his rendering and, if they are black men, grow strong through this moving, having seen their own strength, and weakness; and if they are white men, tremble curse, and go mad, because they will be drenched with the filth of their evil.[12]

"State/ment" extends the protest logic of "The Revolutionary Theater." It contains the seeds of Jones's belief that radical black artists should create exact renderings of society. This call for an art of mimicry, which risked extinguishing the difference between art and reportage, prefigured his later embrace of socialist realism.

Jones's most widely quoted statement of the new Black Arts sensibility was his poem "Black Art." Published in the January 1966 issue of *Liberator*, the initial lines of the poem include "Poems are bullshit unless they are / teeth or trees or lemons piled / on a step . . . Fuck Poems / and they are useful, wd they shoot / come at you, love what you are / breathe like wrestlers, or shudder / strangely after pissing." Such phrases set the stage for the violent imagery that accounted for the poem's notoriety:

> *We want poems*
> *like fists beating niggers out of Jocks*
> *or dagger poems in the slimy bellies*
> *of the owner-jews. Black poems to*
> *smear on girdlemamma mulatto bitches*
> *whose brains are red jelly stuck*
> *between 'lizabeth taylor's toes. Stinking*

Whores! We want "poems that kill"
Assassin poems, Poems that shoot
guns. Poems that wrestle cops into alleys
and take their weapons leaving them dead
with tongues pulled our and sent to Ireland. Knockoff
poems for dope selling wops or slick halfwhite
politicians. . . . Setting fire and death to
whities ass. Look at the Liberal
Spokesman for the jews clutch his throat
& puke himself into eternity. . . .
 . . . Another negroleader
on the steps of the white house one
kneeling between the sheriff's thighs
negotiating coolly for his people
. . . Put it on him, poem.
 . . . Another bad poem cracking
steel knuckles in a jewlady's mouth
. . . Let there be no love poems written
until love can exist freely and
cleanly. Let Black People understand
that they are the lovers and the sons
of lovers and warriors and sons
of warriors Are poems & poets &
all the loveliness here in the world.[13]

An insurrectionary statement of hilarious and demented imagery, "Black Art" is a metaphorical wish list of black transgressions. In turn, the transgressions constitute a cacophony of bohemian violations of bourgeois civilities ("Fuck poems and they are useful wd they shoot come at you"); Jones's personal psychological angst ("poems that smear blackness on mulatto bitches"); desires for political revenge ("Poems that wrestle cops into alleys and take their weapons"); a politically mindless lust for violence, particularly toward the weak ("cracking steel knuckles in a jewlady's mouth"); disdain for bourgeois blacks ("another negroleader . . . kneeling between the sheriff's thighs"); and disgust for white liberals ("Liberal Spokesman for the jews clutch his throat). These images were standard fare for Jones during his Black Arts period. His disdain for light-complexioned blacks and their supposed self-hatred was always most intense when directed at black women. The steel knuckles that he cracked in the "jewlady's mouth" may have been one of his numerous rhetorical assaults on his former wife, Hettie.[14] The rhetoric of "jewlady," much like "jewboy," was a disparaging way of referring to Jews. The idea of a Negro leader kneeling between the sheriff's thighs is a typical use of homosexuality to convey weakness, with the leader supposedly performing fellatio on a white sheriff.[15]

Contrary to a prevalent interpretation of this poem that circulated during the Black Arts era, the poem is nothing more than mere thuggery superimposed on hurt black feelings, impotence, and defeat. To the extent that it is a political wish list and metaphorically displaced political energies, the entire poem is rooted in a present in which none of these acts occurs, at least with the conscious meanings attributed to them by Jones. Worse, it does not make clear how the smashing of black steel knuckles into a Jewish woman's mouth is related to black emancipation. Arbitrary acts of aggression can appear emancipatory only to people like Jones who longed for revenge against whites in general and any individual white in particular. But like protest art, revenge-motivated art is not revolutionary.[16] It's "tit for tat." Besides, does her mere existence as a white Jewish woman make her a justifiable target of a revengeful act? Ironically, despite Jones's intent, there is little difference between writing poems of protest against the racist brutality of Irish American police and poems that invoke cathartic images of murdering such police. Both types of poems are "other directed." Protest art appeals to the conscience of whites, and revenge art attempts to frighten them. Both are parasitic. Although it may be seen as a radical manifesto of the Black Arts movement, "Black Art" was actually an extraordinarily naked testimony to Jones's and, by extension, the black art movement's ressentiment.

Jones's attempt to define an artistic moment/movement while it was evolving constituted a way of providing artistic prescriptions, of determining the scope of black artistic activity. He could not allow the Black Arts to be conceived as merely the artistic products of black Americans, for such an understanding of black art would have allowed too much artistic freedom. In much the same way that he and Karenga later tried to define black authenticity for all black people, Jones tried to project his personal artistic proclivities into an ethnic norm. In the name of black insurgency, artistic uniformity was projected as the desired end. But the dictatorial intentions of Jones's Black Arts formulations should not be overstated. He was attempting to create a black nationalist road map for the diverse intellectual and artistic sensibilities emerging in Afro-American artistic communities. At the same time, he was trying to organize the black nationalist sensibilities raging in the black world. His efforts were both descriptive and prescriptive.

Jones was only one of many black intellectuals defining the Black Arts movement. Larry Neal, cofounder of the Blacks Arts Repertory Theater, was one of the crucial theoreticians of the Black Arts movement. He described the movement:

> The Black Arts Movement is radically opposed to any concept of the artist that alienates him from his community. Black Art is the aesthetic and spiritual sister of the Black Power concept. As such, it envisions an art that speaks directly to the needs and aspirations of Black America. In order to perform this task, the Black Arts Movement proposes a radical reordering of the Western cultural aesthetic. . . . The Black Arts and the Black Power concepts both relate broadly to the Afro-American's desire for self-determination and nationhood.

Like other Black Arts advocates, Neal insisted that black artists needed to divorce themselves from Western aesthetics if they wanted to be creative. The "Western aesthetic has run its course: it is impossible to construct anything meaningful in its decaying structure."[17] But he makes these sweeping claims without ever defining "the Western aesthetic" or his "Decline of the West" thesis. Nonetheless, the Black Arts movement did not need to verify claims about the decadence, immorality, and imminent death of the West, for these beliefs were accepted and propagated much like religious doctrine.[18]

Running throughout all aspects of the Black Arts movement was a quasi-apocalyptic belief in the imminent demise of the West and the simultaneous rise of the black world. Such beliefs may have generated a vicarious sense of empowerment, for they invoked a teleology of black emancipation. But these rhetorical proclamations of imminent change often substituted for rigorous analyses of the plight of blacks in the United States. Why was the demise of the West impending? And why was it assumed that the demise of the West would be accompanied by the ascendance of the black world? Conspicuously absent in the various discourses emerging from the Black Arts movement was any serious discussion of the agent of historical change that would ultimately bring the West to its knees and the African diaspora to ascendance. A century earlier, *The Communist Manifesto* argued that class struggle would be the transformative dynamic of the world. Karl Marx and Friedrich Engels viewed the proletariat as the segment of humanity that, when engaged in a self-interested class struggle, would realize universal human emancipation. Were Jones, Neal, and their followers a black nationalist variant of Marx's proletariat?

Unlike Marx, Jones and his Black Arts compatriots spent enormous amounts of energy issuing one "death of the West" prediction after another. They were not alone, as most Black Power advocates spoke of black revolution as if it were inevitable. The assuredness with which advocates of Black Power and the Black Arts invoked a better "black" tomorrow only hid their shallow diagnosis of the contemporary political-economic situation in the world in general and the United States in particular. The truly radical black nationalist could neither question nor doubt the imminence of the victory of black people. It was as if open-ended analyses of both the black political situation and the strategies for change might introduce doubt into the minds of a people who could not be trusted to act without true-believer convictions.

Contrary to various claims about stepping outside the boundaries of the West, the Black Arts movement was unknowingly premised on the most central of Western narratives, that of the teleological emancipation of the oppressed. This moral narrative originated in the story of Moses and the Jewish Exodus which permeates Jewish and Christian theology. The unstated foundation of the Black Arts movement was a belief in the moral superiority of blacks. When trying to ascertain why Black Arts spokespersons thought that blacks were morally superior, I could only conclude that they granted blacks moral superiority because they were oppressed. According to Addison Gayle,

> From the souls of a great people had come the message of old, shaped and chiseled after the examples of those who had survived numerous holocausts; it was a message embellished with the awe and grandeur of time; it had been sung by black men in the cotton fields . . . heard by Douglass . . . noted by Du Bois . . . issued anew in the call of Garvey . . . sounded aloud in the old biblical inversions of Martin Luther King . . . transformed . . . by the courage and commitment of Malcolm . . . structured and codified through the sensibility, commitment, and devotion of Imamu Baraka. . . . We are an African people and, thus a loving and just people, committed to the salvation of the human spirit, to the improvement of the human condition; we are practitioners of the black arts, advocates of the Black Aesthetic.[19]

The idea that the subjugated are inherently more moral than the oppressor is a central tenet of Jewish and Christian moral discourses. In the case of Judaism, the subjugated Jews have a unique relationship with God and are, when faithful, morally superior (God's chosen). Similarly, Christianity endows the subjugated faithful with a privileged relationship to God as well as moral superiority. In Christianity, the subjugated also possess the key to the redemption of the oppressor. In Christian narratives, Jesus, the subjugated Jew, voluntarily suffers and dies on the cross. In the process, Jesus provides the means to save everyone from eternal damnation. He wins by losing.

In conversations with Martin Kilson, he pointed out that while there may be affirmation for the subjugated in embracing beliefs of moral superiority, there is no reason to view these claims as true. Despite the immorality of oppression, the subjugated could be, and often are, the immoral equals of their oppressors. They may simply be weaker. If oppression was the breeding ground of ethical behavior, the world would have long since been morally perfected.

Insofar as the Black Arts and Black Power contingents of the black intelligentsia were not attempting to redeem "the white man," they were not trying to reconstruct the Christ narrative. For the black literati, that burden had already fallen on the pen of James Baldwin. In Afro-American politics, Christian moral narratives were being used by Martin Luther King Jr., the Congress of Racial Equality, and other nonviolent devotees who subjected themselves to violent attack in order to obtain a moral status that would generate guilt in their white oppressors. Paradoxically, Jones and his Black Arts confreres shared with King the assumption that the oppressed were morally superior. In the case of King, the moral superiority of black Americans had to be earned by their public willingness to suffer, whereas Jones thought that there was no need to intensify blacks' suffering, no matter what benefits could be gained. He thought it was sheer lunacy to deliberately place one's skull within striking distance of a racist, baton-wielding, southern deputy. Four hundred years of racist brutality and oppression had not sufficiently pricked the conscience of white Americans to the point of undermining their commitment to white domination. Besides, oppressors never voluntarily relinquish their superiority.

Jones's thought was confusing and contradictory. While he believed that whites' recognition of their moral culpability in black oppression was irrelevant and contrary to the objectives of the new black assertiveness, he simultaneously celebrated such intentions in manifestos like "The Revolutionary Theater." Blacks, Jones wanted to believe, would be free whether or not whites recognized the legitimacy of their discontent. Unfreedom was not a possibility.[20]

In Jones's writing during the Black Arts era, whites were evil, and blacks were righteous, particularly those blacks who were in touch with their blackness. Black people were creative, community minded, and loving. Unlike whites, blacks did not thrive on the domination of others. Jones, the Black Arts movement spokesman, was a proud racial essentialist. In fact, in a 1967 interview, he even proclaimed himself a racist.

Q: What do you mean when you say you're racist?
A: I'm racist in the sense that I believe certain qualities that are read-

ily observable on this planet have to do with racial types and ar-
chetypes. The identities of peoples are based on their race and
culture....

Q: Do you believe there's a genetic or generic superiority of the
black race over the white?

A: Well yes. The black man was here on this planet first, and he will
be here long after the white man is gone.

Q: Could the white race possibly reverse this trend, by an act of will
or decision, or by social and political changes?

A: It could be, if you had evolved to that state. The next point of evolution for white people seems to me to be dust and ashes.[21]

Perhaps "dust and ashes" was the future for whites, but in the meantime, Jones
had to contend with the reality that evil whites ruled the world. Neither innate goodness nor genetic superiority had liberated black Americans or
Africans. Following in Malcolm's footsteps, Jones pleaded with blacks to
morally sanction whatever actions were deemed necessary for black emancipation. He viewed it as his mission to exorcise those moral sensibilities in
blacks that tolerated subjugation. Like Malcolm, Jones viewed Christianity as
a freedom-retarding culprit. Despite his awareness of the politicized Christianity of Martin Luther King Jr. and others, Jones believed that Christian
morality prevented blacks from recognizing the justness of violent revolution. Maurice Merleau-Ponty, a French phenomenologist, described the political limitations of the Christian worldview in ways that Jones might have
endorsed:

> The Christian always has the right to accept existing evil, but may never pur-
> chase progress with a crime. He can rally to a revolution that is over, he can
> absolve it of its crime, but he cannot start it. Even if a revolution makes just
> use of power, it remains seditious as long as it is unsuccessful. The Catholic
> as Catholic has no sense of the future: he must wait for the future to become
> part of the past before he can cast his lot with it.[22]

In Jones's mind, those white oppressors of blacks who claimed adherence to
Christian morality were sufficient proof of Christianity's uselessness as a
moral system for inducing racial change in America. During a 1968 interview,
he stated, "Most of the Negroes and the 'niggers'—and I use that term because
that's what they are, self-admittedly so—they pray to a god who allows them
to be slaves. Now if you pray to a god who allows you to be a slave, you are a
fool."[23] Christianity created moral ambivalences that could not sustain the

bifurcations needed for a revolutionary consciousness. In Christianity, both the oppressed and the oppressor were sinners, even in the minds of those like Martin Luther King Jr. who believed that God was on the side of the oppressed. In addition, the willingness of most Americanized versions of Christianity to deny the centrality of material conflicts between rich and poor, oppressed and oppressor, created a moral worldview that granted secondary importance to the material preconditions of freedom. A belief based on the equality of the spirit (i.e., equality before God) that gave secondary status to the inequalities of the material world was, ultimately, a reactionary religion.

Jones's valorization of the oppressed blacks' moral character must have forced him to consider the status of Jews. As victims of the worst genocide in modern history, Jews certainly had a justifiable claim to the victim status. Herein lies, I believe, a reason why Jones was overcome by anti-Semitism. He could not grant any white American a high moral character, particularly since he knew that whites, including Jews, were likely to be racist toward blacks. Instead of recognizing the groundlessness of applying Manichaean moral characterizations of peoples, he sidestepped the issue of the historical oppression of Jews by describing their subjugation as proof of their weakness. (Couldn't the same be said about black Americans?) As weaklings, Jews became implicated in their own genocide and thus should be refused entry into the ranks of the morally superior oppressed. Because such fanciful arguments failed to squash their nagging history, Jones tried to silence their humanity by embracing anti-Semitism.

It was no accident that during the Black Arts movement, Jones probed non-Christian based religious and moral systems. After experimenting with Yoruba and Orthodox Islam (Sunni), Jones became a follower of Kawaida, using his talents and craft to convert black Americans to Kawaidan values and practices. But a nagging question lingers. Suppose that miraculously, all black Americans had become dedicated practitioners of Kawaida, then what? Are we to assume that once Kawaidan piety spread to the black masses, a spontaneous emancipation or revolution would follow? Why would alterations in the moral code of a subjugated people necessarily lead to changes in their political and economic circumstances? What Jones could never admit but what seems evident is that he believed in morality as an efficacious agent of political change. His claims for the inevitability of the decline of the West (i.e., the United States) and the ascendancy of blacks (including Africa) were based on an unacknowledged belief in a historical moral teleology. Like Martin Luther King Jr., Jones evidently believed that history bends toward justice. Years later, when he realized that there would be no Kawaidan-inspired black revolution, he converted to a more rigid historical teleology, scientific Marxism.

Jones's manifestos for black art sacrificed his sophisticated understanding of aesthetics. In some sense, the "blacker" that Jones became, the farther he retreated from theory. Theory was thought to be European and therefore unnecessary in order to grasp the immediacy of the Afro-American predicament. More important, theory was seen as a distancing mechanism.[24] Black life was apparent. One did not need Northrop Frye to understand the murder of Emmett Till. Interestingly, the attempt to intellectually stigmatize theorizing as detrimental and inappropriate to Afro-America rests on a black willingness to embrace a long-standing racist discourse that constructed black life as carnal, anticerebral, and self-evident.[25]

Jones viewed the revolutionary theater as the negation of the bourgeois Broadway theater, but it appears that bohemianism continued to inform his art long after he thought that he had escaped its clutches. That is, when Jones referred to the "revolutionary" theater, he actually had little idea of what authentically constituted "the revolutionary" in 1960s America. He did not understand how a culture of consumption with one-dimensional tendencies might absorb and therapeutically use his so-called revolutionary drama.[26] Not only was he ignorant of how the marketplace had successfully co-opted aspects of the avant-garde and marketed them to the mass public as fashionable novelties,[27] but he took insufficient account of the aesthetic temper of his ideal audience. Black Americans were socialized in the prevailing culture to view and accept his drama as they would any drama, as commodified art or, worse, entertainment.

Black art with "positive" political messages affirmed blacks in much the same way that Hollywood made white Americans feel good by marketing to them an image of themselves as the bearers of universal goodness, humor, and vibrancy. Jones's drama was intent on reinforcing the reification of black consciousnesses. After all, how else can we explain the nonsense in his metaphorical proclamations about white men "going mad" and "twenty million spooks storming America with furious cries and unstoppable weapons"? But he failed to recognize that his highly cathartic drama showing black characters acting "revolutionary" against white characters may have encouraged black audiences *not* to be "revolutionary." His plays became rituals of black rebellion. Black audiences could vicariously act out these roles with none of the accompanying social costs (i.e., police repression or imprisonment). Such "rituals of rebellion" often reinforce the status quo by defusing oppositional energies that might have been articulated in authentic rebelliousness.[28]

If black Americans wanted to develop a revolutionary consciousness, Jones's theater may have been precisely what they did not need. That is, he used drama as a form of therapeutic catharsis that allowed blacks to endure yet another day of the status quo. The substance of Jones's political vision was simultaneously reactionary and radical. By traditional leftist criteria, to which he now subscribed, his Black Arts vision for a black revolutionary theater must be considered quite reactionary. In creating dramas that essentialized whites and blacks into Manichaean opposites, Jones minimized the possibilities for depicting progressive political change. Timeless, essentialized racial differences were immune to altered historical circumstances, including those drastic ruptures known as revolutions. Jones's artistic vision employed black nationalism as a mask to cover the class dynamics between whites and blacks as well as the class conflicts in the white and black communities. He appeared to address intraethnic black class divisions through his attacks on the black middle class. But his denunciation of the black middle class usually centered on claims that middle-class Afro-Americans were insufficiently "blackenized." Worse, he sometimes attacked them for having light complexions. In both instances, he used atavistic criteria to define blacks' socioeconomic location. Such formulations were not only backward but specious. Furthermore, such concerns did not address the complex obstacles that racially subjugated blacks, including members of the middle class, had to confront in their daily lives.

The Black Arts movement generally viewed the black middle class as the "sellout" sector of the black community.[29] Given all the invectives hurled at bourgeois blacks by the Black Arts movement, we might believe that the black middle class single-handedly blocked black emancipation. In a community desperate to cope with its political impotence, such ideas gained currency, for they circumvented the need to confront the feared and powerful "white man." Because of the therapeutic allure of dogmatic thinking and the absence of a rich intellectual infrastructure, sophisticated political-sociological analyses had little chance of appearing in black public-sphere discourse. In addition, attacks on the black middle class overstated its inclusion in the mainstream of American society. Finally, the association of economic impoverishment with authentic blackness was based on ontological assumptions about the nature of black existence that were both silly and groundless. Many blacks were poor, and many, if not most, were poor because they were black. They were not black because they were poor.

Certainly, many middle-class blacks were more acculturated and assimilated than many lower-class blacks. It was only reasonable that the Black Power movement would assert as one of its fundamental goals the desire to improve the economic conditions of poor and marginally employed blacks. Ironically, the pursuit of Black Power, if successful, would have reduced the number of poor blacks and therefore the number of "authentically black"

black Americans. If Jones actually thought that an economic status above that of the working class brought into question a black person's ethnic authenticity, then he should have realized that the Black Power struggle was a paradox in which improvements in blacks' living conditions threatened to make "authentic" blacks extinct.

Jones's "revolutionary theater" appeared insurrectionary because it transgressed bourgeois civilities, particularly bourgeois racial etiquette. Such transgressions were thought to release black audiences from those everyday social conventions that induced and authorized their devalued racial status in a liberal, bourgeois social order that often pretended to be nonracist, if not nonracial. Jones's Black Arts–era dramas tried to counter the rationalization of American racial inequality by interrogating and debunking the public valorization of liberal racial equality. In order to do so, Jones overdetermined race, racial identity, and racism by racializing all facets of his dramatic world. Each character and every event are completely racially inscribed. White characters are unceasingly and exhaustively "white." In only a very few instances do the white characters in Jones's Black Arts–era drama step outside their role as inhumane antagonists of black people. Similarly, black characters are always subsumed by their racial selves whether they be Uncle Toms or black nationalist revolutionaries.

Politically oppositional, Jones's art during the Black Arts movement contested the deeply embedded "naturalness" of racial inequality as well as black resignation to that social order. His dramas emphasize the presence of white supremacist intentions behind even those racial prejudices present in the commonplace occurrences of everyday life. Jones also wanted blacks to scrutinize the presence of antiblack racism in their own psyches, to alter the terms of the race debate (at least in black America) from one centered on the unfair racist exclusion of blacks to one in which the socioeconomic and political inclusion of blacks in the American status quo is depicted as destructive of their blackness and thus their humanity. Undoubtedly, Jones stimulated some blacks to question the foundation of their political consciousnesses. The Civil Rights movement did not promote the view that white America was both racist and demented. Such claims were tantamount to labeling racist white Americans as pathological. If as Jones claimed, racially parochial whites (i.e., all whites) were pathological, racial integration would not make sense. Whether or not blacks had viable options other than racial integration was a question that Jones's political vision overlooked. But he knew that black political leaders who viewed racial integration as paramount would not point out the limitations of white America. Their failure of nerve thus gave Jones (and, earlier, Malcolm) an opportunity to appear fearless.

Once legal segregation was declared unconstitutional, the Civil Rights movement became incapable of generating a mass-based interrogation of whiteness. It was somewhat ludicrous that large segments of the white mass public had concluded that all was well once civil rights laws were passed. Jones's demonic depictions of whites raised a question that must have troubled even Martin Luther King Jr. Why were white Americans so wedded to white supremacy? In raising this question, Jones could have opened new veins of black thought. But in attributing the cause of white, antiblack racism to the innate racial characteristics of whites, he precluded the very debate that he could have inspired. Racial essentialism was a reactionary dead end.

In dismissing the possibility that whites' racial attitudes and interests could change or be changed, Jones was left with three political options—separation, revenge, and revolt—which were mentioned individually or in combination throughout most of his Black Power–era political formulations. Black separatism was incorporated into Jones's version of black nationalism. Black revenge against whites for what they had historically done to black peoples became a dominant theme of his black art, including his black nationalist revolutionary theater. Black revolts were celebrated in his valorization of black urban rioters. Though oppositional, revolts were not necessarily intent on overthrowing the status quo. Even if revolution was the intent of black rioters, their actions did not constitute a real threat to the rule of the state. Of these three political alternatives, Jones viewed revenge as the most assertive and certainly the most cathartic. The desire to "get whitey back" implicitly and explicitly saturated the most militant of Black Power sensibilities. The allure of revenge, as opposed to the pursuit of emancipation, gave rise to political sensibilities that devalued strategic thinking and glorified threatening demagoguery. What Jones did not realize was that revenge-oriented art may have been an indication of weakness.

Max Scheler's discussion of ressentiment offers perceptive insights into Jones's so-called revolutionary manifesto and shows why his pronouncements remained mired in the victim status. Even though revenge drives some revolutionaries, it is not a revolutionary sensibility. As Scheler notes, the quest for revenge is reactive. Despite being preceded by an attack, a seeker of revenge does not immediately strike back in self-defense. Instead he or she plots an action that will take place at a later time, precisely because immediate action would be disastrous. Revenge is an admission of weakness ("just wait till the next time").

In describing the impotence fueling the quest for revenge and ultimately ressentiment, Scheler notes, "Revenge . . . leads to ressentiment only if there occurs neither a moral self-conquest (such as genuine forgiveness in the case of revenge) nor an act or some other adequate expression of emotion (such as verbal abuse or shaking one's fist), and if this restraint is caused by a pronounced awareness of impotence." Scheler argues that ressentiment will not arise if the actor desiring revenge *acts*. Persons who are consumed by hate will not experience ressentiment if they actually harm their enemy or even rhetorically "assassinate" the enemy in the presence of others, provided the decision to engage in a rhetorical assault does not stem from a fear of action.

> Ressentiment can only arise if these emotions are particularly powerful and yet must be suppressed because they are coupled with the feeling that one is unable to act them out—either because of weakness, physical or mental, or because of fear. Through its very origin, ressentiment is therefore chiefly confined to those who serve and are dominated at the moment, who fruitlessly resent the string of authority.[30]

Despite the perceptiveness of Scheler's discussion of the characteristics of ressentiment, he may have been incorrect about the types of oppositional assertions that hinder its growth. For example, did Jones's "venting of his spleen" via so-called revolutionary drama or poems that "crack steel knuckles in a jewlady's mouth" succeed in stemming the rise of ressentiment? Certainly, he and numerous other blacks gave whites a "piece of their mind." Scheler may not have anticipated the ways that ressentiment arises and is sustained in liberal democratic societies. If the venting of one's spleen is not repressed by the state, it may become tolerated over time, whereupon it may lose its ability to prevent ressentiment. If screaming at white folks becomes the pattern of black protest "accepted" by the white powers that be, then screaming will not be an effective way of authentically contesting power. In such instances, the scream itself becomes a site of political impotence. Only the act remains authentically oppositional.

BLACK AESTHETIC

Interwoven throughout the Black Arts movement were various announcements of and discussions about the Black Aesthetic, a distinctive approach to and/or methodology for conceiving and appraising the uniqueness of black art. While advocates of the Black Arts movement were frequently advocates of the Black Aesthetic, the two tendencies should not be combined analytically. Advocates of the new Black Aesthetic usually were participants in and supporters of the Black Arts movement, but some advocates of the Black Arts did not embrace the new Black Aesthetic. Poet Nikki Giovanni, for instance, was opposed to the formulation of a Black Aesthetic, although she was an enthusiastic participant in the Black Arts movement.[31] Jones was an emphatic advocate of both.

It is impossible to construct a notion of the Black Aesthetic that would be universally accepted by its adherents. Its legion of advocates championed differing if not conflicting conceptualizations. From the mid-1960s through the mid-1970s, the period when the various concepts of the Black Aesthetic peaked in popularity, there was little impetus to resolve these conceptual differences. To have done so would have necessitated intraethnic critiques and contestations, the types of intraethnic conflict that had momentarily fallen into disfavor among the culturally "blackest" of black artists and intellectuals. In recognition of the open-ended meaning of a Black Aesthetic, Haki Madhubuti wrote: "The Black Aesthetic cannot be defined in any definite way. To accurately and fully define a Black Aesthetic would automatically limit it. . . . After all, that which is called the white (Western) aesthetic is continuously reconsidered every time a new writer, painter, or what they call a musician comes on the scene."[32]

I propose two distinct but fused conceptual tendencies in the Black Aesthetic discourse that emerged during the late 1960s.[33] I call the preponderant theoretical tendency the *politically utilitarian Black Aesthetic* and the other tendency the *culture-premised Black Aesthetic*. These distinctions should not be considered absolute, however, as each tendency has significant conceptual overlap. Consequently, this Black Aesthetic typology should be seen only as a heuristic device to provide order to my discussion.

A POLITICALLY UTILITARIAN BLACK AESTHETIC

The absence of a universally agreed-on meaning of a Black Aesthetic is exemplified in *The Black Aesthetic*, the collection edited by Addison Gayle. In his introduction, Gayle tries to contextualize the emergence of the idea, situating the rise of the Black Aesthetic in black intellectual opposition to racist white intellectual and artistic assessments of blacks and their creations. To illustrate, he refers to the white artistic parochialism in poet Louis Simpson's review of a collection of poems written by Gwendolyn Brooks: "I am not sure it is possible for a Negro to write well without making us aware he is a Negro. . . . On the other hand, if being a Negro is the only subject, the writing is not important."[34] A prominent white poet and critic, Simpson was guilty of one of the central tenets of racist white artistic insularity: he devalued any artistic product that centered on blacks as a subject matter and did so with indifference to the quality of the writing. Black people were of such minor consequence that black writers, however talented, could not rescue from the ranks of the mediocre any art centering on black subject matter. The unstated reason was that serious art dealt with white peoples and that only through a concern with "white" subject matters could an artist address universal human themes. One could also read Simpson as implying that the "whiteness" of white writers was otiose. But even though it was obvious, Simpson's racism never undermined his credibility in mainstream (i.e., white) American literary circles. Despite being less blatant than Simpson, the dominant white American literati agreed that as subjects, blacks were just not artistically compelling.

Had he so desired, Gayle could have documented many more examples of racist parochialism toward black writers by white literary critics. Worse, parochial white critics often had the power to determine the scope and quality of recognition given to black writers by the literary establishment. Such biased evaluations hindered the access of black writers to fellowships, university appointments, and literary prizes. Gayle's ideal white critic of black literature was not only racially parochial but influential. Such traits gave birth to racial arrogance of the worst sort, for white critics were rarely, if ever, compelled to examine their own cultural privileging of whiteness. On those occasions when their minds were publicly caught in the racist cookie jar, they often responded with disdain or dismissal. Whether or not Gayle's focus on Simpson and a few other whites was an honest representation of the prevailing sensibilities of the white American literati, there is little reason to assume that most white literary critics were disinvested of the racism so prevalent throughout the broader society. As guardians of what was thought to be highbrow Western art forms (poetry, novels, drama), white critics could easily become more rationally committed to racial parochialism and Eurocentrism than could many rank-and-file whites. Such critics believed that they were defending not only the pantheon of Western culture but also the richest artistic traditions that humankind had ever produced.

Because of this racial climate in the United States, Gayle challenged black writers to ignore the criticism produced by racist white critics (i.e., all white critics). Black artists, he believed, had to learn to value their own creative productivity, for in seeking the approval of racist white critics, black writers were essentially asking the slave master to view the slave as an equal. Much of the cultural authority of white critics and artists lay in their power to clothe themselves in white Western cultural superiority vis-à-vis racial "others" and even upstart insiders (i.e., poor whites and members of stigmatized white ethnic groups). For most of the twentieth century, it was not only common for white critics to judge blacks but culturally necessary that they find black writers hopelessly deficient or wanting-but-growing.[35] Conversely, white writers could ignore the assessments of their works by black critics.

Despite recognizing the racially premised, parochial assessments of black writers offered by many white critics, Gayle went too far, by concluding that white critics, because they were white, were incapable of honestly and fairly assessing black literature. In his mind, most white critics were culturally too removed from the black world to grasp the nuances of Afro-American creativity. If by chance, some white critics maintained a cultural sensitivity to black life, Gayle assumed that they would still oppose the political goals of emancipatory-minded black writers.

Gayle's belief that white critics of black literature were, like all whites, inherently racist led to an incredible contradiction in his formulation of a Black Aesthetic. He essentialized whites but did not realize that such objectifications could be logical only in a universe that similarly objectified and essentialized blacks. Yet Gayle had no desire to essentialize black writers and critics. He did not view all black critics as inherently steeped in "black culture" or sensitive to literature produced by Afro-Americans. In fact, he claimed that some black critics embraced a "white aesthetic." If Gayle allowed for such volunteerism by blacks, why didn't he allow for it by whites? Couldn't a white critic embrace the Black Aesthetic? In his inability to remedy this faulty reasoning, Gayle cannot define the artistic components of a Black Aesthetic. Accordingly, his Black Aesthetic essentially condones whatever aesthetic concept a Black Arts critic or writer embraces. In his introduction to *The Black Aesthetic*, Gayle notes that each of the contributors to the volume had his or her own definition of the Black Aesthetic. Despite these differences, he hypothesizes that all the contributors would agree that the black artist is at war with America:

> There are few among them—and here again this is only conjecture—who would disagree with the idea that unique experiences produce unique cultural artifacts, and that art is a product of such cultural experiences. To push this thesis to its logical conclusion, unique art derived from unique cultural experiences mandates unique critical tools for evaluation. Further than this, agreement need not go![36]

What Gayle wants us to accept as a rather modest, irrefutable claim is actually riddled with confusion and contradiction. His statement is a rather conventional sociology-of-knowledge pronouncement. Yet like many sociology-of-knowledge claims, Gayle's discussion is far too sweeping and is unable to isolate the specific social factor that functions as the determinant of consciousness. For instance, if, like Gayle, we assume that black Americans share a similar culture, it does not necessarily follow that the creative products emanating from that culture will be aesthetically similar. Such a claim presupposes a strict sociology-of-knowledge vantage point that cannot account for different styles, ambitions, and degrees of creative agency in the community of black writers and artists. More important, there is no reason to assume that all blacks share a similar cultural experience. Finally, even if blacks do share cultural traits, this culture may not be sufficiently different from and/or uninformed by "white culture" to sustain claims of black cultural particularity. To allege that a shared racial/cultural heritage among black Americans leads to a shared aesthetic sensibility among black artists and critics is an unproven and unprovable assertion. Contrary to Mannheim's original formulations, Gayle's sociology-of-knowledge description omits any mention of class as a determining agent of consciousness.[37] His formulation also has difficulty accounting for the significance of gender.

Of the thirty-three entries in *The Black Aesthetic*, only two were written by women, as Gayle did not view black female intellectuals and artists as a meaningful political or artistic subgroup. Notwithstanding Gayle's marginalization of them, black women were active and significant participants in the debates surrounding the Black Aesthetic and the Black Arts. The commitment of the poets Gwendolyn Brooks, Nikki Giovanni, and Sonia Sanchez to the movement cannot be questioned. They were exceeded in popularity only by Jones and perhaps Madhubuti. Carolyn Rodgers, a frequently published critic and poet, founded the Third World Press in partnership with the poet Jewel C. Lattimore (Johari Amini) and Don L. Lee (Haki Madhubuti). Other prominent Black Arts female writers, poets, and critics included Sherley Ann Williams, Julia Fields, Carol Freeman, Jayne Cortez, Mari Evans, Lucille Clifton, Mae Jackson, Toni Cade Bambara, and, to some extent, Audre Lorde. Barbara Ann Teer was an influential figure in the Black Theater movement.[38]

The significant issue here, however, is not whether black women participated in the movement. That is well documented, if no longer well known. Instead, I am concerned with any restraints placed by the male definers of the movement on the scope of the "literary space" that black women writers could occupy and still be deemed legitimate "sisters." Clearly, the prevailing ideological pronouncements of the Black Arts movement did not celebrate black female creative freedom, particularly if black female intellectuals interrogated intraracial sexist behavior of black men. Instead, they privileged the black male angst created by white racist oppression. In the preface to the quasi-feminist 1970 collection *The Black Woman*, Toni Cade Bambara wrote:

> We are involved in a struggle for liberation: liberation from the exploitive and dehumanizing system of racism, from the manipulative control of a corporate society; liberation from the constrictive norms of "mainstream" culture, from the synthetic myths that encourage us to fashion ourselves rashly from without (reaction) rather than from within (creation). What characterizes the current movement of the 60s is a turning away from the larger society and a turning toward each other. Our art, protest, dialogue no longer spring from the impulse to entertain, or to indulge or enlighten the conscience of the enemy; white people, whiteness, or racism; men, maleness, or chauvinism; America or imperialism . . . depending on your viewpoint and your terror.[39]

The invocation of nonracially restricted male chauvinism as an evil comparable to white racism was a major radical statement. That it came from the pen of a "sister" considered quite in tune with Black Power sensibilities must have given pause to some men in the Black Arts who otherwise would have denounced these ideas as racially traitorous.

Gayle's blindness to the significance of gender was only one facet of his conceptual problems. If black art was uniformly unique because it derived from the universally similar cultural experiences of black Americans, there would be little diversity in Afro-American literature. Rather, these arbitrary claims rested on some widely held, commonsense assumptions about the core values of black culture, and black writers who did not fit into this mold were often ignored. If, however, a black writer was too prominent in black intellectual circles to be ignored, he or she could be attacked as pseudoblack, as Ralph Ellison often was.[40] We can only assume, therefore, that Gayle did not really want to advance the claim of black literary uniformity, for he criticizes white critics for both silencing the diversity in black life and thinking that black fiction is single-minded as to content and form. He is caught in an inescapable conundrum. Gayle's assertions about black cultural uniformity and uniqueness can be true only in a world not formed by "other" cultures. Such problematic cultural assumptions should have been dismissed as provincial, but they were not, at least not by large segments of the black intelligentsia. Consequently, a generation of black artists and critics went on a misdirected search for the holy grail of Black Aesthetic purity.

Gayle's concept of a Black Aesthetic is problematic also because it is based on a sociopolitical description of the impact of black literature instead of on qualities inherent in the literature. Gayle states,

> The question for the black critic today is not how beautiful is a melody, a play, a poem, or a novel, but how much more beautiful has the poem, melody, play, or novel made the life of a single black man? How far has the work gone in transforming an American Negro into an African-American or black man? The Black Aesthetic, then, as conceived by this writer, is a corrective—a means of helping black people out of the polluted mainstream of Americanism and offering local, reasoned arguments as to why he should not desire to join the ranks of a Norman Mailer or a William Styron.[41]

By granting literature the power to change lives, Gayle remains ensconced in a Western humanist tradition. His version of this humanist tradition is somewhat crude because he relocates the aesthetic value of a poem from the poem itself to the behavioral response of the reader. This is not as radical a claim as Gayle might have us believe, though.[42] The limitations in his formulation stem from a narrow elaboration of what constituted the nature of beauty for a black person. Curiously, Gayle assumes that "authentically black" listeners to music or readers of poetry would not, could not, or perhaps should not experience beauty through beautiful art. Given the black love of beauty in the form of a well-sung spiritual, a Leontyne Price aria, or a Johnny Hartman collaboration with John Coltrane, Gayle certainly could not have been arguing that contemporary blacks would not or could not experience beauty. Thus we can only conclude that Gayle did not think that black audiences *should be* enraptured by beauty, that appreciation for the beautiful in art was a frivolous activity for oppressed people.

> Man's capacity to appreciate the beautiful, to cultivate a wholesome, healthy aesthetic sensibility, depends upon the security of the environment in which he lives, in the belief in his own self-worth, in an inner peace engendered by his freedom to develop to the extent of his abilities. In a sharecropper's shack in Mississippi, a rat-infested ghetto in Harlem, or a mud hut in Vietnam, a portrait of the Mona Lisa, the strains of a Brahms concerto, the soothing lines of a Keats or a Countee Cullen are ludicrous at best, cruel at worst. In order to cultivate an aesthetic sensibility, given an oppressive society, the first prerequisite is that the oppression must end.[43]

Insofar as Gayle believed that the unfree would be and should be concerned only about attaining freedom, he refused to acknowledge that the oppressed do not live by powerlessness alone. Despite the many conceptual flaws in Gayle's formulation, the idea of a Black Aesthetic was enthusiastically embraced by large segments of the Afro-American intelligentsia. The attractiveness of the idea proved to be far more powerful than the sum of its parts. In 1968, Hoyt Fuller, editor of *Black World*, published a discussion of the Black Aesthetic. When republished as the lead essay in Gayle's edited collection *The Black Aesthetic*, Fuller's "Toward a Black Aesthetic" became another frequently cited essay of the Black Arts movement. Nevertheless, Fuller's formulations of a Black Aesthetic were as theoretically unremarkable as Gayle's. Fuller highlighted the racism of the dominant society and announced that blacks did not want to enter this mainstream. Even though the latter claim demanded empirical verification, Fuller provided none. Undoubtedly, most blacks opposed white racist America (i.e., America as we know it), but it was also probably true that most blacks wanted to enter the mainstream (i.e., greater economic well-being). Nevertheless, Fuller's most important task was to illegitimate white critics of black literature. In so doing, he and other Black Aesthetic critics attempted to cordon off an academic arena from competition from white scholars and, in the process, protect the economic mobility of black critics.

Maulana Karenga contributed to many of the most significant discussions of the Black Arts era, including the debates about the Black Aesthetic. His 1968 essay "Black Art: A Rhythmic Reality of Revolution" promotes an aesthetic with no pretense of being concerned with art:

> All art must reflect and support the Black Revolution, and any art that does not discuss and contribute to the revolution is invalid. . . . Black art must expose the enemy, praise the people, and support the revolution. It must be like LeRoi Jones' poems that are assassin's poems, poems that kill and shoot guns. . . .

Based on this mechanical formula for black creativity, Karenga concluded that the blues as an art form was invalid because it taught political resignation. "We will not submit to the resignation of our fathers who lost their money, their women and their lives and sat around wondering, 'what did they do to be so black and blue.'"[44]

Besides Karenga's obvious willingness to disregard the historical presence of women in the ranks of black sufferers and blues artists, his arrogance in commenting on subjects that he knew so little about (black literature, the blues, aesthetics) was indicative of the priority that he placed on political polemic over substantive dialogue. It was almost acceptable to say anything (and be taken seriously), provided it was couched in terms of black freedom or subjection. After reading Karenga's charlatan formulations on issues of black art, one black writer was sufficiently disgusted to send a response to *Negro Digest* (soon to be *Black World*) that he appropriately entitled "Hemlock for the Black Artist: Karenga Style."[45]

Although he was sympathetic to the Black Arts movement, literary scholar George Kent was repulsed by the proud provincialism of Karenga's claim that "black art must expose the enemy, praise the people and support the revolution." Kent wrote,

> I myself, find Karenga's remarks rather chilling and an extremely tight box for the artist to dwell in. It has all the beauty and the unreality of the Western Syllogism. . . . Whatever Karenga's intention, it is rather difficult not to envision a cultural commissar arriving to enforce upon the artist his version of what fits the people's needs. Or perhaps the version of his superior or committee . . . no careful reading of Jones will suggest that he could be packaged in Karenga's box.[46]

Interestingly, Kent tries to divorce Jones from simplistic pronouncements of the Karenga variety. But nothing that Jones published during the Black Arts era disagreed with Karenga's declarations on art. A discussion in 1967 with black journalist Robert Allen shows Jones's adherence to Karenga's dictates:

> ALLEN: Do you agree with Ron Karenga's statement that black arts must be functional, collective and committing?
>
> JONES: Yes, very much. He certainly is an artist and a political theorist and a cultural theorist of great stature, and I don't think he's been recognized yet.[47]

Because Kent was committed to the Black Arts movement, it may have been difficult for him to admit that Jones agreed with Karenga's pedestrian beliefs. Still, Kent's willingness to sever Jones from Karenga-like sentiments could have stemmed from Kent's awareness that Jones had previously possessed a sophisticated aesthetic sensibility. Karenga, Kent believed, "didn't know," but Jones "knew better." But even if Jones "knew better," his pronouncements on black art were testaments to cultural insularity and crude political utilitarianism. In the name of revolution, Jones had "willed to forget."

In the September 1969 issue of *Black World*, Jones published a short essay, "The Black Aesthetic: We Are Our Feelings,"[48] beginning with the question, "What does *aesthetic* mean?" He answers with a rhetorical question: "Shdn't it mean for us Feelings about reality? . . . We are our feelings. We are our feelings ourselves. Our selves are our feelings. . . . How is a description of Who. So a way of feeling or the description of the process of is what an aesthetic wd be." According to Jones, how black authors write depends on the quality of their being. If they have the proper black feelings, they will write in an appropriately black way. To attain these feelings, they must "Intuit. About Reality" and go "In to selves."[49]

Jones claims that our art reflects our spiritual and life-affirming choices. Accordingly, the greatest achievement for a black writer is not a one-page poem but a life well lived on behalf of the coming black nation:

> . . . Hard work. Brutal work. . . . Build a house, man.
> Build a city, A Nation. This is the heaviest
> work. A poem? One page? Ahhhh man, consider
> 200,000,000 people, feed and clothe them, in the
> beauty of god. That is where it's at. And yeh,
> man, do it well. Incredibly Well.[50]

The purpose of black writing—or perhaps the black purpose of writing—is to aid in the creation of a black nation. By helping unleash the energy of black spiritedness, black authors contribute to the future black nation. Black artists in touch with the Black Aesthetic are not governed by a desire for individual artistic recognition. Rather, their goal is far more ambitious; they aspire to create a just, spirited, and spiritual black nation.

Jones's argument actually extends and perhaps exceeds those of Gayle and Karenga in advocating a utilitarian purpose for black artistic creation. Whereas Gayle, Fuller, and Karenga called on black artists to write in ways that contributed to revolutionary change, Jones proclaimed poetry trivial in the face of harvesting a wheat crop or building decent shelters. If the greatest achievement of the artist under the sway of the Black Aesthetic lay in building schools for black education and growing crops for hungry black stomachs, why did Jones continue to write poems?

We can imagine the problems that a utilitarian aesthetic could create for Jones the artist. If the ultimate success of a poem lies in its contribution to not only the proliferation of a black nationalist consciousness but also the actual building of a material black nation, then the success or failure of an art form becomes dependent on the success or failure of a political movement. But how do we know when a political movement really succeeds or fails? The utilitarian aspects of the Black Aesthetic not only devalued art but sometimes even dismissed art as a distinct entity. When everything becomes art, art as we have known it ceases to exist. This is as true for African art as it is for European art. African art was often valorized by the Black Aesthetic crowd because it was thought that Africans did not separate art from their everyday lives. For instance, African cooking utensils are artistic objects. But the art that emerges from the needs, tasks, and artifacts of everyday life may not be as much African as it is preindustrial or folk art. Similar art can also be found in Afro-American communities, Native American societies, and throughout peasant Europe. This art is quite different from that invoked by the Black Aesthetic circles, precisely because the plays and poems that emerged from that movement were not organically derived from or situated in black everyday life. Black aesthetic art was utilitarian in the sense that it was based on and assessed by motivations outside aesthetic appreciation. Black Aesthetic art was created conspicuously as art by individuals who viewed themselves as creators. This is far different from the work songs created by chain gang members trying to coordinate their lifting of heavy wooden railroad ties and iron tracks. Such songs were not conspicuous artistic creations. In the eyes of their creators, who were usually not individually known, the aesthetic value of these songs was inadvertent and of less significance than their usefulness. The Black Arts crowd were not folk artists, and many had little organic connection to poor black communities.

A CULTURE-PREMISED BLACK AESTHETIC

As stated earlier, Addison Gayle's edited collection *The Black Aesthetic* did not generate or stem from a universally accepted idea of a Black Aesthetic. Instead, Gayle was most attuned to those definitions of the Black Aesthetic based mainly on the political usefulness of black art to the black political struggle. Another, perhaps equally prominent, tendency in Black Aesthetic theorizing de-emphasized the political utility of art for its adherence to black cultural traditions. Unlike the definitions of the Black Aesthetic propagated by Gayle and his supporters, those based on culture often lacked utilitarian political prescriptions. There was, of course, a significant overlap between the definition based on culture and the politicized variant, but they were predicated on different emphases.

The culture-based Black Aesthetic assumed the presence of a distinctly black artistic ethos in the Afro-American tradition. This aesthetic was descriptive, whereas the politicized Addison Gayle variant was prescriptive. The former demanded an extrapolation from existing texts, and the latter provided instructions for future texts. A culture-based Black Aesthetic could be deduced only after rigorous study of the Afro-American literary tradition.

Alain Locke's edited collection *The New Negro* was a precursor of this under-standing of the Black Aesthetic.[51] He sensed a change in black artistic senti-ments in the literature produced by the Harlem-based black writers of the early 1920s. In the essay "Negro Youth Speaks," Locke offers his racialist de-scription of a culture-based Black Aesthetic:

> All classes of a people under social pressure are permeated with a com-mon experience; they are emotionally welded as others cannot be. With them, even ordinary living has epic depth and lyric intensity, and this, their material handicap, is their spiritual advantage. . . . Negro genius to-day relies upon the race-gift as a vast spiritual endowment from which our best developments have come and must come. . . . Our poets have now stopped speaking for the Negro—they speak as Negroes. Where for-merly they spoke to others and tried to interpret, they now speak to their own and try to express.[52]

The culture-based idea of a Black Aesthetic owes a great deal to the Herder-ian belief that all great fine art is an expression and refinement of folk art and/or folk culture. This belief influenced not only the aesthetic sensibilities of Alain Locke but also filtered into the aesthetic ideas of later writers like Richard Wright[53] and Ralph Ellison.

When one thinks of pre–Black Arts era practitioners of a culture-based Black Aesthetic who were still alive and accessible at the time of the Black Arts movement, Sterling Brown and Langston Hughes immediately come to mind. Brown became one of the foundational middlemen linking the New Negro era with the 1960s Black Arts generation.[54] Although politically both men were lifelong integrationists as well as believers in cross-racial artistic fertil-ization, Brown and Hughes were "race men," politically and literarily engaged in the Afro-American freedom struggle. In their writing, Hughes and Brown affirmed black folk cultural traditions and did so without needing to base their affirmations on criteria acceptable to the white literary establishment.[55] Because they were opposed to the idea that art should be primarily propa-ganda, they would have been highly critical of Gayle's politically utilitarian Black Aesthetic. Both men became revered figures in the Black Arts move-ment because they respected black folk art forms long before it was "re-spectable" to do so. Like Jones, many black students at Howard came to know Brown as a professor who critically honored black culture at a time when the university's intellectual ethos was decidedly assimilationist. Also like Jones, many of the young black artists who emerged during the 1960s remembered the generous encouragement that they had received from Hughes early in their writing careers.

In 1973, Sterling Brown's younger colleague in Howard University's English department, Stephen Henderson, edited a collection that reinvigorated debates in Afro-American intellectual circles concerning a culture-based Black Aesthetic.[56] Henderson's *Understanding the New Black Poetry* provides a deeper textual approach to the Black Aesthetic than that offered by Addison Gayle.[57] Henderson's theory of the Black Aesthetic relies on three distinct criteria: *theme, structure,* and *saturation.* He defines theme as "that which is spoken of, whether the specific subject matter, the emotional response to it, or its intellectual formulation."[58] The dominant motifs in black poetry center on the idea of freedom and/or emancipation. This thematic emphasis on black liberation offers an unintentional linkage between Henderson's idea of the Black Aesthetic and Karenga's and Gayle's versions. Henderson claims that black poetry can also be described and criticized according to its structure. For Henderson, structure is defined as those forms and devices (e.g., diction, rhythm, figurative language) that help create a black cultural artifact. Black poetry is "black" to the extent that its structure is copied from Afro-American speech patterns or black music.[59] Henderson's definition of black poetic structure is imprecise and appears to be a residual negation of the more clearly defined English and Anglo-American poetic structures. Most important to Henderson's discussion of a Black Aesthetic is his concept of saturation. According to Henderson, saturation refers to "the communication of Blackness in a given situation" and/or "a sense of fidelity to the observed and intuited truths of the Black experience."

> Saturation may thus be seen as (1) a perception, (2) a quality and (3) a condition of theme and structure. The perception occurs in the reader/audience in a situation of communication involving the poem/poet/reader/performer. If the poem "works," then the reader perceives something in it which he identifies as Black and meaningful. He perceives this as being true to his knowledge of the experience recorded in the poem, according to his observation or according to his intuition. The important thing, at any rate, is that he considers the communication of this "Blackness" to be significant and his reception of it to be significant, whether he agrees with it or not.[60]

Henderson's methodology for aesthetically assessing a poem essentially evaluates the degree of blackness it contains. Some poetic structures are considered blacker than others or, in other words, are more saturated. As an example, he states that the ballad is blacker than the sonnet but that both are less black than the blues. He calls the blues a saturating form and blues imagery, saturated structures. My purpose is not to argue with Henderson's assessments of the degree of blackness that can be assigned to a structure, but it does appear that he is caught in highly subjective assessments of "blackness" that cannot be derived internally from his theory. And need we ask who was qualified to determine what was and was not black? Blacks of course . . . but which blacks?

Henderson's insufficiently formalized aesthetic theories place a tremendous burden on the intuitive "black" sensibilities of black poets, readers, and critics. Concerning this, Houston Baker wrote,

> It should be clear that there were blatant weaknesses in the theoretical framework of the Black Aesthetic. Too often in attempts to locate the parameters of Afro-American culture, Black Aesthetic spokesmen settled instead for romantically conceived boundaries of "race." Moreover, their claims to a scholarly consensus on "culture" sometimes appeared as mere defensive chauvinism.[61]

Henry Gates contends that Henderson's theory appears to be tautological. Gates views Henderson as saying that a poem is blacker when it is more saturated in blackness.[62] If Henderson could determine what structure was blackest, why did he need an interpretive theory? His project became engulfed in racial reification. The idea of "blackness" was a quality or characteristic divorced from the real lives of a culturally diversifying and diversified black community, frozen in time and space and then used to categorize the artistic creations of those ever changing people. A question remains: Why was it significant for Henderson to rank poetry according to its blackness?

In addressing the limitations of the culture-based idea of a Black Aesthetic, David Lionel Smith wrote,

> Again and again the inherent contradictions of racial essentialism undermined efforts to articulate a coherent Black Aesthetic theory. . . . Rather, it seems to me that the theorists of the Black Arts movement erred in their preoccupation with defining a single correct ideology of blackness. What was needed instead of uniformity was a far more pluralist, accurate, and historically detailed understanding of racial identity in American than our culture had previously offered. Thus, the error of the movement's theorists was not that they were too radical but rather that they were too conventional. By remaining in essentialist conceptions of race, they bound themselves to a sys-

tem that was designed explicitly to preclude the revolution they sought. A satisfactory Black Aesthetic would have liberated them to embrace the multifarious particularity of African-American experience. Instead, they subscribed to an ideology of blackness that left them trapped in the fun house of racial essentialism.[63]

In hindsight, it seems clear that the Black Aesthetic advocates tried to replace a constricting view of black writing with one of their own. Much of the intraethnic black literary criticism written during the Black Arts movement was either crass celebrations of black writers, black creativity, and black people or attempts to enforce black artistic conformity. Among others, Ishmael Reed was a constant thorn in the side of Black Arts advocates.[64] His writing was in tune with the historical moment insofar as it affirmed various black cultures and black creative agency. However, Reed did not observe the constrictions of the Black Arts critics. Not as ideologically doctrinaire as Jones, Reed probably was more skillful in engaging black folklore. Nevertheless, he was subjected to ruthless criticism and ridicule. For instance, Joe Goncalves, editor of the *Journal of Negro Poetry*, launched vicious ad hominem attacks on black writers who strayed outside the Black Arts fold. When Goncalves interviewed Ishmael Reed for his journal, Reed referred to the Black Aesthetic as a "goon squad aesthetic" and compared the Black Aesthetic advocates with fascists. He concluded by saying that "this tribalism is for the birds." Goncalves's response to the interview accused Reed of "always serving some white man's purpose." Then Goncalves ended his commentary on Reed in an astoundingly malicious manner: "Reed, drunk, sniffing white girls, dependent, lays dead about the white man's fort."[65] In the Black Arts movement, were vicious and ignorant personal attacks tolerated as legitimate literary criticism?

The emergence of the Black Arts movement led to an intense generational conflict in the black intelligentsia. Many of the most vehement critics of the idea of a Black Aesthetic were black intellectuals and artists who had come of age earlier. Critics of the Black Arts movement included the political scientist Martin L. Kilson, the critic and man of letters J. Saunders Redding, the novelists Ralph Ellison and Albert Murray, the literary critics Nathan Scott, Arthur P. Davis, and Charles Davis, and the poet Robert Hayden. These critics never had a large following among the youthful segments of the black intelligentsia, but they played a crucial role as evaluators of the movement. They spotted major problems in this intellectual formation, some of which led to its demise. While the black critics of the Black Arts/Black Aesthetic did not subscribe to one position, they all believed that the Black Arts movement was parochial and doctrinaire to the degree to which it attempted to place ideological harnesses on black intellectuals and artists. While these critics were conscious of belonging to a devalued racial group in a predominantly white society, they did not believe that black Americans had created a distinct cultural sensibility uninfluenced by whites or that the West was artistically dead or decadent. Finally, they believed in the pursuit and refinement of artistic craft, a pursuit that was devalued by some in the Black Arts movement in favor of valorizing the political message.

Critics of the Black Arts did emerge from the movement, but their criticism was uneven and sporadic. In her excellent study of the Black Arts movement, Sandra Hollin Flowers quotes from the pages of *Liberator* to document the willingness of journals associated with the movement to publish critics of the movement.[66] One black critic had written,

> Does the artist have the right to, and absolute need for, individuality, creativeness and free expression, or doesn't he? If he does, then there's no honest way of making the whim or sociopolitical exaction or appeasement or standards of any particular group the first and last word, the criteria of worth or decisive factor in style and content in the artist's creative life.[67]

In another instance, Clarence Major noted,

> But the Black Literary-Political Establishment is a very curious organization. Hot air at the center, its thrust seems to come in spurts, like that of its white counterpart. Aside from passionately helping white publishers to cultivate blatant mediocrity, many members of the B.L.P.E. go all out to become performers and show personalities in the name of the art of writing. I'm referring to the ones who conduct themselves like comedians. Perhaps they are victims of what Ralph Ellison sees as the sad misunderstanding of the relation between suffering and art.[68]

In *Propaganda and Aesthetics*, Abby and Ronald Johnson claim that one of the few times that Jones was confronted with direct, scathing criticism from the Black Arts movement was in the journal *Black Dialogue*. Appearing in the Winter 1967/68 issue, Askia Toure's "A Letter to Ed Spriggs: Concerning LeRoi Jones and Others" accused Jones of "Reactionary Super-Blackism, a dogmatic nihilism—in Black literature as well as politics."[69] Toure criticized Jones for his antiwhite biases and underdevelopment of "positive perceptions of Afro-American culture. He also stressed the need for internal self-criticism among black writers and advocated a militant, iconoclastic criticism that would be directed toward the sacred cows in our group."[70]

Stanley Crouch, a Black Arts mainstay, criticized fellow black writers from the pages of the *Journal of Black Poetry*. In the Fall 1968 issue, Crouch stated: "One of the major problems in Black Writing today is that most of the people who pass themselves off as writers either cannot write, are capitalizing on something that has moved from true feeling to a name-calling fad masked as 'Revolutionary Black Nationalism,' or, *they have no respect for the craft* [italics in original]."[71] Crouch chastised black writers for not working hard at perfecting their craft and used jazz musicians as the appropriate model for black writers. He noted that even as talented and innovative a figure as the jazz pianist Cecil Taylor was known to practice ten hours a day over long periods of time. According to Crouch, there was no reason that revolutionary black poets could not compose good poetry. A few pages later, in the same issue of the *Journal of Black Poetry*, Crouch reviewed three short volumes of Black Arts poetry. The review essay began,

> I am very concerned about Black Literature and do not believe, as do many others, that we are experiencing a renaissance, but, rather, think that we are falling into the same kind of slump Black Music fell into during the soul-funk fad of eight years ago: A lot of people are bull-shitting under the banner of "getting down."[72]

CONFRONTING ARTISTIC ESTRANGEMENT

The quest for an organic connectedness was a major reason for the Black Arts movement's emphasis on orality and performance. Foregrounding black orality was imagined as African, and it was viewed as a strategy for minimizing estrangement. Black artists had to accept that many impoverished blacks were illiterate and numerous others were functionally illiterate. To privilege the written text, an author would be deliberately excluding many blacks from accessing it. Dramatic performances and public poetry readings therefore became viewed as better ways of reaching black audiences.[73]

The underacknowledged model for the Black Arts writer may have been the black preacher, singer, or blues/jazz musician. All were capable of utilizing sound in ways that not only captured the imaginations of black audiences but often generated a call-and-response dynamic. In the afterword to *Black Fire*, Larry Neal wrote,

> We can learn more about what poetry is by listening to the cadences in Malcolm's speeches than from most Western poets. Listen to James Brown

scream. Ask yourself, then: Have you ever heard a Negro poet sing like that: Of course not, because we have been tied to the texts, like most white poets. The text could be destroyed and no one would be hurt in the least by it. The key is in the music. Our music has always been far ahead of our literature ... the key to where black people have to go is the music. Our music has always been the most dominant manifestation of what we are and feel, literature was just an afterthought, the step taken by the Negro bourgeoisie who desired acceptance on the white man's terms. And that is precisely why the literature has failed. It was the case of one elite addressing another elite.[74]

Even though Neal's comments about black written texts appear to be uncharacteristically banal, his views of the oral centeredness of black culture were pervasive during the Black Arts era. Indeed, Jones had deferred to the creative vitality of black music long before he embraced the Black Arts. In his mind, black music, particularly jazz, functioned as the standard bearer of black creativity and excellence for black writers as well as a black cultural depository for poetic exploration. In other words, it was through the world of sound that black Americans had realized their greatest artistic achievements. It thus is no surprise that a "blacker" Jones would value orality over written texts. Yet as early as 1972, he had criticized the celebration of the oral at the expense of the written: "We talk about the oral tradition of African People ... and it's always as a substitute for the written. What this is is foolfood, because we were the first writers as well. ... Thot is the God of writing, its inventor, and African."[75]

To the extent that the Black Arts movement actually produced artists who were opposed to estrangement from the black masses, it stimulated an artistic ethos that constrained the imagination of the black artists. Such an aesthetic had a negative leveling effect on the black artist. Dudley Randall, a central participant in the Black Arts movement, wrote,

> In the Black Aesthetic, individualism is frowned upon. Feedback from black people, or the mandates of self-appointed literary commissars, is supposed to guide the poet ... this feedback usually comes from the most vocal group, ideologues or politicians, who are eager to use the persuasiveness of literature to seize or consolidate power for themselves.[76]

The issue of artistic alienation from the black mass public was complex. It was one thing to assert that black artists should write for black people, another to say that they were writing for black audiences, and still another to claim that they were writing from the black community. In the first two instances, the writer did not need to be situated in a black community. An example is Richard Wright as described by Sartre:

> To whom does Richard Wright address himself? Certainly not to the universal man. The essential characteristic of the notion of the universal man is that he is not involved in any particular age, and that he is no more or no less moved by the lot of the Negroes of Louisiana than by that of the Roman slaves in the time of Spartacus. . . . But neither can Wright think of intending his books for the white racists of Virginia or South Carolina whose minds are made up in advance and who will not open them. Nor to the black peasants of the bayou who cannot read.[77]

Wright, Sartre argued, viewed himself as writing *for* a reading audience of educated blacks and white Americans "of good will" who were concerned about the plight of blacks.

Sartre's perceptiveness may have been aided by his familiarity with Wright's essay "How 'Bigger' Was Born," in which Wright explains the origins of the novel *Native Son* and particularly its central character, Bigger Thomas.

> I had written a book of short stories which was published under the title *Uncle Tom's Children*. When the reviews of that book began to appear, I realized that I had made an awfully naive mistake. I found that I had written a book which even bankers' daughters could read and weep over and feel good about. I swore to myself that if I ever wrote another book, no one would weep over it; that it would be so hard and deep that they would have to face it without the consolation of tears.[78]

Even though Wright was a celebrated figure among the Black Arts crowd because of his racial militancy, he was not imagined as a model for the Black Arts writer. Not only had he twice married women who were white, but he had chosen to flee the struggles of black American everyday life to become an expatriate in France. Equally important, Wright did not imagine himself situated in a black communal nexus. Instead, he celebrated "homelessness."

For our purposes, it is beneficial to look at the confluences between Sartre's formulation and a Du Boisian double-consciousness. It was this double-consciousness that was continually under attack by the Black Arts advocates[79] who recognized the self-destructiveness inherent in viewing black life through the lens of the white racist sensibility that had taken root in the black psyche. This "from the outside-in" vantage point reinforced the

rationales used to legitimate black inequality. Black writing, these advocates believed, should be concerned only with addressing a black audience
from a black point of view. Likewise, such writing should be judged only by
black critics who write from a black point of view. If the Black Arts had its
way, the response of white readers and critics of black writing would
henceforth be of no literary or political importance to black writers. In this
sense, the Black Arts movement realized that a black double-consciousness
was ultimately an embrace of the black victim status. In an essay published
in the *Liberator*, playwright Charles H. Fuller Jr. addressed the psychological angst that accompanied a double-consciousness for the black writer and
its victim-status implications:

> The reason for the difficulty and many of the sleepless nights has been that
> Black writers . . . tried desperately to explain it [their art] in terms of white
> standards and by so doing to achieve white literary celebration. But art born
> out of oppression can not be explained in the terms of the unoppressed,
> since the condition of the oppressor does not allow him to deal with a form
> that might conceivably make the oppressed his equal. In order for him to re-
> main in power, he must discard any creations of the oppressed people as val-
> ueless even though he has given them the tools to build their creation.[80]

Whites were no longer imagined as capable of humanely responding to black
suffering and thus having the moral character necessary to respond to black
protest literature. Consequently, in the Black Arts, any overt attempt to appeal
to the conscience of white Americans was viewed as an indication of estrangement from and/or lack of faith in black people. The only audience of
political importance for the new black writers was black America.

In trying to disempower the white judgmental gaze, many black writers
mistakenly stigmatized as white (and thus irrelevant) a concern for artistic
form, which lay at the root of all traditional aesthetic concerns. Instead, Black
Arts artists (Jones, Madhubuti) and critics (Gayle, Karenga, Hoyt Fuller) emphasized content.[81] By 1976, Black Arts critic Larry Neal, who also had been
guilty of this conceptual error, recognized the limitations of his previous pro-
posals. In his wonderfully reflective essay "The Black Contribution to American Letters: The Writer as Activist—1960 and After," Neal argued against
those ideas of Karenga, Gayle, and Madhubuti that placed more importance
on the black critic's political and social allegiances than on his or her analytical insights into a discussion of black literature. Madhubuti's error, Neal
asserted, lay in his mistaken emphasis on *art as experience* rather than *art as
method*:

To stress content over form, structure, texture, and conscious craftsmanship is simply a way of stressing questions of social morality over those of abstract aesthetics. (This critical method, as we have noted, has its roots in Marxian proletarian literary criticism.) Hence any writer who evinces a persistent concern for artistic "method" is looked upon as engaging in art for art's sake.[82]

Neal reiterated some of the aesthetic concerns that Crouch, Ellison, and others had previously articulated. When Neal listed the names of those black writers of the Black Arts era who had, "by dint of craftsmanship and study," created "literary works which are uncompromising in their quest of Pan-African forms, yet refuse to sacrifice anything in the way of artistic integrity," he conspicuously omitted Jones and instead named Henry Dumas and Ishmael Reed.[83]

The idea of "art for art's sake" was invoked throughout the Black Arts movement as a code word for decadent Western art. "Art for art's sake" was supposed to represent the epitome of the narcissism and thus purposelessness that governed Western artists' creative sensibilities. While "art for art's sake" certainly opposed the engaged political stance of the Black Arts, it had never been an uncontested norm in Western art worlds.[84] Why, then, did the Black Arts crowd simply erase the existence of Sartre and the idea of a committed literature? Ironically, during the twentieth century, "art for art's sake" had been more influential in bohemian circles, like those inhabited by Jones in the Village, than in mainstream American literary communities. Jones attributed to the entire Western art world a doctrine that he had once been guilty of embracing.

Neither "art for art's sake" nor double-consciousness was the main issue that black writers had to confront in their attempt to minimize their estrangement from the black community. This new direction in black art was conceptually more problematic than its advocates originally perceived. They erroneously viewed the creation of a black-centered art world as a mechanism for overcoming black artistic estrangement from the black community. Contrary to Black Arts announcements, the act of writing for a black audience did not preclude the nurturance of an individual artistic sensibility. After all, the advocates of the Black Arts mistakenly thought that one could write for a black audience only if one were somehow situated in it. They believed that certain subjects were outside the range of mass black interests and accessibilities, thereby making them irrelevant to the black struggle.

For instance, suppose that a black philosopher wrote for a black reading audience a Hegel-influenced defense of black female equality. In addition, let us suppose that her discussion of this philosophical issue was enlightening to black readers. She would still be guilty of writing outside the logic of the Black Arts, in large measure because she used and thus valorized the thought of a European thinker, and a racist one at that. Worse, the author would be guilty of writing only for those blacks familiar with the philosophy of Hegel and Sartre. Clearly this is not what most Black Arts advocates meant when they imagined their proximity to a black public. Rather, they imagined themselves as writing for ordinary black people who had never heard of Hegel. Black arts advocates always construed the idea of being organic to black America as having been influenced by black thinkers to write about blacks, for blacks, and from the black community. Being organic to black Americans always implied being organic to nonbourgeois black Americans, the most authentic blacks, whereas bourgeois Negroes were depicted as the quintessential estranged blacks.

Claims that one wrote for black mass audiences were premised on authorial "inventions" of black reading communities. After all, how did an artist know when her writings were too demanding or too undemanding for a mass black readership? Thus the intended "typical" black audience was often nothing more than a fiction in the black writer's mind, an authorial projection of sorts. In the case of the Black Arts, writers frequently invented the community and then "invented" themselves as being organic to that invented community. What many did not understand is that only folk artists were grounded in the everyday life of a people. The Black Arts writers were not folk artists. Even Gramsci's traditional intellectual who chose to align herself with the struggles of the proletariat became organic to their struggles only voluntarily, a decision that could later be reversed.

In Jones/Baraka's case, the title Imamu signified distance from the real black community and intimacy with the fictitious black community that he constructed. At precisely the moment that the Imamu imagined himself most deeply connected to black urban America, he identified himself in a manner that had no grounding in anything authentically indigenous to black America. His attempt to will himself blacker was responsible for his embrace of the ersatz Africanism of Kawaida, which was organic only to Karenga's fertile imagination. Anyone who saw the Imamu, dressed in his neo-African garb, walking through an ordinary black crowd at a public event would have recognized immediately that he was seen by blacks as certainly different, if not weird. But this response to his image is not often discussed because most critics of Baraka assume that his invented relationship to an invented black community is an accurate portrayal of an empirical phenomenon. It isn't. As Sollors noted,

Despite Baraka's insistence that he was concerned with black culture as Black people live it, his cultural nationalism never allowed much room for Black culture and Black consciousness as it actually existed; instead, he tended to view Black culture as something Black people could *learn*, or even something that might have to be forced on people by intellectuals who had renounced their own backgrounds.[85]

Here is a question for the bourgeois intellectual (e.g., the former LeRoi Jones) who seeks to align himself (as Baraka did) with people of a different and lower socioeconomic status: Can organicity be a willed gesture? I would say yes, but with an immediate caveat. For the bourgeois intellectual seeking to join forces with the less privileged, organic connectedness does not deny estrangement. The bourgeois writer who imagines himself situated in struggle alongside poor blacks must at some point acknowledge his voluntary decision to join the endeavor, a volunteerism that was completely foreign to impoverished blacks. Baraka's willed connectedness was particularly striking, since it came after he had lived in the predominantly white setting of Beat bohemia. The intensity of his black nationalism can perhaps be understood as a way to shorten the immense distance he was trying to cover. First, his virulent antiwhite rhetoric was intended to soothe his private self-doubts concerning the authenticity of his new claims of organic connectedness to disaffiliated blacks. Second, his rhetoric was geared toward convincing his new confreres of his genuineness. Only by appearing to be blacker than the blackest black American could he legitimate the precariousness of his new black allegiances. But even then, his doubts remained, as did doubts about him. Baraka's hyperblackness also signaled his distance from the black community. Try as they might, Baraka and numerous other Black Arts writers could not escape their cultural and intellectual distance from the very people they were supposedly addressing and representing. Sollors wrote:

> The demand for a "collective" art was often a camouflage for individualistic, modernizing artists who feigned collectivity. Despite all the invocations of "the people," despite the claims that alienation has been transcended in Black cultural nationalism, there remains a struggle between the elitist writer and the people who are to learn the right Black consciousness from him. Writing "for the people" may mask a deep seated opposition to the people.[86]

6

Toward a Black Arts Infrastructure

ONE DEFINING ELEMENT of the Black Arts movement was its desire to create the institutional infrastructure necessary to inspire and sustain black creative autonomy. Only through black control of an intellectual infrastructure could the Black Aesthetic become a hegemonic tendency in black intellectual and artistic circles. Throughout the twentieth century, Afro-American intellectuals and artists recognized the need for institutions that could support, nurture, and disseminate their work (e.g., theaters, journals, and book publishers). But the inability of the black intelligentsia and black Americans in general to create elaborate and diversified intellectual and artistic infrastructures has been both a result and a cause of the devalued status of traditional black artists and intellectuals in the eyes of most Afro-Americans. In the absence of such infrastructures, an economic, creative, and political burden of phenomenal proportions was placed on each succeeding generation of ambitious black artists.

In my introduction, I noted that one of the fundamental problems for the black intelligentsia during the twentieth century was its tenuous social location. I referred to this unique status as *social marginality*. Social marginality arises from the limited access of black intellectuals and artists to the material resources that would allow them to nurture their craft, disseminate their ideas, and create in their artistic and intellectual arenas. The racist exclusion of black artists and intellectuals from various levels of national institutional support that historically have supported white American artists and intellectuals (e.g., foundation grants, fellowships, intellectual journals, and faculty positions at research-friendly universities) created black intellectual and artistic communities that were forced to depend on resources in the black community. Such support was usually not forthcoming. Black Americans simply did not have the financial resources necessary to compensate for black artists' lack of access to white-controlled public and private funding. With easy access to communities that did not have the necessary resources to sustain traditional intellectual and fine arts activities but no access to communities that did have these material resources, traditional black intellectuals and artists were often caught in a betwixt-between situation. Despite romanticizations of the poverty-stricken artist willing to neglect meals in order to purchase paint brushes and canvases, far too many twentieth-century black artists involuntarily experienced the torture of poverty and the resulting debilitation of their creativity.

The absence of a rich intellectual and artistic infrastructure in twentieth-century black America was understandable. In pre-1960s America, the disposable wealth of black America was relatively paltry. Perhaps the relatively larger contingent of post-1960s black Americans with money did not view the patronage of black intellectuals and artists as vital. However, to keep matters in perspective, we should remember that during the twentieth century, the stable black working class and the black middle and upper-middle classes were not able to support a diverse political infrastructure, even though such a network of organizations would have benefited their own economic and social mobility. The problems confronting black America throughout the twentieth century relegated the financial neediness of black intellectuals and artists to a secondary status and perhaps justifiably so.[1] But although the general condition of black intellectual and artistic infrastructures has been weak, they have not been nonexistent. During the last quarter of the twentieth century, black intellectuals were given access to mainstream American resources. As I write today, black winners of Guggenheim Fellowships or grants from the National Endowment for the Arts are no longer novelties. Black poets have significantly greater access to various writers' colonies and large publishing houses than they had only thirty years ago. Numerous blacks now teach at elite private colleges and major public and private research universities.

The contemporary black intelligentsia has been the beneficiary of new opportunities spurned by the civil rights and Black Power movements. Before the 1960s, blacks were only occasionally part of broader American intellectual infrastructures. One such occasion was the Harlem Renaissance. Regardless of one's assessment of the quality of the art produced by blacks during the Harlem Renaissance, this movement should be seen as a major cultural and political breakthrough. Black writers associated with that movement entered a broader transracial intellectual infrastructure. White patrons,[2] individual blacks, and black organizations were crucial to the development of this infrastructure. In his study of the Harlem Renaissance, historian David Levering Lewis notes that the black racketeer Casper Holstein, as well as Alain Locke, Charles S. Johnson, and A'Lelia Walker (daughter of Madame C. J. Walker) functioned as creative midwives for black writers.[3]

Throughout the twentieth century, individual as well as small clusters of black intellectuals tried to deal creatively with the weak black intellectual infrastructure. Booker T. Washington immediately comes to mind. Tuskegee

Institute (now Tuskegee University) is a testament to his recognition of the importance of black institutions. But in establishing Tuskegee, Washington founded an institution that devalued art, artists, and humanist intellectuals. Committed to industrial education, Washington believed instead that the key to black advancement was in creating skilled workers. However, Tuskegee outlived Washington and his original pedagogical intentions. By the 1930s, Tuskegee helped train two notable men of letters, Ralph Ellison and Albert Murray. It also served as the institutional home for black intellectuals on its faculty, like musicians Hazel Harrison and William Dawson, sociologist Monroe Nathan Work, and even a scientist, George Washington Carver. Nevertheless, during its formative years, Tuskegee was not an autonomous black institution. Washington essentially gave control of Tuskegee and its curriculum to the local southern white elites and northern white industrialists in return for their endorsement and financial contributions.[4] Although it might appear that Washington did not understand the significance of autonomous black institutions, in the turn-of the century South such institutions were virtual impossibilities except in matters of religious worship.

The spiritual prototype for the idea of "autonomous" black intellectual institutions during the Black Arts era may have been Carter G. Woodson's Association for the Study of Negro Life and History.[5] Biographer Jacqueline Goggin noted that Woodson founded the academic association in 1915, perhaps in anger at the widespread popularity of D. W. Griffith's scandalous film *The Birth of a Nation*. Woodson believed that an accurate and honest historical depiction of the lives and contributions of American Negroes could aid in the battle against the racist hysteria gripping the nation. He surmised that the assault that he wanted to launch on the prevailing orthodoxy of racist, antiblack historiography could be sustained only in institutions free of white racist control. First, he began publishing a scholarly organ, the *Journal of Negro History*, and then he established the Associated Publishers, which published many books by black scholars that would have otherwise never been printed. In 1926, Woodson created Negro History Week, the annual celebration that broadened mass black interest in Negro history. Finally, in 1937 Woodson began publishing the *Negro History Bulletin* as a means of teaching Negro history to black schoolchildren and the broader black community.[6] The pathbreaking successes of the Association for the Study of Negro Life and History relied on funding from sympathetic white individuals and white-controlled foundations. Like Washington's Tuskegee, Woodson's efforts at establishing an infrastructure cannot be considered ethnically autonomous. While Woodson made racial uplift an explicit component of the association's agenda, he was not a black separatist. Had he been, there probably would not have been an association. But when coupled with his vision of influencing scholarly and popular historical discourses, Woodson's progressive racial intentions anticipated the desires of many black intellectuals during the Black Arts movement.

The question of black control over intellectual and political institutions cannot be rigidly confined to the taxonomy that I have presented here. Sometimes individual blacks were able—through sheer nerve and cunning—to create semiautonomous spaces for black creativity and intellectual exchange. Such blacks were able to manipulate whites or at least to steer a controlling white gaze away from what was really happening. For example, for a short moment, Du Bois was able to direct the editorial practices of *The Crisis*. But his control over the journal ended when his editorial ideas conflicted with the opinions of the dominant white hierarchy of the NAACP and its black functionaries who kept a vigilant eye on those practices that might offend white supporters.[7] Despite having federal funding, as a national educational institution, Howard University was a receptive home to the legal theorist and activist Charles Hamilton Houston. At the Howard University Law School, Houston trained black lawyers in the developing field of civil rights law, despite the close congressional oversight (including that of powerful racist southern congressmen) of the university.[8]

The Black Arts movement's attempt to develop an infrastructure had two goals: (1) to try to reach ordinary black people "where they were" and (2) to be ethnically autonomous. No longer would it be sufficient to write, direct, act in, or produce a black play. The new goal was to produce plays about black life in accessible locations in the black community and at prices that black mass audiences could afford. In some instances, the plays would be performed on street corners without charge. On at least one occasion, Gwendolyn Brooks and other black Chicago writers held an impromptu poetry reading in a neighborhood tavern as patrons sitting on bar stools listened attentively and then applauded the poets.

JOURNALS OF THE BLACK ARTS MOVEMENT

Perhaps the clearest indication of the growth of a black artistic and intellectual infrastructure during the Black Arts movement was the appearance of numerous new literary and general black intellectual journals, including the *Journal of Black Poetry, Black Expressions, Black Dialogue, Soulbook, Black Creation, Nommo,* and *Grassroots*. During the height of the Black Theater movement, Ed Bullins edited the journal *Black Theatre*. Published by the New

Lafayette Theater in Harlem, the journal provided a forum for discussions of black theater performances around the nation, interviews with significant figures in the black theater, poetry, short plays, and reviews.

Another important journal of the Black Arts era was *Liberator*. Published between 1961 and 1971 and edited by Dan Watts, *Liberator* was an explicitly political journal, but it also published cultural criticism. At the peak of its influence, *Liberator* published pieces by LeRoi Jones and Larry Neal that were considered essential reading for the Black Arts. During the 1960s, Neal published in *Liberator* a series of provocative essays on various individual black writers (Wright, Baldwin, Ellison, Jones) in attempting to clarify "the role of the black writer."[9]

The dominant black intellectual journal of the Black Arts era (particularly for black literary studies) was *Negro Digest / Black World*. After suspending the monthly publication of *Negro Digest* in 1951, Johnson Publications reissued the monthly journal in 1961. Edited by Hoyt Fuller, *Negro Digest* changed its name to *Black World* in 1970. By the late 1960s, it had become a beacon of black nationalist thought on a wide variety of topics. The journal published numerous articles on Pan-Africanism as a political and intellectual movement and articles on the political situation of black Americans and Africans. Under the editorial guidance of Fuller, *Black World* excelled as a mouthpiece of the Black Arts movement, with extensive coverage of black literature and black theater throughout the United States. According to its publisher, at its peak, *Black World* had a monthly circulation of about 100,000.[10]

Black World exemplifies the contradictions of the black nationalist orientation of the Black Arts movement. The journal was published by black capitalist John H. Johnson, who in 1996 was listed among the richest four hundred people in the United States. Johnson made his fortune publishing frivolous magazines like *Ebony* and *Jet*, which featured obscene displays of black conspicuous consumption. Historically, *Ebony* has aggressively celebrated the anti-intellectual core of black bourgeois ostentatiousness. *Jet*, a modern-day ethnic gossip column, carries ethnic news that cannot be found in other magazines. Both magazines function as de facto press releases for successful black entertainers and athletes. In addition, advertisements for skin-lighteners frequented *Ebony*'s pages even as late as the 1960s. Nothing was more offensive to the Black Arts / Black Power era than the idea of blacks who were ashamed of their Negroid bodies. Nonetheless, despite their vacuousness, criticism of *Ebony* and *Jet* was off limits for articles in *Black World*.

The consequence of being beholden to a company not committed to

Black Power or the Black Arts movement meant that *Black World* would be published only so long as it was profitable. As the publisher of *Black World*, John H. Johnson shrewdly captured a black nationalist market while his flagship publications remained devotedly integrationist. It should not have been surprising, therefore, when Johnson pulled the rug out from under *Black World* in February 1976. In his autobiography, Johnson claimed that he stopped publishing *Black World* when its circulation dropped from 100,000 to 15,000, but this explanation seems disingenuous.[11] Even if the circulation of *Black World* had slipped to 15,000 readers, it might have still been a profitable and viable organ. Johnson should have admitted that *Black World* was not losing money when he chose to shut it down but that its profits were not high enough for him.

In his essay "Blacks, Jews and Henry Louis Gates Jr.," Haki Madhubuti offered a different explanation for John H. Johnson's decision to fire Hoyt Fuller and stop publishing *Black World*. Madhubuti was one of the leaders of a boycott of Johnson's publications that began after his decision to terminate *Black World*.

> We were not an hour into our demonstration when John Johnson, himself, came outside and asked that we come upstairs to talk about his decision. . . . He stated that Fuller was fired because he refused to cease publishing the Palestinian side of the Middle-East struggle and the African support of that struggle. He ceased publication of *Black World* mainly because Jewish businessmen threatened to pull their advertising out of *Ebony* and *Jet* magazines and would have convinced their white friends to do the same if the Middle East coverage did not stop.[12]

It does not seem plausible that Johnson fired Fuller because of *Black World's* advocacy of a pro-Palestinian position, as the magazine published only a very few articles and opinion pieces on the Middle East conflict.[13] Clearly the reasons that Johnson gave Madhubuti for terminating Fuller do not make sense, and moreover, they do not explain why Johnson chose to cease publishing *Black World*. Johnson could have simply fired Fuller as editor and replaced him with someone else. The significance of the controversy over the termination of *Black World* lies in the absence of a class analysis of the Black Arts movement. Because John H. Johnson was black, he was viewed by some black nationalists as having a vested interest in publishing this black nationalist intellectual organ. But they overlooked Johnson's primary desire—to make money.[14]

BLACK ARTS BOOK PUBLISHERS

Though central to the Black Arts movement, black book publishers did not proliferate to a degree comparable to black journals and black repertory theaters, because of the high capital costs of establishing a viable publishing house and the relatively little capital that black publishing houses could generate. Moreover, black book publishers were competing with the large white-owned publishing firms. Unlike the many white literary journals that chose to ignore or debase the Black Arts movement, thus leaving black journals without competition in this arena, the white-owned publishing houses decided that publishing books written by blacks was a lucrative business. Large white-owned publishers not only could offer black authors an established, national distribution network, but they could pay advances and advertise their books in popular organs. Nevertheless, black presses were able to publish inflammatory texts that may not have survived a large book publisher's acquisition process.[15] Small but notable black presses included Emerson Hall, Third Press, Drum and Spear Press, Jihad Press of Newark, Journal of Black Poetry Press, Broadside Press, and Third World Press.

The black presses found that many of the most prominent Black Arts movement writers were not willing to sacrifice their lucrative contracts with white publishing firms in order to help black publishing houses "get off the ground." Recognizing a contradiction in the willingness of Black Arts writers to have their books published by white firms, Ahmed Alhamisi, an editor of the *Journal of Black Poetry*, wrote in 1971, "It is time to refuse to submit our creations to such publishers as Dial, Harper and Row, William Morrow & Company, Bobbs-Merrill Company, Grove Press, Inc., Merit Publishers, Marzani and Munsell, or International Publishers, to name a few."[16] Alhamisi may have had Jones in mind when he wrote this. Although Jones was one of the revered leaders of the Black Arts movement, he used white publishing houses for his "blackest" writings. During the height of the Black Arts movement, Jones had two books published by the black Third World Press, *It's Nation Time* (1970) and *Jello* (1970), and had *Spirit Reach* (1972) published by his own house, Jihad Press. Almost all his other Black Arts movement books were published by white publishers.

Jones was not oblivious to the contradictions between his written words and his choice of publishers. He and Larry Neal, coeditors of *Black Fire*, attacked their publisher, William Morrow, for not allowing them to include the works of more black writers in the paperback edition. They wrote, "The frustration of working thru these bullshit white people shd be obvious."[17] These comments fail, however, to mask the authors' complicity with white publishing houses. If it was so difficult to work with a white publishing firm, why not go to a black press? Ironically, one major writer of the Black Arts era who did take a stand on behalf of black publishers was the poet Gwendolyn Brooks. In 1969, she decided to send her next books to black-owned presses, and until her death in 2000, she remained faithful to this decision.

THE BLACK THEATER MOVEMENT

Though short lived, the greatest expansion of the Black Arts infrastructure was in black theater. There were so many black theater companies and repertory theaters established during the Black Arts movement that some scholars often refer to it as the "Black Theater movement." Behind this expansion was the belief that as an art form, drama could be easily politicized and was aesthetically accessible to the black masses. Moreover, most Black Arts activists understood that a theater politicized on behalf of black liberation would have to be controlled and funded by blacks.

Each April, *Black World* published a special black theater issue that discussed the status of the black theater throughout the nation. In April 1976, the special issue mentioned the activities of more than twenty-five theater groups in New York City alone, including the New Federal Theater, Afro-American Studio, National Black Theater, Amas Repertoire Theater, Harlem Jazz Opera, East River Players, Uhuru Freedom Players, and Barbados Theater Workshop. While the black theater scene in New York City may have been exceptional, similar but smaller groups were cropping up in cities throughout the United States. Although it was not explicitly affiliated with the Black Arts movement, *The Free Southern Theater* was part of the efforts of the time to situate politicized black theater in local black communities.[18] Insofar as its intended audience were ordinary southern blacks, *The Free Southern Theater* was part of the sensibility that gave rise to the Black Arts Repertory Theater and other community drama ventures.

The development of black theaters was not easy, as funding was always scarce.[19] Moreover, most of these theaters were never able to attract large enough audiences to allow them to be self-sustaining.[20] Nevertheless, for a very short moment, blacks committed to the development of the black theater arts created a national infrastructure. This was an astounding achievement.

AFRO-AMERICAN STUDIES PROGRAMS

Undoubtedly one of the most significant developments in the Afro-American intellectual infrastructure during the late 1960s and early 1970s was the creation of Afro-American studies programs and departments.[21] Afro-American studies as a discipline of study was a direct spin-off of Black Power era, white institutions' collective response to the widespread black militancy. The establishment of Afro-American studies as an academic discipline benefited as well from white college students' skepticism regarding the Vietnam War. The emergence of Afro-American studies also was part of a growing groundswell of support among young Americans to democratize their social institutions. Between 1968 and 1971, approximately 150 Afro-American studies programs or departments were established in American colleges and universities.[22]

Historically, black subject matter, black faculty, and black students had usually been excluded from white academia,[23] so predominantly white universities often used Afro-American studies as a way of attracting black faculty. Conversely, the admission of black students to majority-white colleges rose sharply during the late 1960s, and their presence was often used as a rationale for establishing Afro-American studies programs. In other instances, militant black students pressured schools to create these programs, some of which were haphazardly constructed, often in accordance with the university's racist intentions.[24] Others were well planned. Afro-American studies was saddled, however, with the racist stigmatization of being linked to both a devalued subject matter and devalued students and faculty. It was further depreciated because its formative impulses were linked to a mass-based political movement, whereas authentic arenas for academic study supposedly emerged from measured intellectual debate in the academy.

Community outreach was an important component of many of the early Afro-American studies programs. Such programs crossed the university's established boundaries through community-based tutorial programs, extension classes, and locally housed seminars and lectures. They also defied traditional academic criteria in the hiring of faculty. This defiance of entrenched academic practices only intensified the stigmatization of Afro-American studies. Moreover, Afro-American studies did not have enough cultural capital to challenge traditional academic practices. Worse, these programs often were vulnerable to politicized charlatans who were neither interested in scholarship nor committed to informed intellectual exchange. By the mid-1970s, the rising number of black students who had completed doctoral programs, coupled with the rising attraction of "black subject matter" to young white scholars, led to an intensified professionalization of Afro-American studies. As the program gradually emulated established academic departments and disciplines, it lost its oppositional character. Needless to say, in pursuit of academic respectability, careerist Afro-American studies academicians discarded community outreach in favor of departmentalization.

BLACK WRITERS' COLLECTIVES

One strategy that black American intellectuals frequently used to create communities for serious dialogue was the establishment of writers' collectives. These collectives were popular because their success or failure depended less on financial resources than on the intensity of the participants' commitment. Like all intellectuals, black artists needed critical affirmation and sympathetic, informed, and honest criticism.

One of the most important black writers' collectives of the Black Arts was the Umbra Poets' Workshop, even though it technically did not qualify as a Black Arts movement writers' collective because it was formed before the movement. From the summer of 1962 through late 1963, the workshop met weekly in lower Manhattan. One former participant remembered that "the criticism was never harsh—but grown men broke down in tears."[25] Although it stopped meeting regularly after this time, Umbra survived until early 1965. The influence of the Umbra collective on the development of Black Arts is attributed mainly to the prominent role that many of its members later played in the movement. The male-dominated collective also prefigured the male-centered bias of the Black Arts movement. Umbra writers who later attained notoriety during the Black Arts period include Tom Dent, Calvin Hernton, David Henderson, Ishmael Reed,[26] Askia Muhammad Toure (Ronald Snellings), Joe Johnson, Lorenzo Thomas, and Norman Pritchard.[27] The group often participated in public readings, and they sporadically published a literary journal, also entitled *Umbra*.[28]

Perhaps the most prominent black writers' collective to emerge during the Black Arts movement was the Chicago-based Organization of Black American Culture (OBAC).[29] Founded in 1967, the organization was popularly known by its acronym OBAC (o-bah-see).[30] Initially, its leadership consisted of Hoyt Fuller, Gerald McWorter (Abdul Alkalimat), and Conrad Kent Rivers. Unlike Umbra, which marginalized women, black women writers such as Carolyn Rodgers, Ronda Davis, and Jewel Lattimore were prominent members of OBAC from its inception. OBAC was composed of three workshops: the writers' workshop, the visual artists' workshop, and the community workshop. The writers' workshop was founded on the principles of the Black Arts movement, including its quest for a Black Aesthetic. David Smith argues that the OBAC writers, like most of the Black Arts movement, were caught in a vice of racial essentialism that did not allow them to explore the full complexity of Afro-American life. Instead of defining "a single correct ideology of blackness," Smith believes that they should have pursued a Black Aesthetic that "would have liberated them to embrace the multifarious particularity of African-American experience." He notes that the parochialism of OBAC's Black Aesthetic could not have accounted for their own diverse identities:

> Many of the writers used the ideology of essential blackness to mask their own complex backgrounds. OBAC's chair, McWorter, for example, was a University of Chicago doctoral candidate, and Hoyt Fuller was as erudite and cosmopolitan as any American journalist of his generation. To note that they failed to articulate a theory of blackness that could account for how much they themselves owed to white and European culture is not to impugn either their honesty or their theoretical sophistication.[31]

Smith's point here is an excellent one and could be extended to much of the theorizing during the Black Arts movement, particularly as it concerned a Black Aesthetic. But Smith does not want to admit that this parochial concept of blackness impugns the writers' theoretical sophistication. Their notion of the Black Aesthetic, as embodied in the Black Arts movement, was riddled with theoretical vacuities. But this theoretical failure did not diminish OBAC's success as a space where black writers could regularly discuss one another's works as well as those of nonmembers. The OBAC writers' workshop even analyzed the works of white writers when it was thought that something could be learned from them.[32]

The Black Arts Movement established numerous black cultural centers throughout the nation. Baraka's Black Arts Repertory Theater/School and, later, Spirit House were duplicated in various forms throughout urban black America, such as Don Lee's Institute of the Black World in Chicago, Elma Lewis's center in Boston, The EAST in Brooklyn, and Topper Carew's New Thing Art and Architecture Center in Washington, D.C.[33]

The Black Arts movement in partnership with the Black Power movement gave rise to numerous "black-oriented" shows on local television stations, offering so-called black perspectives on news events. Often this meant that these shows discussed "positive" tendencies in various local black communities that were ignored or underreported by the conventional media. Although such shows could not adequately counter the images projected by the mainstream, they did provide information about events, political struggles, and personalities in local black communities.[34] Few of these shows continue to be produced today. In New York City, Gil Noble's *Like It Is* is a reminder of these once heavily politicized talk/news shows, but in other markets, these shows either were canceled long ago or have lost their original political "cutting edge." Their decline stems from the altered politicizations of the black communities as well as the willingness of the mainstream media to cover more "black subjects." Moreover, with the emergence of figures like Oprah Winfrey and Montel Williams, black talk show hosts now cater to the mainstream viewing audience (i.e., white Americans).

OVERVIEW

The Black Arts movement is considered by some literary critics to be one of the most important twentieth-century Afro-American intellectual and artistic movements. But its artistic products seem to have been generally uneven. According to novelist Charles Johnson, "the Black Aesthetic produced preciously little 'good art' and [is] even less capable of lasting."[35] This may be a bit too harsh. But few individual works from that time are read today, except perhaps as period pieces. To most students of black writing, the Black Arts movement has an artistic status far beneath that of the Harlem Renaissance.[36]

Concerning this period in Afro-American arts and letters, Johnson wrote:

> If one had even the slightest concern, or sensitivity, or distaste for injustice, one could not help being caught up in this confusion, the polarization of black and white, young and old, middle class and poor. The pressure to write "politically" was (and still is) tremendous, though little of this fiction survives today, its character—I know from experience—being less that of enduring art than that of journalism hastily written at the front, hammered out in reaction to fast-breaking (bad) news. The age produced . . . a new racial melodrama, or recycled the old ones of the nineteenth century with a new cast: racist spider-bellied cops, noble revolutionaries. You know this crew.[37]

The benefits of the Black Arts movement to black intellectual life cannot be ignored, as it raised questions about the relationship of the black intellectual to the broader black public, as well as the relationship between the black intellectual and the broader society. This is an important question for all intellectuals (note Sartre's *For Whom Does One Write*), but especially for Afro-American intellectuals. Artists from subjugated groups must confront the enticements of utilitarian relevance, for they often lead to vulgar aesthetics. But would our assessment of the Black Arts movement today be different if it had been part of a movement that "emancipated" black America? If we applied Karenga's and Baraka's artistic criteria to the Black Arts movement, we would have to admit that Black Arts writers failed even as utilitarian propagandists.

In the long run, the Black Arts movement increased black artists' artistic freedom. They became both less self-conscious about writing for blacks and more accepting and affirming of black cultural traditions. However, in the short run, when following the dictates of Baraka, Gayle, and others, the Black Aesthetic and the Black Arts movement ultimately constrained black intellectual freedom. Although most Black Arts artists never considered Western artistic traditions to be appropriate for black American artists, in rejecting the West, they cut themselves off from some of their richest cultural resources.

The Black Aesthetic movement lost momentum simultaneously with the decline of Black Power and the incorporation of Afro-American studies into the mainstream academy. This decline signaled the return to dominance of a neo-Ellison aesthetic in black artistic/intellectual circles in which black artistic enterprises are situated in American and Western traditions. American cultural and artistic traditions are viewed as mulatto, the result of racial and ethnic cultural cross-breeding. Unlike Ellison, however, the post–Black Aesthetic black artists, whether integrationists, nationalists, or Marxists, no longer hesitated to proclaim their African connections. In its affirmation of blackness and Africanness, the Black Arts movement helped redefine the Afro-American psyche and, in so doing, empowered Afro-American artists.

One of the long-term benefits of this Afro-American quest for self-determination was the invalidation of the criteria for assessing black life, beauty, and art that were based on Eurocentric models. Extending the critique implicit in "black is beautiful" was the effort to destigmatize African peoples, cultures, and aesthetics, including black bodies. The idea of Africa, however romanticized, emerged as a new source of pride for many black Americans. Yet history had played a cruel trick on them. The historical stigmatization of those aspects of black American identity and life linked to Africa and the simultaneous valorization of "whiteness" that infiltrated historical Afro-American cultural sensibilities stimulated a black response that often simply inverted these evaluative judgments: good Africa, bad Europe. The psychological need of many Afro-Americans for "racial" affirmation was sufficiently great that they often elevated the status of their African lineage and at the same time denigrated their Euro-American heritage. This attempted reversal of the hegemonic white racial hierarchy was understandable given that the Euro-American constituent of Afro-American genealogy was embedded in historical and contemporary practices of racial domination. But in reconfiguring their ethnicity, black cultural nationalists of the late 1960s became imprisoned in Manichaean typological reifications of black versus white. The revalorization of Africa often induced Afro-American nationalists to distort and discard black Americans' actual cultural and physical genealogy. Not surprisingly, Baraka and other black cultural nationalists began to refer to themselves and other black Americans as Africans. As elsewhere, complex identities were thought to impede political mobilization.

Because of the ubiquitous racist devaluations of black creative artifacts, black intellectuals and artists have long protested white American aesthetic determinations and their hegemony over black artistic productivity. Indeed, some black intellectuals viewed the emergence of a political movement for black self-determination as a means of developing a distinct Black Aesthetic. Attracted by the rhetoric of Black Power, many black artists anticipated the creation of black institutions capable of exemplifying these novel, Black Aesthetic assumptions.

The shortcomings of the Black Aesthetic lay in its distortions of black cultural and physiological complexity. Its advocates either did not recognize or chose to ignore the fact that black Americans were bastard children of the West as well as Africa. In addition, black Americans were distinguished contributors to a multiracial American cultural sensibility and aesthetic. Blacks had historically informed what white Americans perceived as white cultural creations. The United States was a dynamic mulatto culture, despite the intentions of its leaders and the wishes of its white cultural commissars. Furthermore, this New World mulatto culture was unlike any European culture. American speech, religious practices, political ideals, humor, music, dance, and fashion all had been "Negroized." Likewise "whiteness" was reflected in the blues and, of course, jazz. Unfortunately, the Black Aesthetic advocates refused to recognize this cross-racial fertilization in favor of mythical claims for a racially circumscribed, distinct black American cultural sensibility. Simply put, they mistakenly thought that the culture of black Americans was an unadulterated black culture.

Early in his intellectual life, Jones recognized the cultural complexity of Afro-Americans. But by the late 1960s, he had chosen to discard and denounce such recognition for political reasons. Informing white Americans that they were, in part, culturally black had not led to better living conditions for blacks. Baraka was not alone among black intellectuals in being bewildered by black Americans' cultural-insider, political-outsider status. For instance, Ralph Ellison was so seduced by the cultural-insiderness of black Americans that he avoided a direct confrontation with their political, economic, and social-outsider status.[38] Unlike Ellison, Baraka was not lured by the mulatto nature of American culture into the trap of believing that there was something deeply democratic about the American experience. Perhaps Baraka understood better than Ellison did that a cultural-insider status does not necessary protect one's political flank. After all, Jews in pre-Hitler Germany were crucial contributors to German culture and society. Historian Peter Gay referred to them as "the outsider as insider," which could also have been a metaphor for black existence in the United States.[39]

Baraka may have perceived the betwixt-between status of black Americans in much the same way. His mistake was assuming that a group's socioeconomic- and political-outsider status necessitated and/or resulted from its cultural-outsider status and attempting to use this mistaken black, cultural-outsider status to generate political and economic inclusion.[40] To do so, he had to attach himself to an ersatz Africanism called Kawaida. Instead of struggling for the economic and political inclusion of black Americans—an outcome desired by the overwhelming majority of blacks throughout American history—Baraka tried to use their economic hell to persuade them to accept his cultural heaven. When black Americans saw that his cultural chicanery was not going to put food on their table, Baraka became a Marxist.

7

Black Arts Poet and Essayist

AS AN ADVOCATE of the Black Aesthetic / Black Arts movement, Jones/ Baraka was quite prolific. It was during this period that he produced much of his work. The plays that he wrote during this period included *Jello* (1965), *A Black Mass* (1965), *Experimental Death Unit #1* (1965), *Madheart* (1966), *Slave Ship* (1967), *Great Goodness of Life* (1966), *Home on the Range* (1966), *The Death of Malcolm X* (1966), *Arm Yourself or Harm Yourself* (1967), and *Police* (1967). A novel, *The System of Dante's Hell*, was published in 1965. *Tales*, a collection of short stories, appeared two years later. Baraka also published several collections of poetry: *Black Magic Poetry* (1969), *It's Nation Time* (1970), *Spirit Reach* (1972), and *African Revolution* (1973). He coauthored with the photographer Fundi a photo-essay, *In Our Terribleness* (1970). And with Larry Neal, he edited an anthology of Afro-American writing, *Black Fire* (1968), which became one of the seminal texts of the Black Arts movement, rivaled, I suspect, only by Addison Gayle's collection *The Black Aesthetic* (1971), Stephen Henderson's *Understanding the New Black Poetry* (1972), and Baraka's earlier essay collection, *Home* (1966). *African Congress* (1972), which Baraka edited, contains the speeches and proceedings of a Pan-Africanist conference held in Atlanta in 1970. Finally, a second collection of social-political essays, *Raise Race Rays Raze*, was published in 1971.

During the height of the Black Arts movement, Baraka also was busy as the titular head of the movement. Besides creating institutions in Harlem and, later, Newark, Baraka traveled throughout the nation giving lectures and readings. He was a particularly popular speaker at colleges. On one occasion during school year 1968/69, Jones was invited by the University of Pennsylvania's Society of African and Afro-American Students to give a lecture to open "Black Week" on the campus. In agreeing to the campus visit, Baraka demanded that the audience for his talk be racially segregated. Black students and other blacks would be seated in the balcony. White students could sit elsewhere. Jones also stipulated that he not be required to interact with whites face-to-face while on campus. Whites also were to be excluded from the stage when he spoke. While Jones's theatrics were moronic, black militancy on campuses was such that a major Ivy League university complied with his demands.[1]

The various stipulations that accompanied the Imamu's appearance were indicative of the petty irrationalisms that marked the black separatism of the late 1960s. The irrationality of mandating a black campus escort seems even humorous today. Are we to assume that the Imamu did not book seats on planes flown by white pilots or serviced by white flight attendants? Did he drink water cleaned by plants in which whites worked? Where did this behavioral attempt to divorce himself from all interactions with whites end? These black separatist antics were impotent campaigns to exert symbolic control over his life. By forcing various white institutions to agree to his conditions, Baraka may have momentarily felt that he was forcing whites to obey his commands. But by acting in a manner that supposedly indicated his disdain for whites, Baraka was actually exhibiting the limitations and impracticality of black separatism.

Baraka was an inspired performance artist. The excitement generated by his lectures and poetry readings was legendary. Insofar as he and other Black Arts artists privileged orality, the performance of poetry was one component of a broader strategy to reach a black mass audience. In her autobiography, poet Gwendolyn Brooks recalls the uproar generated by Baraka's arrival at the Second Black Writers Conference at Fisk University in 1967. On one evening, Brooks was in the audience when Baraka performed "Black People," the poem that had been wrongfully used against him at his trial following the Newark riots. The poem's highly cathartic, violent imagery not only angered the judiciary but on occasion excited black listeners beyond the point of reason. Part of the poem reads:

> you cant steal nothin from a white man, he's already stole it he owes you anything you want, even his life. All the stores will open if you will say the magic words. The magic words are: Up against the wall motherfucker this is a stick up! . . . We must make our own World, man, our own world, and we can not do this unless the white man is dead. Let's get together and kill him my man.[2]

On that evening at Fisk, even the usually reserved Brooks succumbed to Baraka's charismatic presence:

> I was sitting beside a youngish white fellow. He had been very quiet. But when Baraka said at one point, "Up against the wall!" this man jumped to

his feet and said "Yeah, yeah, kill 'em!" And here he was, ordering his own execution. That's how electrified the atmosphere was. "Kill 'em all!" he said.[3]

In her own excitement, Brooks forgot that the white fellow knew that there would be no execution. I suspect that the young man's ability to enter the poem vicariously on the "other side" was a testament to his imagination and Baraka's talent. But someone should inform Brooks that the young man could not order his own execution if there was no executioner. Baraka was merely writing about being an executioner and writing precisely to and for those blacks who would never act. They knew this as well as Baraka did, thus Baraka's cathartic appeal and vicarious power. The joke was on Brooks, for the white fellow knew that this was harmless catharsis. What else was there to do but join the fun?

The performance of poetry and the centrality of orality were thought to have had roots in indigenous black American and African cultures. The model for such performances was supposedly the unassimilated, "gutbucket" black preacher who excelled in exhorting his congregation to fever pitch by using a "call and response" device.[4] The ideal black audience was one whose spontaneous comments showed that the speaker had connected with them. The call and response device may have been distinctly black, but Baraka had been publicly performing his poetry since his days in Beat bohemia.[5] Ginsberg, Kerouac, and Bob Kaufman were known for their theatrical poetry readings. According to Lorenzo Thomas, Ginsberg's first public reading of "Howl," at a San Francisco club in 1955, led Beat poet Kenneth Rexroth to respond, "What happened in San Francisco first and spread from there across the world was public poetry, the return of a tribal, preliterate relationship between poet and audience."[6] Rexroth's assessment resembles the commentaries on Black Arts poetry readings. Baraka's performance poetry thus cannot be traced solely to indigenous black American cultural practices. Nevertheless, one had to hear Baraka in order to experience the Imamu.

BLACK ARTS POET

In 1969, Baraka's *Black Magic Poetry: 1961–1967* was published. It was his most extensive collection of poetry and consisted of three separate poetry collections: *Sabotage* (1961–1963), *Target Study* (1963–1965), and *Black Art* (1965–1966). Appearing during the height of the Black Arts movement, *Black Magic Poetry* contains many of Baraka's most widely read and quoted poems.

Many of the poems in *Sabotage* and *Target Study* had been published before *Black Magic Poetry* came out. By choosing to publish and republish these earlier poems in a single volume, Jones wants us to read the poems in *Black Magic Poetry* as a record of his progression from an entrapment in whiteness to an identification with blackness. The first two subdivisions of *Black Magic Poetry* document Jones's outsider status in bohemia and his movement toward a racially assertive poetics. The final subdivision, *Black Art*, is a testimony to Jones's arrival at a black nationalist sensibility. In chronicling his ideological shifts, the poems in *Black Magic Poetry* are equivalent to the nonfiction essays in *Home*.

Why would Baraka choose to publish *Sabotage* and *Target Study* in a 1969 collection, particularly in light of his admission that these earlier poems were examples of his former attachment to a dying and destructive white ethos? Maybe he had a contractual arrangement with Bobbs-Merrill to publish these earlier collections. Or perhaps his contract called for the publication of a collection larger than his Black Arts poetry alone would have been. It seems more likely, however, that Baraka was enamored with his own ideological development and wanted to make it clear to his readers, particularly those new to his work, that he had undergone a dramatic intellectual change. It was as if in admitting and displaying his former allegiance to a "white aesthetic," Baraka could now be a more honest and committed black nationalist. Furthermore, he used the earlier poems in *Sabotage* and *Target Study* to buttress a hidden narrative in *Black Magic Poetry* in which his earlier selves contained the seeds of his present, hyperblack self. In so doing, he could show his nationalist skeptics that he had never quite been "at home" in white bohemia. Baraka skillfully diverted the reader's attention from the earlier poems and directed it instead to the poet. Previous poetic incarnations of LeRoi Jones were useful, but only to the extent that they illuminated his current identity.

Black Art, the last subsection of *Black Magic Poetry*, explicitly conveys the political implications of Baraka's Black Arts era poetry. "SOS," the first poem, is a rallying call for black people to join the nationalist struggle and was widely read at public events:

> *Calling black people*
> *Calling all black people, man woman child*
> *Wherever you are, calling you, urgent, come in*
> *Black People, come in, wherever you are, urgent, calling*
> *you, calling all black people*
> *calling all black people, come in, black people, come*
> *on in.*[7]

The collection also hints at the death and destruction of all white people. "Black Art," the poem from which the subtitle of the collection's last subdivision is derived, is one of Baraka's most widely recognized poems. In "Attention Attention," Baraka intensifies his appeal for black engagement. But now, instead of poems that kill, Baraka pleads for blacks who are willing to kill whites. Worse, he advocates genocide against whites:

Attention Attention
Attention Attention

All greys must be terminated immediately
Project cutoff date moved up Fifty Years

End of species must be assured. (Repeat)
End of species must be assured.[8]

In the poem "The Deadly Eyes are Stars!" Baraka lambastes the narcissism of the "white man" who is "in love with him self, at everybody else's expense." He concludes the poem in demagogic fashion:

. . . Why don't
somebody kill the motherfucker? Why don't somebody jam his head
in his own shit? Why are all you chumps standing around

doing nothing? Letting this creep tapdance on your dreams.[9]

Among these "death-to-white-people" poems are his various anti-Semitic tracts such as "For Tom Postell, Dead Black Poet":

. . . Smile jew. Dance, jew. Tell me you love me, jew. I got
something for you . . .
. . . I got the extermination blues jewboys. I got
the hitler syndrome figured . . .
So come for the rent, jewboys, or come ask me for a book, or
sit in the courts handing down yr judgments, still I got something
for you, gonna give it to my brothers, so they'll know what your whole
story is, then one day, jewboys, we all, even my wig wearing mother
gonna put it on you all at once.[10]

Baraka's "For Tom Postell, Dead Black Poet" is so morally perverted that it is difficult to accept it as serious poetry. It reveals the degree to which Baraka's hatred of whites and specifically Jews had overwhelmed his ability to focus on blacks' freedom struggle. Furthermore, if he was so immersed in anti-Semitism to state publicly that he had the "extermination blues"—his consciousness so entrapped in a desire for revenge—he could not have possibly projected an emancipatory vision for black people.

Baraka continues his anti-Semitic attack on Jews in the poem "The Black Man Is Making New Gods." It contains another obscene trivialization of the Holocaust:

> Atheist jews double crossers stole our secrets crossed
> the white desert white to spill them and
> turn into wops and bulgarians
> The Fag's Death
> they give us on a cross. To Worship. Our dead selves
> in disguise. They give us
> to worship
> a dead jew
> and not ourselves
> chained to the bounties
> of inhuman
> mad chains of
> dead jews
> and their wishes
> and their escape
> with our power
> with our secrets and knowledge
> they turn into loud signs
> advertising empty factories
> the empty jew
> betrays us, as he does
> hanging stupidly
> from a cross, in an oven, the pantomime
> of our torture,
> so clearly, cinemascope the jews do it
> big, hail the whiteness of their
> waking up unhip
> now
>
> . . . the little arty bastards
> talking arithmetic they sucked from the arab's
> head

Suck your pricks. The best is yet to come. On how
we beat you
and killed you
and tied you up.
And marked this specimen
"Dangerous Germ
Culture," And put you back
in a cold box.[11]

A blasphemous and demonic poem, Baraka accuses Jews of having stolen knowledge from Africa ("arithmetic sucked from the arab's head") and transporting it to Europe ("crossed the white desert") where they became white (i.e., "wops and bulgarians") and claimed the stolen knowledge as their own. Jesus is referred to as both the "fag" and "the dead jew" who, other Jews have falsely convinced us, was God. Baraka argues that Jesus was essentially a Jewish scam on Christians. Why he absolves Christianity of the responsibility for creating Jesus is somewhat baffling. Baraka's anti-Semitism reverses traditional anti-Semitic Christian narratives. Instead of condemning Jews because they did not accept Jesus as the Messiah, Baraka condemns them for tricking the world into falsely accepting him. All along, Jews presumably knew that such claims were nonsense. What makes the poem utterly despicable is Baraka's claim that "the empty jew / betrays us, as he does / hanging stupidly / from a cross, *in an oven*, the pantomime / of our torture"(my italics). On what basis could the murder of Jews in Nazi ovens be considered "the pantomime of our torture"? The indecency of bringing up images of Auschwitz is superseded only by his embrace of the Nazi genocidal image of Jews as a people who embody a "dangerous germ culture."

Baraka's racial essentialism that led him to view blacks as morally superior to innately evil whites permeates this collection. Everything whites create or casually touch is spoiled by their evil nature. In "A School of Prayer," Baraka writes

. . . We are all beautiful (except white
people, they are full of, and made of
shit)

Do Not obey their laws
which we are against God
believe brother, do not
ever think any of that

cold shit they say is
true . . .
. . . Their "laws"
are filthy evil, against
almighty God . . .
. . . they are against
beauty.[12]

This detestable characterization of all things white is pathetic. Undoubtedly, Baraka perceived it as a valid criticism of Western culture and whites. But paradoxically, the infantile and overblown condemnation of whites undermines the credibility of the juxtaposition of praise that he lavishes on blacks.

In the autobiographical meditation "leroy," Baraka provides a metaphorical will for the dispersal of his spiritual assets following his death. He describes his consciousness as part black and part white, racial designations for the moral and immoral aspects of his being. "When I die, the consciousness I carry I will to black people. May they pick me apart and take the useful parts, the sweet meat of my feelings. And leave the bitter bullshit rotten white parts alone."[13]

The collection also contains numerous poems that criticize and revile blacks deemed to be racially obsequious to white America. In "cops," Baraka ridicules by name his former Newark playmates who now were on the Newark police force:

Bowleg Otis played football but was always a prick
he made detective by arresting a dude he knew all his life,
he waited in the cold counting white folks' smiles . . .
. . . Leon parkd in front of the city hospital
bullshitting, but he'd split yr head. He was a bad catcher w/
Baxter Terrace, you slide home head first you get messed up
strong as a bitch . . .
. . . you wanna stand in front of a bar, with a gun
pointed at you? You wanna try to remember why you liked somebody
while the bullet comes. Shit[14]

As a black nationalist, Baraka must have felt betrayed by blacks who willingly did the bidding of the corrupt and racist white power brokers in Newark. Yet he knows that his nostalgia for the days when he played sports with these guys cannot be allowed to make him forget that his friends are now cops.

Black flunkies of the racist power structure were not confined to the ranks of the police department. In "Civil Rights Poem," Baraka berates the head of the national NAACP, Roy Wilkins. Because of his passive demeanor and desire to be inoffensive to whites, Wilkins was a favorite whipping boy of the 1960s black nationalists.

> Roywilkins is an eternal faggot
> His spirit is a faggot
> his projection
> and image, this is
> to say, that if i ever see roywilkins
> on the sidewalks
> imonna
> stick half my sandal
> up his
> ass[15]

During this era when heterosexual machismo was thought to be synonymous with the revolutionary male ethos, no image could have better captured the idea of an obsequious racial weakling than that of the "faggot." Such slurs as "faggot" were common in the black nationalist community. They not only embraced a homophobic stereotype but also conveyed an aggressive dislike for gay men.

The collection also contains the requisite poetry-of-praise to black womanhood, "Beautiful Black Women":

> Beautiful black women, fail, they act. Stop them, raining.
> they are so beautiful, we want them with us. Stop them, raining.
> Beautiful, stop raining, they fail. We fail them and their lips
> stick out perpetually, at our weakness . . .
> . . . Ladies. women. We need you. We are still
> trapped and weak, but we build and grow heavy with our knowledge. Women
> come to us. Help us get back what was always ours. Help us, women. Where
> are you, women, where, and who, and where, and who, and will you help
> us, will you open your bodysouls, will you lift me up mother, will you
> let me help you, daughter, wife/lover, will you[16]

To call this poem trite would be to point out the obvious. Yet such poems flourished during the Black Arts era. Nothing was considered more indicative of a revolutionary black male's commitment to black people than his publicly professed reverence for black women.

Although Baraka's poems in *Black Art* are formulaic harangues against whites and whiteness and celebratory invocations of parochial blackness, they are, by and large, the best poems that Baraka wrote as a black cultural nationalist. What remains striking about his Black Arts verse is that it is overwhelmed by a turgid and all-pervasive ideology. Baraka no longer manifests the ambiguities that made much of his earlier poetry so engaging. Indeed, *Black Art* would have benefited from the self-interrogation central to *Preface to a Twenty Volume Suicide Note* and *The Dead Lecturer*. Certainly there was nothing intrinsic to black nationalist politics that made identity angst obsolete. In Baraka's mind, though, his religious-like devotion to a doctrinaire black nationalism resolved the contradictions in the two-ness of black identity. The black identity paradoxes that had once fueled his creativity were now deemed politically inappropriate, and as a result, his poetry was severely diminished.

Though published in 1967, *Tales* consisted of short stories that had been previously published between the early and middle 1960s. Topically, the collection chronicles Jones's evolution from Beat bohemian to black nationalist. Yet, most of the stories center around the identity ambivalences, angsts and alienations of Jones, a thematic unity that was reminiscent of his bohemian writings. Critics vary widely on their assessments of the artistic value of *Tales,* particularly Jones's attempt to experiment with form. Whether it is "The Alternative" (a description of the bourgeois mindlessness and homoerotic voyeurism of Howard University students), "Going Down Slow" (the hypocritical response of Jones to one of Hettie's affairs), "The Death of Horatio Alger" (a verbally adept young man's inability to physically defend himself against a less verbally adept young man), or "The Salute" (an incident describing the mindless deference of military practices), these short stories appear to be little more than descriptions of events. *Tales* is far less political than Jones's poetry and other fictional writings and thus is of lesser concern to this study.

IT'S NATION TIME

During the early 1970s, Baraka published two collections of poetry, *It's Nation Time* and *Spirit Reach*, as well as *In Our Terribleness*, a coauthored photo-essay that also contained poetry. Consisting of three poems, *It's Nation Time* was only twenty-four pages long. Its title comes from a popular refrain heard throughout black urban America during the late 1960s and early 1970s. For example, a politicized and/or somewhat hip black person might end an informal street conversation with a "black handshake" and the rhetorical question "What time is it?" whereupon the other conversant would respond, "It's nation time."[17] The refrain was also part of the routine for black nationalist political speakers. They would often exhort the crowd to fever pitch with the chant "What time is it?" and the crowd would roar, "It's nation time." Jesse Jackson used in this particular call and response device at the 1972 National Black Political Convention in Gary, Indiana. The invocation of nation referred to a black nation of unified blacks and contained an assertion of black agency.

The first poem in It's Nation Time, "The Nation Is Like Ourselves," is both a description of the mental afflictions that keep blacks from being able to construct a unified nation and a plea to these wayward Negroes to "get their act together." The poem begins as a matter-of-fact statement about our social and political reality. We—that is, black people—are no better or worse than we make ourselves out to be.

> The nation is like our selves, together
> seen in our various scenes, set where ever we are
> what ever we are doing, is what the nation
> is
> doing
> or
> not doing
> is what the nation
> is
> being
> or
> not being[18]

Following this mundane statement of the choices facing black people, Baraka begins to berate those blacks who are not participating in the struggle for a black nation. Clearly, he believes that too many blacks are "not doing" and "not being" and mocks them by referring to them as niggers. It is no accident that he singles out black professionals for criticism.

> doctor nigger, please do some somethin on me
> lawyer nigger, please pass some laws about us.[19]

Baraka's disdain for his black contemporaries who were part of the counterculture movement with its emphasis on drugs, bell-bottom pants, "free love," and indifference to racial identity is evident. Blacks like the singer Sly Stone were probably foremost in Baraka's image of misguided counterculture blacks:

> please mister liberated nigger love chil nigger
> nigger in a bellbottom bell some psychodelic wayoutness
> on YO People, even while you freeing The People, please
> just first free YO people, ol marijuana jesus I dug your last
> record

Even bourgeois black writers are not spared criticism.

> if the rastafarians don't kill you please mr vacationing writer
> man
> write some heavy justice
> about black people
> we waiting
> we starved for your realness
>
> you are our nation sick ass assimilado
> please come back
> like james brown say
>   please please please [20]

After pleading with those Negroes who have used various strategies to avoid confronting their collective plight in racist America, Baraka ends the poem on a funny note by invoking the lyrics of "Please, Please, Please," a hit song by James Brown. The poem can easily be imagined as eliciting laughter and excitement from an audience of black college students.

None of the three poems in *It's Nation Time* is impressive. The redundancy and tendentiousness of the themes make it appear as if Baraka had run out of ideas. Note the following trite lines from "Sermon for Our Maturity":

> you need to get better uh
> you need to experience better times Negro
> We love you negro Love you betta
> if you got betta
> Love yrself betta
> if you got betta.

You can dance Nigger I know it
Dance on to freedom
You can sing Nigger sing
Sing about your pure movement[21]

The final poem in *It's Nation Time* resembles the first poem in the collection, "The Nation Is Like Ourselves":

when the brothers strike niggers come out
come out niggers
when the brothers take over the school
help niggers
come out niggers
all niggers negroes must change up
come together in unity unity
for nation time
it's nation time[22]

Baraka may have done himself a disservice in trying to force his strong polemical impulses into a poetic form. His didactic intentions overwhelm his artistic sensibilities and make the poetry abysmal.

SPIRIT REACH

In 1972, *Spirit Reach* was published by Baraka's own Jihad Press. Its poems resemble those in *Black Art*. For instance, in "Deranged Gutbucket Pigtongue Clapper Heart," Baraka offers his usual admonishments to Negroes who seem too closely wedded to white folks:

cracker you may be wood
and fire is what you need
to change your wooden ways
nigger you might be fire
and need to burn some wood
to live real bright and strong
like you should . . .
but
maybe
may be you wood too-nigger slick butt

turned around blonde twist on yo ass
and here you are bein
wood
steada something
good. Well you get burned too
or if you fire and wont burn wood you might just
burn yourself[23]

Using the word *wood*, as in *peckerwood*, to refer to whites, Baraka rephrases one of his overused Black Arts themes.[24] Perhaps the distinctive element of *Spirit Reach* that is not present in his other Black Arts poetry collections is Baraka's presentation of himself as someone who has integrated higher spiritualism into black nationalism. In the poem "Study Peace," Baraka tells us why he is the Imamu.

Out of the shadow. I am come in to you whole a black holy man
whole of heaven in my hand in my head look out two yeas to ice
what does not belong in the universe of humanity and love. I am
the black magician you have heard of, you knew was on you in you
                                                                now[25]

In the poem "All in the Street," he also alludes to his higher moral consciousness. Now he has become a medium through which Allah speaks.

Listen to the creator speak in me now. Listen, these words
are part of God's thing. I am a
vessel, a black priest interpreting
the present and future for my people
Olorun- Allah speaks in and
thru me now. . . . He begs me to pray for you—as I am doing—He
bids me have you submit to the energy.[26]

It is astonishing that Baraka tried to use verse to legitimate his leadership status in the black community. Perhaps he really did believe that he had reached a higher form of wisdom that was inaccessible to most. But even if he did believe this, it is difficult to understand why he thought that conveying this in his poetry would have been convincing. We can only wonder why such poetic proclamations were not viewed as the bombast of an egomaniacal writer. Baraka's concern for aesthetic innovation was hampered by his belief that he was a bearer of superior wisdom. Any writer who is intimately conversant with God need not trifle with mundane concerns like poetic craft.

IN OUR TERRIBLENESS

In 1970, Baraka's *In Our Terribleness* was published, a text that defies easy description. It is not, strictly speaking, a collection of poetry. Instead, it is a mixture of poetry, polemic, photography, and prose. The book was jointly created with Fundi (Billy Abernathy), a photographer. Baraka's textual partnership with Fundi's photography is somewhat reminiscent of the partnership between Langston Hughes and photographer Roy DeCarava that gave birth to *Sweet Flypaper of Life.*

In Our Terribleness takes its title from the reversals in word meaning often found in urban black American idioms. In such a reversal, a fat person might be referred to as "slim" or "tiny." Likewise, the term *bad* has come to denote something good or positive. To refer to someone who is better than good or something that is stronger than positive, one might borrow James Brown's strategy and use the term *superbad.* In much the same way, Baraka accentuates bad by invoking the term *terrible.*

> *Since there is a "good" we know is bullshit, corny as Lawrence*
> *Welk On Venus, we will not be that hominy shit. We will be,*
> *definitely, bad, bad, as a mother-fucker..*
>
> *To be bad is one level*
> *But to be terrible, is to be*
> *badder dan nat*[27]

In Our Terribleness was an apt name for a photo-essay book celebrating black urban life during the late 1960s and early 1970s. After the title page is a single page of aluminum paper with a cardboard backing. In the middle of this aluminum page is the phrase "in our terribleness." This aluminum page is supposed to function as a mirror for readers, presumably black, to see themselves and recognize their own "terribleness."

Fundi's photographs are quite forceful. He was able to capture moods and situations in black urban life without sentimentalizing them. The black-and-white film offers a starkness to the backgrounds and landscapes of the photographs. Unfortunately, Baraka's accompanying texts too often get stuck in sentimentalism and romanticism. He is so adamant about celebrating black urban life that he attributes profound meanings to every gesture and scene captured in the photographs. For instance, a photograph of a black man at work who has a toothpick in his mouth inspired Baraka to write:

> Like this blood with the tooth pick. . . . Transformed
> wood. A wand. Transmutation. The dumb wood now
> vibrating at a higher rate. With the blood. His
> mouth wand. The toothpick of the blood is his
> casual swagger stick. Sho is hip . . .

As was the male practice during the era of Black Power, black women are referred to as fine, beautiful, strong, and loving. Accordingly, below a photograph of a black woman, Baraka writes, "Hey, man, look at this woman. She is fine. Fine. I cant say nothing else. We need to give her something." Written alongside another portrait of a "sister," Baraka's platitudes become far more expansive: "I love you black perfect woman. Your spirit will rule the twenty first century. That is why we ourselves speed to grace." His professed love of black woman should be interpreted as neither an affirmation of her gender equality nor an indication of respect for her intrinsic value as a human being. Rather, Baraka could see black women only through a hypersexist, black male heterosexual gaze. His Kawaidan philosophy of life endorsed the black male domination of black women. He thus deems a group portrait of female members of the Nation of Islam a "pure image of the black woman." Not surprisingly, this "pure image" is an image of submissiveness. On the page following this photograph, he declares that black women as well as black children must be taught by black men, who must teach themselves. Beautiful but braindead, worshiped but denigrated, black women await guidance from real black men who, presumably, might resemble the Imamu.

In *In Our Terribleness*, Baraka's poetry and prose are sometimes comical, usually overstated, and always doctrinaire in their advocacy of Kawaida. The text is replete with mysticism and symbolic invocations of the black man's unique and potentially unique relationship to God. *In Our Terribleness* strives to be a spiritual text. Insofar as it is too celebratory of the commonplace in black life, it may have been incapable of elevating the consciousness of blacks beyond the confines of their actual lives.

It's Nation Time, Spirit Reach, and *In Our Terribleness* are sometimes referred to as minor collections, and many literary critics and scholarly students of Baraka have chosen not to analyze them. Or they are described as collections of poems that were supposed to be performed. I do not doubt the theatricality of Baraka's performance when reading such poems. But should we expect less from those poems intended for the so-called average blood than those poems written for whites in the Village? Is poetry that was written to be performed intrinsically more hackneyed than poetry written on a printed page to be read? Baraka's Black Arts poetry is frequently so aesthetically uninspiring that it sometimes appears to be a parody of "poetry for the masses." It was as if he did everything in his power to expose blacks to his worst poetry while claiming that such banal verse was nourishment for black minds intent on liberation. If black liberation included the ability to think critically and reflectively, Baraka's poetry for the black masses can only be construed as antithetical to the black freedom struggle. My hunch is that Baraka typically performed these poems before audiences of black activists or black college students, all of whom participated in his vicarious construction of the "average blood" as being one mental stage removed from that of an idiot.

RAISE RACE RAYS RAZE

In 1969, at the height of his involvement with Karenga, Baraka wrote the extended essay "7 Principles of US: Maulana Karenga & the Need for a Black Value System" in which he presented Karenga's doctrine of Kawaida.[28] The essay was issued as a pamphlet which subsequently received widespread circulation in black nationalist circles, including large numbers of black college students.[29] In 1972, Third World Press published Baraka's collection of essays, entitled *Kawaida Studies: The New Nationalism*, which included "7 Principles" and five other essays. A year earlier, five of these six essays (including "7 Principles") were included with numerous others in his Random House essay collection, *Raise Race Rays Raze*.

The initial essay in this collection describes the scene inside a Newark municipal courtroom in 1966. Entitled "Newark Courthouse–'66: Wreck: (Nigger Rec Room)," the essay is an informal courtroom ethnography. As an observer, Baraka was able to describe graphically the social interactions among the arresting police; Narol, the white judge; the accused blacks; and their white lawyers. He imagined the Newark courtroom as a microcosm of the racial divide in the United States. What makes the essay compelling is Baraka's ability to maintain a stoic, matter-of-fact, understated tone when describing the absurd racist humiliations and punishments routinely visited on the blacks accused by a legal system that gave racist judges and police the power to dispense "justice."

Early in the essay, Baraka informs us that he was in the courtroom because he had been arrested the previous night because he dared to ask two

Newark policemen why they had stopped and arrested his two friends who were, at the time, driving to the store in Baraka's car. The cops claimed that the two men looked suspicious. That is, two black men riding in a car were arrested *because they were two black men riding in a car.* In black urban parlance, they were guilty of DWB—"driving while black." Simply for asking why his friends were arrested, Baraka was also taken into custody and charged with "disturbing the peace." Such wanton acts of arbitrary repression by white police have long been the norm in black inner-city neighborhoods. Anyone who has visited municipal courtrooms in any large American city can testify that the charge of "disturbing the peace" is frequently invoked to legitimate the arrest of blacks who have committed no crime. "Resisting arrest" is another charge often similarly used.

Using the ludicrousness of his arrest as a backdrop, Baraka comments on a litany of cases that he witnesses while waiting for his case to be called. One black man has been arrested for getting into an argument while waiting at a bus stop. The black man claims that while "minding his own business," a cop approached him and started "talking rough." He responded in similar fashion. The white arresting cop testifies that he approached the man because he looked suspicious. The judge dismissed the case but told the black man to "watch who you're talking to." There was no admonishment of the arresting white cop. Next Baraka describes the perfunctory "trials" of two different black men, each of whom, while drunk, had fallen asleep in the Newark railroad station. Both men were quickly sentenced to fifteen days in jail. Two weeks earlier, Baraka had watched the same judge presiding over the trial of another black man. When this black fellow mistakenly thought that the proceedings were over, the judge, with obvious disdain, stated, "What, you're a wise guy" and then sentenced him to ten days in jail for the misunderstanding.

Baraka's scorn is also aimed at a black husband and wife who enter the courtroom because of her complaint of domestic violence. He surmises that the white judge and the other white court officials are amused by the spectacle of black-on-black marital discord. Angered at the public display of this "ethnic" dirty linen, Baraka is unable to recognize the gender implications of domestic violence and the court's trivialization of such complaints. Instead, he perceives only racial self-degradation and thus equates the attacking male with the attacked female. The most dramatic episode in Baraka's reportage is a black "33 year old nigger boy name Julius" who was accused of violating his parole. Julius was quickly led in and out of the courtroom as the judge, without ever looking up at the human being standing before him, sentenced him to six months in jail. This mechanical dispensation of justice is perhaps the best example of the routinized injustice confronting black people. Judge Narol has no respect for any of the accused blacks and even patronizingly asks one sixty-year-old black man, "You gonna be a good boy?"

The essay highlights a wretched reality of urban life for blacks. But Baraka's writing is irritating, for in his attempt to describe the legal system's contempt for blacks, he routinely uses ethnic slurs in his descriptions of various white authority figures.

> 9:45 Judge jew is still not in. The few cops in the mostly empty court sit smoking. The youngest, the black haired ginnie-stereotype (too punkish to be Mafioso . . . smokes a long prestige cigar . . .

> Redfaced Oirishmens & swarthy Italians make up the bulk of the force.

> Jewish lawyers come in. (Still connected to us by that desert experience; they follow niggers with wet sucking nozzles stuck in the niggers' throats. The jews love us so.)[30]

Baraka's spits rhetorical venom at Newark's finest, regarding them as the scum of the earth and referring to them as "debased lower animals who think themselves God." His feelings about racist Italian American and Irish American cops is understandable. After all, antiblack racism was the norm for the overwhelmingly white Newark police force. White supremacists in uniform were allowed to roam the streets with the legal right to determine life and death for any black they chose to stop. Thus they patrolled knowing that the legal system existed to defend their actions against black people, even if they included murder.

Baraka's willingness to employ ethnic slurs is troubling despite his justifiable anger at the white racist police. The Irish cops are depicted as drunkards with red noses. Italian American cops are always potential mafioso. Worse, Newark policemen of Italian American ancestry are referred to as ginnie cops and wopcops. This use of ethnic slurs may stem from Baraka's own sense of powerlessness in the face of the real power of these white police. But instead of confronting them in real life, he calls them wopcops on the printed page and in this way shows his contempt for them. Perhaps he believes that he is demeaning them in a way similar to their demeaning treatment of him and other blacks. Nonetheless, ethnic aspersions directed toward Italian American cops and Jewish lawyers do not mitigate Black Powerlessness.

In addition, Baraka violates an implicit ethic when he uses ethnic slurs against even racist whites. Such words are offensive because they are intended to deny or diminish the humanity of others. Why would Baraka want to use words that carry historical memories of the subjugation of other peoples? In denying white police their humanity, Baraka simplifies the world in order to reinforce his Manichaean racial categories.

As the title suggests, the essay "Work-Notes–1966" is about what black communities must do if they are ever going to be able to wage a viable struggle for freedom. Baraka believes that even the necessity of having to work for white men in order to earn a living makes demands on black male psyches that undermine the ability of black men to rely on one another (black females are not mentioned). Blacks, he argues, look at one another through lenses that have been filtered through racist images acquired from whites. Consequently, blacks do not trust other blacks. Even though blacks are disgusted with whites, they still look to them for answers. Instead, Baraka proposes: "We must submit to ourselves. and understand the beauty of our own necessity. It is there. We must submit to each other, and let one of us, as specialists in particular fields, go on out with the rest following. We must see that work gets done."[31]

In pursuit of "getting work done," blacks from all classes must be educated in leadership. They should read, study, and engage in critical discussions with one another. They should not only write and distribute books and pamphlets but do so as cheaply and quickly as possible. Because radio is dominated by whites and television even more so, blacks need to find other ways of disseminating information. Baraka believes that it is possible to produce written words that "have the speed of the electronics media." These quickly written and produced books and pamphlets would allow blacks to distribute information about current events. Baraka's desire for a strategy that would allow blacks to circumvent their lack of power over the electronic media is fine, but he naively assumes that black Americans would read pamphlets just as readily as they would watch the evening news.

Several essays in Raise Race Rays Raze deal with black art and the Black Arts movement. "Poetry and Karma" is the most extensive of these essays and exemplifies Baraka's condemnation of white American poetry. Concealed in this is his attempt to specifically denigrate the creativity and creations of those white poets who were once his friends and mentors. There could be no greater insult to poets like Charles Olson and Allen Ginsberg than to be linked to the mainstream of American mass culture. At some level, the essay must have been an attempt at self-cleansing. Baraka condemns Ginsberg, but he does not tell us why. Perhaps Ginsberg is guilty of being white. To support his assertions, he makes the rather uncontroversial claim that the poetry of a people is a reflection of their spirit.

Denying any singularity to white individuals, Baraka makes white poets the reified embodiments of all white people who, in turn, are granted sole responsibility for America's debased character. In effect, white poets are artistic failures because of their association with whiteness. Earlier, Baraka taught us that white folks lacked humanity, emotional depth, and spirituality and were alienated from themselves and God. The vacuousness of white poetry rivals the vacuity of white music. Baraka notes that "no life has existed in that music for centuries. Perhaps never."[32]

Recognizing their estrangement from God and the accompanying lack of inner spirituality, those few white poets who are devoted to creativity must "masquerade as captive niggers."[33] Other whites (undoubtedly the majority) who are incapable of coping with the superior spirituality of black poetry try to ignore it. Such was the case, Baraka implies, when Donald Allen included only LeRoi Jones among the poets he collected in *New American Poetry, 1945–1960*:

> . . . Only LeRoi Jones in New American Poetry, 1945–1960.
> The Negro! Whose poetry then, only a reflection what
> the rest of that E-X-C-L-U-S-I-V-E club was doing.
> You mean there was no other poetry, you mean there
> were no other spooks, &c. I pass.[34]

Baraka's criticism is significant for what it omits. He is trying to rewrite history. First, he probably knew before its publication that he would be the only black represented in Allen's collection. Why then, did he consent to being a racial token? More important, how does Baraka explain that when he edited a volume of the "new prose writing" three years after the Allen collection, he too included only one black writer, himself. Shouldn't Baraka examine the underlying thinking of LeRoi Jones to figure out why he maintained such an "E-X-C-L-U-S-I-V-E club?" Baraka also does not mention *The Moderns*,[35] for it would undermine his insinuation that white Americans were uniquely incapable of acknowledging black creativity. Perhaps black bohemians also could not contend with the black creative ethos.

"What the Arts Need Now," a short essay first published in *Negro Digest* in 1967, is an example of the short prescriptive tracts concerning the responsibilities of black intellectuals that were frequently published by Black Arts advocates. It is simultaneously a call to arms for the black artist and a commemoration of black people. The essay begins "What's needed now for 'the arts' is to get them away from white people, as example of their culture (of their life, finally, and all its uses, e.g. art) and back where such strivings belong, as strong thrusts of a healthy people."[36] Being a healthy people, as opposed to diseased whites, blacks need to realize that they can and have to create an art that reflects their dynamic humanism. Such art celebrates black life. Much like his calls for poems "that kill," Baraka advocates writing plays that attack whites and whiteness. That is, black playwrights need to write plays that inform and inspire blacks to

> stop bogus so-called urban renewal, which be nigger removal. . . . But at the time of, and at the place of. In the street, at the spot where such disarming is taking place. Have your actors shoot mayors if necessary, right in the actual mayor's chamber. Let him feel the malice of the just. Let the people see justice work out repeatedly.[37]

Black playwrights need to begin to think of the theater as a mechanism for addressing social issues at the time and place that issues arise. Baraka encourages blacks to write plays about the police department or even "Jew plays" (whatever that means). The duty of the black playwright is to show blacks their enslavement and to let "them see the chains fall away."

In "Black Art, Nationalism, Organization, Black Institutions," Baraka defends the natural spiritualness of black people that will become evident once they are conscious of their blackness. The idea of black people's divinity or near divinity is a recurring theme in this essay, as it is in many of Baraka's Black Arts polemics. He proclaims a belief in God, but it is God as a perfected man (undoubtedly a perfected black man). Black creators must strive for this perfection, however unattainable it might be. Baraka contends that black nationalism is the only way that black individuals can get in touch with their true divine-like selves because it is the means for becoming conscious of the glories of black people as a group. As a black nationalist dogmatist, Baraka wished to deny ideological freedom to black artists.

> Art without Nationalism is not Black. . . . The Negro artist who is not a nationalist at this late date is a white artist, even without knowing it. . . . What he does will not matter because it is in the shadow, connected with the shadow, and will die when the shadow dies.[38]

Baraka deliberately links black consciousness with the powers of the universe, asserting a metaphysical link among blackness, creativity, and the universe. Unlike the antinationalist black artist, the black nationalist artist is a creator. More specifically, he is "The Creator." Given such a claim, it is not surprising that Baraka uses a mystical discourse on black nationalism:

Nationalism . . . is important because it is a basic creative function of the universe. If we deny it. We cannot progress or evolve . . . who ever has the value system strong enough to define and develop and defend the essence of their existence will be master of the Planets, Uniters of The Solar System, The Lord Of The Worlds.[39]

Despite the benefits of nationalism to blacks, many still refused to join the nationalist struggle. Instead, they devised numerous lame excuses for remaining uncommitted. In Baraka's mind, political commitment to any program other than black nationalism was the equivalent of being uncommitted. "Lying niggers everywhere. The reason I aint in the program is this, or that, or some other bull shit. Die lying niggers. You fulla shit. Doctors and pimps niggers same ol same ol saying the same jive line. Why they aint. Be somethin for once."[40] Baraka is enormously frustrated by blacks that appear to be content, discontent but passive, too tired to struggle, or too self-absorbed to merge their individual energies with those of other blacks in a collective enterprise. Organizations must be created that in turn will give rise to institutions. Blacks, he believes, should stop fantasizing about freedom. Only through work, the creative enterprise, can the new black reality come into being.

"Negro Theater Pimps Get Big off Nationalism" was originally published as the introduction to Baraka's play *Jello*. The essay is an unfocused condemnation of any and all tendencies within the black theater world that were opposed to a black nationalist political and aesthetic project. Baraka proclaims that any non–black nationalist theater must be white oriented. Because they are white oriented, these black theaters are supported by white foundations intent on turning the black public away from theaters associated with the Black Arts.

The essay opens by criticizing the antinationalist politics of Eldridge Cleaver and the Black Panthers. He refers to Cleaver as a modern-day Yacub who has tried to resuscitate the viability of white humanity. Worse, he accuses Cleaver of rejecting nationalism because of his love for his white female lawyer. Baraka also castigates Cleaver and the Black Panthers ("niggers in French hats") for raising the thoughts of Marx and Lenin "from the tomb again."

In much the same way that Cleaver's willingness to engage in interracial coalition politics undermined the unity of black nationalist politics, some Negroes in the theater world were intent on opposing black nationalist drama. However, in order to proclaim the black nationalist theater as the norm and not a deviant tendency, Baraka is forced to grant himself a centrality to the New York theater world. "When The Black Arts Theater jarred slick newyork and slickamerica thinking about art and reality, many of us who were admittedly jewhypnotized and white committed cut all that jive loose, and made our true move to Home and light."[41] According to Baraka's self-serving narrative, his Harlem theater school generated fear in the white powers that be. In response to BART, powerful whites decided to fund a counterrevolutionary Negro theater that aspired to be white-like.

> The devil had to make his move. . . . He got some niggers, some whiteflesh addicts, to make smoke-dust storms . . . in the name of a negro theater still committed to the same ol same ol . . . whiteness. . . . Like they were in black face, these nigger robots, made homage to . . . and at this very moment, make homage to, Europe, its life, its rule, its degeneracy, and its death; in actuality such theater like white life itself, is part of that death.[42]

This assault is targeted at the most prominent practitioner of Negro Pimp Art, the Negro Ensemble Theater.[43] Not only does Baraka claim that they are white-like, but he calls them inferior artists. Indeed, it is their artistic inferiority that supposedly is responsible for their white support. Baraka even names some of these whitenized Negroes: playwrights Charles Gordone, Lonnie Elder, and Douglas Turner Ward; and actors James Earl Jones and Cleavon Little.

The Imamu is enraged by these individuals and their theater because they rejected black nationalism and thus, by extension, his intellectual and artistic leadership. Worse, they were supposedly supported by whites in order to undermine black cultural nationalism. Surprisingly, these Negroes rejected black nationalism at the very time that their existence depended on it. Foundations, Baraka believes, would have had no use for Negro theater pimps had there not been a nationalist dramatic thrust that they found so threatening and in need of subversion.

Like most of Baraka's essays of this period, this one is a mixture of sense, nonsense, and dogmatic exhortations. First, how can he criticize any black theater that obtains financial support from white foundations when his so-called hyperradical Black Arts Repertory Theater had survived as a beneficiary of the federal government's riot pacification program? Second, Baraka overstates his own significance in the New York art world. On what basis could he honestly claim that his Black Arts Theater/School "jarred the New York art world?" Finally, there was no reason to think that Baraka had any greater claim to authentic blackness than did Douglas Turner Ward, Lonnie Elder, or any of the other accused playwrights and actors. The more that one reads Baraka's essays in this volume, the more one senses that he was an extraordinarily narcissistic writer who was intent on projecting his own neuroses onto all blacks. He writes as if all blacks who associated with whites were governed by the same mentalities that shaped his actions when he associated with whites.

Baraka's "The Need for a Cultural Base to Civil Rites & Bpower Mooments" first appeared in Floyd Barbour's 1967 edited collection, *The Black Power Revolt*. The essay defines Black Power and discusses the centrality of black cultural nationalism to Black Power. Like many others in the collection, this essay is a rehash of many of the ideas that Baraka became famous for championing during the late 1960s.

He begins by claiming that the error of the Civil Rights movement lay in its lack of a black cultural nationalist perspective. Black supporters of civil rights were trapped in a self-defeating fantasy.

> The civilrighter is usually an american, otherwise he would know, if he is colored, that the concept is meaningless fantasy. Slaves have no civil rights. On the other hand, even integration is into the mobile butcher shop of the devil's mind. To be an american, one must be a murderer. A white murderer of colored people.[44]

Negroes who think of themselves as Americans are implicated in the United States' assault on colored peoples throughout the world. Such misguided Negroes are themselves examples of murdered colored people. The foundational aspiration of Black Power is the power of blacks "to control our lives ourselves." Black people in control of themselves will inevitably create a peaceful world. By their very nature, blacks are lovers of peace and universal humanity. Moreover, the black man "is a spirit worshiper as well. The religious-science and scientific-religion is the black man's special evolutionary province."[45] Black power is ultimately rooted in the nature of black people who are, in essence, spiritual beings.

Following a routine denunciation of bourgeois blacks, Baraka appears to throw them a political olive branch. Although he views bourgeois Black Power as the desire of middle-class blacks to mimic the actions of powerful whites, he does not believe that bourgeois blacks actually share the same interests as bourgeois whites. Instead, he discerns in bourgeois black nationalism a way to realize black empowerment:

> Of course the form of Bourgeois black power can be harnessed for heavier ends. The control by black people for their own benefit CAN BE set up

similar to bourgeois black power, but if the ends are actually to be realized, you are talking again about nationalism, nationalization.[46]

To the extent that bourgeois blacks aspire to black control of black people or even the black servicing of black people, Baraka thinks that they can be used to facilitate his black separatist political agenda. Baraka's blindness to the significance of class differences becomes evident here. Even in a black nationalist community, class distinctions would reflect an unequal distribution of power and influence. But in Baraka's mind, the only truly significant division in the world is between blacks and whites, therefore bourgeois blacks who stand against whites are allies.

This essay also foregrounds racial separatism as an intrinsic component of Baraka's black nationalism. Blacks and whites can never live as equals in the same geographical space, for whites would never allow this to happen. To be white is to dominate others. Consequently, anyone who advocates Black Power without endorsing blacks' separation from whites is merely pretending. When Baraka begins to specify the ways that the nature of blacks differs from that of whites, he engages in quasi-mystical descriptions of the black consciousness necessary for the emergence of true Black Power. "Black power cannot be complete unless it is the total reflection of black people. Black power must be spiritually, emotionally, and historically in tune with black people, as well as serving their economic and political ends . . . the seekers of black power must know what it is they seek." The emergence of blacks into established positions of power does not itself constitute Black Power. After all, the election of a black sheriff in Alabama is fine but only if that sheriff is authentically black and thus the bearer of values different from those of his white predecessors. Senator Edward Brooke, the only black in the U.S. Senate, cannot be construed as embodying Black Power. According to Baraka, "He is, for all intents and purposes, a white man."[47]

Many of the blacks who supposedly advocate Black Power are actually frauds.

> There are people who might cry BlackPower, who are representatives, extensions of white culture. So-called BlackPower advocates who are mozart-freaks or Rolling Stones, or hypnotized by Joyce or Hemingway or Frank Sinatra, are representatives, extensions, of white culture, and can never therefore signify black power.[48]

While there were certainly many frauds in the Black Power enterprise, I doubt whether many of them were "mozartfreaks" or "hypnotized by Joyce." Again, we might wonder whether Baraka isn't exorcising his past. Is he, once again, guilty of projecting his own autobiographical journey onto the lives of other black people?

Baraka contends that civil rights and Black Power organizations have failed to attract a widespread following because they do not address the totality of black culture and black consciousness. The Nation of Islam is the only group that he believes has succeeded in addressing this totality. This concern for the total black person lies behind the Nation's success in developing a large mass following.[49] Baraka's belief in the need for a total institution may explain his attraction to Karenga's US and Kawaida doctrine. Yet we must be skeptical when reading Baraka's endorsement of the Nation of Islam's program. As a black nationalist who was comfortable with bourgeois black nationalism, black male supremacy over black women, the goal of black separatism, and a belief in the innate immorality of white people, Baraka should have found the Nation of Islam a welcome home. But he never seriously considered joining the organization. I suspect that the total commitment demanded by the organization would have been too constrictive for him as a black writer, even though he constantly demonized whites and deified blacks. Baraka may have agreed with the Nation's doctrines, but he certainly would not have felt comfortable relinquishing control of his creativity to the dictates of the Honorable Elijah Muhammad. Baraka wanted to be a Malcolm X type of leader, and there was no room for such a figure in the Nation of Islam.

This essay reveals the suffocating insularity of Baraka's black nationalist vision. His notion of blackness is nothing less than an attempt to retard the "modernization" of black people. Because blacks were becoming increasingly diversified and differentiated in this industrial/postindustrial social order (by economic class, education, religion, region, occupation, tastes, sexual orientation, and leisure practices), Baraka viewed black identity as being threatened. His black nationalism was thus an attempt to hold the dike in place, to keep blacks from pursuing their various individual desires. Baraka always viewed individualism as a major deterrent to the realization of authentic blackness. This aversion to individualism was directed to other blacks. Baraka, the Imamu, was singularly individualized.

Baraka's distaste for other blacks' individualism was also extended to creative artists whose unique styles and ambitions precluded the development of a mass black audience. The only valid black artists were those who attempted to reach the broader black community, even if their art had no political content. This new populist, anti-individualist ethic led Baraka into a conceptual wasteland. In "The Fire Must Be Permitted to Burn Full Up: Black 'Aesthetic,'" he wrote:

Jr. Walker's music is superior to Ayler's or that that Ornette's making now, simply because of the world weariness, and corny self consciousness (which is white life hangaround total-ie what you get for being wit dem). Jr. Walker's music existed then and now, as a force describing purity. Ornette and Albert now describe bullshit so are bullshit.[50]

This condemnation of avant-garde black musicians for creating an explicitly self-conscious art speaks volumes about the aesthetic decline of Baraka's writing during this period.

"November 1966: One Year and Eight Months Later" offers brief reflections on the impact of Malcolm's murder on Afro-American life. The essay was written, as the title suggests, one year and eight months after his assassination. It is a blend of anguish, longing, and, ultimately, hope: "His murder, not only critically ruptured American Black connections with the Third World, but crippled his own organization, and turned great numbers of Black People away from The Nation of Islam. There were no black Nationalist or Black Revolutionary organizations that were not affected."[51] According to Baraka, this rupture, this destruction of continuity, was precisely what whites had intended by assassinating Malcolm. Following Malcolm's murder, black America entered a "deep period of reaction." Writing this essay during the winter of 1966, Baraka states that whites are assuming that the cold weather will quell black rebellious energies, at least until the next "long hot summer." He postulates a correlation between the dissipation of white fears of black rioting and the recent failure of Congress to pass a civil rights bill. Nonetheless, he maintains that had this bill become law, life for black people would not have substantially improved. The defeat of even this disingenuous and symbolic response to blacks indicates the new temper of the times. Worse, this moment of black quietude has provided the opportunity for a new generation of Booker T. Washingtons to come to the forefront. These new advocates of accommodationism included Roy Wilkins, A. Philip Randolph, Bayard Rustin, and Whitney Young. Baraka also cites Martin Luther King Jr., although he considers him a bit more shrewd than the others, given King's refusal to join them in signing an advertisement in the *New York Times* denouncing Black Power. Equally troubling is the success that whites have recently had on the international scene. Here Baraka cites the fall of Nkrumah and Sukarno, "two giants."

Certainly, black politics was drastically transformed by the assassination of Malcolm, as his murder was directly implicated in SNCC's decision to become exclusively black. But it is not as clear as Baraka would have us think that Malcolm would have endorsed black separatist politics. The

Malcolm who was killed is the Malcolm that Baraka chose to ignore. By the time of his murder, Malcolm had rejected the Manichaean racial typologies that Baraka continued to embrace. Baraka distorts the historical record when he argues that Whitney Young, Martin Luther King Jr., and the others had come to prominence in the vacuum left by Malcolm's murder in 1965. A Philip Randolph had been an outspoken radical and prominent black labor leader before Malcolm was even conceived. Martin Luther King Jr., Whitney Young, and Roy Wilkins reached the height of their prominence while Malcolm was alive.[52]

The title of the essay "Nationalism Vs Pimp Art" might lead the reader to think that it follows the same argument as "Negro Theater Pimps Get Big off Nationalism." It doesn't. Instead, this short essay offers specific denunciations of the Black Panthers and the white "counterculture" movement. At a more general level, it is a diatribe against any political activity that, while opposing black nationalism, markets itself as beneficial to blacks.

Baraka portrays the white counterculture movement as frivolous and without any real benefit to the black struggle. Regardless of what these young white folks may say about peace and loving their neighbors, they are still white and thus the enemies of black emancipation. Baraka mocks this movement as an effort that will "make Allen Ginsberg and/or Fulton Sheen comfortable with John Bull's grandson." He refers to this cultural front as "a vague, integrated, plastic, homosexual rEVolUTion . . . a conglomerate of words, degeneracy and fake pseudo 'act.'"[53] The strange spelling of the word *revolution* is supposed to indicate the decadent whiteness inherent in the scam radicalism of Ginsberg's so-called revolutionary aestheticism. Baraka's description of the counterculture as a degenerate movement of nakedness, homosexuality, and dope reveals his deep-seated homophobia and is a specific attack on the gay Ginsberg. By condemning drugs, nakedness, and homosexuality, Baraka tries to exorcise from his public identity those bohemian practices that had been central to his life during his days in the Village. Despite his overblown parochialisms toward whites in general and the counterculture specifically, Baraka does make the important point that the counterculture movement was akin to a leisurely act of rebellion (an adolescent rite of passage) for many white youth on their way into the racist mainstream of America. In his essentialist world, white youth—even rebellious white youth—were no different from their immoral white parents or even their evil white grandparents. Whites were white were white.

In Baraka's mind, the Black Panthers did not grasp this simple reality of American life. Because they advocated forming coalitions with progressive whites, the Panthers were really integrationists. "Frankly the Panthers, no matter the great amounts of sincere but purposefully misled brothers, getting shotup because some nigger was emotionally committed to white people, are extreme examples of PimpArt gone mad."[54] Baraka's assumption that the Panther gun cult stemmed from "some nigger's emotional commitment to white folks" is foolish. As he does elsewhere in this volume, Baraka asserts that the embrace of a leftist ideology by any black person is an accommodationist act. Once more, the culprit is Cleaver. Predictably, Cleaver's thoughts are again attributed to his love of a white woman. "And the love of Beverly Axelrod has left terrible Marx on the dirty Lenin Black people have been given by some dudes with some dead 1930s white ideology as a freedom suit. Instead of ol' swishy Bayard Rustin now we get violent integrationists. Wow!"[55] Violent integrationists? Baraka is forced to revise his long-held assumption that only weak blacks (e.g., homosexuals like the "swishy" Bayard Rustin) advocated integrationism. Moreover, he collapses all distinctions among political ideologies into the reductionist typology of nationalist versus integrationist. Integrationists can come in the guise of Marxists, supporters of welfare-state capitalism, followers of Milton Friedman, or even fascists. Whatever their ideology, the only thing that matters to Baraka is that they are sufficiently misguided to work with whites politically.

Any attempt by blacks to follow a white man's theories will ultimately serve the interests of whites. Only "a Black Ideology of change" can free black people.

> Lenin, Marx and Trotsky, or O'Neil, Beckett, and the Marat-Sade dude, are just the names of some more "great white men." There are other dudes who will give you other lists like Washington, Jefferson, Adams, or Paul McCartney, Cream, Grateful Dead, or Mozart, Pinky Lee and the fag with the health tv show. They are just lists of white people.

Baraka claims that he is receptive to being taught by anyone, including, if need be, President Richard Nixon. That is, although he can learn from whites, he will not allow their thoughts to take root in his core identity. The true black man knows that Karenga is correct when he states that "Black is Color, Culture and Consciousness."[56]

According to Baraka, the Panthers are misguided not only because they have romanticized the "pick up the gun" rhetoric but also because they are trapped in the same degenerate values of the slave master. Baraka's condemnation of the Panthers' gun fetish is not an antiviolence statement but a criticism of the Panthers' willingness to use guns before they had developed an emancipatory ideology. This critique of the Black Panthers reflects Karenga's doctrine. The Panthers do not seem to understand that the distinctiveness of black culture is the basis of the black nation. Baraka quotes from Fanon to support the contention that the concepts of nation and culture are inseparable. Yet we can only wonder whether Baraka had actually read Fanon. In *The Wretched of the Earth*, Fanon's discussion of the "pitfalls of national consciousness" could have served as a powerful corrective to Baraka's entire black nationalist agenda.

Once again, Baraka recites his commitment to a religious black nationalism. Once again, Baraka denounces others for tendencies that were once peculiarly his. Once again, this antimodernist demagogue voices his opposition to all differentiation in black America. Perhaps it is easy to understand Baraka's association of integrationism with assimilationism. It is a polemical ploy to construct integrationism as race suicide. But Baraka's political writings rarely, if ever, transcended crude polemic, and he never offers a sustained critique of the limitations of liberal integrationism or a rigorous defense of black nationalism. In the place of rational argument, Baraka substitutes denunciations, slurs, and slanders, all of which solidify his status as a demagogue. Is it therefore surprising that this "thinker" ends this essay by claiming that blacks who criticize black nationalism as a form of racism do so because they are sleeping with whites? Once again Baraka transfers his own neurosis to others. After all, whose psyche was more saturated with the images, fears, and memories of desired white females than that of the hyperblack Imamu?

After this appallingly anemic *Raise Race Rays Raze* appeared, it is amazing that in black nationalist intellectual and artistic circles, Baraka maintained his status as a seminal thinker. His abdication of critical judgment confirmed the absence of any pretense to intellectual/artistic standards in the black intellectual formation that had become mesmerized by the sound of its own political voice. Because *Raise* was written by the Imamu, many black readers and reviewers may have been lulled into an intellectual reenactment of the emperor's new clothes. Larger than life, by the end of the 1960s, Imamu Amiri Baraka was probably the most influential single figure in the black American intelligentsia. Who among black intellectuals was willing to admit that Baraka had become a parody of a serious thinker? Who among those few willing to tell this truth would have been heard? Once heard, who could have retained their ethnic legitimacy as black intellectuals or artists? And how should we regard those black intellectuals who celebrated *Raise* as a major text?

In June 1971, Jan Carew, a prominent West Indian intellectual who was at the time teaching in the United States, reviewed *Raise Race Rays Raze* in the *New York Times Book Review*. Carew was impressed with the collection, particularly "Newark Courthouse–'66 Wreck (Nigger Rec Room)." He writes that

Baraka's courtroom observations give "us vivid and chilling insights into a city's lower depths—black accused and white accusers locked in the throes of a primordial drama."[57] For Carew, the courtroom essay foreshadows the entire collection. Besides this essay, Carew discusses only one other in detail. In deciding not to mention the numerous ill-conceived pieces such as Baraka's essay on the righteousness of black male domination of black women, Carew may have revealed the limitations of his own political vision. Amazingly, he finds Baraka's musings on black art to be stunning and compares them with Yoruba philosophy. The review concludes,

> What is interesting about these collected essays is that they expose the speciousness of the romantic image of Imamu Baraka as a nihilist in a black limbo of his own creation. He emerges, despite some short and incomplete pieces, as a gifted writer with a finely tuned ear. At his best he can make words ignite and burst into flame.[58]

Carew's celebration of such a mundane collection is striking. Maybe he actually thought that he was in the presence of a master essayist. Perhaps he did not want to use the "white" forum of the *New York Times Book Review* to offer serious critical assessments of a self-professed black revolutionary. Whatever the case, it seems apparent that Baraka was deemed a figure worthy of exaltation by those critics who were sympathetic to black nationalist politics.

Addison Gayle, the foremost proponent of a "Black Aesthetic" and a prominent black literary critic, viewed *Raise Race Rays Raze* as one of the most important books written by a black in the twentieth century:

> Look back at the volumes of essays since *The Souls of Black Folk*. All have been footnotes to Du Bois' monumental work. This is as true of *Notes of a Native Son* and *White Man, Listen* as it is of *The Black Situation* and *Home*. None of these essayists had managed to improve on Du Bois' vision; each had merely in some way complemented it. . . . *Raise Race*, however, moves beyond *The Souls of Black Folk* and in so doing, becomes its logical successor. Once and for all, the old question of identity and the conflict of the dual psyche is ended. Salvation for Blacks lay outside the Western orbit! Images, symbols, and metaphors of Blacks are not to be found in the mirrors of Western man.[59]

Gayle evidently believed (or wanted to believe) that the burden of a black double-consciousness as defined by Du Bois and amended by numerous others could be resolved once and for all by merely declaring it to be resolved. Baraka says we are whole, so lo and behold, we are. Hurray for the Imamu! As if to substantiate Baraka's resolution of the black double-consciousness problematic, Gayle quotes directly from *Raise Race Rays Raze*. Baraka had written,

> We have our music. We have our art. We have our athletes. We have our religions. We have our black science, older than any on the planet. We have our beautiful people able to do anything and make anything and bring anything into being. . . . We will make cities . . . beautiful thrones of man and testaments to the ecstatic vision of the soulful.[60]

How could Gayle be so enraptured by this hollow excerpt from *Raise*? The language is ordinary and the ideas are pedestrian. Besides, Baraka the essayist was not an innovative stylist. Perhaps Gayle was trapped in a quasi-religious devotion to the black cultural nationalism symbolized by Baraka. Perhaps he was attracted to Baraka's intellectual and personal charisma. Charismatic and/or religious-like allegiances allow people to confuse foolishness with profundity and the grotesque with the beautiful. Gayle even invoked religious sentiments when he claimed that *Raise Race* "has the distinction of being the literary Koran, the philosophy of the moral and the just, the Ten commandments calling a people to sacrifice, struggle and success."[61]

By the late 1960s, *Home*, Baraka's first essay collection, had become a canonical text in black activist and intellectual circles. Its essays reflected the various attitudinal and political changes in Baraka's life. Because of his example as a black artist who rejected establishmentarian recognition for greater involvement in the black freedom struggle, *Home* was revered as a vehicle for understanding the growth of LeRoi Jones into Amiri Baraka. *Raise* never achieved equal prominence, as it was burdened with the ever-present shadow of *Home*. On its own merits, *Raise* is not as engaging a collection. Its author is more settled and dogmatic in his political, literary, and social beliefs. The personal identity anxieties and unresolved literary tensions that made some of the essays in *Home* so compelling are absent in *Raise*. An insular text, *Raise* is premised on a religious-like advocacy of black nationalism. The essays rarely construct arguments. Instead, Baraka appears to be writing as if the truth has been revealed to him. All that remains is for him to bear witness to it.

As Baraka became more politically engaged, he became increasingly dogmatic. This dogmatism was accompanied by exaggerated articulations of anger and hatred, the same tendencies that had diminished the later essays in *Home*. Baraka's fury against the myriad racist injustices faced by blacks may even have been honorable, but he failed to discover a literary form and authorial voice that would allow him to convey his anger without losing his literary sensibilities. A 169-page primal scream, *Raise* is important because it reflects the political thoughts of a major black intellectual during the height of his intellectual and political influence. Unfortunately, however, screaming is not good writing.

8

Black Revolutionary Playwright

ALTHOUGH BARAKA CONTINUED to write and perform poetry during the heyday of the Black Arts, his poetry became less significant as drama became his preferred genre. Baraka's concern for a revolutionary mass art led him to encourage black artists to privilege those art forms most accessible to the broader black community. In 1972, he published the short essay "Black Revolutionary Poets Should Also Be Playwrights." The essay begins as a condemnation of what Baraka views as pseudoblack black art. He labels as reactionary not only the film *Sweet Sweetback's Badass Song* but all those so-called black poets who romanticize the joy and delight of black life or sentimentalize "the good old days on the block." Such poets refuse to acknowledge that the pervasiveness of white racism is strangling black life. Any art that tries to proclaim blacks as a hip people without showing how they are imprisoned is reactionary.[1]

> Many of the known Black literati should be made to go to Political Education Classes or dismissed from the struggle as enemy sympathizers! Much of our black poetry is imitative at best, and mouths impossible rhetoric rather than concrete instructions for World African Revolution! . . . Also a great many of the theater companies that were once Black are still "Black" but hardly revolutionary. They often become fixed and stylized, and individualistic elitist celebrant cults for gigantic egos, to boot.[2]

Instead of relying on the writings of these deracinated black artists, true revolutionary black poets should organize small drama groups. They should write and even record improvised dramas, plays, skits, songs, and dances about the international black struggle. Poets could write short skits. Actors, singers, and dancers could write short musicals. Regardless of form, the guiding theme should be the need for black unity and self-determination.

Baraka imagines these skits being produced for churches, youth groups, social clubs, fraternities, sororities, and any other black group. Insofar as black Americans do not yet have an identity separate from that of Americans at large, he suggests that these plays and skits be used to teach blacks a new nationalist consciousness. Not surprisingly, the values that he believes consti-tute the core of this new revolutionary group consciousness are found in Kawaida.

As Baraka intensified his commitment to the new Black Arts movement, his drama, like his poetry, became increasingly unambitious. In his attempt to develop a theater audience, Baraka wrote and produced plays that were not only inferior to his earlier efforts but, more often than not, artistically banal. Some scholars have attributed the pedestrian quality of his Black Arts plays to his understandable desire to politicize the black community (i.e., his black au-diences). Such explanations assume that the artistic quality lost in producing agitprop plays was a cost that Baraka was willing to pay for political engage-ment. Assuming that Baraka did not suddenly lose the dramatic sensibility that inspired *Dutchman*, we must presume that his decision to write a string of minor dramatic pieces was intentional. But why?

In 1969 Baraka published *Four Black Revolutionary Plays*, a collection made up of *Experimental Death Unit #1*, *A Black Mass*, *Great Goodness of Life*, and *Mad Heart*. The title of the collection indicates Baraka's belief that the plays followed the dictates of his seminal 1964 essay "The Revolution-ary Theater."

EXPERIMENTAL DEATH UNIT #1 (1964)

Experimental Death Unit #1 was written in 1964 during the height of Jones's anguish over his continued affiliation with the Village scene. It was first per-formed at the fund-raiser for BART held at St. Mark's Playhouse on March 1, 1965. Like many other productions of BART, the production of this play had to overcome the destructiveness of various persons associated with BART. During the rehearsals for *Experimental Death Unit #1*, director Barbara Teer was slapped by one of the Patterson brothers,[3] and so Jones was forced to take her place.

Although the play's content is racially militant, its form reflects Jones's soon-to-be-discarded fondness for the European avant-garde. The three major characters in *Experimental Death Unit #1* are two heroin-addicted white bums and a female black prostitute. The two bums, Duff and Loco, are modeled on Samuel Beckett's characters in *Waiting for Godot*. As they stand on a street corner during a winter storm, they engage in an irrational but eru-dite conversation about beauty and life. Suddenly their conversation is inter-rupted by a once beautiful but now burned-out black prostitute who emerges from the alley. She propositions them. The two white men engage the woman in sexual banter, using sexually explicit images to convey what they would like to do to her. Duff states,

> I am to be used in all your vacancies. All those holes in your body I want to fill. I got meat and mind to do it with. I mean out there in the street. I'll throw you down . . . mount you, giddyap! giddyap! big-assed nigger lady! . . . then I ride you right out through the rain . . . maybe licking your neck.[4]

One of the white men asks her how much she charges. She responds, "I charge just what you owe." Duff is baffled by her answer, but Loco responds to him, "You fool, we owe everything." Loco wants her badly and begs her to let him lick her. Duff is initially disgusted that his friend finds this filthy black whore so enticing. Loco breaks free of Duff's efforts to restrain him and runs to the black woman, on whom he performs oral sex. Duff walks away, stops momentarily, and ultimately gives in to his own sexual desire. He races to the black prostitute and tries to pull Loco away from her. They fight, and Duff beats him unconscious. Throughout the fighting, the woman is cheering on Duff with cries of "kill him, kill him."

With Loco sprawled on the ground, Duff can now have intercourse with the black woman. Duff and the woman begin to copulate in the hallway but are interrupted by a paramilitary group of young blacks marching down the street. At the front of the group we see one of the black youths holding a spike with a severed white head impaled on it. The leader of the paramilitary group orders Duff and the black woman to come out. Unafraid of these "soul brothers," the prostitute comes out of the hallway with Duff behind her. She tells Duff that she will handle this interruption. The leader of the group gives an order for the soldiers to shoot Duff and the black woman. The black woman is killed. Duff screams "niggers, niggers" as he is dying. Beaten and lying on the ground, Loco is heard murmuring something about "a little pussy . . . I need it, baby." He then dies. The black youth cut off the heads of the two white men, place them on poles, and march off.

Experimental Death Unit #1, the first play that Jones wrote after *The Slave*, is a kind of transition play. Although it is the first of Baraka's explicit agitprop plays directed toward a black audience, his borrowing of themes and characters from Beckett testifies to the resilient but soon to be abandoned influence that Western avant-garde playwrights still had on him.

Henry Lacey argued that the black woman in the play must be killed because she is a knowing participant in her own subjugation.[5] She possesses knowledge about the immoral character of whites and their historical participation in her subjugation, and yet she does not change her ways. For

Theodore Hudson, the meaning of the play was clear: blacks who choose to prostitute themselves to whites should be executed.[6] Sollors viewed the play as an attempt by Baraka to exorcise his bohemian demons. That is, what Baraka once considered acts of bohemian freedom he now regarded as the manifestations of decadence. Perhaps each of these commentaries is correct. Nonetheless, the play's meaning remains quite simplistic.

A BLACK MASS (1965)

A Black Mass was first performed in May 1966 at Proctor's Theater in Newark, New Jersey. The play is a dramatic interpretation of the myth of Yacub. According to Nation of Islam mythology, Yacub was the evil scientist who more than 6,000 years ago created white people by genetically altering a black man. One student of the Nation of Islam described Yacub's project:

> By practicing a strict code of birth control, killing all the darker babies and saving the lighter ones and letting them breed, he produced the brown race. By successive gene manipulation, Yacub grafted new races in intervals of 200 years, each lighter than the one before, possessing less and less divine substance. After 600 years, a race of weak-blooded, weak-boned, weak-minded, pale-faced people was finally grafted: the blond, blue-eye white devil. The white man is thus neither truly human nor created by God. He is . . . totally deprived of divine substance, which makes him intrinsically evil by nature.[7]

The opening scene of A Black Mass takes us back in time to an ancient African-Islamic civilization. We see three black scientists/magicians at work in a chemical factory. The signs on the wall are written in Arabic and Swahili. Two of the scientists are swaying to music while working. The third one ignores the music as he intently studies a book. He seems not to be connected to his environment, as if he "lives in his head." His name is Jacoub. The two rhythmic scientists are working on a potion that will inspire blacks to "dance mad rhythms of the eternal universe until time is a weak thing." Time, we learn, had been invented by Jacoub earlier. Considered a form of "white madness," time distorts and dominates life. Because of time, people have discarded the natural flows of their daily and seasonal rhythms.

While the two other scientists are trying to find an antidote to time, Jacoub is at work trying to create a new organism. The work has consumed his life for quite a while. The other two magicians are repulsed by his creation of time, which they view as evil. But Jacoub rejects this assessment of his invention because he does not believe that any knowledge could, in and of itself, be evil. The three scientists debate whether they need to know everything. The two rhythmic scientists believe that they already know everything of value. Jacoub, however, wants to be like God and create something new even though there is not a need for his creations. That is, he believes in the pursuit of knowledge as an end in itself, whereas the others view knowledge as useful only if it contributes to a harmonious, humane life.

Eventually Jacoub admits that he is trying to invent a new kind of person or what he calls a "neutral being." This new being will be in love with time. In response to the questions from the other two scientists, Jacoub describes his creation as "a being who will not respond to the world of humanity. A being who will make its own will and direction. . . . A being like us, but completely separate."[8] The discussion is interrupted by several terrified women who run into the laboratory. The scientists admonish the women for coming in, as females are not allowed in the holy sanctuary of the chemical laboratory. The women are screaming that evil is loose in the world, that the rhythms of life are in disarray. Even the stars are out in the daytime. We then hear a vast explosion and see a blinding light. With the music of Sun-Ra blaring in the background, a beast appears. He is white with a red, lizard-devil mask. Everyone screams at the sight. The beast leaps into the audience and hops around, all the while screaming, "White, white, white." He leaps back onto the stage and continues chanting while hoping around and vomiting.

The other two scientists immediately recognize that Jacoub has created a monster. The creature has neither feelings nor a soul. It is a being capable of killing other humans. Jacoub has created the world's first murderer. In a frenzy, the beast grabs one of the black women by the throat. Soon after, she clutches her throat and turns into a grunting white beast hopping around on stage. She too begins to chant, "White, white, white." The scientists cast a spell that imprisons the two beasts in an invisible cell. Although Jacoub is distressed by the changes in the woman, he still believes it is possible to teach the beast how to feel. The two other scientists disagree, for they know that the beast cannot be taught humaneness. Sure of his ability to teach the beasts, Jacoub breaks the spell and releases the two beasts from their invisible confinements. Once freed, the two beasts attack and kill the two scientists and the women gathered around. Only then does Jacoub recognize his mistake. The beasts attack him. As he is dying, he imposes a curse on the beasts that banishes them to caves. After the beasts leave, we hear the narrator's voice over the loud speaker.

And so Brothers and sisters, these beasts are still loose in the world. Still they spit their hideous cries. There are beasts in our world, Brothers and Sisters. There are beasts in our world. Let us find them and slay them. Let us lock them in their caves. Let us declare the Holy War. The Jihad. Or we cannot deserve to live. Izm-el-Azam, Izm-el-Azam, Izm-el-Azam, Izm-el-Azam.[9]

"Izm-el-Azam" [May God have mercy] is repeated until the stage is black.

Baraka's play about Jacoub follows quite closely the tale of Yacub and the creation of the white race as developed in the Nation of Islam's mythos. Indeed, the play could have been cowritten by Elijah Muhammad! Though entertaining, the play is shallow and reactionary. Its primary message is that whites and blacks constitute morally antagonistic groups owing to their innate racial differences. By thus depicting whites as demonic and blacks as divine, *A Black Mass* celebrates the most banal form of racial essentialism.

Critic Larry Neal, one of Baraka's friends and a partner in the Black Arts Repertory Theater/School, was, however, thoroughly entranced by the play.

This is a deeply weighted play, a colloquy on the nature of man, and the relationship between legitimate spiritual knowledge and scientific knowledge. It is LeRoi Jones's most important play mainly because it is informed by a mythology that is wholly the creation of the Afro-American sensibility.[10]

Why Neal perceived such depth in this play is beyond my powers of explanation. Certainly, the mere fact that the play is based on a cosmological narrative created by black Americans does not in any way enhance the play's meaning.

JELLO (1965)

Like *A Black Mass*, *Jello* was written while Jones was working at the Black Repertory Theater School, but it was not published until 1970. Jones had originally intended to include it in *Four Black Revolutionary Plays*, and in an afterword to that collection is a short explanatory note entitled "Why No Jello."[11] According to Jones, the publisher, Bobbs-Merrill, refused to include the play in the collection, claiming that it attacked the private life of a public figure. Whether or not Jones's explanation is correct, Jack Benny's television show was certainly ripe for dramatic interpretation, however scandalous that might be. In retrospect, one can only agree with Jones's claim that Bobbs-Merrill's refusal to publish it was an attempt at censorship. Interestingly, this censorship may speak to the seriousness that certain white publishers granted to Jones and/or the new black writing. Jones, unwilling to concede defeat, claims that despite the publisher's efforts, the play has become well known throughout the black drama world.

Jello is a spoof on the Jack Benny radio and television show. Jack Benny played the central character whose assistant was Eddie "Rochester" Anderson. Baraka's play focuses on the newly rebellious Rochester. No longer willing to serve as Benny's jokester black flunky, Rochester has acquired a new militant attitude. Even his hair is no longer "conked." The scene is Benny's house which, we are told, is also the setting for the television show. The white comic calls for Rochester and casually orders him to get the car. Rochester responds in a way that Benny had never heard before: "What the hell you want man? Don't be calling me all the time. Damn, can't never get away from you." Benny hears the words coming out of Rochester's mouth but does not perceive them as threatening. He seems to think that Rochester is simply acting weird. It takes Benny a few moments to recognize that Rochester's manner of speech does not reflect his usual obsequiousness. Rochester makes his new attitude clearer. "You wanna go somewhere you get the car out in front yourself, and drive it yourself. Why I have to go with you?"[12] Now angered, Benny orders Rochester to get the car. No longer pretending to be the black man's friend, he has assumed the role of Rochester's white employer. He threatens to fire the Negro and then does so when Rochester doesn't jump at the threat. He predicts that the black man will become a bum now that he has lost his job as a chauffeur. Benny is surprised when Rochester robs him. Not satisfied with the three hundred dollars he has just taken from Benny's wallet, Rochester demands that Benny open his wall safe. Benny, fearful of being assaulted, opens it. A miser, Benny begins to cry inconsolably at the sight of Rochester stealing his money. Soon he is sprawled on the floor kicking and screaming like a "hysterical child." When Rochester asks Benny how he accumulated so much money, Benny answers that he worked hard for it. Rochester knows that not only has Benny underpaid him throughout their years of working together but that he also owns stores in Harlem that overcharge black customers.[13] Benny admits to owning these stores but claims ignorance of their business practices. Rochester clearly knows everything there is to know about Benny's life, and Benny knows little, if anything, about Rochester's. Sounding a great deal like LeRoi Jones, Rochester tells Benny that given the vacuity and sickness of his life, he should commit suicide.

Two other regulars from the show enter the set. One, an explicitly effeminate man, thinks that Benny is trying to fool him when he claims that Rochester has just robbed him. Then Rochester lifts this man's wallet without his realizing it. A white female regular member of the cast enters and also thinks it is a joke but then wonders whether Benny's pleas for help are real. Rochester admits that he has robbed Benny and that he also intends to rob her. She thinks and hopes that Rochester wants her sexually. But when he reaches under her dress, it is only to retrieve her hidden purse. Angered, she falsely accuses him of rape. Finally, the voice of the program's sponsor enters the set and cites Jello as the sponsor of the show. Rochester smacks him on the head, and he too falls near the other bodies. Rochester robs him of his wallet. A car horn is heard, at which Rochester screams out the window that he'll be right out. Rochester leaves. The play ends.

The play is quite hilarious, although it is shallow and lacks any kind of subtlety or complexity. According to Theodore Hudson, "The major point is that in every 'Negro' there is a potential black man—a point which is not missed by most black audiences." The question that Hudson should have asked was whether this play's major point is sufficiently engaging to sustain the drama. One can imagine black folks laughing at the play, but one cannot imagine them leaving with their political consciousness raised. Unfortunately, when coupled with the play's lack of finesse and variation, the weakness of the message led Hudson to conclude that the play would not "often fail to convulse audiences composed of society's common folk,"[14] thereby indicating the ways in which Jones's inferior dramatic productions were often interpreted, if not excused, by traditional black literary intellectuals. The play is unambitious because it is intended for audiences of black common folk. Never stated but clearly implied is the idea that these "common folk" cannot handle a more complex drama.

Literary scholar Werner Sollors analyzed the play in the following manner: "Despite its underlying criticism of art and television Jello does not transcend what Gerald Weales called a 'one-gag play.' Like most of Baraka's nationalist drama, it cannot be measured with the yardstick of *Dutchman* or *The Toilet*."[15] I agree.

GREAT GOODNESS OF LIFE: A COON SHOW

Great Goodness of Life: A Coon Show was first performed in November 1967 by the Spirit House Movers at the Spirit House in Newark. Court Royal, a fiftyish black man, stands bewildered in the center of the stage. He appears to be quite nervous, as if he were in a courtroom. Over a loudspeaker we hear various commands being directed to him. Although we never see the physical

body of the voice, we know that it is white authority. Court Royal tries to figure out the specific charges being brought against him, but Voice repeatedly
tells Court Royal to shut up. When he does, Voice tells him that he has been
charged with harboring a murderer. Court Royal denies the charges and is
puzzled as to how these false charges could have been made. After pleading
innocent, Court Royal states, "Of course I'm not guilty. I work in the Post Office. . . . Didn't you ever see me in the Post Office? I'm a supervisor; you know
me. . . . I'm no criminal. I've worked at the Post Office for thirty-five years.
. . . There must be some mistake."[16] Voice tells Court Royal that he will be assigned a court-appointed attorney. Rejecting the offer, the postal worker says
that he would rather be represented by his private attorney, John Breck. Soon
a buffoon-acting, smiling Uncle Tom figure crawls across the stage. A wire
that runs offstage is attached to his back much like that on an electronic toy.
In the side of his head, we see a huge "wind-up" key. Soon it becomes clear
that this mechanical figure is his lawyer, John Breck. Breck advises Court
Royal to plead guilty. Court Royal protests. Why should he plead guilty to unknown and erroneous charges? Once again the wired and wound-up John
Breck tells Court Royal to plead guilty. Now seeing the key lodged in Breck's
brain, Court Royal wonders why he looks like a human-size toy. Breck tells
him that he has always looked like that.

Suddenly over the loud speaker we hear the voice of Young Victim, who
directs his anger toward Court Royal.

> Now will you believe me stupid fool? Will you believe what I tell you or your
> eyes? Even your eyes. You're here with me, with us, all of us, and you can't
> understand. Plead guilty you are guilty stupid nigger. You'll die, they'll kill
> you and you don't know why now will you believe me? Believe me, half-
> white coward.

Voice orders the police to silence Young Victim. Over the loudspeaker we hear
the sounds of a beating. Young Victim speaks again: "You bastard. And you
Court Royal you let them take me. You liar. You weakling. You woman in the
face of degenerates. You let me be taken."[17] Court Royal hears the voice of
Young Victim and vaguely recognizes it but forgets when the sounds of rapidly firing machine guns come over the loud speaker. Fearful of being shot,
Court Royal pleads for his life. Seeing Court Royal whimpering, Voice erupts
in loud and sustained laughter. Hooded men drag a black woman across the
stage. They pull on her hair and run their hands freely over her body. They tell
Court Royal that she is drunk and ask him if he wants to smell her breath. He

refuses and declares that she "brings our whole race down." The hooded men return carrying the body of a dead black man on a stretcher. The dead man is referred to as "the Prince." When asked by Voice who killed him, the men respond, "a nigger did it for us."[18]

Court Royal continues to maintain his innocence in the face of repeated accusations from Voice. Voice asks him if he knows the man on the screen. When Royal looks at the screen (on the wall behind him) the images of King, Garvey, Medgar, and so forth flash in rapid succession. Court Royal claims that he cannot tell who they are. Voice accuses him of lying. Once again Court Royal claims never to have seen those faces. Voice tells him that he is guilty and must be sentenced. Court Royal, defeated, now awaits his death. At this moment of resignation, Voice suddenly declares him innocent. Court Royal is elated. Voice informs him that he can go after he completes one last task. Court Royal learns that Voice will free him if he shoots the murderer. Even though Court Royal does not realize that the so-called murderer is actually Young Victim, the audience knows. Court Royal does not want to shoot anyone but agrees to do so when Voice convinces him that the young murderer is not really alive but is only a shadow. By shooting the murderer's shadow, Court Royal will free himself from guilt, shame, and blame. For carrying out this act, his soul will be washed "white as snow."

Court Royal aims and shoots the supposed shadow of the so-called murderer directly in the face at point-blank range. As his body collapses, Young Victim utters the word "Papa." He dies. Immediately, Voice declares Court Royal innocent and free. Elated, Court Royal repeats, "My soul is as white as snow, my soul is as white as snow." The play ends as Court Royal, now jovial, asks Louise, his wife, if she knows where his bowling bag is.

Great Goodness of Life is dedicated to Jones's father. The name of the protagonist, Court Royal, is similar to that of Jones's father, Coyette. Moreover, Coyette Jones had been an employee of the Post Office. Jones has admitted that the play was written with his father in mind.[19]

The play can be read on many different levels. On a literal level, the play is about a middle-class black man who, in his haste to do anything and everything demanded of him by white authority, willingly murdered his own son. On a different level, the play might be a statement that the subjugation of blacks can continue only as long as blacks continue to devalue themselves psychologically. By murdering Young Victim, Court Royal has actually murdered blackness and a belief in black people. As Benston notes, "The guilt that he avoids by killing his own son is merely the oppressor's condemnation. The real crime and guilt are the higher sins of moral and spiritual betrayal."[20]

SLAVE SHIP (1967)

Slave Ship was first staged at the Chelsea Theater Center in New York City, on November 8, 1969. The setting is a slave ship. Although the theater is completely dark, the audience can hear sounds of heavy chains, African drums, the splashing of the sea, whips, and guns. There constantly are screams and cries of human agony. We first see white sailors smiling and laughing with one another as they anticipate the riches that will be theirs when they trade the "black gold" in the ship's hold. Chained black women are heard speaking in African tongues calling on African deities. Children are crying. Men are trying to calm the frightened women, although they, too, are crying out for their gods Shango, Obatala, and Orisha. Using the chains, one woman strangles her child and then herself. The others weep and pray to their gods for deliverance and the souls of their dead comrades. One male slave tries to rape one of the women but is thwarted when another African male fights him off. We repeatedly hear the captured Africans calling their white captors "Devils." The African drumming is unceasing. The stage lighting emphasizes the juxtaposition of the gleeful white sailors and the desperate black cargo.

The setting shifts to a group of slaves in the colonies/states. One slave is depicted as a subservient Uncle Tom. Scratching his head in stereotypical fashion, he shuffles to the center of the stage where he speaks to the white man in Willie Best fashion: "I'm so happy I jus don't know what to do."[21] Other slaves are shown discussing rebellion and making plans to slit the master's throat. We learn that the rebellion being planned is Nat Turner's. The Uncle Tom slave tells the white slave master about Turner's plot. All that he asks for in return is a pork chop. At this point, we see scenes depicting the fighting between slaves and masters and the subsequent repression of the Turner revolt. The Uncle Tom is seen happily eating his pork chop.

The scene then changes to more contemporary times. Instead of calling to African deities, we see blacks calling out to Jesus. A Negro preacher (played by the Uncle Tom figure) speaks in an obsequious manner about the need for peace and nonviolence. Interspersed throughout his dialogue is rhetorical gobbledygook that resembles the inarticulate utterances of the white family in Baraka's play *Home on the Range*. The preacher's servile performance is interrupted by a slave woman's crying out for her stolen child, presumably taken away from her and sold to another master. As if depicting the continuing subjugation of black girls, a bloody and burned corpse of a small girl is placed before the Negro preacher. This girl, we are supposed to believe, is one of the victims of the church bombing in Birmingham. The minister grins while he tries to push the girl's corpse behind him. It is apparent that he would rather talk about his Christian ideals than deal with the reality of the girl's murder.

The sounds of a saxophone and drums break through the silence, and the black bodies that were sprawled out on the floor of the stage come to life. The people are rising metaphorically and literally. The singing mixes with the drumming and the screams of the slave ship. The cast breaks into song:

> *Rise, Rise, Rise*
> *Cut these ties, Black Man Rise*
> *We gon' be the thing we are . . .*
> *When we gonna rise up, brother*
> *When we gonna rise above the sun*
> *I mean, when we gonna lift our heads and voices*
> *When we gonna show the world who we really are*
> *When we gonna rise up, brother*
> *When we gonna take our own place, brother*
> *Like the world had just begun.*[22]

The lyrics are repeated. During the singing, black bodies continue to rise from the floor. The arisen blacks form a dance line like that of the Temptations of 1960s Motown fame. Others join the line but do an African dance. Nevertheless, the rhythmic movement of all is clearly seen and felt. The dance and drums have a symbolic power that is distinctly black.

The preacher is afraid of the rising rhythmic black masses, and the music and dance make him aware of his impending doom. He begs the white man for protection. We hear the voice of the white man laughing at the sight of the preacher.

> PREACHER: Please, boss, these nigger goin' crazy; please, boss, throw you' lightin' at 'em, white jesus boss, while light god, they goin crazy! Help! . . . Please, boss, please . . . I do anything for you.

The servile, frightened preacher is surrounded by the blacks. They kill him and then go in search of the white voice. The white voice at first laughs at their intentions and then, upon realizing that the blacks are serious, changes to a plea.

> VOICE: . . . you haha can't touch me . . . you scared of me, niggers. I'm God. You cain't kill white Jesus God. I got long blond blow-

hair. I don't even need to wear a wig. You love the way I look. You want to look like me. You love me. You want me. Please. I'm good. I'm kind. I'll give you anything you want. I'm white jesus savior right god pay you money nigger me is good god be please . . . please don't.[23]

The audience hears the wretched scream of the white voice as it is killed by the empowered, freedom-seeking blacks. The stage is dark again.

The lights of the theater then come up, and the cast members begin to dance on the stage. They go into the audience and recruit blacks to join them in the dancing. Once again we hear the song "When You Gonna Rise." At a point when the dancing is going strong and the audience is relaxed, the severed head of the Uncle Tom preacher is thrown onto the center of the stage floor. After a pause, the dancing resumes even more enthusiastically. The play ends.

Slave Ship has been known to generate intense reactions from the audience. Harry Elam Jr. noted:

> At one performance of *Slave Ship* in Baton Rouge, Louisiana, an aroused audience bolstered by the militant participatory action of the production stood at the end of the performance ready to riot. If not for the fact that the doors of the theater remained bolted until the fervor had subsided somewhat, this audience certainly would have acted on its resolve. At another performance . . . in West Point, Mississippi, the entire audience rose to its feet and joined with the actors, waving fists and chanting, "We gonna rise up!"[24]

Slave Ship's director, Gilbert Moses, claimed in an interview with Harry Elam that in some southern cities, black voter registration increased immediately after a performance of the play.[25] Although Elam hesitated to draw too close a link between the play and political activism, he believed that the audience's participation in the play was in itself a form of political engagement. The intensity of the play was amplified by Moses' clever use of the entire theater as a stage, enabling the action to take place next to where someone was seated or even behind him. By shortening the distance between the performers and the audience, the audience was invited, if not forced, into an emotional engagement with the horrors depicted in the play. At one performance at the Chelsea, slaves were auctioned to members of the audience.

Slave Ship represents the high point of Baraka's allegiance to Artaud's theater of cruelty. According to Leslie Sanders,

> *Slave Ship* embodies the quintessential theater-of-cruelty experience, for it creates for its audience not only the experience of the horror of the Middle Passage and black life in America but also an energy that gathers strength in the course of the play to emerge as celebration in the end.[26]

Baraka's intentions were different from Artaud's desire to purge the audience of the desire to act violently. Instead, Baraka believed that by heightening emotional confrontations through drama, he was helping create and sustain political activism on the part of the blacks in his audience. Elam agreed with Baraka and invoked the theories of August Boal in Baraka's defense.[27] Boal, using Brecht as his model radical artist, believed that the theatrical spectacle was at the beginning of the action. Baraka, however, instead of purging actors of their anger, wanted to intensify it and, in turn, inspire the audience to change the social order. I remain unconvinced that *Slave Ship* transcended a *ritual of rebellion*, a means of articulating a catharsis that ultimately serves to undermine political engagement. Rituals of rebellion can stimulate political activism, but they do so while diffusing an oppositional mentality. It is not an either/or but a both/and proposition.

The racial links between the black performers and the blacks in the audience was reinforced when at the end of the play, the black performers began to chant, "When we gonna rise. Rise, rise, rise, cut the ties, Black man rise."[28] As they chanted, they moved into the audience and shook the hands of blacks only. The performers invited some of the black audience members to dance with them on stage. While some performers and members of the audience were dancing, other performers urged the black audience members to chant along with them, "When we gonna rise. . . ."

Henry Lacey explained the meaning of the play's dance finale:

> The dance serves two vital functions. First, it invites the members of the audience to act out the aggression and violence which they have held in check both during the play and in their everyday lives. In this respect, the "loose improvisation" of this dance provides a real communal exorcism. The dance, with its unifying force, also celebrates the spiritual restoration of the black man. The final scene suggests that the primal energies of the African are now being reasserted, i.e., the former slave has reclaimed those vital elements of his being that were so brutally wrenched from him.[29]

The power of *Slave Ship* lay in its ability to enable the audience, albeit vicariously, to experience the immediate horrors of slavery, particularly as embodied in the wretched hold of a slave-trading vessel. Describing the reactions of New York drama critics to the play, Theodore Hudson wrote:

> Clurman called it a "theatrical phenomenon," *Newsweek*'s Jack Kroll reported the overwhelming intensity of the Free Southern Theater production of it; reviewer Edith Oliver declared, "the music by Archie Shepp and Gilbert Moses, and performed by six instrumentalists, sounds absolutely wonderful." . . . Kroll reported that ". . . slaves reached out clawing for help from the *New York Times*'s Clive Barnes, a nausea-racked slave retched realistically in the lap of Norman Nadel of the Scripps-Howard papers, and during a slave auction a little black boy was "sold" to the *New Yorker*'s Edith Oliver."[30]

It must have been extraordinarily difficult for Baraka to persuade black Americans to confront their slave past and in a manner that did not result in despair, rage, or a paralyzing shame. Many were undoubtedly hesitant to revisit this open historical wound that lay at the very center of their contemporary devalued status. *Slave Ship* was one of Baraka's greatest accomplishments.

AGITPROP PLAYS

In an effort to alter black people's political consciousness, Baraka wrote a series of agitprop plays. Whereas all drama can be construed as somehow didactic, agitprop drama is explicitly didactic. Kimberly Benston described Baraka's use of this genre:

> Every theatrical device is utilized with the primary intention of projecting political idea in an effort to educate black people to their fundamental tasks. This does not mean that these plays are entirely artless or dramatically uninteresting. On the contrary, they reflect Baraka's search for a dramatic experience capable of reaching large numbers of black people as directly as possible. Hence, like most successful agit-prop, these plays are highly contrived and their appearance of simplicity is often gained with much effort.[31]

Even though Benston captures the playwright's ambitions, he is far too generous and uncritical in his artistic assessment of his plays.

Many of the Baraka's most popular plays from this era were agitprop productions, one of the best known being *Arm Yourself or Harm Yourself*. A very short and direct play, it begins in darkness as the police try to force open the door of an inner-city apartment. Once they break down the door, they storm inside and randomly fire their weapons. Next we see two black men and one black woman sitting in the living room of an apartment. Evidently, these three have survived a police assault. The black men begin to argue about how they can resist the racist police assaults. One of them suggests taking up arms, but the other believes that it would be futile. Their argument is interrupted by a black man who stumbles into the room and dies. His wife, the surviving woman, tells the two men that her husband was murdered by the police for trying to protect her from their assault. The argument between the two men continues and eventually escalates into a physical fight. While fighting, white police break down the door and kill the three black people.

Although the play's message is contained in its title, the play also speaks to the dangers to black activists who spend more time arguing and fighting with one another than in preparing for the state's impending assault. In this sense, the play could have been a critique of the U.S.-Panther conflict, but there is little reason to assume that Baraka intended it to be interpreted in this fashion.

A second, though perhaps less well known agitprop play, *Police*,[32] picks up on the theme of police repression against black Americans. This play is about the traitorous behavior of a demented black policeman who indiscriminately murders a black man. The black community then persuades the black murderer to commit suicide. Once dead, his white comrades on the police force eat his body.

CHANT (1968)

Not to be confused with *Black Power Chant*,[33] *Chant* is not really a play but a ritual, a series of choreographed movements interspersed with the performers' chanting. Beyond a nebulous invocation of the power of patriarchal black nationalist unity to defeat white racism, the meaning of *Chant* is unclear.

Black women begin the ritual by shuffling across the stage with their heads bowed. They form circles and perform syncopated movements while loudly humming. Black men enter the stage shuffling as the women depart. They also perform syncopated movements while shuffling and humming aloud. Women are then heard offstage shouting in unison "God God God God God God / Devil Devil Devil Devil Devil Devil." The women reenter the stage shuffling in circular formations and repeating in unison "God God God / Black Truth Black Truth Black Truth / Help us Move, Help us

Move." They then shuffle in a circle around the men who are inside the circle chanting "Black Man's Nation Black Man's Nation." After various other movements and additional chants, the play ends as the men and women engage in a final syncopated movement to the sound of the Impressions' "We're a Winner," a popular song from the late 1960s affirming the ultimate victory of black people.

We can only wonder what was going through Baraka's mind when he composed this chant. It was probably conceived as a piece that could be performed in order to intensify the energy and focus of a political gathering.

HOME ON THE RANGE (1968)

According to the notes in the published version of the play, *Home on the Range*[34] was produced at Spirit House in the spring of 1968 and taken on tour that year by the Spirit House Movers and Players. One of the play's main components is the music of Albert Ayler. A male voice chanting "black" and "blackness" is heard as Ayler's music is played.

The play begins with Black Criminal looking through the window of a house. Inside, a white family is watching television and chatting. The chatter is audible but unintelligible. Black Criminal knocks at the front door and enters with a gun drawn. Despite showing fear and later humor, the family continues to speak in the unintelligible language.

> SON: Gash. Lurch. Crud. Daddoon
> FATHER: Yiip. Vachtung. Credool. Conchmack. Vouty
> MOTHER: Greenchnool crud lurch.

Black Criminal is bewildered by their weird language. At one point, he shouts, "What kind of shit is this? What the fuck is wrong with you people?" The family responds with their unintelligible chatter and even explodes into laughter.

Criminal is then startled by laughter that comes out of the television set. Shocked and momentarily thrown off balance, Criminal points his gun at the television set, but the laughter coming from it intensifies. The family mimics the laughter on the television. They fall on the floor in a state of uncontrolled hilarity. Criminal is still baffled by the family and fires his gun at the television set. The family stops laughing when the television tube explodes. Black Criminal is still intent on persuading the family to speak in an intelligible language.

CRIMINAL: What? Godamit, why do you people talk like that? What kind of language is that? I'm no fool. I been places. What kind of language are you speaking?[35]

Criminal's inability to communicate with Family continues. A voice is heard over a hidden loudspeaker saying, "This is the voice of god . . . everything's cool! Criminal shoots at the hidden loudspeaker. It stops. The family gets up screaming in unison "light, light, light, light." Criminal understands this word but doesn't understand what they mean by chanting it repeatedly. He talks to himself about having entered the house to carry out an honest robbery and instead finds himself at the "funny farm."

After falling asleep and being awakened by the family, Criminal leads them in a rendition of "American the Beautiful" and then a version of "Lift Every Voice and Sing." Tears form in Criminal's eyes when he hears the Negro national anthem. As they all sing, a crowd of blacks crashes through the door. They are acquaintances of Criminal. He wonders why they have come. One of them puts on some records, and they all begin to dance. The family joins the blacks in dancing, but their dances are spastic, crazy, or homoerotic. At this point, Criminal turns to the audience and delivers a soliloquy that encapsulates the meaning of the play. As he talks, he periodically fires his pistol over the heads of the audience.

This is the tone of America. My country 'tis of thee. . . . This is the scene of the Fall. The demise of the ungodly. This is the cool takeover in the midst of strong rhythms, and grace. . . . Run bastards. Run. You grimy motherfuckers who have no place in the new the beautiful the black change of the earth. Who don't belong in the motherfucking world. Faggot Frankensteins of my sick dead holy brother. . . . You betta' get outta here. . . . The World![36]

After the Criminal's speech, the stage darkens. The next scene is in the living room of the house where the exhausted family is lying in a circle in the middle of the floor, and the blacks are asleep around them. Criminal tries once again to engage Father in dialogue. Drowsy Father says that Family are evil ghosts without substance. All the blacks awaken, but the family remains asleep except for nodding Father, who again informs Criminal that the family used to be phantoms. One of the black girls who has awakened looks out the window of the house and says, "Good Morning, Men. Good Morning." The play ends.

Sollors thought that Baraka's use of an unintelligible language for the whites was a reference to the unintelligible "native languages" spoken by blacks in racist movies depicting Africa.[37] The whites are overcome by the energy and dynamism of the black folks, a sign of the superior culture of black Americans over that of the "weird-talking greys." Baraka uses tricks from the theater of the absurd to depict whites as not only mindless but decadent. Benston thought that the play was baffling:

> A collage of absurdity, farce, social satire, mythology, and apocalyptic vision, it seems designed to make a series of quick, catching, and only loosely related impressions on a large audience. It . . . succeeds in making simple fun of "goofy" white Americans. Yet it is diffuse and unfocused, more entertaining than educational.

The youthful Benston, who seemed to be infatuated with Baraka's work, was able to say of this play that it "is probably the least powerful of Baraka's agit-prop pieces."[38] One of Baraka's favorite and most frequently used techniques for symbolizing the power of black people over whites was to depict the cowering of whites in the face of intensifying sounds of black music and rhythms of black dance, bringing to mind Baraka's image of a thousand spooks storming America. What remains unclear about the play is the collusion of the blacks in the irrationality of the whites. If the whites are phantoms of former selves, how do we explain the ease of the blacks' interaction with them? Even if the blacks are authentically alive, they remain confused and depoliticized. It is almost as if Baraka is chiding black people for loving to party in the face of everything. After all, Criminal parties, even though his thieving has been unsuccessful, and his friends come to party for no reason at all. Blacks, we might conclude, are willing to do anything in order to frolic, even if it means dancing and romping with the dead and deadly.

THE DEATH OF MALCOLM X (1969)

No figure throughout Baraka's writing is more revered than Malcolm X, so it was not surprising that Baraka dramatized Malcolm's life or, rather, the circumstances surrounding his assassination.[39] The details of Malcolm's murder will probably never be known. It is a subject that has been an endless source of speculation in black political circles. Malcolm's larger-than-life image, coupled with the avalanche of public suspicions concerning his murder, would seem to make his assassination ripe for dramatic interpretation. Baraka's interpretation of Malcolm's death is governed by the assumption that the U.S. government in partnership with a cabal of powerful whites ordered his assassination. This was and remains a common belief in black activist circles, and given the subsequent exposure of the COINTEL-PRO program, this popular explanation is possible.

The setting of the first scene is Uncle Sam Central, a place where white men in Uncle Sam uniforms are obviously quite busy. In the hallway hangs a sign telling us that this is the Institute for Advanced Black Studies. Seen lying on stretchers are numerous drugged Negroes who are strapped down, awaiting their transfer to an operating room in the institute. Once inside, white surgeons remove their black "mindsouls" and brains and replace them with white ones. We are offered a glimpse into a classroom at the institute where four Negroes who have already been racially lobotomized are being taught to repeat "White is Right." In another room we see a white man rehearsing several black men on their plans for entering the Audubon Ballroom, shooting Malcolm, and escaping during the ensuing commotion. We then look again into the institute's classroom where the Negroes can be seen laughing uncontrollably at movies showing racist caricatures of blacks.

The scene changes. White men are discussing the readiness of their plans, and a Klansman is talking with the President of the United States (dressed as a hippie) about authorization for Malcolm's assassination. He asks what is holding up the authorization. The hippie President answers that the authorization will soon arrive but that in the meantime the Klansman should make sure that his "people" are ready to go, particularly the Negro preacher. The Klansman tells the hippie President that the old nigger (the preacher) is giving them a little trouble but that he will be fine once he is paid.

Back at the institute, blacks can be heard repeating after their white instructor that the Greeks were the "beginning of thought—the beginning of Culture." Soon the Klansman is on the phone with the Negro preacher, who is popularly thought to be a civil rights leader but who is actually on the Klansman's payroll. Evidently the preacher is balking at participating in the plan to murder Malcolm, but the Klansman warns him that he must either go along with the plan or lose his congregation. In a quick succession of scenes, the fat Klansman is depicted in various absurd states of sexual intercourse with a dim-witted white woman. The President finally gets authorization for Project Sambo, the assassination of Malcolm X. The scene then switches to a studio at a television station where Malcolm is speaking into the camera. "No, finally it is the fact that you are evil. Evil. It is that simple fact that will animate the rest of the world against you! That simple alarming fact of your unredeemable evil. You are all disqualified as human beings, disqualified by your inhuman acts." The Klansman sees Malcolm on the television and proclaims, "Yr right nigger but what good will it do you" and then laughs hysterically.[40]

The Negro preacher, disguised as a civil rights leader, is seen leading an interracial march. The marchers are chanting, "Let us be Americans." The marchers, including some of the lobotomized black individuals earlier seen at the institute, are singing "We shall be white." (I suspect that this song was sung to the tune of "We Shall Overcome.") Most of the spectators along the parade route are white. They are either cops or civilians dressed in Uncle Sam outfits. The marchers kneel and pray in unison: "Oh white Northamerican God, help us to be like you and your loved ones." At the very moment that they kneel, the President comes on television denouncing violence, although he cannot do it with a straight face. Soon afterward, the police attack the marchers, but no one lays a hand on the Negro preacher-leader. He stands tall and angelic. Amid the human carnage of the police assault, the preacher proclaims, "Go home my children . . . we have proven our point, that love is stronger than hate . . . we have won, we will be white, we will be whiter than they are . . . whiter, much whiter."[41]

The scene shifts to the next morning and the interior of an airplane flying from Washington, D.C., to New York. On it are the lobotomized blacks who have been trained to assassinate Malcolm. Their white instructor is leading them through a final rehearsal of the plans. When the drill is finished, the "Star Spangled Banner" is played over the address system. As if on command upon hearing the national anthem, the assembled Negroes of the hit squad fall to the floor and proceed to lick the white man's shoes. The scene shifts to Malcolm awakening at home. His wife and children are already up. His aide urges him to hurry so that they won't be late. Malcolm, his bodyguards, and his family engage in friendly banter.

We next see simultaneous depictions of the President, the Klansman, and a corrupt white banker, all of whom appear to be anxiously awaiting an announcement of good news. At the same time, the Negro preacher is standing on stage before an all-white audience receiving an award "for meritorious service." The white audience applauds vigorously.

Malcolm is now seen entering the Audubon Ballroom with his wife and children. Black people are also arriving. White cops are standing around. The hit squad also enters. One of them gives a knowing glance to a policeman. The scene flashes back once again to the Negro preacher on stage now joined by his wife. A close-up of his award is shown, a life-size watermelon made of precious stones and gold.

Now we see the Klansman, the banker, and the hippie President in their offices when the television news interrupts normal programming for a special bulletin. Although Malcolm has not yet been shot, it is apparent that the media are aware of the plans for his murder and so deliver a special news bulletin before it happens. Malcolm begins his speech. Soon he is gunned down as television cameras carry the events live. White men in various offices are seen "howling with laughter or even grinning half embarrassed at their victory." The television announcer states, "Today, black extremist Malcolm X was killed by his own violence."

The assassins disappear into a waiting car and helicopter. As Malcolm clutches his chest, the Negro preacher is seen putting on his Uncle Sam suit. The play ends as all the important white figures in the play are attending a party dressed in Uncle Sam suits. Later they can be heard chanting in unison, "white, white, white."

The play could be viewed as a rather straightforward narrative of the logic behind Malcolm's death. The play combines realism with moments of absurdity, but its principal effect is to hammer home the point that Malcolm was killed on the order of powerful whites who were afraid of the impact of his message on black people. Ironically, the narrative distorts important historical points in order for Baraka to tease out of Malcolm's murder a black separatist message. For instance, the Malcolm who is deemed worthy of assassination in Baraka's play is the dogmatic black nationalist Malcolm of his Nation of Islam days. But in real life, the man who was assassinated was the post–Nation of Islam Malcolm. Many contemporary interpreters of Malcolm believe that his political views became much more subversive to the state when he discarded the racial essentialism that Baraka found so attractive. Baraka's play conspicuously avoids any mention of the Nation of Islam's possible complicity in Malcolm's assassination.

Like so many of his other works from this period, the play is characterized by a simplistic, Manichaean racial/moral divide: good blacks versus bad whites. Baraka could not have sustained this crude formulation if he had included the Nation of Islam as one of Malcolm's foremost detractors during the period before he was killed. In addition, Baraka's desire to maintain the dichotomy of good blacks / bad whites explains why he cannot grant moral autonomy to those blacks who participated in the assassination. The lobotomized blacks of Baraka's plays are essentially white men, for in Baraka's mind, no right-thinking black person could have helped murder Malcolm. Besides, if he had written the script to include the Nation of Islam in Malcolm's murder (or even hinted at the possibility of its collusion in his murder), the play would have tilted toward the tragic or pathetic. Baraka of the Black Arts did not want to portray black life as tragic but as either victorious or heroic. Even though the forces behind Malcolm's assassination are predictable in this play,

Malcolm's heroism is beyond question. Insofar as whites and white-like blacks murdered him, Malcolm's heroism can be imagined as black-group heroism, as opposed to the individual heroism that would have resulted from implicating the Nation of Islam.

The image of the Negro preacher is too simplistic. He comes across like a crude opportunist and a mercenary fool. Instead of being a victim of his own misguided beliefs about the political efficacy of nonviolent civil disobedience, this caricature of King stands for nothing. It is not clear why he is in the play except to show the different reactions of white elites to Malcolm and King. The play also fails to sustain a rationale for the preacher's involvement in the murder of Malcolm. Yes, he is on the payroll of the Klan. Yes, he leads a nonviolent demonstration in which the participants are clubbed by the cops. But at no point does this play tell us why this demonstration was a necessary prelude to Malcolm's murder. Needless to say, Baraka makes all the white characters demonic.

Given the widespread belief in black communities that whites were somehow behind the assassination of Malcolm, it is not clear that this play actually teaches anyone anything; it simply mirrors existing theories. Worse, it does not offer a way out, for in his attempt to create whites as evil controllers of the world, Baraka inadvertently makes them omnipotent.

BLOODRITES (1970)

Bloodrites[42] was first produced by the Spirit House Movers in Newark in 1970. It is not a play in any traditional sense of the term. Instead, one might consider it a ritualized dramatization of the power of black cultural nationalism to confront and defeat the cultural authority of the devils (i.e., white folks).

The ritual begins as a black man and woman enter the stage in various stages of awakening. They stumble, walk fast, stumble again. Black poets enter the stage reciting poetry. The poems awaken the black man and woman into a higher consciousness of sorts. Both of them begin to chant "Black Black Black Black." The poets celebrate this new energy and unity by slapping their palms and repeating "Yeh, Yeh, Yeh."

Uniformed Devils (whites) enter the stage with guns. They proceed to build a nation of blocks and then march around their creation. The poets repeat "Yeh, Yeh, Yeh," but they now are unable to slap palms. The Devils counter their Yehs with "No, No, No." It appears as if the Devils have brought with them a new spirit/force that undermines the connectedness of the black poets. Soon the Devils and the black poets are engaged in a "death struggle." During the struggle, the poets regain their ability to slap hands. Sensing their problematic situation, some of the Devils leave the struggle and begin to sing "Eat of the host . . . love is the answer." A black man and woman succumb to the allure of this devilish Christian message and begin to dance and sing with the Devils. They begin to sing to the other black poets but are interrupted by an unknown and unseen voice over a loudspeaker.

> LOUDSPEAKER: A culture provides Identity, Purpose, and Direc-
> tion. If you know who you are, you will know who your enemy is.
> You will also know what to do. What is your purpose?[43]

The wisdom of the loudspeaker is repeated several times. Afterward, the blacks rejoin the death struggle as they chant "Black People, Black People." The Devils (whites) goose-step like the Nazis. Periodically they stop and identify themselves to the audience as various historical white figures: "I'm Jack Armstrong, I'm John Wayne, I'm FDR, I'm MacArthur, I'm Zeus, I'm the dudes that be with Sly."[44] At this point, the Devils form a goose-stepping chorus line, chanting: "We're Devils, We're Devils, OOOOO, We're Devils, OOO You know, you knew it, you knew it, we knew it, we knew it, we knew it too, We're Devils." The struggle is transformed into a dance. The loudspeaker voice is heard again. "Identity . . . Purpose . . . and Direction . . . our purpose must be the building and maintaining of our communities, and restoring our people to their traditional greatness." A voice over the loudspeaker directs several rhetorical questions to the audience while the actors on stage continue moving. The voice asks, "What can we do . . . who are we? . . . What is the purpose of your life? . . . what will you do with your energy? . . . in what direction?" In response, the heterosexual couples on stage embrace in a loving manner and meander throughout the theater in this embrace. As they walk, they speak to the audience: "We all need each other. If we are to survive. We all need to love each other. How does that sound? It sound good. We all need to sound this good, forever. What about you, sister? What about you, brother, you love somebody?" At this point the song "What Does It Take" by Jr. Walker and the All Stars is played throughout the theater.[45]

Soon brothers start running around on stage very quickly. Now energized by black love and unity, they confront the "crackers." In the background, we hear the seven principles of the Nguzu Saba announced. As the black men run quickly and deftly, the whites move more and more slowly. Baraka's poem "Raise Race Rays Raze" is recited. Whites fall to the floor as if dead. The play ends as a the cast dances around the slain devils. The victorious blacks sing the refrain from "Cool Jerk," a popular song of that time: "Can you do it, can you do it can you do it can you do it."

This dramatization attempts to valorize the strength of the seven principles of the Nguzu Saba. It is interesting to imagine how this play was received by audiences who were not already devout believers of Kawaida. As agitprop drama, the play's message could easily be lost in the various twirls, shuffles, and marches. One of the criticisms of Baraka's agitprop plays is their heavy-handedness. This attempt to use more subtle symbolic statements and body movements to convey the forces of good and evil does not quite work. The subtlety of the symbolic movements does not mesh with the blatant simplicities of the rhetoric. Throughout his agitprop dramas, Baraka repeatedly has white characters chant "white, white, white," as if the audience could not otherwise discern their racial identities. Evidently, black audiences must be convinced that whites are obsessed with their whiteness. Nevertheless, such redundant chanting does not make an engaging drama. Baraka was so entangled in this "hate-whitey" syndrome that even when white characters are mentioned in the script instructions, he employed racial invectives (e.g., devils, crackers, beasts).

JUNKIES ARE FULL OF SHHH (1971)

Like several other agitprop plays written by Baraka, *Junkies Are Full of SHHH*[46] is specifically directed to a Newark audience. The play begins as a member of the Italian Mafia talks about his racist distaste for blacks. He admits that he has now been forced to hire a few niggers to sell drugs because Italian American youth are no longer attracted to the Mafia but are now going to college in pursuit of lawful upward mobility. The mobster is interrupted by a phone call from Hughie, the mayor of Newark (as in Hugh Addonizio). The mayor informs him that blacks in the city's south ward are engaged in political activities. The mayor is angered because the Mafia has not fulfilled its agreement to placate the black community by means of drugs. The mafioso tells the mayor that he will cool out the niggers by flooding the south ward with drugs. The mayor is calmed.

In the next scene, Bigtime, a Negro drug dealer, appears at the office of the mafioso operative to buy more drugs. But he requests smaller amounts than usual, whereupon the mafioso supplier accuses him of using the drugs himself rather than selling them:

Look Bigtime, don't shit me! The south ward ain't high as it shd be. Too much activity going on up there. A guy called me just before you come in. Too much runnin' around, political jazz going on over there, same in central ward. Now you told me you cd get people high.

Bigtime denies using the drugs but the Mafia figure knows that Bigtime is lying. Nevertheless, he needs Bigtime to distribute the drugs and calm the mayor's fears.

The second scene begins with Bigtime on the street selling drugs to regular buyers, including a young boy. A man tries to exchange a stolen television for drugs from Bigtime, but the drug dealer refuses to buy it because the woman who owns the television is chasing the addict with a knife. She confronts Bigtime and curses him for his role in the cycle of drug addiction that led to the theft of her television. While walking down the street, two politically conscious black nationalists who are identified by their Africanized names (Damu and Chuma) run into the young boy, who is high on drugs. They are stunned by this child addict. They threaten him with a beating and demand to know who sold him the drugs. He tells them about Bigtime. Damu and Chuma are next seen devising a plan to rid the streets of Bigtime and his white suppliers. They discuss their plan with a group of Simbas, the black young men who comprised the paramilitary wing of Baraka's CFUN organization.

In scene 3, we see Damu and Chuma talking with Bigtime on the corner. He denies selling drugs. They ask about his supplier, but Bigtime refuses to tell them. Then the two nationalists grab Bigtime and confiscate and burn his drugs while he looks on in shock. The pills that he also sells are taken from his pockets and thrown down the sewer. Bigtime screams, knowing that this theft of his drugs will probably lead to his death at the hands of the Mafia. He knows that he cannot return to the mafioso with the true story of what just happened. In anguish, he tells Damu and Chuma that they might as well kill him, for he is as good as dead. They beat him mercilessly. Writhing in pain, he tells them about his Mafia connection. Damu and Chuma demand that Bigtime take them to his suppliers. At first he refuses, but they trick him into believing that they are interested in selling large quantities of drugs. Bigtime recognizes this motive as valid but tells them that they did not need to steal his drugs or hit him if getting into the business was what they wanted to do. Bigtime calls his Mafia man and arranges a meeting. The Mafia man is elated to hear that even black nationalists are willing to sell dope. Repeating what Damu and Chuma told him, Bigtime tells the Mafia figure that even the brothers in the Committee for Unified Newark are staggering around high.

Unknown to Bigtime, Damu and Chuma hold a strategy session with the Simbas. They secretly devise a plan of action.

The fourth scene begins with the Mafia figures laughing about the prospect of getting black nationalists high on dope. They not only relish the possibilities of the huge profits they could make, but they also believe that the federal law enforcement authorities will treat them favorably if they are successful at "cooling out" the black nationalist activists. The Mafia are awaiting Bigtime and his soon-to-be drug-dealing, black nationalist acquaintances. Bigtime, Damu, and Chuma are seen entering the mafioso's building. When the Mafia man opens the door, he and the other Italian American drug suppliers are killed in a hail of bullets fired from the guns of the Simbas who have run through the door undetected. Bigtime is purposely not killed in the attack. He begs for his life and is reassured by Damu that they are not going to shoot him. Sensing his precarious situation, Bigtime begins to proclaim his aversion to drugs. He even recites the antidrug message that he will now carry to the streets. Instead of shooting him with a gun, Damu and Chuma inject him with an overdose of heroin. Bigtime screams, knowing that the overdose will kill him, and he dies. A sign is pinned to Bigtime's body.

The final scene shows Bigtime and one of the Mafia figures tied to a light pole in the middle of a busy intersection in Newark's black community. The sign on Bigtime's body reads "slave." The sign on the Mafia operative reads "master." A needle is visibly sticking out of Bigtime's arm. Street brothers are seen gazing at the two dead bodies, whispering and then quickly scattering. The stage goes black.

Given the cataclysmic impact of drugs in black urban neighborhoods, the play addressed an important issue. Black urban residents must have found the play compelling. The play is informative in depicting the link between the proliferation of drugs in black communities and white political domination. And the play de-romanticizes black urban drug dealers at a time when such figures were sometimes celebrated as urban folk heroes. In contrast, the play romanticizes the black nationalists, depicting them as selfless creatures who have only the best interests of the community at heart.

An unresolved tension in the play lies in its affected realism. On the one hand, it is a realistic drama of life in black neighborhoods. Yet the play is utter fantasy. It requires nothing less than a "willing suspension of disbelief" to imagine the black nationalists defeating drugs and the Mafia in such a violent and intimidating manner.[47] If the lesson of the play is the need for black nationalists to take violent action against drug dealers, why hadn't Baraka and his Simbas done this? Why create a fantasy of black nationalist agency?

One of the linchpins of the consciousness of the subjugated is the willingness of the oppressed to engage in fantasies of freedom. Black Americans have excelled in this creative endeavor through religious beliefs that depict emancipation in the "by and by." Although Baraka's play does not call for blacks to wait for a drug-free life in heaven, it does encourage the audience toward wishful thinking. It is a play premised on feelings of black impotence. I can imagine people walking out of the theater saying, "Wouldn't it be great if someone really did that?" Ironically, in writing a play about the dramatic defeat of Mafia drug lords by the actions of black nationalists, Baraka effectively admitted that he and his confreres would not do so in real life.

THE SIDNEY POET HEROICAL (1973)

Although *The Sidney Poet Heroical*[48] was not published until 1979, the play is a quintessential Baraka production of the Black Arts era. The central characters in the play are supposed to be close approximations of Sidney Poitier and Harry Belafonte.[49] In this play, Sidney comes from the West Indies seeking fame and fortune. He immediately meets Pearletta, a black woman who aspires to be white. She speaks to Sidney only after she covers her face with a white mask. Not only does she reject Sidney's advances, but she later fraternizes with a white man who has horns and a tail. She impresses the devilish white man with stories of her love of whiteness and disgust for blacks.

Sidney's life changes when he meets Lairee Elephont (later referred to as Elephonty). Lairee introduces Sidney to the world of instant black upward mobility which, in this play, means crass deference to all things white and a vehement desire to escape any attachment to blackness. A chorus warns Sidney to beware of the enticements of whiteness. He might be going in "over his head" into a world of decadence and death. But Sidney, tired of impoverishment and life on the streets, ignores the chorus and proceeds to model himself after Lairee. Throughout the play, one of the major inducements to this self-hatred-driven mobility is both financial gain and greater access to beautiful white women. Lairee is paired with a white woman who is, of course, depicted as possessing a crude and somewhat uncontrollable sexual desire for black men.

Sidney becomes a success. White people love his movies. Baraka even mentions actual Poitier films in the script. After the opening of each picture, Sidney is invited to a party where white people lavish praise on him. White women grab for his body. In the meantime, Sidney has started a relationship with Pearletta, the black woman. She now accepts him, since white people celebrate him as a success. After the opening night of *Defiant Ones* in which Poitier stars with Tony Curtis, the blacks in the audience boo the ending as intensely as the white folks cheer. The ending of the movie sees the Poitier character give up trying to escape in order to rescue the Curtis character. After the parties for *Raisin in the Sun* and *Lilies of the Field*, Sidney abandons Pearletta for white women. Even the nuns from *Lilies of the Field* are rubbing their bodies against Sidney in a sexually promiscuous manner. The blind young white woman who is befriended by Sidney in *Touch of Blue* refers to him as her "nigger helper." She tells him, "I can't see that you're a colored nigger." Baraka reserves his snidest comments about Poitier in regard to Katherine Hepburn, Spencer Tracy, and Katherine Houghton, the white actors in *Guess Who's Coming to Dinner*. In the play's most hilarious scene, Baraka has Sidney act like a hypersexualized buck in the living room before an approving Hepburn and a tolerant dad. Spencer Tracy gives Poitier a "pop-quiz" on the great thinkers of Western civilization. Sidney passes the test with ease, thereby earning Tracy's approval.

Next we see Sidney in bed next to a naked white woman. He is awakened by a talking, life-size Oscar award. The Oscar notifies Sidney that he should take a good look at himself. Sidney goes to the mirror and discovers that his skin has turned white. He is astonished at this development and covers himself with brown makeup so as to retain his black public identity. The chorus reappears and chides him for his new appearance. They remind him of their previous warnings. Sidney gets in touch with Lairee to ask his help in this matter. Lairee tells him that his problem isn't so bad and that he, too, has been wearing skin-darkening makeup for the same reason. Loss of color, in Lairee's mind, is a minor cost for their success in the white world. Sidney is thoroughly disgusted by Lairee and recognizes his sickness.

The turning point in Sidney's understanding of his racial self-hatred comes when he is offered the movie role of a white ape who is taught to read and write. Sidney refuses to play this role on the grounds that it is racially demeaning. Lairee tries to take the role from Sidney, but the movie producers really want Sidney to play White Pongo, the ape. Sidney still rejects it. The chorus appears and helps Sidney return to the black fold, Kawaida style. Predictably, Sidney and Pearletta get back together, but this time both confess their deep love of their black selves and the broader black nation. The play ends with their getting married in a Kawaidan ceremony.

In his review of the play, theater critic Mel Gussow wrote: "This exuberant comedy, written in 1969 but for obvious reasons—too hot to handle—not produced until now (by the Henry Street Settlement's New Federal Theater), permits the author to express himself simultaneously as artist and activist."

Although he believed that the portraits of the two main characters were "malicious, even savage," he thought that the actors playing the roles were able to make them charming. Gussow clearly perceived the play as politically engaged art, but it is not clear that he grasped Baraka's actual political intentions.

> The play is not just a theatrical equivalent of a roman à clef, but also a devastating commentary on the image of the American black in popular culture, the image demanded by whites and delivered, to order, by blacks. Sidney Poet is heroic because society needs him to be heroic. The author's criticism—and the play is an act of criticism as well as a piece of theater—is not directed so much against a specific personality as against a role (and movie roles) thrust upon him. He is projected toward his fate.

Gussow suggested that the play might have been improved had Baraka stepped aside as director. Nevertheless, he concluded that it was "a corrosive indictment of an American dream—and the plundering of that dream by the expectations of society. It makes us realize what a loss it was for the American theater when Mr. Baraka turned his attention primarily to political activism."[50]

Unlike Gussow, who saw a live performance of the play, I only read the script, and so my take on the play was quite different. Although I found it at times funny, the humor is not sustained. The play can easily appear insipid because Baraka was unable to restrain his satire. The lack of subtlety is reminiscent of other didactic plays written by Baraka during this period. The sledgehammer-like satirical overkill makes it more like a farce, thereby turning the play's meaning on its head. In this case, the play's resolution, in which Sidney and Pearletta adopt black cultural nationalism, becomes a ludicrous finale. The characters of Sidney and Lairee are far too overdrawn, plastic, and doctrinaire. There is literally no moment in the narrative that conveys any hint of human complexity. No character is developed. We do not even know why Sidney refuses to play the role of White Pongo, for before his refusal, Sidney had not shown any evidence of a prideful racial consciousness. The narrative of the play is somewhat asinine: success for blacks in mainstream America demands self-hatred and assimilation. The play's conclusion is trite. Imagine the former assimilationist-minded now-reformed black-loving Sidney becoming a practitioner of Kawaida! Tragicomedy has run amok! In his imprisonment in a warped notion of what constituted an authentic black person, Baraka of the Black Arts period was incapable of writing plays that granted any racial integrity to bourgeois blacks. This play is yet another example of the pedestrian art that he produced during the Black Arts period.

Sidney Poitier is ripe for dramatic interpretation. His rise to stardom was based on the role of the unthreatening black male. Poitier became acceptable to mass white audiences precisely because he never showed a sexual desire for any of his white female costars. He was a safe black man, a sort of cultural eunuch. Even in *Guess Who's Coming to Dinner*, Poitier is never seen embracing or even touching his white fiancée in any sexually or nonsexually suggestive manner. But in reversing Sidney's image, Baraka overkills him. Instead of the black eunuch, Baraka's Sidney is momentarily a black beast driven by passion. Yet Sidney, the black buck, does not generate fear in whites. Instead, his sexuality releases whites from their sexual inhibitions.

Before *Sidney Poet Heroical* was published, Baraka worried about being sued for libel.[51] The possibility of a lawsuit evidently became an obstacle to having the play produced. Because the play combines music, dance, drama, and film, the production costs also hindered its production. Evidently, Poitier did not sue Baraka or the theater that produced the play—probably Baraka overestimated the significance of his play to Poitier. Certainly this well-established Hollywood figure knew that his prominence could not be threatened by a marginal play written by a self-anointed Imamu.

Why did Baraka satirize Poitier and Belafonte so viciously? Both men were far more progressive and politically engaged than most other black actors. Belafonte had come to Newark to campaign for mayoral candidate Ken Gibson, and Poitier and Belafonte donated some of the receipts from the Newark premier of their movie *Buck and the Preacher* to the New Jersey delegation preparing to attend the National Black Political Convention in Gary.[52] Baraka could have celebrated them as politically conscious black actors.

CONCLUSION

Because Baraka was not subjected to rigorous critical analyses by those critics sympathetic to his political agenda, he was rarely challenged to realize his considerable talents. Instead, the mediocre was called brilliant and the rote labeled innovative. The tragedy of Baraka's writing lies in the pathos of a black intellectual groupthink that substituted political concerns for artistic quality. I am not sufficiently naive to have imagined Baraka as a man open to critical dialogue. After all, he was the Imamu. Baraka had to wait until he rejected black nationalism to admit that much of what he had written then was quite reactionary, but he never openly admitted that his writing during this period was aesthetically mediocre.

When Baraka moved from the Village to Harlem, he was accompanied by an extraordinary diminishment of his artistic ambitions. When writing for an explicitly black audience, Baraka's art became increasingly simplistic if not overtly asinine.[53] Indeed, Baraka usually wrote his best work when he imagined himself not writing exclusively for blacks. Baraka imagined the black mass populace as less sophisticated than they actually were, and many of Baraka's agitprop plays were downright condescending to black audiences. His image of the backward black community was a crucial fictitious construction, for it allowed Baraka to pretend that he had a superior political consciousness, a consciousness that gave him the right to teach and inform other blacks about their struggle. In hindsight, we can see that much of Baraka's understanding of politics and political change was far less sophisticated and informed than the ideas held by many "average" black Americans.

This is one of the significant paradoxes of Baraka's black art. In order to reach the black masses, Baraka assumed that his plays could not be complex, nuanced, or ambivalent. In his mind, the black community could not adequately engage or interpret complex materials. Ironically, Baraka's Black Arts era art was fundamentally informed by vestiges of the very racism that he thought he was in the vanguard of destroying. When most politically engaged in behalf of blacks, Baraka was most thoroughly estranged from them.

9

Kawaida

Totalizing the Commitment

IN HIS AUTOBIOGRAPHY, Jones writes that the initial days of his return to Newark were spent warding off despair. Part of this was due to the demise of the Black Arts Repertory Theater/School (BART) and his breakup with Vashti, the young "fly" black woman who had been his female companion since the end of his marriage to Hettie. In addition, shortly before he left BART, Jones had unintentionally impregnated Bumi, an eighteen-year-old woman and a member of an African dance troupe. Attracted to her youthful sensuality, Jones desired her only as a momentary sexual liaison.[1] Accordingly, he received the announcement of her pregnancy as dismal news, particularly after she steadfastly proclaimed, against his wishes, that she had no intention of obtaining an abortion. Instead, she expected Jones to take responsibility for her and their child and was devastated by his hesitation to do so. Feeling guilty about his disregard for the young woman's feelings, Jones finally allowed her to join him in Newark, where they lived in a run-down hotel frequented by pimps, prostitutes, and impoverished black migrants. Angry at himself and his irresponsible sexual promiscuity, Jones felt trapped. Depression ensued.

In an attempt to escape his rapidly constricting personal life, Jones returned to his dream of bringing black art to the black masses. He rented a large but inexpensive house in central Newark, and with several friends and neighborhood youths, he cleaned and painted it. They tore down walls and created a theater on the first floor. Spirit House was born. Having learned from the experience of the Black Arts Repertory Theater/School, Jones was far more knowledgeable about the particular demands of a Black Arts center. This time, he was on familiar turf and had fewer illusions about the need to tolerate the frenetic and destructive individuals who might be attracted to his new institution.

Jones organized the Afro-American Festival of the Arts, which was held in a neighborhood public park. Using his BART contacts, Jones was able to attract prominent black artists, critics, and political activists to the event, including Harold Cruse, Stokely Carmichael, and New York's Yoruba Temple Dancers and Drummers. The festival attracted sizable crowds, and equally important, it notified other Black Arts activists in Newark that LeRoi Jones had come home. Soon he began to interact with a group of like-minded, local Black Arts activists. Shortly thereafter, Jones and his Spirit House colleagues began to publish a magazine that featured the Black Arts. A repertory theater followed, and Jones produced two plays that he had written while at BART, *A Black Mass* and *Jello*. One of the lead actresses in *A Black Mass*, Sylvia Robinson, became, in a short time, his second wife and the most enduring and intimate companion of his life.

SYLVIA ROBINSON

Before she met Jones, Sylvia Robinson had been active in the emerging Black Arts movement in Newark. Jones wrote that Robinson, a dancer as well as an actress, "had a whole life as cultural worker in Newark that paralleled what we were trying to do at the black arts."[2] When they first met, Robinson, the mother of two, was in the process of divorcing her husband. Already divorced, Jones was the disengaged father of three children, and another child was on the way. A budding couple, LeRoi and Sylvia also had to decide what to do with the young expectant mother who was living with Jones on the third floor at Spirit House. Jones tried to persuade the two women to enter into a polygamous relationship with him. He later attributed his overtures to his deeply implanted sexism as well as his attraction to Yoruba cultural nationalism.[3] But neither Robinson nor the young woman would consent to Jones's proposal.

Robinson decided to leave Jones, but then tragedy struck. Bumi, the young expectant mother became ill and was rushed to the hospital where she remained in a coma until she died. For LeRoi and Sylvia, her death was a fortuitous calamity, as it enabled them to cultivate an intimate relationship. But Jones claims that for years, he and Sylvia felt extremely guilty about the young woman's death precisely because they knew that they had benefited from it.[4] In her memory, Jones wrote "Bumi," which reads in part:

> *I forgotten who*
> *I is*
> *I wanted to be some body*
> *and lost it*
> *I lost my self*
> *I lost love*

I left a girl
dying
I see her
all the time
I don't know
what
to do [5]

Robinson soon learned that Jones was far from ready to commit himself to a serious monogamous relationship. His chaotic and anarchic bohemian tendencies plus his entrenched male chauvinism must have made her quickly realize that a relationship with Jones would not be easy.

During the spring of 1967 Jones was a visiting professor at San Francisco State University. He had been invited by Jimmy Garrett, the president of its black student union, to organize cultural events at the school, particularly black dramatic productions. Robinson, several months pregnant with their child, accompanied Jones to the West Coast as Mrs. LeRoi Jones. With the aid of Marvin X and Ed Bullins, both of whom became prominent Black Arts movement artists, Jones was able to put together a repertory theater company that produced plays by Jones (*Mad Heart*), Bullins (*How Do You Do*), Ben Caldwell (*Militant Preacher*), Marvin X (*Taking Care of Business*), and Jimmy Garrett (*We Own the Night*). Leaving Jones to his busy creative schedule, Robinson returned to Newark alone to deliver their first child. Not until two weeks after Obalaji Malik-Ali was born did Jones first see his son. Robinson was not impressed by his priorities. [6]

In August 1967, LeRoi Jones and Sylvia Robinson were married. Sylvia later became known as Amina Baraka (Amina means faithful in Swahili). Baraka stated that the marriage fundamentally changed his life, and he credits his wife with forcing him to confront his sexism and the irresponsibility of his "bohemian ways."

> There was no doubt that I regarded Sylvia as a very singular woman, both sensual and intelligent, but I had thought that I would never get married again. I wanted to avoid those kind of forever ties. But I loved this woman, so why all the bullshit? Sylvia Wilson and Everett L. Jones were married the first weekend of August 1967 by the Yoruba priest Nana Oserjeman in a Yoruba ceremony. [7]

Baraka's marriage to a black woman was a decisive step toward ridding himself of the ethnic vulnerability he had endured because of his previous marriage to a white woman. In the eyes of Baraka's black nationalist and separatist confreres, his interracial sexual relationships as well as an interracial marriage were the supreme acts of race betrayal. The white female–black male sexual connection attracted extreme invectives (masquerading as art) throughout the Black Arts era. One example, which bordered on the fanatical and farcical, was the often recited Sonia Sanchez poem, "To All Sisters," in which she rhetorically asks, "What a white woman got cept her white pussy . . . her straight hair covering her fucked up mind . . . her faggoty white man."[8] Sanchez might well have asked what a black man has who evidently finds this vacuous white woman so attractive!

Now that he was married, Baraka could more easily disagree with the majority opinions of his political confreres without becoming an object of suspicion concerning the depth of his commitment to black nationalism. It is difficult to imagine Baraka leaving the confines of black nationalism—as he later did—without first having gained greater security about his ethnic identity. Given the preeminence of his second wife in his life, Baraka is sometimes angered by what he perceives as the media's attention to his first marriage at the expense of his second one. In 1980 he wrote,

> Interestingly, the media has made more of this union [with Cohen] since we split up than while we were together. Biographers never fail to mention it, though they sometimes leave out mention of my present wife of 13 years, Amina, who is Black and our five children. What they are advertising with this slant is the nonexistent "norm" of equality through assimilation rather than equality through national liberation and revolution![9]

Despite Baraka's claim, there is no evidence that the media have spent a lot of time reporting on his life with Hettie. Hettie and Roi were married for only five years and have been divorced for several decades. Certainly, there has been far more time for reporters and scholars to write about his marriage to Cohen since its dissolution. What Baraka cannot acknowledge is that interest in his life with Hettie Jones centers on the fact that his years with her, living among the Village writers and poets, were his most creative. Baraka pretends not to realize that a marriage between an Afro-American male and a white Jewish American female was more exotic than a marriage between a black man and black woman. His case was particularly exasperating inasmuch as he, the black partner in his interracial union, later became a prominent black ethnic chauvinist, racist, and anti-Semite. By treating his marriage to a black woman as normal, the media (whoever they are) silenced his ambivalent identity, denied his desire to return "home," and overlooked the significance of that desire. Nevertheless, it is not clear why Baraka thinks that his marriage to a black woman symbolizes "equality through national liberation and revolution."

Baraka's marriage to a self-assured, ethnically legitimate black woman undoubtedly functioned as a marginality defacilitator. The marriage was a sign of his return to the ethnic fold. Once having returned, Baraka increasingly became a "regular brother." Nonetheless, we must assume that his identity insecurities had not been completely calmed by his marriage to a black woman, for he continued on his journey to what he now refers to as "the university of false blackness."[10]

THE NEWARK UPRISING

Besides the assassination of Malcolm X, several events during 1965 fundamentally redefined Afro-Americans and Afro-American politics. First, the Voting Rights Act of 1965 was passed which established federal mandates and mechanisms to ensure the voting rights of southern blacks. America's political landscape was forever altered as black southerners emerged as highly energized voters. The passage of this law ultimately gave black Americans a more realistic picture of the limitations of voting power. More precisely, only by actively participating in voting could blacks begin to obtain the benefits of liberal democracy and recognize its limitations.

Second, in August 1965, an estimated crowd of 35,000 black Americans rampaged through an area of Los Angeles known as Watts-Willobrook.[11] Whether one considers this a riot or a revolt may depend on one's political orientation. I consider these riots to be moments of insurgency akin to the initial stages of a revolt that never materialized. Regardless of political orientations, most students of American politics agree that what occurred in Watts two years after the March on Washington and one year after the signing of the Civil Rights Act of 1964 was one of the most significant events in the recent history of American race relations. Thirty-four people (mostly blacks) were killed, and a thousand were injured. Four thousand people were arrested. Damage to property was estimated at $200 million. Throughout the United States, Americans were glued to their television sets as news reports showed hordes of black looters running across streets and jumping through broken store windows with stolen goods. The work of arsonists added to these images, as more than 250 buildings were damaged or destroyed by fire. The chant "Burn Baby Burn" became the supposed motto of the rioters. Before it was over, 16,000 National Guard and law enforcement personnel had to be called in to restore order.

The Watts riot signaled the end of the Civil Rights movement. No longer would acts of nonviolent civil disobedience capture the United States' moral imagination. The events in Watts indicated how little legitimacy the traditional black leadership had in predominantly black urban areas. In the aftermath, James Farmer, the national leader of the Congress of Racial Equality, stated, "Civil rights organizations have failed. No one has any roots in the ghetto."[12] Farmer's observation proved to be true in cities throughout the United States. Riots sprang up throughout the latter half of the 1960s, and only in rare instances were the established black political elites in these cities able to control or defuse the situation.

The next major urban conflicts to attract national publicity occurred in Newark and Detroit in July 1967. In Detroit, after several days of rioting, forty-three people had been killed, more than 7,000 persons had been arrested, and about $45 million worth of property had been destroyed.[13] A week earlier, Newark had exploded.

During the 1960s, the two cities most vulnerable to black urban unrest were probably Detroit and Newark. By 1966, Newark's population was almost two-thirds black and Latino, yet the city's power structure was not only overwhelmingly white but also openly racist in its policies and employment practices. The Newark political establishment, led by Mayor Hugh Addonizio, was corrupt to the point of even colluding with the Mafia. The mayor and the city protected the racist police force that regularly brutalized black citizens. It was therefore no surprise when rumors of police brutality against a black cab driver brought a crowd of angry blacks in front of the police station where the driver was being held. During the first night of protest (July 12), the crowd dispersed after minor disturbances (e.g., setting fire to one car). The next day, July 13, 1967, the tension rose again as protesters demonstrated in front of the police station. Later that night, the looting started. In the early morning of July 14, the governor of New Jersey, in response to Mayor Addonizio's request, sent state troopers and units of the New Jersey National Guard into Newark.

The Kerner Commission's investigation of the Newark riot offers a litany of violent acts of repression directed toward the black citizens of Newark by the city police and the New Jersey National Guard. In one instance, a family was watching the looting from the upstairs windows of their apartment. Three carloads of police arrived at the street corner below and yelled at the looters, who then scattered. The police opened fire. Moments later, the three-year-old daughter in the upstairs apartment began crying. A bullet had entered her eye. After spending the next two months in the hospital, she lost the sight in her left eye as well as the hearing in her left ear. In another documented case, a black man who was in front of his house attempting to fix the brakes in his jacked-up car was shot and critically wounded by a state trooper who took aim at him while he was underneath his car. Another black man standing on his porch was shot in the eye. According to the Kerner Commission, in another incident the national guardsmen and state troopers fired at a housing project in response to what they believed was sniper fire:

> On the tenth floor, Eloise Spellman, the mother of several children fell, a bullet through her neck. Across the street, a number of persons, standing in an apartment window were watching the firing directed at the housing project. Suddenly, a federal trooper whirled and began firing in the general direction of the spectators. Mrs. Hattie Gainer, a grandmother, sank to the floor. . . . A block away Rebecca Brown's 2-year-old daughter was standing at the window. Mrs. Brown rushed to drag her to safety. As Mrs. Brown was momentarily framed in the window, a bullet spun into her back. All three women died. . . . At 11 P.M. on Sunday, July 16, Mrs. Lucille Pugh looked out of the window to see if the streets were clear. She then asked her 11 year-old son, Michael, to take the garbage out. As he reached the street and was illuminated by a street light, a shot rang out. He died.[14]

Although the commission did not state that the boy was killed by the National Guard or police, this was clearly implied. As if there was any doubt that the New Jersey National Guard and state troopers were racistly motivated, the report noted the example of the owner of a Chinese laundry who tried to protect his store from looting by placing a "soul brother" sign in the store window. Early in the morning of July 16, his quiet neighborhood was disturbed by the sounds of jeeps and gunshots. The owner peeked out of his upstairs window and discovered that the National Guard and state troopers were smashing windows and shooting into every store that had a "soul brother" sign in it. If the black looters were going to spare black-owned and -identified establishments, the white police and National Guard would even the racial score.[15] Unlike the black rioters who looted white-owned stores, these white destroyers of private property would not be subjected to potential arrest and death. They were *the law*.[16]

During that first night of mass looting in Newark, Jones and two friends piled into his van and drove slowly through the area where the rioting was going on. They assessed both the physical damage caused by the rioters and the responses of the Newark police. There was excitement in the air as black people ran through the streets with goods that they could not otherwise afford. Describing the events twenty years later, Baraka still conveys the frenzy of the moment:

> Boxes of stuff were speeding by, cases of stuff, liquor wine beer, the best brands. Shoes, appliances, clothes, jewelry, food. . . . There were shifts of folk at work. . . . Families worked together, carrying sofas and TV's collectively down the street. All the shit they saw on television that they had been hypnotized into wanting they finally had a chance to cop. The word was Cop & Blow! And don't be slow. . . . Then the fire setters . . . would get on it. . . . Burn it up! Burn it up! . . . These were the most rhythmic, the fire people, they dug the fire caused it danced so tough.[17]

Jones and friends were driving slowly down a main thoroughfare when they realized that the police had begun to shoot at the looters. They saw a young man fall who had been shot in the leg. Acting instinctively, Jones and his two buddies picked him up and took him to a hospital.

Later that night when driving home, their van was stopped by a group of Newark police officers. With shotguns pointed at their heads, Jones and the others were dragged out of the van and beaten. Accusing them of being snipers, the police demanded that they hand over their guns. Jones and his friends denied having any. Then Jones recognized one of the arresting police as an Italian American with whom he had attended high school. Upon telling him "I know you," the policeman hit Jones over his head with the barrel of his revolver. Now semiconscious, Jones was beaten by several police using their nightsticks. Fearing for his life, he screamed, "Allah Akbar. Al Holiah."[18] A black Newark policeman who saw Jones being beaten stated that he

> was standing about thirty feet away when they snatched Jones out of that little truck, knocked him to the ground and began to beat him so viciously that I don't know how that little man is still living today. I started to go over and butt in, but I just knew they were going to kill him from the way they were beating him and I figured they'd just kill me, too. Man, I was crying. That was all I could do without committing suicide.[19]

Fortunately for Jones and his companions, a crowd of people from apartments that overlooked the scene began screaming at the police to stop the beating, and they began hurling objects at the police. Afraid of making an already explosive situation worse, the police took the three men to the local precinct where they beat them again and threw them into cells. After being taken to the police station, Jones was transported to a local hospital. There a white doctor asked the badly beaten Jones if he was a poet. When Jones said he was, the doctor stated, "Well, you'll never write any more poetry!"[20] He then stitched two large cuts in Jones's head without giving him an anesthetic.

While Jones was under arrest, the police and National Guard broke into Spirit House several times, trying to destroy anything and everything. They shot out the windows and damaged the printing machines that Jones had stored in the basement. Unknown to the law enforcers, Sylvia and her baby were hiding on the third floor.[21]

Bail was set for Jones at $25,000, a sum that he referred to as ransom. At his trial, the presiding judge read from one of Jones's poems that appeared in the *Evergreen Review* (December 1967) shortly after his arrest. The poem, "Black People," was used as evidence supporting Jones' guilt.

> *What about that bad short you saw last week on Frelinghuysen, or those*
> > *stoves and refrigerators,*
> *record players, in Sears, Bamberger, Klein's, Hahnes',*
> *Chase and the smaller josh enterprises? . . . You know*
> *how to get it, you can get it, no money down, no money never, money don't*
> > *grow on trees no way, only whitey's*
> *got it, makes it with a machine, to control you*
> *cant steal nothin from a white man, he's already stole*
> *it he owes you anything you want, even his life. All*
> *the stores will open if you will say the magic words.*
> *The magic words are: Up against the wall mother fucker*
> *this is a stick up! Or smash the window at night (these*
> *are magic actions) . . . Just take what you want. . . . Run up*
> *and down Broad Street niggers, take the shit you want.*
> *Take their lives if need be, but get what you want what*
> *you need . . . run through the streets with music, beautiful*
> *radios on Market Street, they are brought here especially*
> *for you. . . . We must make our own World, man, our own world,*
> *and we can not do this unless the white man is dead.*
> *Let's get together and kill him my man . . . let's make a*
> *world we want black children to grow and learn in do not*
> *let your children when they grow look in your face and*
> *curse you by pitying your tomish ways.*[22]

Although the poem conveys Jones's support of rioting and looting, that is not illegal. It would be a gross misreading of the social dynamics of the rioting to suggest that a poem written by LeRoi Jones could instigate black mass unrest in Newark. Furthermore, because the poem was not published until after the riot, such charges were obviously ludicrous. What is appalling is that the presiding judge introduced the poem into the legal proceedings. Fortunately for Jones, the judge was so thoroughly committed to finding him guilty that he was unable to sustain even a veneer of impartiality.

On the second day of his trial, a handcuffed and screaming Jones was dragged from the courtroom. The incident began when Jones tried to walk away from the defendant's table, shouting to the courtroom, "This is not a court of justice and you are not qualified to try this case. I will not be judged by you or one hundred white people. . . . They are not my peers . . . they are my oppressors. I will not be judged by this kangaroo court. I am leaving."[23] In response to his trial for gun possession, a group of his former, Village-based, white literary confreres issued a public statement in his behalf:

We believe LeRoi Jones, not the Newark Police, that the poet carried no revolvers in his car, no revolvers in the car at all; that the police beat Jones up and then had to find a reason, thus found phony guns; that after the double-whammy of his beating and rabbit-in-hat guns, his trial before an all-white jury was triple-whammy. Lo and behold, fourth execrable whammy"—the judge recited LeRoi's visionary poem to the court, (a butchered version) . . . and gave him a long 2½ to 3 year sentence because of it.

Mr Jones; white kind is that self-same demon we call tyranny, injustice, dictatorship. As poet he champions the black imagination; as revolutionary poet his revolution is fought with words. He scribes that the police carried the guns. Lyres tell the Truth!

We herald to literary persons: Get on the ball for LeRoi Jones, or else get off the poetic pot. LeRoi Jones is not only a black man, a Newark man, a revolutionary, he is a conspicuous American artist imprisoned for his poetry during a crisis of authoritarianism in these states.

The statement was signed by John Ashbery, Gregory Corso, Robert Creeley, Diane Di Prima, Robert Duncan, Lawrence Ferlinghetti, Allen Ginsberg, Kenneth Koch, Denise Levertov, Michael McClure, Charles Olson, Joel Oppenheimer, Peter Orlovsky, Gil Sorrentino, Philip Whalen, and John Wieners.[24] His former white associates from the village chose not to abandon him, even though by this time Jones had denigrated them both publicly and privately.[25] In particular, Allen Ginsberg remained resolute in his support of his old friend Roi. Believing that Roi was being framed, Ginsberg helped raise money for his trial and successfully appealed to the members of the PEN Club of New York to issue a statement on his behalf, particularly since the judge was using Jones's writing against him.[26]

Jones was convicted and sentenced to three years in prison for possession of the two revolvers that the police claimed to have found in his van. Jones and his friends steadfastly denied this allegation. In any case, the sentence was far too harsh for the alleged offense.[27] Although it was not sympathetic to Jones, *Newsweek* had to concede that it "was plain that Kapp [the judge] had indeed held Jones's poem against him and given it, in the process, far wider publication than the *Evergreen Review*."[28] Because of Kapp's bias in introducing Jones's poem to the court as proof of his guilt, an appeal was granted, and in the second trial, the conviction was overturned.

Jones initially regarded the riot in Newark and the others that took place throughout black urban America between 1964 and 1968 as the cornerstones of the black liberation movement. The riots demonstrated that large numbers of urban blacks were frustrated with their lives and the pace and direction of those policies supposedly intended to enhance their socioeconomic inclusion in American society. The looting that accompanied the rioting flaunted the widespread black disrespect for American property laws, which many blacks viewed as mechanisms to legitimate their poverty in a land of abundance. The looting also showed that black rioters viewed consumer goods as indices of freedom. Perhaps more important, the willingness of some of the rioters to engage in gunfights with state authorities indicated their rebellious disposition. Accordingly, Jones mistakenly but understandably believed that the riots were indications of an awakening revolutionary spirit in the black urban masses.

What remains awkward about Jones's trials and the events that led up to them is the ease with which he could claim then, as he emphatically does today, not to have been guilty. Baraka has repeatedly stated that the urban riots of the 1960s, like the one that took place in Newark, were political rebellions and therefore constituted the vanguard of the black liberation movement. Why, then, wasn't a self-proclaimed black revolutionary like Jones guilty of those charges against him and much, much worse? Like that of Angela Davis, Jones's revolutionary stature rested in large measure on being viewed as having done something that he claims never to have done. That is, he and Davis were seen as revolutionary not because they behaved in a revolutionary fashion but because they were unjustly charged by the state for acting "revolutionary."[29]

During the 1960s and early 1970s, the rite of passage for some blacks into the status of revolutionary required nothing more than to have been pursued by the police. The paranoid racism of FBI director J. Edgar Hoover and other functionaries of state repression thus succeeded in granting many blacks the status of "revolutionary." In effect, we witnessed the creation of state-certified revolutionaries. Yet it was reasonable for Jones to fear that he and other black militant activists had been targeted for death by various levels of the state police apparatus. Indeed, many were targeted, and more than a few were killed. But being targeted for harassment or death by the state does not make one a revolutionary.[30]

Similarly, Jones's revolutionary image was exposed as a media posture when he publicly displayed his expectation that the police and legal system would treat him fairly according to his rights as a citizen of the United States. Never once did Jones realize that his bid for justice was predicated on and reinforced the legitimacy of the state that he claimed was illegitimate. This predicament of being simultaneously protected and assaulted by the state was a conundrum faced by many activists during the 1960s. In the case of black militant activists, this paradox confirmed their peculiar insider-outsider status as Afro-American citizens of the United States. Essentially, Jones was a reformer hiding behind revolutionary rhetoric. Fortunately for him, the American legal system occasionally allowed justice to prevail.

I am not implying that Jones should have given up his legal rights and gone to jail. It was reasonable for him to try whatever means were available to remain out of prison. But his behavior and thought exhibit a deeper psychological fusion with the idea of America than he would have us believe. He was not and would never be a true revolutionary. A psychic break, a rational severance from society and its political and ideological infrastructures, is a necessary stage in the psychological development of all authentic revolutionaries. Jones never entered that realm of willed "homelessness" in which the existing state and social order are seen as the "total" enemy.

The so-called black revolutionary who seeks the protection of the legal system is one variant of the victim-status appeal. It is like the child who claims to be old enough to make up her mind but who does so hoping that her mother does not accept her announcement of independence just in case she fails at being independent. One cannot imagine Castro pleading for justice in Batista's courtroom. Concerning the so-called black revolutionary who was actually nothing more than a protester operating in the confines of established American political expectations and channels, Harold Cruse wrote in 1966:

> In America today there has flowered a young black breed in the ghettos of the North who says that Negroes must be prepared to die for their "free-

dom," and that they themselves are prepared to do just that. Many of them also talk avidly of "revolution," but aside from their volatile activist proclivities their "revolution" is a borrowed term abstracted out of the revolutionary ideologies of the "Third" or "Bandung" world. It is the revolutionary sentiments of identification with movements as close as Cuba and as distant as China, but its native methodology is one of pure and simple protest, both non-violent and violent.[31]

While Cruse does not specifically mention Baraka, the description fits him all too well. Moreover, recall that Cruse had accompanied Baraka on the trip to Cuba that resulted in "Cuba libre." He might have noticed how Baraka's subsequent romanticization of that event had mistakenly led him to think that he understood the nature of revolution.

In his autobiography, published approximately two decades after the urban riots of the 1960s, Baraka's discussion of those events remains mired in romanticism. He did not, and perhaps cannot, deal with the pain and suffering inflicted on the black community as a result of the riots of the 1960s. When talking about the riots, he ignores the plight of the rioters:

> Rebellions popped like dearly firecrackers in city after city that summer. But the week after the Newark rebellion, Detroit went up in even more flames. Forty-three dead, over 7,000 people arrested, $44 million damage. They brought in 14,000 paratroopers and National Guard. Yeh, even the airborne, with machine guns, because bloods in Detroit had come up with automatic weapons, not just the pop-pop of 22's.[32]

Conspicuously absent from these comments is the recognition that most of those forty-three persons killed in Detroit were black rioters. Many more were maimed. Life for many black inner-city dwellers became a bit more unbearable when the local businesses were destroyed. But little of this mattered to Baraka, for the "bloods" were fighting back and revolution was primarily a question of imagery. Even death could be objectified, romanticized, and marketed as an icon of an imaginary revolution.

BLACK POWER CONFERENCE

On July 20, 1967, the National Conference on Black Power commenced in Newark. Plans for this four-day conference had been made at a meeting called by Congressman Adam Clayton Powell (D-NY) in the fall of 1966. At this planning session, Congressman Powell appointed Nathan Wright to chair a "continuations committee" which was responsible for planning the first National Black Power Conference. Wright, the executive director of the Department of Urban Work of the Episcopal Diocese of Newark, was a longtime liberal political activist and Episcopal priest. Besides Wright, the planning committee consisted of four other black men, including Chuck Stone, a congressional assistant to Powell, and Maulana Karenga of Los Angeles.

At Wright's insistence, the Black Power conference was held in Newark, as his position in the Newark Episcopal diocese gave him access to a pool of workers who could help manage the conference. Scheduled to begin on July 20, just four days after the rioting ended, Wright was pressured by the Newark and New Jersey authorities to cancel the gathering. He refused. Against a backdrop of smoldering rubble and the "occupation" troops of the New Jersey National Guard, the conference began. According to Robert Allen, approximately 1,300 people attended the conference, representing 190 organizations from forty-two cities and thirty-nine states. It was the first of several major Black Power conferences held during the 1960s. Allen also noted that the conference was held at a white-owned hotel in downtown Newark, with a registration fee of $25 per participant, and thus limited participation to mainly middle-class blacks or full-time black activists.[33]

According to Chuck Stone, the driving question behind the conference was how the new wave of black militancy, as expressed by the concept of "Black Power," could be mobilized into an actionable unity involving the black masses and then translated into constructive programs of black empowerment.[34] To answer this question, the conference focused on certain key areas of policy and politics such as urban electoral politics and economic development. Delegates to the conference could choose among numerous workshops.

The range of resolutions that the conference produced represented the diversity of the participants. For instance, to improve economic well-being, the conference decided to (1) endorse "buy black" policies in all black communities, (2) establish neighborhood credit unions, and (3) urge the establishment of a guaranteed income for all people, with the alternative that black people would disrupt the country's economy. Regarding education, the conference passed a resolution requiring all black educational jurisdictions to be administered and controlled by black boards of education. Concerning politics, the conference agreed to (1) help the blacks of Newark in the recall election of Mayor Addonizio; (2) establish a Black Power lobby in Washington, D.C.; (3) hold a national black grassroots political convention; and (4) demand that Adam Clayton Powell be given full seniority in

Congress. In regard to international affairs, the conference endorsed (1) the establishment of an international employment service to serve as a skills bank for exchanges by Africans and black Americans and (2) the support of the freedom struggles of all nonwhite peoples throughout the world against their white oppressors.[35] Finally, the conference issued some miscellaneous resolutions such as (1) initiating a national dialogue on the desirability of partitioning the United States into racially homogeneous, separate, and independent nations; (2) assigning only black police captains to predominantly black neighborhoods; and (3) boycotting all sponsors of televised boxing until Muhammad Ali's title was restored.

This listing does not include all the resolutions made by the conference, but it does show that the gathering lumped the serious with the frivolous. Did the conferees truly think that the federal government would be frightened by their threat to damage the American economy if all Americans were not given a guaranteed income? Although Muhammad Ali had been wrongfully stripped of his title, why was such a inconsequential issue brought up at a conference formulating national black priorities?

What was striking about the Newark Black Power conference is that it was extensively funded by white corporate America. Nathan Wright, the primary organizer of the event, stated that these white-controlled companies had not been pressured into contributing but did so to help powerless blacks obtain greater social and political efficacy. The white corporate sponsorship of radical black gatherings continued throughout the 1960s and early 1970s,[36] and the Newark Black Power conference became the prototype for numerous gatherings held during the next decade. Throughout the continental United States, various congresses, conferences, and assemblies developed strategies and resolutions for black emancipation. The participants argued about various positions, voted on them, and then went home. It was as if the mere gathering of black people to discuss politics constituted a radical or militant praxis. All too often, these resolutions were forgotten, discarded in someone's wastebasket, or superseded by the resolutions made in the next, even more radical, conference.

The theatrical highlight of the Newark conference came during a speech by Karenga. Looking menacingly at the audience, he inquired, "Any white people here who oppose our demands? Any Negroes who want to stand up for their white masters? *We're giving you a chance to die for your white master*"[37] (my emphasis). Maybe there were no whites in the audience who were opposed to "our demands," but they could easily have been found just outside the conference doors in Newark. All that Karenga and his thugs had to do was go outside and present their demands to Police Chief Spina and his confreres on the Newark police force. But instead they chose to terrorize those at the conference while remaining a safe distance away from authentic white opposition. Such cowardice, masquerading as militance, was commonplace.

The phony bravado in Karenga's threats of violence was just one of the many that took root during the Black Power era. These threats were supposed to both intimidate those gathered and enhance Karenga's image, since he had the power to order a person's death. But they also showed the degree to which the thug image had come to be seen as revolutionary by black nationalists. Karenga frequently invoked this image during the Black Power era, and the former LeRoi Jones soon adopted the practice.

RIOT DETERRENCE 1968

In his autobiography, Baraka discussed his behavior during the 1967 Newark riots but conspicuously omitted his behavior during the 1968 Newark riots.[38] After the assassination of Martin Luther King Jr. in April 1968, Newark, like many large urban areas, was beset by black rioting, but the riots were not as large as those in 1967. Jones played a crucial role in containing the 1968 riots, not only because he believed in the efficacy of pragmatic black electoral politics, but also because he recognized that the repressive forces of the state were far better armed, trained, and willing to destroy the black insurgents. By 1968, Jones viewed rioting in Newark as hindering black electoral control of the city. He believed that the election of a black mayor would radically alter the living conditions of blacks in Newark.[39]

Only tangentially related to the community of rioters, Jones used his previous beating and arrest during the 1967 riots as ethnic political capital to "purchase" media attention in 1968 to speak for the needs of those Newark blacks that he did not actually represent. He used his access to the media to install himself as a black political middleman between the black rioting populace and the white power elite while publicly marketing himself to whites and blacks as an indigenous black political spokesperson. This rather clever power play was repeated throughout the United States as bourgeois blacks discovered the political utility in black ethnic militancy. The success of this strategy depended on the white establishment's recognition of specific black middlemen. This recognition was usually granted when the white establishment determined that (1) the middlemen could control the rioters and (2) the cost of the middlemen's demands was lower than the cost of responding to the rioting blacks.[40]

To cultivate a client status with Newark's white power elite, Jones employed a strategy of tactical acquiescence, discarding political principle. On April 12, 1968, he appeared on a local television broadcast accompanied by Police Chief Spina and Anthony Imperiale, the racist right-wing leader of Newark's racially recalcitrant white ethnic communities. In partnership with Imperiale, Jones denounced white leftist community organizers in Newark and suggested that white leftists like Tom Hayden had instigated the April 1968 riots.[41] Concerning these remarks, a Newark police Department official told the House Committee on Un-American Activities that "it was a very happy occasion for me to find myself in total agreement with LeRoi Jones."[42]

Tom Hayden, a nationally known antiwar activist and one of the founders of the Students for a Democratic Society (SDS), had come to Newark in July 1964 to organize the poor. SDS wanted to develop a northern chapter of the Student Non-Violent Coordinating Committee (SNCC) and had chosen Newark as the site because it was a large city with a majority-black population. Newark's mayor, Hugh Addonizio, was known as a liberal, which, given the horrible material conditions of black Newark, spoke to the limitations of white liberalism. Concerning the Newark that greeted him in 1964, Hayden wrote:

> White or black city officials were widely perceived as corrupt. Construction costs of city contracts were higher than anywhere in the United States. Gambling was the city's biggest business and the narcotics trade flourished. ... With a total population of 400,000 people, Newark ranked highest in the country in crime, maternal and infant mortality, tuberculosis, and venereal disease. Unemployment citywide was 15 percent, and much higher in the black community. One third of the city's children dropped out of school, and less than 10 percent achieved normal reading levels.[43]

Hayden and his group of grassroots organizers created the Newark Community Union Project (NCUP, pronounced en-cup) to organize black neighborhoods in that city. Utilizing SNCC's Southern strategies, NCUP tried to recruit local black residents as leaders. They lobbied for neighborhood traffic lights, better social services in poor neighborhoods, and the like. Members of NCUP attended various local hearings and organized demonstrations. The hours were long, the work was arduous, and the victories were few. It would be difficult to consider NCUP's efforts as detrimental to black Newark and utterly ridiculous to suggest that this marginal group of organizers and their black recruits controlled the energies of the entire black community of Newark. Nonetheless, Jones made these ludicrous claims and did so in association with the most reactionary forces in Newark.

Thoroughly unprincipled, Jones expediently employed red-baiting tactics to stigmatize the presence of white leftist organizers. He did not want whites influencing the direction of black Newark politics, even if those whites were politically progressive. Jones was now a black nationalist and a separatist black nationalist at that. His antagonism toward Hayden and his leftist peers did not stem solely from their "whiteness," however. Rather, their group competed with the one Jones wanted to establish and control. LeRoi did not want political competition. It did not matter to him if Hayden and his peers were helping blacks in that community. Jones alone had decided that the white left was not wanted in Newark. Cleverly, he marketed his private desires for power and the elimination of the white community organizers as the collective desires of Newark's black community. Once again, Jones's deeply embedded antidemocratic tendencies came to the fore.

In his autobiography, Baraka sidesteps any discussion of how he came to denounce white leftists and close ranks with reactionary racist whites. In this case, the whites whom he chose as allies, the Newark police and Imperiale, were those most antagonistic to the needs of black Newark.[44] How did Jones's black nationalism tolerate a working partnership with Imperiale? Was Jones more antagonistic to white leftists than to white racist reactionaries like Imperiale? In any event, Jones participated in an explicitly racist narrative to explain black discontent: white "Commies" were behind it! We must conclude that the soon-to-be Imamu was not above crass opportunism. In a fit of understatement, Baraka later referred to his behavior on this occasion as "asinine."[45] The opportunistic quality of Jones's attack on Hayden and his colleagues becomes more obvious when we realize that Jones did not attribute the 1967 Newark riot to them. Instead, Jones proclaimed the 1967 riot as an act of black revolutionary assertion. Had Hayden and his colleagues claimed responsibility for the 1967 riot, Jones would have been among the first to call them racists for assuming that black protests needed white instigation. But in 1968, Jones presented such an argument to white racists all too eager to believe it.

Shortly after Jones had appeared on television with Imperiale, he explained his political agenda:

> Our aim is to bring about black self-government in Newark by 1970. We have a membership that embraces every social area in Newark. It is a wide cross-section of business, professional and political life. I'm in favor of black

people taking power by the quickest, easiest, most successful means they can employ. Malcolm X said the ballot or the bullet. Newark is a particular situation where the ballot seems to be advantageous. I believe we have to survive. I didn't invent the white man. What we are trying to do is deal with him in the best way we can. . . . Black men are not murderers. . . . What we don't want to be is die-ers.[46]

In exchange for bringing peace to the black community, Jones demanded a black mayor, feeling that this was a price that the Newark establishment could afford. Jones was both right and wrong. The white elite's toleration of a black-run city came only after a long, hard, black-led struggle against rank-and-file white ethnics who were far less amenable to the idea. In 1970, Kenneth Gibson became the first elected black mayor of Newark. Years later, Baraka expressed shock and resentment that Gibson's election had not substantially altered black life.[47]

Jones's commitment to urban electoral politics as a mechanism for black economic advancement and ethnic self-determination was widely shared in black nationalist and integrationist circles during the middle and late 1960s and early 1970s. A few remaining black nationalists believed that any involvement in electoral politics was tainted. Some black nationalists imagined that predominantly black urban areas would become mini-black nations in the United States. Others, like James Boggs, naively assumed that black city administrators would "naturally" be more concerned about the well-being of black city residents than the white politicians they replaced.[48] In a 1968 interview, Jones described black community control: "In the cities it means the mobilization of black people with black consciousness to take control over that space which they already inhabit and to achieve programs so that they can defend and govern that space and survive the onslaughts of white society."[49] Despite what they assumed to be novel and insurrectionary politics, the black nationalists who called for black control of city hall were reminiscent of earlier generations of white ethnic political activists. Many black nationalists, including Baraka, would probably have shuddered at the accusation that they were participating in a rite of American political incorporation. They were attempting to give ethnic political succession a radical veneer by referring to predominantly black urban areas as colonies of the United States. "Internal colonialism" became a frequently invoked description of the power relations between black urban enclaves and white America.

To interpret Baraka's 1968 behavior as that of a political novice would be to ignore the previous times that he had attached his political/artistic aspirations to the misery of black rioters. I am not arguing that Jones's behavior in

Newark was dictated solely by his peculiar style of self-promotion. Instead, I am pointing to his intellectual and artistic self-interests when analyzing his political behavior. Despite his ever present self-interest, Baraka's intentions in Newark were far more attuned to the perceived needs and aspirations of the local black community than his Harlem agenda was. His demands for a black mayor, a black city council, and a black board of education were part of a commonly held desire of black Newark residents to improve their lives.

TOWARD A BLACK RELIGION

As the director of BART, Jones regularly interacted with other black nationalist organizations in Harlem, including the Yoruba Temple. But the Yoruba religion did not influence his personal beliefs until shortly after his return to Newark, where, in Spirit House, Jones constructed a small Yoruba religious altar.[50] The former bohemian in pursuit of race purification had become, in his own words, a "super-African." Another factor that seemingly influenced Jones's attraction to Yoruba was its sanctioning of polygamy. While his specific fondness for Yoruba may have ebbed and flowed depending on the number of women in his life, the late 1960s was a moment of general spiritual inquisitiveness for him.

Shortly after the 1967 Newark riots, Jones became increasingly attracted to the Sunni Muslim faith. Malcolm X had been a Sunni Muslim at the time of his assassination, and in 1967, Jones was approached by several Sunni Muslim priests who persuaded him to give their religion a chance. Once again, Spirit House became a religious site, an unofficial *jamat*, "or gathering place for Islamic believers." For a short while, Spirit House offered classes on Islam and Arabic. Jones felt deeply honored that he had been approached by Haij Heesham Jaaber, the same Islamic priest who had officiated at Malcolm X's funeral. It was around this time that LeRoi Jones, then an eclectic practitioner of the Sunni Muslim religion, acquired the name Ameer Barakat (blessed prince), which was later "Swahilized" under Karenga's direction to Amiri Baraka.[51] His wife Sylvia was simultaneously renamed Ameena (faithful) which later became Amina. According to Baraka, "The name change seemed fitting to me . . . and not just the meaning of the name Blessed Prince, but the idea that I was now literally being changed into a blacker being. I was discarding my 'slave name' and embracing blackness."[52] The name change is emblematic of Baraka's dramaturgic approach to politics. In ridding himself of his American name, Baraka tried to eliminate the ambivalence in his Afro-American identity. Like Malcolm X, he would no longer be known by a "slave name."[53] Perhaps, however, Baraka attributed too much significance to changing his name. Jones's excitement at substituting his white "slave name" for an Arabic slave name and, later, an Arabic-influenced Swahili slave name speaks to the irony and pathos of black attempts during the 1960s to ritualistically create a more thorough outsider identity. At that time, it was necessary just to do something symbolically related to Africa to indicate one's opposition to the United States or whites in general.

Jones's adoption of Yoruba and, later, Islam was not undertaken simply to alter his identity. He became, however momentarily, a true believer in these faiths. For instance, in a 1968 interview, Baraka appears to have been momentarily enraptured by Islamic mysticism, arguing that religious beliefs were important to a non-brainwashed black man. The "black man who is an Oriental, an Eastern man, is a naturally religious man."[54] Always Manichean, Baraka claimed that whites were naturally irreligious but that in order to perpetuate their dominance of the world, they paid homage to the god that maintained them in that position. In the 1968 interview, Baraka conveyed his mystical bent:

> If you look at the most powerful Masons and Shriners, you will see they are wearing tarbooshes and fezzes on their heads. They understand the scientific utilization of religion and they know how it keeps them in power. The highest-degreed masons make *salats* (prayers), you know—they face the east and make *salats* to Allah—and when they reach their thirtieth or thirty-first or thirty-second degree, they are actually praying to Allah. They are actually aspiring to be Muslims! . . . But don't tell that to the man in the street because it's not for his advantage to know. Why would a president have to be a thirty-third degree Mason? Even in Kennedy's case he was a member of the Catholic Knights of Columbus which is analogous. *Otherwise he couldn't rule.*[55] [my emphasis]

This fantastic and weird commentary on Masonic power sheds light on a tendency in Jones that is rarely discussed. That is, he was quite vulnerable to mystical doctrines, and his Spirit House was home to numerous forms of spiritual engagement as Jones discarded one religious sensibility for another.

KARENGA'S DISCIPLE

Jones first met Ron Karenga shortly before the Newark rebellion/riot of 1967. Karenga had come to Newark to attend a planning session for the forthcoming Newark Black Power conference. Unannounced, he visited Jones at Spirit House with two other men who not only had Swahili names like Karenga but duplicated him in attire (bald heads and an African sculpture hanging around their necks). Even though he said he liked Jones's book *Blues People*, Karenga pontificated about the reactionary nature of the blues.[56] Jones disagreed but listened to this fascinating character: "He went on, elaborating his theories on culture and nationalism, talking at high speed nonstop, laughing at his own witticisms and having two members of a chorus, yea-saying, calling, 'Teach' when Karenga made some point he considered salient."[57]

Karenga was born in Parsonburg, Maryland, in 1941, the son of a Baptist minister. His name at birth was Ronald McKinley Everett.[58] Like Baraka, he changed his name gradually, first becoming Ron Ndabezitha Everett-Karenga, then Ron Karenga, then Maulana Ron Karenga, and finally Maulana Karenga. According to Baraka, Maulana meant "master teacher" and Karenga meant "nationalist." The self-named Maulana Karenga was the master teacher of nationalism.[59] Armed with a master's degree from UCLA, Karenga was the leader and "theoretician" for a Los Angeles–based black nationalist group called US (which many believe stood for United Slaves but others say it meant "us," as opposed to "them"). An extraordinarily talented individual, Karenga displayed many of the traits of the black paraintellectuals who, according to Martin Kilson, emerged as a major force in the black intelligentsia during the Black Power era in the late 1960s and early 1970s:

> These "para-intellectuals," now a major force in the Negro intelligentsia, are largely upper-lower-class, though sometimes lower-middle-class in background. They possess at best secondary schooling, and more commonly are drop-outs from high-school. But they are usually persons of high talent, and they display a high degree of motivation in the context of Negro lower-class culture. In general, they are adept at verbal and other skills, which enables them to become what may be called "cultural celebrities" in the Negro lower class.[60]

Karenga was certainly better educated than the persons Kilson had in mind, but he resembled Kilson's paraintellectual in his mastery of a "street rap" rhetorical style and in his willingness to market it as a new intellectual genre. More important, Karenga claimed to be more in touch with the black masses than were the "traditional" black intellectuals. If this claim was true, it was only because the traditional black intelligentsia had virtually no mass base, particularly among nonbourgeois blacks. Karenga excelled in producing clever pop-conceptualizations of a new Afro-American cultural nationalism that would supposedly advance the emancipatory politicization of blacks. Whether or not Karenga was reasoned or informed remains a matter of debate and is perhaps of less significance than the ways in which he simultaneously appropriated and rejected a scholarly air.

The 1960s Karenga had a distinctly charlatan component, as revealed in the ridiculously trite aphorisms that Clyde Halisi, one of his closest followers, collected and published as *The Quotable Karenga*.[61] In the US organization, the collection was viewed as a source of wisdom. Modeled on the popular collection of quotations from "Chairman Mao," *The Quotable Karenga* showed Mao-like aspirations toward a cult of leadership. From Karenga's collected aphorisms we learn:

> The Seven-fold path of Blackness is to Think Black, Talk Black, Act Black, Create Black, Buy Black,
> Vote Black and Live Black.
> All *Negroes* want to be capitalists—and ain't none of them got any capital.
> The fact that we are black is our ultimate reality. We were Black before we were born.
> The only real things *Negroes* produce are problems and babies.[62]

It is difficult to reconstruct the sociohistorical context in which these aphorisms were interpreted as profound. We can justifiably wonder whether the "cult of leadership" that informed Karenga's charismatic hold over his followers created a version of groupthink in which his followers' repeated collective affirmations of his wisdom deluded them into thinking that Plato was in their midst. This might also explain how Karenga came to view himself as profound.

At a 1967 Yale University symposium on the intellectual viability of Afro-American studies, Karenga argued for a new historiography that would affirm black equality rather than document black inferiority. Instead of proclaiming Marcus Garvey as a "Black Moses," the new black historiography would not tacitly inferiorize Garvey by granting a comparative priority to Moses. Perhaps this new historiography would generate descriptions in which Moses would be referred to as a Garvey-type figure. He had a valid argument in claiming that a historiography that created black inferiority would have a frame of reference different from that of a historiography that invalidated it. Even though Karenga did not substantiate his claim that in 1967 the prevailing historiography of blacks created a discourse of black inferiority, it was clear to all in attendance that racist historiography had yet to become a memory.[63] Karenga's paraintellectual qualities became evident when he suggested that this reference could be altered merely by modifying the descriptive nomenclature. Karenga's new historiography was black hagiography.

> Now, we have developed another type of interpretation in which we say that none of our black heroes fail. We believe in progressive perfection: they did as much as they could given the time and circumstances. I would never expect Garvey to do as much as I am doing, if for no other reason than that he didn't have this mike or tape.[64]

It is astounding that Karenga, an advocate of history-as-functional-mythmaking (otherwise known as propaganda), would be asked to participate in a symposium at Yale University whose stated goal was to address the intellectual and scholarly validity of the emerging discipline of Afro-American studies. His invited presence at the Yale gathering reveals the degree to which blacks and whites in the mainstream liberal academy during the late 1960s accepted black paraintellectuals as a valid sector of the black intelligentsia.[65] Responding to black mass insurgency, whites in the liberal academy sought out those blacks deemed to be spokespersons of the restless masses. Blacks in elite white academia probably had similar desires. In addition, black academicians may have had doubts about their ethnic legitimacy, a vulnerability that could have led them to valorize the Karengas in the black world. In both instances, the Karenga who was invited to Yale was probably a creation of their imaginations. After all, who were the black masses that Karenga supposedly represented? How many? Where?

Karenga invented cultural artifacts that were marketed to black Americans as the keys to touching base with Africa and their authentic ethnic selves. These artifacts were supposedly African in origin but were actually the products of Karenga's fertile American imagination.[66] The Maulana believed that the message contained in these cultural artifacts was as important as the function of such artifacts as ethnic unification rituals. For instance, Karenga devised what he considered to be an authentic, normative, Afro-American value system called Kawaida. Kawaida was based on seven principles, the Nugzo Saba, also invented by Karenga. The seven principles were *umoja* (unity), *kujichagulia* (self-determination), *unima* (collective work and responsibility), *ujamaa* (cooperative economics), *nia* (purpose), *kuumba* (creativity), and *imani* (faith).[67] These seven principles were supposed to encompass an emancipatory black way of life distinct from white European cultural norms and grounded in an African élan. The Nugzo Saba thus would be the basis for any program in the black community for emancipating black Americans.[68]

Karenga also devised the holiday Kwanzaa as an alternative to Christmas celebrations.[69] At first, he falsely marketed Kwanzaa as an African harvest festival. When later explaining his deliberate deceit about the origins of Kwanzaa, Karenga stated, "I said it was African because you know black people in this country wouldn't celebrate it if they knew it was American. Also I put it around Christmas because I knew that's when a lot of people would be partying."[70] Perhaps Karenga's deceit was merely a strategic marketing plan. Nevertheless, it was indicative of a mood of uncritical black acceptance of all things designated as African. But Karenga's deception may have been an error of youth. After all, the man who invented Kwanzaa and captured the allegiance of LeRoi Jones was only twenty-six years old. Kwanzaa remains extremely popular today, though without the insurgent imagery it originally possessed. Its resilience as an established Afro-American cultural institution testifies, however, to Karenga's awareness of the psychopolitical needs of Afro-Americans.

Baraka admits to having been somewhat amazed at the ingeniousness of Karenga's cultural doctrines. Karenga wanted to alter Afro-American cultural rituals because he believed that a "cultural revolution" in the minds of black people was a necessary precondition for the political revolution. Baraka came to share this doctrine. This belief in the priority of "culture" as a political tool lay at the heart of black cultural nationalism. The Karenga conception of culture as reified artifacts allowed for the easy mass production of "authentically black" cultural commodities. It paved the way for undermining the ethnic autonomy that these cultural artifacts were supposed to encourage. Blackness in the guise of "African" cultural artifacts—geles, Kente cloth, dashikis, Afro hairstyles, African jewelry—became profitable commodities for white and black capitalists and hip novelties for white consumers (Bo Derek's corn rows and terms such as *right-on, heavy,* and *get down*).[71] Although imported African clothes were quite expensive, one could buy cheap, made-in-America, mass-produced dashikis at K-Mart or Sears. I did.

In his autobiography, Baraka explains his immediate and intense allegiance to Karenga's doctrines.[72] First, Baraka was introduced to Karenga's philosophy and organization shortly after the Black Arts Repertory Theater School collapsed, mainly because it lacked a working organizational structure and culture. Second, Baraka admired the clearly delineated hierarchy in Karenga's organization. He envied Karenga's status as an uncontested leader, the one who issued commands that others followed. Baraka's antidemocratic sensibilities had earlier been exposed in his romanticization of Malcolm X. Baraka also was impressed by Karenga's authority to name the advocates,[73] marry them, name their children, and even suggest their place of work. Instead of being repulsed by these despotic practices, Baraka felt that Karenga "seemed to me to be the kind of next-higher stage of commitment and organization as compared to the Black Arts or what was going on in the Spirit House in Newark."[74] And Baraka admired the ideological uniformity of Karenga's organization. Karenga created various lists to facilitate the memorization of his ideological posturings. Such lists included Three Criteria of a Culture, Three Aspects of a Culture, Two Kinds of Revolution, and Seven Aspects of Malcolm X.[75] Members of US were drilled on these lists and were supposed to be able to recite them when asked.

Third, Baraka was enthralled by the paramilitary style of Karenga's organization. The male followers of US were members of Karenga's paramilitary corps known as the Simba Wachanga (young lions). They provided security for Karenga and punished Karenga's political enemies (though never the police). Karenga's intricate organizational infrastructure indicated to Baraka the seriousness of their preparation for the coming revolution. Vulnerable to delusions of grandeur, Baraka must have known that Karenga's minions were no match for the United States military or even the FBI. Apparently Baraka believed that a "revolutionary appearance" was a crucial component of being revolutionary. Most important to the revolutionary image was the sight of strictly disciplined cadres in "uniform." For Baraka's political accomplices, this uniform was traditional African garb. Uniforms were important because they helped distinguish the group from the rest of society and instill in the members the belief that they constituted one collectivity.[76] Style was central to Afro-American political efforts during the Black Power era. For instance, the seriousness of the Nation of Islam was conveyed in its members' neat but unfashionable clothing. Men in "the Nation" had closely cut hair and wore drab suits, white shirts, bow ties, and leather shoes. Women in the Nation wore long dresses/gowns and head wraps. Likewise, the mystique of the Panthers was in part created by their uniform of big "natural" Afro-hair styles (for women), berets (for men), and dark sunglasses, leather coats/jackets, and dark pants for everyone. Black power lay in unity and uniforms.

Mimicking Karenga, Baraka tried to eliminate any spontaneous individuality in his organization by adopting authoritarian forms of decision making. He may have sensed that the antidemocratic ethos of the air force had given him the discipline essential to his development as a writer. Yet it remains baffling that Baraka—or, for that matter, Karenga himself—could find anything edifying about leading a cadre of men who mindlessly took orders and repeated memorized sayings. These cultural nationalists projected a vision of a black community as potentially revolutionary at precisely the moment that blacks chose to repress the possibility for individual critical enlightenment. In the name of revolutionary discipline, thought conformity became black freedom.

During the 1960s, the presence of highly visible bodyguards was de rigueur for any would-be black revolutionary leader. Karenga and, later, Baraka were surrounded by armed security teams. Part of the excitement of seeing these "revolutionary leaders" was the crowd of menacing protectors that surrounded them as they strolled through an airport lounge or down the isle of a lecture hall. A cadre of ominous bodyguards was also clever dramaturgy, for it created a public image of significance for the guarded person.

Baraka and Karenga were deeply critical of the American pretense of egalitarianism and democracy in the face of historical and contemporary Afro-American subjugation. But their nationalist vision did not generate a serious critique of the flawed nature of American democracy, for that would have been tantamount to admitting the possibility of an interracial or multiracial society. More precisely, discussing the possibilities for democracy in the United States would have assumed that the political system, however defective, could be improved. This idea of historical contingency was incompatible with Baraka's belief that whites were intrinsically racist and immoral. Baraka and Karenga regarded democracy as a white idea and of little relevance to authentic blacks. Whether the political system was called democratic, communist, authoritarian, or oligarchical was inconsequential. The salient issue was that whites controlled black life.

The authoritarian aspirations of Baraka and Karenga were supposedly a response to the chaos evident in the lives of the black lower classes, which provided a sizable number of their recruits. Baraka and Karenga viewed themselves as offering their followers a sense of direction. The discipline would inevitably be reactionary insofar as it required a renunciation of the individual's critical faculties. Similar to Elijah Muhammad's agenda in the Nation of Islam, in which total obedience was demanded of the members and used to propel their entry into the world of petty capitalism or the labor market, the total obedience demanded of the cultural nationalists around Baraka facilitated organizational efficiency. This was evident in the crucial role that Baraka's followers played at the Atlanta Congress of African Peoples and later at the National Black Political Convention in Gary.

The failure of the capitalist labor market to absorb large numbers of the black lower class resulted in the growth of a populace that had never been systematically socialized into modern American society. The absence of market-inspired but self-imposed order in the lives of large numbers of urban blacks hindered their ability to articulate their discontent in a politically viable manner. Marx, we must remember, counted on capitalist exploitation to create a proletarian consciousness. Paradoxically, the failure of American capitalism to homogenize the black lumpen and lower classes made it all the more difficult for them to rebel against that marketplace in an organized fashion. Under the pretense of being revolutionary, Baraka and Karenga attempted to homogenize and rationalize the black urban working classes. Ironically, the successful homogenization of their followers only made them more vulnerable to a predatory marketplace that was willing to sell blacks any "black" identity they so desired.[77]

Accordingly, the subculture of black militancy that arose during the mid-late 1960s and early 1970s was one that celebrated the gun.[78] As if to add black names to the frontier imagery of American heroes, Karenga, Baraka, Huey Newton, and others acted as if bearing arms was the only authentic passport to freedom. The idea of using violence as a means of establishing one's free identity was just another variation of the mythic American adherence to what Richard Slotkin called "regeneration through violence" and/or a "gunfighter nation."[79]

KARENGA'S DECLINE

Whereas some of the militant black writers of the Black Arts movement may have been members of gangs during the 1950s, many of the members of the Black Panther Party and Karenga's US were recruited directly from gangs.[80] In many instances, the recruits retained their gang mentality. What Baraka perceived as the discipline of Karenga's followers was thus both true and untrue. They were disciplined insofar as they apparently acted as a unit. Still, there is little to suggest that they ever gravitated to anything higher than disciplined thuggery masquerading as revolutionary praxis. It is one of the paradoxes of the Black Power era that many of the so-called black revolutionaries were actually murdered by other supposed black revolutionaries. Explanations for such anomic behavior are often shuttled aside in favor of the convenient excuses of COINTELPRO.[81] While COINTELPRO did violate the legal rights of many black activists and did coordinate the murder of others, the intense competitive disdain held by one radical black group for another was not only common but deadly. The federal police apparatus could not have instigated such black-on-black fratricide if the tendencies toward that behavior were not already present in the various organizations. Concerning this phenomenon, Baraka wrote:

It is proven now from Freedom of Information Act files that the FBI orchestrated much of this discord between the two organizations. But certainly Cleaver's arrogance and shallow bohemian anarchism which he
passed off as Marxism, plus Karenga's Maulana complex, helped speed up
the tragic collision that finally saw Bunchy and Huggins dead.[82]

Baraka's "explanation" for the violence between US and the Black Panthers is
disingenuous, the typical Orwellian "doublespeak" that masquerades as honesty whenever American political figures are asked to confront issues they
want to elude. The strategy is to invoke clever non sequiturs. What does
Cleaver's supposed bohemian anarchism or Karenga's Maulana complex have
to do with the murder of Carter and Huggins? In many black nationalist and
radical circles, Karenga is suspected of having colluded with the state, particularly the Los Angeles Police Department and the FBI. There is, to my knowledge, no definitive proof for these charges. However, at various times Karenga
did act in concert with the will of the police agencies.[83] First, Karenga was part
of a group that met with Governor Ronald Reagan in the aftermath of the
Watts riots. Recognizing Karenga's opportunistic sensibilities, the *Wall Street
Journal* referred to him as "typical of many militants who talk looting and
burning but usually are eager to gather influence for quiet bargaining with the
predominantly white power structure."[84] Second, the program of US was decidedly nonrevolutionary. That is, Karenga's organization was more committed to controlling the behavior of other black activists than to confronting the
authority of the state. Beyond his desire to be an ethnic autocrat, Karenga had
no viable political praxis. Instead of engaging in political actions to improve
blacks' living conditions, Karenga recommended their wearing African
clothes and using African languages. He also, as previously mentioned, tried
to convince blacks that memorizing and reciting his trite ditties was somehow
emancipating, but it is not clear how. Third, various state agencies (e.g., California Social Welfare) allowed Karenga to participate openly in the antiriot,
pacification programs that were established after the 1965 Watts riot. As a result, Karenga was not only invested with state legitimacy but had access to financial resources that allowed him to increase his following. For instance,
Karenga, as opposed to the Panthers, had ready access to the Los Angeles
Human Relations Commission (HRC).[85] Why? Didn't the Human Relations
Committee know that Karenga was a revolutionary? His connection to the
HRC is all the more perplexing because Karenga was not a community organizer. Instead, one might consider Karenga a secular priest who tried to sell
black folks a false, other-worldly blackness and ersatz Africanisms.

It was widely speculated concerning Karenga's ties to the repressive wing of the state that key figures in his organization were government agents. Perhaps Karenga did not know this, although this seems highly unlikely given his close scrutiny of his followers. In his 1980 doctoral dissertation, "War Against the Panthers: A Study of Repression in America," Huey Newton quotes a man who had informed on the Black Panthers for the FBI.[86] This informant, D'Arthard Perry, claims to have seen three of Karenga's followers at the FBI offices in Los Angeles. He again saw these same three men, Claud Hubert and brothers Larry Stiner and George Stiner, at the FBI offices immediately following the murder of two Black Panthers. The informant maintained that Claud Hubert was the actual murderer and that he learned from his contacts in the FBI that Hubert was an FBI agent and had been transferred to an East Coast FBI office after the killing.[87]

Of course, it is possible that this informant was not telling the truth, although the Stiner brothers were arrested and charged with the murders. It also is true that the Stiner brothers were key members of US. They were subsequently convicted of murder and sentenced to prison at San Quentin. After four years, the brothers had become such model prisoners that they earned the right to have conjugal visits. During one such visit, they escaped and have never been heard from again.

The story of US and the Stiner brothers would have been forever buried in the paranoia and mystery that surrounds so many incidents from the 1960s had it not been for the guilty conscience of a former FBI agent. In *FBI Secrets: An Agent's Exposé*, former agent M. Wesley Swearingen gives credence to Perry's tale. He reveals that soon after he had been transferred to the Los Angeles racial squad (the FBI had special units in major cities whose mission was to keep blacks under surveillance), he was told by one agent that another agent had arranged for his informers to assassinate Bunchy Carter and John Huggins. According to Swearingen, following FBI instructions, FBI informants George Stiner and Larry Stiner murdered Carter and Huggins on the UCLA campus on June 17, 1969. Swearingen also confirms Perry's belief that the FBI arranged the escape of the Stiner brothers from San Quentin: "As of 1992 the Stiner brothers were still listed as fugitives. Either the FBI has disposed of them or they are in the FBI's Witness Protection Program. I know that Darthard Perry was an FBI informant and that he is telling the truth about the FBI." Swearingen also claims to have found several other cases in which members of US who were informers for the FBI were paid to assassinate members of the Black Panther Party. He does not mention a single instance in which Panthers were paid to kill members of US.[88] The crucial point missed by people like Baraka who tried to take the middle ground between the Panther–US conflict is that the state was much more concerned about the Black Panthers than US. Contrary to Baraka's ahistorical and inaccurate insinuations that the state used US and the Black Panthers to destabilize each other, the truth is that the state used Karenga and his followers to derail the Panthers. There is little evidence to suggest that the state viewed US as a threat. Whether or not the Panthers were actually capable of "going anywhere" politically is another issue but that does not erase Karenga's complicity in their demise.

In the final analysis, Karenga's influence in the black community ultimately rested on his control of men, who would threaten, beat, and even murder if it were deemed necessary. When Baraka now comments on Karenga's activities during the 1960s, he never mentions that this revolutionary black nationalist and his cronies succeeded in murdering only black men.

Following the highly publicized murders of the two Black Panthers, Karenga's organization went into decline. According to Baraka, Karenga became paranoid at the possibility that the Panthers would try to retaliate, and his paranoia led to drug dependence. During this period, Karenga's personal influence on Baraka significantly weakened, even though Baraka continued to be a practitioner of Kawaida. It was during this time that Karenga tried but failed to intimidate Baraka into canceling the Atlanta Pan-African Congress.

Karenga finally disappeared from national prominence when he and three of his followers were charged with torturing two black women, Gail Davis and Debra Jones, who lived in Karenga's home. Karenga had accused them of trying to poison him with "crystals" that had been placed in his water and clothes and throughout his home. In May 1971, Karenga and three members of US were convicted, although Karenga denied all charges. The testimonies of Gail Davis; Debra Jones; Karenga's wife, Brenda Karenga; and George Armstrong-Weusi, the former head of Karenga's personal security, were sufficient for a conviction. Afraid for their lives, Jones and Davis fled to Jamaica and returned only to testify at the trial. Brenda Karenga moved to Virginia.[89] The Maulana spent the next four years of his life in prison. After his release, Karenga did return to prominence in certain sectors of the black intelligentsia. His return was testimony to both his resilience and the short historical memory of black activists.

While Karenga was absorbed in his various conflicts with the Black Panthers, Baraka became a political organizer on both the local and national levels. Then, when Karenga was imprisoned, Baraka no longer had any challengers to his status as the preeminent black cultural nationalist in America.

CONCLUSION

Despite the fantasy in elevating Kawaida—a derivative set of practices—to the realm of emancipatory thought, the impetus behind Baraka's embrace of black cultural nationalism was understandable. Karenga and Baraka believed that their political opposition to black socioeconomic subjugation necessarily contained a cultural component. They recognized that having been damaged by racism, black psyches were probably incapable of sustaining an oppositional political engagement. Following in the footsteps of Elijah Muhammad and Malcolm X, Baraka and Karenga knew that many blacks had internalized racism and were locked in a self-hating mind-set. As true idealists, they thought that the principal barrier blocking the journey from self-defeat to self-assertion lay in the recesses of the black mind. If black people realized their true human value, they would not tolerate or submit to their devaluation by white America.

Unfortunately, Karenga and Baraka mistakenly assumed that an emancipatory psyche could be created anew. They incorrectly believed that the substance of this new emancipatory black mind-set could be based on the recuperation of traditional African cultural beliefs and practices. Their cultural formulation had numerous conceptual shortcomings. First, Baraka and Karenga were imprisoned in a Manichean world in which everything white was bad and everything African was good. In creating this Manichean world, Baraka essentially was reacting to "white" practices and beliefs. He and Karenga were caught in a vice of knee-jerk antiwhite reactionism that prevented them from admitting that some aspects of American society and culture were worth maintaining even after the death of white supremacy. Were black folks to forsake polio vaccine or laser surgery for cataracts? In addition, Baraka and Karenga were insufficiently dialectical in their understanding of cultural change. Evidently, they did not grasp that cultural beliefs could be substantively altered only in an engagement with the materiality of the lives of oppressed blacks.

As stated earlier, their racial essentialism created a severely constrained future. In a world in which blacks and whites could not evolve or change, the potential for viable social transformation was minuscule. It was, therefore, not surprising that racial essentialism gave rise to a worldview in which an apocalyptic intervention by God would be necessary for social change. This simple lesson could have been learned from an examination of the Nation of Islam. Because Elijah Muhammad believed that white people were genetically incapable of treating blacks fairly, he was forced to establish a religious teleology in which white behavior toward blacks did not matter. But where, when, or how could this happen in the United States? Ironically, in confronting white domination, Elijah Muhammad created a theology in which whites were powerless over blacks. He devised various ways in which God would intervene on the side of blacks and destroy the naturally wicked white peoples of the world. In the meantime, he asked the wicked white folks to give him a black nation in the South where blacks could live in peace. But why would wicked white people do anything beneficial for black people?

Bizarre as it may appear to some, it did not take much imagination for many blacks to view whites as innately evil or warped. For hundreds of years, European peoples had tried to control the lives of nonwhite peoples around the world. Their colonization of Africa, Latin America, Asia, and India testifies to this. Hitler's dream of a world dominated by Aryan people was only one episode in the long history of European desire to control all nonwhite peoples. On those historic occasions when whites settled among nonwhite peoples, their intentions soon turned to domination, for example, the white racist domination of New Zealand, Australia, South Africa, Rhodesia, Canada, and the United States. Despite their conceits about who is and is not civilized, white Europeans and their descendants do not have an impressive history of getting along with other peoples. Accordingly, we can perhaps understand why Baraka and Karenga viewed whites as intrinsically antihumanistic. Their error was their inability to distinguish white people as a biological race from whiteness as a cultural construct. Certainly something deeply pathological about whiteness had developed over the last five centuries, but it was not embedded in white genes or skin cells.

Their inability to distinguish whiteness as a cultural construct led Baraka and Karenga to accept a simplistic worldview in which they could not acknowledge the pathologies often found in black societies. Instead, they spent an enormous amount of time trying to claim that any immorality and pathology in blacks was taught to them by whites. In so doing, they created a passive image of blacks. Racial essentialism pretended to explain differences in "racial natures," but it could not explain racial inequalities. Paradoxically, at the very moment that Karenga and Baraka believed that they were being most radical, they were incapable of escaping their reliance on moral discourses. Simply put, when one scratched below the surface of their rhetoric about black militancy, one discovered pleas to whites for better treatment of blacks.

In their desire to create a nostalgia for a black past that never was, Baraka and Karenga had to avoid confronting the African past or present. A serious engagement with history would not have allowed them to create the innocent black noble savages that saturated their ontology of black people. Had Africans been as loving, peaceful, and communally oriented as Baraka's and

Karenga's mythology maintained, the African slave trade would have failed. Considering the extent to which the Africanism valorized by Baraka and Karenga was an ersatz Africanism created by Karenga's Hollywood-influenced mind, Baraka and Karenga never really tried to engage Africa. Their willingness to replace history with myth allowed Baraka to create Islam as a black African religion, free of the evil legacy of Christianity. Ironically, however, Islam had an equally valid claim to the mantle of "slave religion."

In sum, Baraka and Karenga were unable to escape the identity problem that had ensnarled generations of black thinkers before them. This dilemma was rooted in the peculiarly unstable identity of black Americans. Simultaneously bastards of the West and Africa, black Americans could find true homes only in a hybrid "new-world" American identity, which even for white Americans was the norm, whether or not they recognized it. Baraka's attempt to embrace a "pure" African identity was a bid to create an uncompromising oppositional identity. He wanted to cleanse himself of the complex identity given to him by an accident of birth. Through the mere assertion of his individual will, he thought that he could walk away from the Du Boisian problematic of Afro-American duality. But appropriating a true black identity made sense only in an environment in which that identity was not protected by existing cultural boundaries. Even those Africans embedded in European acculturation à la Senghor did not have to purchase a black identity. The quest for a blacker self was possible only in a society saturated with norms of whiteness. In this sense, black Americans are descendants of the West in ways quite foreign to black Africans, however culturally Westernized the Africans might be. Ignorance of Hegel, Flaubert, or Bach does not marginalize black Americans from the West in the same ways that knowledge of them granted Senghor access to a francophone identity. Like white Americans, black Americans are inscribed with Westernism, however far they may be from highbrow European culture.

10

The Slave as Master

Black Nationalism, Kawaida, and the Repression of Women

CONTEMPORARY SCHOLARSHIP OF twentieth-century black political formations has documented the historical devaluation of issues pertaining to the specific plight of Afro-American women. Besides the male dominance of black ethnic institutions (e.g., churches, black colleges, black insurance firms, professional organizations), the absence of much concern about black women's issues stemmed from an overarching ethnic belief that the enemy of black progress was white supremacy. In this view, white supremacy did not differentiate according to gender. Thus, to champion issues that presupposed a unique plight for black women was tantamount to undermining race unity. Despite the historical marginalization of such issues, black women have played crucial roles in all social movements toward black emancipation.

Black women, for example, were essential participants in the Civil Rights movement. They could be found among the demonstrators and even in its leadership circles. From the refusal of Rosa Parks to give up her seat on a Montgomery, Alabama, bus to the women who organized the subsequent bus boycott to women like Septima Clark who worked in citizenship schools, black women "carried their weight." Despite not being supported by the Democratic Party's leadership, Fannie Lou Hamer, an uneducated Mississippi sharecropper, challenged the Mississippi racial oligarchy at the 1964 Democratic National Convention in Atlantic City. Ella Baker, a lifelong political activist and organizational genius helped construct the community empowerment model adopted by the organizers of SNCC. In SNCC, women like Gloria Richardson, Diane Nash, Faye Bellamy, Ruby Doris Smith-Robinson, and Joyce Ladner were important participants and leaders. Earlier, Daisy Bates, president of the NAACP chapter in Little Rock, Arkansas, managed the highly contentious desegregation of Central High School.[1]

Nonetheless, the debate continues over the degree to which women in SNCC were subjected to sexist treatment by male activists. Similarly, there are questions about whether the experiences of black women in the Civil Rights movement generally were different from those of their white female peers. In *How Long? How Long? African-American Women in the Struggle for Civil Rights*, Belinda Robnett shows that black women were crucial as leaders and rank-and-file participants in the Civil Rights movement, although they usually were not given formal leadership roles.[2] Black women often became leaders on the strength of their individual personalities and or during crises when their competence could not be as easily ignored. Therefore, even though black women were not equally represented in the formal Civil Rights movement leadership, their participation marked the peak of female participation in black political movements of the twentieth century. Then, the decline of the Civil Rights movement and the subsequent rise of the Black Power movement signaled a massive retreat in the already minuscule ability of black women to shape national and local black political agendas.

Robnett notes that the rise of the Black Power movement out of the ashes of the Civil Rights movement meant more rigid hierarchies "and fewer free spaces for women's leadership." Concerning the gender implications of the emergence of the non-southern-based Black Power movement, Robnett writes:

> And in the North, the exhibitionism of manhood was not mitigated by the strength of Black institutions whose most vital resource was women. Both black men and radical-chic white men-women, too applauded the machismo of leather-jacketed young men, armed to the teeth, rising out of the urban ghetto. The theme of the late sixties was "Black Power" punctuated by a knotted fist . . . common ethos between northern and southern blacks. Although it may not have been consciously conceived out of the need to affirm manhood, it became a metaphor for the male consciousness of the era. As Floyd McKissick . . . explained: "The year 1966 shall be remembered as the year we left our imposed status as Negroes and became Black men."[3]

The Black Power movement's emphasis on men also coincided with the valorization of violence as the means for attaining freedom. The physical aspects of struggles for freedom were considered a male domain insofar as warriors were deemed to be males.[4] In turn, the idea of a violent black struggle was enhanced by the example of the Vietnamese, who at the time were waging a devastating struggle against the United States military. The Vietnam example was an important influence on the Black Power era, for not only were the Vietnamese nonwhite but they also were successfully waging war against the "white man" without having access to the phenomenal technologies of war used by the United States. Throughout the nation, militants wondered whether blacks could do the same.

Many blacks, however, regarded the adoption and the rhetoric of violence as reversing the acquiescence and docility of passive nonviolent resistance, the dominant praxis of the Civil Rights movement. By 1965, Martin Luther King Jr.'s image had begun to dim in the eyes of many northern black political activists, although he remained popular with the black rank-and-file. In the eyes of the national media, after the Watts riot of 1965 Martin Luther King Jr. and his disciples lost much of their ability to influence the moral image of blacks. Black protesters were no longer depicted as respectful citizens in search of what was rightfully theirs. Having lost their association with religiosity, Black Power activists appeared on American television screens as would-be destroyers of the social order. Instead of appealing to the conscience of white Americans, the dominant public spokespersons of the Black Power movement, including figures like Stokely Carmichael and H. Rap Brown, rhetorically assaulted and threatened white America. The writings of Baraka, Karenga, Huey Newton, Julius Lester, Eldridge Cleaver, and George Jackson reiterated these threats.

Even though the rhetoric of Carmichael and Brown and the writing of Baraka and Cleaver were ominous, they were overshadowed by and dependent on the images of looting, arson, and gunfire that dominated television news broadcasts as city after city exploded in urban rioting. Not only were urban police forces incapable of quickly subduing the disorder, but it also became clear that many blacks on the streets were challenging the legitimacy of the state's authority. The black urban riots of the late 1960s underscored the rhetorical threats of violent revolution by Black Power spokespersons. Ironically, the consequent increase in the cultural authority of Black Power spokespersons allowed many of them to feign a role in these urban explosions that they really did not possess. That is, Baraka and the others must be seen as clever elements in the black bourgeois intelligentsia who used the urban riots to enhance their own political capital and voice.

The Black Power movement was seen as a moment when black men would rise as men. Cleaver referred to the history of black America as "four hundred years minus my Balls."[5] The days of Step 'n Fetchit had been replaced by the presence of armed black men in berets and black leather jackets who were willing to kill police. Images of angry and armed black men who seemed not to fear their own deaths or those of others momentarily replaced the ubiquitous Soviet Communists as mainstream white America's worst nightmare.[6]

Perhaps no single figure embodied the new black male assertiveness more than Malcolm X. His straightforward and forceful rhetoric cut against

the grain of the bourgeois civility that had governed the public pronouncements of King, Roy Wilkins, James Farmer, and other civil rights leaders. His
stridence inspired many blacks who had grown tired of the pleas of the traditional civil rights leadership sector. Moreover, he appeared to be beyond compromise. Fearless, Malcolm told "the white man" precisely what "whitey" did
not want to hear and, in so doing, vicariously empowered a generation of
blacks. Many black men found in Malcolm a surrogate for their manhood.

In no small measure, Malcolm's status was enhanced by his membership
in the male-dominated, highly organized Nation of Islam. Under the direction of Elijah Muhammad, the Nation tried to initiate a cultural revitalization
movement among urban blacks. The centerpieces of this effort were (1) a
blackened version of the Protestant work ethic for men, (2) an essentialist belief in black racial superiority and the necessity of black unity, (3) the reha-
bilitation of criminals and otherwise incarcerated black men, (4) the promotion of a black patriarchal family structure, and (5) the rejection of the immoral white man's values and cultural influences (e.g., smoking, drinking,
dancing, drugs, sexually provocative clothing). Furthermore, Elijah Muhammad advocated puritanical heterosexual relationships before and outside
marriage. (Of course, not everyone practiced what he preached!)

Many black women were drawn to the Nation of Islam precisely because of its conservative cultural practices. As members, they could expect
to be treated respectfully by male members and even male nonmembers
who respected the possibility of male retribution from the Fruit of Islam.
When these women married men who belonged to the Nation, they had
reason to believe that they would not be abandoned or otherwise left to
fend financially for themselves and their children. Because the Nation of
Islam instilled in its male members the importance of fatherhood, it appears to have attracted black women seeking a stable, patriarchal family.
What may have appeared to many outside the organization as its endorsement of female subservience was frequently viewed by female members of
the Nation as a respite from the chaotic heterosexual relationships prevalent in urban black communities.

Women in the Nation were taught to excel at the domestic "arts" of cooking, sewing, and mothering. Equally important, they were taught to dress
conservatively and to refrain in public from interacting informally with men.
A student of the Nation of Islam described the peculiar status of women in
the organization:

> The image of virtuous womanhood presented to the public through Mus-
> lim displays of chivalry and propaganda often gave outsiders the impression

that female believers actually held a superior place in the temple. However, the reality of Muslim power arrangements and gender relations confirmed for the insider and the keen observer that the pedestals on which woman were placed had been constructed by men and could be cast aside when a female believer needed a good "smack in the face" for challenging the will of her male counterpart.[7]

The reasons for the religiously sanctioned sexism of the Nation of Islam may have been similar to those in black American Christian churches. In Christianity, it was thought that as descendants of Eve, women were more susceptible to sin than men. Elijah Muhammad maintained:

> Allah, Himself, has said that we cannot return to our land until we have a thorough knowledge of our own selves. The first step is the control and the protection of our own women. There is no nation on earth that has less respect for and as little control of their woman as we so-called Negroes in America. . . . Our women are allowed to walk or ride the streets all night long, with any strange men they desire. They are allowed to frequent any tavern or dance hall that they like, whenever they like. They are allowed to fill our homes with children other than our own. Children that are often fathered by the very devil himself.
>
> . . . Our women have been and are still being used by the devil white race, ever since we were first brought here to these States as slaves.[8]

Elijah Muhammad's teachings influenced Malcolm's views on women. In his autobiography, Malcolm stated that all women "by their nature are fragile and weak: they are attracted to the male in whom they see strength."[9] Malcolm's sexism did not diminish his popularity among Black Power activists (including, probably, most female Black Power proponents). To the contrary, Malcolm's sexism was one of the core components of his appeal. He became the living reversal of the emasculated black male. Malcolm had "balls." The eulogy delivered by Ossie Davis at Malcolm's funeral captured the significance of his life as a black man:

> And if you knew him you would know why we honor him: Malcolm was our manhood, our living, black manhood! This was his meaning to his people. And, in honoring him, we honor the best in ourselves.
>
> . . . And we will know him then for what he was and is—a Prince—our own black shining Prince!—who didn't hesitate to die, because he loved us so.[10]

Malcolm's militant black manhood inspired Huey Newton and Bobby Seale to form the Black Panthers and intensified the political energies of LeRoi Jones. Following Malcolm's lead, Jones became a public truth teller who was willing to incur the wrath of whites. Ultimately, however, Jones confused the goal of telling truths that might upset whites with the goal of upsetting whites.

Jones had been hurling threats and invectives at whites long before it became de rigueur for Black Power advocates. He had become particularly entranced by the idea of frightening white Americans. It was as if he had deliberately chosen to be Jimmy Baldwin's antithesis. Whereas Baldwin was writing about the suffering of black folks and the subversion of white humanity in white supremacy, Baraka spoke of killing whites. He was not concerned about their moral redemption. His unstated aspiration was to rhetorically decimate whites in a manner comparable to their historical persecution of blacks.

Jones's maniacal desire to frighten whites reached a peak with the publication of "American Sexual Reference: Black Male." Republished and widely read in *Home*, the essay originally appeared in *Cavalier Magazine* in January 1966. The cover of the magazine reads "LeRoi Jones Tells It Like He Sees It: The White Man Is Obsolete." Accompanying the article is a photograph of Jones casually posed in a sports coat, tie, and tennis shoes. He holds the proverbial writer's cigarette in his hand. This relaxed photo was placed against his bombshell essay, an irony not lost on the magazine's editors, who wrote below the published photo, "This pleasant, affable young man has a message for you."[11] Jones's decision to publish this vitriolic article in a predominantly "white" magazine revealed the parasitic status of those victim-status blacks who were locked into a quest for white recognition by means of fear. The smug picture of Jones accompanying the article does not indicate his awareness of his dependence on whites. If anything, Jones looks as though he actually believes that he has written something quite provocative and radical.

This essay reveals Jones's willingness to use vicious and vulgar sexism and sickening racist depictions of blacks in order to terrify whites. He argues that because of their history in America, black men were more in touch with their sexuality than white men were and that recognition of this black male predicament had led to white women's sexual desire for black men.

> The reason the white woman was supposed to be intrigued by the black man was because he was basic and elemental emotionally (which is true for the nonbrainwashed black, simply because there is no reason he should not be; the black man is more "natural" than the white simply because he has fewer

things between him and reality, fewer wrappings, fewer artificial rules), therefore "wilder," harder, and almost insatiable in his lovemaking.[12]

When one realizes that "fewer things between him and reality, fewer wrappings, fewer artificial rules" is, for Baraka, a description of the black male's distance from Western civilization, the similarities between his comments and Mailer's "White Negro" become astonishingly apparent. Most repugnant are the affinities between Baraka's "almost insatiable" black man and the black beastly creatures in the novels of Thomas Dixon.[13] Jones's statements may help us understand why he had not earlier responded to Podhoretz's claim that Kerouac and the Beats in general had racistly romanticized black sensuality and sexuality. Perhaps Jones had not disagreed with Kerouac's stereotypes of black sensuality. Consequently, his objection to the "Crow Jane" sexual ethic in the Village was not the white woman's perceptions of the sexual superiority of black men. Those perceptions were supposedly accurate. Rather, Jones's anger was directed at her desire to sap the vitality from the black man. Although Jones does not say so, his anger was also implicitly directed at the eagerness with which black men relinquished their virility to her.

The black man of "American Sexual Reference" was simultaneously morally innocent and apelike in his uncontrolled libido. Jones's new black man was the authentic Noble Savage and morally superior to the white man, for as a victim he had no access to the power to do evil. In addition, he was blessed with the inadvertent sexual superiority of the beast. As an oppressed being, the black male had sidestepped those anxieties of modern life that had dampened the eroticism of his white male victimizers. The result was sexually impotent white men. "Most American white men are trained to be fags. For this reason it is no wonder their faces are weak and blank. . . . Can you, for a second, imagine the average middleclass white man able to do somebody harm?"[14]

In Jones's homophobic eyes, the association of white males with homosexuality confirmed their weakness and impotence. Gay men were always imagined as feminine. Given his devaluation of women, this association was a hypernegative stigmatization. But Jones could not explain why the so-called weak white man was able to so thoroughly subjugate blacks, including the hypermasculine black male.

The literary scholar Robyn Wiegman viewed such rhetoric as an attempt to invert the "representational economy that depicts the black man as either literally or metaphorically less than a man." Baraka, she noted, "aligns feminization with whiteness, defining white men as 'effeminate and perverted.'"[15] Jones's homophobic diatribes against white men were critical to his explanation of why the white man wanted to oppress the black man. In lieu of a socioeconomic, political, or psychological theory to explain the rationality of the racist oppression of black people, Jones adopted a myth-like tale that white men had invented technology as a means to control black men because black men were their sexual masters and thus their superiors. White men were too scared and too weak to confront black men in face-to-face penis duels, and evidently the white woman knew this.

Jones used a "state of nature" argument to situate heterosexual potency as the central dynamic in race relations. Effeminate white homosexuals (i.e., all white men) were no match for black men. For similar reasons, black homosexuals were considered incapable of participating in the Black Power struggle. Even more despised than the idea of the black female mistress to a powerful black-male-hating white man was the black male homosexual who longed to be "fucked" by white men. Black homosexuals were by their very nature weaklings and thus tempted to become whores and race traitors for the white man. They were therefore, incapable of being free, that is, free to act in the manner of victimizers.[16] Only real men could lead the freedom struggle. Women and those men who acted like women would have to follow.

Perhaps the most vicious statements that Jones ever wrote concerning women were those assertions in "American Sexual Reference" that attempted to legitimate the black male rape of white women. "That is the average ofay [white person] thinks of the black man as potentially raping every white lady in sight. Which is true, in the sense that the black man should want to *rob the white man of everything that he has*" [my emphasis]. Sounding a great deal like a script writer for "Birth of a Nation," Jones continued:

> But for most whites the guilt of the robbery is the guilt of rape. That is, they know in their deepest hearts that they should be robbed, and the white woman understands that only in the rape sequence is she likely to get cleanly, viciously popped, which is a thing her culture provides for only in fantasies of "evil." . . . The black man, then, because he can enter into the sex act with less guilt as to its results, is freer. Because of the robbery/rape syndrome, the black man will take the white woman in a way that does not support the myth of the Lady, thus *springing an outside reality that will seem either beast like or god like, depending on the lady's psychological connection with the White American Crime.*[17] [my emphasis]

Baraka's inability to view white women as other than objects owned by white men was classically sexist. His willingness to state that white women could justifiably be raped by black men engaged in the act of stealing property from white men was racist-inspired misogyny. According to this argument, the black man could supposedly take whatever he wanted from the white man, whether it be televisions, shoes, or "his women." Such was the nature of the unequal distribution of private property. Of course, for a black nationalist like Jones to suggest that the "revolutionary" black man would even want to rape a white woman demands an explanation, unless rape was less an act of sexual desire than an act of violence against the white man whose task it was to protect this woman. Jones's crude logic is confusing, for if he viewed rape as merely an act of violence, he would have to view the woman, not "her man," as the subject of the violence.

Jones implies that the violated white woman would enjoy being raped by a virile black man, for he would undoubtedly give her the thrill of her sexual life. Such an argument was vicious and vulgar, once again indicating his racist misogyny. Jones contended that whereas a black man would rape a white woman for reasons of retributive violence against the white man, the non-racist white woman would experience her rape as sexually exhilarating—a God-like gift that no white man could give to her. Only a racist white woman would perceive her rape by a black man as a beast-like violation. At no point does Jones admit that rape is an assault on a woman.

bell hooks correctly perceived the warped logic of Baraka's belief in the revolutionary nature of the virile black man, regarding it as ironic that Baraka would accept as valid and then glorify the very stereotypes that had been used by racist whites as a pretext for lynching black men:

> Ironically, the "Power" of black men that Baraka and others celebrated was the stereotypical, racist image of the black man as primitive, strong and virile. Although these same images of black men had been evoked by racist whites to support the argument that all black men were rapists, they were now romanticized as positive characteristics.[18]

Historian Martin Duberman dismissed Baraka's moronic but passionately articulated vulgarity:

> My main reaction to these ravings is not anger or fright but boredom. They are so obviously the effluvium of a disturbed man that they cannot even be taken with the seriousness we accord polemics. Jones is pursuing private catharsis, not communication; there is no room at all for exchange—and apparently Jones couldn't care less.

As if to inform Jones that his outlandish attempts to frighten whites have been exposed as a fraud, Duberman continued:

> No doubt my boredom is what he hoped for; it confirms his expectations of how a decadent, "dead-loined," smug materialist (i.e., a White) would react to the hip, soulful, virile truth-seeking of a POWERFUL BLACK WRITER. To which I can only repeat—I'm bored. Bored by categories. Bored by pretense. Bored by lectures. Bored by bearded oracles.[19]

It was certainly Jones's intention to use these writings to frighten white readers. Because the black rapist remains a feared stereotypical image in the psyche of white and black America, Jones believed that the image of the rapist could be given a radical ethos.[20] His image of the revolutionary as rapist prefigured the emergence of an actual rapist as a would-be revolutionary, Eldridge Cleaver. In *Soul on Ice*, Cleaver wrote,

> I became a rapist. To refine my technique and modus operandi, I started out by practicing on black girls in the ghetto . . . and when I considered myself smooth enough, I crossed the tracks and sought out white prey. I did this consciously, deliberately, willfully, methodically. . . .
>
> Rape was an insurrectionary act. It delighted me that I was defying and trampling on the white man's law, on his system of values, and I was defiling his woman—and this point, I believe, was the most satisfying to me because I was very resentful over the historical fact of how the white man has used the black woman. I felt I was getting revenge.[21]

Like Jones, Cleaver was utterly incapable of granting any human dignity and autonomy to white women.[22] In Cleaver's case, he also did not recognize human dignity in black women. At some deep level, he simply hated women. His attempt to rationalize rape as an insurrectionary act was nonsense. His claim to have raped white women out of revenge is disingenuous. First, it does not explain why he raped black women. Second, Cleaver's admission of rape appears in his book immediately after he discusses his phobic attraction to white women. Third, the rape of a white woman in no way hurts white men who rape black women. But it is not surprising that a common but clever hoodlum like Cleaver would try so hard to rationalize his unethical behavior. The differences between Cleaver and Jones is the reader's knowledge that Cleaver actually committed rapes. While I cannot vouch for Jones's behavior toward women, his writing appears to be a rhetorical strategy for scaring white folks, and it does morally sanction rape. What remains striking about

Cleaver is that his admissions and third-rate moral evasions granted him a revolutionary status in the eyes of many Americans. Perhaps the subtitle to *Soul on Ice* should have been *Reflections on How a Monster Became a Revolutionary by Admitting to Thuggery.*

Cleaver's successful bid to occupy the status of Beast/Gorilla did translate into lucrative royalties, public appearances, and widespread notoriety, however, all of which testified to the dominance of irrationality and image politics during the Black Power era. Despite his embrace of an image that was dependent on the reactions of whites, Cleaver mistakenly believed that he embodied a new, revolutionary, black male ethos. Precisely when he thought he was being most assertive, he was most parasitically dependent on recognition from whites. "Thus, articulating a political agenda of nationalist power, Black Power asserted black masculinity as coterminous with racial emancipation."[23]

Like Cleaver, Jones was incapable of realizing that the events and images that terrorized white America were not necessarily the events and images that would emancipate black America. Baraka has always had an infantile, Hollywood-like understanding of social change. Reminiscent of his days in the Village, Jones once again mistook parasitic, ad hoc societal rejectionism for revolutionary praxis. Alarming threats substituted for revolutionary theory and practice.

The significance of the black male rape of the white woman is that it was one of those rare instances to which Baraka could point in which the black man had become an intimate exploiter of a white person—in this case, the white woman and, by default, her overseer, the white man! By acting like the victimizer, the rapist supposedly glimpsed black freedom. Scheler would have recognized in this the deceit of ressentiment.[24] Black freedom meant little more than reproducing the behavior of the white oppressors. Baraka had not understood Fanon.[25] To those who responded that rape had nothing to do with obtaining freedom, Baraka would retort that white men had historically raped black women and did so in order to deny black men their manhood. Black men were demeaned and emasculated by their inability to protect their women. As a result, black women ceased to look to black men, their rightful protectors, for protection. It was now black America's turn to change places with whites. Women were but the ground on which battles over manhood—that is, freedom—would be waged.

While hooks and other critics are correct in condemning Jones's embrace of the worst stereotypes of black men, they are inadvertently participating in and reinforcing his attempt to obfuscate his own sexuality. Jones's endorsement of the rape of white women and his homophobic attacks on white men were part of his broader strategy to bury his own homosexual past under black sexual exotica and sexist venom. He knew that popular knowledge of his homosexuality would have undermined the credibility of his militant voice. By becoming publicly known as a hater of homosexuals, Jones tried to defuse any claims that might surface linking him with a homosexual past. Was there a better way to "pass" for heterosexual than to embrace images of the hyper-heterosexually sexed black male beast who preyed on white women? What is amazing about "American Sexual Reference" is that it did succeed in masking Jones's homosexual past. When discussed, the essay is usually treated solely as an attempt by Jones to appropriate a racist stereotype in order to scare whites, when in fact scaring whites may have been the sleight of hand that hid his homosexual desire.[26]

KAWAIDA AND THE REPRESSION OF WOMEN

It is not surprising that the cultural nationalism propagated by Baraka and Karenga during the late 1960s and early 1970s was sexist. Baraka pointed out that Karenga's doctrines not only failed to challenge his male chauvinism but granted it a revolutionary legitimacy. Women and men were not viewed as equals but were "complementary," that is, slightly more equal than master and slave.

In her autobiography, former Black Panther Elaine Brown describes a social gathering that she attended in San Diego at which Karenga and numerous members of US were present. Brown was talking with a female acquaintance when a young woman, presumably a member of US, approached the two women and asked if they wanted to contribute to the group collection being taken to buy some Kentucky Fried Chicken. Brown and her female friend (neither of whom were members of US) contributed money to the collection. When the food finally arrived, Brown and her friend walked toward the kitchen. They were stopped by another female and informed that women were not allowed to eat until all the men had been fed. Brown remembers the woman as saying, "Sisters you will have to wait until our Brothers are served. Yeah, our Brothers are our warriors. Our warriors must be fed first, Sisters." Brown remembers responding that no one had mentioned that order of eating when her money was solicited for the collection. Later, one of the male members of US explained the "rules" to her. "Sisters, he explained, did not challenge Brothers. Sisters, he said, stood behind their black men, supported their men, and respected them. In essence, he advised us that it was not only unsisterly for us to want to eat with our Brothers, it was a sacrilege for which blood could be shed."[27]

Angela Davis had a similar experience with members of US. While helping organize a rally in San Diego in 1967,

> I was criticized very heavily, especially by male members of Karenga's organization for doing "a man's job." Women should not play leadership roles, they insisted. A woman was supposed to "inspire" her man and educate his children.... The constant harangue by the US men was that I needed to redirect my energies and use them to give my man strength and inspiration so that he might more effectively contribute his talents to the struggle for Black liberation.[28]

The mention of these incidents should not be interpreted as proclaiming that by default, the Black Panther Party was a bastion of gender egalitarianism. It wasn't. But the Black Panthers never formally instituted rituals that underscored females' subservience to males. Whereas women members of US were required to cross their arms over their breasts and bow down before the men of the organization, the Panthers never elevated to doctrine the need for the black male dominance of the black woman. As if to register uneasiness with this female ritual of submission, Baraka reformed the practice in his Newark organization, the Congress of Afrikan People (CAP), so that female members had to bow down only for the organization's officers, all of whom were apparently male. As the Imamu, Baraka certainly thought that he was worthy of female submission.

> Karenga also had wild stuff in his doctrine about how women ought to dress.... He said they should show flesh to intrigue men and not be covered up so much. I could never adjust to Karenga's thing with women either on paper or in the flesh. He was always making "sexy" remarks to women, calling them "freaks" and commenting loudly on their physical attributes. In LA [Los Angeles] Karenga even sanctioned "polygamy."[29]

Even though Baraka can now admit that he was sexist, he does not explain how male chauvinism ever came to be a central component of his and other black "revolutionary" agendas. The depth of the sexism in Baraka's and Karenga's organizations went far beyond that sanctioned in the existing black community, thus eliminating the possibility of claiming that it was merely a romanticized carryover from Afro-American folk culture. Had their sexist practices been rooted in Afro-American folk culture, with its myriad of patriarchal practices and beliefs, it would still have to be considered reactionary. It remains unclear just what Baraka meant when he stated that he "could never adjust to Karenga's thing with women,"[30] for Baraka uttered sexist claptrap and objectified women with an ease unsurpassed by Karenga. Moreover, Baraka tried to introduce polygamy into his life.

In a 1970 issue of *Black World*, Baraka published an essay, "Black Woman," in which he asserted that the black man and woman had become alienated from each other.[31] This disaffection had supposedly arisen as a result of slavery and the subsequent persistence of white racism. In hopes of restoring unity to black men and women, Baraka called for the revalorization of African values and the adoption of African identities. By returning to the traditions of African life before the slave trade, black male-female relationships would surmount the divisiveness caused by subjugated life in the diaspora. "We must erase the separateness by providing ourselves with healthy African identities. By embracing a value system that knows of no separation but only of the divine complement the black woman is for her man." At no point does Baraka tell us how these precapitalist African identities could be transported to the United States or why traditional African male and female relations constituted a model worth emulating in the United States during the second half of the twentieth century. Instead of interrogating traditional African gender roles and relationships, Baraka chose to cast demonic aspersions on what he viewed as white American norms. "We do not believe in 'equality' of men and women. We cannot understand what the devils and the devilishly influenced mean when they say equality for women. We could never be equals . . . nature has not provided thus."[32]

During the height of his allegiance to black nationalism, Baraka used the designation "devil" when referring to whites in order to reverse the deeply embedded white Western association of blackness and/or darkness with evil. Such labeling was also convenient for his dogmatic ideology. If he could successfully label certain beliefs and behaviorisms as creations of the demonic whites, it would preclude the necessity of explaining why such beliefs should be loathed and the behaviors spurned. Essentially, whatever was deemed "white" was bad. Baraka's ad hoc rejection of all things white was but the latest installment of his parasitic attachments to the parent society. The negative stigmatization of whites had simply replaced his Beat-era demonization of the philistine bourgeoisie.

White feminists (the devils) and their black counterparts (the devilishly influenced) would have been astonished to find out that gender equality had become a white American norm. Perhaps the pervasiveness of gender inequality in most white communities in the United States should have led Baraka to view his celebration of gender inequality for blacks as "devilishly influenced"! For Baraka to retreat to claims of "nature" to justify his assertions of male-female inequality appears somewhat myopic, given the historical in-vocations of "nature" to support claims for white supremacy. Baraka correctly perceived the struggle for women's equality as an assault on male hegemony, but he assumed that men were by their very nature destined to rule women and concluded that it was the weakness of the white man that allowed him even to think of women as his equal. Black men, the nation's only "real" men, would have nothing to do with such foolishness.

Baraka's formulations of gender relations unequivocally called for the black realization of idealized, traditional American, patriarchal family rela-tionships. Like other black cultural nationalists, Baraka was able to delude himself into thinking that there was something oppositional in the black pa-triarchal family. As bell hooks states in *Ain't I a Woman*, Baraka "did not use terms like patriarchy or male rule; instead he discussed the formation of a black male-dominated household with its inherent antiwoman stance as if it were a positive reaction against white racist values."[33] Baraka's support of pa-triarchy is not surprising, given that his hero Malcolm X also tried to market as revolutionary the installation of patriarchal norms in the black family. Like Malcolm and Malcolm's teacher, Elijah Muhammad, Baraka championed or-thodox gender roles. Note the domesticity in Baraka's ideal black revolution-ary woman: "We say that a black woman must first be able to inspire her man, then she must be able to teach our children, and contribute to the social de-velopment of the nation."[34]

In the essay "Black Woman," Baraka elaborates on the three duties of the revolutionary black woman. She should inspire the black man by joining him in the creation of a new black nation. For her to succeed, the black woman must have a revolutionary black consciousness that is part of her everyday life. The life that the black man and woman create for themselves and their children will be a microcosm of the life of the future black nation.

> The house we live in, the clothes we wear, the food we eat, the words we speak, must reinforce our move for National Liberation and the new con-sciousness of the million year old African personality, and it is the woman who must reinforce these thrusts. She is the creator of the environment, if she is conscious.[35]

The task of teaching the children is significant because the children are the fu-ture of the new black nation. The women must teach black children the val-ues of emancipation developed by Maulana Karenga, and in so doing, they help ensure revolutionary continuity. The revolutionary black man has many other important tasks, one of which is to educate the revolutionary black woman: "It is Black Fathers who must teach Black Mothers, and Black Families, but it is Black Mothers, who are the earliest living memory closest, therefore, of perhaps deepest value as teachers."[36]

Women are the leaders in creating a new, emancipated sense of community among blacks:

> The woman must encourage the seeds of liberation in her every act. Social Development means education, health, the home, the community—how it relates to the theme of National Liberation. . . .
>
> . . . *Social Development means to re-create the life style of a free people,* evolving it from the life style of a conquered, colonized, people.[37] [emphasis in the original]

In some crucial respects, Baraka's idea of social development parallels Gramsci's notion of a counterhegemonic community. Despite being caught in an oppressive system, the revolutionary black woman helps create an oppositional culture and an affirming community that prefigure the life that blacks will live once they are emancipated.

Amina Baraka headed a women's division in the daily operations of the Newark CAP. She was in charge of social development classes and wrote a regular column, entitled "Social Development," in the CAP newspaper. Under her leadership, the women of the Newark CAP founded the African Free School. Despite the devalued status of women in CAP, the organization realized some of its greatest successes in those areas controlled by black women. Because of Amina Baraka's obvious competence in executing her duties in Newark, it is astounding to read her call for black female subservience that was issued at the Atlanta Congress of African People in 1970. As coordinator of the section on "Social Organization," she announced that once black women rid themselves of Western influences, they would discover their natural roles as complements of black men: "As Maulana points out, 'What makes a woman appealing is femininity and she can't be feminine without being submissive.'"[38] She then revealed that black women have to be taught the proper ways of being submissive (once again according to Maulana's dictates). True to her devotion to Karenga, Amina defined the three core duties of revolutionary black women as inspiration, education, and social development.

In "The Black Family," a resource paper for the Atlanta Congress of Afrikan People, Akiba ya Elimu stated:

> We understand that it is and has been traditional that the man is the head of the house. He is the leader of the house/nation because his knowledge of the

world is broader, his awareness is greater, his understanding is fuller and his application of this information is wiser. The accepting of the Black man's leadership has involved the understanding of the African personality which has no superior or inferior, only a complement. The man has any right that does not destroy the collective needs of his family. After all, it is only reasonable that the man be the head of the house because he is able to defend and protect the development of his home.[39]

Akiba ya Elimu's statement was a condensed version of the CAP's formal position on gender relations. In 1971, the Committee for a Unified Newark (CFUN), Baraka's CAP affiliate in Newark, published a short pamphlet about black women. Entitled *Mwanamke Mwananchi* (The Nationalist Woman), the pamphlet is as reactionary as any statement issued by the Maulana.

> We understand that it is and has been traditional that the man is the head of the house. . . . Women cannot do the same things as men—they are made by nature to function differently. Equality of men and women is something that cannot happen even in the abstract world. Men are not equal to other men, i.e., ability, experience, or even understanding. The value of men and women can be seen as in the value of gold and silver—they are not equal but both have great value. We must realize that men and women are a complement to each other because there is no house/family without a man and his wife. Both are essential to the development of any life.[40]

The cultural nationalism propagated by Karenga and Baraka during the late 1960s and early 1970s was intentionally sexist. In line with the rest of the Black Power movement, their nationalism was embedded in a validation of black male agency. Such male assertiveness was viewed as radical when juxtaposed against stereotypical images of black men as cowering weaklings before "the white man." The hidden premise of the idea of black male revitalization was that racism had been more deadly and disabling to black men than to black women. The fact that the black male could not protect the black woman from white male sexual exploitation was both the cause and the effect of undermining black male authority.

The desire to return the black male to his rightful status was the reason for much of the cultural nationalist project. While the purported primary agenda of black cultural nationalism was the emancipation of black America, an essential ingredient of that emancipation was the reconstruction of black patriarchy. Ironically, Baraka's and Karenga's understanding of the debased black male could have been lifted verbatim from Daniel Patrick Moynihan's

Moynihan Report. Baraka also seems to have constructed his ideal for gender relationships after reading the report.[41] Moynihan argued that the black man needed not only steady employment but also the discipline of the military and an area in which he could realize his universal male desire to "strut." Kawaida and the various neomilitary groups around Spirit House were Baraka's version of the military and discipline, and the ritualized female adulation of her gender superiors provided the stage for the male strut.

After evaluating a 1971 position paper issued by the Sisters for Black Community Development (an organizational affiliate of Baraka's) entitled "Black Woman's Role in the Revolution," sociologist Robert Staples concluded:

> The position of writer and cultural nationalist, Imamu Baraka (LeRoi Jones), is a clear-cut call for Black female subordination. His organization has a doctrine concerning the Black woman's role in it. Women should not smoke, drink, wear slacks, or have abortions. They should not be involved in men's discussions except to serve refreshments. While the men are busy making decisions, women should occupy themselves with ironing, sewing and cooking. The rationale for this sexual segregation . . . is the necessity for developing a unique Black culture that is bereft of all white concepts.[42]

Jones's sexism had already been manifested in his creative works written before and during the Black Arts era.[43] In *Madheart*, one of his four black revolutionary plays, he dramatized the use of violence as a method for controlling the black woman. In a scene where a black woman is urging a black man to leave white women alone and come to her, the black male "hero" of the play demonstrates his power to use force to subdue her."[44]

In the play, the character BLACK WOMAN chides and mocks the attempts of BLACK MAN to reclaim her as his woman. She essentially tells him that he is in no position to claim anyone, not to mention BLACK WOMAN. Not one to tolerate her disrespect, BLACK MAN intends to show her that he, unlike other black men she has known, is a real BLACK MAN. In the eyes of a real BLACK MAN, BLACK WOMAN has "gotten out of line."

BLACK MAN: I'll get you back. If I need to.

BLACK WOMAN: *(laughs):* You need to, baby . . . just look around you. You better get me back, if you know what's good for you . . . you better.

BLACK MAN: *(looking around at her squarely, he advances):* I better?

. . . (he wheels and suddenly slaps her crosswise, back and forth across the face.)
BLACK WOMAN: What??? What . . . oh love . . . please . . . don't hit me. *(He hits her, slaps her again.)*
BLACK MAN: I want you woman, as a woman. Go down. *(He slaps her again)* Go down, submit, submit, . . . to love . . . and to man, now forever.[45]

After pleading with the man not to strike her again, the black woman tells the black man that she has been waiting for him to assume his strong black male identity. She has missed him and has been waiting for him to become strong enough to merit her submission. She acknowledges the humiliation he has had to endure in the face of white racism. She has seen him "crawl for dogs and devils." He then acknowledges her suffering, for he has seen her "raped by savages and beasts, and bear bleach-shit children of apes." She tells him that he permitted this to happen to her but that she understands that he was powerless to intervene.

BLACK MAN: But now I can *(he slaps her . . . drags her to him, kissing her deeply on the lips)*. That shit is ended, woman, you with me, and the world is mine.

Kissing and slapping her, BLACK MAN says to BLACK WOMAN:

BLACK MAN: You are my woman, now, forever, BLACK WOMAN.
BLACK WOMAN: I am your woman, and you are the strongest of God. Fill me with your seed. *(They embrace . . .).*[46]

The absurdity of the dialogue between BLACK MAN and BLACK WOMAN might lead one to conclude that *Madheart* was a comedy or even a parody of the sexism present in black male-female relationships. Unfortunately, it wasn't. A primitive sexism was fundamental to the cultural nationalism of Baraka and Karenga. An important freedom for black men was to be able to dominate "their women" in a manner similar to the way that the white man controlled "his woman." That is, black freedom meant reproducing the behavior of white men. The subjugated black male envisioned freedom as his ability to dominate others. Once again, we see evidence of the victim status and its accompanying ressentiment.

In black nationalist circles of the late 1960s and early 1970s, black women were frequently less than forceful defenders of gender equality. Trapped in the belief that black male needs were superior to their own, they often participated in subservient activities in order to enhance the black male's image of himself. Not only was feminism seen as racially divisive, but sexism was viewed as a more frivolous form of political subjugation than racism. Even so-called militant black female writers often ignored the specific plight of the black woman. The poet Nikki Giovanni wrote about one version of the antifeminist logic present in militant black female circles:

> I think that it's a moot issue. Just another attempt of white people to find out what black people are doing or to control what we are doing.... They [white women] want "equality" to deal with black women because they've certainly dealt with black men. They're so upset about black women not coming in because they're ultimately trying to control us. There aren't any other reasons why they could be upset. Black people consider their first reality to be black, and given that reality we know from birth that we are going to be oppressed—man, woman, or eunuch![47]

Less prominent but nonetheless politically engaged black nationalist female artists also expressed antifeminist sentiments. *Black Theatre #5*, a journal produced by the New Lafayette Theater in Harlem and edited by Black Arts playwright Ed Bullins, interviewed Roberta Raysor, a black actress with the New Lafayette. In answer to a question about the role of black women in the revolution, she stated:

> You want to do as much as you can and the most you could do, you think, would (be to) give your life to the revolution. You know, gonna fight side by side with your man. But that's not the way ... that's not what you have to do. What you have to do is be a woman. And have babies (LAUGHS). Be women for the men. So the man ... men ... let the men be the men, because that's where the problem is too, in the Revolution. That the men weren't allowed to be men. And the only way they can be is if we be their women. And fighting side by side with them is not going to help ... it's not going to do ... the women are doing things now ... talking about what? Women's rights? And equal rights.... That stuff is all a fantasy. (LAUGHS) All part of the white people's sick, crazy fantasy.... That's what they do. Because the men are faggots, and the women are all ... you know ... want to be men. But that's not our revolution. Our revolution is for women to be women; men to be men and that's going to make it (the revolution) stronger. That's the natural way. The secret is nature. The secret is doing it the natural way, 'cause like it's always the right way.[48]

All the code words are here: white women are lesbians and white men are homosexuals. It is only because of her manliness and his femininity that white women and men can even consider the possibility of gender equality. A real woman—in this case, the real black woman—has babies and encourages her man to be a revolutionary.

CONCLUSION

In his autobiography, Baraka praises his wife Amina for struggling against his male chauvinism. It was she, he claims, who "stopped us from getting too far out in Kawaida." Nevertheless, he admits that both with and without Karenga's influence, his black nationalist politics projected a crude sexism.

> All the black women in those militant black organizations deserve the highest praise. Not only did they stand with us shoulder to shoulder against black people's enemies, they also had to go toe to toe with us, battling day after day against our insufferable male chauvinism.[49]

Although we should respect Baraka's contrition, we do not need to support his unwillingness to question these distorted gender relations, or to explain why black women, who were supposedly empowered as political activists, tolerated such demeaning treatment by black men. But even more conspicuously, he does not discuss the psychological deformation of black men who demanded obsequious deference from black females in order to bolster their egos.

Like many American male intellectuals, Baraka began to wrestle with the question of women's oppression only after the women's liberation movement of the 1960s and 1970s placed the oppression of women before the body politic. After years of making a virtue out of the worst sexist practices, Baraka now admits to having been a chauvinist. In hindsight, Baraka elevated to the status of heroic those women in black nationalist organizations who simultaneously endured and opposed the deep sexism found there. What he cannot admit is that it might have been far more heroic for these black women to have refused to join such sexist circles. Had women spurned these male-centered black nationalist organizations, their reactionary sexist nonsense would have been far more vulnerable to attack.

After becoming a Marxist, Baraka began to view women's oppression as a fundamental derivative of capitalist oppression. To be opposed to sexism is to be against capitalism. Any antisexist struggle that does not confront capitalism is a fraud. Even though the notion of oppressed women remains vaguely defined and ultimately tangential to most of his Marxian political ideas, Baraka must be given credit for the enormous distance he has traversed to rid himself of his vulgar sexism. One testimony to Baraka's changed views on women's issues was his decision to coedit with his wife an anthology of pieces by black American women, *Confirmation: An Anthology of African American Women*, published in 1983. Baraka explained the rationale behind the book: "The purpose of this volume is to draw attention to the existence and excellence of black women writers."[50] This supposed rationale for the publication of *Confirmation* is perplexing given the enormous visibility that many black women writers were enjoying by the early 1980s.

In his introduction to *Confirmation*, Baraka offered one of his most comprehensive statements about the "black woman question" from the vantage point of his Marxist-Leninist-Maoism:

> Black women in the United States are at the very bottom of the American social ladder—as someone has said, "the slaves of slaves." But even this bitter characterization hides the real nature of the evil we are confronting. Black working women are *triple* losers . . . they must face the violent attacks of class exploitation, as workers under monopoly capitalism; national oppression as African Americans . . . and as well the horrors of sexual oppression as women.[51]

What is significant about Baraka's reflections on the status of women is that he analyzes sexism in the same way that he analyzes racism. Sexism, like racism, cannot be completely overcome until the economic structure that causes it is demolished. Once this economic structure is demolished, sexism and racism will still exist, but only as ideas without material bases.

Although I have been tempted to characterize Baraka's movement since the middle 1960s as a journey from crude nationalism to vulgar Marxism, this description would unjustly silence his growth on the "women's question." It would be more precise to say that Baraka abandoned a vehemently sexist, crude black nationalism for an antisexist, vulgar Marxism. Yet the memories of Baraka's sexism linger. In his autobiography, he mentions the anger that can overtake his wife Amina, years after the fact, when she reflects on the sexism that she endured from him and others in black nationalist organizations during the Black Arts era.

> For Amina, the shattering impact of our move to socialism brought a self-awareness of this intense and formal male chauvinism disguised as

African traditionalism that disfigured our movement. The more we saw the atavism and cultural nationalism as backward, so the male chauvinism, in all of its ugly disguises and pretense, the more—she will tell you this—she felt used and made silly by the whole of our ideological trend.[52]

Regardless of the various arguments that Baraka now invokes to explain his vulgar sexism, the black community suffered at the hands of black activists who advocated the subservience of black women. Black women were demeaned and humiliated, and the weak psyches of black men were propped up rather than challenged. False empowerment in the guise of "controlling our women" became the seedbed of reactionary politics.

11

New-Ark and the Emergence of Pragmatic Nationalism

HAD BARAKA NOT been involved in any other political struggle, his activities in Newark alone would have solidified his status as one of the best-known black activist intellectuals of the Black Power era. His involvement in community organizing was critical to the election of Kenneth Gibson as Newark's first black mayor. Gibson's election was considered a momentous national event because it was one of the first successful efforts at electing a black mayor in a large city. During the late 1960s, the mainstream national media marketed the elections of black mayors as proof of American democratic possibility and racial progress. Often, these new black mayors were depicted as the culmination of the Civil Rights movement. In black America, the ecstatic public responses to the elections of Richard Hatcher in Gary, Indiana; Carl Stokes in Cleveland, Ohio; and Kenneth Gibson in Newark were overblown. In most instances, the elections of these figures were merely indications of the changing demographics of urban centers. The euphoria also concealed the fact that the newly elected black mayors were usually inheriting financially destitute cities. Nevertheless, given the history and breadth of the white racist dominance over Newark city politics, Gibson's election was an outstanding achievement. In Newark, a succession of white ethnic mayoral regimes had utterly ignored the needs of its black residents. Unlike Chicago, where black voters had a long tradition of electoral activism, the hegemonic machine in Newark neither needed nor courted the black vote.[1] As a result, blacks in Newark over time had become "beaten down" into a fatalistic acceptance of the racist status quo. Coming only three years after the colossal riot of 1967, Gibson's victory in Newark became a symbol of change in black America. Black power rhetoric was becoming a reality.

In Afro-American intellectual circles during the Black Power era, blacks in Newark had a political notoriety unrivaled by that of blacks in other cities. After all, Newark was the home of Amiri Baraka, the former LeRoi Jones and the preeminent black writer of the Black Power era. Angry but deliberate,

Baraka successfully channeled his justifiable rage by becoming the mastermind behind the 1970 black takeover of Newark. The city was an example of black possibility, a model that inspired activists in other cities. It had metaphorically become the New-Ark, the vessel for the regeneration of black America. Newark's rebellion, a metaphorical and literal "fire next time" gave birth to Imamu Baraka, our modern-day Noah.

Despite the romanticism and exaggeration often associated with this narrative of Baraka's political journey, his activities in Newark between 1967 and 1974 were marked by a quality of political engagement that has rarely been rivaled in the twentieth century by traditional American intellectuals. It was unremarkable for poets to write poems and essays about political issues. But joining picket lines was rare. It was exceptional for an American poet to be arrested and imprisoned as a political prisoner. It was unheard of for an established poet/playwright of Baraka's stature to take the lead in formulating political actions (e.g., establishing picket lines, leading boycotts, disrupting school board meetings, organizing electoral candidates, trying to build needed public housing) while continuing to write. Baraka, the writer who was politically engaged, became indistinguishable from Baraka, the political activist who wrote. Baraka became the model of the revolutionary black man.

Baraka's political activism in Newark becomes even more astounding when compared with the political activism of other, well-known twentieth-century American literary figures (e.g., James Baldwin, James Farrell, Randolph Bourne, Adrienne Rich, Alice Walker, Lilian Smith, Charles White), most of whom used their artistic talent in their political pursuit. Conversely, Baraka put his efforts to work in a nonliterary political realm. In this sense, Baraka's political activism is more reminiscent of the site changes of people like Joel Spingarn, a literary scholar who became head of the NAACP, Professor Alpheus Hunton of the Committee on African Affairs, or the many-talented W. E. B. Du Bois. Unlike these others, though, only Baraka chose to shuttle between a solitary literary existence and popular immersion in the sloppiness of mass politics.

BLACK NEWARK: A COMMUNITY IN TROUBLE

Like many northern industrial centers, Newark's black population dramatically increased during the United States' involvement in the two world wars. In the case of Newark, the greatest changes in the black population occurred after World War II. In 1910, blacks accounted for only 2.7 percent of a city population of 347,469,[2] but by 1920, the black population had grown to

16,977. By 1940, Newark was approximately 11 percent black. As a result of the southern black migration north during and following World War II, Newark's black population rose to 17 percent by 1950. By 1970, the percentage of the city's black population had risen to 54.4, and at the same time, the white population had fallen to 36.6 percent, with Puerto Ricans making up approximately 9 percent. During the 1960s, approximately 100,000 whites left Newark, many for nearby suburbs, and the black middle class left Newark for predominantly black or integrated suburban towns like East Orange and Montclair.[3]

Before 1940, the black population was distributed throughout many of the city's wards. As long as the black population was very small, whites did not object to blacks' residential mobility. But as the black population grew, whites' opposition to blacks' dispersion intensified throughout the city. Blacks' housing options became increasingly restricted, which subsequently led to their concentration in the Third Ward (also known as the Central Ward). This concentration of black residents was not merely the result of racist white neighborhood responsiveness to prospective black neighbors. Rather, the concentration of blacks in the Third Ward was the intended result of a policy deliberately pursued by Newark's powers that be.

The intersection of racism and city housing policies in Newark vaguely resembled Chicago's, as chronicled in Arnold Hirsch's *The Making of the Second Ghetto*. By 1940, Newark's power elite, as did Chicago's, decided to restrict blacks to certain areas of the city. Given the growth of the black population, this restriction led to incredible overcrowding in the black neighborhoods, which worsened in 1939 when the city began to construct several massive housing projects in the Central Ward.

As was the case in many black ghettos in northern cities, the Central Ward was initially dominated by white organized-crime syndicates. The powerful East Coast crime boss Abner Zwillman, a native of Newark's Third Ward, had an extensive organization throughout New Jersey, including Newark. From the 1930s through the 1950s, Zwillman used organized crime to control Newark's politics, including that of the predominantly black Central Ward. The overlap between the ward's political leaders and organized-crime figures was extensive. Black politicians were bought off in exchange for police protection of various rackets in the black community. Voting rolls were amended and ballot boxes were stuffed. Many blacks relied on underworld jobs for occupational opportunities that were closed to them in the noncriminal world. Nonetheless, the black political association with the white underworld prevented the emergence of political leaders committed to blacks' inclusion in the socioeconomic mainstream. The white underworld had a vested interest in maintaining black despair. When the Jewish Zwillman was imprisoned in the early 1950s, his Jewish American crime syndicate disintegrated, and Italian American crime syndicates moved into the Central Ward. Soon thereafter, the leading black political figures, including the up-and-coming Irvine Turner (elected Newark's first black city councilman in 1954), switched their political allegiances from Ellenstein, the leading Jewish politician (and friend of Zwillman), to Villanie, a prominent Italian American politician and reported friend of the Italian mob. In the pragmatic logic of black political leaders, a change in the ethnic identity of the city's mob boss necessitated a change in political loyalties. Yet the new organized-crime bosses continued to oppose blacks' economic and political progress.

In 1963, political scientist Harold Kaplan published a study of the politics of urban renewal in Newark. Although he mysteriously concluded that it had been a highly successful city in this area, his study actually documents the growing intransigence of its racial conflict.[4] Kaplan describes the efforts by the Newark Housing Authority between 1949 and 1960 to build both affordable private housing and federally subsidized housing projects in Newark. Not surprisingly, he discovered that the policies of the Federal Housing Authority effectively denied loans for private home ownership and business development in areas designated as "Negro slums." The federal government institutionalized the presence of absentee landlords in Newark's predominantly black areas, while the Federal Housing Authority subsidized white flight into the suburbs.

Kaplan's study describes a peculiar political situation. White ethnics in Newark did not have enough power to completely block the spread of the black population. Consequently, Newark's powers that be did not quite succeed in establishing a "second ghetto," as Chicago did between 1940 and 1960. This is not to say that the Newark Housing Authority did not try to maintain the segregated boundaries of Newark's neighborhoods but to suggest that the white ethnic communities were neither powerful nor politically mobilized enough to prevent the dispersion of the black population. But Newark's white ethnic collusion with the underworld was able to bar blacks from public service employment. The contradictory governing dynamic in Newark was premised on the inability of poor and working-class whites to prohibit black residential incursion, although working-class and middle-class white ethnics were able to monopolize the city's public-sector job market. Robert Curvin notes that in 1953, there were only 27 blacks in a police force of more than 1,000 and only 120 teachers, including one black full-time secondary teacher, in the entire Newark school system. As late as 1954, there were no black doctors on the staff of Newark City Hospital.[5]

This all changed when the city's black population ballooned. In 1950, seven of Newark's ten wards had a black population of less than 14 percent, but by 1960, only one ward was less than 14 percent black. Thus the Newark that Jones returned to in 1966 was significantly blacker than the Newark he knew growing up. It was also far poorer.

Federal funds were used to clear substandard housing in the black neighborhood of Newark (the Central Ward), and new housing units were built there, although not enough to house all the displaced blacks. So when housing "projects" were constructed in other locations in Newark, prosegregationist protests from neighborhood whites erupted. These whites, often Italian Americans, tried to persuade the Irish American mayor to restrict access to these new non–Central Ward units to people from the immediate neighborhood (i.e., whites only). They generally succeeded, though not completely. The federally subsidized housing that was built conformed largely to the city's existing segregated residential patterns. Yet unlike Chicago's, Newark's housing authority was forced to place some blacks in housing outside the Central Ward. The white ethnics' inability to block the spread of the black population during the 1940s and 1950s ultimately resulted in the enormous white flight from Newark during the 1960s.

As whites departed the city for the segregated suburbs, so did many of the stable working-class jobs in Newark's traditional manufacturing sector. Between 1950 and 1960, Newark lost 250 manufacturers, and during the 1960s, 1,300 manufacturers closed up shop. Between 1958 and 1970, Newark lost 20,056 manufacturing jobs, a drop of 24.2 percent.[6] The departure of white residents to the suburbs was both the cause and effect of the flight of industrial jobs. On the one hand, many industries still wanted to restrict their employment pool to whites, a desire more easily realized in white-only suburbs. But even those firms that were not restricting employment to whites fled to the suburbs in search of tax relief. Consequently, many black Newark residents had to commute out of the city to their jobs.

Once the industries, manufacturing firms, and providers of services moved out of Newark, the city's tax base began to erode, which in turn affected the quality of social services provided by the city (e.g., schools, parks). In response, Newark's property tax rates rose dramatically. White residents and business firms thereupon relocated to the more hospitable tax rates of the suburbs. Once the departures began, they snowballed, and by the mid-1960s, Newark was one of the poorest big cities in the United States, even though property owners were subject to tax rates that were among the highest in the nation. The whites who fled to the suburbs continued to monopolize the remaining employment opportunities in Newark. In the daylight hours, Newark appeared to be a predominantly white city, but by night, the city became black and Latino.

The combination of a corrupt city government and a disempowered black community gave rise to a black submachine in which a black ward boss controlled the black vote for the city's racist power structure. Combining militant black rhetoric with passive political acquiescence, Irvine I. Turner ruled the Central Ward from 1954 to 1970.

> Turner, in many ways, was the classic ethnic boss who served as broker between the voters and the political leaders (machine). The machine took care of the boss, and the boss, in turn, assured voter support. He helped soothe, co-opt, or challenge any opposition to the white leaders to whom he was loyal. It was not that Turner avoided issues that would embarrass the political leaders or challenge the status quo; rather, after the issues were raised, he made no organized effort to insure that they were discussed or acted on. It was an effective way of preempting leadership on any issue, while assuring that nothing would be done.

Again the comparison with Chicago is instructive, for the racistly restrictive housing policies in both cities relied on the collusion of black leaders. In the case of William Dawson in Chicago and Turner in Newark, restrictions on black housing choices created majority-black residential areas (and thus political jurisdictions) that were easy for black "bosses" to control. In effect, the initial vestiges of black political inclusion in Newark city politics (e.g., Turner's election to the city council) were based on black residential exclusion.[7]

In 1962, Hugh Addonizio, a Democratic congressman, challenged the incumbent "reform" mayor Leo Carlin and won in a landslide election. Addonizio based his electoral bid on Italian American and black voters, promising blacks an end to police brutality and discrimination in the educational system. In addition, he pledged to hire more blacks in city jobs and strengthen the Mayor's Commission on Human Rights. During his first term in office (1962–1966), Addonizio appointed more blacks to political office than had ever been the case in Newark.[8] But despite his promises, achievements, and perhaps even his initial goodwill toward blacks, Addonizio could not reverse the tide of black disenchantment. The prevailing perception was that he had not done enough, which, of course, was easy to document. His actions on behalf of blacks were never intended to reverse their exclusion from all levels of policymaking in the Newark city government. Although blacks were part of his electoral coalition, they were excluded from his governing coalition. That is, Addonizio wanted to appease blacks, but not at the expense of Newark's white residents. Worse, his civic mindedness in regard to blacks and even Italian Americans took a back seat to his criminal activities and associations.

Founded in 1961, by the mid-1960s, Newark's chapter of CORE (Congress of Racial Equality) had become the most active organizational voice for black Newark concerns. As expected, Turner, the machine's black functionary, was an outspoken critic of CORE. Yet the daily televised reports of the southern-based Civil Rights movement generated a sense of responsibility and empowerment in many Newark blacks that Turner (and thus Addonizio) could no longer manipulate so easily. Owing to its growing political assertiveness, Newark's ever expanding black population was slowly reshaping the environment in which Addonizio governed.

The mayor was caught in a political bind. He had to respond in some visible way to the blacks' new assertiveness. However, he did not want to be seen as giving too much to them, so as not to alienate his antiblack, white ethnic constituencies. Addonizio tried to walk this fine line by appointing a few blacks to highly visible but powerless, symbolic positions. The basic concerns of the black community were ignored. The mayor thus tried to address blacks' needs without violating the corrupt and racist contours of established Newark city politics. But he could not do this, for the racist dominance of black Newark was fundamental to the operation of the city's economic and political hierarchy. Consequently, after four years of Addonizio, black unemployment remained high, housing terrible, and police brutality rampant.

Although Addonizio easily won reelection in 1966, the election contained the seeds of his demise. One of Addonizio's challengers in 1966 was a black engineer, Kenneth Gibson. A relatively unknown black candidate, Gibson nevertheless won 16,000 votes, placing him third in the balloting.[9] This surprising showing planted a seed in the heads of Gibson and other black politicos. For the first time, they realized that if sufficiently organized and funded, a black candidate might be able to challenge the incumbent mayor.[10]

Despite Gibson's strong showing in 1966, Addonizio believed that he controlled enough of the key political players in black Newark to maintain adequate support among black city residents for the indefinite future. His "political reach" was sufficiently long that he even controlled the Newark chapter of the NAACP. Nevertheless, the mayor was fighting a losing battle, as he was committed to the patron-client control of Newark's blacks at the very moment that the political dynamics of black Newark were quickly changing. Perhaps the key ingredient in the emergence of a sustained black opposition to the politics as usual in Newark was the influx of financial resources from federal antipoverty programs, particularly the Office of Economic Opportunity (OEO), a centerpiece of Lyndon Johnson's urban "war on poverty." While Addonizio was able to control much of the poverty program's money entering Newark, local community groups also were able to obtain a substantial share. These community groups in turn became conduits for the emergence of antiestablishmentarian, black political leadership.[11] Turner and other Addonizio "front men" could no longer ensure black compliance.

Three central issues exacerbated Newark's racial tensions. First, in early 1967, the white secretary of the board of education announced his plans to retire. Many black residents viewed his retirement as an opportunity to appoint the city's first black secretary, and by 1967, the schools were at least 70 percent black. Wilbur Parker, a black civil servant, announced his desire to fill the vacancy. The black community thought he was highly qualified for the job. The first black certified public accountant in New Jersey, Parker was Newark's budget director. Nonetheless, ignoring the desires of his black constituents, Mayor Addonizio announced that he intended to fill this vacancy with his friend and longtime political ally, city councilman James Callaghan. Addonizio miscalculated the outrage from the black community when they discovered that he had decided to appoint a man who had never completed high school, instead of an obviously qualified black man. It was clear that Addonizio was more concerned about plum patronage jobs for his cronies than about the quality of education provided to the majority-black student populace. Indeed, blacks' protests against the appointment of Callaghan became so vociferous that Addonizio rescinded the appointment. But instead of appointing Parker, he persuaded the secretary to withdraw his request to retire. Many blacks thought that Addonizio's refusal to appoint Parker stemmed from a racist disregard for him and black Newark. While racism was certainly a factor in Addonizio's choice, it may have also been the case that Callaghan shared the mayor's desire to siphon funds and contracts from the school budget. In Newark, it was sometimes difficult to determine whether Addonizio was more committed to white supremacy or to corruption.

The second issue that galvanized black political discontent was the proposed location of a new New Jersey College of Medicine and Dentistry. Mayor Addonizio and the Newark Housing Authority had designated 155 acres of the Central Ward for the school's construction. As proposed, the medical school complex would require the removal of more than 20,000 black residents of the Central Ward. What made the proposal so absurd in the eyes of black protesters is that the medical school would be much larger than any other medical school in the nation. For instance, Johns Hopkins University Medical School was situated on only one and a half acres. The attempt to use the construction of a medical school complex as a reason for tearing down a black neighborhood upset black Newark. Many people, including Baraka, believed that the real purpose of the proposed medical school project was simultaneously to undermine a majority-black city council district and to reduce the number of black residents of Newark.[12]

The third issue that galvanized the black community was the recurring problem of police brutality. Newark's police force was notorious for its abuse of black and Puerto Rican residents. Addonizio had done little to make the police force more professional and law-abiding. The frequency of the brutalizations of black Newark residents by the police had created the climate of anger and distrust that subsequently led to the massive riot/rebellion of 1967.

As was the case in many other cities, the rebellion in Newark was ignited by reports of the police brutalization of a black civilian. The rioting destroyed millions of dollars in property and resulted in the deaths of many, most of whom were murdered by the Newark police and the New Jersey National Guard. For Addonizio, the riot undermined the image of Newark that he had tried to project to the media. In its aftermath, the mayor was quoted as saying, "I don't care if a Negro sat here as mayor, he couldn't do anything more for the Negro than I've done."[13] Politically, the riot heightened racial tensions in the city, leading to an even greater white flight and a greater retrenchment of those whites who remained. Many whites in Newark became increasingly fearful of the "rising black menace." As the leader of the racist white retrenchment mood, Anthony Imperiale rose to national prominence. The riots similarly intensified the militancy of black activists. Few were more affected than Amiri Baraka.

CULTURAL NATIONALISM ENTERS THE ELECTORAL ARENA

Taking advantage of the energy unleashed by the 1967 Newark rebellion and the second Black Power conference that followed, Baraka and a few confreres sponsored weekly meetings to discuss the political situation of blacks in Newark. Hosted at Spirit House, these meetings attracted an ideologically diverse spectrum of black male Newark residents, including bourgeois black integrationists, bourgeois black nationalists, true-believing black cultural nationalists, and numerous less doctrinaire but Black Power–minded folks associated with Spirit House. This group called itself the United Brothers and later became the core of the Committee for Unified Newark (CFUN). At the same time that the United Brothers was taking shape, Amina Baraka was helping organize the United Sisters in order to raise the political consciousness of black women. The black nationalist sensibilities sweeping through urban black America were ever present in Newark. Blacks wanted change and would no longer accept the token representation of the past.

By early 1968, Baraka began considering using elections to effect a black takeover of political power in Newark. As a first step, he called on blacks to become involved in the November 1968 special elections to fill vacant seats on the Newark City Council. This special election would be a practice run for the mayoral race in 1970. In April 1968, Baraka was quoted in the *New York Times* as saying,

> We've come to conclude that the city is ours anyway, that we can take it with ballots. We've issued a call for a black convention to pick black candidates for every city office . . . what we want to do is nominate one black candidate for each office to insure that there will be black self-government.[14]

In June 1968, the United Brothers sponsored a black political convention in Newark, an attempt to organize the united front necessary to contest elections in Newark. The convention provided a mechanism by which candidates were agreed on and supported so as to prevent the emergence of other minority candidates who could dilute the voting strength of black Newark. The convention decided that it would endorse only one candidate for each office. Candidates who wanted the convention's endorsement thus would have to attend the convention and be subjected to its scrutiny.

Baraka delivered one of the keynote speeches at the convention, in which he announced a collective black desire for self-government. The next day, Maulana Karenga addressed the group and encouraged them to deepen their involvement by organizing and registering the black community. But perhaps the most provocative address of that first convention was delivered by Phil Hutchins, one of SNCC's national leaders during its last days. He stated, "You won't have control of Newark unless you take over the whole country. The honkies still would maintain control over you through the state and federal government."[15] Hutchins clearly understood that Baraka's vision of a black-controlled, autonomous entity called Newark, New Jersey, was a dangerous and ill-conceived fantasy.[16] He warned his listeners that they had to understand the workings of the capitalist economy if they were to understand the black political condition.

Yet even Hutchins was captured by the euphoria of the moment, for despite his astute recognition of the limits of urban electoral politics for blacks, he emphatically endorsed the so-called black takeover of Newark politics. Most dramatically, he implored that this takeover occur with either the "ballot or the bullet." Perhaps the "bullet or ballot" rhetoric should be viewed as a bombastic ploy of those who wanted to be linked to Malcolm's legacy, but the idea contradicted Hutchins's own thinking. Even if blacks were able to take Newark by the ballot or the bullet, the city would still be controlled by the state of New Jersey, the federal government, the American economy, and global capitalism. I mention the contradiction because such conceptual confusion was common in black radical circles of that time.

What is remarkable about the 1968 black convention is that despite all the militant and contentious rhetoric, the United Brothers was a liberal reformist organization. The two black candidates who received its endorsement were not racially assertive, and the convention ended with a spirit of unity.[17] It appeared that blacks would finally be able to overlook small differences in order to form a broader, more effective electoral coalition.

Baraka's willingness to interact with establishmentarian-minded bourgeois black politicos in order to create a viable coalition speaks to his pragmatic instincts. His goal was to begin the process by which black Newark residents would obtain substantive representation. If it meant momentarily closing ranks with nonmilitant blacks, then he was willing to do so. But Baraka was somewhat naive about the operating motives of many in the United Brothers discussion group. Perhaps it is understandable that he did not grasp how opportunistic many of these black political figures were. Even Baraka assumed that liberal-minded black politicos were interested in helping the black poor and ending police brutality. Only later did he realize that cynicism and amorality were the basis of the power ambitions of many blacks, even many who espoused Black Power.

In late August 1968, Baraka and other participants in the United Brothers' Black Convention went to Philadelphia to attend the Third National Black Power Conference. As had been the case at the Second Black Power Conference, which had been held in Newark in 1967, the participants at the Philadelphia meeting discussed strategies for black political advancement. Once again, most of the resolutions passed were symbolic statements.[18]

On the advice of Maulana Karenga, the name United Brothers was discarded in favor of a less contentious one. The members did not want to alienate any of the various voting constituencies in black Newark, some of which may have objected to the popular black nationalist rite of referring to black males and females as "brothers" and "sisters." The new name of the group was Committee for Unified Newark (CFUN).

On November 5, 1968, Newark went to the polls. The candidates endorsed by the United Brothers (CFUN) lost. If that was not enough of a blow to the political egos of Baraka and his confreres, Anthony Imperiale, the leader of white ethnic backlash politics in Newark, was elected to the city council, along with a former Newark policeman of similar racist sensibilities and "law and order" rhetoric. Imperiale was a known leader of vigilantes who operated with the tacit assent of the Newark Police Department. He and his associates patrolled the streets in cars and assaulted blacks and Puerto Ricans who crossed the borders of their respective ghettos. He did not hide his hatred of blacks, and in 1968, Imperiale chaired George Wallace's campaign in New Jersey.

The candidates on the United Brothers slate received the overwhelming majority of those votes in predominantly black wards that were cast for city council candidates. In the Central Ward, however, almost half the blacks who had voted for a presidential candidate did not cast votes for any city council candidate. In another black ward, almost 63 percent of the blacks who voted for the president did not vote for the city council. The very novelty of the United Brothers' effort may have left many black Newark voters with a sense of apprehension about their agenda. Others probably had never heard of the United Brothers or CFUN. The defeat of the United Brother's candidates was a wake-up call for CFUN and black activists in Newark, that it would take greater work, greater commitment, and far more organizational discipline if they were to realize their goal of electing black candidates.

Nikki Giovanni believed that the macho-militancy of Baraka and his confreres led to the defeat of the black candidates in 1968, that their aggressive style often led to mindless confrontations with the very nonmilitant blacks on whom they were so dependent. Citing the exaggerated warlike ambience of the United Brothers' headquarters, Giovanni described an incident involving a black man donating money to the 1968 black campaigns. With a check for $600, he entered the headquarters of the United Brothers asking to speak with Jones. The male guards at the headquarters questioned the man, and when they did not receive the expected answers, they physically manhandled him. Giovanni wrote:

> It was a disaster. If that kind of treatment was accorded a man with as much prestige as he had, we shudder to think what happened to those who just drifted in to see. They offered an apology to the offended brother, but that missed the point entirely. The people of Newark became more afraid of the Black candidates and their organization than they were of the present scandal ridden, Black-hating administration.[19]

This episode was just one example of how so-called militant blacks often treated other blacks. These symbolic articulations of power became part of the legacy of Black Power militancy as black-on-black violence claimed many more lives than black-on-white violence.

Following the defeat of the CFUN ticket in 1968, Baraka realized that it had been a mistake to have tried to mobilize blacks exclusively at the expense of the city's other nonwhite peoples. His new attitude toward coalition building with other subjugated groups became evident during the planning of the 1969 political convention in which candidates for the 1970 elections would be nominated. Instead of holding an exclusively black nomination convention, participants in the 1969 convention decided to form a black and Puerto Rican coalition.

The convention selected Kenneth Gibson as its mayoral nominee and numerous candidates for the city council. The understanding was that this black and Puerto Rican ticket would run coordinated candidacies under the banner "The Community's Choice." The goal of Baraka and the others who had devised the convention strategy was to minimize bickering among their candidates as well as the energy spent mending internal conflicts. One of the first conflicts that Baraka and his colleagues had to navigate was the desire of some in the Gibson camp to separate the mayoral candidate from some of the endorsed city council candidates, so as not to lose the support of voters who favored other candidates for the council. Several years later, Baraka acknowledged that Gibson's entourage was solely committed to winning the mayoralty and that they would do whatever it would take. Baraka and others, in contrast, viewed themselves as part of a social movement to reallocate political power in Newark. Electing Gibson was fine but only if progressive black candidates were elected to the city council, for a black mayor without a supportive city council would be unable to pursue new "problack" initiatives in public policy.

An engineer by training, Gibson was not a smooth politician. Unlike the charismatic Carl Stokes in Cleveland, Gibson projected a competent, decent, but dull and inoffensive presence that may have made him more acceptable to some whites. Gibson was not particularly gifted in matters of pressure politics. He often seemed ready to compromise and "act reasonable" even before the fight started. It would be difficult to find a time when Gibson fought deeply entrenched white power brokers over an issue of importance to blacks. Perhaps the first indication that Gibson was governed by a different ethic than were CFUN and the black and Puerto Rican convention was his firing his first and second campaign managers, both of whom were black. He replaced them with a professional white campaign manager and his white associates.[20] As a result of Gibson's actions, the campaign split into two distinct but affiliated parts. One was run by whites in search of the white and bourgeois black vote.

The other was administered and staffed by those affiliated with the black and Puerto Rican convention. Baraka and his black nationalist buddies thought that the pursuit of white votes was a waste of time and resources. Moreover, they worried about the political implications of Gibson's apparent yearning for white voter support.

Gibson campaigned on the basis of his competence and the need to restore integrity to a corrupt mayoral regime. Shortly before the campaign, Addonizio was indicted for corruption, rumors of which had persisted throughout his tenure. During the final weeks of the campaign, Addonizio traveled daily to and from his trial in Trenton. Whenever time allowed, he would campaign in Newark. Addonizio's negative press greatly enhanced the possibilities of a Gibson victory. Gibson campaigned as a reformer, and equally important, he marketed himself as a black, although he did so in a manner that minimized the possibility that whites would view him as racially assertive. One reporter who covered the 1970 campaign quoted Gibson as saying, "The poor and disenfranchised can no longer tolerate being controlled by machine politicians, and politics must become synonymous with social and civil rights."[21] In a few instances Gibson embraced more racially militant lingo: "Today, black people select their own leaders and their own political candidates. They won't be happy about other groups trying to put up puppets and Uncle Toms."[22]

Even though Gibson was not a black nationalist, the white nationalist Imperiale (who also was running) tried to paint him as a follower of Amiri Baraka. In white Newark, Baraka was known as a black extremist who wanted to destroy what whites had created. Worse, Baraka was the black man who wanted to rape white women and otherwise do to whites what whites had historically done to blacks. At public functions, Imperiale frequently read from Baraka's poem in which he calls for "black dada nihilismus" to rise up and rape their daughters.[23] Gibson refused to denounce Baraka, but he repeatedly told audiences that he was running to make Newark a better place for everyone.

Once Gibson received the nomination of the black and Puerto Rican convention, Baraka used his national connections to solicit contributions, guest appearances, and endorsements from prominent Afro-Americans and whites of goodwill. Visits to Newark by celebrities attracted press attention and gave voters a sense of the national significance of the Gibson campaign.

Under Baraka's direction, the election of Kenneth Gibson in Newark became a national Black Power crusade. Answering Baraka's call, hordes of black college students from around the nation descended on Newark to help with the campaign effort. These ideologically motivated students as well as the black nationalists around Baraka and Spirit House were among the most dedicated workers on the entire campaign. On May 12, 1970, Kenneth Gibson received 40 percent of the total vote, a percentage that placed him first in a field of seven candidates. Addonizio came in second with 20 percent of the vote. Imperiale finished third. The Gibson showing was strong but short of the 50 percent necessary to avoid a runoff on June 16 against Addonizio. Addonizio changed his political strategy for the runoff. No longer willing to assume the moderate position between the "extremes" of Baraka and Imperiale, Addonizio now understood that he could win only if he had the white vote solidly behind him. His new strategy thus was simultaneously to embrace Imperiale and frighten whites about the ramifications of a black takeover of the mayor's office. One reporter noted,

> Addonizio, who said that he had "never used the issue of race in my twenty-two years of public life," went on repeatedly to inflame his supporters by warning that "Gibson is part of a raw and violent conspiracy to turn this city over to LeRoi Jones and his extremist followers." At times the mild and methodical Gibson was almost lost amid the flurry of anti-Jones rhetoric and a stranger might have received the impression that the fiery poet-playwright was in fact Addonizio's political opponent . . . the mayor unrelentingly used him, as part of a strategy of desperation, to generate fear and hatred among whites. "I want to make it clear," he said, "that I haven't brought race into this campaign. My opponent has, though. I wasn't selected by a *white* convention, but he was selected by a *black convention*. I'm not identified with extremists, but he is."[24]

On June 16, 1970, Kenneth Gibson defeated Addonizio by a vote of 55,097 to 43,086. The majority-black wards voted in unprecedented numbers. The city council candidates on "the Community's Choice" ticket did not fare as well. Earl Harris was the only one of its candidate to win an at-large seat on the city council. Sharpe James (a future mayor) was victorious in the South Ward. In the Central Ward, Dennis Westbrook defeated Irvine Turner, the longtime incumbent and Addonizio crony. All the other Community Choice candidates lost. There was now a minority of three blacks on the seven-person city council. A recalcitrant white majority on the city council spent the next several years trying to undermine Gibson's administration. But on election night, the reality of the city council results took a back seat. When it became clear that Gibson had won a decisive victory, many blacks exploded in glee.

The carnival-like mood among blacks following the announcement of

Gibson's victory was understandable given the history of black disempowerment in Newark. Perhaps many black Newark residents had not really believed that a black person could become mayor. Baraka and his allies had long understood that one of their most important tasks during the campaign was to convince black and Latino voters that Gibson could actually win, so they had to make the election seem like a life-and-death issue. As a result, the preelection enthusiasm could only produce postelection expectations of change that did not match reality. Predictably, the result was disappointment when black voters realized that they had been betrayed by those they just elected.

CONFRONTING THE LIMITS OF BLACK POWER

Despite his self-perception as being more politically sophisticated than the average black resident of Newark, Baraka also was a victim of unrealistic expectations. Unlike most black voters in Newark, Baraka's unrealistic expectations derived from his conceptually confused ideology. Shortly before the Gibson victory, Baraka announced:

> Newark, New Ark, the nationalist sees as the creation of a base, an example, upon which one aspect of the entire Black nation can be built. We will build schools or transform present curriculum to teach National Liberation. We will create agencies to teach community organizing, national and local politics, and send brothers all over the country to re-create the model. We will nationalize the city's institutions as if it were liberated territory in Zimbabwe or Angola. There are nations of less than 300,000 people. . . . We will build a "city-state," or make alliances throughout the area to develop regional power in the scatter of Black cities of northern New Jersey.[25]

Clearly, Baraka's understanding of urban political power was a fantasy. The election of a black as mayor and a black majority on a city council could never set the stage for "nationalizing" anything in the United States. Baraka's idea of a confederated black nation made up of separate, black-governed, majority-black cities could not be taken seriously. In his reified way of conceptualizing race, Baraka saw blacks as having similar goals and values, provided that they got in touch with their essential blackness. He imagined black communities as uniform in character and ambitions. As a cultural nationalist, his mission was to teach blacks an authentically black value system which, predictably, was Karenga's Kawaida. The idea that blacks should have and could have a unified value system allowed Baraka to marginalize the salience of divergent class interests in black America. Class differences would not matter if all blacks thought alike, and all blacks could think alike if they just adopted Kawaida.[26]

Like most black Americans, Kenneth Gibson never became a follower of Kawaida. As mayor, Gibson's "blackness" remained in dispute for Baraka until he abandoned the reified racialisms of black cultural nationalism for Marxism. It should not have been surprising that shortly after Gibson was sworn in as mayor of Newark, he and Baraka began to clash. Unlike Baraka, Gibson believed that a good black mayor would govern the entire city fairly. Shortly after he was elected, Gibson wrote: "I am elected to represent all of the people of the city of Newark. This responsibility I recognize and will do my best to fulfill. Of course, there are people whose political motives will not allow them to understand or believe this."[27] In a similar vein, Gibson also stated that when he spoke of community, "I do not speak of the middle class, the lower class, the poor or the hungry. I speak of an entire community."[28] Diametrically opposed to Gibson's "I play no racial or class favorites" mayoral ideal, Baraka believed that good black mayors governed in favor of their historically neglected black constituents. Although both men had been able to agree on the task of electing a black mayor, they never agreed on the political meaning of that election.

A year after Gibson's election, Baraka had become one of his most vocal critics, and by the end of Gibson's first term in office, he and Baraka were political enemies. Gibson was a dogmatic integrationist; Baraka was a devout black nationalist of romantic proportions. He viewed the goal of black politics as the creation of a black nation, a semiseparate state. Gibson was a crude pragmatist, a man who felt compelled to choose between the lesser of two evils without ever trying to broaden the scope of options or challenging his limited choices. He was the typical technocrat—a man of limited vision who believed that good government was efficient government. In Newark, with its history of corruption and bureaucratic inefficiency, an efficient government was sorely needed, but efficient government alone could not redress the history of black exclusion.

Baraka was less interested than Gibson was in efficient government. Rather, he wanted an administration that was as biased toward blacks (in terms of services, programs, employment) as previous administrations had been against them. In Baraka's mind, Gibson's commitment to governing Newark without favor not only was ludicrous politics but did not take into account why black people had voted for him. Inefficiency had not been the reason that blacks had received so little from previous Newark mayoralties. Ironically, the technocratic Gibson may have overstated the Newark government's legacy of inefficiency. After all, the history of various mayoral administrations testified to the efficient exclusion of blacks and black community interests. Newark mayors like Addonizio may have been corrupt, but their corruption was never arbitrary in its targets or beneficiaries.

Baraka did not recognize that Gibson had become associated with the United Brothers and later CFUN and the black and Puerto Rican convention for only tactical reasons. Gibson knew that Baraka could give him an image of racial assertiveness. There is little reason to think that Gibson would have ever been associated with black nationalists had he been able to win without them. In addition, Baraka did not understand the political and economic structures that governed Newark. In his version of black cultural nationalism, any change in the composition of the city's political elite would lead to changes in the city's policies. Ignorant of the political economy of capitalism, Baraka worked under a naïve belief in elite volunteerism.

Upon becoming mayor, Gibson recognized the structural limitations on his range of public policy options. First, Newark was in a state of economic decline, a position that would be difficult to reverse. A city in economic despair grants a great deal of authority to those large industries and companies that have remained but threaten to move out. Because of its declining economic condition, the city's tax base was undermined. A declining tax base leads either to higher taxes on property, which can drive people to the suburbs, or to a loss of city services, which also can lead to suburban flight. In both instances, the poor who remain in the city are hit the hardest.

Many of the most pressing problems facing Kenneth Gibson stemmed from the city's increasing impoverishment and its lack of financial resources. Regardless of his intentions, urban decline in Newark could not have been reversed without a coordinated national urban policy. When Gibson took office in 1970, Newark had the highest percentage of substandard housing of any city in the nation. In addition, it had the honor of registering the country's highest rate of crime, venereal disease, tuberculosis, maternal mortality, and infant mortality.[29] Policy analyst Bette Woody concluded that "there is little question that the Gibson administration probably inherited the worst public fiscal crisis in recent times in the United States."[30]

Though massive, the problems confronting the black poor in Newark were not beyond public policy redress, but Gibson's impoverished city did not control the resources necessary to do so. And those in the federal government, state government, and corporate sector who did control sufficient resources did not possess the will. Mayor Gibson observed:

> Structurally, we cannot provide improved services without the help of the
> national government. We hoped that this help would be forthcoming. The

city needs help which is not complicated or encumbered. The Newark administration can certainly tell the federal government what we need and what should be done. Whether or not it will be done is beyond our control.[31]

If I am correct that Gibson could have done little to improve black living conditions in Newark, then why did he stay in office once he realized the futility of his efforts? Gibson may have been content to function as a symbolic leader. If Baraka and his black nationalist confreres could be accused of engaging in "rituals of rebellion," Gibson could be viewed as having orchestrated a "ritual of inclusion." In a twist of dialectical irony, black mayors may have inadvertently or even intentionally discouraged more substantive black political inclusion by posturing as powerful in the absence of power.

Another issue that Baraka did not understand was that his connection to Gibson made Baraka vulnerable to the mayor's failure to honor promises made during the campaign. That is, Gibson's failure and/or inability to deliver benefits to blacks and Puerto Ricans would ultimately undermine Baraka's credibility in Newark, for one of the sources of Baraka's public prominence was his political efficacy and access to the mayor. The weak impact of Gibson's mayoralty on the quality of black life in Newark threatened the national euphoria associated with Baraka's vision of black nationalist control over urban America. A nagging doubt about the importance of electoral politics to the black nationalist project was introduced.

Once in office, Gibson maintained a vested interest in portraying Baraka as an extremist and using this portrayal to depict himself as a black man of reason and moderation. Gibson occasionally even marketed himself as the only person in Newark who could keep the black militants in check. It was not as easy for Baraka to use Gibson to validate himself and his political beliefs. At some point early in Gibson's term, the mayor decided that he no longer needed Baraka. Gibson calculated that once in office, he could be reelected without Baraka's support. Unfortunately for Baraka, Gibson was correct. Not only did the incumbent mayor boycott the next black and Puerto Rican convention, which was held in 1974, but he also won reelection that year without the convention's endorsement. Gibson was elected to four terms as mayor of Newark. Baraka had been important only in the first race. Nevertheless, Baraka and CFUN could never openly oppose Gibson's reelection, for they realized that if they did, they would lose their legitimacy in the eyes of black Newark. Baraka's admission of defeat was his renunciation of black nationalism in late 1974.

Baraka had realized by 1972 that Gibson would not be an innovative mayor for the black and Puerto Rican communities. He also knew that he would not have any influence in the Gibson administration. Despite his rage at this apparent betrayal, he did not give up but instead threw himself into an almost manic attempt to create a model black nationalist community in Newark.

SPIRIT HOUSE'S ACTIVITIES

By the late 1960s, Baraka's Spirit House had become the center of the Black Arts movement and also a center for black cultural creativity and political assertiveness. Having learned from his mistakes in Harlem, Baraka was far less tolerant of those chaotic individuals who might be drawn to Spirit House in pursuit of power or personal acclaim. Unlike the Black Arts Repertory Theater/School, most of the participants in Spirit House were members of Baraka's organization, and they were subjected to rites of initiation and behavioral codes that had not been demanded of participants in the school in Harlem. When David Llorens visited Spirit House in 1969, Baraka's organization had only about 100 active members. A few years later, Curvin estimated Baraka's active members to number approximately 300.[32]

In accordance with his own semifanatical devotion to Karenga, Baraka demanded that the members of CFUN become devotees of Karenga's Kawaida doctrines. Historian Komozi Woodard, a former member of CFUN, noted that Baraka made the members recite Karenga's seven principles several times a day. When members of CFUN spoke at their group meetings, they ended by stating, "If I have said anything of value or beauty, all praise is due to Maulana Karenga, and all mistakes have been mine."[33] Such cultist rituals were certainly intent on generating "groupthink" in CFUN. Baraka successfully created a cult of personality around Karenga, which shortly thereafter he extended to himself. Baraka's devotion to Karenga cooled somewhat when the Maulana retreated from public life after two Black Panthers were murdered on the UCLA campus by members of Karenga's organization. Fearing retaliation from the Black Panthers, Karenga became less visible and less willing to journey to Newark to offer guidance to Baraka and CFUN, and as a result, his influence on Baraka waned. While Baraka continued to be a devoted follower of Kawaida, he no longer acted as if CFUN had to be a replica of Karenga's US. In addition, he changed some organizational rules in recognition of his differences with Karenga. According to Woodard, one of the first and most significant revisions that CFUN made was admitting black women as full members.[34] Full membership did not, however, mean equal membership.

Beginning in the late 1960s, Amina Baraka started a discussion group composed of black female associates of CFUN. Even during the height of Karenga's influence on CFUN, Amina Baraka and other women in the organization tried to break out of the constrained gender roles mandated by Karenga's various doctrines. Calling themselves the United Sisters, this group of black women became some of the most active members in CFUN. One of the cornerstones of CFUN's efforts to create institutions to promote Kawaida was the African Free School. Under the direction of Amina Baraka, Spirit House founded the school to educate and supplement the education of young black students who lived in the neighborhood around Spirit House.[35] Besides teaching the children the values of Kawaida, it also exposed them to African culture. The school assumed that an emphasis on Africa would facilitate the mastery of crucial skills like reading, writing, and math. Moreover, this destigmatization of Africa was thought to help students develop a positive image of themselves and thus expand their sense of intellectual authority and self-worth. The idea of using African culture as a way of learning and self-development prefigured by decades the use of Afro-centric educational pedagogies in inner-city schools.

The African Free School was accredited by the state as an elementary school. The school did not charge any tuition, but the parents of the students had to participate in various activities to help keep the school alive. Instead of the traditional pledge of allegiance to the American flag, a typical day in the African Free School began with a pledge of allegiance to the black liberation flag. In September 1970, the African Free School's pedagogical success led to the establishment of an African Free School class in the Robert Treat Public School. Financed by a grant from the U.S. Department of Health, Education and Welfare, the class was viewed as an experiment to determine whether the novel pedagogy could improve the academic performance of students who had been previously designated "problems" and "slow learners."

The purpose of the African Free School and its class at Treat was to create a learning experience that valorized cooperative learning over individual competition and achievement. The teacher of the class at Treat commented on the pedagogy: "It teaches collectively, not individually. The students don't have to feel left out or in competition. Individualism is a white man's idea. We want to reduce the conflict that individualism and competition produce and achieve consensus." The principal of the Robert Treat school considered the African Free School class "an important alternative to traditional education. We recognized that what we did in the past was a failure, that we had to do something different. . . . Now we hope that by inculcating new values we are making some progress."[36] Although the principal hoped that this alternative class would improve the students' test scores, its impact could not have been gauged accurately by their performance on standardized tests, for the year-long class was only a small segment of their entire educational experience. It could be argued that any improvement in the students' sense of intellectual self-efficacy should be interpreted as a significant achievement. I was not able to find any evidence showing whether the students enrolled in the African Free School class at Treat benefited from it.

Besides sponsoring various theater and dance troupes, the Newark CAP also had a publishing house, Jihad Publishers. Founded in 1967, this publishing component of CFUN issued works written by Sekou Toure, Julius Nyerere, and Amilcar Cabral. Jihad Publications also issued most of the theoretical and political writings written by the Imamu as the head of CAP. Another of CAP's publishing ventures was the biweekly newspaper *Black New-Ark*, which was later renamed *Unity and Struggle*. This newspaper featured local news and events throughout the African diaspora. In addition, the Political School of Kawaida was established to train activists from around the country in the organizing methodology of Karenga's philosophy. In a similar vein, Amina Baraka began a pedagogical class in order to teach activists the methods of the African Free School. Finally, CFUN also ran a store that sold African clothing and various artifacts from Africa. The CFUN members' collective contributions helped fund these activities.

In addition to the $39,000 grant that CFUN received for the African Free School class at Treat, CFUN received other grants from foundations and government agencies. But CFUN had trouble raising money. According to Baraka,

> We get grants from foundations, not as many as we'd like because people have said we're anti-Semitic, we're this and that, we're gonna buy guns. I means all kinds of bad stuff so we have not got the kind of grants from these foundations that a whole lot of other people have got.[37]

Even though Baraka may have been correct in attributing CFUN's fund-raising difficulties to distortions of its political positions, he does not seem to realize that he had made obscene statements about Jews and other whites while based in Newark. Still, it is baffling why Baraka would try to obtain funding from corporate and governmental agencies, given his public pronouncements concerning the revolutionary intentions of CFUN and himself. Once again, it is curious that Baraka did not choose to create a black-funded and -controlled infrastructure, however small.

Spirit House and CFUN were the centers of a vibrant community held together by a black nationalist ideology and praxis. As the charismatic head of the group, Baraka's role was central in maintaining group unity and a continuity of purpose and practice. The weekly meetings held at Spirit House and later at the CFUN headquarters became known as "soul sessions." Modeled on Karenga's US in southern California, the soul sessions regularly included some type of cultural production (drama, music, or dance) and political speeches. Usually Baraka gave a speech. Afterward, the attendants performed the popular line dances.[38] CAP became a world unto itself. Indeed, when reflecting on the "good ole days of CAP" in his autobiography, Baraka admitted that the organization may have become too insular.

By the early 1970s, a cult of personality had developed around Baraka. Curvin writes:

> To his followers, Baraka has extraordinary powers and abilities to lead the Black masses out of poverty and despair. He counsels his followers on family and personal matters, mediates in family disputes and officiates at wedding ceremonies for his adherents.... According to a former member of the Committee, if a person questioned something said by Baraka, that person would be considered, "inept, counter-revolutionary, or not committed."[39]

A 1972 CAP position paper, "The Beginning of National Movement," describes Baraka as an "innovative sage and guiding light of the new nationalism, Kawaida, whose profound words of magnificence turn immediately into deeds of divine significance." Deeds of divine significance? By the early 1970s, a photograph of Baraka was placed on the cover of all CAP publications. As if plastering his photograph on everything was not sufficient to sustain his cult of personality, beginning in the early 1970s, Newark CAP celebrated Baraka's birthday in a manner fit for a divine presence. This celebration was announced in a 1973 edition of the organization's newspaper, *Black New Ark*.

> *Leo Baraka*, October 7th is the Birth Date of our leader and teacher of Revolutionary Afrikan Nationalism, Imamu Amiri Baraka. We advocate this day as our HIGH HOLY DAY. Imamu Baraka's works are his best teacher.
>
> We, the advocates of Imamu Amiri Baraka's works and studies use this day as a day of absolute work and study. We work and study to strengthen our commitment to the building and developing of our community and restoration of our people to their traditional greatness. On *Leo Baraka*, we

wear Black because Black is for our faces and the work we must do. Our food intake consists of fruit and juice from fresh fruits.[40]

Why would anyone engage in these sophomoric rituals? How did these rituals come to be seen as having anything to do with revolutionary change? The elevation of Baraka's birthday to a high holy day in the organization speaks to the degree to which the organization was run as a fiefdom of the Imamu.

Despite Gibson's growing rift with Baraka and his allies, the mayor had not turned a totally deaf ear to all of Baraka's desires. Under Gibson, the Newark Housing Authority allowed CFUN to use several city-owned buildings rent free, and the board of education recognized and subsidized the African Free School class at Treat school. One of Baraka's major political initiatives came in the attempt to build low- and moderate-income housing with federal and state funds made accessible to community organizations for such projects. It is a testimony to Baraka's realpolitik instincts that he was able to obtain HUD approval and funding for this housing project. Equally significant, Baraka and his colleagues were able, with Mayor Gibson's support, to obtain from the Newark City Council a tax abatement for the land that the housing was to be built on. Despite the need for housing, the tax abatement was a great achievement insofar as the proposed housing was to be located in an integrated neighborhood in the predominantly Italian American North Ward, home of Anthony Imperiale. The name of the proposed housing was Kawaida Towers, a name that made it apparent to all that the project was linked to Amiri Baraka.

In March 1972, Baraka attended a meeting in Mayor Gibson's office in which officials from the New Jersey Housing Finance Agency approved an application for a forty-eight-year mortgage for $6.4 million. In hopes of minimizing Italian American protests against the building of Kawaida Towers, Baraka hired an Italian American construction company. Excavation of the site began in September 1972, and the formal groundbreaking ceremony was held in October. In early November, Anthony Imperiale, head of the North Ward Citizens Committee, led demonstrations at the site. With the active participation of numerous Newark police officers in uniform, the construction workers and supporters of Kawaida Towers were physically attacked. John Redden, Gibson's police chief who had been chosen by the mayor to replace the hated racist Dominic Spina, refused to protect the construction workers. Instead of fulfilling the duties of his job, he resigned rather than rein in his own police force. Shortly thereafter, the city council voted six to three to retract the tax abatement that had been given to the building only a year earlier.

Even though canceling the abatement was illegal, the intensity of the protests were such that the political will to pursue the project had been lost. Work on the project came to a standstill.

In March 1973, Mayor Gibson was still expressing public support for the project and was quoted in the *New York Times* as saying, "The sponsors of the project have fulfilled every legal requirement and I am still firmly resolved that Kawaida Towers be built."[41] By this time Baraka was beginning to have doubts about the mayor's willingness to confront the racist white demonstrators, for even though Gibson issued public statements of support, he did not mobilize his city government behind the project. By August, Baraka was calling Gibson a "puppet" of the business community.

By 1974, it was clear that Gibson was not willing to expend his political capital to build Kawaida Towers. Moreover, it soon became apparent that Earl Harris, one of the black city councilmen who owed their election to the black and Puerto Rican convention, was now doing everything in his power to undermine its construction. The reasons for Harris's change of heart is unknown, but it appears that he may have quietly joined some of the corrupt forces in Newark that historically had dominated the building industry. After the 1974 municipal elections, Harris became the first black city council president, and as such, he issued orders denying tax abatement to anyone or any organization affiliated with LeRoi Jones. A housing plan that had taken Baraka and CFUN three years to devise was now being scuttled in a matter of minutes.

In early February 1975, Baraka and a few other members of CFUN were arrested during a meeting of the Newark City Council on the orders of the council president Earl Harris, who charged them with disturbing the peace. Baraka and the others had come to the meeting in order to show support for the passage of tax abatement for Kawaida Towers. While they were being booked in a local precinct, the Newark City Council voted seven to one to deny tax abatement to Kawaida Towers. Only Councilman Sharpe James voted to build it.

The defeat of Kawaida Towers was perhaps the hardest one for Baraka and his confreres in CFUN. A few months after the council's vote denying tax abatement to Kawaida Towers, the funding for Kawaida Towers, Kawaida Community Development, the African Free School, and other programs was withdrawn, and the programs were dismantled. The Newark Housing Authority also rescinded its offer to CFUN for the free use of those buildings housing various CAP functions. Mayor Gibson must have been behind these events. Shortly thereafter, the buildings that had housed various functions of CAP were demolished. In 1976, even the foundation of Kawaida Towers was finally buried.

CONCLUSION

Baraka's experiences in Newark, particularly his immense disappointment with the Gibson mayoralty, ultimately led to a crisis of faith in black nationalism. As a result of his Newark experiences, Baraka concluded that changes in the racial identity of those in power were insufficient to alter the city government's priorities. Specifically, he surmised that an emphasis on the racial identity of black candidates hid their class interests. We might conclude that Baraka was quite astute in rejecting black nationalism. Whatever one may think of Baraka's version of black cultural nationalism, it was quite honorable for him to willingly discard an ideology and entire way of life once he decided that it was hindering the black struggle for emancipation. Yet in hindsight, it seems apparent that Baraka misdiagnosed the problem of black electoral politics.

Gibson's embrace of establishmentarian politics was situated in his technocratic approach to governing. As mayor, Gibson could have used his office to generate a protest movement against state policies that made Newark financially destitute. Once he realized that so-called efficient government would not help black Newark, he could have used more activist means to campaign for Newark's needs. But he did not do so.

Once Baraka recognized that Gibson would not be a progressive mayor, he tried to work around him on many cultural and political issues. Spirit House and CFUN became oppositional political operations in Newark. Although they were responsible for many important social improvements in Newark, these black activists realized that without the support of the mayor's office and city council, they would never be able to reach a large segment of society. Thus once the mayor's office and city council actively turned against them, CFUN could no longer survive.

Baraka's inability to alter the direction of Newark city politics cannot be viewed as a failure, as the forces aligned against him were too powerful. Paradoxically, Baraka became the antidemocratic, charismatic leader of an organization that tried to broaden the scope of political participation in Newark's civic affairs. Having rejected democratic decision making as an inefficient and "white" organizational practice, Baraka may have mistakenly believed that he was opposing whites in instituting autocracy in CFUN/CAP. In their attempt to change Newark, Baraka and CFUN discovered the depths of the charade of American democracy, and in the process, they discovered the normality of their autocratic sensibilities.

12

Pan-Africanism

THE VEHEMENCE OF white resistance to the expansion of the Afro-American civil rights struggle during the 1950s intensified the ethnic-political consciousness of Afro-Americans throughout the nation. During the mid-1950s, black citizens of Montgomery, Alabama, decided to boycott the local public transit system rather than continue to tolerate the racist seating practices on buses.[1] That such an action would occur in the very "heart of Dixie" indicated a new sense of black political assertiveness. The Supreme Court's landmark 1954 ruling, *Brown vs. Board of Education*, removed the legal mandate for "separate but equal" schooling in the South. But opposition to the *Brown* decision showed Afro-Americans that white supremacy in the United States would not be crumble because of judicial mandate alone.[2] For example, in Prince Edward County, Virginia, the local white population was so incensed by the Supreme Court ruling that they closed the county's public schools from 1959 through 1964 rather than desegregate them.[3] And because of the international embarrassment caused by the refusal of the governor of Arkansas to obey not only the highest court in the nation but also widely publicized presidential requests, President Dwight D. Eisenhower, a racist in his own right and opponent of the *Brown v. Board of Education* decision, deployed troops from the U.S. Army's 101st Airborne Division to escort nine black teenagers to the formerly all-white Central High School in Little Rock.[4]

The foot-dragging of the federal government regarding domestic violations of black American rights, including lynchings, amplified blacks' recognition of the tenuousness of "racial progress." No single public event better highlighted the resilience of white American racism than the brutal murder of fourteen-year-old Emmett Till.[5] During the summer of 1955, Till, a native of Chicago, was visiting relatives in Mississippi. Accused by a white woman of whistling at her, Till was shot, dismembered, and discarded in the Tallahatchie River. Even though there was overwhelming evidence against the two white men charged with the vicious crime, they were quickly and routinely acquitted by an all-white Mississippi jury.[6] Because of the tenacious efforts of Till's mother to publicize the crime and the subsequent miscarriage of justice, the brutalized body of young Emmett was presented for public viewing in a

Chicago funeral home. Thousands of people came to see the mutilated corpse. But even this media attention did not bring an end to the violence against Mississippi blacks.

The feeble responses of the federal government to the Till murder, the slaying of numerous other blacks, white southern "massive resistance" to the *Brown* decision, and the continued political disenfranchisement of southern blacks only increased skepticism of the United States' intentions toward its black citizenry. In turn, this skepticism was important to creating the conditions in Afro-America for critically assessing the behavior of the United States toward black people elsewhere. Like that of many black intellectuals who matured during the late 1950s and early 1960s, Baraka's political coming of age included a growing consciousness of the Afro-American connection to Africa. For many black Americans, this renewed interest in Africa was stimulated by African anticolonial movements as well as the United States' complicity in the European colonial dominance of Africa.[7] In 1956, the Gold Coast became the first European colony in Africa to win its independence. The new free nation of Ghana was led by the highly charismatic Kwame Nkrumah, who gave new vitality to the dream of an emancipated African continent. Nkrumah was popular in black American intellectual circles because of his advocacy of Pan-Africanism. Moreover, he had been educated in the United States at the predominantly black Lincoln University in Pennsylvania and later at the University of Pennsylvania.[8]

According to Harold Isaacs, "What came new out of Africa in the late 1950s for a great many Negro Americans was indeed the chance for the first time to identify in a positive way with the continent of their black ancestors."[9] Black Americans began to write a great deal about Africa and their African ancestry and to participate in events that conveyed their respect for and pride in the new African nations.

The late 1950s was a time of black awakening. Although Jones was not yet politically engaged or captivated by the new developments on the African continent, in the late 1950s he began to take steps in that direction. In mid-February 1961, much of the world was startled by the news from the former Belgian Congo that Patrice Lumumba, the duly elected president of the new African nation of Congo, had been assassinated. During the months preceding his murder, Lumumba had become an internationally recognized African symbol of resistance to colonialism and neocolonialism for his efforts to keep his emerging country unified.[10] Western governments and multinational businesses had attempted to finance the secession of Katanga Province from the Congo because of its valuable mineral deposits. Staunchly opposed to the secessionist movement and highly angered by the Belgians' viciousness and

Machiavellian machinations, Lumumba threatened to turn to the Soviet Union for support. In response, the United States set about trying to assassinate him.[11] But before it could do so, he was killed by secessionist forces working in partnership with Belgium and the CIA. The United Nations was also complicit in his overthrow and murder by neither recognizing him as the sovereign leader of the new nation nor protecting him.

Following Lumumba's assassination, Jones participated in a demonstration outside the United Nations' headquarters, protesting the Belgian and U.S. governments' conspiracy with the United Nations in not recognizing Lumumba's legitimate authority. The demonstrators also recognized that Western capitalist interests, including various American companies, had helped instigate the secessionist movement in Katanga Province, which ultimately led to the murder.[12] Along with other protesters marching in front of the U.S. mission, Jones was attacked and arrested by the police.[13] His arrest was his first exposure to political repression by the state, and the experience strengthened his political commitment.

Pan-Africanism has a long and complex history in Afro-American political life and intellectual thought, and it is a difficult concept to define.[14] For instance, the black historian John Henrik Clarke wrote that "Pan Africanism is about the restoration of African people to their proper place in world history,"[15] and he noted that the purpose of this historical restoration was to reinvigorate black respect. Historian Manning Marable defined Pan-Africanism as follows:

> Pan-Africanism . . . expressed the historic cultural unity between blacks in the United States, the Caribbean, and Africa. Politically, Pan-Africanism stood for the continuity of worldwide racial struggle—against colonialism, neo-colonialism and apartheid abroad and against "domestic colonialism" at home.[16]

Finally, St. Clair Drake, an Afro-American sociologist and lifelong participant in Pan-African politics, defined Pan-Africanism as "the idea that Africans and peoples of African descent in the New World should develop racial solidarity for the purpose of abolishing discrimination, enforced segregation, and political and economic exploitation of Negroes throughout the world."[17]

Clark's definition of Pan-Africanism confuses a description of Pan-Africanism with one of its goals. Although Marable's definition is an improvement on Clarke's, he is wrong to suggest that Pan-Africanism universally presupposed cultural unity among blacks throughout the world. Marable is also incorrect to attribute to traditional Afro-American Pan-Africanist sentiments the belief that black Americans constituted a domestic colony. Of these three definitions, therefore, Drake's is the most amenable to my discussion.

I define Pan-Africanism as the political actions and/or intellectual thought by Africans and/or people of the African diaspora that regard Africa and the peoples of African descent throughout the world as constituting an interrelated political unit with a shared core of political interests and/or cultural values. Pan-Africanism is somewhat like a transnational ethnic identity that is grounded in tenuously shared histories and/or cultures ("we all have African origins") or in shared phenotypical characteristics (a darker skin pigmentation).[18] Unlike black nationalism, Pan-Africanism indicates an affinity and not a political strategy. An individual could have a transnational ethnic affinity with blacks and yet not endorse black nationalism as a viable strategy of emancipation. Historically, Pan-Africanism arose in opposition to the European colonization of Africa, the partition of Africa into arbitrarily defined colonies, and the political plight of the descendants of those Africans who were transported as slaves and exploited as laborers throughout the world. For most of the twentieth century, Pan-Africanism has been the preserve of a small segment of the black intelligentsia throughout the diaspora.

Traditionally, Pan-Africanism has had numerous and distinct components. For instance, liberal Pan-Africanism counterbalances radical Pan-Africanism. In emerging African nations, liberal Pan-Africanism strove for the replacement of white colonialists with black political leaders and "captains of industry." Marcus Garvey advocated a liberal Pan-Africanism during the 1920s. This is the tradition of Pan-Africanism exemplified in the defense of the Americo-Liberian domination of indigenous Africans in Liberia presented by W. E. B. Du Bois and the Nigerian Benjamin Nnambi Azikiwe during the 1930s. The tradition of liberal Pan-Africanism is also associated with heroic African figures like Jomo Kenyatta. Despite being a militant opponent of British colonial rule in Kenya, when he assumed power Kenyatta turned Kenya into one of Africa's most extensive neocolonial, capitalist client states.[19]

The goal of radical Pan-Africanism is to fundamentally change the economic order initiated by the colonial powers, because the economic order under colonialism did not serve the interests of the majority of the colonized. To replace colonial white faces with newly independent black ones does not automatically alter the distribution of economic benefits and political power. Consequently, more often than not, radical Pan-Africanism advocates some form of socialism and is wary of the hegemonic world capitalist order. The tradition of radical Pan-Africanism includes people like Julius Nyerere of Tanzania, Sekou Toure of Guinea, the later Du Bois, Amilcar Cabral of Guinea-Bissau, and Walter Rodney, a Guyanan intellectual.[20]

Likewise, cultural Pan-Africanism can be juxtaposed with political Pan-Africanism.[21] Cultural Pan-Africanism views Africa and the peoples of the African diaspora as constituting a shared cultural core, as shown in the works of Cheikh Anta Diop and the Negritude artistic movement (e.g., Leopold Senghor, Leon Damas, Aime Cesaire) and the contemporary Afrocentric intellectual movement in the United States. Such tendencies also were present in the early work of W. E. B. Du Bois. Political Pan-Africanism views Africans and the diaspora as constituting a shared political struggle against a common enemy (i.e., European colonialism or white racism). Less emphasis is placed on international black cultural similarities than on the various struggles against European racist colonization and white racist practices throughout Africa and the African diaspora. This is the Pan-Africanism of George Padmore, the later Du Bois, and C. L. R. James.[22]

In its broadest and most colloquial usage, Pan-Africanism indicates a social consciousness, a political temperament that generates and sustains affective links to all black peoples. A Pan-African consciousness can inspire bourgeois black Americans to tour Bahai in Brazil while on expensive vacations. It can lead blacks in Britain to worry about the plight of Haiti and blacks in Canada to have a political concern for the genocide in Rwanda. Pan-African sensibilities led the South African revolutionary Nelson Mandela to keep abreast of events in Harlem while he was in prison. Pan-Africanism allows a "black person" to define himself or herself as a member of a larger "we" group. In the United States, Pan-Africanism became important to some activists as a way of stepping outside the construction of themselves as members of an American minority group.

Whereas Baraka's mature Pan-Africanism combined its cultural and political tendencies, his initial Pan-Africanist posture was liberal. As a black cultural nationalist, Baraka explicitly valorized the cultural motifs and practices of indigenous African cultures, even though his art does not seem to have been significantly influenced by Africa. He engaged in a crude romanticization of traditional African societies, believing that there was something radical about appearing to live like a traditional African (whatever that is) in Newark, New Jersey, during the late 1960s and early 1970s. The Africa with which Baraka identified was a fictitious revival of an illusory historical moment. His ideal Africa lay somewhere in the past or far distant future. It did not have a present, hence its escapist tendencies! Baraka was a crucial participant in the Afro-American "invention of Africa" during the 1960s and 1970s. This Afro-American invention of Africa was grounded in the therapeutic and political needs of black Americans and was expressed primarily through the consumption of "African-oriented" consumer goods such as clothing, foods, and pseudo-African doctrines like Kawaida.[23]

Baraka and other adherents to Karenga's Kawaida intentionally distorted and fictionalized an African past and then pretended to revive those distortions and fictions as if in so doing they were returning to their traditional African selves. Ironically, this hyperinvention of Africa was based not only on black American ignorance of Africa but also on Afro-American disrespect for authentic traditional African cultures. Had Karenga truly valued traditional Africa, he would not have invented that California hype known as Kawaida. Instead, he might have gone to Africa, studied, and spared many black Americans a great deal of identity confusion. Instead, Karenga, Baraka, and their comrades were mainly interested in using the *idea of Africa* to the extent that it served an Afro-American political and cultural function.

They invoked an attachment to traditional Africa as a means of appearing to have purged European cultural influences from their lives. The Africa of Karenga and Baraka was a functional fantasy that did little to encourage Afro-Americans to confront the reality of twentieth-century African pathos and possibility. Traditional African cultures had historically failed to stem the tide of European colonial domination. Why, then, did Baraka and his accomplices think that a revitalization of these cultures would help Afro-Americans succeed in abolishing white American racism in the latter part of the twentieth century? Recognizing their history of subjugation at the hands of Europe, the emerging independent black African nations were not necessarily opposed to escaping their traditional pasts. Rather, black African nations were more interested in modernizing (i.e., Westernizing), precisely when many Westernized black American intellectuals were celebrating their newly discovered "premodern" (i.e., non-Western) status.

Given Baraka's quasi-religious attachment to a romantic idea of Africa via the fabricated neo-African culture of Kawaida, he could not interrogate African societies, particularly traditional African societies. In this sense, the novelist Richard Wright was Baraka's polar opposite. Unlike Baraka, Wright was not ideologically inhibited from engaging in a ruthless critique of Africa. At the Presence Africaine Conference (the First Congress of Negro Artists and Writers) in Paris in 1956, Wright questioned the role of indigenous African cultural traditions during the colonial period. Incapable of pro-African (or Pan-African) romanticism, Wright described the inability of traditional African cultures to generate and sustain opposition to European dominance. During the following question-and-answer session, Wright made the following controversial comments:

Might not the vivid and beautiful culture that Senghor has described . . . have been a fifth column, a corps of saboteurs and spies of Europe? . . . The ancestor cult religion with all of its manifold, poetic richness that created a sense of self-sufficiency—did not that religion, when the European guns came in act as sort of aid to those guns? Did that religion help the people to resist fiercely and hardly and hurl the Europeans out? I question the value of that culture in relationship to our future; I do not condemn it, but how can we use it? . . . I want to be free and I question this culture, not in its humane scope but in relationship to the Western world as it meets the Western world.[24]

Critical of European colonialism, Wright seemed to have been too enamored of Western modernity to consider that African societies may have had indigenous traditions worthy of respect and retention. Nonetheless, he understood that a viable emancipatory politics could not rest on the shoulders of romantic distortions of a defeated past.

Despite his immersion in the ersatz Africanism of Kawaida, Baraka believed that the political struggle against white racism in the United States was linked to the emancipation of Africa from European and American domination. Insofar as his early liberal Pan-Africanist ideology assumed that white racism was the principal obstacle to worldwide black emancipation, it did not include an economic critique of colonialism, neocolonialism, or the class hierarchies in precapitalist Africa. Baraka condemned neocolonialism, but only as a form of power by which whites manipulated blacks. He saw African neocolonial leaders as international versions of Uncle Toms. Unlike Baraka's conception, another tradition of Pan-Africanist discourses viewed capitalism as hindering the freedom of blacks throughout the diaspora as much as antiblack racism did. But Baraka gave short shrift to critiques of capitalism. He was a victim of his own knee-jerk antiwhiteism that led him to devalue white thinkers, including Karl Marx.

Liberal Pan-Africanists often were incapable of criticizing the power hierarchies in African societies and diasporic communities. This is evident in Baraka's earliest pronouncements on Africa. He condemned white racist domination in South Africa and Rhodesia and neocolonial domination in other African States, but he had little to say about the pathetic autonomous behavior of indigenous African elites toward their nations' masses. Rather, Baraka attributed all problems in Africa to white racist dominance and the collusion of obsequious African elites. He ignored the possibility that these indigenous African elites had no desire to link their plight to that of their impoverished compatriots. He did not seem to understand that self-interest and greed were not confined to European cultures. This blindness allowed him to view exploitative blacks as minor pawns in the greater exploitative schemes of the white world.

According to Manning Marable, by 1971 most black nationalists in the United States had discarded the term *Black Power* for *Pan-Africanism*. The idea of Black Power had been compromised by Richard Nixon's promotion of "black capitalism" as "Black Power." In addition, Black Power had been commodified in apolitical notions of blackness such as "soul." Marable did not consider that Black Power rhetoric was discarded because it now meant nothing and everything. Prevailing definitions of Black Power were often a hodgepodge of eclectic subjective desires (e.g., Black Power is black people having the right to live in decent housing"). Such claims were more descriptive than analytical and did little to advance the cause of black politics.

Black militant spokespersons could describe what an emancipated black America would look like, but they could not tell us how to get from "here to there." The absence of strategic thinking became so commonplace in black militant circles that Pan-Africanist political ambitions and visions, such as a United States of Africa, ultimately superseded discussions of realizing them. Political fantasies of a Pan-Africanist world hid the strategic confusions of Pan-Africanist activists. Dreams of a "free" African diaspora became more important than strategies for effecting change. When one thinks of Malcolm X, the Black Panthers, the Republic of New Africa, Karenga and US, and Baraka and CAP, one realizes the weaknesses of their strategic thinking. For instance, Malcolm X believed that the newly independent black nations of Africa and the Caribbean, when linked to the colored nations of Asia and Latin America, could band together in the United Nations to confront the American domestic racial problem. Malcolm not only underestimated the international power of the United States, but he overestimated the degree to which foreigners would be concerned about black Americans.

There is no greater testimony to Baraka's commitment to utopian Pan-Africanist visions at the expense of strategic Pan-Africanist thinking than the Pan-African congress that he helped organize in Atlanta in 1970. Though flawed strategically, Baraka tapped into a political consciousness that was waiting to be mobilized.

ATLANTA CONGRESS: IN SEARCH OF PAN-AFRICAN POSSIBILITIES

Baraka was instrumental in organizing a conference that he subsequently referred to as the "first modern Pan-African Congress."[25] Held in Atlanta in

September 1970, the meeting was promoted as an offspring of those early-twentieth-century Pan-African congresses called by Du Bois, Padmore, and others. About 2,700 people attended this so-called Congress of African Peoples. Besides approximately 350 delegates from Africa and Third World countries, many prominent Afro-American elected officials attended the Atlanta meeting, including mayors Kenneth Gibson of Newark and Richard Hatcher of Gary, Indiana, and Georgia State legislator Julian Bond. Also in attendance were prominent Afro-American civil rights leaders such as Ralph Abernathy (Southern Christian Leadership Conference), Jesse Jackson (Operation Bread Basket), and Whitney Young (National Urban League). The presence of these prointegrationist political leaders at a conference organized and facilitated by Baraka and his black cultural nationalist peers made it one of the most ideologically diverse black political gatherings of the mid-twentieth century. More than any other accomplishment of the Atlanta congress, the mere physical presence of such ideologically antagonistic Afro-American political leaders inspired those in attendance to believe that they were participating in a grand historical event. Baraka's ability to engineer highly publicized moments of symbolic ethnic unity served him well in Atlanta, as it would two years later at the National Black Political Convention in Gary.

Baraka's "Ideological Statement of the Congress of African Peoples" described the congress's various themes. Not surprisingly, the statement was explicitly black nationalist and liberal Pan-Africanist. Given its ideological tenor, it is unclear why Whitney Young and other integrationist-minded black leaders were invited to speak to the gathering. Its purported ideological diversity was evident, however, only on a rhetorical level. For programmatic matters, black nationalism was the only acceptable creed. Indeed, the ideological statement included the claim that "Pan-Africanism is thus the global expression of Black nationalism."[26]

Baraka coordinated the workshop on political liberation, whose purpose was to devise strategies for an international black political praxis. True to his Kawaida influence, Baraka continued to insist that cultural change was a necessary prerequisite for political change.

> We must *separate the mind*, win the mind, wage the revolution to win the Black man's mind so we will begin to move *together* as a people conscious that we are a people, struggling for national liberation. Separation must come *mentally* before any physical movement can begin. Separation away from assimilation or brain-washing or subjugation by the mind of the white nation.[27] [italics in original]

Despite Baraka's Karenga-inspired, mechanistic understanding of cultural change as the first step to liberation, his comments as the coordinator of the political liberation workshop appeared to be pragmatic. He called for building black political institutions, particularly a political party. The ultimate goal of his Pan-Africanist institution building was to construct an international Pan-African party for all members of the diaspora. It would lead not only to a unified black world but also to an international governing body of blacks. Details of this fantasy were never spelled out.

Ironically, when Baraka tried to explain the workings of such a party, he used his experiences in Newark electoral politics as the model. These experiences were, however, too provincial to function as a model for an international political organization. For instance, Baraka did not account for the relative absence of democracy in Africa. So how could the worldwide Pan-African party register voters and run candidates for office? Many African nations had no elections, and if Baraka had been living in one of these nations (including Toure's Guinea) when he issued his proclamation advocating democratic participation, he might well have been put in prison.

In calling for the Pan-Africanist party to prefigure the emancipated worldwide African nation, Baraka was trying to create counterhegemonic political institutions and practices. The Italian Marxist Antonio Gramsci argued that revolutionary institutions must encourage those practices that they hope will prevail in the emancipated society. Instead of devising procedures for decision making and holding discussions that could have empowered the political consciousnesses of his Pan-African confreres, Baraka skimmed over procedures and empowerment and opted for public declarations of positions on issues. In proclaiming its policy goals, the Atlanta congress made declarations and plans that could have had real meaning only if it had had a viable infrastructure in which to pursue these ends. Simply put, the resolutions had no bite. They were merely symbols that created a false sense of empowerment and offered a momentary catharsis for all in attendance. As a consequence, there was little that was counterhegemonic about the practices of CAP, despite its opposition to white racism and European colonialism.

With this unifying party in mind, the Atlanta Congress of African Peoples was formalized as a permanent organization, the Congress of African Peoples (CAP). CAP would be an international umbrella organization composed of local black nationalist political organizations. Furthermore, CAP would be a Kawaida organization.[28] In the aftermath of the Atlanta congress, Baraka's Newark organization, the Committee for Unified Newark (CFUN), would henceforth be known as the Newark chapter of CAP. To proclaim Kawaida as the guiding principle of a supposed international black political party indicated the degree to which Baraka's Pan-Africanism was actually more American than international. It would have been lunacy to have tried to persuade African political activists to endorse the tinsel-town, ersatz African principles of Kawaida.

By the time of the Atlanta congress, Baraka had become a charismatic figure in his local Newark organization and throughout much of black nationalist America. His followers spoke about him with reverence. He demanded of his immediate confreres complete loyalty if not blind obedience. In assuming the mantle of charismatic leader, Baraka appropriated one of the most anti-democratic traditions in American and Afro-American political cultures. The discipline of Baraka's followers and the efficiency of his autocratic rule facilitated the organization of a such a massive venture as the Atlanta Congress. Baraka's CFUN was given the crucial task of maintaining order at the Atlanta congress, which included providing security.

In Atlanta, Baraka was particularly concerned about the disruptive potential of Karenga's US followers. On several occasions, Karenga had spoken to Baraka about his desire to postpone the congress. Baraka disagreed and went ahead with the Atlanta congress despite Karenga's absence from its planning sessions. Predictably, Karenga tried to disrupt the gathering. The armed US members he sent to the congress tried to intimidate the participants. But Baraka's security measures prevented Karenga's men from trying anything blatantly disruptive. Karenga's displeasure with the Atlanta congress is curious given the intellectual deference paid to him throughout the proceedings.[29] Indeed, his desire to undermine the assemblage may have stemmed from the realization that his prize disciple now had gained greater prominence than himself.

Historian and former CAP member Komozi Woodard argues that the Atlanta congress was important because it signaled a new level of unity on the black political front.[30] I disagree. Despite the warmth and camaraderie among the political leaders at the conference, this momentary collegiality did not translate into an enduring or even endurable substantive political unity. Had this event led to the unity of black leadership across the ideological spectrum, there would still be little reason to assume that this unity in itself would have resulted in significant black political advancement. Unity or no unity, the only black political leaders at the Atlanta congress who had even marginal access to the resources necessary to affect American and Afro-American political outcomes were disproportionately in the ranks of the antinationalist leaders. Even these integrationist leaders (Whitney Young, Ralph Abernathy, Jesse Jackson, Richard Hatcher) knew that they did not control substantial resources.

Perhaps the most memorable moment of the Atlanta gathering was when Hayward Henry stood between Whitney Young and Louis Farrakhan and held their hands aloft as a symbol of unity. But regardless of who clasped hands or shouted in unison, "it's nation time," the conceptual problems undergirding the entire Pan-Africanist project did not disappear. To wit, Louis Farrakhan delivered a speech in which the only agenda he could offer the delegates was to declare their allegiance to Elijah Muhammad and join the Nation of Islam. What debate over tactics and strategies could Farrakhan have had with any of the other speakers? Certainly he had nothing to say about an international Pan-African party. At the time, he did not even vote and would not do so until Jesse Jackson's 1984 campaign.

Baraka had yet to confront the fact that black Americans constituted only one-ninth of the U.S. population. Therefore, for blacks to have an impact, through elections, on the policies governing the United States, they would have to enter coalitions with other Americans, including whites. There was no escaping this fact. Even a unified black America would, at best, be numerically marginal. If whites and blacks in the United States became completely balkanized in the way that Baraka recommended, blacks would inevitably lose. But blacks were losing anyway, even when they played coalition politics. White Americans were not in a democratic mood. The exhaustion of realpolitik options for black advancement could thus culminate in a black nationalist variant of political escapism that masked black American desperation. Those blacks who were playing politically "by the rules" were engaged in escapism as well. They pretended that the antidemocratic tendencies in the American political-economic system were errors of implementation and not structurally grounded in the system. If Baraka and the black cultural nationalist project were subjected to criticism, it certainly could not have emanated from the NAACP or the Edward Brookes of the world. White racism offered no escape even to pro-American black ideologues.

The Congress of African Peoples was an organization without a strong financial or popular base. Baraka still had not learned how to limit his political ambitions to goals that could be realized, given the real constraints of black life in America (e.g., lack of money). Instead he opted once again for the grand stage. The size of the Atlanta congress and its broad list of diverse speakers took precedence over the arduous task of forming an autonomous, self-supporting political organization. In his autobiography, Baraka still does not discuss how CAP was supposed to have survived without funding.[31]

In regard to the Atlanta congress, in his study of black nationalism in the

United States, *Red, Black and Green*, sociologist Alphonso Pinkney recognized that CAP's lack of financial resources would be a major obstacle to its effectiveness, and he argues that the issue of fund-raising should have been given a higher priority. Although Baraka and his colleagues appeared to recognize the limitations of an underfunded organization, they nevertheless made plans for programs that far outstripped CAP's resources. The congress's inability to resolve the issue of organizational funding is indicative of political escapism and naïveté. Not only did Baraka and his nationalist peers not deal with the question of financing the CAP organization, but most of the bills for the Atlanta gathering itself were paid by "white" institutions and government agencies. Pinkney concluded: "It seems unlikely that such agencies will continue to finance an organization which is fundamentally opposed to a system which permitted them to amass these resources in the first place."[32] It was not merely unlikely that such agencies would refuse to finance CAP, it was inevitable. No viable black separatist political articulation could have white money as its primary financial support base. It was irresponsible for black nationalists to have either wanted or accepted white funding for their nationalist political agendas.

Thirty years after the fact, I raised this point with several black activists who had participated in the Atlanta gathering. I was told that a prevailing argument at the time was that white funding of these gatherings was a form of "reparations." This is a pathetic rationalization of a severely flawed political strategy. The necessity for economic self-sufficiency is so obvious that we can only assume that Baraka was not as interested in creating an authentic black nationalist movement as in wanting *to be seen* as having created such a movement. Why would Baraka participate in such theatrics? We must remember that the dramatic had always been a core component of Baraka's political sensibility.

The Atlanta meeting once again demonstrated Baraka's less than astute political mind. Perhaps he simply did not understand the connection between an authentic black nationalist movement and financial self-sufficiency. The Congress of African Peoples lasted for almost a decade, but it never again reached the heights of symbolic importance and enthusiasm that it attained between the Atlanta congress in 1970 and the Gary convention (National Black Convention) in 1972 (discussed in the next chapter). CAP had not only successfully organized a major Pan-African Congress, but it was instrumental in realizing one of the goals established in Atlanta, the creation of a separate black political organization (i.e., the National Black Convention).

CAP: A NATIONAL POLITICAL ORGANIZATION

In the hope that the Atlanta Pan-African Congress would not be a symbolic, one-shot gathering, those attending decided to make CAP an ongoing political organization. Hayward Henry, one of the leaders of the Atlanta gathering, became its first chairperson. An instructor in the Afro-American studies program at Harvard University, Henry was also the chairman of the National Black Caucus of the Unitarian-Universalist Church.

The appointment of Henry symbolized CAP's attempt to unify black integrationists and black nationalists in order to form a national black political party. CAP decided to open independent offices in black communities in cities with large black populations. When this could not be done, CAP tried to attract existing community organizations into a national federation. This federated structure, which had been created at the Atlanta congress, was supposed to prepare for the emergence of a national all-black political party.

Most of the black groups, affiliates, and organizations that participated in the original Atlanta congress never became formal members of the new Congress of African People. It even is doubtful that many maintained significant working relationships with CAP after the Atlanta meeting. In fact, the Atlanta congress may have been the high point of Baraka's attempt to develop a national, black nationalist, organizational infrastructure. Given the powerful allure of symbols for many activists during the heyday of black cultural nationalism, CAP's greatest importance may have been that it provided Baraka with a national vehicle that made his charismatic authority appear more rational. Given the centrality of Baraka to CAP, it was not surprising that the Newark CFUN became the national prototype for local branches of CAP. During the early 1970s, CAP had branches in San Diego; Wilmington, Delaware; Washington D.C.; Chicago; South Bend, Indiana; Indianapolis; Baltimore; Boston; Detroit; St. Louis; Camden and East Orange, New Jersey; Newark; Albany; the Bronx; Manhattan; Brooklyn; Cleveland; Oberlin, Ohio; Philadelphia; Pittsburgh; and Houston. The Chicago CAP was headed by Haki Madhubuti, and in Brooklyn, the local community center, called The East, became the local CAP affiliate.

The Second International Assembly of the Congress of African People met on Labor Day 1972 in San Diego. At this gathering, Baraka was elected the national chairman of CAP. Not only was he its most prominent member, but he seemed to be able to maintain his black cultural nationalist orientation while working with less militant, more establishmentarian black leaders and groups. Baraka was both pragmatic and ideologically doctrinaire. However, he was quite autocratic in the way that he administered CAP as the self-anointed master thinker of the organization.[33] During its short life span, CAP published numerous position papers, most of which Baraka wrote himself. These papers were printed and issued by CAP's publishing house, Jihad Production, were distributed to CAP branches throughout the country, and served as the basis of individual reflections and organizational discussions. The degree to which Baraka's ideas became the actual views of individual CAP members remains unclear. Because CAP was a federation of locally based organizations, the authority of the national office to impose strict ideological conformity was severely constrained.

AFRICAN LIBERATION SUPPORT COMMITTEE

Perhaps the most active phase in the Pan-Africanist sentiments of the late 1960s and early 1970s was the attempt by some black Americans to mobilize public protest against the United States' foreign policy toward Africa. Of particular importance to these protests were the arms shipments that Portugal received from the United States which it then used against anticolonialist movements in Angola, Mozambique, and Guinea-Bissau. The ultimate insult was that black Americans (through their taxes) were funding the murder of black African freedom fighters and the continued subjugation of African peoples.[34] In addition, the United States did not support the international trade embargo against the racist minority regime in power in Rhodesia. Finally, many politicized black Americans opposed the continuation of apartheid in South Africa.

Black American activists decided to use African Liberation Day to demonstrate for black freedom on the African continent. African Liberation Day was created by Kwame Nkrumah upon Ghana's independence. Shortly thereafter, the Organization of African Unity (OAU) named May 25 of each year as African Liberation Day. Each year on that day, observances were to be held in each of the OAU member states in support of the liberation movements in various locations throughout Africa.

To coordinate the national protest activities, the African Liberation Support Committee (ALSC) was founded, a coalition of national and local Pan-Africanist and black nationalist organizations. According to political scientist and Pan-African activist Ronald Walters, a relatively small celebration of African Liberation Day took place in 1971,[35] but on May 27, 1972, a large political protest was held in Washington, D.C. According to Walters, approximately 50,000 people came to the demonstration. The speakers included

Congressmen Charles Diggs and Walter Fauntroy, poet Don L. Lee (Haki Madhubuti), and Baraka. Another demonstration was held simultaneously in San Francisco which attracted approximately 10,000 marchers. In 1973, a total of 100,000 persons participated in African Liberation Day marches in various parts of the United States. In addition, the ALSC claimed to have raised $40,000 to send to the freedom fighters.[36] Unfortunately, the momentum behind these successful national demonstrations was short lived.[37]

In 1974, an ideological conflict in the ALSC's executive committee threatened the entire movement. Once again, black Marxists and black nationalists were engaged in ideological fisticuffs. At the time of the initial conflict, Baraka was in transition between Pan-Africanist nationalism and Marxism. By late 1974, he had entered the Marxist camp. Although both ideological sectors remained committed to the African liberation movements, their loyalty to different dogmatic ideologies prevented them from working together. The conflict among different factions of the former African Liberation Support Committee became so intense and self-destructive that in May 1975, three different African Liberation Day marches were held simultaneously in Washington, D.C. One march was organized by the All African Peoples Revolutionary Party, led by Stokely Carmichael. Another was led by Abdul Alkalimat (formerly Gerald McWhorter) and was sponsored by the Socialist Workers Party. The third march was led by Baraka under the mantle of Marxist-Leninist-Maoism.[38] This divisiveness again resulted in three marches in 1976. It is unfortunate that the African Liberation Day movement was allowed to disintegrate on the basis of ideological differences in its leadership ranks. After all, the purpose of the African Liberation Day protests was to generate both support for African liberation movements and criticism of the United States' complicity in the colonial dominance of Africans. In pursuit of these goals, the ideological discord of the ALSC leadership should have been irrelevant, and probably was, to the majority of the participants in the protests. In any event, the ALSC's leaders saw themselves as theoreticians and came to believe that holding the correct ideology was paramount to joining forces to sustain the protest activities.[39]

What remains so puzzling about black nationalist activists of the late 1960s and early 1970s is that their dogmatic ideological allegiances often caused enmity between former black compatriots (who now adhered to different ideologies) that rivaled and at times even surpassed the antipathy felt for the supposed "enemy," be it white, capitalist, or both.[40]

The significance of fanatical ideological adherences for individual activists lay in the roles that such ideological beliefs played in the construction of personal identities. Ideological postures were worn like identity tags and signaled to all concerned whether its wearer was friend or foe. In adopting Pan-Africanism, Baraka shifted the edifice of his moral discourse and critique. No longer merely a member of an American minority group protesting white American injustice, a Pan-Africanist-minded black American had entered a social group and political formation that was not based on an appeal to white Americans. Ironically, he could continue to wage the same struggles that he had embraced before appropriating Pan-Africanism, but now the criteria for determining success or failure were different. For Baraka, Pan-Africanism was an important facilitator of ethnic marginality. By adopting Pan-Africanism and redefining his field of struggle, Baraka was trying to escape an Afro-American victim status and perhaps would have had he remained in the Pan-African fold. But Baraka was fickle, simultaneously invoking the worldwide self-determination of African peoples and writing protest poetry to frighten or prick the guilt of white Americans. But if whites were as amoral and innately intent on black domination as Baraka contended, there would be little reason to try to scare them with feeble black threats. Such people would not have the consciences required to feel guilt for their cruel deeds.

Despite its theoretical incongruity and highly contradictory meanings, Pan-Africanism has at times functioned as a mechanism for generating an international constituency of concern about certain local issues. As a political movement, it has not had a major impact on Afro-American politics. Moreover, the accomplishments of Pan-Africanism as an intellectual movement are not obvious. Its historical attractiveness to black thinkers has had as much to do with its therapeutic benefits as its political efficacy. Through an allegiance to Pan-Africanism, black Americans have been able to redefine themselves as part of a larger community and, in so doing, have been able to vicariously and emotionally participate in political successes in other parts of the diaspora when political struggles were not going so well at home.

In appropriating Pan-Africanism as a way out of the debilitations of the Afro-American victim status, Baraka stumbled on an international black existential quandary. Everywhere in the world, black people confronted subjugation. Pan-Africanism helped Baraka confront an Afro-American victim status, but it could not shield him from the worldwide subjugation of black people and their eclectic attempts to occupy a victim status vis-à-vis the world's whites. Similarly, throughout the world, different populations of blacks were engaged in protest politics against white domination. The difficulty of using Pan-Africanism as an ethnic marginality facilitator is that it allowed individual black intellectuals and activists from various locations throughout the world to redefine (i.e., broaden) their particular locus of struggle but did not allow blacks as a worldwide corporate body to do so.

THE INFLUENCE OF AFRICAN PAN-AFRICANISTS

Baraka's increasing exposure to prominent African social thinkers prompted him to reexamine his liberal Pan-Africanism. More precisely, Baraka was inspired by his exposure to African Pan-Africanist thinkers to reevaluate his attitude toward Marx. Because these thinkers were African, Baraka could not dismiss them as insufficiently black or dupes of whites. In particular, Baraka was influenced by the Pan-Africanism of Nkrumah, the African socialism of Toure and Nyerere, and the African Marxism of Amilcar Cabral.

In Pan-Africanist circles, Kwame Nkrumah was and remains a revered figure. As the first president of Ghana, Nkrumah was postcolonial Africa's most illustrious and charismatic advocate of Pan-Africanism. The former British colony of the Gold Coast, Ghana was the first sub-Saharan African nation to become independent, and Nkrumah was the first African head of state.[41] Great Britain granted Ghana independence in March 1957, and almost immediately, Ghana became a repository for all the repressed hopes and frustrations of colonized Africa. While many positive things can be said about Kwame Nkrumah, he was not an effective administrative leader. His rhetoric outstripped his considerable accomplishments. In fairness, however, he had tremendous problems to confront as the leader of a small, economically underdeveloped new nation. Nevertheless, it is curious that his image remained so untarnished among Afro-American Pan-Africanists of the 1960s and 1970s. Nkrumah was not a creative thinker, although in Baraka's Pan-Africanism, Nkrumah reigned as an intellectual giant of African independence. When Nkrumah was overthrown after a decade in power, legions of Pan-Africanists throughout the diaspora viewed it as a tragedy, but inside Ghana, there was rejoicing.[42]

Sekou Toure, leader of the small nation of Guinea on the west coast of Africa, became a hero to Pan-Africanists and anticolonialists throughout the world for his defiant stand for African freedom from European colonial dominance. Under President Charles de Gaulle, France offered colonies in Francophone Africa a choice between complete independence from France or autonomy in a French commonwealth. Most of the Francophone African leaders (e.g., Leopold Senghor of Senegal and Félix Houphouët-Boigny of the Ivory Coast) agreed to become members in a French-dominated commonwealth. On September, 28, 1958, France held a referendum throughout French West Africa for membership in the French community. Calls for a vote of yes were heard throughout the French African colonies except Guinea. Willing to stand alone, Toure asked the Guineans to vote no.[43]

On October 2, 1958, Guinea became an independent nation, with Sekou

Toure as its president. Typical of the patronizing racism of European colonialism, de Gaulle's France immediately set out to punish Guinea. French administrators were withdrawn, often taking with them supplies such as typewriters and telephones. Telephones lines were destroyed. French medical doctors also left, taking with them medical supplies. In other offices, the departing French smashed furniture, broke windows, and destroyed everything they could (e.g., toilets, lights). In Paris and Dakar, Guinean students lost their French government scholarships. France also tried to prevent private firms from investing in Guinea. But to de Gaulle's disappointment, Guinea did not collapse. Rather, France's assault on Guinea only solidified Toure's heroic stature in Africa and the African diaspora.[44]

Pan-African circles in the United States during the late 1960s and early 1970s initially admired Toure for his defiance of France, but he was also popular because he, among all African leaders (save perhaps Nyerere), was the strongest advocate of Pan-Africanism after the overthrow of Nkrumah. Baraka was drawn to Toure first because Toure saw himself as a poet and man of letters, an African philosopher-king.[45] In addition, Toure was a master rhetorician who aspired to be a radical political theorist and reinforced his charisma. Toure remained in power from the inception of Guinea as an independent nation until his death.

Guineans paid a steep price for his early resistance to de Gaulle. Toure was autocratic and did not tolerate private or public criticism. His words carried the authority of state decrees. Worse, Guinea's elite had to memorize and recite Toure's writings in order to secure employment.[46] Following the defeat of an invasion force of Portuguese mercenaries and Guinean exiles in 1970, Toure proclaimed the existence of a "permanent plot" to overthrow him, a condition that gave rise to a paranoid state of vigilance. Human rights abuses proliferated, and Toure even murdered some of his closest political confreres. According to journalist David Lamb:

> By the best count available, seventeen of Toure's cabinet ministers were shot or hanged between 1958 and the late 1970s, eighteen others were condemned to life in prison at hard labor.... Toure's murdered victims included Diallo Telli, the secretary-general of the Organization of African Unity. As many as two million Guineans—a staggering total of 40 percent of all the Guinean people—have escaped their homeland to live in exile in other African and European countries.[47]

Even though Toure marketed his regime internationally as socialist, Manning Marable's characterization of it as "authoritarian state capitalism" is more accurate.[48] What is striking is that Baraka and his Pan-Africanist accomplices viewed Toure as the ideal radical African leader and were willing to overlook the impact of his rule on his black African subjects. Baraka was a proponent of the Pan-Africanist strain in the United States that looked at the world from an Afro-American vantage point. That is, the *idea of Sekou Toure* was useful for Pan-Africanists in the United States, even if that idea had little resemblance to the actual demagogue. Baraka and Karenga, two black American autocrats, modeled themselves after a cruel megalomaniac African dictator.

From the vantage point of the Pan-African sensibilities that flowered in the United States during the late 1960s, the most honored leader in Africa was probably Julius Nyerere of Tanzania.[49] Nyerere recognized that his nation confronted a world political-economic order committed to maintaining it in a state of poverty and powerlessness. Not interested in neocolonialism, Nyerere also encouraged his nation to struggle with poverty and other problems without making threats and sweeping overstatements about the imminent decline of the West or the future power of Africa.[50] Nyerere's Tanzania was idealized as a place where the future of Africa was being correctly set in motion. In a 1972 issue of *Black World*, Baraka published a short article celebrating Nyerere and Tanzania: "The United Republic of Tanzania is one of the most progressive countries in Africa . . . it was truly inspiring for African Americans to be present to observe intimately and in great detail the dynamic and courageous social evolution which the Republic of Tanzania is undergoing."[51] After Nkrumah was overthrown, Tanzania replaced Ghana as the primary site of Afro-American romanticization of Africa. Swahili, the Tanzanian national language, became the most popular African language in a black America reaching back for cultural roots. Symbolic of this fact was the scene one day in 1968 during the second Black Power conference in Philadelphia when an awestruck crowd watched Karenga and Baraka hold a thirty-minute discussion completely in Swahili.[52]

Nyerere was fundamental to the Pan-Africanism that emerged in the United States during the late 1960s because of his valorization of traditional African society. Afro-Americans used the ideas of this respected African leader to support their claims for the superior humanity of black peoples. In *Ujamaa—The Basis of African Socialism*, a pamphlet published in 1962, Nyerere "described" traditional African society:

> Both the rich and the poor individual were completely secure in African society. . . . Nobody starved, either of food or of human dignity, because he lacked personal wealth; he could depend on the wealth possessed by the

community of which he was a member. That was socialism. That is social-ism. . . . In the old days the African had never aspired to the possession of personal wealth for the purpose of dominating any of his fellows. . . . In tra-ditional society, the individuals or the families in a tribe were "rich" or "poor" according to whether the whole tribe was rich or poor. . . . The foun-dation, and the objective, of African socialism is the extended family. . . . We in Africa have no more need of being "converted" to socialism than we have of being "taught" democracy. Both are rooted in our own past—in the tra-ditional society which produced us.[53]

All the code words are here. Nyerere's romanticization of indigenous African socialism persuaded Baraka to gradually add a progressive economic agenda to his cultural nationalism. Using Nyerere's ideas, Baraka could confront is-sues of class and economic inequality without having to resort to the "white ideas" of men such as Marx, Lenin, or Trotsky. According to Nyerere, to be truly African was to be socialist. Increasingly, however, Baraka recognized that Nyerere's claims about the "natural" socialism of traditional African societies did not explain the lack of socialism in contemporary Africa. Although he never expressed his doubts openly, Baraka realized that Nyerere's celebration of traditional African society was insufficient for understanding the dynam-ics of the African diaspora and particularly the economic issues facing black Americans.

SIXTH PAN-AFRICAN CONGRESS

Between June 19 and 27, 1974, the Sixth Pan-African Congress was held in Dar es Salaam, the capital of Tanzania, the first Pan-African Congress held on the African continent. The Sixth Pan-African Congress was also the first to which most of the delegations from Africa and the Caribbean were represen-tatives of black-run states. But because the political elites in each of the black-run states chose the members of their nation's delegations, many radical and independent-thinking Pan-Africanists were barred from attending.

The tension between the governing elites and independent thinkers was not resolved. Whereas the governing elites controlled the resources necessary to subsidize the congress, the banned independent thinkers were the only ones who would have criticized the shortcomings of the black-run nations. Such shortcomings were obvious and a major factor in the decision to hold a Pan-African congress. It was clear from the early moments of the welcoming address by Tanzania's President Julius Nyerere that this would be an atypical

Pan-African congress. First, Nyerere praised the pantheon of Pan-African heroes now departed. But then he stated:

> The Pan-African movement was born as a reaction to racialism. And racialism still exists. Nowhere has it been completely defeated. . . . The evil which required the birth of the Pan-African movement has not yet made meetings like this irrelevant. . . . We oppose racial thinking. But as long as black people anywhere continue to be oppressed on the grounds of their color, black people everywhere will stand together in opposition to that oppression, in the future as in the past.[54]

He also asserted that an exploitative economic system (and not racism) was the "real problem." "We are neither poor, nor are we kept poor because we are black. We remain poor because of the world trading and monetary systems—and these whatever their other disadvantages, are colour blind. They adversely affect the whole of the Third World."[55] The black people of the world must remove their insular race consciousness and align themselves with the Arab world, Latin America, and so forth, since they all are victims of the capitalist world economy. Perhaps for tactical reasons, Nyerere chose not to mention that the oil-producing Arab and Islamic OPEC states did not sell their oil more cheaply to African and other Third World countries.

Sekou Toure did not attend the gathering but instead sent a welcoming message that was read to the gathered delegations. In much more forceful language than Nyerere used, he called for the end of racial parochialism in the black world. Indeed, it seemed to some that he called for an end to race consciousness:

> The racists of southern Africa and the poets of Negritude all drink from the same fountain of racial prejudice and serve the same cause—the cause of imperialism, exploitation of man by man, and obscurantism, which is the most effective anesthetic utilized by imperialism against nations.

This was probably directed at Toure's longtime adversary, Leopold Senghor of Senegal. Then, to remove all doubt as to the political implications of his attack on race-based politics, Toure wrote,

> Is it not true that our friend, the great revolutionary leader of Cuba, Fidel Castro, is more hated by the imperialists, colonialists, segregationists and fascists than black leaders who have become the accomplices and devoted

and servile agents of those who exploit their brothers and cynically scoff at the rights of African peoples? . . .Was not Allende closer to the exploited Blacks than certain Afro-American or African "leaders"?[56]

That several of the African leaders most revered by Baraka could announce that race-based politics was inherently parochial undoubtedly helped him resolve to escape the confines of black cultural nationalism. By the time of the Sixth Congress, it was well known in his former black nationalist circles that Baraka had departed their ranks for a new ideological home, Marxism. During the year before the congress, Baraka had issued public announcements to that effect (see chapter 13).

Because of his prominence, Baraka was invited to address the congress, and he entitled his speech "Revolutionary Culture and the Future of Pan-African Culture." One of its main purposes was to describe the significance of culture to a revolutionary struggle. Baraka claimed that in any struggle or unequal social order, culture was a crucial site of conflict. It could either tame the subjugated into accepting their plight or sustain them in their revolutionary struggle. A second purpose of his speech was to proclaim the necessity of a "radical Pan-Africanist vision." Before this, Baraka has been an advocate of liberal Pan-Africanism. His statement thus was an announcement of sorts, part of an extended ideological coming-out in which he demarcated his new posture. Baraka was not merely conveying ideas but was redefining himself. Although he did not specifically mention his own culpability in racially essentialist Pan-Africanism, his speech constituted a moment of severe self-criticism of his previous advocacy of a parochial black nationalism. Baraka argued that any nationalism (including Afro-American nationalism) that did not aspire to socialism was as reactionary as the European nationalism that helped inspire the domination of Third World peoples. He referred to such nationalism as "superficial nationalism," and he asserted that black nationalists who did not advocate socialism were often trying to corner a capitalist market for themselves.

Although most of Baraka's speech was unremarkable, he must have surprised a few in the audience when he grouped UNITA (National Union for the Total Liberation of Angola) leader Jonas Savimbi with President Nyerere as "the most progressive leaders in Africa." His endorsement of Savimbi once again blatantly displayed the absence of rigor and sophistication in his political thinking. The celebration of Savimbi was bizarre, since the UNITA leader was not only opposed to socialism but was also a manipulator of the worst type of race-based, skin-color politics. One of the attractions of UNITA to many Afro-Americans, including Baraka, was that it was seen as *the* organization of authentically black Angolans (i.e., dark complexioned). The leadership of the MPLA (Popular Movement for the Liberation of Angola) consisted of many mulattoes and "assimilados," thus making their intentions suspect in the minds of black Americans who transposed their domestic skin color angsts to the international arena. By exploiting Afro-American skin-color neuroses, Savimbi was able to generate support from black Pan-Africanists as the representative of the authentic black Africans in Angola. Also overlooked in Baraka's celebration of Savimbi was Savimbi's history of opportunistic alliances with the apartheid government of the Union of South Africa against MPLA. Indeed, one would have had difficulty locating a black figure who embodied African neocolonialism more thoroughly than Jonas Savimbi.

Undoubtedly he recognized the invitation to speak as a great honor. Nonetheless, Baraka's prominence at the congress may have been elevated by the absence of elected and appointed Afro-American government officials in the U.S. delegation. Except for his criticisms of Afro-American nationalism and the liberal Pan-Africanism of so many Afro-American nationalists, his speech would not have attracted much notice. What little controversy it did cause was in the Afro-American delegation, many of whom remained champions of positions Baraka once held but now condemned. Given his ever present fear of being dislocated from the black masses, radical Pan-Africanism may have offered him the perfect cover for retreating from the parochialness of black cultural nationalism. Once enveloped by the legitimating cloak of Pan-Africanism, Baraka was able to change his own race consciousness and, by extension, his domestic race agenda.

Crucial questions remained unanswered. Could Pan-Africanism exist without race consciousness (blackness) as its core organizing principle? On what basis could a Pan-African conference grant delegate status to whites? Could a white South African be designated as a Pan-Africanist?

The Pan-Africanism advocated at the Sixth Pan-African Congress was a redefinition of the struggle of black people against class oppression and international capitalism. Traditional "race-based" Pan-Africanism appears to have exhausted its analytical utility for those African nations now being governed in wretched fashion by their own people. In these independent black nations, traditional Pan-Africanism no longer was able to offer internal economic and political critiques of the prevailing social order. Yet to highlight class as the core principle around which blacks would organize essentially dismissed the struggles of blacks in England, the United States, the Sudan, and other places around the world where race was still a major factor in subjugation. And what about apartheid? Displaying a simplistic, Manichaean grasp of the race-class dialectic, the congress's General Declaration included the following naive statement:

> In certain capitalist countries there are indications that the advanced sections of the white working class have gained in class consciousness, and therefore should be encouraged as political allies in the struggle against racism and imperialism, which are the common enemies of all people of the world. However, we recognize that in the advanced capitalist countries such as the U.K. and the U.S.A., the material base of racism distorts class consciousness and sets white workers against black workers. Where advanced class consciousness does not exist it is our duty to encourage it and work for a movement of the working masses to defeat monopoly and finance capitalism and the forces of racism, imperialism, colonialism and neo-colonialism.[57]

One could have left the Sixth Pan-Africanist Congress with the understanding that the future of Afro-American politics depended on a transracial, class-based coalition with the white working class. Moreover, "it was the duty of blacks" to take the lead in this endeavor. Perhaps these ideas were politically valid. But if they were, the emancipation of black America would be delayed until the return of the Messiah! But why go to Africa to discover a truth that many in the American delegation could have learned at a local fire and brimstone tabernacle? Perhaps Nyerere and Toure were unaware of the political dynamics of multiracial societies, even though their nations were ethnically diverse. Their Marxist-influenced analyses were crudely economistic and could not therefore approach race as anything other than the ideological superstructure of a capitalist economy. In their minds, race consciousness was false consciousness. For Baraka and his colleagues to think that socialism would weaken race consciousness was simply wishful thinking. Certainly this had not happened in the Soviet Union or China. Even the plight of blacks in Castro's Cuba was a question of open debate, at least to some in attendance at the congress.[58] Why was an international Pan-Africanist congress not able to understand that it did not need to be based on either race or class but both and ...?

In the end, the highly emotional debates had little or no effect on the real problems faced by black people throughout the world. Like so many events central to Baraka's political life, rhetorical postures were mistaken as political events. If the rhetorical flights from reality at this congress were merely the well-intentioned misunderstandings of naive individuals, we could at least celebrate their spirit of ethical concern and hopefulness. Certainly, many of the delegates sincerely wanted to improve the black world. However, the ultimate fallacy of the Pan-Africanist discourse lay in the dishonesty and guile displayed at the congress. President Nyerere set the tone for such deception, perhaps inadvertently. That is, he played host to a congress that highlighted economic neocolonialism as the main problem facing Africa (besides colonial dominance and South Africa). Although neocolonialism was repeatedly condemned, such condemnations had little to do with the realpolitik of the African economic situation. For while neocolonialism was rightfully condemned as exploitative, it was a fact of economic life in Africa that should have been discussed and analyzed. Given the existing international economic order, what real choices did poor African nations have? Had Nyerere and other Africans been able to talk about their economic dependence instead of issuing romanticized ideological pronouncements and condemnations, the congress might have stimulated a serious dialogue.

Less forgivable was the congress's moral evasiveness. This ethical elusiveness was incorporated in the very presumption of a "bounded discourse" that repressed mention of the bankruptcy of much of so-called free black Africa. Baraka was complicit in this moral evasion. For instance, at the very moment that the congress was taking place, Idi Amin, reigning "next door" in Uganda, was ruthlessly enveloping his nation in violent and murderous barbarity. But in none of Baraka's voluminous commentaries on Pan-Africanism and African freedom that were published during Amin's tenure is there is a single mention of his butchery and barbarity, even though the Ugandan situation was widely covered by the press. This was not an innocent oversight. Baraka's reluctance to condemn Amin was shared by many Afro-Americans in the Pan-African community. It was as if by criticizing Amin, they would betray a black African leader who had been subjected to criticism and ridicule by whites. So as not to join forces with whites (i.e., racist whites), these black American intellectuals either defended or pretended to ignore Amin. Their greater concern about the image of Africa in the eyes of whites than about the actual living conditions of black Africans was indicative of a parasitic, reactive, victim-status syndrome. And as if Baraka's silence on Uganda was not sufficient, the entire Sixth Pan-African Congress chose to ignore Amin's carnage. Even more astounding, during the final days of the congress James Turner, head of the American delegation, tried to organize a group of Americans to visit Uganda as guests of Idi Amin. Amin even sent his private jet to pick them up. Despite the thousands of corpses littering the country, these black Americans were thrilled to be invited by the dictator/butcher.[59]

Amin was just one blight on a pathos-ridden continent. During a three-month period in 1972, the Watusi-controlled government of Burundi massacred 200,000 Hutus. In the Central African Republic, Jean-Bedel Bokassa was

spending $20 million from his country's meager treasury for his own corona-
tion, this in a nation with only 170 miles of paved roads. The despotic rulers
of Equatorial Guinea engaged in systematic terror and murder. In such company, Sekou Toure looked like a benevolent democrat. Dictatorships and mass
butchery should have been, but were not, central to the discussions at the congress. Exhausted, Pan-Africanism could not sustain a moral critique of those
African and Caribbean nations ruled by indigenous blacks.

Baraka wrote a retrospective on the congress in which he criticized the
ineptitude of its organizers. He deplored the exclusion of progressive delegates by the neocolonial regimes in power in the Caribbean nations and
maintained that these governments acted in this repressive manner in response to pressure from the United States. Moreover, he believed that the FBI
had unsuccessfully tried to cancel the charter flight that was to bring the U.S.
delegation to Dar es Salaam. If this is true, it speaks to the FBI's paranoia, for
there was little political significance in the U.S. delegation's attendance at the
congress. Once again, the agency was invoked to certify Baraka's radical credentials. What was most striking about Baraka's retrospective is his claim that
he and his so-called progressive confreres dominated the conference: "The
Imperialists thought that by excluding the Caribbean progressive and trying
to disrupt the North American delegation that the neocolonial forces would
take over the Sixth PAC." He contends that "the skin nationalism, that most of
us have gone through, was completely exposed as reactionary and supportive
of the world ruling class of imperialism."

> The progressive faction clearly won out in Dar es Salaam, despite the nu-
> merical superiority of the reactionary nationalist and comprador elements
> which clearly dominate politics in the Afrikan world. The Sixth PAC Gen-
> eral Political Statement is a dramatically progressive document. It calls for
> an end to colonialism, but also an end to neocolonialism. It says Afrikan
> Unity is impossible without class struggle in the Afrikan world![60]

Once again, Baraka overstated the importance of the rhetorical. The political
statement that came out of the Sixth Pan-African Congress had literally no
impact on the political discourse among blacks in the United States. I suspect
it went similarly unnoticed in other nations. Baraka's ability to delude himself surfaced once again. Although no longer enveloped in parochial blackness, Baraka was still wedded to the power of rhetoric and spectacles. His politics had changed, and yet they remained the same.

13

National Black Political Convention

AFTER THE ATLANTA congress, Baraka's appetite for pragmatic political involvement grew. Empowered by Gibson's successful campaign in Newark, Baraka wanted to give substance to the symbolic unity displayed in Atlanta. Blacks, he thought, were on the brink of a new political moment if only they could be organized. During the early 1970s, such optimism was widespread among black activists and political observers, much of which stemmed from their electoral success at the city and local levels. The victories of black mayoral candidates in Cleveland (1967), Gary (1967), and Newark (1970) seemed to be harbingers of a new day. By 1970, twelve blacks were serving in the U.S. House of Representatives,[1] and in 1971, in hopes of maximizing their power through coordination, they formed the Congressional Black Caucus.[2]

Spurred on by these electoral successes, Baraka began talking with established black political figures about organizing a preelection black political gathering that would have two strategic goals: (1) creating a national mechanism to register black voters and (2) providing blacks with a national organization to work with the two dominant American political parties. He attended numerous meetings with various black political leaders to discuss the possibility. On September 24, 1971, a planning conference was held, chaired by Mayor Richard Hatcher of Gary, Indiana and including Baraka; Roy Innis of CORE; Julian Bond; Manhattan Borough President Percy Sutton; Congressmen John Conyers (D-Mich.), Augustus Hawkins (D-Calif.), and Walter Fauntroy (D-Wash., D.C.); SCLC's Andrew Young; Atlanta Vice-Mayor Maynard Jackson; and Chairperson of the National Urban League Vernon Jordan.[3] They endorsed Baraka's idea of holding an independent black political convention in 1972.[4]

In March 1972, the independent black political convention was held. Gary had been chosen as the site because it was a predominantly black city governed by an elected black mayor, who was able to ensure a welcoming environment for the thousands of black delegates and visitors to the convention.

Because many black Americans believed that the established American political system was not responsive to their needs, those at the convention suggested starting a distinctly black political movement. Some even thought that blacks should create a separate black political party. Despite the electoral success of various black candidates, the early 1970s was also a period of immense backlash against black Americans' political aspirations. First, the demise of President Lyndon Johnson's Great Society left many politicized blacks feeling bereft. Even during its most liberal years (1963–1968), the United States appeared incapable of comprehensively confronting racism and its impact on blacks' lives. Doubt and distrust were particularly evident in those sectors of the black community least affected by the Civil Rights movement.

Numerous aspects of Johnson's Great Society, however, had benefited the lives of the black poor. The Office of Economic Opportunity, Head Start, the Jobs Corps, the Comprehensive Employment and Training Act, child nutrition programs, and school lunch programs were substantive interventions in poor people's lives. But Johnson's unwillingness to end the war in Vietnam not only restricted the federal funds that could be allocated to domestic poverty programs[5] but inspired a national antiwar movement that eventually pushed him into early retirement. In addition, the association with Johnson's war policies also sealed the defeat of his anointed successor, Vice-President Hubert Humphrey.[6] Enter a reconstituted Richard Nixon.

The successful 1968 presidential campaign of Richard Nixon was based on the simultaneous arousal of racist white southerners through his "southern strategy" and the racist resentments of white ethnic northerners, many of whom lived in white ethnic ghettos bordering predominantly black neighborhoods. Nixon won the presidency by not conceding the racist white vote and the white backlash vote to the third-party candidacy of the white supremacist Alabama governor, George Wallace. Furthermore, Nixon's victory made black Americans realize that most white American voters were no longer committed to liberal public policies for blacks' advancement.[7] Nixon also let it be known that as president, he would not view black Americans as a justifiable claimant group. Rather, he would be president of the "silent majority."[8] He tried, illegally, to impound funding that Congress had previously allocated to the Office of Economic Opportunity, the flagship program of Johnson's "war on poverty." Soon after, he disbanded it, thus ending the Great Society dream of "maximum feasible participation."[9] In addition, the Justice Department relaxed the enforcement of civil rights laws, particularly those relating to desegregating public education in the South.

Paradoxically, the liberalism of the Johnson presidency and the moderate, though racist, conservatism of the Nixon presidency sustained the belief of the broader black electorate that there were significant differences between the Democratic and Republican Parties on issues pertaining to blacks' socioeconomic advancement and civil rights. The Democratic Johnson had not only presided over the most extensive package of civil rights legislation since Reconstruction, but he had appointed more blacks to higher positions in government than any previous president. Johnson was the first president to appoint a black American to his cabinet when he selected Robert Weaver as the first Secretary of Housing and Urban Development. In addition, Johnson nominated former NAACP lawyer Thurgood Marshall to the U.S. Supreme Court, the first black to ever occupy a seat there. As a result of these appointments and the civil rights legislation, many blacks felt that the Democratic Party and thus the political system was finally responding to their needs. Nixon, however, was clever. He shrewdly threw a plum to bourgeois blacks by establishing the Office of Minority Business Enterprise (OMBE) which helped coordinate a minority business set-aside program that granted small black businesses special access to government contracts.

The idea of black capitalism was marketed as the true realization of Black Power. Former militant black activists like Floyd McKissick rushed to participate in Nixon's program, using the Nixon administration's funding for Soul City, an all-black, planned residential development in North Carolina. Ironically, the same Floyd McKissick who had sat next to Karenga, H. Rap Brown, and others at the 1967 Newark Black Power conference had successfully used his militant posturing to become a black capitalist.[10] Because of the failure of liberal politics to stem the development of "two societies, one black, one white—separate and unequal,"[11] and the clever co-optation of Black Power by Nixon's black capitalism offensive, there were, by the early 1970s, significant political factions within the black community. These cliques were present in Gary.

When the National Black Political Convention began in Gary in March 1972, many of those attending hoped that they could agree on an agenda. Approximately 8,000 black community activists, elected officials, bureaucrats, and political hacks of all stripes came to Gary. They ranged from nonviolent integrationists to militant black separatists. This diversity could also be found in the convention's leaders: Jesse Jackson, Mayor Richard Hatcher, Congressman Charles Diggs, and Imanu Amiri Baraka. Notwithstanding the diversity, black nationalism was the convention's prevailing ideological tone. As such, the slogan "unity without uniformity" was resurrected as the rallying cry of a black nationalist–minded audience. The Gary convention was an attempt to generate a black nationalist presence in American electoral politics. As a strategy, it was full of paradoxes. Gary embodied the insider-outsider contradictions in black life, that two-ness that Du Bois once eloquently invoked. Although many blacks were angered by the political system's reluctance to treat them like accepted members of the American polity, they still wanted to use their outsider status to obtain assistance from the inside. Many of those present at Gary wanted to act pragmatically but did not want to be associated with the "dirty hands" of conventional politics. Among the participants were the pragmatic and the dogmatic, political bargainers and ideological purists.

No one better embodied these contradictions than Amiri Baraka. Once again, he tried to harness his militant black nationalist ideology and his rhetorical skills to his goal of mobilizing black Americans for political inclusion. As he had done so skillfully in Newark, Baraka was trying to walk a thin line between the two dominant political formations: the compromise-oriented pragmatists versus the ideologically dogmatic black nationalists. Both factions viewed the other as naive and illegitimate. As he had done in Newark, Baraka relied on bourgeois black nationalists like Hatcher and Jesse Jackson to mediate this ideological cleavage. These men represented those in the black political establishment who used black nationalist rhetoric, dress, and symbols while supporting liberal integrationist agendas. Yet even these bicultural black politicians found few universally shared political objectives at Gary that they could stress in order to unite the various factions. Whereas in Newark, the election of a black candidate to political office was the objective of both black integrationists and black nationalists, the goal of establishing a issue-based consensus at Gary did not address the interests of all gathered there.

The convention's leadership decided not to formally place before the delegates the issue of supporting one of the white presidential candidates. They also refused to endorse the presidential candidacy of black congresswoman Shirley Chisholm. Chisholm did not attend the Gary convention because she believed that this male-dominated body would not seriously consider her candidacy, and she was correct. But fear of a sexist rejection may not have been the only reason for Chisholm's absence. In trying to generate a transracial electoral appeal, Chisholm had linked her candidacy to the emerging women's movement. She did not want to be viewed by the broader American public (i.e., white Americans) as the candidate of blacks. Consequently, she may have used the sexism issue as an excuse for avoiding a potentially damaging public association.[12]

As had been the case at the Atlanta congress, the ideological diversity of the Gary convention made the gathering too diffuse and unruly to be more than symbolically significant. Although "unity without uniformity" may seem to be a slogan that valorizes toleration for diversity, it actually presupposes the primacy of a black nationalist praxis. On what basis, except common racial identity, could these diverse delegates claim unity? By momentarily ignoring the political divisions within the black community in order to create the appearance of a working unity at Gary, the convention leaders laid the groundwork for the convention's irrelevance to the future of black politics. Instead, they became more interested in appearing to be unified than in debating important issues. Indeed, debate and disagreement should have been encouraged if the actual goal of the gathering was to generate a functional unity.

Even if the delegates agreed on certain issues while they were at the convention, their support of that position could not be guaranteed once they left the convention hall. The first reason was that many of the delegates who had participated in floor fights at the convention were already committed to certain presidential contenders. Regardless of how they voted at the Gary convention, many of them already knew that they would ultimately support the presidential candidacies of George McGovern, Hubert Humphrey, or Shirley Chisholm. Some were even committed to Richard Nixon's reelection. This inability to adhere to a unified position was a particularly difficult problem for this convention. It had no way of punishing those who did not "hold the line" or rewarding those who did. Rather, its principal means of gaining political allegiance was the euphoric belief that this was a singularly significant moment in black history. The convention planners soon discovered, however, that such euphoric emotions were transitory. One of its greatest problems was the weaknesses in the black nationalists' political infrastructure. That is, the black nationalists who attended the gathering generally had no formal representative relationship with blacks beyond their informal black nationalist networks. Of the three formal leaders of the conference, Baraka was the only one who had not ever had his leadership qualifications certified by a mass black public. Only once had Baraka sought electoral office, in Newark, and he had been soundly defeated.[13] Not beholden to any large-scale representative process, nonelected black activists like Baraka were free to support virtually any issue position without cost. But because elected officials were accountable to electorates that could remove them from office, they were not as free as Baraka was to endorse contentious issues.

Be that as it may, many of the black elected officials at Gary were indeed beholden to the Democratic Party and were loyal to the party in order to gain greater influence. In his keynote address, Mayor Richard Hatcher criticized the Democratic and Republican Parties for being racist and unresponsive to black American interests, but he did not go so far as to completely break ranks with them, stating, "I for one, am willing to give the two major political parties one more chance in the year 1972. But if they fail us, a not unlikely prospect, we must then seriously probe the possibility of a third party movement in this country."[14] Despite his disgust, the Democrats seemed more likely than Baraka-style black nationalists to aid Gary's fiscal plight.[15]

The Gary convention had two functions. First, it was supposed to set in motion the creation of a permanent black political infrastructure, the National Black Political Assembly. Second, it was supposed to establish a national black political platform, the National Black Political Agenda. Individual state delegations[16] were responsible for drawing up state platforms to be submitted to the platform committee of the Gary conference before the gathering. Once all the states had submitted their platform requests, they would be compiled and presented to the delegates for discussion and then subjected to ratification. Amendments could be added from the floor. Once ratified, this document would be issued as the National Black Political Agenda, presumably representing the collective political will of Afro-Americans. The leaders of the Gary convention would then take this agenda to the Democratic and Republican National Conventions to determine which one of the two presidential candidates was more sympathetic to blacks. They then would tell black people which candidate to support. Once elected, the president of the United States was supposed to use the National Black Political Agenda to guide his relationship with black Americans.

Not having any historical precedents, the Gary convention improvised rules and procedures as problems arose. Because of the novelty of the convention process and the diversity of the participants, the many glitches did not come as a surprise. Most of the state delegations had failed to submit their platform before the convention. As a result, the conventioneers had to spend much of their time holding hearings with the state delegations. The National Black Political Agenda was a disjointed document that reflected its rushed completion. Nonetheless, it was presented to the delegates as a finished document. This was a major tactical error.[17] Instead, it should have been used as a draft to open a discussion and debate that would lead to revisions and, finally, the creation of the finished agenda. Instead, this document was distributed to the convention delegates for expeditious, *pro forma* endorsement. The head of the Michigan delegation, Coleman Young, a Michigan state senator, was opposed to having the agenda unceremoniously rammed through the convention: "After some inane discussion, we were handed a black agenda, as the Baraka people called it—a document about the size of the *New York Daily News*—and told that we had two hours to digest it before the vote."[18] Young also protested the brevity of the deliberation and discussion process, arguing that the delegates should be allowed to take the fifty-five-page document home for a few weeks, study it, and then come back together for further discussion and a final vote. Young claimed that the Baraka crowd was adamant about endorsing the document right away. He suspected that they were aware of its conceptual and strategic weaknesses and thus tried to minimize serious discussion of it.

> The platform was completely off-target and unacceptable. It was a bla-
> tantly separatist document, the obvious work of Baraka, the misguided
> ramblings of a so-called artist who would be dictator. It consisted of bull-
> shit like taking over five states for black people. . . . I didn't have much use
> for Baraka. I made him mad when I told him that behind that fancy-ass
> name he was still LeRoi Jones to me, a half-assed poet in a flowing gown
> and patent-leather shoes.[19]

Baraka's armed henchmen, who were serving as the security for the convention, tried to intimidate the Michigan delegation when, following Young's
lead, they decided to walk out of the convention. According to Young, Baraka's
followers backed off when they saw that the Michigan delegation was well
armed. Two years later, Young was elected mayor of Detroit.

Despite Young's criticism of Baraka's leadership at Gary, most observers
and participants considered the Newark activist singularly responsible for
holding the convention together.[20] Moreover, Coleman Young's motivations
for leaving the convention were not solely based on his love of democratic values. Instead, the Michigan delegation had been challenged at the convention
by other Michigan activists on the grounds that it did not represent the black
political spectrum in Michigan. According to political scientist Ronald Walters, Young's delegation "was dominated by trade unionists and professionals."[21] Young, who was deeply immersed in trade union politics, had seen to it
that black nationalist–minded activists were a minority among the Michigan
delegation. But then, when he and his delegation left the convention, their
black nationalist challengers from Michigan took over their seats in the convention hall.

One problem with the idea of the convention was that it did not allow average black Americans at home to engage in public dialogue and debate about
the National Black Political Agenda's position on various issues. Equally important, the absence of public discussion meant that the Gary convention
missed being able to educate black Americans about political issues that concerned them. Writing shortly after the convention, political commentator Bill
Strickland mentioned some of these shortcomings:

> The National Black Convention will make a grievous error if it rushes to
> consolidate the proposed continuation structure at the existing level of par-
> ticipation. For the meaning of Gary, as the Black Panthers, for example,

correctly understand it (see the April 20 issue of the Black Panther newspaper in which they reprinted the entire Gary document), is that the Black Agenda means nothing unless it is ratified by Black people. The meaning of Gary must be taken to the broader masses of Black people, for up to this point they have not yet been reached by the Gary process . . . no truly independent Black political movement can be based solely upon either Black elected officials as a class or group, or upon some of the sectarian nationalists, who were in attendance.[22]

Strickland's advice was ignored. The inevitable messiness of a democratic procedure in which the black public could participate in discussions, forums, and debates was not compatible with the euphoria surrounding the convention. Most of the Gary convention's participants wanted immediate action. Furthermore, exposing the resolutions of the Gary convention to public debate and input would undermine the authority of those activists who viewed themselves as the vanguard of the new black political front. Finally, the Imamu would not be beholden to discussions in neighborhood barber shops.

As stated earlier, the proposed National Black Political Agenda was dominated by black nationalism. Accordingly, the NAACP, under the direction of its autocratic patriarch Roy Wilkins, attacked the Gary convention as violating the organization's commitment to an integrated society. But Wilkins was naive about the ways in which black political inclusion would occur, and the NAACP was ignorant of the history of American ethnic politics. To generate broader social and ethnic inclusion, white ethnic groups have historically based their political appeals on solidarity. For example, Italian Americans wanting greater ethnic diversity on New York City's school board had to form an Italian American political bloc. The NAACP, however, projected a political vision implying that when blacks acted self-consciously as an ethnic/racial collective, they were practicing segregationist politics.[23]

Curiously, the preamble to the National Black Political Agenda that was so offensive to the NAACP was written by Congressman Walter Fauntroy and Illinois State Senator Richard Newhouse, two avid integrationists. As head of the SCLC's Washington, D.C., chapter, Fauntroy had been one of the main organizers of the historic 1963 March on Washington. He appears to have assumed that the NAACP would endorse the agenda. A draft of the preamble was sent to the NAACP and other black civil rights organizations for their comments. It read in part:

We come to Gary in an hour of great crisis and tremendous promise for black America. While the white nation hovers on the brink of chaos, while its politicians offer no hope of real change, we stand on the edge of history and are faced with an amazing and frightening choice. We may choose in 1972 to slip back into the decadent white politics of American life, or we may press forward, moving relentlessly from Gary to the creation of our own black life. The choice is large, but the time is very short.[24]

Clearly the preamble contains wording that the NAACP would not have chosen. Fauntroy and Newhouse realized that those in established black politics (like themselves) had to accept some of the new nomenclature of the Black Power movement if they were to maintain popular ethnic legitimacy. But in refusing to tolerate such rhetoric, the NAACP essentially indicated its disaffection from the prevailing black political mood.

Reminiscent of the Atlanta congress, the National Black Political Convention passed numerous resolutions that were essentially articulations of black political fantasies. According to sociologist Paulette Pierce,

the agenda demanded either a full employment policy at decent wages or a guaranteed annual income and adequately funded governmental programs to insure quality housing, health care and education to every American. The Agenda called for the creation of a National Black Development Agency to help finance projects like a black owned and controlled communication media. It also proposed a constitutional amendment guaranteeing 15 black Senators and 66 representatives in the US Congress, as well as "a proportionate black employment control at every level of the Federal Government structure."[25]

In addition, the National Black Political Agenda demanded community control over the police, schools, and other institutions affecting the lives of blacks; the release of all political prisoners; the creation of a black commission to calculate the amount of reparations due blacks because of slavery and racial discrimination; free academic and technical education for all blacks up to their highest attainable level; home rule for the District of Columbia; and an end to the political surveillance of blacks by the FBI, the CIA, and the Justice Department. It seems highly unlikely that any presidential candidate would have or could have agreed to all of these demands. The National Black Political Agenda had created electoral criteria that no presidential candidate could possibly have met.[26]

According to Pierce, the most radical aspect of the National Black Political Agenda was its attempt to push the U.S. Constitution once again to recognize group rights, as opposed to individual rights. That is, black Americans as a group had needs that could not be adequately addressed through the recognition of individual rights. This assumption was the core of the Gary convention's agenda, that blacks shared an experience that made them fundamentally different from white Americans and fundamentally similar to one another. The problem lay in defining this black similarity. Who would be the judge? Such arguments did not acknowledge that if individual rights were not recognized, blacks would become the subjects of whoever had the skills and power to shape and manipulate black ascriptive allegiances. Besides, the recognition of group rights was not a radical idea. Black Americans had a long history of subjugation that had been reinforced by legally recognized group rights. Simply put, before the Civil Rights movement, the group rights of black Americans were not equal to the group rights of white Americans.

In foreign policy, the National Black Political Agenda called for a 50 percent cut in the defense budget, the immediate withdrawal of the United States from Vietnam, and an end to the deployment of U.S. military forces to protect private American corporations. Obviously, the Gary document was black hallucination made concrete. Had the agenda been the utopian statement of a political movement, its lofty goals would have been understandable. Instead, it was supposed to be a document around which pragmatic black inclusion in the American political arena would be negotiated. The agenda called for a revolutionary change in the character of the nation, a change that would supposedly satisfy black voters. Yet there was no reason to assume that Gary spoke for all or most blacks. Incredibly, in calling for the immediate withdrawal of the United States from Vietnam, the document appeared to ignore the failure of an intense popular mobilization of Americans in this effort. Though politically fanciful, the demand for an end to the military protection of American capital investment in foreign countries was admirable. But why stop there? The document could have just as easily demanded that each black family be guaranteed an annual income of $50,000 as reparation.

The National Black Agenda was more romantic than pragmatic, although any demand for universal black equality would have appeared as utter fantasy in the context of American history and politics. In hindsight, the Gary convention needed a leadership figure who knew how to explain to the delegates that the agenda was an ideal that should be pursued but that would never be realized. As an ideal, it should not be so unrealistic as to be unrealizable. Gary represents a huge lost opportunity. It was a moment when a formidable collection of black Americans were energized by the possibility of stepping outside the confines of the hegemonic political discourses that had historically governed racial politics in the United States. Black Americans have rarely en-

gaged in mass-based politics that did not internalize the hegemonic boundaries of acceptable discourse.

One of the two principal issues of contention at the convention was busing. Although polls indicated that black Americans were fairly evenly divided
over the use of school busing, black elected officials tried to maintain a united
front in support of busing for reasons having as much to do with the education of black students as with the antiblack sentiments that usually accompanied whites' antibusing sentiments. Roy Innis, the conservative black nationalist leader of the Congress of Racial Equality (CORE), circulated an antibusing resolution on the convention floor that called for community-controlled
schools. Political scientist Robert C. Smith noted that predictably, an antibusing resolution was introduced once the platform was opened to amendments
from the floor.[27] Introduced by the South Carolina delegation, the resolution
read like a Roy Innis speech:

> We condemn forced racial integration of schools as a bankrupt, suicidal
> method of desegregating schools, based on the false notion that Black chil-
> dren are unable to learn unless they are in the same setting as white children.
> As an alternative to busing of Black children to achieve total racial balance,
> we demand quality education in the Black community through the control
> of our school system, school districts and a guarantee of an equal share of
> that money.[28]

The resolution was adopted. Veteran black news reporters Barbara A. Reynolds and Ethel Payne reported that some of the delegates thought that Innis
had been sent to the convention by President Nixon (or his henchmen), either
to divide the delegates or to provide a nonracist cover for the president's antibusing position.[29] If these veteran reporters were right, Nixon should have
congratulated Innis for a job well done.

The second issue that caused dissension at the convention was a resolution calling for the dissolution of the state of Israel. Like the school-busing
amendment, this amendment was passed in the final hours of the convention,
long after many of the delegates had returned home. Some defenders of the
convention argued that the white media placed far too much emphasis on the
busing and Israel resolutions, both of which were marginal to the weekend's
events. The white media were depicted as having a vested interest in minimizing the significance of the Gary gathering. These accusations may have been
true. But many defenders of the Gary convention failed to realize that in their
efforts to describe the marginality of the antibusing and anti-Israel amendments to the main work of the assemblage, the convention did not provide

any substantive "checks and balances" on frivolous political positions. For instance, Innis and Douglas Moore (who proposed the dissolution of Israel) were allowed to influence amendments that everyone must have known would be received as controversial and divisive. It was ridiculously naive for convention planners not to take into account the ways that the media might target these controversial positions. Unlike the busing issue, which directly pertained to black American politics, the Israeli-Palestinian conflict was not of obvious interest to large numbers of black Americans. Why did a convention intent on developing the National Black Political Agenda even take a position on an issue of tangential importance? It could easily appear that black nationalist intellectuals and activists were obsessed with Israel and Jews. Although they knew that passage of this amendment would not affect Middle East politics, they also knew that such a resolution would anger American Jews. The anger of Jews, traditional liberal supporters of civil rights legislation, had become a knee-jerk insignia of the new independent black politics. Jewish anger and disapproval were erroneously thought to certify black autonomy. Such antics were a precursor to those of Louis Farrakhan during the 1990s. But the black nationalists' obsession with Jews had a deleterious effect on the Gary convention. First, two of the convention's three chairman, Mayor Hatcher and Michigan Congressman Charles Diggs, immediately issued public disclaimers from the anti-Israel amendment, thereby undercutting the image of black unity at Gary.[30] Second, the controversial anti-Israel and antibusing resolutions kept many other established black political figures from endorsing or even affirming the Gary convention.

In the days immediately after the convention, the antibusing component of the national black agenda was rigorously attacked. Some critics accused the convention of playing into the racist hands of President Nixon, who after all, was using his opposition to racial integration via school busing as a symbolic appeal to antiblack voters. Washington's nonvoting delegate to Congress, Walter Fauntroy, publicized a Gallup poll indicating that 80 percent of black Americans supported busing to advance integration. In response to criticism of the convention's stances on busing and the Middle East, the steering committee met two weeks after the Gary gathering and altered the language of both amendments.

To control damage to its public image as a result of its support of the Gary convention, the Congressional Black Caucus (CBC) issued its own National Black Declaration of Independence and Black Bill of Rights.[31] Political scientist Ronald Walters described the CBC documents as "watered-down versions of the Gary agenda," adding that the Congressional Black Caucus had reneged on its agreement to endorse the Gary agenda. This sense of betrayal was widespread among black nationalist participants,[32] whereas more established black political figures viewed the CBC documents as necessary to restoring black political legitimacy. Contrary to Walters's assertion, I could find no proof that the Congressional Black Caucus ever formally endorsed the Gary convention or the National Black Political Agenda.[33] It is difficult to imagine U.S. congresspersons endorsing the platform of a convention before knowing what it said. In addition, congresspersons usually do not blindly lock themselves into agreements to endorse whatever issue positions are championed by activists like Roy Innis or even Amiri Baraka. As established political figures, the Congressional Black Caucus had to make public their differences with the National Black Agenda.

Despite all the tensions and fissures, Baraka steadfastly adhered to the strategy devised at the Gary convention. Although he was not pleased with the dismantling of the spirit of black political unity after the convention, he was adamant about trying to incorporate blacks into American national politics. According to this strategy, Baraka would lead a delegation in bargaining with the Democratic and Republican Parties as the representative broker for all of black America. In this capacity he traveled to the Democratic National Convention in Miami, taking with him the National Black Political Agenda. Unfortunately, Baraka self-destructed on the eve of this effort. Rhetorical excess was, once again, the cause.

Coinciding with the start of the Democratic National Convention, *Newsweek* published a short opinion essay written by Imamu Amiri Baraka. Entitled "Black and Angry," the essay was a typical Baraka jeremiad.[34] It begins: "When Americans are happiest, it seems, is when they can pretend that black people do not exist." The sickness of white Americans is evident in their ability to construct their victims as nonhuman beings. As examples of this general white American tendency, Baraka points to the enslavement of blacks as well as the genocide against Native Americans. But, he argues, the historical strategies employed by white America to ignore its victims behind a veil of silence no longer work. "The system created to justify and perpetuate the enslavement of Africans, and the genocide committed on Native Americans, not only has injured its perpetuators permanently as it has injured its victims but in the end will almost certainly destroy one or the other or both."[35] Baraka claims that the assassinations of the major leaders of the United States (e.g., John Kennedy, Robert Kennedy, Martin Luther King Jr., and Malcolm X) told the entire world about the pathological nature of American society. Black Americans suffer most under this pathological state of affairs. The example of the Gary convention, however, indicates that black Americans are becoming increasingly aware of their subjugated status and are trying to change it.

Accordingly, Baraka endorses the National Black Political Agenda. He then uses the rest of the essay to spell out some of the issues and proposed solutions raised by the Gary convention, including the $6,500 minimum guaranteed family income, proportional representation in all governing bodies, and the withdrawal of American investments from the Republic of South Africa.

The essay is full of threatening rhetoric, such as the claim that the United States will be destroyed if it does not change. Blacks, Baraka warns, will riot with a heretofore unseen abandon if these changes are not implemented. "The riots of the '60s would be as football Saturdays to the swell of absolutely scientific disruption that would seethe through American cities, rendering American society useless for anything but obituaries." Baraka's scare tactics hide a confusing argument. He states that either America will change or it will be destroyed, and yet he predicts, as a foregone conclusion, the destruction of the American system of white supremacy. He states that the inevitability of the demise of white supremacy is obvious to most people. Those who do not recognize this inevitability are "too sick to see anything clearly." Worse, they could be "colored caucus-ians defending Israel. Bought and paid for like them sleepy ho's on Lexington Avenue near Grand Central."[36] This is a straightforward attack on the Congressional Black Caucus. Baraka calls them pseudo-whites, an immense condemnation for the hyperblack Imamu. The designation supposedly indicates their self-hating collusion in white supremacist politics. And why are they subject to such vitriol? Obviously, Baraka is angry at their criticism and disavowal of the resolution on Israel that was passed at the Gary convention. He does not even allow them to hold legitimately pro-Israeli positions but instead calls them political whores (much like the prostitutes on Lexington Avenue) who have responded to (unnamed but ubiquitous) Jewish money.

This essay must have sent shock waves through the ranks of those black elected officials who had momentarily entered into a working partnership with him in Gary. Baraka was now, as he had always been, a rather apocalyptic loose canon. These elected officials may have felt betrayed by his return to crude attempts to intimidate whites, but they probably understood that his sophomoric theatrics scared no one, except perhaps Mom and Pop back in Peoria. Can one imagine President Nixon or Attorney General John Mitchell quaking in their shoes after reading this essay? In all likelihood, had they even read the essay, they would probably have been cynically amused. Baraka must not have understood how comical such an essay made him appear to the powers that be. From his first day on the campaign trail, candidate Nixon had made it clear that he saw no need for restraining repressive forces against black rioters. Perhaps this explains why black urban riots ceased during his years as president.

Despite composing such an inflammatory essay, Baraka continued to believe that he still had enough credibility to bargain with America's political elites at the national conventions of the two major parties. Why did he write such an apocalyptic, parochial essay at precisely the moment of his deepest involvement in realpolitik electoral strategizing? Was this essay a proclamation of a black nationalist integrity, an occasion to demonstrate that he had not been compromised by Gary? Did it reflect the resilient schizoid nature of his political consciousness, a desire to be simultaneously inside and outside? Did he actually believe what he stated? Or finally, did he believe that such threats would increase his bargaining authority? In offering him a national forum during the week of the 1972 Democratic National Convention, *Newsweek* had provided Baraka with sufficient rope to hang himself. The repercussions for accepting the magazine's bait soon became evident. Black political leaders, even those who attended the Gary convention, felt little reason to maintain their ties to him.

In Miami, Baraka hoped to meet with various candidates for the Democratic Party's presidential nomination in order to ascertain their positions concerning the National Black Political Agenda. He immediately discovered that the black elected officials, including some who had actively participated in the Gary convention, were now negotiating their own deals with the candidates. Jesse Jackson, co-chair of the Illinois delegation; Congresspersons Clay, Fauntroy, and Stokes; and Willie Brown, head of the California delegation competed with one another to become McGovern's black "kingmaker" and broker with black Democratic delegates.[37] All these men had attended the Gary convention. There, Jackson initially called for the creation of a separate black political party. But at the Democratic National Convention, when he and the others found themselves in the presence of powerful white establishmentarians, their individual power ambitions took over. The Gary convention was all but forgotten.

In the absence of strict racial unity, which would have been impossible even if all the Gary participants had remained loyal to the National Black Political Convention, Baraka's strategy was doomed. First, most of the black delegates to the Democratic Party National Convention had neither attended the Gary convention nor promised any allegiance to it. Second, the majority of the most prominent black elected officials had not attended the Gary convention and so did not feel beholden to it. Instead, they viewed Baraka as a highly energized nuisance. Worse, the masses of black voters who held long-term allegiances to the Democratic Party hardly noticed the National Black Political Agenda.

Baraka met with similar failure at the 1972 Republican National Convention. He was not able to gain access to any significant Republican Party power brokers. It is doubtful that Nixon even knew that he existed. Black Republicans blocked his efforts to obtain a public or private hearing with anyone powerful. It had been almost impossible for the black Republicans to get themselves on the convention's agenda, so why would they spend political capital on Baraka's behalf?

Baraka's belief that he was in a position to bargain for all black Americans indicates not only incredible naïveté but self-delusional tendencies. On what basis could Baraka speak for millions of people? At the height of his influence he had chaired only one convention of about 10,000 delegates. It seems likely that Baraka's self-image as the Imamu may have distorted his political sensibilities. While he had tremendous charismatic power in black nationalist circles, his influence with black America as a whole was miniscule. Most blacks had probably never heard of him. But despite his naïveté and power ambitions, Baraka was undoubtedly correct concerning the opportunism displayed by those black politicians at the Democratic and Republican Party conventions. In Baraka's eyes, their refusal to accept his leadership was proof of their opportunism. He was wrong. Their opportunism did not lie in their behavior at their party's national conventions but in their behavior at Gary.

The Gary convention taught Baraka a crucial lesson. He had erred grievously in his reading of black elected officials. In his commitment to black nationalism, Baraka had assumed that race loyalty would be steadfast. He misread establishmentarian black political leaders and erroneously attributed to them a commitment to black nationalism similar to his own. From the vantage point of a black nationalist strategy, a major strategic error at Gary was allowing black elected officials such a dominant role in shaping the agenda and determining the image of the convention. Several of the convention's leaders were not strongly committed to its ideological tenets. This should have been apparent in Hatcher's opening speech in which he listed the years that the Democratic Party had betrayed blacks, only to call for "giving them one more chance." Without the participation of black elected officials, though, the Gary convention would probably have never been held.

Baraka and the black nationalists at the Gary convention should have vigorously promoted the National Political Agenda in every nook and cranny of black America. They should have realized that their influence directly depended on the size of the constituency that supported the document. There was no reason to assume that they could not have attracted a sizable following, but they did not try. Such behavior would have contradicted Baraka's understanding of himself and his black nationalist colleagues as the vanguard of the black political agenda.

A smaller but financially self-sufficient convention of black nationalist activists and loyalists would have received less official news coverage but would have laid the groundwork for an authentic black nationalist political organization. As was the case in Atlanta, Baraka's fondness for immense spectacles of black unity and political assertiveness overwhelmed his strategic sensibilities. Furthermore, instead of holding a conference to produce a national political structure that would "bargain" with the two major political parties, Baraka and his colleagues should have held a convention that had as its goal the pressuring of local black elected officials. The power of most black political figures was their ability to sway black voters. In any event, before the Gary convention, Baraka would not have entertained this strategic possibility, given his weak understanding of internal differences in the black community. But the lesson of Kenneth Gibson as well as the lesson of Gary forced him to recognize that it was not enough to close ranks merely ethnically and racially. Class allegiances emerged as important predictors of political behavior even in those who claimed allegiance to black advancement. It took Baraka a long time to learn this lesson but once mastered, he remedied the situation. Once again, he changed his ideology.

POSTSCRIPT TO GARY

During the two-year lull following the Gary convention, Baraka and his followers worked behind the scenes to see that black nationalists would make up the majority of the delegates in Little Rock. To do so, they altered the process of selecting delegates, by changing the rule that granted automatic delegate status to black elected officials. When they were announced, these rule changes indicated to everyone that the National Black Convention was moving even deeper into the ranks of sectarian black nationalism. Not surprisingly, the 1974 National Black Convention in Little Rock was a decided disappointment following the euphoria of Gary. The most visible difference between the Gary and the Little Rock conventions was the very small number of black elected officials in attendance in Little Rock and significantly fewer important black politicians there.[38] Even the Gary convention's president, Congressman Diggs, chose not to attend the Little Rock convention. Diggs's absence may have been a response to the chicanery of the Baraka crowd. He had probably realized by then that it was fruitless to try to maintain a working relationship with Baraka. Mayor Richard Hatcher, the chairman and host of the convention in Gary two years earlier, continued to play on the boundaries of the "unity without uniformity" game plan. In his opening address, he criticized prominent black political figures for not being at Little Rock. His lambasting of absent black politicians only momentarily hid his own ambivalence at continuing to participate in these gatherings, for he, too, sensed that Baraka and other ideologues were trying to control the entire process. Unlike the Gary convention, black nationalist ideologues at Little Rock like Owusu Sadaukai protested its association with establishmentarian black elected officials. He told one journalist covering the convention that "neo-colonialist, petit bourgeois black elected officials are as much the enemy as their white counterparts."[39]

It was little wonder that after Little Rock, Hatcher began to question his continued association with the convention. At Little Rock, Mayor Hatcher was quoted as saying:

> I will have to reevaluate my future with the convention in light of the unity motto. We need to revive that motto. My future depends on the willingness of some to be tolerant of people when you disagree with them. Part of my reevaluation will be to see if the unity motto is still intact. . . . I don't think we can be effective unless we have an organization in which elected officials, nationalists, conservatives, liberals and civil rights activist can feel comfortable and work in.

As if to make matters very clear, Hatcher commented on the differences in his political agenda and that of Baraka. "I happen to think that the convention is about basic things—political organizing, electing people to office and although we get along personally, Baraka has a grander design in terms of revolution."[40]

Given the tensions with Baraka that became evident in Little Rock, it was not surprising that in November 1975, Baraka was ousted from his position as secretary-general of the convention. Concerning the reasons for his dismissal, Robert Smith writes:

> His authoritarian and confrontational leadership style, his rhetorical bombast and vitriol and his unwillingness to abide by the Assembly's recently adopted "Statement of Principles" were all factors in his ouster, but a critical factor was his formal adoption shortly after the Little Rock convention of the ideology of Marxist-Leninism.[41]

Robert Smith believes that it was unfair but understandable that Baraka was ousted as a result of his new Marxist allegiances. He argues that on pragmatic considerations alone, Baraka's Marxism would have alienated the black mass public. While I understand Smith's argument, it strikes me as inherently paradoxical. The black churchgoing people that Smith imagines as alienated from Baraka's Marxism would probably have been alienated by many of the militant black nationalists whom, Smith seems to believe, retained their pragmatic validity. Despite Baraka's best efforts to undermine the "unity without uniformity" ideal, why didn't this ideal, once reinstated, apply to black Marxists? Perhaps it would even have applied to Baraka had he been less doctrinaire in his ideological assumptions and less absolutist in his praxis. If, as Baraka argued, black elected officials were the lackeys of monopoly capitalism, it made sense that he could not have agreed to close ranks with them under the rubric of black unity. Why, then, did Baraka even want to continue to be involved with the National Black Convention? According to Smith, without Baraka and his committed followers, the convention no longer had an infrastructure that could have continued its work. Concerning Baraka's centrality to the National Black Convention, Smith stated,

> Whatever prospects for success it had were substantially undermined by its moving force—Baraka. Thus, in some sense the wound of his departure was beside the point; the process could not survive with him or without him. This is a harsh judgment; but Baraka must share both the praises for the creation of the convention and also the heavy burden of blame for its destruction.[42]

Baraka's ability to alienate everyone was not a testimony to his powerful or intimidating persona. By this time, most serious political actors viewed him as politically frivolous if not destructive. As Congressman William Clay (D-Mo.) once pointed out, "My district is 49 percent black and 51 percent white and I get elected every two years. Baraka's district is 65 percent black and they send Peter Rodino, a white man, to Congress. Now tell me, what business do I have letting him tell me about political power and political organization?"[43] Although Baraka never succeeded in generating a mass political support base, he was quite skillful at undermining existing political organizations. Baraka, the revolutionary black nationalist turned hyperrevolutionary Marxist, had helped create and then destroy two black political formations: African Liberation Day and the National Black Political Convention. Had his actions rescued blacks from misguided political journeys, or had he destroyed what he could not dominate?

14

Ever Faithful

Toward a Religious Marxism

REJECTS BLACK NATIONALISM

By 1974 it had become generally accepted by all but his most devout black nationalist followers that Baraka had renounced black nationalism in favor of "scientific socialism."[1] No longer committed to Kawaida, Baraka had become a disciple of what he called "Marxism-Leninism-Mao Zedong" thought. What may have appeared to be a rather sudden move to the left was actually a change of heart that had been developing for several years. Baraka's disappointment with Newark Mayor Kenneth Gibson and the National Black Convention led to his conclusion that black nationalism served primarily the black bourgeoisie and thus the white elite. He was stunned by the establishmentarian policies of Newark's first black mayor, who had been elected in part through a black nationalist appeal that Baraka himself had fashioned.

Although to his credit Gibson had never identified himself as a black nationalist, the black nationalist sentiments then sweeping throughout black urban America, including Newark, created the political climate for his initial electoral success. By using his organization to register and transport voters to the polls, Baraka had played a critical role in Gibson's first election. But Baraka had naively assumed that once in office, a black mayor would run city hall for Newark's black and Puerto Rican residents. Then, when he discovered that Gibson intended to govern the largest city in New Jersey according to liberal pragmatic political strategies—which meant not alienating those corporate interests left in Newark—Baraka realized the limitations of his nationalist analytical framework. That is, his adherence to black nationalism had blinded him to the significance of class differences in the black community as well as the different political interests arising from these class distinctions.[2] Baraka's black nationalist thought did not take account of the prevailing economic and social structures that limited the political options confronting blacks like Mayor Gibson who had entered establishmentarian power circles. Black cultural nationalism, including Kawaida, had no theory of the state.

Baraka had assumed that the United States was governed by a power elite that had unlimited powers over the whole range of social policies. His black nationalist political involvement in Newark was based on the idea that a change in the skin color of the person occupying the mayor's seat would necessarily result in radically revamped city policies. Any understanding of the structural constraints on Mayor Gibson or any other black mayor was lost in Baraka's accusations of race betrayal.

Baraka's experiences with the National Black Convention allowed him to see at first hand the opportunism governing so much of the political behavior of established black elected officials. The rush of some black elected officials to renege on their commitment to the Gary convention taught Baraka that Mayor Gibson was not an aberration. Rather, the problem lay in the logic of electoral politics in which candidates sought personal gain and influence through compromise. Compromises meant engineered consensus, and consensus in American politics consistently excluded the protection of those concerns most dear to impoverished black Americans. Gibson's unwillingness to try to expand the boundaries of Newark's governing consensus ultimately rendered his mayoralty of little benefit to the city's poor.

During this period of disillusionment with black electoral politics, Baraka was increasingly exposed to theories of African socialism, particularly those of Nkrumah, Toure, Nyerere, and Cabral.[3] The writings of these African thinkers convinced him that there was nothing racially demeaning in appropriating the ideas of Karl Marx. In response to his new fondness for Marxist thought, Baraka repudiated the political ideology of *Raise Race Rays Raze* in which he had labeled Marx as just another racist white man.[4] He was particularly drawn to Cabral who, unlike Toure, Nyerere, and Nkrumah, was an avowed Marxist.

Baraka's former black nationalist colleagues were furious with his ideological reversal.[5] Realizing that any changes in his ideology would mean a modification in the ideology of the Congress of African Peoples, many black nationalists resigned from the organization. In an extraordinarily insightful article, Kalamu Ya Salaam warned black activists about the long-run danger inherent in an organization run by an autocratic leader:

> The ideology of the leader is the ideology of the organization which works as long as the leader is strong and positive; but what usually happens is that ideological development is resultantly tied to the personal development of the individual leader rather than to the collective development of the entire organization.[6]

One would have hoped in vain for Baraka to understand the truth of this essay, which had been prominently published in *Black World*. Former confreres of Baraka, who were closely acquainted with his leadership style, should not have been surprised by his autocratic desires to mold the organization in his own image. Baraka might well have told them "CAP, c'est moi!" Indeed, he conveyed such sentiments in his autobiography: "*We* were going to the Left, *I* was reading Nkrumah and Cabral and Mao . . . it was clear now where CAP was going, *at least to me*[7] [my emphasis]. It was evident that Baraka was not functioning in a democratic political structure or a democratic organizational subculture. In 1975, Baraka changed the name of the Congress of African Peoples to the Revolutionary Communist League. No longer an "Imamu," Baraka became a "chairman"! Autocracy still reigned.

Why did Baraka, who had previously been so antagonistic to white Marxists, now claim to be a devout follower of Marx? His autobiography does not adequately explore the reasons for the abrupt turnabout. Baraka could have simply reformed his black nationalistic outlook to include a sensitivity to class distinctions. Perhaps the reasons for the reversal had a psychological origin as much as a political one, given Baraka's history of revoking ideologies when faced with psychopolitical dilemmas. According to Gerald Early,

> Baraka does not seek to make any sort of peace with any part of the world as it is; hence his rebellion is not only against governments, oppressive political ideologies, false prophets, and bad artists but against the present itself. . . . It is obvious to anyone even slightly familiar with Baraka's writings that he needed and continues to need these sleight-of-hand identity swaps in order to create the psychological tension he must have to write.[8]

Early's comments are not entirely accurate. Baraka has not made as many identity swaps as Early insinuates. He has now been committed to a rather orthodox Marxist position for more than a quarter of a century. Early does not consider the possibility that some "identity swaps" were more intellectually fruitful than others. Baraka may have thought that he needed to create new "psychological tensions" in order to write, but it is not apparent that such changes were beneficial to his artistic creativity. Indeed, Baraka's art may have been consistently undermined by his constant quest for engagement and the resulting feelings of estrangement. It would not be surprising if his embrace of Marxism stemmed primarily from a desire to escape his claustrophobic black nationalist world and only secondarily from an attraction to Marxism. At some point, he must have recognized the mediocrity of many of the black nationalist intellectual and artistic undertakings, including much of what he had written during this period.[9] This latter point is mere speculation, for Baraka has never issued a critical aesthetic appraisal of the Black Arts movement. Rather, most of his post–black nationalist commentaries on the Black Arts movement have been concerned with the ideological presuppositions of the art created during this period. Yet to argue, as Baraka the Marxist often does, that the principal problem of the Black Arts movement was its erroneous ideological focus is to sidestep a serious intellectual engagement with the movement. It was precisely Baraka's inability or unwillingness to engage in rigorous aesthetic and artistic self-criticism that rendered him irresponsible in the eyes of many.

During the Black Arts period, Baraka had been a proponent of ethnic cheerleading black art, provided that it helped "liberate" black people. This rationalization for even mediocre art was based on the belief that the only black art of value was black nationalist propaganda. The litmus test for the value of propaganda was political efficacy, not aesthetics. When it became apparent to Baraka that there would be no black nationalist revolution in the foreseeable future, his political rationalization for tolerating black artistic mediocrity was severely undermined. He thus might have concluded that until the revolution appeared on the horizon, he might as well be a serious artist, or he might as well "just be."

Similarly, the failure of the Black Arts movement to create and/or sustain a black nationalist political front brought before Baraka and other black artists the question of the usefulness of their propaganda. What tangible benefits had accrued to blacks as the result of poetry that sent the tongues of cops back to Ireland? Had Irish American cops stopped beating black heads? The Black Arts movement was a movement of and for intellectuals, and like most political formations dominated by intellectuals, Black Arts intellectuals never admitted to having insular self-interests.

In leaving black nationalism for Marxism, Baraka claimed to have intensified his commitment to the emancipation of black America, arguing that Marxism was the logical next step for any sound thinking, revolutionary, black nationalist. That is, instead of depicting his adoption of Marxism as a rejection of black nationalism, Baraka publicly marketed the alterations in his ideology as a "natural" progression. The same love of black people that inspired him to become a black nationalist ultimately led him to adopt Marxism.

By adopting Marxism and declaring it superior to black nationalism, Baraka was able to abandon his nationalist disciples without ever having to offer critical statements concerning their work. Mired too deeply in ethnic insularity to escape by gradual means, Baraka converted. Conversion allowed

Baraka to leave "the past" behind and become, in effect, a new person. The "born again" aspects of Baraka's conversion to Marxism help explain why he never felt the need to apologize to former associates whom he had helped "lead astray" into the depths of black nationalism. Baraka had made a similar conversion when he left Beat bohemia for Harlem. Like his earlier conversion, Baraka's adoption of Marxism was accompanied by vicious and unfair personal attacks on his former associates. That is, Baraka became ultra-Marxist and intensely antinationalist, treating his former nationalist peers as if they had become the vanguard of the enemy camp. Indeed, his defection dealt black cultural nationalism a devastating blow from which it never recovered.

Baraka was not able to persuade many blacks to follow him into the ranks of the Stalinist left.[10] Quite the contrary: Baraka's influence in Afro-American political and intellectual circles quickly subsided when he became a Marxist. In Baraka's mind, however, the weakness of his Marxist appeal to his former nationalist comrades did not signify his growing political irrelevance but testified to the revolutionary authenticity of his new ideological home. Once again, he had become too radical for his peers.

TRANSITIONAL ESSAYS: WRITHING TOWARD MARXISM

Baraka explained his shift to the left in a series of essays that he began to publish in late 1973. Some of these essays were position papers for CAP members, and others were directed to his broader Afro-American intellectual and political audiences. These essays allow us to see not only his growing disillusionment with black cultural nationalism as expressed in Kawaida but also his creeping attachment to Marxism. *Creeping* is the key word here, for Baraka's initial flirtation with scientific socialism contained numerous quotations from international heroes of the black freedom struggle, as if by mentioning them he was legitimizing his right to appropriate the ideas of "white Europeans." Baraka had supported a form of socialism long before he became a Marxist. However, his pre-Marxist socialism was based on a romantic depiction of traditional African society, as if one could create a postcapitalist society in the United States modeled on African feudalism. This "back-to-the-future" character of Kawaidan socialism was unadulterated romanticism.

In March 1974, Baraka delivered a short speech at a CAP regional meeting in Chicago.[11] Little did he know that this speech, "National Liberation and Politics," would be received as a bombshell by some of the black nationalists in the audience.[12] Today, the speech does not seem to substantively redefine CAP's mission. Instead, it appears to have been a call to arms, a speech of encouragement. The speech begins with three quotations from Amilcar Cabral, followed by a quotation from Lenin and one from Mao. The essay includes the requisite deferential references to the thought of Karenga. Baraka concludes with his often-repeated ideas that the revolutionary black movement must consist of (1) revolutionary nationalism, (2) Pan-Africanism, and (3) socialism (*ujamaa*). Given the utter predictability of the speech, Baraka could only assume that his mere mention of Lenin and Mao was what threw the doctrinaire CAP members into a state of disarray.

Soon after the Chicago speech, Baraka delivered another, "Revolutionary Party: Revolutionary Ideology," at the Midwestern Conference of the Congress of Afrikan People. This speech/position paper was one of the most explicit transition statements in Baraka's writing of that period. First, as was the case in Chicago, Baraka still identified himself as the "Imamu." The essay begins by stating that "our ideology" is revolutionary Kawaida, an ideology built on an African cultural base based on empirical facts and not mythology, idealism, or metaphysics. This essay is principally a critique of black nationalism rather than a positive assertion of Marxism. Baraka observes that the nationalism that he championed, Karenga's Kawaida, was a revolutionary nationalism, as opposed to a bourgeois black nationalism. He criticizes those "who would celebrate the old Afrikan feudalistic culture while refusing to struggle to create a new revolutionary socialist one."[13]

Baraka calls for the creation of a united black front, modeled perhaps after the left's popular front of the 1930s. Even though they are participants in this united black front coalition, advocates of revolutionary Kawaida must recognize that they are in the advance of the black struggle and must therefore assume the responsibilities of the vanguard. Here, Baraka confuses the role of the vanguard party with the role of the working class as the agent of universal human emancipation. Because blacks are at the "bottom of the American heap," Baraka contends that their liberation would necessarily lead to the emancipation of everyone. But he mistakenly thinks that the centrality of their struggle to all others means that blacks are the vanguard of the revolutionary movement. This is a misreading of Marx and Lenin. Baraka must have known that Marx assigned to the working class the role of universal emancipator, despite the existence of people who were lower in economic and social status than the proletariat. Conspicuously, he sidesteps Marx's discussion of the lumpenproletariat but believes that many of the blacks who would participate in and benefit from a socialist revolution are members of the lumpen. Instead of grappling with this troubling aspect of Marx's thought, he simply ignores it. He also must have known that Lenin was not among the most subjugated of Russian citizens before the revolution. So if the vanguard must come out of the lowest of the low, on what grounds could Lenin have been the leader of the vanguard movement? More pertinent, by what justification could the bourgeois Baraka lead a contemporary revolutionary movement?

The speech/position paper ends with a description of the specific theories that must be taken into account when determining the ideology and strategy of the vanguard revolutionary party. Baraka says that such a party must be influenced by the thought of Marx, Lenin, Mao, Nkrumah, Nyerere, Toure, Cabral, and Maulana Karenga. Although Karenga still holds the preeminent position in Baraka's thought, Marx and Lenin have been added to his pantheon of emancipatory thinkers. This speech was far more explicit than the earlier "National Liberation and Politics" in declaring the usefulness of Marxism to the black struggle. Concerning his thought at this time, Baraka wrote, "By March of 1974 I was now openly including elements of Marxism in this 'Revolutionary Kawaida,' but I was still unwilling or unable to cut Karenga's doctrine, at least the main thrust of it, loose."[14]

In April 1974, CAP issued "Black People and Imperialism," a position paper written by Baraka in which he had now shed most references to Kawaida and Karenga. Although Baraka's picture continued to appear on the cover of the position papers, he was now referred to as Chairman Amiri Baraka instead of Imamu Amiri Baraka. Like many of his essays of this period, this one begins with an extended quotation from Lenin. The rest of the essay is essentially a paraphrasing of Lenin's and Mao's ideas on capitalism, with repeated invocations of Cabral. The essay ends a statement that the black American liberation struggle should be recognized by blacks and whites alike as the vanguard of the forthcoming American revolution. Likewise, Third World countries, including those on the African continent, were the vanguard of the international struggle for socialism. But once again, Baraka offers neither explanation nor substantiation of his assertions.

In the November 1974 issue of *Black World* is an essay written by Imamu Amiri Baraka entitled "Toward Ideological Clarity: Nationalism, Pan-Africanism, Socialism." Originally presented in May 1974 as a CAP position paper, the version published in *Black World* was quite abbreviated. Interestingly, Baraka still identifies himself by his nationalist title, Imamu, although he had earlier discarded that title in some of his CAP working papers. This inconsistency in his self-identification may have stemmed from his ambivalence about the changes he was making. A more likely possibility is that Baraka viewed the publication of his essay in *Black World* as different from that of his CAP position papers. Consequently, he might have been trying to use his popularly known black nationalist title as a means of softening the changes that he was introducing. "Toward Ideological Clarity" is essentially an explanation of his reconceptualization of the political problem of Afro-America as one of capitalist oppression and racism. Because Baraka had long identified racism as the main reason for black people's subjugation, the novel formulation in this essay is his identification of capitalism as an equal if not superior cause. He argued that racism could best be understood as a tool of capitalist oppression, even though sometimes racist oppression conflicted with and superseded market exploitation.[15] The slave trade and the subsequent division of the African continent into European-controlled colonies was deemed a result of racism operating in a framework of capitalist profiteering.

As the focal theorist for his reflections, Baraka now placed Lenin in the role he once reserved for Karenga. "Toward Ideological Clarity" begins with an extended quotation from Lenin's "Imperialism: The Highest Stage of Capitalism."

> Imperialism is capitalism in that stage of development in which the dominance of monopolies and finance capital has established itself; in which the export of capital has acquired pronounced importance; in which the division of the world among the international trusts has begun; in which the division of all territories of the globe among the great capitalist powers has been completed. . . . Imperialism as interpreted above, undoubtedly represents a special stage in the development of capitalism.[16]

For Baraka, imperialism and its first cousin, colonialism, were the dominant forms of capitalist oppression that originally brought Africa and the African diaspora to their knees. The imperial conquest of Africa by Europe is significant not only because Africans were forced to submit to an economic system in which Europe thrived at Africa's expense but also because colonialism was accompanied by a virulent antiblack racism that morally legitimated the dominance of black Africa by white Europe. Racist colonialism wreaked havoc on African identities as it attacked and distorted the continent's indigenous cultural traditions.

Baraka's appropriation of Marxism gave him a framework for understanding the plight of blacks, even though his categories and teleology remained rigid and doctrinaire. In "Toward Ideological Clarity," Baraka repeatedly quotes from Amilcar Cabral's writings. This is not surprising, for Baraka was deeply influenced by Cabral before leaving the ranks of black cultural nationalism. Indeed, Cabral may well have been the only Marxist that black cultural nationalists during the 1960s and early 1970s deemed worthy of reading. Because Cabral was a respected African revolutionary and an unabashed

Marxist, Baraka may have believed that invoking his name might serve his post–black nationalist quest for ethnic legitimation.[17] In addition, Cabral regarded indigenous culture as a major site of conflict between capitalist/European domination and "the people's" emancipatory resistance. In this sense, Cabral appeared to function for Baraka as a para-Gramscian thinker.[18] By invoking the centrality of cultural struggles, Baraka believed that Cabral provided a conceptual schema for situating aspects of his former black nationalist political activities in a revolutionary cloak. Baraka quotes Cabral:

> History teaches us that, in certain circumstances, it is very easy for the foreigner to impose his domination on a people. But it also teaches us that, whatever may be the material aspects of this domination, it can be maintained only by the permanent organized repression of the cultural life of the people concerned.[19]

But Baraka misinterpreted Cabral's thought as applicable to the political-cultural conditions of blacks in the United States. First, Cabral's unique theoretical contribution to Marxism stemmed from his analyses of colonialism and imperialism.[20] Second, it is far too simplistic to claim, as Baraka does, that black Americans were forced to "relinquish" their indigenous culture in the same way that a colonized people did. Rather, Afro-American culture was created simultaneously with and in the history of black subjugation. Except for a few phenomena, the vastness of modern Afro-American culture does not predate Afro-American subjugation. In addition, Afro-American culture has been thoroughly informed by white Americans in much the way that "white American culture" has been informed by blacks. To speak of a "black culture" in the United States is to speak of the cultural beliefs and practices of the majority of black Americans, not a culture that is distinct from that produced by white Americans. In this sense, there is no "white culture." Land was central to Cabral's understanding of colonialism. Because black Americans did not own a separate piece of land before white domination, Cabral did not consider the Afro-American struggle to be an anticolonial struggle. Baraka, however, ignored these aspects of Cabral's formulations, which contributed to the theoretical confusion in Baraka's nascent Marxism.

We must assume that Baraka was familiar with the informal talk that Cabral held in New York City with a group of black Americans in October 1972, as a transcript of the lecture and discussion was widely disseminated in black nationalist and Pan-Africanist intellectual circles. Baraka may even have been there. During the talk, Cabral mentioned a discussion that he had had with Eldridge Cleaver, who was then living in exile:

We agreed on many things but we disagreed on one thing. He told me your condition is a colonial condition. In certain aspects it seems to be, but it is not really a colonial condition. The colonial condition demands certain factors. One important factor is continuity of territories. There are others which you can see when you analyze.[21]

Although the majority of black Americans moved out of the South, Baraka continued to insist that the Black Belt South remained the national homeland of black Americans and used this supposedly black land to satisfy Cabral's requirement of continuity of territory. Cabral contended that black Americans, though subjugated, were not a colonized people. Baraka, he reasoned, was not oppressed by a foreign power.

By using Cabral's understanding of culture, Baraka was able to recognize some of the conceptual errors in his previous ahistorical, black nationalist concept of culture. He saw that culture could not be understood as simply a repository of what has gone on in the past but had to be viewed as always changing. In an effort at self-critique, he wrote: "The mistake made by so-called cultural nationalists, in their use of culture, a mistake still being made, is to take the concept of culture as a static concept that had only partially . . . to do with the Afrikan in North America as we find ourselves."[22]

Baraka was caught in a quandary. He no longer wanted to be linked to the idealistic and romantic conceptions of an African feudal past contained in Karenga's thought. But he also did not want to give up black nationalism completely. His response, therefore, was a conceptual compromise. He now held capitalism primarily responsible for the subjugation of Afro-Americans, but he continued to view blacks as culturally oppressed. To the extent that black Americans were a distinct cultural group, they constituted a nation. Although black nationalism remained necessary, it was no longer sufficient for emancipating Afro-America. Perhaps the most publicly apparent change in Baraka's understanding of the plight of black America was that he now acknowledged that blacks could not free themselves without joining forces with emancipatory-minded whites. The natural white allies of blacks were, of course, the white working class, despite the ways in which racism had blinded many white workers to their true self-interests and nonwhite class comrades. In black nationalist circles, the racism of the white working class was legion. Most black political activists, left or antileft, would not stake their political lives on the viability of a class coalition with white workers.

Black nationalism was vulnerable to manipulation and control by the capitalist economic order. Capitalists were quite adept at using black nationalism to establish a "neocolonial"-like black elite whose mission was to keep the masses of blacks subdued by diverting their attention away from the class struggle. In Baraka's mind, Kenneth Gibson, the NAACP's Roy Wilkins, and the Congressional Black Caucus were exemplary members of this black neo-colonial elite.

Baraka's essay "The Congress of Afrikan People: A Position Paper" appeared in the January/February 1975 issue of *The Black Scholar*. It contains little if anything new. Baraka wades through his favorite themes: monopoly capitalism, the capitalist basis of the African slave trade, the Soviet Union as an imperialist power, the inevitable decline of capital, the need for a revolutionary vanguard party, and the inevitable rise of revolutionary peoples. What is striking about this essay is his expanding pantheon of Marxist heroes: "Nationalism is backward when it says that we cannot utilize the revolutionary experience of the world . . . the theories and experience of men like Marx, Engels, Lenin, Stalin, Mao Tse Tung . . . or Ho Chi Minh, Fidel Castro, Enver Hoxha of Albania, Kim Il Sung of North Korea."[23]

In March 1975, Baraka published a lengthy CAP position paper entitled "Black Nationalism and Socialist Revolution," a shorter and more widely read version of which was published in the July 1975 issue of *Black World* under the title "Black Nationalism and Socialist Revolution: Why I Changed My Ideology." Baraka begins the essay in a manner that foretells his inability to distinguish CAP from himself: "One question to which we must constantly respond is why did we change our ideology. We, meaning the Congress of Afrikan People, but also specifically Amiri Baraka."[24] Baraka's willingness to publish the essay under the title "Why I Changed My Ideology" belies his usage of the royal "we" throughout the essay. Those familiar with CAP knew that Baraka was its theoretician and autocratic leader. Most CAP members were not included in the decision to alter CAP's ideology. Yet it is clear that Baraka was under pressure to show that CAP was more than his personal fiefdom. Baraka's need to explain the change in his politics almost a year after he first embraced Marxism testifies to the continuing problems he was having convincing blacks that he was still politically relevant to the black struggle.

"Why I Changed My Ideology" does not tread on new ground but restates themes that Baraka routinely made in his speeches at this time. He again admitted that the cultural nationalism that he had once admired had been a flawed political program, since it not only was guilty of celebrating African feudalism but also was divorced from the indigenous culture of Afro-Americans. In addition, Baraka admits that it was an error to have acted as if black people could have freed themselves without affecting or being affected by the political status of nonblacks, particularly oppressed whites. But he continued to insist that despite these errors in theory, CAP had remained true to its revolutionary calling.

> We changed our views from cultural nationalists because we have always viewed ourselves as revolutionaries, black people struggling for national liberation. We have not ever thought we needed to be fixed at any point or intractable on any view, except the view that we must be totally dedicated to the liberation of black people in North America.[25]

Baraka distorts the truth here. One could read this and conclude that the black cultural nationalist leader Imamu Baraka had been ecumenical in his politics. But he was as doctrinaire and dogmatic a black nationalist as any figure that emerged from the Black Power movement of the 1960s. Few black political figures spent as much time hurling invectives at other politicized blacks who did not adhere to his cultural nationalist program. It did not matter whether they were bourgeois integrationists or self-professed Marxist-Leninists. Baraka had been a religious nationalist and, worse, a fundamentalist religious nationalist.

Baraka once again declared that CAP changed its ideology because it realized that many blacks in the United States and Africa were functioning as the agents of white capitalist domination. Whether they were neocolonial elites in Africa and the West Indies or black elected officials in the United States, the new Black Power holders were the means by which international capitalism had acquired a softer and ethnically legitimate image.[26] The color of the elites had changed, but the masses were still exploited. As long as capitalism existed, racism would thrive. In the final analysis, racism existed to serve the interests of capitalism. For this reason, Baraka proclaimed the Congress of Afrikan People to be a revolutionary communist organization.[27]

After ushering the reader through a rudimentary rendition of Marx's notion of capitalist exploitation, Baraka again asserts that blacks in the United States constitute an oppressed and colonized nation. Although he recognizes the nationalist aspects of the "Negro question," he rejects black nationalism for Marxism because Marxism is scientific. As a science, it is applicable to everyone, anywhere and everywhere.

> There are people, for instance, who tell us that we cannot learn from international revolutionary experience. They tell us we cannot use Marx-Engels-Lenin-Stalin because they were white. Why is it that Mao Tse-Tung in China, Ho Chi Minh in Vietnam, Kim Il Sung in Korea, Amilcar Cabral, Kwame Nkrumah and Sekou Toure in Afrika, all could use these

theories and practices to advance the struggles and make revolution for their people? It is because scientific truth is universally applicable. Just as gravity and relativity do not just function in Europe, but everywhere, so do the scientific discoveries of men like Marx, Engels, Lenin and Stalin.[28]

According to Baraka, it is necessary for blacks to recognize their collective interests with white workers. But they cannot do so until America develops a truly revolutionary vanguard party. Baraka knows that capitalism cannot be defeated peacefully or through gradual reform. Rather, a violent revolution is needed. In pursuit of that revolution, in 1975 the Congress of Afrikan People became the Revolutionary Communist League M-L-M.[29]

THE MARXIST AS POLITICAL ESSAYIST: THE FOOTSTEPS OF LU XUN

In 1984, Baraka published *Daggers and Javelins*, his third major collection of sociopolitical essays. The essays were written from 1974 to 1979, and some had previously been published. The title of the collection is derived from the words of Lu Xun (Lu Hsun), a radical Chinese writer who lived from 1881 to 1936, who wrote: "The living essay must be a dagger, a spear [javelin], something with which it can cut through a blood path to survival with the readers."[30] A primary instigator and influence in prerevolutionary, left-wing Chinese literary circles, Lu Xun supported the developing Communist movement, even though he was always too independent and idiosyncratic to join the party.[31] Lu Xun excelled in the writing of short stories, prose poetry, and classical Chinese poetry, but it was his use of the polemical, political essay to which Baraka was first attracted.

Lu Xun's nonfiction prose, or what he called *zawen*, consisted of scholarly treatises, prose poetry, reminiscences, and essays. The term *zawen* comes from the related terms *zagan* (miscellaneous impressions) and *zatan* (miscellaneous discussions).[32] Lu Xun became a highly stylized and prolific writer of *zawen*, whose purpose was to incite debate. For polemical purposes, Lu Xun employed vicious satire. According to one critic, his essays were "cutting, pugnacious, devastating, even venomous and directed against real and imagined enemies." Borrowing from Harriet Mills, Leo Ou-fan Lee, another scholar of Chinese literature, described Xun's satirical style as

> the *reductio ad absurdum* technique, the use of paradox and argument by analogy or authority, the repetition of key words or phrases, and finally the

terse but lethal punch line to finish off his opponent. To this may be added his intentional twisting, often out of context, of quoted statements from his opponents—whose positions he also purposely inflates.[33]

Baraka does not inform us how he came to admire Lu Xun, but we can hypothesize that the celebration of Lu Xun by Mao Zedong, one of Baraka's Marxist deities, influenced Baraka's perceptions of the writer. On one occasion, Mao called Lu Xun "the major leader in the Chinese cultural revolution. He was not only a great writer but a great thinker and a great revolutionist."[34]

The significance of Lu Xun for Baraka is that the Chinese writer was explicitly politically engaged. In addition, Baraka has claimed an affinity with Lu Xun because he too had encountered censorship because of his radical political ideas.[35] The essay form that Lu Xun mastered may have inspired Baraka's polemical energies, but it did not significantly influence Baraka's style. Despite the collection's title, most of the essays published in *Daggers and Javelins* were not reminiscent of Lu Xun's essays. Instead, Baraka included in this volume several attempts at what he thought were informed, semischolarly analyses of significant issues in the contemporary world. The essays that most resemble those of Lu Hsun were published in CAP's newspaper, *Unity and Struggle*, and only a few of those were republished in this volume.

The essays in *Daggers and Javelins* are divided into four themes. One theme is Baraka's Pan-Africanist sensibilities. The second concerns the political plight of Afro-American intellectuals. The third theme is Baraka's views of certain international radical intellectuals and artists. Finally, the fourth type is concerned with the general Afro-American political predicament. The essays are highly repetitive and quickly become monotonous. In more than half, Baraka invents a past in which the so-called revisionism of the Communist Party USA prevented it from assuming its role as the guiding vehicle of black political emancipation. Also frequently repeated is the claim that the former Soviet Union practiced social imperialism.

One does not read Baraka in order to understand Marx or a Marxist intellectual tradition. Indeed, it is not clear that he has read much of Marx. His essays do not indicate a familiarity with Marx's writings. Second, it also is apparent that Baraka has not grappled with the Western Marxist intellectual tradition. Baraka is as removed from sophisticated Marxist thought as Jerry Falwell is from Paul Tillich. Whereas Falwell adheres rather dogmatically to a crude neofundamentalist tradition of Christian thinking, Baraka adheres to an equally dogmatic, neofundamentalist Marxism. Both men are devoutly religious, but Baraka hides his faith in the language of scientific socialism. In

Baraka's mind, Marxism is a set of rules that can be applied to any situation, any place, at any time.

ON INTERNATIONAL POLITICS

The initial essay in *Daggers and Javelins*, "Africa, Superpower Contention and the Danger of World War," offers a glimpse of Baraka's Marxian view of international politics prior to the collapse of the Soviet Union. Embracing an ideological line advanced by China, Baraka believed that the Soviet Union was far more dangerous to Third World nations than the United States, for the United States was clearly in decline, as shown by its defeat in Vietnam.

As proof of Soviet imperialism, Baraka cites the Soviet domination of Eastern Europe and its behavior during the Angolan civil war. After Portugal's colonial rule ended, the three major Angolan independence factions that had fought against the Portuguese began to fight among themselves. Baraka considers the Soviet Union's aid to only one faction in the civil war, the Marxist MPLA (Popular Movement for the Liberation of Angola), to have been an unjust attempt to influence the outcome of the war. He contends that the Soviets encouraged the introduction of Cuban mercenaries into the struggle after "agitating a civil war" and that the Soviet Union and Cuba entered Angola "only after the three Angola liberation movements had agreed amongst themselves to administer the post colonial Angola state."[36]

Unfortunately, Baraka was not above dishonesty and distortion. All of the groups fighting in Angola were externally funded and armed. UNITA (National Union for Total Liberation of Angola) received arms from the United States and South Africa while FNLA (National Front for the Liberation of Angola) received arms from Zaire, the United States, and Communist China. In March 1975, an agreement between the three warring factions was violated when FNLA attacked MPLA. With the aide of Cuban advisers, MPLA repelled the FNLA attack. However, in October 1975 South Africa, in partnership with UNITA, intervened in the civil war. Within one week, five thousand South African soldiers had advanced five hundred miles up the Angolan coast. Fearing defeat, MPLA asked for Cuban troops. During the next six months, Cuba sent approximately twenty-two thousand troops to Angola. The South African invasion was repelled. Because of the intervention of the hated South Africans on the side of UNITA, most African nations became opponents of UNITA, allies of MPLA, and supporters of Cuban intervention. Baraka, however, writes as if South Africa never intervened.

Baraka enters the realm of pure propaganda when he refuses to comment on the irrationality of China's policy toward Africa. In knee-jerk fashion, China opposed whatever the Soviets did. By 1973, Chariman Mao was hosting right-wing African dictators such as Mobutu Sese Seko of Zaire precisely because Mobutu was opposed by the Soviet Union. Evidently, it did not matter to Mao that Mobutu was despotic with his own people.

DOMESTIC POLITICS

Baraka's analytical sophistication did not improve in his essays about the United States' domestic politics. The mechanistic anti-intellectualism of his Marxism can be seen in "Marxism and the Black Community," in which he denounces various "Marxist" and communist parties in the United States for their failure to proclaim black America a subjugated nation within a nation. By rejecting the position of the "white communists" on the "Negro question," Baraka believes that they reveal their racial chauvinism.

The essay "Black Liberation / Socialist Revolution" continues with the claim that the most important political policy concerning black Americans is "self-determination for the African-American nation in the black belt South." Baraka asserts that an autonomous black belt in the American South is the only way to ensure freedom for blacks, "the only guarantee of equality, the only guarantee that the demand for equal rights and democratic rights for the black oppressed nationality scattered throughout the United States will be satisfied." Astonishingly, Baraka does not explain how or why a separate black nation in the American South would guarantee the rights of blacks living in Philadelphia or Detroit. And why would such a nation necessarily be progressive? He also argues that the possibility of realizing an independent, socialist black belt nation is (in the 1970s) better than at any time since the abandonment of the black masses by the Communist Party of the United States. The vacuum left by the political opportunism of the American communists had allowed the black bourgeoisie to capture the black liberation movement. The dynamic leadership of Malcolm X had rescued the black masses from the black bourgeois leadership. Malcolm, according to Baraka, was not only the spokesperson for the black working class but was, "without a doubt, the most influential black leader of his time." The Black Liberation movement, we are told, has never recovered from Malcolm's assassination. Baraka concludes the essay by maintaining that the liberation of black Americans and the creation of a separate black nation can come about only through an armed, violent revolution: "It should be clear that the reason the black rebellions of the 1960's could not become revolution is that there was no Marxist-Leninist leadership in the form of a revolutionary party."[37]

Following in the footsteps of the self-professed "black Bolshevik," Harry Haywood, Baraka contends that those black Americans who live in that area of the southern United States historically referred to as the "Black Belt" constitute an oppressed nation within the United States.[38] Much like his earlier espousal of Kawaidan black cultural nationalism that appropriated reified constructs from an African feudal past and magically transformed them into bulwarks of freedom in a late capitalist society, Baraka's Marxism brings ideological positions from the past into the present without taking into account historical changes.

Baraka's attempt to reinvigorate the black nation thesis indicates his continued unwillingness to confront the needs of black Americans at this time. Indeed, the Communist Party's support of a Negro nation was viewed by most blacks as somewhat ludicrous and unrealistic.[39] Today, the concept is beyond silly. Most black Americans no longer live in the Black Belt. Moreover, it would be difficult to substantiate the claim that most blacks are partner to a shared culture distinct from that of whites. When the Communist Party initially issued its call for a black nation, one could have argued that blacks had created a distinct folk culture in the Black Belt South. This shared folk culture was mainly expressive (e.g., music, dance, language cadence). It is one thing to state that blacks created a unique music in America but quite another to insist that all blacks are musical. Even if this latter claim were true, it would still beg the question: How would a black nation contribute to the well-being of the millions of blacks who live outside the Black Belt? How would it benefit those who live within it?

In addition, in *Daggers and Javelins*, Baraka makes blatantly dishonest claims about the political significance of Marxism in the United States: "What is developing swiftly in the U.S.A., and with growing influence on the masses, is the movement to build a new Marxist-Leninist communist party, an anti revisionist communist movement, which can lead the working class and oppressed masses in making socialist revolution."[40] Why did Baraka distort the significance of Marxism in the United States? Perhaps he could not be honest about its marginality because that would have revealed his own political feebleness.

Baraka's essays contain the usual imprecisions and unsubstantiated assertions that routinely appear in his political polemics. For example, he erroneously assumes that Martin Luther King Jr. had a smaller working-class following than Malcolm X did. There is no proof of this. Furthermore, the Malcolm that Baraka celebrates is the Malcolm of the Nation of Islam. Whatever one might argue about Malcolm, he spent most of his mature political life advocating the neo–Booker T. Washington bootstrap philosophy of Elijah Muhammad. Malcolm also believed in Elijah Muhammad's divine descent from God on Earth, Master Fard. Worse, Malcolm endorsed the ridiculous narrative of Yacub, the mad scientist who invented white people. When Malcolm left the Nation of Islam, he continued to practice the Muslim faith. But Baraka condemns only Martin King for harboring metaphysical beliefs, as if Malcolm were a less religious man. Finally, Baraka cannot bring himself to admit that most of the black urban riots/rebellions during the 1960s erupted spontaneously, often in response to some local event. Instead of a realistic analysis, Baraka creates a tautology. Had there been a vanguard party "in control" of the black masses, then the riots would not have occurred spontaneously. That they failed to lead to a revolution indicates that the rioters were not sufficiently disciplined by a revolutionary vanguard. If there had been a revolutionary vanguard with the power to discipline the black masses, the "riots" would not have been riots—which, for me, means that they never would have occurred.

MARXIST LITERARY CRITICISM

Several of the essays in *Daggers and Javelins* are attempts at Marxist literary criticism. As if caught in a fifty-year time warp, Baraka's Marxist criticism resurrects and revalorizes socialist realism.[41] But not surprisingly, his Marxist literary criticism is as reductionist as his Marxist political commentaries.[42] And given his idolization of Stalin, Baraka can find value in Stalin's cultural policies regarding the arts. Marxist literary criticism, at least of the Stalinist variety, assumed that the writer's duty was to use his or her art for the advancement of the proletariat. Stalin thus tried to force Soviet artists/writers to create a purely proletarian culture devoid of bourgeois artistic influences.[43]

> The transition from the revolutionary to the totalitarian phase in Soviet cultural policy was a life-and-death struggle in which physical terror played the decisive role, as is attested to by the murder of men like Meyerhold, Babel, Pilnyak, and Mandelsham, by the restrictions imposed on Shostakovich and Prokofiev, and by the banning of the films of Eisenstein and Pudovkin.[44]

Stalinistic artistic directives reached their bureaucratic apex in 1934 when the All Union Congress of Soviet Writers adopted the artistic policy of socialist realism. Jointly devised by Stalin and Maxim Gorky, the policy was included in the original statutes of the Union of Soviet Writers:

> *Socialist realism* is the basic method of Soviet literature and literary criti-cism. It demands of the artist the truthful, historically concrete representa-tion of reality in its revolutionary development. Moreover, the truthfulness and historical concreteness of the artistic representation of reality must be linked with the task of ideological transformation and education of workers in the spirit of socialism.[45]

It has long been held by most students of Soviet literature that socialist real-ism was an unequivocal artistic disaster, not only for Russian writers, but for all artistic supporters of the Communist Party. Commenting on the calami-tous impact of this policy on Soviet writers, Terry Eagleton wrote: "There is no space here to recount in full the chilling narrative of how the loss of the Bol-shevik revolution under Stalin expressed itself in one of the most devastating assaults on artistic culture ever witnessed in modern history."[46] In Stalin's eyes, however, socialist realism was a mechanism for maintaining the spirit of the revolution in a postrevolutionary society. Paradoxically, Baraka and many other Stalinist-influenced writers viewed socialist realism as a mechanism for inspiring a revolutionary fervor among workers in a capitalist society.

Baraka's Marxist literary criticism is not truly intent on interpreting texts except to determine whether or not they valorize revolutionary activities and/or the plight of the working class. Much like his aesthetic pronounce-ments during the Black Arts period, the Marxist Baraka remains trapped in a utilitarian aesthetic. He continues to divide texts into Manichaean moral cat-egories of good (pro-proletariat) versus bad (pro-bourgeois) black art. Only the criteria for making these assessments have changed. Baraka's Marxist lit-erary criticism describes the ideological intentions of a text rather than its artistic merits. As a result, Baraka's mode of criticism cannot distinguish be-tween excellent bourgeois art and crude bourgeois propaganda.

Baraka declared that the best Marxist literary theory that he had ever read was in a series of speeches delivered by Mao in 1942 at the Yenan Forum.[47] In a 1978 interview, Baraka stated,

> The best book of literary criticism that I have ever read is Mao Tse Tung's book, the *Yenan Forum on Art and Literature*, in which he says that art has to be not only politically correct but artistically powerful . . . he also says that just because you are a Marxist doesn't mean that when you write a play it is necessarily going to be great art. . . . Mao says that if the thing is

not artistically powerful, no matter how correct its political statement is, it is going to fail.[48]

We should not be surprised that Baraka would praise literary criticism from the leader of a revolutionary movement of peasants in a preindustrialized nation engaged in a war of national liberation against the Japanese occupation of the Chinese mainland. As stated earlier, Baraka appears to respect the thought of only those Marxists who had engaged in successful revolutionary praxis.[49] Nonetheless, we should be surprised that he treats Mao's cultural pronouncements as if they were timeless and directly applicable to the United States during the 1970s. Mao's lectures at the Yenan Forum were not literary criticism but a literary call to arms. Although he offers prescriptive statements about the role of revolutionary writers, his lectures contain very little specificity. How could Baraka believe that they were the best literary criticism that he had ever read?[50]

In "The Revolutionary Tradition in Afro-American Literature," Baraka begins with the literary scholar Bruce Franklin. Franklin had written that the term "American literature" as used in American literary studies had historically excluded the writings of Afro-Americans and other subjugated American peoples. He asserted that any concept of "American literature" that excluded Afro-American slave narratives was an ideological distortion and factual error. As part of the ideological superstructure buffering the material realities of American capitalism, the literature celebrated under the rubric "American literature" tended to valorize the status quo in all its sexist and racist glory. Baraka then scans the history of Afro-American literature from the vantage point of his dogmatic materialist Marxist framework and evaluates literary figures according to the political-economic interests purportedly served by their writing.

Baraka states that there are essentially two traditions in Afro-American literature: the reactionary tradition and the revolutionary tradition. Phyllis Wheatley and Juniper Hammon are deemed reactionary because they viewed slavery as beneficial to blacks. Baraka argues that they are celebrated in most literary histories of Afro-American literature as the founders of Afro-American literature because of their reactionary tendencies. Too often ignored are the true progenitors of the Afro-American literary tradition, the slave narratives of Frederick Douglass, Henry Bibb, Moses Roper, Linda Brent, William Wells Brown, the Krafts, Henry "Box" Brown, and numerous others.[51]

As the Civil War approached, a revolutionary tendency emerged in Afro-American literature. Baraka calls these individuals "pre–Civil War revolutionary black nationalists." In these ranks he places David Walker,

Henry Highland Garnet, Charles Lenox Remond, C. H. Langston, and William Wells Brown. Unsurprisingly, Baraka places Chestnutt in the reactionary tradition. Dunbar is situated in both camps, and James Weldon Johnson is condemned for his desire to create "high art."[52]

> *High art* is by definition slavemaster bourgeois art and that what was and is needed by all artists, or by those artists who intend for their works to serve the exploited and oppressed majority in this country, is that they be artistically powerful and politically revolutionary![53]

According to Baraka, Du Bois was the fountainhead of the emerging twentieth-century revolutionary tradition in Afro-American literature. This is a rather confounding assertion, for few black intellectuals were more committed than Du Bois to the pursuit of high art. The *Souls of Black Folk* is written in aristocratic, arcane language, yet Baraka does not admonish Du Bois's artistic ambitions in the same way that he denounces James Weldon Johnson. Why did he spare Du Bois? Perhaps Baraka realized that a discussion of Du Bois and high art would have forced him to revise his argument. In any case, the question of Marxism, high art, and its relationship to a capitalist economy is far more complicated than Baraka implies.

Following a perfunctory mention of the Harlem Renaissance and the communist sympathies of Langston Hughes and Claude McKay, Baraka discusses Richard Wright. He is ambivalent about the later Wright, although he views the early Wright as a hero of revolutionary writing. "His early works, *Uncle Tom's Children*, *Native Son*, *Black Boy*, including the long-suppressed section of this book called *American Hunger*, are among the most powerful works written by any American writer of the period."[54] Without explanation, Baraka then declares that Wright's individualism and idealism finally sabotaged his art. How? Perhaps Baraka meant that Wright's individualism and idealism were responsible for his rejection of communism and his subsequent embrace of existentialism. Baraka's inability to construct precise arguments weakens his assessment of Wright.

Predictably, Baraka condemns Ralph Ellison for his *Invisible Man*, contending that the novel became prominent because the "work puts down both nationalists and Marxists, and opts for *individualism*."[55] Despite the novel's elegance, Baraka views *Invisible Man* as an attempt to devalue the black protest activities of the 1930s and early 1940s. He further claims that Ellison was celebrated by establishmentarian literary circles (i.e., white literary circles) as the most formidable black novelist of his day only after they had rejected James Baldwin's play *Blues for Mr. Charlie*. This is a curious assertion given that Ellison won the National Book Award for *Invisible Man* before Baldwin had published his first novel and certainly before he had published *Blues for Mr. Charlie*.

The essay could have been more engaging had Baraka been less formulaic, as it suffers from the use of an overly simplistic moralistic categorization of "good art versus bad art." The broad sweep of the essay also hides numerous other weaknesses. Black women are conspicuously ignored. Who could have been more central to the black revolutionary literary tradition than Ida Wells-Barnett? And where is Anna Julia Cooper or even Lorraine Hansberry? Once again, Baraka's condemnation of high art is hollow. Are we to believe that a black person concerned about the plight of Afro-Americans cannot aspire to play Debussy? The essay reads like an introductory lecture delivered at the beginning of the semester, announcing the subjects to be discussed. But he never discusses them. Worse, the essay does not define what he means by a "revolutionary literature." Much like the misnomer "revolutionary theater" that he earlier attached to the plays *Dutchman*, *The Toilet* and *The Slave*, Baraka's claim that he is discussing a revolutionary tradition in Afro-American literature serves to mask the fact that he is actually discussing black protest literature.

Baraka revisits the politics of black writing in his essay "Afro-American Literature and Class Struggle," which is, in most respects, a restatement of "The Revolutionary Tradition in Afro-American Literature." No longer satisfied by the two-tier bracketing of black literature that structured his analysis in "The Revolutionary Tradition in Afro-American Literature," Baraka argues that most black writers "fall somewhere between those two poles." Nonetheless, he states that most of the major black writers have been revolutionary and, once again, that the Afro-American slave narrative constitutes the beginning of Afro-American literature as a distinct tradition. Du Bois is granted a centrality insofar as he supposedly bridged the nineteenth and twentieth centuries.

> His *Souls of Black Folk*, and indeed Du Bois's constant *forward movement* ideologically, from isolated democrat to black capitalist and yea-sayer for the "talented tenth" and the emerging black bourgeoisie (its militant national wing as opposed to the comprador wing of Booker T. Washington) to Pan-Africanism and socialist and finally to Marxist communist, is the underlying dynamic of all of our intellectual and political journey.[56]

Although Du Bois was an immense figure and chronicled many of the political struggles of black Americans in his life's narrative, Baraka cannot bring himself to acknowledge that Du Bois's politics were filtered through an elite veneer. On what grounds, therefore, can Baraka pretend that Du Bois's life is representative of "our" journey? Certainly, Baraka's political journey does not mirror Du Bois's, even though Baraka may want the reader to see Du Bois's repeated ideological changes as similar to his own. Rather, the real question concerns the quality of the political engagement generated by Du Bois and Baraka in any given ideological position.

According to Baraka, Langston Hughes and Claude McKay were the premier talents of the Harlem Renaissance. But this assessment is all too predictable given Baraka's valorization of any black writer who held leftist political positions. Toomer and Hurston are accordingly less important not because of their Harlem Renaissance writings but because of their subsequent political postures. Toomer, we are told, later repudiated blackness and Hurston succumbed to writing against voting rights for blacks in the South during the 1950s. Whatever one thinks of Toomer or Hurston, it is inappropriate to criticize their writing of the 1920s and 1930s by invoking their later political lives. After all, in later life, McKay became a devoutly conservative Catholic, and in the 1950s, Langston Hughes repudiated his progressive writings during the McCarthy hearings.

Richard Wright is celebrated for *Uncle Tom's Children*, which Baraka considered to be a depiction of the "national oppression of the Afro-American nation."[57] Once again, he denounces Ellison and Baldwin as agents of the white literati's desire to enfeeble Wright during the McCarthy era. Baraka lists Ellison's essay "Richard's Blues" as one example of these anti-Wright putdowns. Perhaps Ellison did write an essay by that title, but I have never found any reference to it. In 1945, years before the onslaught of McCarthyism, Ellison published an essay, "Richard Wright's Blues," in which he offered an unbridled defense and celebration of Richard Wright, author of *Black Boy*.[58] It is perplexing to find in Baraka's essay a complete misreading, if not outright invention, of a text.

Baraka then rehashes his usual fare concerning the Black Arts movement and how it was on the right track but just not far enough to the left. Unfortunately, he continues his ad hominem attacks on those black writers who chose not to embrace the Black Arts movement or not to endorse Marxism-Leninism. And he criticizes black feminist writers Michelle Wallace and Ntozake Shange for not realizing that the only solution to the sexist oppression of black women is socialist revolution.[59] Here Baraka's economistic Marxism rears its dogmatic head. As if engaged in self-parody, Baraka ends one essay with the chant: "Long live revolutionary artists and writers! People of the world unite against United States Imperialism and Soviet Social Imperialism!

Marxist-Leninists unite, win the advanced to communism! Liberation of the black nation! Socialist revolution! Victory to all oppressed people!" (Baraka, *Daggers and Javelins*, p. 52).

It would be an understatement to conclude that *Daggers and Javelins* was not an impressive essay collection. In actuality, it was extraordinarily pedestrian on matters of Marxist theorizing and sophomoric on issues of praxis. Baraka's belief that he had mastered the science of Marxism—in the way that one understands the rules of algebra—undoubtedly led him to forget that he still needed to argue on its behalf. Instead, Baraka's collection is composed of highly repetitive essays that are themselves assemblages of linked assertions. Perhaps Baraka's failure to write sophisticated Marxist polemics stems from his frustration at having to show incrementally what he knows to be universally true. If one thinks that God (i.e., timeless truth / laws of nature) has revealed itself in the disguise of a Vladimir Lenin, a Joseph Stalin, and a Mao Zedong, then there is no need for rational or logical argument. The truth, at least in the eyes of the believer, is obvious and irrefutable. In such minds, sophisticated arguments are essentially admissions of doubt.

The essays in *Daggers and Javelins* show Baraka to be a ceaseless conveyor of unsophisticated "Marxist" claptrap. The "Marxism" espoused by Baraka is not informed by the work of any major twentieth-century Marxist thinkers except for Lenin, Mao, and Cabral. It was as if Jean-Paul Sartre, Herbert Marcuse, Antonio Gramsci, Louis Althusser, Max Horkheimer, or Lucien Goldmann never existed.[60] Their work does not inform his "Marxism." Accordingly, Baraka does not address most of the problems of twentieth-century Marxism that were central to the intellectual agendas and theoretical reformulations of the post–World War II Western Marxists, including the more humane alterations in modern capitalism and the antiemancipatory nature of socialism in existent socialist countries.

There is little of intellectual or political value to be acquired from reading Baraka's "Marxist" essays in *Daggers and Javelins*. Instead, this collection of essays shows the extent to which a once serious and creative artist deteriorated intellectually after attempting to become a political thinker and activist. Baraka, the former advocate of a dogmatic black nationalism, was now a dogmatic exhorter of left-wing ditties. His style was more reminiscent of mimeographed leaflets announcing forthcoming demonstrations than serious, Marx-influenced reflections on important issues.

15

The Artist as Marxist / The Marxist as Artist

MARXIST PLAYWRIGHT

No consideration of Baraka the Marxist would be complete without a discussion of his Marxist-influenced art. Shortly after his 1974 conversion to Marxism, Baraka began to write a series of Marxist-influenced plays, the best known of which are *The Motion of History, S-1,* and *What Was the Relationship of the Lone Ranger to the Means of Production.*

In the William Morrow edition of his collection of plays, *The Motion of History and Other Plays,* is an epigraph from the *Peking Review* which serves as an ideological preview of the plays:

> The emergence of Marxism brought to light for the first time the objective laws governing the development of mankind's history; it scientifically proved the great truth that history is made by the slaves. Reversing the history the exploiting classes have reversed, Marxism thus brought about the utter bankruptcy of the idealist conception of history and uprooted the theoretical basis of thousands of years of reactionary rule by exploiting classes. Chairman Mao in leading the Chinese revolution has from time to time educated all Party members and cadres, the proletariat and other working people in the basic viewpoint of historical materialism, i.e., the masses are the makers of history.[1]

Baraka's belief that "the masses are the makers of history" meant that his Marxist plays would focus on the lives of the exploited, particularly the working class. No longer would he write plays about the identity crises of bourgeois black Americans, as he had done with Clay in *Dutchman* and Walker Vessels in *The Slave.* In accordance with his belief in the scientific nature of Marxism, all significant human dilemmas were collapsed into a teleological struggle between capitalists and workers that would inevitably result in the workers' victory. Baraka's understanding of Marxism prevented him from exploring the interior lives of the working classes except in relationship to economic exploitation. Instead, Baraka's Marxist drama tried both to affirm the workers' recognition of their own exploitation and to inspire them to realize their human destiny by joining the class struggle. Much like a black preacher who instilled hope in his congregation by asserting that God was on their side, Baraka marketed a secularized form of divine intervention.[2] In this instance, Baraka's gospel was scientific Marxism.

THE MOTION OF HISTORY (1975–1976)

The Motion of History is composed of thirty scenes, each of which depicts a certain historical event in which blacks and/or whites are involved in political actions opposing different forms of repression. The events are not chronological.

The play's first scene begins with a dialogue between a bourgeois Negro man and a 1960s white male hippie. While they talk, a screen behind them shows film clips of the political repression of liberation struggles. White American police are seen beating black civil rights demonstrators; Third World people are being beaten by the police and military forces of repressive regimes; and striking white European workers are being clobbered by their own policemen. Commenting on the events in the film, the white fellow appears to be slightly sexually aroused by the intense energy of the clashes. The black guy, somewhat disengaged or perhaps even jaded, appears not to feel any direct connection to the struggles on the screen. In the next scene, the same black character is seated at his desk in a posh office. He has a look and demeanor indicating that he is, as he claims, a professional Negro on his way "to the top." The white fellow is now seen sharing a joint with a counterculture white woman. His comments repeatedly reinforce his attraction to the energy on the screen. Quite excited by the scenes of white police clubbing black and white demonstrators, the white fellow refers to them as a choreographed dance.

Several scenes later, we are situated in Rev. Chaney's house or church. He is obviously a southern black minister living in a town gripped by Civil Rights movement activities. He is praying to God and asking why it is that heathens run the world. A younger man, the minister's son (played by the same actor who was the "bourgeois Negro"), questions his dad's belief in God's justice. Opposed to metaphysical invocations of God, the son advocates a materialist understanding of social change.

A white male figure (played by the same actor that previously played the hippie) enters and volunteers to help Rev. Chaney and the other blacks in their struggle. He claims that he was drawn to the struggle because it gives vitality and purpose to his life. Accompanying him is another white fellow. Both the white men decide to accompany Rev. Chaney's son to a local civil rights meeting where political strategies will be discussed. While riding in a car to the meeting, the three young men are intercepted by the Klansmen and brutally murdered. The final scene of the act shows Rev. Chaney and other church activists at the riverside where the mutilated bodies of the three young men have been found.

The second act begins with our overhearing a conversation between a white executive of Man River Textile Mills (supposedly Dan River Mills), his wealthy lawyer friend, and two local, economically marginal, white laborers. The laborers have been invited to the rich lawyer's house. It immediately becomes evident that the white laborers have never been to the lawyer's house before, even though they have known him for a very long time. The executive and his lawyer have invited the two poor men to the house in hopes of convincing them that whites need to band together against the struggle for black civil rights. The poor white men have always worked hard in cotton fields overseeing blacks picking cotton. The business executive and his lawyer friend try to convince the white workers that all whites share the same pre-dicament and thus have a similar interests in repressing the blacks. Although the impoverished white workers are impressed by the grandeur of the lawyer's house, it makes them suspicious of the men's claims. If they were really in the same boat, how is it that the lawyer lives "high on the hill" while they have remained poor? One of the poor whites points out that it is highly unlikely he'll ever live in a big house, since the lawyer inherited both it and a great deal of money. Reese, one of the poor whites states, "You got all this from your father before ye, and him from his father. You all had a thousand niggers humpin their ass off for all this, huh." The wealthy lawyer responds, "What the hell are niggers for . . . or fathers either for that matter?" The poor men are not convinced.

> My father was there with you. Stride for stride under the same damn hot sun. In fact, we run the niggers for you. We held the bastards down so they'd work steada running off or murderin you. Made em bring that goddamn cotton up out of the ground, and strip the branches bare. And all this time we ain't said doolysqat to each other, yet we been knowin each other a whole lifetime. Strange world ain't it?[3]

The wealthy white men are relentless in their attempts to convince the poor whites that giving civil rights to "niggers" would prevent poor whites from getting to the top. Even the poor white men cannot tolerate the idea of sending white girls to school with black boys. The discussion is not resolved, but it seems likely that the cultural appeal of white supremacy to the white workers will win over their resentment of intraracial class exploitation.

Next is a very short depiction of a ceremony celebrating the opening of school for black youth during Reconstruction. We hear celebratory words of the extension of the franchise to blacks and poor whites as well as commemorations of the importance of free public schools and social legislation. Reconstruction is depicted as a progressive moment in American history.

In scene 3 of act 2, we revisit the Man River Textile Mills, except that this time, it is almost a century earlier, during the latter part of Reconstruction. Poor whites are talking with a former white landowner who is trying to convince them that Reconstruction is bad for all whites. One of the poor whites comments about the quality of his life as a poor white man during the pre-Reconstruction years. "We couldn't vote before either. . . . Didn't have no school either till them niggers got to rootin around like they was somebody. Funny how much we seem to be in the same boat. Yet we ain't . . . I guess not really."[4] Hearing about life for poor whites in the antebellum South, the white former landowner is enraged that any poor white could consider himself as sharing interests with "niggers." He accuses the poor white man of being a "nigger lover" and screams that the niggers and northerners were responsible for the impoverishment of poor whites. The two men debate their previous fortunes under the old order. The former landowner browbeats them into submission with images of "niggers" strutting around as the master of white folks. As a strategy for changing this insulting new order, he silently displays a Klan hood.

Next we see three well-dressed white men discussing the economic viability of returning the South to white racist domination. The northern banker is not concerned about the plight of blacks; his sole desire is for the southern white elite to establish a social order conducive to profitable investments. In this new partnership, the white southern aristocrats have agreed to rule the South in accordance with the economic interests of white northern capitalists. The final scene shows a discussion among several black southerners when they find out about the Hayes-Tilden Compromise of 1876. This compromise ended the northern occupation of the South and also ended Reconstruction and set the stage for the reemergence of white supremacist rule in the South.

The blacks recognize that their interests have been betrayed in the compromise but vow to continue to fight.

The entire play consists of similar dramatic reconstructions of historical events in which racism is used either to divide the common interests of whites and blacks or to resolve them by some kind of unifying, transracial, class appeal. In several scenes, Baraka depicts Bacon's rebellion, in which black slaves and white bond servants banded together against Virginia's colonial elite. He also charts the divide-and-conquer response by the colonial elite to the rebellion in which slavery and bond servitude become restricted to blacks only. Other scenes depict the planning of the slave revolts of Denmark Vessey, Nat Turner, and Gabriel and their betrayal by slave informers. In the stage directions, Baraka suggests that the intermission be used to discuss the events that have been depicted. An announcer should come out from behind the curtain and ask two questions: "What is the future of the United States?" and "What is the main thing we have learned so far?" Baraka instructs that "at least one plant in the audience must give correct line":[5]

> The future of America is in the hands of the people. But it's more and more clear that the only change will come from violent revolution. To end Capitalism and build Socialism. That's clear. One thing we keep seeing is that it will take all the people together to make any real change, any revolutionary change in this system. Also we keep seeing how the negative ruling-class forces were always very clearly aware that they had to keep working-class people divided along national and racial lines.[6]

Baraka's distrust of the discussion that might be generated by his play led him to orchestrate a phony dialogue, as if all that mattered was what the audience heard. Nothing better illustrates Baraka's disrespect of the mental faculties of the "average American" than his script directions calling for a plant to offer the "correct line." Once again, in his overvaluing the political importance of rhetoric, Baraka apparently believed that radical ideas, clearly articulated, would persuade those who hear them.

Similar scenes follow the intermission. First we see a member of the American Communist Party call for black self-determination in the Black Belt South. Next we hear him reverse that position in favor of closing ranks with President Franklin Roosevelt and the AFL-CIO. Another scene shows Robert Williams's advocacy of armed reprisals against Klan violence. Later we see Roy Wilkins receiving a report of Williams's actions and deciding to suspend him. Another scene is a collage of Martin Luther King Jr. delivering his "I Have a Dream" speech followed shortly by a depiction of the bombing murder of the four black girls in a Birmingham church. In the aftermath of their murder, Malcolm X appears as a denouncer of the "white devil" and a vociferous critic of the false benefits of civil rights legislation. Malcolm's assassination is depicted in juxtaposition with a robotic-like Elijah Muhammad who seems to be incapable of muttering anything other than "the white man is the devil."[7] Other scenes reveal the police murder of Fred Hampton and the advocacy of Black Power by Stokely Carmichael and H. Rap Brown.

The play's final scenes are extensive dialogues between contemporary white and black workers who are trying to determine the ways that racial differences have been used historically to divide them and keep them from struggling together for their common class interests. These scenes are not grounded in historical events but are fictional creations. In all likelihood, Baraka may have viewed these scenes as the most important in the play, for they convey his proposed solution, which is socialist revolution. These scenes are uniformly weak, however, perhaps the weakest in the entire play, as Baraka uses these interracial dialogues to lecture his audience. One character recites the differences between use value and exchange value. Another explains the Marxist interpretation of exploitation in the capitalist production process. Still another offers a recitation of Mao's thought. As do many of Baraka's Marxist essays, the play ends with the characters repeatedly chanting "Forward to the Party! Long Live Socialist Revolution."

The Motion of History is probably Baraka's most successful Marxist play written before 1980. His use of historical events to dramatize the intersections of race and class are sometimes engaging. Perhaps the best vignettes are those dealing with Bacon's rebellion and the end of Reconstruction. But even when he successfully captures historical moments, Baraka's Marxist-Leninism more often than not overwhelms the dramatic form. The play fails miserably when Baraka addresses contemporary race and class politics, as he does in the latter scenes. In those scenes, Baraka advocates a crude scientific Marxism, and character development is nonexistent. Instead, characters are proxies for the articulation of various bits and pieces of a Marxist theory. The plot lines are flimsy, underdeveloped, and far too predictable.

From a Marxist vantage point, the play suffers because it has no understanding of the aesthetic uses of dramatic form. Form is sacrificed for rhetorical dogma. Baraka's didacticism undermines the dialectal tensions in his drama, for it leads to a linear and predictable narrative. Nonetheless, the historical scenes in *The Motion of History* might have been informative and engaging to some people, although I suspect that significantly fewer were inspired by Baraka's attempt to be a political tactician.

S-1 (1975)

S-1[8] was first performed at the Afro-American Studio in New York City in July 1976, and it was directed by Baraka. The play's name is from an omnibus crime bill that was being debated by Congress at that time.

The play begins as Red and Lil, a married radical couple, are talking about the bankruptcy of American politics. Both are members of the Central Committee of the Revolutionary People's Union. Red answers a phone call from a comrade in Cleveland. The Cleveland organizer tells Red about the police murder of a sixteen-year-old girl who was shot in the back during an altercation between her mother and their landlord. Red is heard instructing the Cleveland operative to immediately mobilize a coalition to protest this murder. When discussing their own inability to form a coalition, Red and Lil mention the two main obstacles as being bourgeois nationalists and communist revisionists:

> RED: By now everybody should see the go-fer suit you get runnin
>   that devil jive, Rocky be laughin all the way to the oil well and
>   back to the bank, niggers and white folks fightin over who's the
>   devil, when the real devil is the capitalist beatin both they asses.[9]

Clearly, this is included as a critique of the Nation of Islam's ideological line. It also is a self-critique of Baraka's former allegiance to Manichaean racial categories and their correlated essentialisms.

Scene 2 shifts to the chambers of the Supreme Court, in which the justices are debating the merits of S-1. One conservative justice claims that the bill should be passed because it would discourage anarchy. Carter Dougs (supposedly William Douglas), the most radical of the justices, views the bill as a move toward fascism because it authorizes the imprisonment of communists and anarchists without their being charged. The Negro justice, Thurman Marsh (supposedly Thurgood Marshall) is opposed to the bill but not as adamantly as Justice Dougs is. Dougs announces that if the Court declares the bill to be constitutional, he will be forced to speak directly to the American people about its dangers. When he solicits Justice Marsh to join him in this endeavor, Marsh demurs. Justice Dougs observes that the law in this nation has always served the interests of the rich, including himself. Shaken by the horror of the bill, Dougs suffers a stroke.

Next we go inside the Senate office building where a capitalist is talking with two U.S. senators, one liberal and one conservative. The conservative senator is celebrating Justice Dougs's stroke. The capitalist reminds the conservative senator that the presence of the liberal justice is important, for he makes people believe that there is balance on the Court. Even the liberal Senator Bay (probably Edward Kennedy of Massachusetts) argues for the necessity of maintaining a "semblance of balance" on the court; otherwise middle-class Americans might get upset. The conservative does not care about the appearance of democracy; he believes in capitalist oligarchy. The liberal believes that the rich should rule but that their rule must be hidden from the masses.

The following scene shows striking bus drivers and communist organizers confronting management and the police. This is followed by a short vignette of a judge in seventeenth-century England sentencing poor English folk to the colony of Georgia where they must work to pay off their debts. In another brief scene, we see an undercover federal agent notifying local police authorities about his intention to infiltrate radical political activists. We then move to a meeting of a local unit of the Revolutionary People's Union. Red and Lil deliver speeches explaining why Marxist-Leninism-Mao Zedong thought is the only viable path to emancipation. The next scene occurs on the floor of the House of Representatives where a liberal representative is condemning S-1 as fascist legislation, and a conservative legislator is ridiculing the liberal's claims. A black legislator opposes the bill and attacks the character of the racist conservative legislator from Mississippi. The conservative legislator responds by calling the black congressman a phony black militant. Baraka uses his speech to attack his old adversary, Congressman William Clay from Missouri. The conservative legislator announces:

And you, sir, Representative from Missouri, you have a reputation among certain of the people in this body and in Washington as a militant, a man of the people, but that, sir, I submit, is a joke. The black militants say you are a sellout, that you are to, quote them, "A rip-off specialist." They say you are part of this system you so scathingly denounce, that you represent the narrow interests of the black middle class and upper class.[10]

Following the passage of the crime bill, we are taken to a rally at which Red delivers another forceful speech in which he calls for the violent destruction of the capitalist state. Using scientific Marxism, he predicts that the United States will soon be at war with the other imperialist superpower, the Soviet Union, for the imperialist intentions of both nations have placed them on a collision course. The undercover policeman is also at the rally, posing as a reporter from a local newspaper. Red is not fooled and convinces an honest but naive reporter from a local radio station that the other so-called reporter is really a police informant. Although the federal authorities are monitoring the demonstration, they do not intervene then but wait until later to arrest Lil and Red at home. Other radicals are seen being arrested in their homes and at public places. After their arrest we hear a news bulletin announcing that NATO forces are fighting with Soviet troops. A courtroom scene follows in which Lil and Red are charged with various offenses, both real and trumped up.. Red is even charged with treason. Despite obvious violations of the couple's constitutional rights, the presiding judge upholds the prosecutor's arguments. The courtroom scene conveys a witch-hunt atmosphere, which is now legal, given the passage of S-1. President Gerald Ford delivers a speech to the nation explaining the war. The honest radio reporter tapes a scientific Marxist commentary by the recently released Lil, which accurately predicted and explained this conflict between the imperialist superpowers. To the surprise of the radio station's owners, the reporter plays Lil's comments on his news show. Red, in jail, hears Lil's recorded commentary and is pleased. The play ends with people filing by unsuspecting police and entering a church where they will hold a party congress. The anthem "America" is heard.

Baraka's play may have struck a chord at the time the S-1 crime bill was being debated. As proposed, the S-1 crime bill terrified civil libertarians and authentic democrats, for it would eliminated numerous civilian legal protections against the police and state authorities. The bill was cosponsored by none other than the liberal Senator Ted Kennedy. Although not all of the proposed bill became law, parts of it passed that did give more authority to the police. I wonder, though, how those audiences reacted who were not familiar with the proposed legislation. To those familiar with the bill, Baraka's inability to take into account dramatically that the S-1 bill was never passed as proposed may have revealed his inability to address the nuances of oppression under the American capitalist order.

Baraka probably did not convince his audiences that the United States was either fascist or on the verge of becoming a fascist state. Indeed, it is not even clear why he brought up fascism. Evidently, he believed that members of his audience could not see themselves as economically exploited or politically manipulated. But instead of condemning the status quo of monopoly capitalism, Baraka invents a far worse fictitious picture of American fascism and then tries to argue that the only viable opposition to that fictitious moment of fascism is communist revolution. In his bid to create an extremely repressive America, he sacrifices a realistic portrayal of contemporary American society. The proposed bill, S-1, was not sufficient proof for the existence of American fascism. In the real world of American politics, many of the worst aspects of the proposed legislation were defeated or discarded. Worse, Baraka writes as if the only true opponents to fascism were revolutionary communists. He ignores liberals and civil libertarians, even though it was the liberal Supreme Court Justice Dougs who first opposed the bill.

Baraka's need to condemn both the Soviet Union and the United States leads to his creation of a war between the superpowers. At no point in the play, however, is it made clear why the two superpowers were fighting. How did this supposedly inevitable military conflict enhance the play's political message? What was scientific about its prediction?

Because the dialogue is either too forced or too plastic, the play is a highly uneven attempt to dramatize the radicals' opposition to the federal government's increasing repression. In the era of Reagan-Bush and Newt Gingrich, Clarence Thomas, Edward Meese, Antonio Scalia, and William Rehnquist, the play appears quite timely. Liberties have become increasingly restrictive. Nonetheless, one wonders whether Baraka would have been more persuasive had he written a polemical essay instead, for his didacticism overwhelms his ability to create a drama that is both intellectually stimulating and artistically engaging.

WHAT WAS THE RELATIONSHIP OF THE LONE RANGER TO THE MEANS OF PRODUCTION (1978)

The play *What Was the Relationship of the Lone Ranger to the Means of Production*[11] takes place on the shop floor of a large automobile manufacturer, Colonel Motors. The time is now. Workers are busy on the production line when they see a masked man enter the factory and walk toward them. One of the workers laughingly refers to him as the "Lone Ranger." The masked man begins to address the workers. A press agent for free-market capitalism, the masked man tells the workers that they have entered a new "poststrike, post-revolutionary" era. In appreciation of all who have helped bring about this new age, this spokesman for capitalism offers thanks to "Marcuse, CPUSA, Jesse Jackson, NAACP, all who urge righteous moderation!"[12] He informs the workers that they are lucky to be employed at Colonel Motors. The workers still do not know who he is. Humorously, they ask where Tonto is. In a serious tone, he replies that Tonto is dead, a victim of hostile Indians of the Geronimo and Crazy Horse variety. The masked man asks the workers to call him MM. Later, he tells them that his real name is Money Master and admits to being the collective spirit of all owners and capitalists.

Two of the workers, Donna and Reg, are quite politically aware of their exploitation as workers, whereas Clark, another worker, is completely naive and ignorant. Donna reads MM's appearance as just another capitalist attempt to allay the workers' discontent by offering them escapist films of monsters and spectacles of sex, nostalgia, and metaphysics. MM agrees with Donna and tells her and the others that if they looked closely, they would see MM in all the scenes of Hollywood movies, including the furniture. This is Baraka's use of a standard economics symbol for capital. In simple economic analyses, M-M means money that is used to make money, which is otherwise known as capital. MM, Money Master, is the symbol of capital.

MM claims responsibility for the workers' livelihood as if their employment were a gift from him and his kind. He tells the workers that strikes don't really accomplish anything. In fact, he is there to give them a raise—a raise in spirit. The workers protest that they want a raise in salary. MM informs them that money isn't everything. Instead, they should take pride in their accomplishments as workers. They have a stake in the system. Moreover, he even denies that there are any socioeconomic classes in the United States. When Donna inspects his hands, it becomes clear to all that he has never done any manual labor.

Tuffy, the compromised union representative, appears. An accomplice of MM, he urges the workers to listen to the masked man. He is pushing a wheelbarrow holding the dead body of one of the workers. The workers are stunned and perplexed by the dead body. Tuffy tells them that they are lucky to be Americans and lucky to have jobs. He is crude and uses overtly racist and sexist language. MM calls Tuffy aside and tells him that such language should be used only in private meetings with him. Tuffy tells the workers that they should love MM because MM loves them. Like MM, Tuffy announces that the day of strikes is over. Workers should be concerned only with working.

MM interrupts, proclaiming that without strikes, a new era of peace has emerged. The only thing the workers need to do is sign the "New Agrees," a new contract between laborers and management. Reg and Donna laugh when they hear the stipulations in the New Agrees: MM is always right; women must become redomesticated; there can be no complaining, bitching, or striking; coloreds, Mexicans, and Puerto Ricans will get slightly less money than the cheap wages paid to the white workers; fascism needs to be "momentarily" implemented; and commies are poison. MM tells them that they either must sign the New Agrees or join the unemployment line. Cops enter the factory. MM reminds the workers that there are more than enough unemployed workers to take their places. Jobs are scarce and most of their former coworkers have already been fired and sent home. They can work or die impoverished. Their wages will be reduced. Hearing this, Clark, the naive worker, finally realizes that MM is not his ally but his enemy. More cops enter the factory.

Donna and Reg walk over to the dead body in the wheelbarrow and discover that it is Felipe, a fellow worker and union organizer. He has been shot in the head. The masked man suddenly becomes the Lone Ranger, and the dead body of Felipe momentarily comes to life as Tonto. Tonto tells the Lone Ranger that his days as the ranger's flunky are over. He predicts the death and destruction of the Lone Ranger and all that he represents, whereupon MM, now the Lone Ranger, shoots and kills Tonto. The surreal scene ends and the dialogue and characters return to "reality." MM threatens to kill all of them in the same way that he killed Tonto. The police surround the workers, but in the background we hear the voices of the recently fired workers who have gathered outside the factory doors. The workers, many of whom are armed with clubs, pistols, and rifles, crash through the factory door while chanting "Strike, Strike, Strike." They rescue the three captive workers. Realizing their vulnerability, MM, Tuffy, and their police flunkies retreat. The play ends with the workers chanting in unison, "Strike, Strike, Strike."

Even though the dialogue is not subtle, the play has less of a sledgehammer quality than the scenes depicting the contemporary workers in *The Motion of History*. It is not clear what the interplay between The Lone Ranger and Tonto has to do with the play's overall theme. Although Tonto is depicted as racially obsequious to the white supremacist Lone Ranger, the interplay between the two has little to do with capitalist-worker relations except perhaps to insinuate that workers who passively accept the dictates of capitalism are metaphorical Tontos.

The play might have been more provocative had Baraka presented a more comprehensive discussion of the plight of American workers in regard to the globalization of the workforce and the international fluidity of capitalism. Instead of confronting the new relationship between labor and capital, however, Baraka romanticizes the efficacy of the strike as if we were living in the 1930s.

It is difficult to view Baraka's Marxist drama as other than dismal. These plays are basically propaganda. As was the case in his Black-Arts-era agitprop plays, Baraka seems not to believe that his audience can understand a more thoughtful and aesthetically rich drama. Once again, his strict didacticism reveals his distance from them. Baraka is less interested in stimulating their minds than in telling them how to view the world and act politically. As was the case during his Kawaida days, Baraka wants followers, not independent thinkers. Instead of stimulation, his dramas offer instructions.[13]

Concerning Baraka's Marxist drama, critic C. W. E. Bigsby wrote:

> Baraka's is a sensibility that apparently craves submission to ideology. Confronted with the ambiguities that are the birthright of the black American

and the natural inheritance of the writer who wishes to transform the world which he inhabits by reinventing it, he has always been tempted to resolve this by opting for a single interpretation, by being drawn to one pole of experiences. It remains true, however, that his most impressive and honest work remains that which he wrote when poised in hesitation, when he could still acknowledge not merely the strength but also the legitimacy of the competing demands on his mind and imagination . . . he has laid aside a talent which might have made him one of America's leading writers and which had already established his command of theatrical form and idiom . . . he has replaced metaphor with statement, ambiguity with simple assertion, character with role and a painful attempt to sift an authentic language from inherited forms with mere rhetoric and party slogans.[14]

MARXIST POET

In 1975, Baraka published a small book of poetry, *Hard Facts*. The introduction is a short explanation of Baraka's Marxist aesthetics, including many of the ideas that he explores in the essays on art contained in *Daggers and Javelins*. He contends that the American academy valorizes middle-class poetry, which he defines somewhat tautologically as poetry that reflects not only middle-class life and interests but also "bourgeois social and production relations":

> The poetry, art or writing reveals the class stand, and attitude of the writer, reveals the audience to whom the writer and artist addresses themselves, it also reveals what work they have been active in and what studies they are involved in. There is no art that is above the views or needs or ideology of one particular class or another, though the rulers pretend that art is classless and beyond political definition. That is why we aim at an art that serves the great majority of people, the working masses of people. That is why we make an art that praises what helps the people and puts down mercilessly what oppresses or exploits them.[15]

The goal of the revolutionary poet is to write poems that educate and intensify the class consciousness of the working class. To do this, the revolutionary poet must develop a writing style that is accessible to the masses. Such a poet is the creator of a popular mass art. Writers who write for other writers and intellectuals are bourgeois. According to Baraka, any bourgeois writer who writes with and for the working class can attain a working-class artistic identity. Revolutionary writers recognize that "the people" do not need ambiguity or pessimism but "odes of strength, attack pieces, bomb, machine gun and rocket poems. Poems describing reality and methods of changing it."[16] Baraka regurgitates images from his poem "Black Art" his Black Arts manifesto in which he calls for "poems that kill, assassin poems, poems that shoot guns."

Although Baraka's Marxist writing borrows extensively from his writings during the Black Arts / Black Power era, he uses his new Marxist framework to assess his black nationalist activities.

> Earlier our poems came from an enraptured patriotism that screamed against whites as the eternal enemies of Black People. . . . The same subjective mystification led to mysticism, metaphysics, spookism, & c., rather than dealing with reality, as well as an ultimately reactionary nationalism that served no interests but our newly emerging Black bureaucratic elite and petit bourgeois, so that they would have control over their Black market.[17]

The poem "Revolutionary Love" is a tribute to the idealized character of his wife, Amina. Given the absolute centrality of his wife to his political involvements since returning to Newark, Baraka repeatedly praised her as his foremost political companion and life partner.

> *Black Revolutionary Woman*
> *In love w/ Revolution*
> *Your man better be a revolution*
> *for you to love him . . .*
>
> *. . . Black Revolutionary Woman*
> *were you my woman, and even in the pit*
> *of raging struggle, we need what we love,*
> *we need what we desire to create, were you*
> *my woman, I'd call you companion, comrade,*
> *sister, black lady, Afrikan faith, I'd call you*
> *house, black Revolutionary woman*
> *I'd call you wife*[18]

Even though it is included in *Hard Facts*, this testimony to Amina Baraka could have been written or published during the Black Arts era, as it does not contain the trademarks of Baraka's Marxist poetry. There is neither mention nor hint of communism or scientific Marxism.

In the poem "When We'll Worship Jesus," Baraka maintains his scathing denunciation of black religious beliefs, particularly Christianity, that had been present in his work during his Black Arts days. But now, as a Marxist, Baraka does not urge an alternative black cosmology. Furthermore, he is less concerned about the complicity of Christianity in white domination, even though he condemns that as well. Mainly he emphasizes that Jesus should be understood as a repository of hopes and energies that could better be directed to engaging the real, material world. Only by acknowledging the existing world can believers in Jesus realize what they pray for. Praying to Jesus is a waste of time.[19]

> We'll worship Jesus
> When jesus do
> Somethin
> When jesus blow up
> the white house . . .
>
> . . . we'll worship Jesus when
> he get bad enough to at least scare
> somebody—cops not afraid
> of jesus
> pushers not afraid
> of jesus, capitalist racist
> imperialist not afraid
> of jesus shit they making money
> off jesus[20]

In his post–black nationalist era, Baraka now feels free to criticize Islam, something he never would have done five years earlier. Allah, too, is a metaphysical fantasy.

> jesus need to be busted
> jesus need to be thrown down and whipped
> till something better happen
> jesus aint did nothin for us
> but kept us turned toward the
> sky (him and his boy allah
> too, need to be checkd
> out!)[21]

Given the black community's pervasive belief in Jesus (or respect for those who hold such beliefs), it is hard to imagine Baraka reading this before a rank-and-file black audience unless, of course, he wants to shock them.

Many of the poems in *Hard Facts* are personal attacks on prominent black entertainers and political figures. But instead of accusing them of being white-like, as Baraka had once done, he now depicts them as flunkies of the capitalist order. One poem, "At the National Black Assembly," is an assault on Hannah Atkins, the Oklahoma state official who resigned her position in the National Black Convention because of the demagogic behavior of the Marxist Baraka. Baraka, of course, feels the need to humiliate her. Baraka disparages Newark Mayor Kenneth Gibson in several of the poems. Another poem criticizes Congressman William Clay, Baraka's antagonist in the Gary convention. *Niggy the Ho*, the most vicious poem in the entire collection, was reserved for the poet Nikki Giovanni. Evidently, Baraka was enraged by her growing political moderation. He writes,

> . . . *a mediocre flunky, now she say she really dig President Ford.*
> *Yahoo, what else is new, . . . Hi Ho, her butt for sale everywhere, Hi Ho, ugly*
> *American, sell out bitch scribbler, athletic supporter of imperialism*
> *all the perfume in the world cant cover the farts*
> *of the maggots*
> *in your soul.*[22]

After reading *Hard Facts*, one can easily understand why Baraka's early Marxist poetry has often been dismissed or ignored. The poetry is embarrassing.

Besides the viciousness and artlessness of the poetry in *Hard Facts*, Baraka seems to have run out of ideas when he composed the collection. The themes are so repetitive and insipid that one could easily read the collection as a parody of political poetry. Or perhaps he thought that scandalous and offensive statements would be sufficiently shocking to give artistic life to this shoddy work. Baraka's next venture into Marxist poetry, *Poetry for the Advanced*, was equally banal.[23]

Concerning Baraka's Marxist poetry, Werner Sollors wrote,

> Baraka's poems have not regained the strength of his early work. Although Baraka has renounced the reactionary anti-Semitic and antifeminist excesses of the nationalist poems, his postnationalist, Maoist work admits only occasional flashes of poetry, which are often overshadowed by hammering political slogans. What Baraka perceives as a political strength in his new

commitment may well be a crucial poetic weakness; he knows exactly what he wants to say at all times.[24]

CONCLUSION

Baraka is not the typical vulgar Marxist, for his Marxism does not seem to be informed by any desire to engage Marx's writing. Rather, it is a Marxism that respects and draws on only those Marxists who were, except for Stalin, successful political revolutionaries—Lenin, Mao, and Cabral. Baraka mistakenly believes that he is appealing to a tradition of Marxism that is vehemently anti-intellectual and interested solely in seizing power for the proletariat.[25] But even within the confines of American Marxism and its traditionally antitheoretical bent, Baraka's "Marxism" is pedestrian. He has appropriated Marx—and, worse, Lenin, Stalin, and Mao—in much the way that he appropriated Karenga, by memorizing key phrases and reciting them where applicable. Baraka, the secular religious fanatic, left the confines of black nationalism for the security of a more omnipotent God, "scientific socialism."[26] In a 1978 interview, Baraka made the following "religious" statement concerning his Marxism:

> Now, as I came more and more in contract with dialectical materialism and Marxism, I began to understand very clearly that change is constant and also that reality moves from a lower to a higher level—that ultimately the motion of society and humanity is always onward and upward, from ignorance to knowledge, from the superficial to the in-depth and the detailed. Once you understand clearly that this is the nature of reality you will see that your own development has to be in that direction.[27]

It is this quasi-religious element in his appropriation of Marx that makes Baraka incapable of functioning creatively in the Marxist intellectual tradition—of subverting while reinforcing.

Baraka's move to Marxism is fundamentally different from that of Richard Wright during the 1930s. Wright became a communist primarily because of the intellectual community in the American Communist Party. Wright, a black novice writer from Mississippi with less than a high school education, found that he could apprentice as a writer in the Communist Party. Membership in the party gave him access to the guidance of many notable American literary figures. The party functioned for Wright in much the same way that Beat bohemia functioned for Baraka, as a marginality facilitator. Baraka's conversion to Marxism was not linked to any attempt to broaden his intellectual community. He has not been a participant in any significant leftist intellectual dialogue or community. Unlike Wright, Baraka views himself as a potential American Lenin or Mao, a dream reflected in his decision to establish his own vanguard party.[28]

Baraka's Marxist-influenced plays are as disappointing as the essays in *Daggers and Javelins*. They do not indicate that he has studied any masters of the Marxist dramatic form. Instead, he erroneously believes that he is and has long been a master of politically engaged drama. All that he needs to do with his Marxist plays is change the ideology. Unfortunately, the Marxist plays are often as disastrous as those abominable agitprop plays that he wrote during the height of the Black Arts movement.

Perhaps critic Lloyd W. Brown said it best:

> As a scientific socialist he is in the least imaginative phase of his life as a political writer. This relative lack of creativity is not really the fault of the ideology itself. It seems, more likely, to be the reflection of a certain intellectual flabbiness on Baraka's part. Not only in the forgettable poems of *Hard Facts* but also in the plays and essays of the later years, Baraka seems to find it increasingly difficult to go beyond the accepted clichés of political dogma. It has appeared progressively easier for him to offer hackneyed and literal statements in lieu of artistic forms that are both imaginative and sociopolitically significant.[29]

What happens to a charismatic figure when he loses his charisma? In Baraka's case, the loss of his intellectual clarity—which was both the cause and effect of his charismatic authority in black nationalism—left him unprepared to confront a new historical situation. Those outside the nexus between the charismatic Baraka and his nationalist followers have long viewed his political beliefs as a mixture of sense and nonsense. Yet the scope of the black nationalist appeal and the legitimacy of some of the issues it raised gave the movement a degree of rationality that in turn was granted to the movement's leaders. But because Marxist-Leninist politicizations do not currently have a popular presence or legitimacy that demands explanation and discussion, the thoughts of Baraka, America's would-be Lenin, are viewed without the cover of rationality invested in a social movement. In reading the now-naked Baraka, one might easily conclude that he is writing to and for himself. This conclusion may not be absurd as it sounds, for Baraka could be less interested in influencing a reading audience than in proclaiming a new political identity. Such an interpretation would be consistent with Baraka's repeated efforts to purchase a new identity by projecting a new image. Reification has run amok, once in black face, now in red.

Baraka's shift from the black nationalism of *Raise Race Rays Raze* and *Madheart* to the "Marxism" of *Daggers and Javelins* and *The Motion of History* was not accompanied by greater political, analytical, or aesthetic sophistication. The fundamental shortcomings in Baraka's "Marxism" are its profound anti-intellectual and antitheoretical currents, problems that were present as well in *Raise Race Rays Raze*. The anti-intellectualism of Baraka's "Marxism" allows him to dodge explanations of why the thought of Marx, Lenin, Stalin, and Mao hold the keys to black emancipation. Simply put, he never clarified why black nationalism was no longer the correct strategy, except for asserting that he had been duped by black politicians who used nationalistic appeals in order to win black votes and then pursued policies that were not in the interest of the broader black community. One could rebut my criticism by pointing out that Baraka had never convincingly argued why blacks ever should have adopted black cultural nationalism. Why, then, should I expect him now to tell us why we should now reject it?

In calling for the rise of the working class, Baraka neglects to acknowledge the changes that have occurred in the American capitalist economy (consumerism, mass culture, globilization) that make it far more difficult to define the working class and equally difficult to isolate and politicize a non-hybrid, working-class consciousness. Why does he overlook the long-standing racial parochialism of the white American working class? Likewise, he ignores the historical collusion of the American working class in U.S. neocolonialism toward the Third World. He also does not address the intense American jingoism of large numbers of black Americans. In addition, Baraka overlooks the large percentage of black Americans who would be labeled members of the lumpenproletariat, which, according to his strict application of "scientific socialism," might ultimately necessitate their destruction.

On what grounds does Baraka assume that Stalin could inspire a revolutionary movement in the United States? Stalin, the fanatical tyrant, killed and imprisoned millions of people. When asked during a 1977 interview, "Is rightist rule any worse than Stalinism?" Baraka responded, "Yes, absolutely. Stalin upheld the dictatorship of the proletariat. Stalin upheld the dictatorship of the *majority*. Capitalism was restored in the Soviet Union in the late '50s, so obviously Stalin's purges didn't reach far enough."[30] Nearly two decades after Khrushchev's revelations, Baraka's willingness to consider Stalin an ally of working-class emancipation is dumbfounding. His claim that Stalin did not murder a sufficient number of people is despicable and morally vulgar. But dogmatic scientific socialists like Baraka do not believe in morality.

And what about China's increasing drift into monetary alliances with the Rockefellers of the world? These and many more questions are not addressed in Baraka's "Marxism."

Once again, Baraka has willingly diluted his artistic ambitions in order to serve the right side of history. It is sad to witness the decline of an artist of Baraka's talents. Once a creative dramatist, he is now content to place polemical essays into the mouths of his characters. A former artistic innovator, he is now trying to revitalize the dreaded aesthetic uniformities of socialist realism. Baraka's commitment to political art has undermined his creativity, but not because political art is intrinsically weak. The problem with Baraka's political art is Baraka. Whenever Baraka has imagined himself as politically engaged, it has always been as a self-anointed leader of the masses. In his case, the masses are always figments of his imagination, figments that are far more simplified, pacified, and dim-witted than the real living people. Baraka, the politically engaged artist, has always written for his "idea of the people," an idea that often had little relationship to actual Afro-Americans (or whites) of any economic class.

The results have been travesties. In the name of black nationalism and later Marxist-Leninist-Mao Zedong thought, Baraka has created intellectual styles that allow him to appear "at home" at precisely those moments that he is most estranged. No matter how he dresses, walks, or speaks, the clue to Baraka's alienation from poor blacks and the working class is his inability to imagine them as intelligent as himself.

Conclusion

ALTHOUGH THIS STUDY is limited to Baraka's political beliefs and actions through the middle 1980s, I do not want to imply that his more recent work is unworthy of critique. But by ending my study with the mid-1980s, I have been able to concentrate on Baraka's creative life and political involvements during the height of his prominence.

During the past fifteen years, Baraka has continued to write and publish prolifically. He has published several new collections of older and more recent work, a fact that testifies to his continued significance as a literary artist, despite his decline in political significance. A collection of essays on music, published in 1987 and entitled *The Music: Reflections on Jazz and Blues*, is reminiscent of his earlier collection, *Black Music*. The 1991 publication of *The Leroy Jones / Amiri Baraka Reader*, edited by William J. Harris, author of a previous study of Baraka's poetry, is the most comprehensive single collection of Baraka's work yet published. *Transbluesency*, a collection of Baraka's selected old and newer poetry was published in 1995.[1] In addition to collections of older and newer pieces, Baraka has continued to publish new work, including two collections of poetry: *Why's, Wise, Y's* and *Funk* Lore. *Eulogies*, the most unusual and captivating of Baraka's recent publications, is a collection of his written and spoken tributes to various individuals. Published in 1996, the collection contains several eulogies for political figures that he admired (e.g., Malcolm X, Amilcar Cabral, and William Kunstler) as well as testimonies to writers (Toni Cade Bambara, Larry Neal, Bob Kaufman, James Baldwin) and jazz musicians (John Coltrane, Miles Davis, Dizzy Gillespie, Don Pullen, Sun Ra). The eulogy that he delivered at James Baldwin's funeral service was an eloquent testimony to Baraka's growing appreciation of Baldwin as a major emancipatory voice in the black freedom struggle. Many of the most engaging eulogies honor black "common folk," including former political confreres and civic-minded Newark residents. The most touching was delivered at the funeral for his murdered sister, Kimako Baraka, the former "Lanie Poo."[2]

Baraka has continued to write occasional essays for popular journals. His profile of Miles Davis, which appeared in the *New York Times Sunday Magazine*, was a uniquely "Barakian" tribute to this idiosyncratic artist. On another occasion, Baraka fought a polemical duel with the conservative essayist Shelby Steele. Baraka was one of the featured narrators and writers of a four-part 1995 PBS documentary on the life of W. E. B. Du Bois, and he was also the subject of a filmed profile by St. Clair Bourne.[3] His journalistic pieces regularly appear in the newspapers and journals published by his sectarian Marxist organization.

Baraka has long believed in the virtue of the political act and statement. Political acts need not be grounded in prior political understanding but are thought to lead to inevitable understanding. The unity of theory and praxis for the Barakas of this world has always meant the unity of tactics and praxis. Philip Rieff commented, in *Fellow Teachers*, that "at cross purposes with any revolution, theory carries a repressive implication. Theory admits no blind obediences."[4] If Rieff is correct, then Baraka is temperamentally incapable of being a serious theorist.

But is he a revolutionary? Baraka can be said to be a revolutionary only in the sense that anyone who considers himself revolutionary and is somehow committed to sweeping political and economic change is a revolutionary. He cannot be said to be a revolutionary if it includes being a part of a mass political movement with both the desire and a potentially viable strategy for challenging the authority of the existing social order. Even at the height of his involvement with black cultural nationalism, Baraka could not accurately be viewed as having been a member of a movement that threatened the power of the state. A revolutionary must possess a normative vision, one that appears simultaneously utopian and realizable given the constraints of the status quo. Such a dialectical vision has never been present in Baraka's thought.

Once Baraka decided to take a full-time job as a professor of Africana Studies at the State University of New York at Stony Brook, his continuing claims to be a "revolutionary" could be interpreted as the legitimation cries of someone who has made his "subsistence peace" with a recalcitrant status quo. His move into the academy signaled a degree of pessimism. Whereas his previous adherence to black nationalism called for imminent revolution, the "revolution" was no longer impending. Marxism thus gave Baraka a chance to maintain his optimism while recognizing that a revolution would not occur in the foreseeable future. Baraka's version of scientific Marxism objectifies existing oppression by placing its resolution in a strict linear teleology. In this way, he can continue to argue that the situation will change only when the historical conditions are right. In the meantime—that is, until the working class rises up, which it cannot do until a vanguard party is in place to lead it, which in turn cannot happen until "the conditions are right"—Baraka has decided that he might as well live.

Baraka retired from SUNY Stony Brook in 1988 and then accepted a temporary appointment at Rutgers University. Baraka had been considered for a joint appointment in English and Africana studies, but in early 1990, Rutgers's English department voted not to give him a permanent, tenured appointment. The Rutgers job would have been far closer to Newark and his family than the job at SUNY Stony Brook had been. It is not known publicly why Baraka was denied the position. But in characteristic fashion, Baraka condemned the English department. At a campus rally to protest his rejection, Baraka stated:

> The power of these Ivy League Goebbels can flaunt, dismiss, intimidate and defraud the popular will. We must unmask these powerful Klansmen. These enemies of academic freedom, people's democracy and Pan American culture must not be allowed to prevail. Their intellectual presence makes a stink across the campus like the corpses of rotting Nazis.

In response to Baraka's tirade, the department chairman, who was one of Baraka's supporters, replied, "Once you start labeling people Nazis and Klansmen, basically you're saying there can no longer be conversation or dialogue."[5]

In his autobiography, Baraka never admits to feeling pessimistic, perhaps because he has never admitted to being defeated. In his autobiography when he talks about his involvement with black cultural nationalism, he never concludes that he was on the losing side of history. Rather, Baraka views these earlier involvements as necessary learning experiences that led him to a more scientific understanding of revolution. Baraka's strict teleological views of historical change allow him to link his anti-Marxist nationalism to his anti-nationalist Marxism. The unifying, self-validating undercurrent that Baraka uses to legitimate his various political guises is that he was then, and is now, engaged in political struggle. Nationalism was but a moment's error in a continuum of political struggles. Simply put, he had been captured by the wrong ideology. He now has the correct one.

The movement of Baraka from black cultural nationalism to Marxism has impeded his access to a black victim status. Although Jones continues to chant and scream about class struggle in much the same way that he once threatened America with a race war, he now instills far less fear into the hearts of the accused and less excitement in the minds of other potential accusers.[6] The mass populace, black and white, is not as easily aroused by threats clothed in a rhetoric of class struggle as those clothed in the image of the black man as a sexual beast seeking racial retribution and revenge. The sexual beast image was a feared racial stereotype and a central icon of "American political demonology," whereas the collapse of the Soviet Union and the end of the cold war significantly weakened the national fear of Communism.[7]

White Americans often have been incapable of perceiving this nation as anything other than their self-governed entity. Because of the tremendous difficulties throughout American history of developing and sustaining class-oriented political articulations, most American left-wing activists and intellectuals would not be attracted to Baraka's "Johnny-come-lately," frivolous left-wing antics. At best, Baraka has a tiny following among those Americans drawn to Marxist-oriented politics. He probably has even fewer followers of a non-Marxist socialist bent. At the height of his Marxist influence, Baraka was the autocratic leader of a miniscule revolutionary party with no real base of support in a society with a large working class that had shown few proclivities toward revolution. But despite the ebbs and flows of his sectarian political involvements, Baraka remains absurdly fixated on acting like a political leader laying the groundwork for an American-style Bolshevik revolution.

But has Baraka successfully confronted his former imprisonment in the victim status? He is certainly not as firmly rooted in a race-based victim-status appeal as he was during the days when he draped himself in "blackness" and continually "screamed wolf" at white Americans. The success of his appeal then was superficially determined by the guilt and fear that he instilled in whites. Ultimately, the entire enterprise rested on the willingness of white America to grant a victim status to militant blacks. One cannot grasp the limitations of the Baraka-led black nationalist appeals of the 1960s and 1970s without recognizing that these projects rested on the ability and desire to project a militant black face to a supposedly timid white America and, in doing so, to convince whites and other blacks that black nationalists secretly possessed a serious political game plan and would act on it if not appeased. Image was everything. Behind all the "hate whitey" rhetoric, Baraka and his colleagues were modern-day black clients in search of white patrons.[8] Booker T. Washington would probably have been amazed at their ingenuity. Baraka's appropriation of the lingo of scientific socialism has steered him away from patron-client, victim-status appeals. He has abandoned much of the rhetoric concerning the moral superiority of the black victim and replaced it with rhetoric proclaiming the moral superiority of the working class. The working class does not occupy a victim status in America, however, even when it is imagined as the black working class.

Perhaps the principal reason for Baraka's willingness to relinquish a black victim-status appeal was that by the early 1970s, it was clear that the efficacy of the black militant appeal was declining. By 1974, the year when Baraka "changed his ideology" from black nationalism to scientific socialism, the second-term Nixon presidency had black militants fearing for their freedom, if not their lives.[9] Whites were no longer responding to black militant antics with fearful concessions. They had seen through the charade of so-called revolutionaries like Karenga and Baraka. By 1972, even the Imamu was compelled to admit that "a billion rhetorical bullets have killed too few enemies and built too few actual black institutions."[10]

Following the backlash of white conservative sentiment to the black urban riots of the late 1960s, white America in the early 1970s no longer felt as guilty about racial matters. The collective white guilt toward blacks had arisen only in response to the media coverage of white southern racist brutality and the black nonviolent response. As a consequence of rioting and urban crime, blacks, once perceived by many whites as victims of American racism, became increasingly seen as victimizers. As a result, blacks were cut from liberal white America's short-lived financial conduit for the black militants' fear-induced, victim-status benefits. The riots became a symbol of black political autonomy when in fact, blacks, even those advocating rioting, were far from autonomous creatures. The riots created an image of blacks as revolutionaries, which ultimately undermined the ability of militant blacks to maintain access to liberal white funding, the "sugar daddy" for their militancy.

The journey from the image of victim to the image of victimizer was complex and unpredictable. While the urban riots ultimately gave rise to the white American image of blacks as victimizers, there was an momentary interim status in which black urban rebelliousness was widely interpreted as an indication of the desperation of black victims. For a moment, H. Rap Brown and friends were perceived as strengthening the guilt-induced, black victim-status designation. Established black victim-status ideologues of the Martin Luther King Jr. and Ralph Abernathy variety tried to incorporate the riots into their reservoir of guilt-mediated, victim-status moral capital, and for a short while they succeeded, but ultimately King and Abernathy lost this ideological contest. The media had been captivated by the rhetoric of vitriolic black speakers such as Carmichael and the revolutionary imagery of the Black Panthers. Over time, Cleaver, Carmichael, H. Rap Brown, Bobby Seale, Huey Newton, Karenga, Baraka, and other militants were temporarily successful in undermining and replacing the Martin Luther King, guilt-induced, victim-status appeal. The militants momentarily generated a black victim status premised on fear. Fear of rebellious blacks, a long-standing current in white American sensibilities, soon gave rise to white support for black repression. Besides President Johnson's Vietnam War policies, the 1968 presidential election was a referendum on white responses to black militancy. On the one hand, the Democratic candidate, Vice-President Hubert Humphrey, still operated in a guilt-mediated, black victim-status syndrome. His opponents, Independent George Wallace and Republican Richard Nixon, viewed the victim status of blacks as either undeserved or anti-American.

Richard Nixon and Spiro Agnew campaigned against black claims to the victim status. Nixon had decided that his rejuvenated political future lay in reaching out to a white "silent majority" of law and order–minded white citizens. As president, Nixon did not completely dismantle welfare-state interventions in the black community, although he did undermine black moral claims to such intervention.[11] Lyndon Johnson, who, more than any other American president, had granted legitimacy to black claims to the victim status, probably went to his grave dumbfounded and angered at the apparent black rejection of his patronage.[12] More important, the defeat of Hubert Humphrey in 1968 brought to an end the federal funding of black reform and "revolutionary" activities. Nixon was not going to fund a privately run, black revolutionary theater/school in Harlem. He barely wanted to fund Harlem's public schools.

The lesson that Baraka and his black nationalist peers should have learned was to never feign ethnic autonomy before becoming self-sustaining. If the fictitious image is erroneously perceived as fact, the substantive benefits of the victim status will be withdrawn before the political benefits of being autonomous are obtained. This is easier said than done, for the forces behind the creation of the mass media's images of black militants lay far outside their control. While Carmichael, Rap Brown, and others may have relished the media attention and their national celebrity statuses as "revolutionaries," they were clearly unprepared for the media manipulation of their images. They had not developed what sociologist Alvin Gouldner called a "media-critical politics."[13]

Baraka's search for and creation of an absolute timeless truth in "Marxism" does not mean that he has ceased to be a radical intellectual. In a broadly defined sense, Baraka remains a radical intellectual precisely because he still has a normative vision of society that is neither hegemonic nor realizable in the existing political-economic parameters of the social order. However, radical does not necessarily mean progressive. Instead, it signifies an extreme distance from or difference with the status quo. Baraka was a radical intellectual during the period of his cultural nationalist allegiances *precisely because* he advocated a return to African-based feudalistic social formations. He was the "radical-as-reactionary," trapped in a race-based romantic nostalgia for a "past that never was." In his Marxist and cultural nationalist phases, Baraka failed to acquire a Gramscian critical consciousness. That is, he does not recognize "himself as the product of a historical process that has deposited its traces in him."[14]

How should we analyze this crude and simple-minded political thinker? Should he be excused on the grounds that he is, after all, only a poet? What makes him worthy of being listened to at this time?

These questions are difficult. The main reason for reading Baraka's political pronouncements at this stage in his life is to examine how a former serious and creative artist has intellectually deteriorated since attempting to become a political thinker and activist. One might well learn nothing more than the obvious, that minds that function well in one genre may function horribly in another. However we approach these questions, it is imperative that we not abandon our critical faculties in favor of descriptive commentary. The demise of Baraka as a creative writer can be partly attributed to those mainstream critics who totally ignored him while he wrote mundane polemics, propagandistic poetry, and agitprop dramas and to those nonmainstream white and black critics who treated everything he wrote as the "emperor's new clothes."

Since leaving the Village, Baraka has been aesthetically hurt by the absence of a critical intellectual community. This absence was often self-inflicted. During the period when he was a cultural nationalist and an advocate of the Black Aesthetic, Baraka was beyond criticism, for he became, in effect, the standard for himself. There was criticism of his work, but it was often easily dismissed as the mutterings of the reactionary. White critics could be rejected as racist. Black critics were insufficiently "black." Even today, Baraka continues to repudiate black critics of his work.[15]

In recent decades, as Baraka has become increasingly politically marginalized because of his advocacy of a dogmatic Marxism, his polemical and political writings have been ignored. As a "Marxist," he no longer commands a large audience of writers and is virtually ignored as a serious thinker. The effects of this isolation are evident. But to dismiss Baraka out of hand because his Marxism is vulgar is too easy. His politics are indeed simplistic, but this may be because his political involvements, unlike those of most ambitious intellectuals, are immediate and not mediated through texts. If Sartre is a model of the politically engaged writer, Baraka is a model of the politically engaged individual who writes. Although he is similar to Richard Wright in his obsession with political writing, Baraka has remained in the "belly of the beast" to fight in arenas not accessible to the pen. Wright, however, overwhelmed by American racism and class exploitation, left America. Therefore, when criticizing Baraka's various political positions, it is only appropriate that we recognize the heroism in his will to engage.

Baraka views traditional intellectuals as politically irrelevant, if not counterrevolutionary, to progressive change, given their usual disdain for working with "the people." In attempting to be aligned with the "masses," Baraka believes that it is his duty to lead them, whether its through a political organization like CAP, his various vanguard Leninist parties, or messages contained in his art. Like most traditional intellectuals who protect their privileged positions "to speak," Baraka holds tenaciously to one of the key privileges of the bourgeois Western intelligentsia.

When Edward Said wondered whether a Marxist reading of a minor novel by Balzac could "shake the foundations of capitalism," he was forced to conclude that it does not and cannot.[16] Baraka pondered a similar question when he tried to assess the political relevancy of his Yeats-influenced poetry and his Dante-inspired novel. He concluded that "high" avant-garde art was politically useless to the class/race struggle. Unable to provide a political defense of his intellectual tastes and ambitions, he decided that the unattached, traditional intellectual life was reactionary.

Of the major black intellectual figures in the twentieth century, Baraka was for years one of the least politicized. It is difficult to imagine a Langston Hughes, Richard Wright, or even Alice Walker as divorced from politics as LeRoi Jones was during his Beat bohemian days. Yet it was during this period that Jones grew as a writer. Jones, the most prominent black nationalist intellectual/artist of our generation was also the most prominent black intellectual to emerge in recent times outside an Afro-American intellectual lineage. He was artistically nourished in Greenwich Village.

Once issues pertaining to the actual living conditions of black America became central to Jones's consciousness, he saw in his white peers a reflection of himself as a self-possessed intellectual divorced from the plight of black America. Like his white Village peers, Jones tried to use the "safety" of his bohemian displacement to proclaim himself "the poor Negro's best friend." But this "head-in-the-sand" strategy was destined to fail, and soon he became overwhelmed with guilt. I suppose that Baraka was also seriously hurt by the viciousness of white supremacy. Any sane black person in the United States, particularly an artist as sensitive to human pain as LeRoi Jones, is continually forced to devise new ways of dealing with the psychic, spiritual, and material assaults of white racism, or else be destroyed by them. Jones subsequently articulated this combination of repressed hurt and internalized pain as black rage. But hurt is a difficult emotion to acknowledge, particularly in public. For a black man confronting white racism, hurt leads to feelings of racial gullibility, for hurt can exist only if he expected better treatment from whites. Thus even though hurt was an understandable reaction, it also hampered many of the black strategies for coping with racism. That is, one of the most devastating aspects of black life under white supremacy is that in order to survive, blacks are not always allowed to express the full range of human emotions. Certainly Baraka has never admitted to believing that the United States would live up to its professed principles in its treatment of blacks. Yet the resilience of his political involvement cannot be understood without also recognizing that he was motivated primarily by hope and outrage.

In becoming politicized on behalf of blacks, Richard Wright wrote primarily for a white audience and lived among white intellectuals. Baraka, however, in becoming politicized on behalf of blacks, wrote for both blacks and whites but lived most of his intellectual life among black intellectuals and black nonintellectuals. He was thus exposed to the depth, intransigence, and pettiness of white racism. It is the ubiquity of racism that one immediately senses when living among black people in an inner-city neighborhood. Not only does one discover the horrible living conditions but one also finds high school seniors who can barely read, youths without adequate legal aid who are forced to plea-bargain for crimes they did not commit, talented musicians who cannot afford piano lessons at the local YMCA, and children mentally deficient from birth because of their mother's undetected or untreated sexually transmitted disease. Writing about black life from Riverside Drive (Ellison), exile in France (Wright), or a predominantly white, elite college (myself) is very different from writing about black inner-city life while living next door.

In response to Said's question concerning the political significance of Marxist literary criticism, fellow literary critic Frank Lentricchia answered,

> The question that Said and Eagleton raise projects the sardonic, irritated tone of engaged intellectuals who have seen reams of ineffectual prose pumped out by their humanist colleagues. The irritation is understandable, but in this case it is not only misdirected: it lurches toward despair of the useful work that might be done in the academy, and maybe even toward personal disintegration. The difficult truth that Said and Eagleton know above most others (but it's easy to forget in our exhausted academies) is that struggles for hegemony are sometimes fought out in (certainly relayed through) colleges and universities; fought undramatically, yard for yard, and sometimes over minor texts of Balzac: no heroes, no epic acts.[17]

Would Lentricchia argue that an engaged intellectual who views black emancipation as a priority be satisfied with this academic assault on capitalist hegemony? I don't think so. Given the extraordinary outsider status of many blacks in the United States and the devalued status of black intellectuals within the community of American intellectuals, it may be difficult for many black intellectuals to accept responses like Lentricchia's. Because the black community's political neediness is so great, we might conclude that only the most insular black intellectuals can ignore nonscholarly political calls. Not true! Such calls are routinely dismissed, especially by black academicians. Black intellectual insularity is not unusual. Baraka's inability to remain a bohemian in the Village, although similar to Du Bois's inability to remain in the archives, cannot be understood as a black intellectual norm.

Lentricchia is correct in rejecting as naïve the belief that all intellectuals should be politically engaged and that such engagement can be total. It is Gramsci-influenced Marxism that teaches us the inevitability of political ambivalence. No matter how committed a writer may be to the destruction of a given status quo, he or she will act in ways that reproduce some aspects of the status quo. One can never stand outside society. In this sense, all intellectuals are, at some level, organic, although organic to differing class locations. Recognizing this, Lentricchia can be understood as calling for radical intellectuals to battle in those arenas in which they are best suited to fight. Baraka's inability to recognize such ambivalence and endure it emotionally and morally led to his attempts to be politically pure. His politics changed, but they never became more sophisticated. His dogmatism remained.

Lentricchia asked, "Can a literary intellectual . . . do radical work as a literary intellectual?"[18] He, of course, answered yes. But he should have raised other questions. Under what circumstances would a radical literary intellectual do his primary radical political work as a literary intellectual? Are there circumstances in which the radical literary intellectual should put down her pen and leave her desk? Given the self-interests of radical literary scholars (and all radical academics), it is likely that no political concern in contemporary America will ever be sufficiently compelling to demand nonliterary activism.

The problem of Baraka is in part a problem inherent in the project of the politicized black intelligentsia: the problem of sharing an ethnic identity with an oppressed group that understandably does not have the resources to facilitate the traditional intellectual's life. Insofar as black America has yet to develop a political and cultural infrastructure that allows for and encourages the participation of Afro-American traditional intellectuals as intellectuals, those black intellectuals who do decide to link themselves actively to a political struggle with the broader black populace must haphazardly journey to the "people." This often necessitates putting down the pen. More precisely, the black populace often demands that the intellectual cease to function as a creative intellectual and instead become a "spokesperson" or an ideologue. Commenting on this predicament, Harold Cruse wrote,

> Negro creative intellectuals must not become political leaders or mere civil rights spokesmen in the traditional sense. To do so, means that intellectuals who are creative will be forced to subordinate their potential to the narrow demands of the politics of nationalism and civil rights. The only real politics for the creative intellectual should be the politics of culture. The activist of race, nationalism and civil rights will never understand this, hence this dilemma becomes another ramification of the manifold crisis of the Negro intellectual.[19]

Without understanding the political significance of the traditional intellectual and artistic life and unable to endure the isolation of such an existence, Baraka has continually sought an organic intellectual home among dispossessed blacks. But no matter how much he wants to be organically linked to poor blacks, he can never be, a fact that Baraka cannot accept.

POSTSCRIPT

My exploration of Baraka has led me to wonder whether a traditional intellectual can choose to become politically engaged with nonintellectuals and still function in a democratic, antielitist manner without forsaking his or her critical spirit. This question goes to the root of the politicized intellectual project, and it dogged politicized traditional intellectuals throughout the twentieth century. Sartre, for instance, never claimed to be organic to the French working classes, even though he spoke for them. Although Fanon played a crucial role in the Algerian struggle for independence, he remained a bourgeois outsider to the general Algerian populace. Even so thorough an activist-intellectual as Martin Luther King Jr. never relinquished his autocratic voice when dealing with the southern black masses.

The history of Western intellectuals' involvement with communism is a history of people tortured by questions of organicity. In pursuit of a utopian, egalitarian society, many intellectuals who joined various communist parties silenced their critical voice or curbed their artistic ambition in order to produce art and ideas that could help achieve their socialist utopia. The experiences of Richard Wright as chronicled in the now famous collection *The God That Failed* speak to the attempt of one intellectual to adhere to Marxist ideological dogmas and party discipline only to find both too confining and disrespectful of his intellect. The writer who viewed her political mission as embodied in her ability to produce enlightening art was viewed as suspect, if not corrupted by bourgeois individualism.

In his writings on intellectuals, political theorist Michael Walzer raises similar questions about the allegiances of intellectuals to the very communities that they criticize. He celebrates the "connected critic," the one who does not break ranks with his own people.[20] Although Walzer admires intellectuals who are grounded in a community, his ideas are not wholly convincing, for he does not recognize the key role that Simmelian-type "strangers" have played as critics of societies. Indeed, it often is the pariah intellectual who is the only one sufficiently brave and free to offer critical commentary on his home community, whether it be an ethnic group or a nation. Ironically, in celebrating the connected critic, Walzer denies the importance of Jewish critics in post-emancipated Europe who often felt alienated from other Jews as well as the broader gentile society. Whereas he views as honorable Albert Camus's inability to break with the French community in Algeria, I would argue the reverse. Camus's ethical (and ethnic) parochialism prevented him from situating his self-interests and private desires within a broader human context. As a result, he chose his mother over Algeria's freedom.[21]

Walzer raises significant issues concerning the relationship between the intellectual's sense of political responsibility and his or her social linkages. But he only touches on the question that haunts me: Can the politicized intellectual live a democratic life and be responsible to his or her intellectual calling? This question is perhaps most relevant to intellectuals from subjugated groups. The cultural capital of a traditional intellectual is valuable to that person's group; that is, he or she may be able to articulate the group's needs and desires in ways denied to the rank and file. But must her views be ratified by the people before she speaks? Do the masses not place any checks on their supposed intellectual spokespersons? It is this absence of such checks that makes me wary of the new generation of black "public intellectuals," despite my agreement with many of their positions. Because they belong to a subjugated group, it is easy for them to appear connected to the group when they take an oppositional political stand, no matter how unreasonable it may be. This is the source of my problematic view of Baraka.

When the absence of commitment to a democratic intellectual project is joined with the weakness of a black American intellectual/political infrastructure that does not provide sufficient "checks" on intellectuals' pronouncements, an ambitious black intellectual has an unobstructed pathway to demagoguery. Add to this the power of the media to create spokespersons, and we have a recipe for gross irresponsibility. After all, Ronald Karenga and

Amiri Baraka anointed themselves as a Maulana and an Imamu, respectively, and, in so doing, attracted intellectual and nonintellectual followers who viewed these titles as authoritative. Those black intellectuals who did not respect the voices of Karenga and Baraka were nevertheless forced to respond to them. But Baraka has never accepted responsibility for his authoritative voice and its impact on black political discourses. Instead, he acts as if he were only one person "speaking his mind."

The myopia of Baraka is never more evident than in his autobiography when he acts as if his political activities and ideological conversions were merely private choices and decisions. This claim is disingenuous and irresponsible, for Baraka knows that his vicious assaults on white humanity had important ramifications far beyond his personal station in life. While verbal assaults on white and black peoples may have emanated from sources deep in his individual psyche, he chose a public forum as his Freudian couch. But he writes as if he has to account for his past behavior only in terms of his personal motivations and effects.

Black Americans never certified Baraka's leadership status, but then he knew that this step was unnecessary, provided that he was able to obtain recognition from whites and white-controlled institutions as a "black spokesperson." It is one of the most pathetic aspects of black subjugation that most black Americans do not demand to participate in deciding who will represent their interests. Such a demand would not necessarily prevent illegitimate leaders from arising, but its absence speaks to the self-deprecation in the group's collective consciousness. Blacks are now and have been vulnerable to irresponsible individuals who use a racist disrespect for the views of "ordinary" black Americans to monopolize what appears to be black oppositional discourses. Baraka has never and perhaps could never admit that the form of his political praxis indicated various degrees of disregard for black people.

The problematic aspects of Baraka's political engagements are not simply that he has more often than not championed "backward" visions of black emancipation (from African feudalism to Stalinism) but that he felt no inclination to certify his leadership status in black America. Using the antidemocratic rhetorical cover of being a revolutionary, Baraka followed his whims wherever they led with disregard for their impact on black Americans.

Unfortunately, black Americans seem to be too tolerant of irresponsible and unrepresentative political leaders, white and black. It is therefore not surprising that one of the dominant forms of black political leadership is autocracy. In many instances, the very concentration of power in the hands of a very few individuals creates a charisma around them that gives some blacks a vicarious sense of empowerment. Charismatic leadership, however, is inherently antidemocratic and is usually incapable of generating authentic mass empowerment.

Baraka owes many black Americans a debt that he cannot pay. Because of his public actions, many political opportunities were either lost or distorted beyond viability. Yes, he was committed to black freedom. And yes, he was seemingly inexhaustible in his commitment to the struggle. But yes, he advanced a political line that was socially retarded even for the times. The viciousness of his sexism, the obscenity of his anti-Semitism, and the ridiculousness of his pipe dream to usher black Americans into African feudalism demand a day in the public court. Baraka and Karenga came far closer to advocating an atavistic, black neofascism (including the valorization of a racially cleansed "black space" and pure black blood) as any black leaders in American history. *It is not enough to say that Baraka meant well.*

Despite his role as an advocate of an utterly reactionary political vision, Baraka has continued to play an important emancipatory role as a black intellectual defender of black humanity. In this sense, Baraka has worn two different hats which sometimes conflict and other times reinforce each other. Simultaneously, he has been hegemonic in the black America and counterhegemonic in broader American society. He is a political outsider who is an insider in his group of outsiders.

In many respects, Baraka is the outsider as subjugated native who has chosen both not to make himself at home and not to depart. While maintaining fluid and ambiguous ties of responsibility to the social order around him, he still manages to "stick his nose" into everyone's social affairs. Instead of leaving or shutting up, he has become a thorn in the ass of American pretensions, a demystifier of American conceits. Baraka is a bearer of scandalous commentary who dares society to ignore him but, through his resilience and talent, touches many nerves. Try as it might, society cannot easily dismiss or silence him. Baraka's unique outsider identity could not be contained in Beat bohemia or even Afro-America. A master of maintaining and combining numerous outsider identities, Baraka gravitated to Beat bohemia where he joined a group of "outsiders" only to become an outsider himself. He then left bohemia for "the black community" where his hyperblack identity simultaneously stimulated and hid his marginalization from other blacks.

At some moment, even Baraka's marginalized community of hyperblack blacks became too confining, and he left only to reemerge in yet another deviant American subculture, the left. But because Baraka's leftism was hypersectarian and dogmatic, he was sent once again to the margins of the marginals. In each of his new invocations, Baraka chose to embrace and/or accentuate his individuality.

Baraka's response to his plight as a black man and writer in twentieth-century United States was to continually pursue an individuality beyond co-optation by the prevailing culture and political order. Although he can never achieve this goal, he has not stopped trying. The carcasses of former allies and political causes are scattered along his life's journey. The priority of maintaining his individuality has made him a uniquely irresponsible political ally. Baraka can champion a cause, but the moment enough other supporters come aboard, he abandons the cause and turns to another. What remains striking about Baraka is his inability to admit that his life has been a romantic quest to live as an authentic individual.

During his earliest Beat bohemian days, Baraka could admit to harboring such a goal. But even then he realized that his individuality often appeared narcissistic and thus bourgeois. Since these early days of honest self-introspection, Baraka has chosen to mask his individuality behind proclamations and even actions intent on affecting a larger community. Nevertheless, Baraka has never ceased to be self-absorbed. For a brief moment—at some point while he was a disciple of Karenga—he thought that his political concerns could be reconciled with his individuality. Karenga's influence on Baraka and Baraka's devotion to him can be understood only as quasi-religious. Baraka was able to relinquish his quest for pure individuality only to the extent that he relinquished his rationality to the charisma of an individual who had attained world-historical status. In the same way, Baraka followed another extraordinary individual, Malcolm X, who relinquished some of his individuality to a superior, divine-like figure in Elijah Muhammad. But just as Malcolm had to break with Elijah, Baraka had to break with Karenga.

This does not mean that Baraka's commitment to the black freedom struggle has ever waned, but it has always taken a form that protected his individuality. Some critics have confused Baraka's quest for individuality with a constant desire to change. But change benefits Baraka only to the extent that it protects his individuality. Consequently, Baraka's embrace of the most dogmatic and disreputable tradition of Marxist-Leninist-Stalinism has endured for more than a quarter of a century, and I suspect that Baraka will remain a Stalinist for the remainder of his life. It gives him an outsider identity that cannot be incorporated into the mainstream of America. Moreover, his opposition to a more theoretically sophisticated Marxism precludes his absorption by even those Marxist and neo-Marxist circles still found in academia.

All outsiders remain attached to their parent society, which even Baraka, who defines individuality as "difference" or "uniqueness," must know. As an outsider who is immune to co-optation, Baraka is nonetheless a parasite on the parent social order. Being unlike the others is as conforming as being like the others. His quest for a purely self-determined, authentic individuality without social influences cannot be realized. Baraka appears to have returned to the approach to society that he took during his Beat bohemian days. It may be crazy to believe that Baraka has returned to his bohemian roots, but I don't think he ever left.

Notes

NOTES TO INTRODUCTION

1. Jerry Gafio Watts, *Heroism and the Black Intellectual: Ralph Ellison, Politics, and Afro-American Intellectual Life* (Chapel Hill: University of North Carolina Press, 1994).

2. Harold Cruse, *The Crisis of the Negro Intellectual* (New York: Morrow, 1967).

3. We can divide the black urban riots of the 1960s into three phases: (1) the early phase, which includes Harlem (1964) and Watts (1965); (2) the middle phase, which includes Newark (1967) and Detroit (1966); and (3) the third phase, which includes those riots that took place after the assassination of Martin Luther King Jr. (1968).

4. By civil rights intelligentsia, I mean individuals like Bayard Rustin, Robert Weaver, Kenneth Clark, John Hope Franklin, Thurgood Marshall, J. Saunders Redding, Martin Luther King Jr., Sterling Tucker, Roy Wilkins, and Whitney Young, as well as other intellectuals affiliated with organizations involved in the civil rights movement.

5. Stokely Carmichael left the United States for Guinea in West Africa. He also changed his name to Kwame Toure to honor Kwame Nkrumah of Ghana, a father of Pan-Africanism, and Seko Toure of Guinea, a leader who advocated freedom for his country from French colonial and neocolonial domination.

6. The National Conference of Black Political Scientists (NCOBPS), a black political science organization, was founded in March 1969. The NCOBPS is a separate organization from the American Political Science Association, and its annual meetings are not held in conjunction with the larger organization.

7. Surprisingly, to date, there is no comprehensive study of the history and status of black studies programs in American academia, although historian Nathan Huggins wrote a brief and rather cursory report on black studies for the Ford Foundation. See Nathan Huggins, *Afro-American Studies: A Report to the Ford Foundation* (New York: Ford Foundation, 1985).

8. The William J. Harris, ed., *The LeRoi Jones / Amiri Baraka Reader* does not contain a single sample or excerpt from *Raise Race Rays Raze*. It is as if Baraka were ashamed of those essays.

9. Martin Kilson, "Black Power: Anatomy of a Paradox," *Harvard Journal of Negro Affairs* 2, no. 1 (1968): 30–34.

10. Imamu Amiri Baraka (LeRoi Jones), *Raise Race Rays Raze: Essays since 1965* (New York: Random House, 1971), p. 98.

11. For a discussion and critique of the black aesthetic movement, see Houston A. Baker, *The Journey Back: Issues in Black Literature and Criticism* (Chicago: University of Chicago Press, 1980), chap. 5, and *Blues, Ideology, and Afro-American Literature: A Vernacular Theory* (Chicago: University of Chicago Press,1984); Charles Johnson, *Being and Race: Black Writing since 1970* (Bloomington: Indiana University Press, 1988).

12. Some of these important works are Karl Mannheim's *Ideology and Utopia: An Introduction to the Sociology of Knowledge*, trans. Louis Wirth and Edward Shils (New York: Harcourt, Brace and World, 1936); Alvin Gouldner's *The Future of Intellectuals and the Rise of the New Class* (New York: Seabury Press, 1979); Pierre Bourdieu's *Homo Academicus*, trans. Peter Collier (Stanford, CA: Stanford University Press 1988); Edward Shils's *The Intellectuals and the Powers and Other Essays* (Chicago: University of Chicago Press, 1972); Robert Merton's *The Sociology of Science: Theoretical and Empirical Investigations* (Chicago: University of Chicago Press, 1973); Lewis Coser's *Men of Ideas: A Sociologist's View* (New York: Free Press, 1965); Daniel Bell's *The Winding Passage: Essays and Sociological Journeys, 1960–1980* (New York: Basic Books, 1980); Norman Birnbaum's *The Radical Renewal: The Politics of Ideas in Modern America* (New York: Pantheon, 1988); Seymour Martin Lipset's *Political Man: The Social Bases of Politics* (Baltimore: Johns Hopkins University Press, 1981); Zygmunt Bauman's *Legislators and Interpreters* (Ithaca, NY: Cornell University Press, 1987); Robert Nisbet's *Tradition and Revolt: Historical and Sociological Essays* (New York: Random House, 1968); and Raymond Aron's *The Opium of the Intellectuals* (New York: Doubleday, 1957).

13. A much more elaborate discussion of the victim status can be found in Jerry G. Watts, "Victims' Revolt: Afro-American Intellectuals and the Politics of Ethnic Ambivalence" (in progress).

14. Orlando Patterson, "The Moral Crisis of the Black American," *The Public Interest*, no. 32 (Summer 1973): 52.

15. During his Black Arts days, Baraka mistakenly believed that the use of words that frightened whites would help emancipate blacks. What he could not acknowledge is that his most vociferous and vicious voice as a black nationalist was often directed to whites and, as such, remained dependent on their recognition.

16. The key texts in this area are by Frantz Fanon, *Black Skin, White Masks*, trans. Charles Lam Markmann (New York: Grove Press, 1967), and *The Wretched of the Earth*, trans. Constance Farrington (New York: Grove Press, 1968); Albert Memmi, *The Colonizer and the Colonized* (Boston: Beacon Press, 1967); Jean-Paul Sartre, *Anti-Semite and Jew*, trans. George J. Becker (New York: Schocken Books, 1948); and Paulo Freire, *Pedagogy of the Oppressed*, trans. Myra Bergman Ramos (New York: Seabury Press, 1974).

17. Ever concerned about the impression of whites, Wright stated that he had made a mistake in writing *Uncle Tom's Children*. He wrote, "When the reviews of that book began to appear I realized that I had made a terrible mistake. I found that I had written a book which even bankers' daughters could read and weep over and feel good

about. I swore to myself that if I ever wrote another book, no one would weep over it; that it would be so hard and deep that they would have to face it without the consolation of tears." See Richard Wright, "How 'Bigger' Was Born," introduction to his *Native Son* (New York: Harper & Row, 1966), p. xxvii.

18. The idea of ethnic marginality is derived from Robert Park's notion of the "Marginal Man." I have updated the term to take into account the drastic changes in the quality of acculturation for black Americans.

19. For a discussion of Toomer and Gurdjieff, see Rudolph P. Byrd, *Jean Toomer's Years with Gurdieff: Portrait of an Artist, 1923–1936* (Athens: University of Georgia Press, 1990).

20. For a short introduction to this unique Afro-American intellectual, see Herbert Hunter and Sameer Y. Abraham, eds., *Race, Class, and the World System: The Sociology of Oliver C. Cox* (New York: Monthly Review Press, 1987), esp. Cox's essays and the editors' excellent introduction.

21. Jones's estrangement from poor Negroes is mentioned in the first half of *The System of Dante's Hell*.

22. Jean-Paul Sartre, *What Is Literature?* trans. Bernard Frechtman (New York: Harper & Row, 1965), p. 17. Sartre's idea of words as loaded pistols sounds a great deal like Baraka's late 1960s call for "poems that kill."

23. *Témoignage* constitutes a competing rationale to engagement, for engagement presumes an intent to change the world. After all, *témoignage* easily justifies willed martyrdom. See David L. Schalk, *The Spectrum of Political Engagement: Mounier, Benda, Nizan, Brasillach, Sartre* (Princeton, NJ: Princeton University Press, 1979), pp. 18–21. Although *embrigadement* has no English equivalent, the term could be understood as fanatical devotion, a devotion that is too emotional or suprarational.

24. Schalk, *The Spectrum of Political Engagement*, pp. 24–25.

25. Werner Sollors, *Amiri Baraka / LeRoi Jones: The Quest for a Populist Modernism* (New York: Columbia University Press, 1978), p. 1.

26. Addison Gayle Jr., *The Way of the New World: The Black Novel in America* (New York: Doubleday, 1976). p. 306.

27. Jean-Paul Sartre, *Black Orpheus*, trans. John MacCombie, in *Black and White in American Culture: An Anthology from The Massachusetts Review*, ed. Jules Chametzky and Sidney Kaplan (Amherst: University of Massachusetts Press, 1969), p. 415.

NOTES TO CHAPTER I

1. Throughout this manuscript, I use either Amiri Baraka or LeRoi Jones, although I try to coordinate my use of the names with the name he was using at the time under discussion. See Theodore Hudson, *From LeRoi Jones to Amiri Baraka: The Literary Works* (Durham, NC: Duke University Press, 1973), p. 3 and chap. 1. Many students of Jones mistakenly claim that he was born Everett LeRoi Jones. Jones describes his name change from LeRoy to LeRoi in *The Autobiography of LeRoi Jones / Amiri Baraka* (New York: Freundlich Books, 1984), p. 87. This book is henceforth cited as

The Autobiography. In 1997 a longer, uncut edition of his autobiography appeared, entitled *The Autobiography of LeRoi Jones* (Chicago: Lawrence Hill Books, 1997). This later edition is cited as *The Autobiography II*. In the eyes of black Americans, the black lower-middle class and upper-working class often constitute the black middle classes.

2. LeRoi Jones, *Blues People* (New York: Morrow, 1963), p. 58.

3. Barbara J. Kukla, *Swing City: Newark Nightlife, 1925–1950* (Philadelphia: Temple University Press, 1991), p. 1.

4. Jones's boyhood is described in detail in *The Autobiography*, pp. 1–41, quotation from p. 33.

5. Hudson, *From LeRoi Jones*, p. 9.

6. Although far more affluent and conspicuously consuming than the stable upper-working-class blacks that Jones knew in Newark, the "black bourgeoisie" that he discovered at Howard did not constitute an authentic bourgeois class in the sense in which Marx and other classical sociologists used the term. After all, the overwhelming majority of these Negroes had neither significant capital investments nor ownership of any means of production. Instead, I use the term *black bourgeoisie* here to refer to a black social stratum that functioned as the "elite" of black America. Undoubtedly, their tenuous class location sometimes led to immense efforts to reinforce their status through displays of wealth and economic frivolity. See Walter Dyson, *Howard University: The Capstone of Negro Education* (Washington, DC: Graduate School of Howard University, 1941); and Rayford Logan, *Howard University: The First Hundred Years* (New York: New York University Press, 1969).

7. Describing his days at Howard, Baraka wrote: "In fact, like I said, the only thing that I know I did a lot of at school was sit around and bullshit. Tell jokes, lie, insult people, and try to get out of schoolwork. . . . I learned to drink at school, to smoke cigarettes, and something else a little deeper but then I wasn't even aware of that part of it" (*The Autobiography*, p. 74).

8. Hudson, *From LeRoi Jones*, p. 9. Jones marketed an image of Howard University that explains his lack of intellectual seriousness and political awareness. Howard University, though traditionally regarded as a social retreat, has also produced generations of serious black professionals, many of whom have contributed to the black struggle for equality. Less than a decade after Jones left Howard, many of its students became leaders of the Student Nonviolent Coordinating Committee (SNCC). What Jones cannot seem to admit is that there may have been politically aware students at Howard (certainly among its many international students) but that he was simply not attracted to them.

9. See LeRoi Jones, "Philistinism and the Negro Writer," in *Anger and Beyond: The Negro Writer in America*, ed. Herbert Hill (New York: Harper & Row, 1966), pp. 51–52.

10. Hudson, *From LeRoi Jones*, p. 10.

11. Owen Dodson was the chairman of the drama department at the time that the Baldwin play was produced at Howard, and perhaps Baraka's comments were a description of Dodson.

12. James Hatch described this infamous dean of music: "The Howard director of music, Warner Lawson, son of a concert pianist, was an elitist. Under his directorship the choir by 1951 had become the unofficial chorus of the National Symphony Orchestra in Washington. Lawson forbade the playing of jazz in the music department, banning the saxophone completely. Gospel he excoriated. His approach to spirituals can be inferred from his remark to the National Music society; 'I work entirely from the point of view of diction and concentration on consonants rather than vowels.' He belonged to those teachers who determinedly pulled Blacks up and away from rural or ghetto roots." James Hatch, *Sorrow Is the Only Faithful One: The Life of Owen Dodson* (Champaign-Urbana: University of Illinois Press, 1993), p. 206.

13. Jones, "Philistinism and the Negro Writer," p. 52. Jones refers to Kenton's "progressive jazz" style as a white reaction to bebop. Referring to "progressive jazz" as self-consciously intellectual, Jones called it "probably the 'whitest' music given the name *jazz* to appear in recent times." Jones, *Blues People* (New York: Morrow, 1963), p. 206.

14. Jones, "Philistinism and the Negro Writer," pp. 51–52.

15. See *The Autobiography*; pp. 63–93, esp. p. 85; quotation from p. 94.

16. See Baraka's discussion of one of his initial attempts at "revolutionary" organizing in *The Autobiography*: "I also thought it should be a paramilitary organization" (p. 197).

17. Ibid., p. 92.

18. Ibid., pp. 94–123. Also see Hudson, *From LeRoi Jones*, p. 11.

19. Jones, "Philistinism and the Negro Writer," pp. 52–53.

20. *The Autobiography*, pp. 103–4.

21. Not surprisingly, Jones was ashamed at having flunked out of Howard University. He wrote, "I never thought clearly about it [enlistment in the air force], I just acted. That was how I could get away, get off these streets, disappear again and be somewhere else other than being stared at by people who were putting together their own explanations of what had happened to me" (*The Autobiography*, pp. 94–95).

22. See Jake Ryan and Charles Sackrey, *Strangers in Paradise: Academics from the Working Class* (Cambridge, MA: South End Press, 1984); and C. B. Barney Dews and Carolyn Leste Law, eds., *This Fine Place So Far from Home: Voices of Academics from the Working Class* (Philadelphia: Temple University Press, 1995).

23. *The Autobiography*, p. 156.

24. Ibid., pp. 114–15.

25. Ibid.

26. Jones emphatically denied these accusations. See "Confessions of a Former Anti-Semite," *Village Voice*, December 17–23, 1980, p. 19.

27. This is the term that Jones uses in his autobiography to refer to the air force.

28. Jones acknowledges that the "Little Rock" crisis was a transitional historical moment. See *The Autobiography*, p. 128.

29. Ibid., p. 125.

30. Ibid., pp. 91, 119. Bohemia refers to a geographical region in what is now

the Czech Republic. The term *bohemian*, referring to an artistic subculture, was first used in France in reference to gypsies, who were thought to have come from Bohemia. Bohemian artists lived a precarious, gypsy-like life without predictability and conformity.

31. Werner Sollors, *Amiri Baraka / LeRoi Jones: The Quest for a "Populist Modernism"* (New York: Columbia University Press, 1978), pp. 18–19.

32. Ibid., p. 19.

33. Ibid., p. 20.

34. I borrowed the use of Mary Pratt's notion of contact zone from Jon Parish, *The Color of Jazz: Race and Representation in Postwar American Culture* (Jackson: University Press of Mississippi, 1997), p. 23.

35. Once in the Village, Jones learned that the image of interracial harmony was not quite accurate. For the racial underside of the Village bohemian scene, see Panish, *The Color of Jazz*, chap. 2.

36. In a 1970 interview, Baraka commented on the class location of his family: "I would say that we were not so much middle-class as working class. I think black people who had jobs, as my parents did, could be considered middle-class, but certainly not middle-class compared to what America is. . . . My parents had jobs, yes, but they were working class people. As I said, my father worked in the post office. My mother was a social worker, but she started out working in sweat shops before they started giving black women jobs. Then during the World War she got a job as, you know, in the government and after that she sort of maintained the social worker thing." See Charles Reilly, ed., *Conversations with Amiri Baraka* (Jackson: University Press of Mississippi, 1994), p. 71.

37. Of course, in 1950s America, there were a few wealthy black Americans but not enough to constitute a meaningful social formation.

38. A clue to Jones's distance from the daily life of the black middle class was his uncritical reliance on E. Franklin Frazier's distorted polemic *The Black Bourgeoisie* as a primary source of knowledge about this segment of black America. Several generations of black American intellectuals seeking to validate their supposed distance from black bourgeois values have invoked Frazier's book as an accurate empirical depiction. For a critique of Frazier's *Black Bourgeoisie* from the vantage point of a black leftist, see Oliver Cox's introduction to Nathan Hare's *The Black Anglo-Saxons* (New York: Marzani and Munsell, 1965).

39. Norman Podhoretz, "The Know-Nothing Bohemians," *Partisan Review* 25, no. 2 (Spring 1958): 305–318.

40. One of Podhoretz's most popular works is an autobiographical self-celebration entitled *Making It* (New York: Random House, 1968). Interestingly, many of my black graduate school peers found it a fascinating read (I did too), perhaps because Podhoretz's reflections captured a parvenu intellectual sensibility, a sensibility that was a fundamental component of our lives. For an insightful discussion of Podhoretz's reaction to the Beats, see Alexander Bloom's *Prodigal Sons: The New York Intellectuals and Their World* (New York: Oxford University Press, 1986).

41. See Bloom, *Prodigal Sons*, pp. 303–4.

42. Norman Podhoretz, "The Know-Nothing Bohemians," in his *Doings and Undoings* (London: Rupert Hart-Davis, 1965), p. 146.

43. Ibid., p. 147.

44. Ibid.

45. See Leslie Fishbein's *Rebels in Bohemia: The Radicals of "The Masses," 1911–1917* (Chapel Hill: University of North Carolina Press, 1983); Christopher Lasch, *The New Radicalism in America, 1889–1963: The Intellectual as a Social Type* (New York: Knopf, 1965); Henry May, *The End of American Innocence: A Study of the First Years of Our Time, 1912–1917* (Chicago: Quadrangle Books, 1964).

46. For a discussion of Jean Toomer's attachment to bohemian Gurdjieff circles, see Rudolph P. Byrd, *Jean Toomer's Years with Gurdjieff: Portrait of an Artist, 1923–1936* (Athens: University of Georgia Press, 1990).

47. Wini Breines, *Young, White, and Miserable: Growing up Female in the Fifties* (Boston: Beacon Press, 1992), chap. 4.

48. Hazel Barnes, *An Existentialist Ethics* (Chicago: University of Chicago Press, 1978), chap. 7.

49. This is a liberal use of Murray's construct. For its original meaning, see Albert Murray, *The Hero and the Blues* (Columbia: University of Missouri Press, 1973), p. 39.

50. Stuart D. Hobbs, *The End of the American Avant Garde* (New York: New York University Press, 1997), p. 159.

51. Barry Miles, *Ginsberg: A Biography* (New York: Simon & Schuster, 1989), p. 248.

52. See "Correspondence," *Partisan Review* 25, no. 3 (Summer 1958): 472–73.

53. Podhoretz, "The Know-Nothing Bohemians," pp. 151.

54. Ibid., pp. 151–52.

55. Ellis Amburn, *Subterranean Kerouac: The Hidden Life of Jack Kerouac* (New York: St. Martin's Press, 1998).

56. Podhoretz, "The Know-Nothing Bohemians," pp. 151–52.

57. Jones, "Correspondence," p. 473.

58. According to biographer Barry Miles, by the early 1960s Kerouac had become openly anti-Semitic and racist. Miles finds this "shocking" because of Kerouac's friendships with LeRoi Jones and Ted Jones and his love of jazz. But Miles certainly overstates the "friendship" between Jones and Kerouac. A fondness for jazz has absolutely no correlation with a fondness for or a hatred of actual living black people! Miles reports that by the early 1960s, Kerouac was a supporter of the Klan. In the summer of 1962, he helped build a cross and then burned it on the border of a Negro neighborhood. While it was burning, he jumped up and down, all the while hollering racist obscenities. Miles also reports that during Kerouac's earliest years in New York, he would sometimes refuse to go to parties "if Negroes were going to be there." See Barry Miles, *Jack Kerouac: King of the Beats: A Portrait* (New York: Henry Holt, 1998), p. 278.

59. This is mere speculation, but the viciousness of Jones's later attacks on white bohemians could be construed as the articulation of repressed anger at them and himself for tolerating bohemian racists like Kerouac.

60. *The Autobiography*, p. 210.

61. Ibid., pp. 124–201; Sollors, *Amiri Baraka / LeRoi Jones*, p. 3, chaps. 1 and 2.

62. By "Village scene," I mean the bohemian/artistic/deviant art worlds and intellectual circles that were thriving in the Village. I am not implying that the geographical space and urban residential area known as Greenwich Village was any less racist than any other neighborhood in New York. Indeed, in his autobiography Baraka describes several encounters with local racist street thugs in the Village.

63. See Norman Podhoretz, *Making It* (New York: Random House, 1968), and *Breaking Ranks: A Political Memoir* (New York: Harper & Row, 1979).

64. See Wayne Cooper's excellent study, *Claude McKay: Rebel Sojourner in the Harlem Renaissance: A Biography* (Baton Rouge: Louisiana State University Press, 1987) chaps. 3 and 5, and also see Cooper's introduction to *The Passion of Claude McKay*, ed. Wayne Cooper (New York: Schocken Books, 1973); Mae Gwendolyn Henderson, "Portrait of Wallace Thurman," in *The Harlem Renaissance Remembered*, ed. Arna Bontemps (New York: Dodd Mead, 1972); and Byrd, *Jean Toomer's Years with Gurdjieff*.

65. Harold Cruse, *The Crisis of the Negro Intellectual* (New York: Morrow, 1967), p. 355. Other black intellectuals then living in the Village included musicians Cecil Taylor and Archie Shepp, writers A. B. Spellman and Samuel Delaney, painters Vincent Smith and Bob Thompson, and theater producer Ellen Stewart.

66. Elias Wilentz, *The Beat Scene* (New York: Corinth Books, 1960), p. 101.

67. Sollors, *Amiri Baraka / LeRoi Jones*, p. 25.

68. Podhoretz was correct in claiming that Kerouac was engaged in a Crow-Jimism romanticization of blacks. Furthermore, it was far too predictable that Kerouac could romanticize blacks and Charlie Parker and yet do literally nothing to advance the cause of black civil rights. Kerouac was a jingoistic conservative, much like Podhoretz later became. Kerouac opposed the confrontational aspects of the civil rights movement. See Charles Jarvis, *Visions of Kerouac* (Lowell, MA: Ithaca Press, 1974), pp. 158–59.

69. As an aside, I cannot overlook the possibility that one of the issues that most infuriated Podhoretz about the Beat scene was the prevalence of interracial couples. In an essay published in 1963, Podhoretz admitted that there were certain social phenomena that forced him to recognize his own racism toward blacks. "How do I know that this hatred has never entirely disappeared? . . . I know it from the disgusting prurience that can stir in me at the sight of a mixed couple." See Norman Podhoretz, "My Negro Problem—And Ours," in his *Doings and Undoings* (London: Rupert Hart-Davis, 1965), p. 367.

70. Sollors, *Amiri Baraka / LeRoi Jones*, p. 25. It is important to note here that the "Crow-Jane" that describes the interracial sexual reversal is not the "Crow-Jane" that

appears as the subject of several of the poems in *The Dead Lecturer*. The "Crow-Jane" mentioned in Jones's poems refers to a Western muse, a riff on a blues song by Mississippi Joe Williams and the "Crazy Jane" poems of William Butler Yeats. Kimberly Benston discusses Jones's "Crow Jane" poems in *Baraka: The Renegade and the Mask* (New Haven, CT: Yale University Press, 1976), pp. 115–20.

71. From "For Crow Jane," in LeRoi Jones, *The Dead Lecturer* (New York: Grove Press, 1964), p. 49.

72. Leslie Fiedler noted that some black bohemians created themselves in the image of Crow-Jimism in order to reap the "benefits" of bohemia's racial patronage: "Moreover a new generation of Negroes is presently learning in Greenwich Village, or in Harvard College, to be what the hipster imagines it to be, imitating its would-be imitators." Leslie Fiedler, *Waiting for the End* (New York: Stein & Day, 1964), p. 133.

73. Fishbein, *Rebels in Bohemia*, p. 162.

74. Ibid., p. 162. Though racist in his views of blacks as cultural exotics, Van Vechten was a serious supporter of black artists and writers. He is responsible for establishing the James Weldon Johnson Collection at Yale University, which now houses the papers of Richard Wright, Langston Hughes, Claude McKay, and Jean Toomer, among black writers. Van Vechten deposited his own papers in the library at Fisk University.

75. Norman Mailer, *The White Negro: Superficial Reflections on the Hipster* (San Francisco: City Lights, 1957).

76. James Baldwin, *Nobody Knows My Name* (New York: Dell, 1961), p. 230.

77. Bernard Rosenberg and Norris Fliegel, *The Vanguard Artist: Portrait and Self-Portrait* (Chicago: Quadrangle Books, 1965), pp. 291–92. Rosenberg and Fliegel made the classic racially parochial error of granting universality to whites and racial specificity to blacks. When they wrote "artists are convinced," what they really meant is "the *white* artists that we interviewed are convinced." The omission of a racial designation for white artists indicates the degree to which the authors granted these artists the authority to make supposedly unbiased assessments of black artists, as if these white artists were somehow beyond the racial parochialism that dominated American society. Moreover, this study is so methodologically flawed that the entire chapter on the Negro artist is based on the summarized impressions of white artists concerning black artists. Worse, the authors use these white impressions to construct a psychological portrait of the Negro artist and do so without talking to even one black artist. This speaks to a racial superiority so thoroughly ingrained in the psyches of the artists and scholars as to be beyond consciousness.

78. Seymour Krim, "Anti-Jazz: A Question of Self-Identity," in *The Village Voice Reader*, ed. Daniel Wolf and Edwin Fancher (Garden City, NY: Doubleday, 1962), pp. 98–103.

79. For an extraordinary discussion of the political implications of a parvenu status for intellectuals, see Zygmunt Bauman, *Postmodernity and Its Discontents* (New York: New York University Press, 1997), chap. 5.

NOTES TO CHAPTER 2

1. Werner Sollors, *Amiri Baraka / LeRoi Jones: The Quest for a "Populist Modernism"* (New York: Columbia University Press, 1978), p. 3.

2. Theodore R. Hudson, *From LeRoi Jones to Amiri Baraka: The Literary Works* (Durham, NC: Duke University Press, 1973), p. 12.

3. Hettie Jones, *How I Became Hettie Jones* (New York: Dutton, 1990). Hettie Jones also wrote a dozen children's books, helped write the history of an antipoverty agency, and raised two daughters. see Steven Watson, *The Birth of the Beat Generation: Visionaries, Rebels, and Hipsters, 1944–1960* (New York: Pantheon Books, 1995), p. 269.

4. Watson, *The Birth of the Beat Generation*, p. 15.

5. LeRoi Jones / Amiri Baraka, *The Autobiography of LeRoi Jones / Amiri Baraka* (New York: Freundlich Books, 1984), p. 151. This book is henceforth referred to as *The Autobiography*.

6. See the 1979 Debra L. Edwards interview with Baraka republished in Charlie Reilly, ed., *Conversations with Amiri Baraka* (Jackson: University Press of Mississippi, 1994), p. 147.

7. Hettie Jones, *How I Became Hettie Jones*, p. 74.

8. See the reprints of *The Floating Bear: A Newsletter*, nos. 1–37, 1961–69, ed. Diane di Prima and Le Roi Jones (La Jolla, CA: Laurence McGilvery, 1973), p. vii.

9. Watson, *The Birth of the Beat Generation*, p. 269.

10. Ibid. Jones's relationship with Diane Di Prima was also at one point a sexual one, resulting in the birth of a son, for whom Jones evidently did not take responsibility. See *The Autobiography*, pp. 163, 180; and Aldon L. Nielsen's *Writing between the Lines: Race and Intertexuality* (Athens: University of Georgia Press, 1994), p. 234. Di Prima also mentioned an abortion that she had as a result of her sexual liaison with Jones. See Diane Di Prima, "Spring Thoughts for Freddie: A Memoir," *Evergreen Review* 12, no. 55 (June 1968): 65–69, 82–83.

11. See Reilly, ed., *Conversations with Amiri Baraka*, p. 148.

12. In a newspaper article concerning the obscenity charges and his arrest, Jones complained that he could have spent the time sitting in jail writing but that they refused to give him a pen and paper. Moreover, he compared the arrest with his discharge from the army on false charges of subversive activity. He stated, "This is just the latest in a series of minor annoyances at the hands of the government. It's getting to be a drag." See "A Poet Laments Time Lost in a Courthouse," *New York Post*, October 19, 1961.

13. *The Floating Bear*, no. 20.

14. For the Totem Press series, Jones edited *The Scripture of the Golden Eternity*, by Jack Kerouac, and *Empty Mirror*, by Allen Ginsberg.

15. In *Amiri Baraka / LeRoi Jones*, Sollors provides an example of the explicit influence of Eliot's *The Love Son of J. Alfred Prufrock* on Jones's earliest poetry.

16. William J. Harris, *The Poetry and Poetics of Amiri Baraka: The Jazz Aesthetic* (Columbia: University of Missouri Press, 1985), p. 35.

17. Reilly, ed., *Conversations with Amiri Baraka*, pp. 6–7.

18. LeRoi Jones, *Preface to a Twenty Volume Suicide Note . . .* (New York: Totem/Corinth Books, 1961), p. 13.

19. Kimberly Benston, *Baraka: The Renegade and the Mask* (New Haven, CT: Yale University Press, 1976), p. 98.

20. Jones, *Preface to a Twenty Volume Suicide Note*, p. 15.

21. Ibid., p. 16.

22. Ibid., p. 17.

23. From the poem "The Death of Nick Charles," in ibid., p. 32.

24. Although black women regular appear in Jones's work as bourgeois straw women, in this instance he is specifically commenting on his sister.

25. From the poem "Hymn for Lanie Poo," in Jones, *Preface to a Twenty Volume Suicide Note*, p. 6.

26. Ibid., p. 11.

27. Jones, *Preface to a Twenty Volume Suicide Note*, p. 47.

28. *The Autobiography*, p. 161.

29. Mayfield was a well-known black novelist and essayist. His novels include *The Hit* (1957), *The Long Night* (1958), and *The Grand Parade* (1961). He was one of the leaders of the expatriate black American colony in Accra, Ghana, during Nkrumah's years in power. Wright was the author of a collection of poetry, *Give Me a Child* (1955), and a prize-winning novel, *This Child's Gonna Live* (1969). Williams was the head of the NAACP chapter in Monroe, North Carolina. He had become nationally prominent as a result of his advocacy of black self-defense in Monroe. As a result of his advocacy of militant self-defense, he was suspended from his NAACP office by Roy Wilkins. Clarke was a black historian who attempted to inspire Afro-Americans to engage their African past. He was a mainstay in Harlem's black intellectual community.

30. For a discussion of the Fair Play for Cuba Committee, see Van Gosse, *Where the Boys Are: Cuba, Cold War America and the Making of a New Left* (London: Verso, 1993). An excellent study, the Gosse text has, unfortunately, not been widely disseminated.

31. Ibid., p. 140.

32. See James Campbell, *Exiled in Paris: Richard Wright, James Baldwin, Samuel Beckett, and Others on the Left Bank* (New York: Scribner, 1995), p. 205: "Gibson's troubles continued after leaving Paris. He came to be regarded by certain other people involved in the Fair Play for Cuba Campaign, such as the poet LeRoi Jones (later Amiri Baraka), as being a government agent." I could find nothing to substantiate Campbell's claims concerning Jones's suspicions of Gibson. Unfortunately, Campbell does not offer documentation for the claim.

33. For discussions of Gibson's treachery in Paris, see Michel Fabre, *From Harlem to Paris: Black American Writers in France, 1840–1980* (Champaign-Urbana: University of Illinois Press, 1991), pp. 249–50, and *The Unfinished Quest of Richard Wright*, trans. Isabel Barzun (New York: Morrow, 1973), pp. 461–71; and Ollie

Harrington, *Why I Left America and Other Essays* (Jackson: University Press of Mississippi, 1993), pp. 13–14, 19.

34. Sollors, *Amiri Baraka / LeRoi Jones*, p. 165.

35. *The Autobiography*, p. 163.

36. LeRoi Jones, "Cuba Libre," in his *Home: Social Essays* (New York: Morrow, 1966), p. 42.

37. Ibid., pp. 61–62.

38. Ibid., pp. 63–67.

39. Ibid., pp. 65–66.

40. Ibid., p. 64.

41. Ibid., p. 83.

42. Sollors, *Amiri Baraka / LeRoi Jones*, p. 177.

43. Jones, *Home*, p. 86.

44. See Isaiah Berlin, "Two Concepts of Liberty," in his *Four Essays on Liberty* (Oxford: Oxford University Press, 1969), pp. 118–72.

45. Jones, *Home*, p. 85.

46. Ibid., p. 92.

47. See Cheryl Lynn Greenberg, *"Or Does It Explode": Black Harlem in the Great Depression* (New York: Oxford University Press, 1991).

48. Gerald Horne, *Black Liberation / Red Scare: Ben Davis and the Communist Party* (Newark: University of Delaware Press, 1994). For a description of the presence of the Communist Party in Harlem affairs, see Mark Naison, *Communists in Harlem during the Depression Years* (New York: Grove Press, 1983).

49. Jones, *Home*, p. 93.

50. See W. E. B. Du Bois, "Criteria of Negro Art," *The Crisis*, no. 32 (October 1926). For a discussion of this essay and Du Bois's aesthetic outlook concerning black writing, see Ronald A. T. Judy, "The New Black Aesthetic and W. E. B. Du Bois, or Hephaestus, Limping," *Massachusetts Review*, Summer 1994, pp. 249–82; and Keith E. Byerman, *Seizing the Word: History, Art, and Self in the Work of W. E. B. Du Bois* (Athens: University of Georgia Press, 1994), chap. 5.

51. LeRoi Jones, "Myth of a Negro Literature," in *Home*, p. 107.

52. David Lionel Smith, "The Black Arts Movement and Its Critics," *American Literary History* 3, no. 1 (Spring 1991): 98.

53. Ibid.

54. Jones, *Home*, p. 118.

55. Ibid., p. 120.

56. Jones's attitude toward Baldwin changed over time. The eulogy delivered by Baraka at the funeral service for Baldwin in 1987 is an unfettered and eloquent song of praise. See Amiri Baraka, *Eulogies* (New York: Marsilio Publishers, 1996), pp. 91–98.

57. Jones, *Home*, p. 164.

58. Ibid., pp. 164–65.

59. Theodore W. Allen documents the racist colonial domination of the Irish in

The Invention of the White Race, vol. 1, *Racial Oppression and Social Control* (London: Verso, 1994).

60. See Ian Crump, "'A Terrible Beauty Is Born': Irish Literature as a Paradigm for the Formation of Postcolonial Literatures," in *English Postcoloniality: Literatures from around the World*, ed. Radhika Mohanram and Gita Rajan (Westport, CT: Greenwood Press, 1996), p. 40.

61. LeRoi Jones, ed., *The Moderns: An Anthology of New Writing in America* (New York: Corinth Books, 1963), pp. xiii–xiv.

62. Ibid., p. ix.

63. Jerry Tallmer, "Across the Footlights," *New York Post*, March 24, 1964. The column was entitled "LeRoi Jones Strikes Again."

64. LeRoi Jones, *The Baptism* and *The Toilet* (New York: Grove Press, 1967), pp. 17, 21.

65. Benston, *Baraka: The Renegade and the Mask*, pp. 200, 201.

66. Harold Clurman, *The Naked Image: Observations on the Modern Theatre* (New York: Macmillan, 1966), p. 90. Many critics have assumed that the play's title is taken from the myth of the Flying Dutchman, who was condemned to sail forever with a crew of the living dead.

67. LeRoi Jones, *Dutchman* and *The Slave* (New York: Morrow, 1967), p. 11.

68. Ibid., p. 18.

69. Ibid., pp. 29–31.

70. Ibid., p. 33.

71. Ibid., p. 34.

72. Ibid.

73. Ibid., p. 35.

74. LeRoi Jones, "A Poem for Willie Best," in his *The Dead Lecturer* (New York: Grove Press, 1964), p. 26.

75. Clurman, *The Naked Image*, pp. 90, 91.

76. Jones, *Home*, pp. 187, 188.

77. Howard Taubman, "The Theater: *Dutchman*," *New York Times*, March 25, 1964.

78. C. W. E. Bigsby, *A Critical Introduction to Twentieth-Century American Drama*, vol. 3, *Beyond Broadway* (Cambridge: Cambridge University Press, 1985), p. 399.

79. Jones, *The Baptism* and *The Toilet*, p. 53.

80. Ibid., pp. 58–59. It would have been a grand insult for a black homosexual to have expressed desire for the gang leader. That the homosexual love letter was written by a white boy only intensified the collective shame felt by the gang members. Jones uses the whiteness of Karolis both to intensify his homosexuality and his homosexuality to intensify his whiteness.

81. Sollors, *Amiri Baraka / LeRoi Jones*, p. 110.

82. Gerald Weales, *The Jumping-off Place: American Drama in the 1960s* (London: Macmillan, 1969), pp. 141–42.

83. Clurman, *The Naked Image*, p. 92.

84. Langston Hughes, "That Boy LeRoi," *New York Post*, January 15, 1965, p. 38.

85. Sollors, *Amiri Baraka / LeRoi Jones*, p. 112.

86. Reilly, ed., *Conversations with Amiri Baraka*, pp. 130–31.

87. Jones, *Dutchman* and *The Slave*, pp. 43, 44.

88. Amiri Baraka, *Selected Plays and Prose of Amiri Baraka / LeRoi Jones* (New York: Morrow, 1979), p. 105.

89. Jones, *Dutchman* and *The Slave*, p. 60.

90. Ibid., pp. 66, 67.

91. Ibid., p. 72.

92. Ibid., p. 73.

93. Weales, *The Jumping-off Place*, pp. 142–43.

94. Clurman, *The Naked Image*, pp. 92–93.

95. Ibid., p. 93.

96. Reilly, ed., *Conversations with Amiri Baraka*, p. 14.

97. Ibid., p. 134.

NOTES TO CHAPTER 3

1. Van Gosse, *Where the Boys Are: Cuba, Cold War America and the Making of a New Left* (New York: Verso, 1993), p. 187.

2. LeRoi Jones / Amiri Baraka, *The Autobiography of LeRoi Jones / Amiri Baraka* (New York: Freundlich Books, 1984), p. 168. This book is henceforth cited as *The Autobiography*.

3. Ibid., p. 169.

4. Harold Cruse, *The Crisis of the Negro Intellectual* (New York: Morrow, 1967), p. 363.

5. On Guard was short lived. In some respects, it had no political purpose outside of addressing the idiosyncratic needs of some black intellectuals to "do something." The organization did become deeply involved in the struggle to defend Robert Williams, an NAACP official and self-defense advocate. But the Williams issue never captured the imaginations of most Harlemites.

6. Perhaps one indication of the marginalization of black intellectuals in the Village intellectual scene is their complete absence from the staff of the news weekly, the *Village Voice*, which began publishing in 1955. Billed as an alternative newspaper, its racial orientation was parochial. See Ellen Frankfort's devastating critique *The Voice: Life at The Village Voice* (New York: Morrow, 1976).

7. Renato Poggioli, *The Theory of the Avant-Garde*, trans. Gerald Fitzgerald (New York: Harper & Row, 1971), pp. 97, 127.

8. Theodore R. Hudson, *From LeRoi Jones to Amiri Baraka: The Literary Works* (Durham, NC: Duke University Press, 1973), p. 117.

9. Charlie Reilly, ed., *Conversations with Amiri Baraka* (Jackson: University Press of Mississippi, 1994), p. 100.

10. Ibid., pp. 91–92.

11. LeRoi Jones, *The System of Dante's Hell* (New York: Grove Press, 1965), p. 7.

12. Ibid., p. 153.

13. Ibid., p. 11.

14. Ibid., pp. 11–12.

15. Ibid., p. 13.

16. Ibid., pp. 13, 21.

17. Ibid., pp. 31, 49.

18. In a review of the novel, the novelist John A. Williams made a similar point. "Sometimes . . . the novel becomes too personal. It is as if the writer were thinking: I'll be damned if you're going to understand this, reader. The writer's symbols have little relationship to what we know or understand." See John A. Williams, "LeRoi Jones' Novel: Not a Novel," *New York Post*, November 18, 1965, p. 34.

19. Jones, *The System of Dante's Hell*, p. 79.

20. Ibid., p. 80.

21. Werner Sollors, *Amiri Baraka / LeRoi Jones: The Quest for a "Populist Modernism"* (New York: Columbia University Press, 1978), pp. 95–102, 139–146; and Kimberly Benston, *Baraka: The Renegade and the Mask* (New Haven, CT: Yale University Press, 1976), pp. 10–30. Lloyd Brown's discussion of *The System of Dante's Hell* is also excellent. See Lloyd W. Brown, *Amiri Baraka* (Boston: Twayne, 1980), pp. 59–83.

22. Jones, *The System of Dante's Hell*, p. 108.

23. Ibid., pp. 128, 139.

24. Ibid., p. 140.

25. LeRoi Jones, *Black Magic: Collected Poetry, 1961–1967* (Indianapolis: Bobbs-Merrill, 1969), unnumbered inside page.

26. Ibid., p. 6.

27. Ibid.

28. For a discussion of Jones's violation of bohemian ethics, see Isabel Eberstadt, "King of the East Village," *New York Herald Tribune*, December 13, 1964, pp. 13–15.

29. Jones, *Black Magic*, p. 27.

30. Ibid., p. 9

31. Ibid., p. 10.

32. Ibid., pp. 10, 11.

33. Ibid., p. 17.

34. Ibid., p. 41.

35. Ibid., pp. 29–30.

36. LeRoi Jones, *The Dead Lecturer* (New York: Grove Press, 1975), p. 11.

37. Ibid.

38. Ibid.

39. Ibid. Sollors believes that the phrase "you are no brothers, dirty woogies" was directed against the black middle class, but I believe that Jones was expressing his alienation from the "typical" black.

40. Jones, *The Dead Lecturer*, p. 11.

41. Ibid., p. 15.

42. It was common for Jones to write as if white women were the property of white men.

43. Jones, *The Dead Lecturer*, p. 16.

44. Ibid., p. 26.

45. Ibid.

46. Ibid., p. 25.

47. Reilly, ed., *Conversations with Amiri Baraka*, p. 174.

48. Jones, *The Dead Lecturer*, p. 29.

49. LeRoi Jones, "The Politics of Rich Painters," in *The Floating Bear*, no. 22, p. 246–47, 1962. Reprinted in Jones, *The Dead Lecturer*, pp. 32, 33.

50. Diane Di Prima and LeRoi Jones, *The Floating Bear: A Newsletter*, nos. 1–37, compiled in a serial book (La Jolla, CA: Laurence McGilvery, 1973), p. 569. Rivers was a bohemian mainstay in the Village. A painter, jazz musician, and designer of drama sets, Rivers was a friend of Jones. See Larry Rivers (with Arnold Weinstein), *What Did I Do? The Unauthorized Autobiography* (New York: HarperCollins, 1992).

51. Stuart D. Hobbs, *The End of the American Avant Garde* (New York: New York University Press, 1997), p. 153.

52. Ibid., p. 160.

53. Jones wrote a series of poems concerning his personal confrontation with the Western muse. Referring to this muse as "Crow Jane," Jones addresses the terrifying and debilitation influence of Crow Jane on his psyche as writer. In attempting to grapple with an "anxiety of influence," Jones wanted to sustain his creative ambitions without being overcome by a debilitating silence as the weight of tradition bore down on his verse. See Jones, *The Dead Lecturer*, pp. 48–53.

54. Ibid., p. 59.

55. Ibid., p. 60.

56. Ibid., p. 79.

57. Ibid.

58. Ibid.

59. Jones, *Black Magic*, unnumbered preface.

60. Ibid., p. 68.

61. Ibid., p. 93.

62. Ibid., p. 54

63. Ibid., p. 55.

64. Ibid., p. 108.

65. Ibid., p. 111.

66. Ibid., p. 112.

67. For a discussion of the relationship between the Beats and jazz, see Jon Panish, *The Color of Jazz: Race and Representation in Postwar American Culture* (Jackson: University Press of Mississippi, 1997); and David Rosenthal, *Hard Bop: Jazz and Black Music: 1955–1965* (New York: Oxford University Press, 1992), pp. 73–84.

68. For a good discussion of the appropriation of jazz by white "hipsters" in

search of a vicarious marginal identity, see Andrew Ross, *No Respect: Intellectuals and Popular Culture* (New York: Routledge, 1989), esp. chap. 3.

69. LeRoi Jones, *Black Music* (New York: Morrow, 1967), p. 69.

70. Ibid., p. 70.

71. Ibid., p. 71.

72. See Noam Chomsky, "The Responsibility of Intellectuals," in his *American Power and the New Mandarins* (New York: Pantheon Books, 1969), pp. 323–66.

73. Jones, *Black Music*, p. 13.

74. I cannot attest to the correctness of Jones's claim that criticism that uses musical notations is inherently incapable of revealing anything significant about jazz. But I suspect that Jones is just displaying his ignorance of the formal musical qualities of jazz. Moreover, the claim can also be understood as a swipe against white critics. Although many white jazz critics did not use musical notation, the "idea of the white critic" is nevertheless cleverly invoked by Jones's implication that formal musical techniques do not offer an insight into jazz. Besides, is the work of Gunther Schuller and other white jazz critics who concentrate on musical notations really useless?

75. Jones, *Black Music*, pp. 14–15.

76. Ibid., pp. 15–16.

77. Ibid., p. 20.

78. LeRoi Jones, *Blues People: Negro Music in White America* (New York: Morrow, 1963). Although it was published in 1963, Jones claimed that the book was written in 1961. See Reilly, ed., *Conversations with Amiri Baraka*, p. 156.

79. Jones, *Blues People*, p. 65.

80. Ibid., pp. 17–18.

81. Since its publication in 1963, numerous works have appeared that have advanced the scholarship in this area. Some of the better-known studies are Charles Keil, *Urban Blues* (Chicago: University of Chicago Press, 1966); Norman E. Whitten Jr., and John F. Szwed, eds., *Afro-American Anthropology: Contemporary Perspectives* (New York: Free Press, 1970); Ben Sidran, *Black Talk: How the Music of Black America Created a Radical Alternative to the Values of Western Literary Tradition* (New York: Holt, Rinehart and Winston, 1971); Lawrence Levine, *Black Culture and Black Consciousness: Afro-American Folk Thought from Slavery to Freedom* (New York: Oxford University Press, 1977); Robert Farris Thompson, *Flash of the Spirit* (New York: Random House, 1983); and Sterling Stuckey, *Slave Culture: Nationalist Theory and the Foundations of Black America* (New York: Oxford University Press, 1987).

82. Reilly, ed., *Conversations with Amiri Baraka*, p. 250.

83. Jones, *Blues People*, pp. 123–24.

84. One of the problems in Jones's analysis is that he uses the designation "middle class" far too liberally. The so-called black middle class that emerged in the late nineteenth century and early twentieth century was disproportionately working class. As such, many of its members were employed in positions that were designated as "colored jobs." Although they may have wanted to whitenize themselves, their jobs often were predicated on their ability to stay within the existing racial parameters.

85. This is the accusation that Norman Podhoretz, in *Know Nothing Bohemians*, leveled against black Beats.

86. Jones also thought that the acculturation of Jews and white ethnic Americans was a cultural disaster and something to fight against. Of course, he was never forced to devise a social theoretical outlook that could explain how white ethnic groups and blacks could resist the homogenizing tendencies of the capitalist marketplace.

87. Robert Stepto, *From behind the Veil: A Study of Afro-American Narrative* (Champaign-Urbana: University of Illinois Press, 1979).

88. In discussing the appropriation of jazz by whites, Jones continually charts how the dynamism, innovation, and spontaneity of the jazz as played by black musicians turned into watered-down imitations and commodities in the hands of whites. He titled the chapter in *Blues People* in which he discusses this phenomenon "Swing— From Verb to Noun." Its arguments later appeared in Jones's 1964 essay on the greater importance of "arting" over the artifact. See Jones, "Hunting Is Not Those Heads on the Wall," in his *Home: Social Essays* (New York: Morrow, 1966), pp. 173–78.

89. For an excellent discussion of this verb/noun distinction in Jones's thought, see Nathaniel Mackey, "Other: From Noun to Verb" in *Jazz among the Discourses*, ed. Krin Gabbard (Durham, NC: Duke University Press, 1995), pp. 76–99.

90. Wasn't it significant that even in bebop, Dizzy Gillespie and Charlie Parker made a point of hiring white musicians for some of the earliest bands? See the discussion of white jazz musicians in bebop in Scott DeVeaux, *The Birth of BeBop: A Social and Musical History* (Chicago: University of Chicago Press, 1997), pp. 18–19. For a discussion of the problematic treatment and status of white jazz musicians in the jazz community as well as the critical literature on jazz, see Charley Gerard, *Jazz in Black and White: Race, Culture, and Identity in the Jazz Community* (Westport, CT: Praeger, 1998). Gerard also contests Jones's inability to grant white jazz musicians their proper respect and recognition.

91. According to one student of avant-garde jazz, Jones was instrumental in creating the sense of the music as politicized. See David G. Such, *Avant-garde Jazz Musicians: Performing "Out-There"* (Iowa City: University of Iowa Press, 1993), pp. 26–28.

92. One study that reiterates Jones's discussion of the centrality of politics to bebop and other forms of black music is Frank Kofsky's *Black Nationalism and the Revolution in Music* (New York: Pathfinder Press, 1970). For a more nuanced discussion of the politics of bebop, see Eric Lott's "Double V, Double Time: BeBop's Politics of Style," in Gabbard, ed., *Jazz among the Discourses*, pp. 243–55.

93. Lisa E. Davenport, "Jazz and the Cold War: Black Culture as an Instrument of American Foreign Policy," in *Crossing Boundaries: Comparative History of Black People in Diaspora*, ed. Darlene Clark Hine and Jacqueline McLeod (Bloomington: Indiana University Press, 1999), pp. 282–315.

94. This does not mean that black jazz musicians did not have an oppositional political consciousness. It does, however, mean that Monk, Diz, and others were not interested in creating propaganda. They were far too committed to their craft to subsume art under political directives. For a discussion of the links between politics and

jazz, see Charles Hersch, *Democratic Artworks: Politics and the Arts from Trilling to Dylan* (Albany: State University of New York Press, 1998), esp. chap. 4. Also see David Rosenthal, *Hard Bop: Jazz and Black Music, 1955–1965* (New York: Oxford University Press, 1992).

95. This aspect of heroin addiction is discussed in Ben Sidran, *Black Talk: How the Music of Black America Created a Radical Alternative to the Values of Western Literary Tradition* (New York: Holt, Rinehart and Winston, 1971), pp. 112–14, 120–21.

96. Jones, *Blues People*, pp. 201–2.

97. Sidran, *Black Talk*, p. 112.

98. For an additional discussion of the role of heroin in jazz communities, see Gerard, *Jazz in Black and White*, pp. 84–90.

99. Ralph Ellison, *Shadow and Act* (New York: Vintage Books, 1964), pp. 247–58.

100. LeRoi Jones, "The Changing Same (R & B and New Black Music)," in Jones, *Black Music*, pp. 180–211.

101. While Ellison offers a perceptive critique of *Blues People*, he also deliberately misreads the text in order to bolster his polemical intentions. See Kimberly W. Benston, "Ellison, Baraka, and the Faces of Tradition," *Boundary 2*, vol. 6, no. 2 (Winter 1978): 333–54.

102. Andrew Ross, *No Respect: Intellectuals and Popular Culture* (New York: Routledge, 1989), p. 76.

103. *Newsweek*, April 13, 1964, p. 60.

104. Raymond Vernon, "A 'Dialogue' with White Liberals," in his *The Black Revolution and the White Backlash* (New York: Merit Publishers, 1964). This pamphlet was a collection of articles from *The Militant*.

105. Reilly, ed., *Conversations with Amiri Baraka*, p. 8.

106. Ibid., p. 10.

107. Ibid.

108. Ibid., p. 11.

109. Jack Newfield, "LeRoi Jones at Arms: Blues for Mr. Whitey," *Village Voice*, December 17, 1964, pp. 1, 12.

110. Ibid., p. 12.

111. Isabel Eberstadt, "King of the East Village," *New York Herald Tribune*, December 13, 1964, p. 13.

112. Jones, *Home*, pp. 179–80.

113. Ibid., p. 183.

114. Ibid.

115. Ibid., p. 186.

116. Ibid., p. 190.

117. Ibid., pp. 192–93.

118. Ibid., p. 197.

119. Ibid., pp. 208–9.

120. For a short description of the militant voice of Archie Shepp, see Such, *Avant-garde Jazz Musicians*, pp. 25–26.

121. In her autobiography, Hettie Jones refers to set of the play *The Slave* as the "ingenious collapsing scenery by Larry Rivers." See Hettie Jones, *How I Became Hettie Jones* (New York: Dutton, 1990), p. 220.

122. In his autobiography, Larry Rivers described the incident somewhat differently: "There was a Life versus Art symposium at the Village Vanguard, featuring LeRoi and Archie Shepp, the jazz saxophonist, myself, and some other white artists. The Vanguard evening began with talk about the art-lit-jazz scene. Soon things began to get wild. LeRoi told me I was making art for a bunch of uptown fags. Archie brought up the twelve million blacks in the Congo annihilated by slavery and the Belgians. I began to make an allusion to the Holocaust, trying to see just exactly what I felt about Germans. Before I finished half a paragraph, Archie pointed his finger at me and shouted, 'there you go again, always bring up the fucking Jews.' He couldn't talk about his pain without Jews bringing up theirs! The intimidated moderator threw the ball to the audience. LeRoi's and Archie's responses to the questions amounted to: There's only one kind of white—Whitey who hates Negroes." See Larry Rivers, with Arnold Weinstein, *What Did I Do? The Unauthorized Autobiography* (New York: Harper-Collins, 1992), p. 432.

123. Cruse, *The Crisis of the Negro Intellectual*, p. 486. In his autobiography, Larry Rivers noted that after this occasion, he and Jones did not speak to each other for more than twenty years. See Rivers, *What Did I Do*, p. 432.

124. Cruse, *The Crisis of the Negro Intellectual*, p. 486.

125. Ibid. While these whites were in Mississippi assuaging their consciences, Shepp remained in New York City, away from the fray.

126. *The Autobiography*, pp. 189, 193. Neither Cruse nor Jones provides specific dates for Jones's "angry black man" harangues. It is therefore somewhat difficult to determine whether they are referring to similar events. Cruse claimed that the one he attended was held at the Village Vanguard. Jones comments on two different events, one held at the Village Gate and the other at the Village Vanguard. I have assumed that the event that Cruse witnessed at the Village Vanguard was the same one that Jones describes as having been held at that club because both mentioned Jones's attack on Larry Rivers as having taken place there.

127. LeRoi Jones / Amiri Baraka, *The Autobiography of LeRoi Jones* (Chicago: Lawrence Hill Books, 1997), p. 285 (*The Autobiography II*).

128. *The Autobiography*, pp. 193, 194.

129. Jones acknowledged that part of his motivation for speaking in such inflammatory tones was the fact that he was not strong enough to act. See *The Autobiography*, p. 189.

130. Ibid., p. 193.

131. Ibid.

132. David Burner, *Making Peace with the 60s* (Princeton, NJ: Princeton University Press, 1996), p. 58.

133. Ibid.

134. *The Autobiography*, p. 161. The excerpt is from "A Poem Some People Will Have to Understand," in Jones, *Black Magic*, p. 6.

135. Thomas Wolfe, *Radical Chic and Mau-Mauing the Flak Catchers* (New York: Harper & Row, 1970).

136. This excerpt from the interview with Cecil Taylor was published in Alfred Willener's *The Action-Image of Society: On Cultural Politicization*, trans. A. M. Sheridan Smith (New York: Pantheon Books, 1970), p. 254.

137. Stephen Schneck, "LeRoi Jones, or Poetics and Policemen or, Trying Heart, Bleeding Heart," in *Five Black Writers*, ed. Donald Gibson (New York: New York University Press, 1970), pp. 193–94.

138. *The Autobiography*, p. 198. Unable to accept full responsibility for his unprincipled actions, Jones typically attempted to mask his irrationality behind the mention of social deterministic claims. His claims could be non sequiturs. For instance, he tells us that "we carried the fanaticism of the petty bourgeoisie." When did the petty bourgeoisie become intrinsically fanatical? Why is fanaticism only a petty bourgeois affair? Why can't he simply say, "we were fanatics?"

NOTES TO CHAPTER 4

1. See Jones's discussion of the breakup in LeRoi Jones / Amiri Baraka, *The Autobiography of LeRoi Jones / Amiri Baraka* (New York: Freundlich Books, 1984), pp. 190–201. This book is henceforth cited as *The Autobiography*. Throughout his autobiography, Jones displays his anxiety not only over not being psychologically "black" enough but also over the possibility of being exposed as such by other blacks. He talks about his fear that he could no longer dance after having lived with whites in the Village and after having been laughed at by blacks in Harlem when dancing at a party. He was, of course, afraid of being accused of dancing like a "white boy" (p. 210).

2. The shallowness of Jones's reflections on Cohen is disturbing, and the entire autobiography is unreflective. Gerald Early aptly stated, "Ultimately, the autobiography is most revealing in letting us see how little a certain kind of black intellectual can understand himself." Gerald Early, *Tuxedo Junction: Essays on American Culture* (New York: Ecco Press, 1989), p. 205.

3. *The Autobiography*, pp. 144, 146. The actual quotation is more mean-spirited. "Maybe we liked sleeping with each other, but there was never any passion."

4. Ibid., p. 142.

5. I mention his beard and sunglasses only to substantiate my general point that Jones was overly concerned, if not obsessed, with projecting the "correct" style as a means of telling others just who he was. Concerning his group of Village-based black nationalist activists-in-waiting, Jones wrote, "I had a cap, hunting jacket and round dark glasses, the dress of our little core" (*The Autobiography*, p. 200).

6. Ibid., p. 148.

7. LeRoi Jones, *Home: Social Essays* (New York: Morrow, 1966), p. 223.

8. This emphasis on ethnic identity essentially prohibited Jones from viewing the vast cultural differentiations within black America as legitimate. Ironically, this idea that "blackness" inhabits only those spaces from which whites are absent gives whites an infinitely richer range of options for "authentic existences" and a far more resilient and potent ethnicity. Martin Kilson understood this dynamic when he discussed the ways in which black ethnicity was often externally defined. See Kilson's "Blacks and Neo-Ethnicity in American Political Life," in *Ethnicity: Theory and Experience*, ed. Nathan Glazer and Daniel P. Moynihan (Cambridge, MA: Harvard University Press, 1975).

9. In the preface to *Home*, Jones informs the reader of his reified identity. "By the time this book appears, I will be even blacker" (p. 10).

10. Hettie Jones, *How I Became Hettie Jones* (New York: Dutton, 1990), p. 223.

11. Eugene Victor Wolfenstein, *Psychoanalytic-Marxism: Groundwork* (New York: Guilford Press, 1993), p. 338.

12. See Frantz Fanon, *Black Skin, White Masks*, trans. Charles Lam Markmann (New York: Grove Press, 1967), chap. 2. Fanon's arguments became sacred scriptures for militant Afro-American activists during the middle and late 1960s. Brilliant and provocative, Fanon was more than occasionally wrong or muddled. Unfortunately, all too often Fanon's ideas were incorporated by fundamentalist black militants with a literalness that would compare favorably to the Southern Baptist Convention's interpretation of the Bible.

13. Amiri Baraka, "Confessions of a Former Anti-Semite," *Village Voice*, December 17, 1980, p. 20.

14. See the discussion of the renegade and renegadism in Lewis Coser's *The Functions of Social Conflict* (New York: Free Press, 1966), pp. 67–71.

15. *The Autobiography*, p. 147.

16. In a moment of generous reflection on LeRoi's decision to leave her, Hettie Jones compared her husband with her father: "Both these men, Cohen then Jones, first loved me for myself and then discarded me when that self no longer fit their daughter/wife image. If I hadn't been myself all along I might have been left next to nothing. Still, while they loved me they sometimes saw in me more than I did, and for those times I owe them." She was absolutely correct in her formulation that LeRoi left her after she no longer fit his *image* of a wife. See Hettie Jones, *How I Became Hettie Jones*, p. 216.

17. Baraka, "Confessions of a Former Anti-Semite," p. 20.

18. Ibid.

19. Theodore R. Hudson, *From LeRoi Jones to Amiri Baraka: The Literary Works* (Durham, NC: Duke University Press, 1973), p. 15.

20. Baraka, "Confessions of a Former Anti-Semite," p. 19.

21. From the poem "For Tom Postell, Dead Black Poet," in LeRoi Jones, *Black Magic: Collected Poetry, 1961–1967* (Indianapolis: Bobbs-Merrill, 1969), p. 154. The poem was written in 1965 or 1966.

22. Werner Sollors, *Amiri Baraka / LeRoi Jones: The Quest for a "Populist Modernism"* (New York: Columbia University Press, 1978), p. 199.

23. When asked by an interviewer in 1981 if there were any misconceptions about his life and work that he wanted to clarify, Baraka answered, "No, except that people are always catching you where you were." That is, Baraka is implicitly asking us to ignore his past as if his present were a progressive culmination of all that went before and therefore the negation and erasure of his past. See D. H. Melhem, *Heroism in the New Black Poetry: Introductions and Interviews* (Lexington: University of Kentucky Press, 1990), p. 259.

24. *Liberator* 6, no. 1 (January 1966); reprinted in Baraka's *Black Magic*, p. 116.

25. Isaac Deutscher, "The Ex-Communist's Conscience," in his *Heretics and Renegades* (Indianapolis: Bobbs-Merrill, 1969).

26. *The Autobiography*, pp. 210, 215.

27. In the second edition of his autobiography, Baraka lambastes Hettie Jones's memoir of their life together, contending that it is full of lies. He refutes her claims that her desire to write was put "on hold" in order to raise their two daughters and to allow him time and space to create. Moreover, he asserts that she thoroughly overstated her commitment to political activism. Baraka even chides Hettie Jones for her "racist dismissal of what I went on to do" after he left her and the two children. Now it may be true that *How I Became Hettie Jones* is full of lies. I am certainly in no position to vouch for its accuracy, but her claims seem far more plausible than Baraka's refutations. For Baraka's severe commentary on Hettie Jones and her memoir, *How I Became Hettie Jones*, see LeRoi Jones / Amiri Baraka, *The Autobiography of LeRoi Jones* (Chicago: Lawrence Hill Books, 1997), pp. xxi–xxii. This later edition is henceforth cited as *The Autobiography II*.

28. The marriage separation is discussed in *The Autobiography*, pp. 167–201. Hettie Jones provides a more nuanced discussion of the "messy" departure of Jones from his family and life in the Village. See her *How I Became Hettie Jones*, pp. 217–39.

29. Michael Dyson briefly describes the sexism of Malcolm X in his *Malcolm X: Myth and Reality* (New York: Oxford University Press, 1994). Also see the short commentary by bell hooks concerning Malcolm's sexism in her essay collection, *Teaching to Transgress* (New York: Routledge, 1995).

30. Eugene Victor Wolfenstein, *The Victims of Democracy: Malcolm X and the Black Revolution* (New York: Guilford Press, 1993), pp. 336–37.

31. Jones claims to have met with Malcolm in January 1965, one month before his murder. Jones says that on that occasion, Malcolm told him that black activists like himself had to begin to create a viable united front among blacks. See Joe Wood, ed., *Malcolm X: In Our Own Image* (New York: St. Martin's Press, 1992), p. 29.

32. The Baraka play *A Black Mass* is based on the Nation of Islam's Yacub myth.

33. See Amiri Baraka, ed., *African Congress: A Documentary of the First Modern Pan-African Congress* (New York: Morrow, 1972), pp. 44–56.

34. *The Autobiography*, p. 202.

35. Jones used the idea of the prodigal son to describe his life journey. In the preface to *Home*, he wrote, "And there is a sense of the Prodigal about my life that begs to be resolved" (p. 9).

36. Harlem in this sense refers not only to a specific neighborhood in upper Manhattan but also metaphorically to all the black inner-city areas in America's largest cities.

37. Like many other writers, the French critic Genevieve Fabre claims that Jones and BART received $40,000 from the federal government. See Genevieve Fabre, *Drumbeats, Masks, and Metaphor: Contemporary Afro-American Theatre*, trans. Melvin Dixon (Cambridge, MA: Harvard University Press, 1983) p. 19. In his autobiography, Jones states that there were many differing reports as to the amount of money they received: "We must have got away with a couple hundred grand and even more in services when it was all over" (*The Autobiography*, p. 211).

38. See Allen J. Matusow, *The Unraveling of America: A History of Liberalism in the 1960s* (New York: Harper & Row, 1984), pp. 257–60.

39. Michael L. Gillette, *Launching the War on Poverty: An Oral History* (New York: Twayne, 1996), p. 209.

40. *The* Autobiography, p. 212. Michelle Wallace, noted feminist, cultural critic, and native of Harlem, recalled that in 1965 as a young teenager, she, her sister, and her mother, the artist Faith Rheingold, "took classes at Amiri Baraka's newly inaugurated School of Black Arts in Harlem." See Michelle Wallace, *Invisibility Blues: From Pop to Theory* (London: Verso, 1990), p. 194.

41. *The Autobiography*, p. 213.

42. Fabre, *Drumbeats, Masks, and Metaphor*, p. 20.

43. See Matusow, *The Unraveling of America*, p. 259; and Daniel P. Moynihan, *Maximum Feasible Misunderstanding: Community Action in the War on Poverty* (New York: Free Press, 1970), p. 150.

44. "Tax Funds a 'Hate The Whites' Project," *U.S. News and World Report*, December 13, 1965, p. 16.

45. *The Autobiography*, pp. 211–15.

46. *Time*, March 18, 1966, p. 28.

47. *The Autobiography*, p. 214.

48. In admitting to his immaturity without calling it such, Jones reflected on BART's loss of HARYOU funding, stating that had he and others around BART had "a good grasp of skating on the thin ice of government grants and with a smart grantsman around we could have not only bit deeper into the federal pie, we could have gotten some of the foundation money . . . we made it easy for them [federal government] to take us off—we acted so wild and woolly" (*The Autobiography*, pp. 214–15).

49. See Lewis Coser's *Greedy Institutions: Patterns of Undivided Commitment* (New York: Free Press, 1974) Greedy institutions demand total commitment from their members and have historically been attractive to those who are isolated, deprived, or uprooted. Such institutions can included the priesthood of the Catholic

Church or the community that perished in Jonestown, Guyana, under the leadership of Jim Jones.

50. *The Autobiography*, pp. 231–32.

51. See *The Autobiography of Malcolm X* (New York: Grove Press, 1965); and Wolfenstein, *The Victims of Democracy*, chaps. 6 and 7. Malcolm X documents how he began to think reflectively only after he left the Nation of Islam. Concerning his newly founded intellectual freedom, he stated, "And that was how after twelve years of never thinking for as much as five minutes about myself, I became able finally to muster the nerve, and the strength to start facing the facts, *to think for myself*" (*The Autobiography of Malcolm X*, p. 306).

52. The idea of "cultural capital" is most often associated with the work of Pierre Bourdieu. However, my usage of the term is derived from Alvin Gouldner's discussion in *The Future Intellectuals and the Rise of the New Class* (New York: Seabury Press, 1979).

53. LeRoi Jones, "Philistinism and the Negro Writer," in *Anger and Beyond: The Negro Writer in the United States*, ed. Herbert Hill (New York: Harper & Row, 1966), p. 54.

54. Ibid.

55. Ibid., pp. 58–59.

56. Jones, *Home*, p. 107.

57. Martin Kilson, "Black Power: Anatomy of a Paradox," *Harvard Journal of Negro Affairs* 2, no. 1 (1968).

58. Martin Kilson, "Politics and Identity among Black Intellectuals," *Dissent*, Summer 1981, p. 340.

59. Ironically, Baraka is the best refutation of this position. His current Marxism is as intellectually confining as his previous black nationalism was. Surprisingly, Kilson shares Baraka's belief that his movement to "Marxism" indicates intellectual growth.

60. The discussion of ideology in J .G. Merquior's *The Veil and the Mask: Essays on Culture and Ideology* (London: Routledge & Kegan Paul, 1979) is illuminating and has the added virtue of being free of jargon. My conception of ideology has also been influenced by Raymond Williams's *Marxism and Literature* (New York: Oxford University Press, 1977); Terry Eagleton's *Literary Theory: An Introduction* (Minneapolis: University of Minnesota Press, 1983), and *Ideology: An Introduction* (London: Verso, 1991); and the excellent discussions of John B. Thompson in his *Studies in the Theory of Ideology* (Berkeley and Los Angeles: University of California Press, 1984).

61. See Irving Howe's *World of Our Fathers* (New York: Touchstone Books, 1976), pp. 204–8.

62. For insightful discussions of various forms of Afro-American nationalism, see the work of historian Wilson Moses, particularly *The Golden Age of Black Nationalism* (Hamden, CT: Archon, 1978), *Alexander Crummell: A Study of Civilization and Discontent* (New York: Oxford University Press, 1989), and *The Wings of Ethiopia: Studies in African-American Life and Letters* (Ames: Iowa State University Press, 1990).

63. For a perceptive discussion of the problematic relationship between Baraka and the broader black community, see the contentious essay by Jennifer Jordan, "Cultural Nationalism in the 1960s: Politics and Poetry," in *Race, Politics and Culture: Critical Essays on the Radicalism of the 1960s*, ed. Adolph Reed (New York: Greenwood Press, 1986).

64. "Interview: Imamu Amiri Baraka," *The Black Collegian*, March/April, p. 30.

NOTES TO CHAPTER 5

1. The white critics on the panel included Richard Gillman of *Newsweek* and Gordon Rogoff of the *Tulane Drama Review*. See Genevieve Fabre, *Drumbeats, Masks, and Metaphor: Contemporary Afro-American Theatre*, trans. Melvin Dixon (Cambridge, MA: Harvard University Press, 1983), p. 23.

2. "The Revolutionary Theater" was originally published in *Black Dialogue*. When it appeared in *Liberator*, it did so as a reprint. I can only assume that *Liberator* had a much larger audience. See Abby Arthur Johnson and Ronald Maberry Johnson, *Propaganda and Aesthetics* (Amherst: University of Massachusetts Press, 1991), p. 177. Later, the article was included in Jones's essay collection *Home: Social Essays* (New York: Morrow, 1966).

3. Jones, *Home*, pp. 210–11, 213, 214.

4. Ibid., p. 215.

5. According to one theater scholar, *The Conquest of Mexico* tears "away the civilizing aspirations of colonialism by presenting the realities of conquest and revealing its essential evil through the psychological effects of the conquistadors on a people whom Artaud believed to be 'natural.'" See Christopher Innes, *Avant Garde Theatre: 1892–1992* (London: Routledge, 1993), p. 89.

6. Jones, *Home*, p. 211.

7. Daphne S. Reed, "LeRoi Jones: High Priest of the Black Arts Movement," *Educational Theatre Journal* 22, no. 1 (March 1970): 58.

8. Robert Brustein, *The Theatre of Revolt: Studies in Modern Drama from Ibsen to Genet* (Boston: Atlantic Monthly Press / Little, Brown, 1964), pp. 369–70.

9. Ibid., p. 370.

10. According to John Peter, Artaud's idea of theater was centered on theatrical events. Theater was supposed to generate an ecstatic union with a stunning and dazzling event that appealed to the mind but not to reason. Peter wrote, "I do not know another piece of writing about the theatre that reminds one so strongly of the atmosphere of a Nazi rally." Artaud dedicated his pamphlet *The New Revelations of Being* to Adolph Hitler. See John Peter, *Vladimir's Carrot: Modern Drama and the Modern Imagination* (London: Andre Deutsch, 1987), pp. 296–97.

11. For an extensive collection of Artaud's writings, see Antonin Artaud, *Selected Writings*, ed. Susan Sontag (New York: Farrar, Straus & Giroux, 1976), pp. 215–76.

12. Jones, *Home*, p. 251.

13. LeRoi Jones, *Black Magic Poetry: 1961–1967* (Indianapolis: Bobbs-Merrill, 1969), pp. 116–17.

14. This idea may have originated in my reading of David L. Smith, "Amiri Baraka and the Black Arts of Black Art," *Boundary 2*, vol. 15, nos.1–2 (Fall 1986/Winter 1987): 248.

15. For a discussion of the centrality of homophobia in Jones's black arts writing, see Phillip Brian Harper, *Are We Not Men? Masculine Anxiety and the Problem of African-American Identity* (New York: Oxford University Press, 1996), chap. 2.

16. By revenge art, I mean art that is intended to wound someone in retaliation for a previous action. I want to distinguish "revenge art" from revenge-motivated art, for one can be motivated by revenge but not create revenge art.

17. Larry Neal, "The Black Arts Movement," in *The Black Aesthetic*, ed. Addison Gayle (Garden City, NY: Doubleday, 1971), pp. 257, 258.

18. The idea of the "death and/or decline of the West" has a long and varied history in Western intellectual thought. For a survey of this tradition, see the tendentious history of this idea written by Arthur Miller, *The Idea of Decline in Western History* (New York: Free Press, 1997).

19. Addison Gayle, *The Way of the New World: The Black Novel in America* (Garden City, NY: Doubleday, 1976), p. 313. Note the silent comparative invocation of Jews: We "had survived numerous holocausts."

20. Because the teleology of the black power and black arts crowds did not depend on appeals to or changes in the collective conscience of white Americans, it was able to appear more secular and racially autonomous than the Christian-influenced teleologies of black social change as advanced by Martin Luther King Jr. Such appearances were false, however, for all teleological systems of thought grant the ultimate authority for social change to some transhistorical, suprahuman force like God or History.

21. Charlie Reilly, ed., *Conversations with Amiri Baraka* (Jackson: University Press of Mississippi, 1994), pp. 32–33.

22. Maurice Merleau-Ponty, *Sense and Non-Sense*, trans. Hubert L. Dreyfus and Patricia Allen Dreyfus (Evanston, IL: Northwestern University Press, 1964), pp. 177–78.

23. Interview with Austin Clarke, in Reilly, ed., *Conversations with Amiri Baraka*, p. 37.

24. According to Philip Rieff, theorizing is a distancing mechanism. When comparing Norman Mailer with Herbert Marcuse, Rieff wrote, "'The White Negro' (1957) is not a work of theory but of tactics. Marcuse's work remains intractably theoretical; at cross-purposes with any revolution, theory carries a repressive implication. Theory admits no blind obediences. Being tactical, Mailer's work is more useful." See Philip Rieff, *Fellow Teachers* (New York: Harper & Row, 1973), p. 103.

25. Jones had previously argued that the reasons that the white woman was sexually attracted to the black man "was because he was basic and elemental emotionally

(which is true for the nonbrainwashed black, simply because there is no reason he should not be; the black man is more natural than the white simply because he has fewer *things* between him and reality, fewer wrappers, fewer artificial rules)." See LeRoi Jones, "American Sexual Reference: Black Male," in his *Home*, pp. 221–22.

26. I am, of course, referring to the arguments presented by Herbert Marcuse in *One-Dimensional Man* (Boston: Beacon Press, 1964); and by Philip Rieff in *The Triumph of the Therapeutic: Uses of Faith after Freud* (New York: Harper & Row, 1966).

27. Renato Poggiolo, *The Theory of the Avant-Garde* (New York: Harper & Row, 1971).

28. The idea of "rituals of rebellion" came from my reading of Martin Kilson's work on political development, particularly *Political Change in a West African State* (Cambridge, MA: Harvard University Press, 1964). Kilson attributes the idea to Max Gluckman.

29. As a Marxist, Baraka referred to them as *compradors*.

30. Max Scheler, *Ressentiment*, ed. Lewis Coser and trans. William W. Holdheim (New York: Schocken Books, 1961), p. 48.

31. When asked if there was a black aesthetic, Giovanni responded, "As the black-aesthetic criticism went, you were told that if you were a black writer or a black critic, you were told *this* is what you should do. That kind of prescription cuts off the question by defining parameters. I object to prescriptions of all kinds. In this case the prescription was a capsulized militant stance. What are we going to do with a stance? Literature is only as useful as it reflects reality." See Claudia Tate, ed., *Black Women Writers at Work* (New York: Continuum Press, 1985), p. 63.

32. Don L. Lee, "Toward a Definition: Black Poetry of the Sixties (after LeRoi Jones)," in *The Black Aesthetic*, ed. Gayle, p. 232.

33. My distinctions are simplistic and intended only for use as heuristic devices.

34. Gayle, ed., *The Black Aesthetic*, p. 4.

35. Morris Dickstein argues that during the 1960s, white critics of black literature engaged in racial patronization of black writers, resulting in inflated praise of inferior works. Although this may have been the case, Dickstein unfortunately does not mention any specific instances. Given the significance of his claim, the absence of documentation is irresponsible. One could read Dickstein and think that Donald Goines was nominated for a National Book Award. I did not uncover this tendency. See Morris Dickstein, *Gates of Eden: American Culture in the Sixties* (Cambridge, MA: Harvard University Press, 1997), p. 158.

36. Gayle, ed., *The Black Aesthetic*, p. xxxiii.

37. Karl Mannheim, *Ideology and Utopia* (London: Routledge, 1968).

38. Discussions of Bambara, Brooks, Clifton, Evans, Giovanni, Rodgers, Lorde, and Sanchez can be found in Mari Evans, ed., *Black Women Writers (1950–1980): A Critical Evaluation* (Garden City, NY: Doubleday, 1984). An excellent discussion of Cortez can be found in Aldon Lynn Nielsen, *Black Chant: Languages of African-American Postmodernism* (Cambridge: Cambridge University Press, 1997). Extended interviews with Cortez, Sanchez, and Brooks can be found in D. H. Melhem, *Heroism in the*

New Black Poetry (Lexington: University Press of Kentucky, 1990). For a discussion of Teer, see Barbara Lewis, "Ritual Reformulations: Barbara Ann Teer and the National Black Theatre of Harlem," in *A Sourcebook of African-American Performance: Plays, People, Movements*, ed. Annemarie Bean (New York: Routledge, 1999), pp. 68–82.

39. Toni Cade Bambara, ed., *The Black Woman: An Anthology* (New York: Penguin Books, 1970), p. 7.

40. See "Ralph Ellison: His Literary Work and Status," a special issue of *Black World* 20, no. 2 (December 1970).

41. Gayle, ed., *The Black Aesthetic*, p. xxii.

42. In some respects, Gayle's claims represent a rudimentary variant of reader-response criticism. For a description of the major theorists and theoretical tendencies in this arena, see Vincent B. Leitch, *American Literary Criticism: From the 30s to the 80s* (New York: Columbia University Press, 1988), chap. 8.

43. Gayle, *The Way of The New World*, p. 379.

44. Ron Karenga, "Black Art: A Rhythmic Reality of Revolution," in *The Black Aesthetic*, ed. Gayle, pp. 31–32, 36.

45. James Cunningham, "Hemlock for Black Artist: Karenga Style," *Negro Digest* (January 1968); reprinted in *New Black Voices: An Anthology of Contemporary Afro-American Literature*, ed. Abraham Chapman (New York: New American Library, 1972), pp. 483–89.

46. George Kent, *Blackness and the Adventure of Western Culture* (Chicago: Third World Press, 1972), p. 200.

47. Reilly, ed., *Conversations with Amiri Baraka*, p. 22.

48. Ameer Baraka, "The Black Aesthetic: We Are Our Feelings," *Black World* 18, no. 11 (September 1969): 5–6, and Amiri Baraka, *Raise Race Rays Raze* (New York: Random House, 1971), p. 118.

49. Baraka, *Raise Race Rays Raze*, p. 117.

50. Ibid., p. 123.

51. For an insightful discussion of Locke and aesthetics, see George Hutchinson, *The Harlem Renaissance in Black and White* (Cambridge, MA: Harvard University Press, 1995), chaps. 6 and 14. For additional pieces by Locke concerning issues related to a black aesthetic, see his *The Negro and His Music and Negro Art: Past and Present* (New York; Arno Press, 1969).

52. Alain Locke, "Negro Youth Speaks," in *The New Negro*, ed. Alain Locke (New York: Atheneum, 1977), pp. 47–48.

53. Richard Wright, "Blueprint for Negro Literature," in *Richard Wright Reader*, ed. Ellen Wright and Michel Fabre (New York: Harper & Row, 1978), pp. 36–49.

54. Sterling Brown, the critic, wrote *Negro Poetry and Drama and The Negro in American Fiction* (New York: Atheneum, 1978). For an overview of his poetry, see Sterling Brown, *The Collected Poems of Sterling Brown* (New York: Harper & Row, 1980). For a discussion of Sterling Brown, see Sterling Stuckey, *Going through the Storm: The Influence of African American Art in History* (New York: Oxford University Press, 1994), chap. 8. Any discussion of the influence of Langston Hughes on a subsequent

generations of black writers must begin with the two-volume biography of Hughes by Arnold Rampersad: *The Life of Langston Hughes,* vol. 1, *1902–1941, "I, Too, Sing America"* (New York: Oxford University Press, 1986), and vol. 2, *1941–1967, "I Dream A World"* (New York: Oxford University Press, 1988); the excellent biography by Faith Berry, *Before and beyond Harlem: A Biography of Langston Hughes* (New York: Wings Books, 1992); and Charles Nichols, ed., *Arna Bontemps-Langston Hughes Letters: 1925–1967* (New York: Dodd, Mead, 1980). For a representative sample of Brown's writings on Afro-American politics, literature, music, and folklore, see Mark A. Sanders, ed., *A Son's Return: Selected Essays of Sterling A. Brown* (Boston: Northeastern University Press, 1996).

55. A comprehensive and informative treatment of Brown can be found in Joanne V. Gabbin, *Sterling Brown: Building the Black Aesthetic Tradition* (Westport, CT: Greenwood Press, 1985). Also see the special Sterling A. Brown issue of *Callaloo* 21, no. 4 (Fall 1998).

56. For a celebration of Sterling Brown, see Stephen E. Henderson, "A Strong Man Called Sterling Brown," reprinted from *Black World* (September 1970) in Dudley Randall, ed., *Homage to Hoyt Fuller* (Detroit: Broadside Press, 1984), pp. 156–63.

57. Stephen E. Henderson, ed., *Understanding the New Black Poetry, Black Speech and Black Music as Poetic References* (New York: Morrow, 1973), esp. Henderson's introduction.

58. Henry Louis Gates Jr., *Figures in Black: Words, Signs, and the "Racial" Self* (New York: Oxford University Press, 1987), p. 33.

59. Henderson, *Understanding the New Black Poetry*, p. 80.

60. Stephen E. Henderson, "Saturation: Progress Report on a Theory of Black Poetry," in *Homage to Hoyt Fuller*, ed. Randall, p. 198.

61. Houston A. Baker Jr., *Blues, Ideology, and Afro-American Literature* (Chicago: University of Chicago Press, 1984), pp. 84–85.

62. Gates, *Figures in Black*, pp. 32–35.

63. David Lionel Smith, "Chicago Poets, OBAC, and the Black Arts Movement," in *The Black Columbiad: Defining Moments in African American Literature and Culture*, ed. Werner Sollors and Maria Diedrich (Cambridge, MA: Harvard University Press, 1994), pp. 257–58.

64. For a discussion of Reed's relationship to the Black Aesthetic movement, see Patrick McGee, *Ishmael Reed and the Ends of Race* (New York: St. Martin's Press, 1997); and Reginald Martin, *Ishmael Reed and the New Black Aesthetic Critics* (New York: St. Martin's Press, 1988). Reed makes many statements "off the cuff" which, when reviewed, do not stand true. He excels at generating controversy. However, in his non-fiction and interviews, Reed often displays a superficiality of thought that is quite stunning. For proof of this, read any three of the interviews in Bruce Dick and Amritjit Singh, eds., *Conversations with Ishmael Reed* (Jackson: University Press of Mississippi, 1995).

65. Joe Goncalves, "'When State Magicians Fail': An Interview with Ishmael Reed," *Journal of Black Poetry* 1, no. 12 (Summer/Fall 1969): 73, 76, 77.

66. Sandra Hollin Flowers, *African American Nationalist Literature of the 1960s* (New York: Garland, 1996), pp. 44–45.

67. Timothy Phoenix, "Black Writers Must Be Free," *Liberator* 7 (August 1967): 10.

68. Clarence Major, *The Dark and Feeling: Black American Writers and Their Work* (New York: Third Press, 1974), p. 19.

69. Abby Arthur Johnson and Ronald Maberry Johnson, *Propaganda and Aesthetics: The Literary Politics of Afro-American Magazines in the Twentieth Century* (Amherst: University of Massachusetts Press, 1991), p. 183. Toure's "open letter" to Baraka originally appeared in *Black Dialogue* 3 (Winter 1967/68): 3–4.

70. Johnson and Johnson, *Propaganda and Aesthetics*, p. 183.

71. Stanley Crouch, "Toward a Purer Black Poetry Esthetic," *Journal of Black Poetry* 1, no. 10 (Fall 1968): 28.

72. Stanley Crouch, "Books," *Journal of Black Poetry* 1, no. 10 (Fall 1968): 90.

73. Lorenzo Thomas, "Neon Griot: The Functional Role of Poetry Readings in the Black Arts Movement," in *Close Listening: Poetry and the Performed World*, ed. Charles Bernstein (New York: Oxford University Press, 1998).

74. Larry Neal, "And Shine Swam On," in his *Visions of a Liberated Future: Black Arts Movement Writings*, ed. Michael Schwartz (New York: Thunder's Mouth Press, 1989), pp. 20–21.

75. Amiri Baraka, introduction to *Beer Cans, Bullets, Things & Pieces*, by Arthur Pfister (Detroit: Broadside Press, 1972), and republished in Nielsen, *Black Chant*, p. 19.

76. Dudley Randall, "The Black Aesthetic in the Thirties, Forties, and Fifties," in *The Black Aesthetic*, ed. Gayle, pp. 213–14.

77. Jean-Paul Sartre, *What Is Literature?* trans. Bernard Frechtman (New York: Harper & Row, 1965), p. 72. An extended discussion of Wright can be found in the chapter "For Whom Does One Write?"

78. Richard Wright, *Native Son* (New York: Harper & Row, 1966), p. xxvii. "How Bigger Was Born" appears as the introduction to this volume.

79. One scholar wrote, "Whereas to preceding generations, the Negro's 'double consciousness' had been his unique resource, to Baraka's young contemporaries it became the primary symptom of his malady. In their writings, derogatory references to Du Bois's Idea were frequent, even as they embraced him and included him in their pantheon of heroes. Instead was projected the ideal of a unified non-Western sensibility, merging ideas of a distinctive and peculiar racial *Geist*, a separate culture, and a Black Nation." Sigmund Ro, "'Descerators' and 'Necromancers': Black American Writers and Critics in the Nineteen-Sixties and the Third World Perspective," *Callaloo 25*, vol. 8, no. 3 (Autumn 1985): 573.

80. Charles Fuller, "Black Writing Is Socio-Creative Art," *Liberator*, April 1967, p. 8.

81. One of the ironies of the celebration of jazz and the blues that was so prevalent during the Black Arts period was the unwillingness of many black arts literary

critics to concede that black musicians had phenomenal respect for artistic forms and their craftsmanship. In a fit of honest dogmatism, Baraka even began to criticize black jazz musicians for their concerns for artistic form. He even claimed that Junior Walker and the All Stars, a popular Motown group known for its complex and intriguing musical scores (e.g., *Shotgun* and *Road Runner*), was engaged in a more substantive artistic venture than were Albert Ayler and Ornette Coleman. And Baraka wasn't joking. See Baraka, *Raise Race Rays Raze*, p. 120.

82. Larry Neal, "The Black Contribution to American Letters: Part II, The Writer as Activist—1960 and After" in *The Black American Reference Book*, ed. Mabel Smythe (Englewood Cliffs, NJ: Prentice-Hall, 1976), p. 783.

83. Ibid., p. 784. Neal and Baraka were cofounders of the Black Arts Repertory Theater/School and coeditors of *Black Fire*. Consequently, his omission of Baraka is all the more conspicuous and significant.

84. For a rather extensive discussion of the idea, see Gene H. Bell-Villada, *Art for Art's Sake and Literary Life: How Politics and Markets Helped Shape the Ideology and Culture of Aestheticism, 1790–1990* (Lincoln: University of Nebraska Press, 1996).

85. Werner Sollors, *Amiri Baraka / LeRoi Jones: The Quest for a "Populist Modernism"* (New York: Columbia University Press, 1978), p. 193.

86. Ibid., p. 194.

NOTES TO CHAPTER 6

1. I do not know why the black middle class has not been more supportive of black intellectual infrastructures. In a provocative, often quoted, but deeply flawed essay, Cornel West makes the mistake of listing his speculations as if they are empirical facts that can suffice as proof for various assertions: "In addition to the general anti-intellectual tenor of American society, there is a deep distrust and suspicion of black intellectuals within the black community. This distrust and suspicion stem not simply from the usual arrogant and haughty disposition of intellectuals toward ordinary folk, but, more importantly, from the widespread refusal of black intellectuals to remain, in some visible way, organically linked with African American cultural life. The relatively high rates of exogamous marriage, the abandonment of black institutions and the preoccupation with Euro-American intellectual products are often perceived by the black community as intentional efforts to escape the negative sigma of blackness or are viewed as symptoms of self-hatred." Cornel West, "The Dilemma of the Black Intellectual," in his *Keeping Faith: Philosophy and Race in America* (New York: Routledge, 1993), p. 71. There is no proof that most or even many black Americans think of black intellectuals as racially self-hating.

2. Among the best studies of the various "white" intellectual infrastructures that helped produce the Harlem Renaissance are those by George Hutchinson, *The Harlem Renaissance in Black and White* (Cambridge, MA: Harvard University Press, 1995); and Ann Douglas, *Terrible Honesty: Mongrel Manhattan in the 1920s* (New York: Farrar, Straus & Giroux, 1995).

3. David Levering Lewis, *When Harlem Was in Vogue* (New York: Knopf, 1981).

4. For a thorough discussion of Tuskegee, see Louis Harlan, *Booker T. Washington, II: The Wizard of Tuskegee, 1901–1915* (New York: Oxford University Press, 1983); and James Anderson, *The Education of Blacks in the South, 1860–1935* (Chapel Hill: University of North Carolina Press, 1988).

5. For glimpses of Carter G. Woodson as a developer of a black intellectual infrastructure, see August Meier and Elliott Rudwick, *Black History and the Historical Profession, 1915–1980* (Champaign-Urbana: University of Illinois Press, 1986), esp. chap. 1.

6. Jacqueline Goggin, *Carter G. Woodson: A Life in Black History* (Baton Rouge: Louisiana State University Press, 1993), pp. 32, 114.

7. For Du Bois's experiences at *The Crisis*, see David Levering Lewis, *W. E. B. Du Bois: Biography of a Race, 1868–1919* (New York: Henry Holt, 1993), chaps. 15–19. I do not want my discussion of Du Bois's treatment as editor of *The Crisis* to suggest that he should have been given a free hand to run the magazine according to his personal whims. After all, it was the house organ of an organization.

8. See Genna Rae McNeil, *Groundwork: Charles Hamilton Houston and the Struggle for Civil Rights* (Philadelphia: University of Pennsylvania Press, 1983); Richard Kluger, *Simple Justice: The History of Brown v. Board of Education and Black America's Struggle for Equality* (New York: Knopf, 1976); and J. Clay Smith Jr., *Emancipation: The Making of the Black Lawyer, 1844–1944* (Philadelphia: University of Pennsylvania Press, 1993).

9. Some of these essays are reprinted in Larry Neal, *Visions of a Liberated Future: Black Arts Movement Writings*, ed. Michael Schwartz (New York: Thunder's Mouth Press, 1989). Neal's writings on Jones are not included in this collection.

10. John H. Johnson, with Lerone Bennett Jr., *Succeeding against the Odds* (New York: Warner Books, 1989), p. 289.

11. In his autobiography Johnson wrote, "Later, when the Freedom Movement ebbed, the circulation of *Black World* dropped from 100,000 to 15,000 and I discontinued the renamed *Negro Digest* for the second time" (ibid.).

12. Haki Madhubuti, "Blacks, Jews and Henry Louis Gates, Jr.," in his *Claiming Earth: Race, Rage, Rape, Redemption* (Chicago: Third World Press, 1994), p. 68.

13. I could uncover only very scanty evidence to suggest that any anti-Israeli sentiments were ever prominently displayed in *Black World*. The October 1975 issue published a copy of an appeal by a group known as Black Americans in Support of Israel Committee (B.A.S.I.C.). The appeal had been previously published in the *New York Times*. It was entitled "An Appeal by Black Americans for United States Support to Israel" and was attributed to the A. Philip Randolph Institute, which was under the directorship of Bayard Rustin. *Black World* viewed this appeal as an affront and republished it with a response entitled "A Resolution Condemning the Appeal by So-Called Black Leaders Calling for United States Support to Israel." It was written by Jomo Logan, who belonged to an organization called A.F.R.I.C.A. The response argued that because the Organization of African Unity

(OAU) had endorsed the Arabs in the Middle East conflict with Israel, black Americans should endorse the Arab position. In addition, it condemned Israel for the role it was supposedly playing in the exploitation of black diamond miners in South Africa. Logan stated that "the Zionists have been the allies of imperialism in all its activities in Africa, Asia, Latin America and the African-American communities in the United States. Thus by so doing, the Jews have denied and continue to deny the right of self-determination for Black people that they are trying to force in the Middle East for themselves." Jomo Logan, "A Resolution Condemning the Appeal by So-Called Black Leaders Calling for United States Support to Israel," *Black World*, October 1975, p. 41. Perhaps this article was seen as anti-Semitic, although it is more accurate to refer to it as anti-Zionist.

14.   When interviewed by the literary critic Robert Stepto, novelist Ralph Ellison was asked to comment on the special issue of *Black World* on his work. Annoyed by the journal's treatment, Ellison's response points to the contradictory impulses of the journal's political slant, given the class orientation of the journal's publisher. Unfortunately, Ellison seems to have believed that the highly uneven criticism of him in that one issue made the entirety of the journal useless. Concerning his critics in that issue, he wrote, "But I can say this for them. Safe behind the fence provided by a black capitalist, they had one big 'barking-at-the-gate' go at me. They even managed to convince a few students that I was the worst disaster that had ever hit Afro-American writing. But for all of their attacks I'm still here trying—while if I'm asked where is *Black World* today my answer is: Gone with the snows of yester-year / down the pissor—Dadaa, Da-daa, and good riddance!" See "Study and Experience: An Interview with Ralph Ellison," in *Chant of Saints: A Gathering of Afro-American Literature, Art, and Scholarship*, ed. Michael S. Harper and Robert B. Stepto (Champaign-Urbana: University of Illinois Press, 1979), p. 461.

15.   For a discussion of the fate of small black publishing firms during the early 1980s, see Melba Joyce Boyd, "Out of the Poetry Ghetto: The Life/Art Struggle of Small Black Publishing Houses," *Black Scholar*, July/August 1985, pp. 12–24.

16.   Ahmed Alhamisi, "On Spiritualism and the Revolutionary Spirit," *Journal of Black Poetry* 1, no. 15 (Fall/Winter 1971): 89.

17.   LeRoi Jones and Larry Neal, eds., *Black Fire: An Anthology of Afro-American Writing* (New York: Morrow, 1968), p. xvi. Jones maintained his relationship with his white agent, Sterling Lord, throughout the Black Arts era.

18.   Thomas C. Dent, Richard Schechner, and Gilbert Moses, eds., *The Free Southern Theater* (Indianapolis: Bobbs-Merrill, 1969).

19.   For a discussion of the problems of funding black theaters, see Errol Hill, ed., *The Theater of Black Americans*, vol. 2, esp. the essays by Ellen Foreman, "The Negro Ensemble Company: A Transcendent Vision" (pp. 72–84), and Lindsay Patterson, "Black Theater: The Search Goes On" (pp. 147–52). Also see Mance Williams, *Black Theatre in the 1960s and 1970s: A Historical-Critical Analysis of the Movement* (Westport, CT: Greenwood Press, 1985), esp. chap. 3.

20.   See Thomas D. Pawley, "The Black Theatre Audience," in *The Theater of Black*

Americans, vol. 2, ed. Hill, pp. 109–19; and Williams, *Black Theatre in the 1960s and 1970s*.

21. Studies of black studies include Johnnella E. Butler, *Black Studies: Pedagogy and Revolution* (Lanham, MD: University Press of America, 1981); Armstead Robinson, Craig C. Foster, and Donald Ogilvie, eds., *Black Studies in the University* (New Haven, CT: Yale University Press, 1969); Nathan Huggins, *A Report to the Ford Foundation on Afro-American Studies* (New York: Ford Foundation, 1985); Robert L. Harris Jr., Darlene Clark Hine, and Nellie McKay, *Three Essays: Black Studies in the United States* (New York: Ford Foundation, 1990); Molefi Asante, "A Book Review Essay: A Note on the Nathan Huggins Report to the Ford Foundation on African American Studies," *Journal of Black Studies* 17, no. 2 (December 1986): 255–62; and John Blassingame, ed., *New Perspectives on Black Studies* (Champaign-Urbana: University of Illinois Press, 1971).

22. Vincent B. Leitch, *American Literary Criticism: From the 30s to the 80s* (New York: Columbia University Press, 1988), p. 360.

23. When black subjects were included in the curriculum, it was usually in reference to problems in need of solution. Need we remember Du Bois's question in *The Souls of Black Folk*, "How does it feel to be a problem?"

24. For a scathing, polemical critique of the failure of black studies programs at white institutions, see Don L. Lee, "The New Pimps / or It's Hip to Be Black: The Failure of Black Studies," in his *From Plan to Planet: Life Studies: The Need for Afrikan Minds and Institutions* (Detroit: Broadside Press, 1973), pp. 55–61. Just as I was about to celebrate the intelligence of this critique, I read the following nonsensical statement "We need original thinkers who can politically deal with the *right* and the *left* (p. 59). Perhaps it was my stupidity to have assumed that even a dogmatic, religious nationalist like Lee could have recognized variation in the thoughts of white intellectuals. Moreover, in this essay, Lee refers to the fictitious *The Report from Iron Mountain* as if it were an authentic report of a hidden white plot in the making.

25. For an extensive history of Umbra, see Michel Oren, "The Umbra Poets Workshop, 1962–1965: Some Socio-Literary Puzzles," in *Studies in Black American Literature*, vol. 2: *Belief vs. Theory in Black American Literary Criticism*, ed. Joe Weixlmann and Charles J. Fontenot (Greenwood, FL: Penkevill Publishing, 1986), pp. 177–223, 180.

26. Of course, it is debatable whether or not Ishmael Reed should be considered a participant in the Black Arts movement.

27. Oren, "The Umbra Poets Workshop," p. 177.

28. Abby Arthur Johnson and Ronald Maberry Johnson, *Propaganda and Aesthetics: The Literary Politics of Afro-American Magazines in the Twentieth Century* (Amherst: University of Massachusetts Press, 1991), p. 164.

29. See David Lionel Smith, "Chicago Poets, OBAC, and the Black Arts Movement," in *The Black Columbiad: Defining Moments in African American Literature and Culture*, ed. Werner Sollors and Maria Diedrich (Cambridge, MA: Harvard University Press, 1994), pp. 253–64.

30. For a more expansive introduction to OBAC, see Carole A. Parks, ed., *Nommo: A Literary Legacy of Black Chicago (1967–1987)* (Chicago: OBAhouse, 1987).

31. Smith, "Chicago Poets, OBAC, and the Black Arts Movement," pp. 259, 257, 258.

32. Ibid., p. 260.

33. See "An Interview with Topper Carew," *Saturday Review*, July 18, 1970, pp. 46–48.

34. Tony Brown's show *Black Journal* was a national version of these types of programs.

35. Charles Johnson, *Being and Race: Black Writing since 1970* (Bloomington: Indiana University Press, 1988), p. 120.

36. I say this not to imply that academic literary criticism is the ultimate arbiter of what is or is not good writing. After all, for most of the twentieth century, academic literary taste relegated blacks and most white females to an artistic scrap heap. Yet because even black critics also now "ignore" these works, the Black Arts movement is slowly being forgotten. The reason could, however, be the result of the professionalization of black literary studies, a professionalization that gains more cultural capital from situating black writing in established traditions, as opposed to celebrating those who intentionally remained outsiders.

37. Johnson, *Being and Race*, p. 22.

38. See Jerry G. Watts, *Heroism and the Black Intellectual: Ralph Ellison, Politics, and Afro-American Intellectual Life* (Chapel Hill: University of North Carolina Press, 1994), esp. chap. 2.

39. Peter Gay, *Weimar Culture: The Outsider as Insider* (New York: Harper & Row, 1968).

40. In this sense, Baraka was following some of Harold Cruse's dictates, as described in his *The Crisis of the Negro Intellectual* (New York: Morrow, 1967).

NOTES TO CHAPTER 7

1. Gerald Weales, "The Day LeRoi Jones Spoke on Penn's Campus: What Were the Blacks Doing in the Balcony?" *New York Times Magazine*, May 4, 1969, pp. 38–40.

2. LeRoi Jones, *Black Magic Poetry: 1961–1967* (Indianapolis: Bobbs-Merrill, 1969), p. 225.

3. Gwendolyn Brooks, *Report from Part One* (Detroit: Broadside Press, 1972), pp. 168. The episode is also mentioned on p. 85.

4. The Black Arts crowd was of two minds concerning the authenticity of traditional black religious worship. On the one hand, they viewed the black Christian Church as a model for reaching the black masses. On the other hand, they viewed the message of the church and even its fever pitched emotionalism as antithetical to the black emancipation struggle.

5. For a discussion of performance poetry in Beat bohemia, see Lorenzo Thomas's excellent "Neon Griot: The Functional Role of Poetry Readings in the Black

Arts Movement," in *Close Listening: Poetry and the Performed Word*, ed. Charles Bernstein (New York: Oxford University Press, 1998), pp. 300–23.

6. Ibid., p. 306.

7. Jones, *Black Magic Poetry*, p. 115.

8. Ibid., p. 135.

9. Ibid., p. 142.

10. Ibid., p. 154.

11. Ibid., pp. 205–6.

12. Ibid., p. 121.

13. Ibid., p. 217.

14. Ibid., p. 186.

15. Ibid., p. 140.

16. Ibid., p. 148.

17. I remember that some black activists in Washington would say, "it's nation time," while others would assert, "it's nation-building time."

18. Imamu Amiri Baraka, *It's Nation Time* (Chicago: Third World Press, 1970), p. 7. On the title page, the author's name is listed as Imamu Amiri Baraka, but immediately underneath this is the name LeRoi Jones, in smaller letters and enclosed in parentheses. Why did a black nationalist publishing firm like Third World Press feel compelled to clarify Baraka's historical identity?

19. Ibid., p. 8.

20. Ibid., pp. 8, 10, 11.

21. Ibid., pp. 15, 16.

22. Ibid., p. 22.

23. Amiri Baraka, *Selected Plays and Prose of Amiri Baraka / LeRoi Jones* (New York: Morrow, 1979), p. 202.

24. Stiff, wooden, dead-in-life white folks need to be destroyed (burned). Blacks, dynamic fire, need to destroy them. However, a black who doesn't understand that white folks need to be burned is probably as dead-in-life as they are and either needs to be burned or might burn himself.

25. Baraka, *Selected Plays*, p. 204.

26. Ibid., pp. 212–13.

27. Imamu Amiri Baraka and Fundi, *In Our Terribleness* (Indianapolis: Bobbs-Merrill, 1970). There are no printed page numbers in *In Our Terribleness*, so I will not use notes for my discussion of this text.

28. The essay originally appeared in the journal *Black Scholar* in 1969.

29. I remember receiving a copy of this booklet during the summer before my first year at Harvard College, sent to me by Harvard's black student organization. Fascinated, I was nevertheless baffled by the booklet precisely because I did not know why I was supposed to pay attention to the arbitrary views of this unfamiliar person who called himself Imamu. Besides, I wondered just what this return to traditional African values had to do with my desire to attend Harvard. Only later did I discover that these African values were, in fact, "California African" names. That aside, the booklet was

useful as a centerpiece of numerous late-night dorm conversations about the responsibility of black students to the black community. It is not clear to me that the nationalist penchant, as embodied in Baraka's booklet, for raising such important questions was ever supplanted (for later generations of black students) by an equally effective alternative discourse. However, the discussions generated by texts like Baraka's were often based on a limited range of ethnically legitimate answers. The subcultures that arose around such texts produced a "constrained inquisitiveness."

30. Imamu Amiri Baraka, *Raise Race Rays Raze: Essays since 1965* (New York: Random House, 1971), pp. 4, 5.

31. Ibid., pp. 11–12.

32. Ibid., p. 19.

33. Ibid., p. 18.

34. Ibid., p. 25; see also Donald M. Allen, ed., *New American Poetry, 1945–1960* (New York: Grove Press, 1960), p. 25.

35. LeRoi Jones, ed., *The Moderns: An Anthology of New Writing in America* (New York: Corinth Books, 1963).

36. Baraka, *Raise Race Rays Raze*, p. 33.

37. Ibid., pp. 33–34.

38. Ibid., p. 98.

39. Ibid., pp. 98–99.

40. Ibid., p. 99.

41. Ibid., p. 112.

42. Ibid., pp. 112–13.

43. Part of the Black Arts movement intellectuals' animus toward the Negro Ensemble Theater stemmed from the theater's decision to locate outside a black community, which they considered to be an admission of the difficulty black theaters faced in trying to attract a sustaining audience. This approach to theater also differed drastically from the community development ethos championed by the Black Theater movement.

44. Baraka, *Raise Race Rays Raze*, p. 39.

45. Ibid., p. 40.

46. Ibid., p. 41.

47. Ibid., p. 42.

48. Ibid. p. 43.

49. The Nation of Islam had a smaller black membership than the NAACP. The Nation of Islam had a much larger following of "sympathetic" black nonmembers than actual members. Many of these nonmember sympathizers had been drawn to the Nation through Malcolm, so when Malcolm was assassinated, many of them ceased to be as sympathetic to the organization. Certainly, Baraka was an example of such a sympathizer. Baraka's discussion of the reasons for the Nation's appeal is wrong. First, the Nation of Islam was relatively small for the very reasons that Baraka erroneously claimed lay behind its appeal. That is, its totality was too demanding for most blacks. Claude Andrew Clegg III, a biographer of Elijah Muhammad, estimated that at its

height during the early 1960s, the Nation of Islam had about 20,000 members nationally. However, Clegg notes that estimates of the Nation's membership have ranged from 5,000 to 250,000. See Claude Andrew Clegg III, *An Original Man: The Life and Times of Elijah Muhammad* (New York: St. Martin's Press, 1997), p. 115.

50. Baraka, *Raise Race Rays Raze*, p. 120.

51. Ibid., p. 30.

52. Perhaps Baraka was so devoted to his quasi-religious, black nationalist worldview that he actually believed his rewriting of history. If so, he rewrote history *as he wished it had been.* According to Baraka's mythical narrative, (1) Malcolm was the uncontested leader of black people; (2) white America trembled at the sound of his voice; and (3) Martin Luther King Jr., Roy Wilkins, and Whitney Young were popularly recognized by blacks as well-intentioned weaklings at best and Uncle Toms at worst.

53. Baraka, *Raise Race Rays Raze*, pp. 125, 126.

54. Ibid., p. 129.

55. Ibid., p. 130.

56. Ibid., pp. 130, 131.

57. Jan Carew, review of *Raise Race Rays Raze*, by Amiri Baraka, *New York Times Book Review*, June 27, 1971, p. 4.

58. Ibid., p. 31.

59. Addison Gayle Jr., *The Way of the New World: The Black Novel in America* (Garden City, NY: Doubleday, 1976), pp. 310–11.

60. Ibid., p. 311.

61. Ibid., p. 312.

NOTES TO CHAPTER 8

1. Apparently Baraka did not use these criteria when writing *In Our Terribleness*, a text that romanticizes black life "on the block." Devoid of self-reflection, Baraka can state simultaneously that "a slave cannot be hip—it is a contradiction" and yet, a slave could be "terrible."

2. Amiri Baraka, "Black Revolutionary Poets Should Also Be Playwrights," *Black World* 21, no. 6 (April 1972): 5.

3. Charlie Reilly, ed., *Conversations with Amiri Baraka* (Jackson: University Press of Mississippi, 1994), p. 236.

4. LeRoi Jones, *Four Black Revolutionary Plays* (Indianapolis: Bobbs-Merrill, 1969), pp. 7–8.

5. See Henry C. Lacey, *To Raise, Destroy, and Create: The Poetry, Drama, and Fiction of Imamu Amiri Baraka (LeRoi Jones)* (Troy, NY: Whitston Publishing, 1981), pp. 133–39.

6. Theodore R. Hudson, *From LeRoi Jones to Amiri Baraka: The Literary Works* (Durham, NC: Duke University Press, 1973), p. 164.

7. Mattias Gardell, *In the Name of Elijah Muhammad: Louis Farrakhan and the*

Nation of Islam (Durham, NC: Duke University Press, 1996), p. 148. For the complete story of Yacub and the invention of white people, see Elijah Muhammad, *Message to the Blackman in America* (Chicago: Muhammad's Temple no. 2, 1965), pp. 103–22.

8. Jones, *Four Black Revolutionary Plays*, pp. 27–28.

9. Ibid., p. 39.

10. Larry Neal, *Visions of a Liberated Future: Black Arts Movement Writings*, ed. Michael Schwartz (New York: Thunder's Mouth Press, 1989), p. 73.

11. Jones, *Four Black Revolutionary Plays*, p. 89. "Why No *Jello*" is signed Ameer Baraka, even though the name LeRoi Jones appears on the title page and cover of the collection.

12. LeRoi Jones, *Jello* (Chicago: Third World Press, 1970), pp. 11, 13.

13. It is not incidental that Benny was identified as a Jew earlier in the play, thus targeting him as one of the exemplary targets of Jones's antiwhite invectives against exploitative Jewish store owners in black neighborhoods.

14. Hudson, *From LeRoi Jones*, p. 165.

15. Werner Sollors, *Amiri Baraka / LeRoi Jones: The Quest for a "Populist Modernism"* (New York: Columbia University Press, 1978), p. 210.

16. Jones, *Four Black Revolutionary Plays*, p. 47.

17. Ibid., pp. 50–51. Note that Baraka considers it is an invective of the highest order to call a man "woman." This is a common rhetorical practice among urban black males.

18. Ibid., p. 55. (Presumably this is supposed to represent Malcolm X.)

19. Reilly, ed., *Conversations with Amiri Baraka*, p. 72.

20. Kimberly Benston, *Baraka: The Renegade and the Mask* (New Haven, CT: Yale University Press, 1976), p. 213.

21. Amiri Baraka, *The Motion of History and Other Plays* (New York: Morrow, 1978), p. 138.

22. Ibid., p. 143.

23. Ibid., pp. 144, 145.

24. Harry J. Elam Jr., "Social Urgency, Audience Participation, and the Performance of *Slave Ship* by Amiri Baraka," in *Crucibles of Crisis: Performing Social Change*, ed. Janelle Reinelt (Ann Arbor: University of Michigan Press, 1996), p. 13.

25. Ibid.

26. Leslie Catherine Sanders, *The Development of Black Theater in America: From Shadows to Selves* (Baton Rouge: Louisiana State University Press, 1988), p. 171.

27. Augusto Boal, *Theatre of the Oppressed* (New York: Theatre Communications Group, 1985).

28. Elam, "Social Urgency," p. 23.

29. Lacey, *To Raise, Destroy and Create*, p. 157.

30. Hudson, *From LeRoi Jones to Amiri Baraka*, p. 171.

31. Benston, *Baraka*, p. 217.

32. Published in *Drama Review* 12, no. 4 (Summer 1968).

33. Published in *Black Theatre*, no. 5 (1971): 16–17. A shorter ritual piece, "Black

Power Chant," was first published in *Black Theatre*, no. 4 (1970): 35. "Chant" was first published in *Black Theatre*, no. 5 (1971): 16–17.

34. Published in *Drama Review* 12, no. 4 (Summer 1968).

35. Ibid., p. 108.

36. Ibid., pp. 110–11.

37. Sollors, *Amiri Baraka / LeRoi Jones*, p. 207.

38. Benston, *Baraka*, pp. 219–20.

39. The script of the play can be found in Ed Bullins, ed., *New Plays from the Black Theatre* (New York: Bantam Books, 1969), pp. 1–20.

40. Ibid., p. 9.

41. Ibid., p. 10.

42. Published in Woodie King and Ron Milner, eds., *Black Drama Anthology* (New York: Columbia University Press, 1972), pp. 25–31.

43. Ibid., p. 27.

44. Ibid. Once again he is referring to Sly Stone of Sly and the Family Stone singing group.

45. Ibid., pp. 27, 28.

46. Published in King and Milner, eds., *Black Drama Anthology*, pp. 11–23.

47. The defeat of the Mafia at the hands of militant blacks was a common theme in "blaxploitation" films of the 1960s and 1970s. Recall the plot of *Shaft*.

48. Published in book form as *The Sidney Poet Heroical: in 29 Scenes* (New York: I. Reed Books, 1979).

49. It is not clear why Baraka attacks Belafonte so viciously in this play, because Belafonte had been one of the most active black entertainers in the civil rights movement. Moreover, he had come to Newark in 1970 to help Kenneth Gibson's campaign. Perhaps Baraka disapproved of Belafonte's and Poitier's interracial marriages. In his autobiography, Baraka mentions a earlier confrontation with Belafonte during his days at BART: "We pulled some thoroughly juvenile delinquent shit on Harry Belafonte—after demanding some money which he wouldn't give up, writing his name on some paper and then tearing the paper up as if that signified his imminent disposal. But it didn't work, Belafonte wasn't cowed by such shallow theatrics." LeRoi Jones / Amiri Baraka, *The Autobiography of LeRoi Jones / Amiri Baraka* (New York: Freundlich Books, 1984), p. 217.

50. Mel Gussow, *Theatre on the Edge: New Visions, New Voices* (New York: Applause, 1998), pp. 118, 119.

51. Mel Gussow, "Baraka Discusses Politics as an Art," *New York Times*, March 13, 1973, p. 30.

52. See Komozi Woodard, *A Nation within a Nation: Amiri Baraka (LeRoi Jones) and Black Power Politics* (Chapel Hill: University of North Carolina Press, 1999), pp. 148, 194, 200.

53. Baraka was not adverse to creating frivolous "black art." One need only read the rite that he created for the coronation of black queens. A black version of the coronation of the Rose Bowl queen, Baraka's ersatz-African ritual is resplendent with

libations, Swahili chants and stools, and African attire. Not surprisingly, even this supposedly female-centered ritual ends with the former Negro woman, now the African Queen, chanting "sifa ote mtu" (all praises to the black man). That Baraka can state that this ritual should be used instead of the "derivative European-oriented rites" is beyond credulity. Doesn't the entire project of crowning these ceremonial queens on college campuses emanate from white American practices? Actually, Baraka's ritual is a paradoxical admission of the "Americanness" of its creator and the black students participating in it, but evidently this paradox was lost on the Imamu. Nevertheless, after reading this, I was led to wonder whether someone had created ersatz-African debutante balls or even ersatz-African Greek fraternities and sororities. See Imamu Ameer Baraka's "The Coronation of the Black Queen," *Black Scholar*, June 1970, pp. 46–48. The fact that this silliness was published in the *Black Scholar* is just more evidence of the degree that this supposedly serious black nationalist intellectual organ was captured by a vapid blackness at the expense of rigor.

NOTES TO CHAPTER 9

1. LeRoi Jones / Amiri Baraka, *The Autobiography of LeRoi Jones* (Chicago: Lawrence Hill Books, 1997), pp. 320–21. This longer, uncut edition of Jones's autobiography, which was published in 1997, is henceforth cited as *The Autobiography II*.

2. LeRoi Jones / Amiri Baraka, *The Autobiography of LeRoi Jones / Amiri Baraka* (New York: Freundlich Books, 1984), p. 239. This book is henceforth cited as *The Autobiography*.

3. Ibid., pp. 240–41.

4. Despite his admission of guilt about the death of this young woman, Baraka does not discuss the reasons. Why did she die? Did she have access to decent prenatal health care? Did she practice some sort of alternative health care as a result of her attachment to the Yoruba religion, New York style? Did Baraka? Was there any attempt to save the unborn child? See ibid., p. 241.

5. LeRoi Jones, *Black Magic: Collected Poetry, 1961–1967* (Indianapolis: Bobbs-Merrill, 1969), p. 196. The poem "The World Is Full of Remarkable Things" was also dedicated "for little Bumi" (p. 193).

6. *The Autobiography*, pp. 248, 256.

7. *The Autobiography*, pp. 268–69.

8. The poem was reprinted in Houston Baker's essay "Our Lady: Sonia Sanchez and the Writing of a Black Renaissance," in *Studies in Black American Literature*, vol. 3: *Black Feminist Criticism and Critical Theory*, ed. Joe Weixlmann and Houston A. Baker Jr. (Greenwood, FL: Penkevill, 1988), p. 184.

9. Amiri Baraka, "Confessions of a Former Anti-Semite," *Village Voice*, December 17, 1980, p. 20.

10. *The Autobiography*, p. 327.

11. Gerald Horne, *Fire This Time: The Watts Uprising and the 1960s* (Charlottesville: University Press of Virginia, 1995), p. 3.

12. Lewis M. Killian, *The Impossible Revolution, Phase II: Black Power and the American Dream* (New York: Random House, 1975), p. 94.

13. Kerner Commission, *Report of the National Advisory Commission on Civil Disorders* (Washington, DC: U.S. Government Printing Office, March 1, 1968), pp. 60–61. For a more extensive report of the Detroit riot, see Sidney Fine, *Violence in the Model City: The Cavanagh Administration, Race Relations, and the Detroit Riot of 1967* (Ann Arbor: University of Michigan Press, 1989); and Thomas J. Sugrue, *The Origins of the Urban Crisis: Race and Inequality in Postwar Detroit* (Princeton, NJ: Princeton University Press, 1996).

14. Kerner Commission, *Report*, pp. 30–38; quotation from pp. 37–38.

15. According to the Kerner Commission's report, the New Jersey National Guard numbered only 303 blacks in a force of 17,529.

16. Kerner Commission, *Report*, p. 38.

17. *The Autobiography*, p. 260.

18. Ibid., p. 262. At his trial, Jones claims to have repeatedly prayed "All praise to Allah" while being beaten by the police. See *Village Voice*, November 11, 1967, p. 3.

19. Ron Porambo, *No Cause for Indictment: An Autopsy of Newark* (New York: Holt, Rinehart and Winston, 1971), pp. 34–35.

20. *The Autobiography*, p. 265.

21. Ibid.

22. Jones, *Black Magic*, p. 225.

23. *Minneapolis Star*, October 24, 1967, p. 5a.

24. The statement was written by Di Prima, Ginsberg, Olson, and Corso. A copy can be found in Beinecke Library, Yale University (LeRoi Jones Pamphlets, Box 6). P.E.N. took a position opposing the sentence given to LeRoi Jones, and a LeRoi Jones defense committee was established. An advertisement for the defense committee stated that it was "urgently in need of funds to carry on its work." *Freedomways* 8, no. 1 (Winter 1968): 6.

25. In a 1963 essay entitled "Black Writing," Jones wrote, "The Negro writer writing about his own life is in trouble too—so that some maniac can say to you as Gregory Corso said to me recently, "Black writers are stuck because they're always talking about their people." See LeRoi Jones, *Home: Social Essays* (New York: Morrow, 1966), p. 163.

26. Ginsberg's resilient loyalty and fondness for Baraka are conveyed in an interview that was taped for the St. Clair Bourne documentary film, *In Motion, Amiri Baraka*. The interview was published in James B. Gwynne, ed., *Amiri Baraka: The Kaleidoscopic Torch* (New York: Steppingstones Press, 1985), pp. 76–83.

27. *The Autobiography*, pp. 269–72.

28. "Poetic Justice," *Newsweek*, January 15, 1968, p. 24. *Time*'s coverage of the trial included a picture of Baraka, Amina, and their child. The article does not take the position that the trial or the sentencing was unjust or unusual.

29. The peculiar case of Angela Davis was that she was considered both revolutionary and unjustly prosecuted. She became a cause célèbre for her assumed role or

lack thereof in the 1969 California courtroom shoot-out that involved the younger brother of George Jackson. Her incarceration was seen by many as a miscarriage of justice. But she was popularly granted a revolutionary status for having participated in the incident, even though she claimed she had not. Either way, as a victim of injustice or as a revolutionary, her image was enhanced. For a more extensive discussion of the Angela Davis affair, see her autobiography, *Angela Davis: An Autobiography: With Freedom on My Mind* (New York: Bantam Books, 1975), and the collection of essays that she edited while in prison, *If They Come in the Morning* (New York: Signet Books, 1971). There is, of course, the possibility that Jones and Davis were guilty as charged but proclaimed their innocence for obvious reasons.

30. As late as 1981, Baraka still thought that the state might attempt to kill him. See the interview with Baraka in D. H. Melhem, *Heroism in the New Black Poetry: Introductions and Interviews* (Lexington: University Press of Kentucky, 1990), pp. 244–45.

31. Harold Cruse, *Rebellion or Revolution* (New York: Morrow, 1968), p. 188.

32. *The Autobiography*, p. 266.

33. Robert L. Allen, *Black Awakening in Capitalist America* (Garden City, NY: Doubleday, 1969) p. 133.

34. Chuck Stone, "The National Conference on Black Power," in *The Black Power Revolt: A Collection of Essays*, ed. Floyd B. Barbour (Boston: Porter Sargent, 1968), pp. 189–98.

35. Evidently places like Haiti and Liberia did not exist for these conference participants.

36. Allen, *Black Awakening*, p. 138. Allen describes how the Black Power conference held in Philadelphia one year later was even more closely tied to corporate America. The call to the Philadelphia meeting was sent out on the letterhead stationary of the Clairol Company.

37. K. Komozi Woodard, "The Making of the New Ark: Imamu Amiri Baraka (LeRoi Jones), the Newark Congress of African People, and the Modern Black Convention Movement. A History of the Black Revolt and the New Nationalism, 1966–1976" (Ph.D. diss., University of Pennsylvania, 1991), p. 108.

38. For a description of the 1967 Newark riot, see Tom Hayden's *Rebellion in Newark: Official Violence and Ghetto Response* (New York: Vintage Books, 1967).

39. Allen, *Black Awakening*, pp. 114–19.

40. Ibid., p. 136–39.

41. Ibid., p. 115.

42. House Committee on Un-American Activities, Charles Kinney, testimony, *Hearing before the Committee on Un-American Activities, Subversive Influences in Riots, Looting, and Burning: Part 4 (Newark, N.J.)*, 90th Cong., 2d sess., April 23 and 24, 1968, p. 1944.

43. Tom Hayden, *Reunion: A Memoir* (New York: Random House, 1988), p. 127.

44. Interestingly, while Jones was trying to pacify Newark blacks, Karenga was doing the same on the West Coast. Robert Allen writes: "Following the assassination

of Martin Luther King, Karenga met secretly with Los Angeles Police Chief Thomas Reddin, and he played an important part in preventing the outbreak of riots in that city." Allen, *Black Awakening*, p. 139.

45. *The Autobiography*, p. 274.

46. Allen, *Black Awakening*, p. 115.

47. See *The Autobiography*, pp. 230–313. In fairness, I should note that even the most critical observers of black nationalist politics (except for Robert Allen and a very few others) did not at this early date foresee the limitations of black mayors and black electoral activities. Furthermore, who could have known that Gibson would have been so weak kneed and visionless? Compared with others in this first generation of black mayors, Gibson was one of the worst.

48. See James Boggs, "The City Is the Black Man's Land," in his volume of collected essays, *Racism and the Class Struggle: Further Pages from a Black Worker's Notebook* (New York: Monthly Review Press, 1970), pp. 39–50.

49. Allen, *Black Awakening*, p. 115.

50. *The Autobiography*, p. 240.

51. Ibid., pp. 266, 267.

52. Ibid. Jones changed his name on several occasions. Everett LeRoy Jones became Leroy Jones who became LeRoi Jones, who became Ameer Barakat, who became Amiri Baraka, who later became Imamu (Spiritual Leader) Amiri Baraka and is now once again Amiri Baraka. Jones's penchant for acquiring new names may be a sign of his objectified self-identity. To alter one's identity, one need only to call oneself by a different name.

53. We should not overlook the irony of acquiring an Arabic name. Arabs were deeply implicated in the African slave trade. Second, Swahili was a language created when the Arabs dominated black East Africans.

54. Charlie Reilly, ed., *Conversations with Amiri Baraka* (Jackson: University Press of Mississippi, 1994), p. 36.

55. Reilly, *Conversations with Amiri Baraka*, pp. 37–38.

56. For a discussion that engaged and disputed Karenga's understanding of the blues, see Larry Neal, "The Ethos of the Blues," *Black Scholar* 3, no. 10 (Summer 1972): 42–48.

57. *The Autobiography*, p. 248.

58. Horne, *Fire This Time*, p. 200.

59. *The Autobiography*, p. 253.

60. Martin Kilson, "The New Black Intellectuals," *Dissent*, July/August 1969, p. 306. The Kilson formulation is somewhat ingenious and can be enhanced by an understanding of Antonio Gramsci's concept of the *organic intellectual*. When revised for the contemporary American context, Gramsci's formulation allows us to place these "paraintellectuals" in a richer political context. Kilson's paraintellectuals are the organic intellectuals of the black urban lower-classes. See Antonio Gramsci, *Selections From the Prison Notebooks*, ed. Quintin Hoare and Geoffrey Nowell Smith (New York: International Publishers, 1971), pp. 3–23; Also see the discussion of intellectuals in

Christine Buci-Glucksmann's *Gramsci and the State*, trans. David Fernback (London: Lawrence and Wishard, 1980); and Carl Boggs's *The Two Revolutions: Gramsci and the Dilemmas of Western Marxism* (Boston: South End Press, 1984).

61. *The Quotable Karenga* (Los Angeles: Saidi Publications, 1967).

62. An excerpt from *The Quotable Karenga* can be found in Floyd Barbour, ed., *The Black Power Revolt* (Boston: Porter Sargent, 1968), pp. 162–70.

63. For a discussion of racism in American historiographical studies of black Americans, see David Novick, *That Noble Dream: The "Objectivity Question" in American History* (Cambridge: Cambridge University Press, 1988).

64. Armstead Robinson, Craig C. Foster, and Donald Ogilvie, eds., *Black Studies in the University* (New Haven, CT: Yale University Press, 1969), pp. 45–46.

65. Since his emergence as a "paraintellectual" during the mid-1960s, Karenga has increasingly found acceptance in academic circles, particularly in black studies programs. Legitimated by a Ph.D., Karenga now lectures in black studies programs and to black students throughout the United States. His *Introduction to Black Studies* (Los Angeles: Kawaida Publications, 1982) has become a standard text in many black studies courses. In the winter of 1984 I first met Karenga when he served as a discussant on a panel for which I delivered a paper as part of the annual meeting of the Western Political Science Association. Karenga did not bring up having once been a militant black cultural nationalist, and he has long since changed his rhetorical style and mastered the lingo of the academy. Today, therefore, one could not accurately label Karenga a paraintellectual, for he does engage in serious intellectual exchange and argues and writes without being dominated by his utilitarian political sensibilities. Yet he has chosen to remain his individual self by retaining his name/title Maulana and his African attire. Still an advocate of Kawaida, Karenga's political vision has become far more expansive and progressive than it was during the 1960s. In recent years he has been studying ancient African civilizations.

66. For a discussion of Karenga's cultural Pan-Africanism, see Nagueyalti Warren, "Pan-African Cultural Movements: From Baraka to Karenga," *Journal of Negro History* 75, nos. 1–2 (Winter/Spring 1990): 16–28.

67. *The Autobiography*, p. 252.

68. The Nugzo Saba had a significant impact on black college students, as many of the black student centers created on white campuses during the late 1960s were given names like Umoja House or Ujamaa Center.

69. Maulana Karenga, *Kwanzaa: Origin, Concepts, Practice* (Los Angeles: Kawaida Publications, 1977); and Haki R. Madhubuti, *Kwanzaa: A Progressive and Uplifting African-American Holiday* (Chicago: Third World Press, 1972).

70. Robert Weisbrot, *Freedom Bound: A History of America's Civil Rights Movement* (New York: Penguin Books, 1991), p. 229.

71. For an excellent discussion of the commodification of black culture during the Black Power era, see William L. Van Deburg, *New Day in Babylon: The Black Power Movement and American Culture, 1965–1975* (Chicago: University of Chicago Press, 1992).

72. In a 1975 *New York Times* article discussing the ideological shifts then occurring among Jones and his nationalist peers, one black intellectual commented, "To know Baraka's position tomorrow read Karenga today." See Charlene Hunter, "Black Intellectuals and Activists Split on Ideological Direction," *New York Times*, April 28, 1975, p. A1.

73. It is perhaps not incidental that Karenga, like Father Divine and Elijah Muhammad, had the desire and authority to rename his followers, as if to give them totally new existences. Black autocracy, particularly black religious autocracy, has a tradition.

74. *The Autobiography*, pp. 253–54.

75. Ibid.

76. Nathan Joseph and Nicholas Alex discussed the importance of uniforms to the maintenance of a group: "For his peers . . . the uniform underscores a common membership, allegiance to the same set of rules, and the probability of similar life experiences. If he is an outsider, the uniform stresses the differences in status, norms and way of life. It serves, then, to bind the wearer to his peers and to separate him from outsiders . . . from his own group he will obtain self-esteem through conformity: from other groups, he may obtain self-prestige by conflict." See "The Uniform: A Sociological Perspective," *American Journal of Sociology* 77, no. 4 (January 1972): 726.

77. See Adolph Reed, "Black Particularity Reconsidered," *Telos*, no. 39 (Spring 1979): 71–93.

78. From interviews with several members of Baraka's former security detail, I learned that both Karenga's and Baraka's followers were usually armed. Moreover, before the installation of FAA metal detectors at airports, Karenga's followers would travel by plane completely "strapped."

79. See the impressive trilogy by Richard Slotkin, *Regeneration through Violence* (Middletown, CT: Wesleyan University Press, 1973), *The Fatal Environment* (New York: Atheneum, 1985), and *Gunfighter Nation* (New York: Atheneum, 1992). To make this analogy work in the case of urban blacks and Baraka, we must change the context and perhaps view the urban landscape (Baraka's black internal colonies or nations) as divinely ordained "black space" that both is occupied by whites (in terms of economic control) and serves as the geographical and mythical backdrop for the realization of black freedom and manhood.

80. As a young person in Newark, Jones had never formally joined a gang, although he had been on the periphery of one.

81. Kenneth O'Reilly, ed., *Racial Matters: The FBI's File on Black America, 1960–1972* (New York: Free Press, 1989), and *Black Americans: The FBI Files* (New York: Carroll & Graf, 1994); and Ward Churchill and Jim Vander Wall, *Agents of Repression: The FBI's Secret Wars against the Black Panther Party and the American Indian Movement* (Boston: South End Press, 1988).

82. *The Autobiography*, p. 279.

83. A comprehensive and damning appraisal of Karenga's behavior in post-riot Watts can be found in Bruce Michael Tyler, "Black Radicalism in Southern

California, 1950–1982" (Ph.D. diss., University of California at Los Angeles, 1983). Tyler documents Karenga's role as a state functionary who spent more time trying to control oppositional black organizations than he did confronting the racist social order. While I cannot confirm many of Tyler's claims concerning Karenga, it does seem clear that Karenga and US wanted to be recognized by the powers that be as the only valid black militant organization. Once having obtained that status and the police protection that accompanied it, Karenga's organization could effectively neutralize other black groups. In effect, Karenga and US functioned as adjunct arms of the state but did so under the guise of being revolutionary—a good hustle, indeed. Unfortunately, Tyler's thesis is based on the silly idea that had Karenga and the cultural nationalists not been present, a revolutionary struggle might have broken out in Watts in the guise of more riots or even war. This is patently nonsense. Perhaps there would have been more rioting, but there is no reason to think that it would have been elevated to "revolutionary" actions. Karenga was not crazy in trying to squash urban rioting in Los Angeles. After all, the second time around, the state would have been more deeply invested in asserting its control. However, Tyler convincingly argues that the cultural nationalism espoused by Karenga functioned in a therapeutic fashion. This may have been rational on Karenga's part, but it was not the image that Karenga was marketing of himself and his organization nationally. For a sophomoric and ultimately pathetic attempt to defend Karenga against all accusations of complicity with the police, see Scot Ngozi-Brown's "The US Organization, Maulana Karenga, and Conflict with the Black Panther Party: A Critique of Sectarian Influences on Historical Discourse," *Journal of Black Studies* 28, no. 2 (November 1997): 157–70.

84. Allen, *Black Awakening*, p. 139.

85. For a discussion of Karenga's open participation in antiriot pacification programs, see Horne, *Fire This Time*.

86. Newton's dissertation was written for the History of Consciousness program at the University of California at Santa Cruz. It was later published in book form. See Huey P. Newton, *War against the Panthers: A Study of Repression in America* (New York: Harlem River Press, 1996).

87. I have no way of verifying Perry's claims concerning Hubert.

88. M. Wesley Swearingen, *FBI Secrets: An Agent's Expose* (Boston: South End Press, 1995), p. 83.

89. Tyler, "Black Radicalism in Southern California," pp. 374–77.

NOTES TO CHAPTER 10

1. David J. Garrow, ed., *The Montgomery Bus Boycott and the Women Who Started It: The Memoir of Jo Ann Gibson Robinson* (Knoxville: University of Tennessee Press, 1987); Cynthia Stokes Brown, ed., *Ready from Within: Septima Clark and the Civil Rights Movement: A First Person Narrative* (Trenton, NJ: Africa World Press, 1990);

Kay Mills, *This Little Light of Mine: The Life of Fannie Lou Hammer* (New York:

Plume, 1994); Carol Mueller, "Ella Baker and the Origins of "Participatory Democracy," in *Women in the Civil Rights Movement: Trailblazers and Torchbearers, 1941–1965*, ed. Vicki L. Crawford, Jacqueline Anne Rouse, and Barbara Woods (New York: Carlson, 1990); Annette K. Brock, "Gloria Richardson and the Cambridge Movement," in *Women in the Civil Rights Movement*, ed. Crawford et al. For an extensive treatment of Robinson, see Cynthia Griggs Fleming, *Soon We Will Not Cry: The Liberation of Ruby Doris Smith Robinson* (Lanham, MD: Rowman & Littlefield, 1998); and Daisy Bates, *The Long Shadow of Little Rock: A Memoir* (Fayetteville: University of Arkansas Press, 1987).

2. Sara Evans, *Personal Politics: The Roots of Women's Liberation in the Civil Rights Movement and the New Left* (New York: Vintage Books, 1980); Mary King, *Freedom Song* (New York: Morrow, 1987); Belinda Robnett, *How Long? How Long? African-American Women in the Struggle for Civil Rights* (New York: Oxford University Press, 1997), pp. 99–121.

3. Robnett, *How Long? How Long?* pp. 180–82.

4. Note that the black power era was before the American military accepted females into its ranks.

5. Eldridge Cleaver, *Soul on Ice* (New York: Dell, 1968), p. 189.

6. Phobic white responses to black militancy occasionally linked black assertiveness to communism. Anthony Imperiale, the leader of white ethnic backlash in Newark during the late 1960s and early 1970s, sometimes publicly referred to LeRoi Jones and his black nationalist peers as "communists." See L. H. Whittemore, *Together: A Reporter's Journey into the New Black Politics* (New York: Morrow, 1971), pp. 197–98. Perhaps this should not be surprising, since many white southerners viewed the civil rights movement as communist inspired.

7. Claude Andrew Clegg III, *An Original Man: The Life and Times of Elijah Muhammad* (New York: St. Martin's Press, 1997), p. 102.

8. Elijah Muhammad, *Message to the Blackman* (Chicago: Muhammad's Temple no.2, 1965), pp. 59–60.

9. Patricia Hill Collins, "Learning to Think for Ourselves: Malcolm X's Black Nationalism Reconsidered," in *Malcolm X: In Our Own Image*, ed. Joe Wood (New York: St. Martin's Press, 1992), p. 74.

10. Ossie Davis, "Our Shining Black Prince," in *Malcolm X: The Man and His Times*, ed. John Henrik Clarke (New York: Macmillan, 1969), p. xii.

11. *Cavalier Magazine*, January 1966, p. 23.

12. LeRoi Jones, "American Sexual Reference: Black Male," in his *Home: Social Essays* (New York: Morrow, 1966), pp. 221–22.

13. Perhaps I need not mention that had a white person written such vulgarity, he or she would have been resoundingly condemned by the newly blackenized black literati. Instead, Baraka's foolishness was often accepted as raw and disturbing but undoubtedly insightful and ethnically authentic.

14. Jones, "American Sexual Reference," pp. 216–17. The idea of the white man as an effeminate, intellectual weakling is dramatized in Jones's play *The Slave*.

15. Robyn Wiegman, *American Anatomies: Theorizing Race and Gender* (Durham, NC: Duke University Press, 1995), p. 107.

16. Besides insisting that his rapes of black and white women were acts of political rebellion, Cleaver's *Soul on Ice* also provided us with vicious homophobic commentaries on black homosexuals, particularly James Baldwin. Michele Wallace accurately states that one of Cleaver's "most dubious contributions was the idea that black homosexuality was synonymous with reactionary Uncle Tomism." See Michele Wallace, *Black Macho and the Myth of the Superwoman* (London: John Calder, 1979), p. 67. Cleaver, whose homophobia exceeded that of Jones, could not possibly have denounced James Baldwin more viciously than to have claimed that Baldwin wished to have a white man's baby. It was an indication of the degree to which "black macho" nonsense had become hegemonic in the black power era that a thug like Cleaver was allowed to denounce an ethnic treasure like Baldwin and receive very little criticism from the black intelligentsia. Jones's denunciations of homosexuality may originate from the same roots as his diatribes against interracial sex/marriage. That is, he might have been guilty of attempting to exorcise a haunting past. In a letter from Peter Orlovsky to Allen Ginsberg dated September 25, 1963, Orlovsky wrote, concerning Jones, "I hope Leroy is happy and alright. Sorry I didn't make love with him when he wanted me to. John was right when he said I was scared." Winston Leyland, ed., *Allen Ginsberg and Peter Orlovsky: Straight Hearts' Delight: Love Poems and Selected Letters* (San Francisco: Gay Sunshine Press, 1980), p. 216.

17. Jones, *Home* pp. 227, 228.

18. bell hooks, *Ain't I a Woman: Black Women and Feminism* (Boston: South End Press, 1981), p. 96.

19. Martin Duberman, *The Uncompleted Past* (New York: Random House, 1969), p. 135.

20. Literary scholar Robyn Wiegman argues that Jones's mention of the black rapist of white women is part of a larger tradition: "Throughout the twentieth century, black male writers have repeatedly turned to the figuration of the black rapist as both a protest and warning, purposely revising the mythic encounter between black men and white women as part of a challenge to the history of mutilation." She includes Richard Wright's Bigger Thomas in this tradition as well as an episode in Ralph Ellison's *Invisible Man*. See Wiegman, *American Anatomies*, p. 104.

21. Cleaver, *Soul on Ice*, p. 14.

22. In *Soul on Ice*, Eldridge Cleaver quotes from Jones's poem "Black Dada Nihilismus," chiefly those lines calling for the raping of white girls and their fathers and the cutting of their mothers' throats. Cleaver then comments on the poem: "I have lived those lines and I know that if I had not been apprehended I would have slit some white throats. There are, of course, many young blacks out here right now who are slitting white throats and raping the white girl. They are not doing this because they read LeRoi Jones' poetry, as some of his critics seem to believe. Rather, LeRoi is expressing the funky facts of life" (p. 15). It remains one of the sickest legacies of the 1960s that the moral perversion expressed in Jones's poem would be considered somehow "rev-

olutionary" and, worse, that the pathology expressed in Cleaver's behavior did not undermine his revolutionary credibility. The opposite occurred; Cleaver's past as a rapist enhanced his revolutionary credibility.

23. Wiegman, *American Anatomies*, p. 107.

24. Max Scheler, *Ressentiment*, ed. Lewis Coser and trans. William W. Holdheim (New York: Schocken Books, 1961). Concerning his attitude during this period in his life, Jones wrote: "There was a deep anti-white feeling I carried with me that had grown deeper and deeper since I left the Village . . . to the extent that I merely turned white supremacy upside down and created an exclusivist black supremacist doctrine, that was bullshit." See LeRoi Jones / Amiri Baraka, *The Autobiography of LeRoi Jones / Amiri Baraka* (New York: Freundlich Books, 1984), p. 245. This book is henceforth cited as *The Autobiography*.

25. The crucial texts in this regard were Fanon's *Wretched of the Earth* and *Black Skin, White Masks*. In his autobiography, Baraka states: "But we made the same errors Fanon and Cabral laid out, if we had but read them, understood them. . . . Crying blackness and for all the strength and goodness of that, not understanding the normal contradictions and the specific foolishness of white-hating black nationalism. The solution is not to become the enemy in blackface" (p. 323).

26. For a discussion of Jones's homosexual past and his inability to accept this aspect of his identity, see Ron Simmons, "Baraka's Dilemma: To Be or Not to Be," in *Black Men on Race, Gender, and Sexuality: A Critical Reader*, ed. Devon W. Carbado (New York: New York University Press, 1999), pp. 317–23.

27. Elaine Brown, *A Taste of Power: A Black Woman's Story* (New York: Pantheon, 1992), p. 109.

28. Angela Davis, *An Autobiography: With My Mind on Freedom* (New York: Bantam, 1974), pp. 159–60.

29. *The Autobiography*, p. 275.

30. Ibid.

31. This essay was republished in Baraka's essay collection *Raise Race Rays Raze: Essays since 1965* (New York: Random House, 1971).

32. Baraka, *Raise Race Rays Raze*, p. 148. Note also that in this essay, Baraka was quite comfortable with the idea of complementary sexes, even though he is quoted earlier as calling "complementary" a Karenga play of words that, in reality, meant unequal.

33. hooks, *Ain't I a Woman*, p. 95.

34. Jones, *Raise Race Rays Raze*, p. 148.

35. Ibid., p. 149.

36. Ibid., p. 151.

37. Ibid., p. 152.

38. Imamu Amiri Baraka, ed., *African Congress: A Documentary of the First Modern Pan-African Congress* (New York: Morrow, 1972), p. 177.

39. Ibid., p. 179.

40. This quotation is found in *The Combahee River Collective Statement* written

by the Combahee River Collective and reprinted in Barbara Smith, ed., *Home Girls: A Black Feminist Anthology* (New York: Kitchen Table, Women of Color Press, 1983), p. 278.

41. See Lee Rainwater and William L. Yancey, *The Moynihan Report and the Politics of Controversy* (Cambridge, MA: Massachusetts Institute of Technology Press, 1967).

42. Robert Staples, *The Black Woman in America: Sex, Marriage and the Family* (Chicago: Nelson-Hall, 1973), p. 176.

43. One scholar offered a rather sophisticated argument in support of the claim that misogyny was present in *Dutchman* and *The Slave* in ways the prefigured the sexism in Baraka's black arts dramas. See Beth McCoy, "A Nation's Meta-language: Misogyny in Amiri Baraka's *Dutchman* and *The Slave*," in *Staging the Rage: The Web of Misogyny in Modern Drama*, ed. Katherine H. Burkman and Judith Roof (Madison, NJ: Fairleigh Dickinson University Press, 1998), pp. 54–75. While I find McCoy's arguments compelling, they also strike me as hyperacademic and pedantic in the style of so much of the theory in the humanities today. In order to substantiate her readings of these two plays, McCoy is forced to create an analytical narrative that goes far beyond the impressions conveyed by these plays to a "normal" and reasonable audience. That is, she is so concerned with discussing the hidden meanings of the play that she appears to overlook the fact that its message also had to be apparent to the audience if it was to convey a political statement.

44. hooks, *Ain't I a Woman*, p. 106.

45. LeRoi Jones, *Four Black Revolutionary Plays* (Indianapolis: Bobbs-Merrill, 1969), p. 81.

46. Ibid., pp. 82, 83.

47. James Cone, *For My People: Black Theology and the Black Church* (Maryknoll, NY: Orbis, 1984), p. 131.

48. "Black Theatre Discovers the New Lafayette," *Black Theatre*, no. 5 (1971): 37.

49. *The Autobiography*, p. 276.

50. Amiri Baraka and Amina Baraka, eds., *Confirmation: An Anthology of African American Women* (New York: Quill, 1983), p. 15.

51. Ibid., p. 16.

52. LeRoi Jones / Amiri Baraka, *The Autobiography of LeRoi Jones* (Chicago: Lawrence Hill Books, 1997) (*The Autobiography II*), p. xvi.

NOTES TO CHAPTER 11

1. See Harold Gosnell, *Negro Politicians* (Chicago: University of Chicago Press, 1935); Dianne Pinderhughes, *Race and Ethnicity in Chicago Politics: A Reexamination of Pluralist Theory* (Champaign-Urbana: University of Illinois Press, 1987); and William J. Grimshaw, *Bitter Fruit: Black Politics and the Chicago Machine, 1931–1991* (Chicago: University of Chicago Press, 1992).

2. Robert Curvin, "Black Ghetto Politics in Newark after World War II," in *Cities*

of the Garden State: Essays in the Urban and Suburban History of New Jersey, ed. Joel Schwartz and Daniel Prosser (Dubuque, IA: Kendall Hunt, 1977), p. 146.

3. George Sternlieb and Robert W. Burchell, *Residential Abandonment: The Tenement Landlord Revisited* (New Brunswick, NJ: Rutgers University, Center for Urban Policy Research, 1973), pp. 5, 41.

4. Harold Kaplan, *Urban Renewal Politics: Slum Clearance in Newark* (New York: Columbia University Press, 1963). In explaining the criteria that led him to conclude that Newark had been highly successful at urban renewal, Kaplan wrote, "Throughout this study the term 'success' is used synonymously with high levels of clearance activity. Defined in this way, success may be measured by the number of blocks cleared, the number of new dwelling units constructed, or the total amount of funds spent. It is a quantitative, not qualitative index; it deliberately avoids questions involving the appropriateness of particular versions of renewal policy" (p. 2).

5. Robert Curvin, "The Persistent Minority: The Black Political Experience in Newark" (Ph.D. diss., Princeton University, 1975), pp. 22, 25.

6. Ibid., p. 21.

7. Ibid., pp. 36, 33.

8. Ibid., p. 42. For a list of these positions, see pp. 47–49.

9. Ibid., p. 89.

10. In 1966, Gibson had no organization and only $2,000 in campaign funds. See Bette Woody, *Managing Crisis Cities: The New Black Leadership and the Politics of Resource Allocation* (Westport, CT: Greenwood Press, 1982), p. 77.

11. Throughout urban America, community action agencies became infrastructures for the emergence of community leaders. See Frances Fox Piven and Richard Cloward, *Regulating the Poor: The Functions of Public Welfare* (New York: Vintage Books, 1972), esp. chap. 10.

12. LeRoi Jones / Amiri Baraka, *The Autobiography of LeRoi Jones* (Chicago: Lawrence Hill Books, 1997), pp. 349, 350. This later edition is henceforth cited as *The Autobiography II*.

13. Leonard Cole, *Blacks in Power: A Comparative Study of Black and White Elected Officials* (Princeton, NJ: Princeton University Press, 1976), p. 140.

14. This quotation from the *New York Times*, April 14, 1968, is found in Curvin, "The Persistent Minority," p. 68.

15. K. Komozi Woodward, "The Making of the New Ark: Imamu Amiri Baraka (LeRoi Jones), the Newark Congress of African People, and the Modern Black Convention Movement. A History of the Black Revolt and the New Nationalism, 1966–1976" (Ph.D. diss., University of Pennsylvania, 1991), p. 164.

16. Hutchins further developed his critique of Baraka and the United Brothers' strategy in an unpublished essay that was circulating at the time: "If there is a weakness in the United Brothers approach it is the question of whether or not black control of Newark by 1970 can actually fundamentally change the lives of blacks in the city. It is no secret that economic power is moving to the suburbs. . . . In the long run Newark (though now a pace setter) cannot be separated from what happens around

the nation. . . . Black control of some cities where blacks are the majority (or have a plurality) is not the answer to racism in 20th century America. It may be that black people will have to have blacks in power over them within the confines of this system before they can truly recognize the necessity to organize against capitalism as well as the racist aspects of America." See Robert L. Allen, *Black Awakening in Capitalist America* (Garden City, NY: Doubleday, 1969), pp. 119–20.

17. Curvin noted that a third black candidate was later endorsed as a United Brothers candidate when a second at-large city council seat became vacant. Ironically, this third candidate had at first been considered too close to Addonizio. See Curvin, "The Persistent Minority," p. 68.

18. For example, one of the symbolic resolutions called for "staunch resistance by draft-age black youth against being used as cannon fodder for this racist imperialistic war," which was passed unanimously. See K. Komozi Woodard, *A Nation within a Nation: Amiri Baraka (Leroi Jones) and Black Power Politics* (Chapel Hill: University of North Carolina Press, 1999), p. 108.

19. Nikki Giovanni, "Black Poems, Poseurs and Power," *Negro Digest* 18, no. 8 (June 1969): 31.

20. Some of them remained top aides to Gibson once he became mayor.

21. L. H. Whittemore, *Together: A Reporter's Journey into the New Black Politics* (New York: Morrow, 1971), p. 103.

22. Ibid., p. 103. According to Whittemore, this latter comment was directed to the white business establishment of Newark which had somehow let it be known that according to their informal plans, 1974, and not 1970, would be the year of a black ascension to the mayoralty. In their minds, 1970 was too soon, whatever that meant. Gibson's comment about "puppets and Uncle Toms" supposedly let the white power structure know that it was not their choice to make.

23. Baraka believes that the energy spent by Imperiale, Addonizio, and their supporters denouncing him as a black racist and extremist backfired. Not only did their attacks on him help unite blacks, but it also kept the focus of their energy and scrutiny away from candidate Gibson. Moreover, when juxtaposed with Gibson's more issue-oriented campaign, the hysteria of their ad hominem attacks on Baraka made Gibson appear even more "mayoral." See Amiri Baraka, "The Creation of the New Ark," chap. 12. This unpublished manuscript is housed in the Amiri Baraka Collection of the Moorland-Spingarn Research Center, Howard University.

24. Whittemore, *Together*, p. 105. Perhaps it is significant that Addonizio ignored the Puerto Ricans in his description of the convention. Blacks, I presume, occupied a more central position in white racist demonology.

25. Amiri Baraka, *Raise Race Rays Raze* (New York: Random House, 1971), p. 163.

26. Baraka uses this racial reification of black Americans throughout his analysis in his unpublished manuscript "The Creation of the New Ark," in which he calls black politicians who did not follow his black nationalist agenda "white-like."

27. Nathan Wright Jr., ed., *What Black Politicians Are Saying* (New York: Hawthorn Books, Inc.1972), p. 111. Gibson's essay is entitled "Newark and We," pp.

110–25. It is not clear to whom Gibson is referring as constituting "those whose political motives will not allow"—perhaps his white antagonists on the city council or Anthony Imperiale or even Baraka.

28. Ibid., p. 124.

29. Ron Porambo, *No Cause for Indictment: An Autopsy of Newark* (New York: Holt, Rinehart and Winston, 1971), pp. 7–8.

30. Woody, *Managing Crisis Cities*, p. 105.

31. Wright, ed., *What Black Politicians Are Saying* , p. 116.

32. David Llorens, "Ameer (LeRoi Jones) Baraka," *Ebony*, August 1969, p. 80; Curvin, "The Persistent Minority," p. 203.

33. Woodard, *A Nation within a Nation*, p. 120.

34. Ibid., p. 122.

35. David Llorens, "Ameer (LeRoi Jones) Baraka," *Ebony*, August 1969, p. 78.

36. Fox Butterfield, "Experimental Class in Newark School Is Indoctrinated in Black Subjects," *New York Times*, April 10, 1971, p. 42.

37. Interview with Imamu Amiri Baraka in *The Black Collegian* 3, no. 4 March/ April 1973): 30–33.

38. Woodard, *A Nation within a Nation*, p. 132.

39. Curvin, "The Persistent Minority," p. 200.

40. *Black New Ark* 2, no. 11 (October 1973): 7.

41. *New York Times*, March 7, 1973, p. 47; and Leonard A. Cole, *Blacks in Power* (Princeton, NJ: Princeton University Press, 1976), p. 171.

NOTES TO CHAPTER 12

1. Martin Luther King Jr., *Stride towards Freedom: The Montgomery Story* (New York: Harper Bros., 1958).

2. In what must be construed as a phenomenally naive statement, NAACP attorney Thurgood Marshall was quoted in the *New York Times* only a day or two after the *Brown* decision as saying that school segregation would be completely ended within five years and that all forms of segregation would be eliminated by the hundredth anniversary of the Emancipation Proclamation (1965). See Richard Klugar, *Simple Justice* (New York: Knopf, 1976), p. 714.

3. Instead of desegregating public schools, whites opened "private" all-white academies subsidized by county funds. See Bob Smith, *They Closed Their Schools: Prince Edward County, Virginia, 1951–1964* (Chapel Hill: University of North Carolina Press, 1965); Daniel Berman, *It Is So Ordered: The Supreme Court Rules on School Segregation* (New York: Norton, 1966); and Kluger, *Simple Justice*, p. 778.

4. For a description of Ike's pathetic immorality on racial issues, see Earl Ofari Hutchinson, *Betrayed: A History of Presidential Failure to Protect Black Lives* (Boulder, CO: Westview Press, 1996), chap. 4. Also see Kenneth O'Reilly, *Nixon's Piano: Presidents and Racial Politics from Washington to Clinton* (New York: Free Press, 1995). In his memoirs, Chief Justice of the U.S. Supreme Court Earl Warren reminisced about

a moment during the *Brown* deliberations when he was invited to the White House for dinner. The president had also invited John W. Davis, the lead attorney for the forces wanting to maintain racial segregation. Clearly, the president was trying, inappropriately, to influence the man whom he had appointed as chief justice. Warren described the moment: "During the dinner, the President went to considerable lengths to tell me what a great man Mr. Davis was. At the conclusion of the meal . . . we filed out of the dining room to another room. . . . The President . . . took me by the arm, and, as we walked along, speaking of the Southern states in the segregation cases, he said, 'These are not bad people. All they are concerned about is to see that their sweet little girls are not required to sit in school alongside some big overgrown Negroes.' . . . Shortly thereafter the *Brown* case was decided, and with it went our cordial relations." Earl Warren, *The Memoirs of Earl Warren* (Garden City, NY: Doubleday, 1977), pp. 296–97.

5. A comprehensive discussion of the Emmett Till lynching can be found in Stephen J. Whitfield's *A Death in the Delta: The Story of Emmett Till* (New York: Free Press, 1988).

6. Robert Weisbrot, *Freedom Bound: A History of America's Civil Rights Movement* (New York: Plume, 1991), p. 93.

7. I use the term *renewed* because historian Penny Von Eschen convincingly showed that during the 1940s there was significant agitation in the Afro-American community about African decolonization. See Penny Von Eschen, *Race against Empire: Black Americans and Anticolonialism, 1937–1957* (Ithaca, NY: Cornell University Press, 1997).

8. For a short discussion of the history of African students at Lincoln University, see the essay by Lincoln's former president, Horace Mann Bond, "Forming Afri-can Youth at Lincoln University," in *Black Homeland, Black Diaspora: Cross Currents of the African Relationship*, ed. Jacob Drachler (Port Washington, NY: Kennikat Press, 1975), pp. 114–19. Like Howard University, Lincoln University has a tradition of educating Africans.

9. Harold Isaacs, *The New World of Negro Americans* (New York: John Day, 1963), pp. 288–89.

10. See Jean Van Lierd, ed., *Lumumba Speaks: the Speeches and Writings of Patrice Lumumba, 1958–1961*, trans. Helen R. Lane with an introduction by Jean-Paul Sartre (Boston: Little, Brown, 1972). As Sartre notes, the United States' desire to murder Lumumba is somewhat baffling, since he was not trying to nationalize Western business interests in the Congo (contrary to what Baraka, in his autobiography, later claimed concerning Lumumba). Moreover, Lumumba's speeches show that he was not a sophisticated political thinker. But how could Lumumba have been a sophisticated political thinker, given the meager exposure and education offered to him and other colonized Africans in the Congo?

11. Madeleine G. Kalb, *The Congo Cables: The Cold War in Africa—From Eisenhower to Kennedy* (New York: Macmillan, 1982). According to Kalb, the United States supposedly feared a Communist takeover of the Congo should Lumumba become its

first head of state and was in the process of planning Lumumba's assassination when he was killed.

12. The Belgian Congo's Katanga Province was the region richest in natural resources and minerals. If Katanga had seceded from the rest of the Congo, the new nation would have lost much of its wealth.

13. LeRoi Jones / Amiri Baraka, *The Autobiography of LeRoi Jones / Amiri Baraka* (New York: Freundlich Books, 1984), p. 181. This book is henceforth cited as *The Autobiography*.

14. Some of the major studies of Pan-Africanism are George Padmore, *Pan-Africanism or Communism* (New York: Doubleday, 1972); W. E. B. Du Bois, *The World and Africa* (New York: International Publishers, 1965); Imanuel Geiss, *The Pan-African Movement: A History of Pan-Africanism in America, Europe and Africa*, trans. Ann Keep (New York: Africana Publishing, 1974); Colin Legum, *Pan-Africanism: A Short Political Guide* (New York: Praeger, 1962); Ronald W. Walters, *Pan-Africanism in the African Diaspora: An Analysis of Modern Afrocentric Political Movements* (Detroit: Wayne State University Press, 1993); and American Society of African Culture, ed., *Pan-Africanism Reconsidered* (Berkeley and Los Angeles: University of California Press, 1962).

15. John Henrik Clarke, "Pan-Africanism: A Brief History of an Idea in the African World," *Présence Africaine* 145, no. 1 (1988): 28.

16. Manning Marable, *Blackwater: Historical Studies in Race, Class Consciousness and Revolution* (Dayton, OH: Black Praxis Press, 1981), p. 102.

17. Walters, *Pan Africanism in the African Diaspora*, p. 43.

18. But even this is not a sacred category. Even though racial designations often vary according to area, membership in the Pan-African world was usually extended to any person of African descent, without regard for the quantity of African "blood" in his or her veins. As it emerged in the United States, Pan-Africanism often internationalized the criteria for determining black racial identity prevalent in the United States.

19. For an example of Du Bois's liberal Pan-Africanism, see his essays "Liberia, the League and the United States," *Foreign Affairs* 11, no. 4 (July 1933): 682–95, and "Pan-Africa and New Racial Philosophy," *The Crisis* 40 (November 1933): 247–62; and Benjamin Nnambi Azikiwe, *Liberia in World Politics* (London: A. W. Stockwell, 1935). Azikiwe later became the first president of the newly independent nation of Nigeria. Also see Cedric J. Robinson, "W. E. B. Du Bois and Black Sovereignty," in *Imagining Home: Class, Culture and Nationalism in the African Diaspora*, ed. Sidney Lemelle and Robin D. G. Kelley (London: Verso, 1994), pp. 145–57; and I. K. Sundiata, *Black Scandal: America and the Liberian Labor Crisis, 1926–1936* (Philadelphia: Institute for the Study of Human Issues, 1980). Finally, see Colin Leys, *Underdevelopment in Kenya: The Political Economy of Neo-Colonialism, 1964–1971* (Berkeley and Los Angeles: University of California Press, 1975).

20. See President Nyerere's welcoming speech to the delegates attending the Sixth Pan-African Congress in Dar es Salaam in 1974 in *Resolutions and Selected*

Speeches from the Sixth Pan African Congress (Dar es Salaam: Tanzania Publishing House, 1976), pp. 3–10; and Seko Toure's speech at the Sixth Pan-African Congress in ibid., pp. 11–17. See also Amilcar Cabral's "Connecting the Struggles: An Informal Talk with Black Americans," in his collection of essays, *Return to the Source: Selected Speeches of Amilcar Cabral*, ed. Africa Information Service (New York: Monthly Review Press, 1973). Walter Rodney wrote a highly contentious speech condemning liberal Pan-Africanism that he intended to give to the Sixth Pan-African Congress. Although he recognized liberal Pan-Africanism as the dominant form of Pan-Africanism on the African continent, he claimed that it was the Pan-Africanism of the African petty bourgeoisie. See Walter Rodney, "Towards the Sixth Pan-African Congress: Aspects of the International Class Struggle in Africa, the Caribbean and America," in *Resolutions and Selected Speeches from the Sixth Pan African Congress* (Dar es Salaam: Tanzania Publishing House, 1976), pp. 21–34.

21. Adelaide M. Cromwell, ed., *Dynamics of the African Afro-American Connection: From Dependency to Self-Reliance* (Washington, DC: Howard University Press, 1987), pp. 43–45.

22. During the late 1960s and early 1970s, the ideas of Senegal's Cheikh Anta Diop influenced the thought of black Americans who favored black cultural nationalism and/or Pan-Africanism based on shared cultural cores. See Diop, *The African Origins of Civilization: Myth or Reality* (New York: Lawrence Hill, 1974), and esp. *The Cultural Unity of Negro Africa* (Paris: Presence Africaine Press, 1970). See Kwame Anthony Appiah, *In My Father's House: Africa in the Philosophy of Culture* (New York: Oxford University Press, 1992), esp. chap. 2. Padmore's ideas on Pan Africanism can be found in his many books, including *How Britain Rules Africa* (London: Wishart Books, 1936), *Africa and World Peace* (London: Secker and Warburg, 1937), *Africa: Britain's Third Empire* (London: Dennis Dobson, 1949), *Pan-Africanism or Communism* (London: Dennis Dobson, 1956), and a book he edited, *Colonial and Coloured Unity, a Programme of Action: History of the Pan-African Congress* (Manchester: Panaf Services, 1947). For a discussion of Du Bois's Pan-Africanism, see Imanuel Geiss, *The Pan-African Movement*, chaps. 12 and 18; Manning Marable, *W. E. B. Du Bois: Black Radical Democrat* (Boston: Twayne, 1986); and Robinson, "W. E. B. Du Bois and Black Sovereignty," pp. 145–57. For a collective discussion of the Pan-Africanist politics of Robeson, Du Bois, Alpheus Hunton, and others who created the Council on African Affairs, see Penny M. Von Eschen, "African Americans and Anti-Colonialism, 1937–1957: The Rise and Fall of the Politics of the African Diaspora" (Ph.D. diss., Columbia University, 1994). A revised version of this dissertation was published as *Race against Empire*. For James's ideas on Pan-Africanism, see C. L. R. James, *A History of Pan-African Revolt* (Washington, DC: Drum and Spear Press, 1969), and his essay "Towards the Seventh: The Pan-African Congress—Past, Present and Future," in his essay collection *At the Rendezvous of Victory* (London: Allison and Busby, 1984), pp. 236–50.

23. For a discussion of the mass marketing and consumption of African artifacts during the Black Power era, see William L. Van Deburg, *New Day in Babylon: The Black*

Power Movement and American Culture, 1965–1975 (Chicago: University of Chicago Press, 1992).

24. The lecture that he delivered at the congress was subsequently published as "Tradition and Industrialization" (chap. 2) in Wright's essay collection, *White Man Listen* (New York: Doubleday, 1957). See also Michel Fabre, *The World of Richard Wright* (Oxford: University Press of Mississippi, 1985), p. 201.

25. The proceedings of this congress are published in Imamu Amiri Baraka, ed., *African Congress: A Documentary of the First Modern Pan-African Congress* (New York: Morrow, 1972).

26. Ibid., p. 108.

27. Ibid., pp. 117–18.

28. The Congress of African Peoples is discussed in *The Autobiography*, pp. 289–312.

29. In his autobiography, Baraka notes that at the time of the Atlanta congress, Karenga was either mentally unstable or in a drug-induced stupor as a result of stress following the murder of two Panthers by members of Karenga's US on the UCLA campus. Karenga was paralyzed with fear of retaliation by the Panthers.

30. K. Komozi Woodard, "The Making of the New Ark: Imamu Amiri Baraka, the Newark Congress of African People, and the Modern Black Convention Movement: A History of the Black Revolt and the New Nationalism, 1966–1976" (Ph.D. diss., University of Pennsylvania, 1991), or Woodard's *A Nation within a Nation: Amiri Baraka (LeRoi Jones) and Black Power Politics* (Chapel Hill: University of North Carolina Press, 1999), esp. chap. 5.

31. At no point in his discussion of CAP in his autobiography does Baraka reflect on any of its shortcomings other than its various positions on issues.

32. Alphonso Pinkney, *Red, Black and Green: Black Nationalism in the United States* (Cambridge: Cambridge University Press, 1976), p. 135.

33. In private conversations, I asked two members of his Newark coterie if they ever questioned Baraka on matters of "theory" or strategy, and both told me that they did not engage in give-and-take discussions with him. Rather, their task was to listen to him.

34. On December 8, 1970, the United States along with France, Great Britain, and Spain abstained from voting on a UN Security Council resolution that condemned Portugal's November 22, 1970, invasion of the Republic of Guinea. The United States formally accepted the findings of the UN special mission that determined that Portugal had in fact invaded the country. The United States claimed, however, that such behavior did not merit UN sanctions against Portugal. For a more extended discussion of U.S. complicity in Portuguese colonialism, see Congressman John Conyers's essay, "Portugal Invades Guinea: The Failure of U.S. Policy towards Africa," in *What Black Politicians Are Saying*, ed. Nathan Wright Jr. (New York: Hawthorn Books, 1972), pp. 94–109.

35. Walters, *Pan-Africanism in the African Diaspora*, p. 71.

36. Manning Marable, *Race, Reform and Rebellion: The Second Reconstruction in*

Black America, 1945–1990 (rev. 2d ed.) (Jackson: University Press of Mississippi, 1991), p. 134.

37. Donald R. Culverson, "The Politics of the Anti-Apartheid Movement in the United States, 1969–1996," *Political Science Quarterly* 111, no.1 (1996): 127–49.

38. Walters, *Pan-Africanism in the African Diaspora*, pp. 84–85.

39. I am not claiming that the problem with the "theorists" associated with the leadership of the African Liberation Support Committee was that they were "ideological." Instead, I am claiming that their ideology was problematic because it was dogmatic and constituted a totalizing truth, much like a fundamentalist religious belief.

40. Although their aggressiveness toward one another is baffling to me, such behavior was not unusual for highly politicized, marginalized formations. After all, such internecine warfare was commonplace throughout the history of the American Communist Party.

41. Of course, Ethiopia and Liberia were "independent" African nations at the time of Ghana's founding.

42. For a discussion of Nkrumah as a charismatic leader, see David E. Apter, "Nkrumah, Charisma, and the Coup," in *Philosophers and Kings: Studies in Leadership*, ed. Dunkwart A. Rustow (New York: Braziller, 1970), pp. 112–47. And for a brief but critical description of the Nkrumah regime in Ghana, see Manning Marable, *African and Caribbean Politics: From Kwame Nkrumah to the Grenada Revolution* (London: Verso, 1987), chap. 2. After the coup, Nkrumah lived the remainder of his life in exile in Guinea where Seko Toure gave him the honorary title of Joint Head of State of Guinea. After a long bout with cancer, Nkrumah died in Bucharest, Romania, on April 27, 1972. On July 7, 1972, his body was flown to Accra where it lay in state before being buried.

43. Ronald Segal, *African Profiles* (rev. ed.) (Baltimore: Penguin Books, 1963), p. 312.

44. Dorothy Shipley White, *Black Africa and De Gaulle: From French Empire to Independence* (University Park: Pennsylvania State University Press, 1979), pp. 201–11. This book is useful for factual data, but the author's interpretative presuppositions are so closely wedded to the belief that de Gaulle was a great figure that she seriously entertains the racist idea that France colonized Africa out of a benevolent desire to give it the richness of French culture and that Africans needed French culture whether they knew it or not. Also see Wole Soyinka, *The Open Sore of a Continent: A Personal Narrative of the Nigerian Crisis* (New York: Oxford University Press, 1996), p. 36.

45. For a discussion of Toure's political thought and behavior, see Charles F. Andrain, "The Political Thought of Seko Toure," in *African Political Thought: Lumumba, Nkrumah, and Toure*, ed. W. A. E. Skurnik (Denver: Monograph Series in World Affairs, University of Denver, 1968), pp. 101–35; R. W. Johnson, "Seko Toure and the Guinean Revolution," *African Affairs* 69, no. 277 (October 1970): 350–65; Ladipo Adamolekun, *Sekou Toure's Guinea: An Experiment in Nation Building* (London: Methuen, 1976); Claude Riviere, *Guinea: The Mobilization of a People*, trans. Vir-

ginia Thompson and Richard Adloff (Ithaca, NY: Cornell University Press, 1977); and Lansine Kaba, "Rhetoric and Reality in Conakry," *Africa Report* 23, no. 3 (May/June 1978): 43–47. For examples of Toure's thought, see Ahmed Seko Toure, *Africa on the Move* (London: Panaf Books, 1979), and his Pan-Africanist manifesto, *The United States of Africa* (Conakry, Guinea: Government Press Office, 1977).

46. A typical narcissist in his overestimation of the "brilliance" of his own mind, Toure was the precursor to Karenga and Baraka. Of course, Toure always feared that he might actually be an unremarkable thinker, which of course he was. Karenga and Baraka certainly had similar fears and justifiably so. After all, one does not imagine secure thinkers believing in the need to induce followers to defer to them intellectually in the manner devised by Toure, Karenga, and Baraka.

47. David Lamb, *The Africans* (New York: Random House, 1982), p. 223.

48. Marable, *African and Caribbean Politics*, p. 182.

49. Walters, *Pan-Africanism in the African Diaspora*, p. 66.

50. For examples of Nyerere's writings and speeches, see his *Freedom and Unity: A Selection from Writings and Speeches, 1952–1965* (Oxford: Oxford University Press, 1967), *Freedom and Socialism: A Selection from Writings and Speeches, 1965–1967* (Dar es Salaam: Oxford University Press, 1968), and *Freedom and Development: A Selection from Writings and Speeches, 1968–1973* (Dar es Salaam: Oxford University Press, 1973).

51. Imamu Amiri Baraka, "'Towards Pan-Africanism': Tanzania Independence Anniversary," *Black World*, March 1972, pp. 65–67.

52. Walters, *Pan-Africanism in the African Diaspora*, pp. 66–67.

53. Julius K. Nyerere, *Ujamaa: Essays on Socialism* (New York: Oxford University Press, 1968), pp. 1–12.

54. Lerone Bennett Jr., "Pan-Africanism at the Crossroads: Dreams and Realities Clash as Delegates Debate Class and Color at Historic Congress in Tanzania," *Ebony*, September 1974, pp. 148–52, 154–60.

55. Julius Nyerere, "Opening Speech," in *Resolutions and Selected Speeches from the Sixth Pan African Congress* (Dar es Salaam: Tanzania Publishing House, 1976), p. 8.

56. *Resolutions and Selected Speeches from the Sixth Pan African Congress*, p. 16.

57. Ibid., p. 88.

58. Carlos Moore attended as a representative of the International Committee to the Second World Black and African Festival of Arts and Culture in Lagos. According to Hoyt Fuller, at President Nyerere's reception at the state house, Moore, a critic of Castro and Cuban racism, had a confrontation with the Cuban delegation that almost turned violent. The Cuban delegation lodged a protest against Moore's presence, and he was soon on a plane to Lagos. See Hoyt Fuller, "Notes from a Sixth Pan-African Journal," *Black World*, October 1974, p. 80.

59. Fuller, "Notes," p. 81.

60. Imamu Amiri Baraka, "Some Questions about the Sixth Pan-African Congress," *Black Scholar*, October 1974, pp. 45, 46.

NOTES TO CHAPTER 13

1. There was one black member of the U.S. Senate, Republican Edward Brooke from Massachusetts. Brooke did not formally join the Congressional Black Caucus.

2. For a discussion of the origins of the Congressional Black Caucus, see Congressman William L. Clay's *Just Permanent Interests: Black Americans in Congress, 1870–1992* (New York: Amistad Press, 1993), chap. 5.

3. Manning Marable, *Race, Reform, and Rebellion: The Second Reconstruction in Black America, 1945–1990* (rev. 2d ed.) (Jackson: University Press of Mississippi, 1991), p. 122.

4. The National Black Assembly was the name given to the grassroots infrastructure that was supposed to be created by the National Black Political Convention. For the sake of consistency, I refer to it here as the latter.

5. Peter Marris and Martin Rein, *Dilemmas of Social Reform: Poverty and Community Action in the United States* (2d ed.) (Chicago: University of Chicago Press, 1982), pp. 241, 252.

6. The defeat of Hubert Humphrey in 1968 was particularly devastating to black liberal Democrats and supporters of civil rights. Humphrey was "Mr. Civil Rights," a title earned from his earliest days as mayor of Minneapolis when he pushed for and won a civil rights plank on the 1948 Democratic Party platform. A comprehensive discussion of Humphrey and the black freedom struggle can be found in Timothy N. Thurber, *The Politics of Equality: Hubert H. Humphrey and the African American Freedom Struggle* (New York: Columbia University Press, 1999).

7. Reg Murphy and H. Gulliver, *The Southern Strategy* (New York: Scribner, 1971); Joseph A. Aistrup, *The Southern Strategy Revisited: Republican Top-Down Advancement in the South* (Lexington: University Press of Kentucky, 1996); Kevin P. Phillips, *The Emerging Republican Majority* (Garden City, NY: Doubleday, 1970); and see Dan T. Carter's *From George Wallace to Newt Gingrich: Race in the Conservative Counterrevolution, 1963–1994* (Baton Rouge: Louisiana State University Press, 1996) and *The Politics of Rage: George Wallace, the Origins of the New Conservatism, and the Transformation of American Politics* (New York: Simon & Schuster, 1995).

8. Earl Ofari Hutchinson, *Betrayed: A History of Presidential Failure to Protect Black Lives* (Boulder, CO: Westview Press, 1996), chap. 7; and Kenneth O'Reilly, ed., *Nixon's Piano: Presidents and Racial Politics from Washington to Clinton* (New York: Free Press, 1995), esp. chap. 7.

9. See Daniel P. Moynihan, *Maximum Feasible Misunderstanding: Community Action in the War on Poverty* (New York: Free Press, 1970).

10. Even *Liberator* magazine, a voice of black nationalism, endorsed Nixon's "black capitalism" agenda.

11. In July 1967 President Lyndon Johnson issued an executive order creating a national commission on civil disorders. Its mission was to explain the causes of the urban rioting. Chaired by Otto Kerner, the former governor of Illinois, the commis-

sion issued the *Report of the National Commission on Civil Disorders* (1967). On p. 1, the "two-nations" wording appears.

12. I am speculating that Chisholm may have used sexism as an excuse. But she held no such reservations about participating in the Democratic National Convention, although it too was run by sexist males, who in this instance happened to be white and much more powerful.

13. During the summer of 1968 while out on bail (for his arrest during the Newark riot), Baraka ran for a seat on a Newark Community Council. The council was responsible for overseeing the spending priorities of the Federal Model Cities Program in Newark. He came in twelfth in a field of nineteen candidates who were competing for four positions. See the interview of Baraka by Tish Dace, "LeRoi Jones / Amiri Baraka: From Muse to Malcolm to Mao," *Village Voice*, August 1, 1977, p. 13.

14. Hatcher's speech was printed in *Black Scholar* 4, no. 1 (September 1972): 17–22. The quotation is from p. 21.

15. In his opening address, Jesse Jackson, head of PUSH, asserted the need for a black political party. Unlike Hatcher, Jackson was not an elected official and therefore was somewhat "freer." Smith argues that a majority of the delegates probably supported the creation of a black political party. However, Jackson soon moderated his position, asserting that mass political mobilization would have to come before a black political party could be formed.

16. For a report on the platform debate in the New York State delegation, see "Platform Formed by State Blacks: They'll Present It to Parley Opening in Gary on Friday," *New York Times*, March 6, 1972, p. 28.

17. The official version of the National Black Political Agenda was issued on May 19, Malcolm X's birthday.

18. Coleman Young and Lonnie Wheeler, *Hard Stuff: The Autobiography of Coleman Young* (New York: Viking Press, 1993), pp. 189–90.

19. Ibid., p. 190.

20. I attended a lecture at the Yale Law School in the mid-1970s in which Mayor Richard Hatcher explicitly cited Baraka as the moving force in and organizational key to the success of the Gary gathering.

21. Ronald W. Walters, *Black Presidential Politics in America: A Strategic Approach* (Albany: State University of New York Press, 1988), p. 87.

22. Bill Strickland, "The Gary Convention and the Crisis of American Politics," *Black World*, October 1972, pp. 22–23.

23. For criticism of the NAACP's warped understanding of ethnic pluralist politics, see Harold Cruse, *Plural but Equal: Blacks and Minorities in America's Plural Society* (New York: Morrow, 1987), pp. 351–63. Cruse's understanding of cultural pluralism is equally flawed, for he writes as if ethnic groups have an "unofficial official" status as political units in American politics. That is, he confuses American pluralism with what political scientists have sometimes called "consociational politics." Robert C. Smith describes the thinking of Roy Wilkins and his

attempt to control the convention agenda even before it took place in *We Have No Leaders: African Americans in the Post–Civil Rights Era* (Albany: State University of New York Press, 1996), pp. 46–47.

24. Thomas A. Johnson, "N.A.A.C.P. Aide Opposes Draft of Black Preamble," *New York Times*, March 10, 1972, p. 20.

25. Paulette Pierce, "The Roots of the Rainbow Coalition," *Black Scholar*, March/April 1968, p. 11.

26. Although I am commenting on Pierce's specific analysis of the Gary convention, her article provides an important discussion of the historical linkages between the political energies unleashed by the 1972 Gary convention and Jesse Jackson's decision to run for the Democratic presidential nomination in 1984.

27. Smith, *We Have No Leaders*, p. 50.

28. Walters, *Black Presidential Politics*, p. 88.

29. Barbara A. Reynolds, *Jesse Jackson: The Man, the Movement, the Myth* (Chicago: Nelson-Hall, 1975), p. 249; and Ethel Payne, "The Moment of Truth at Gary and Beyond," *Chicago Defender*, March 18–24, 1972.

30. See the special to the *New York Times*, March 16, 1972, entitled "Hatcher Reviews Parley of Blacks: Seeks Softer Busing Stand—Deplores Vote on Israel." Hatcher claims in this article that the Israeli amendment "snuck through" late in the convention after most of the delegates had left the floor. He said, "I did not see any strong anti-Israeli sentiments on the floor . . . it was a very unfortunate resolution."

31. Walters, *Black Presidential Politics*, pp. 91–92. These two documents are found in abbreviated form in William Clay's *Just Permanent Interests*.

32. Walters, *Black Presidential Politics*, p. 92.

33. Congressmen William Clay writes, "Although Congressmen Charles Diggs and Walter Fauntroy played leading roles in planning and executing the Gary Convention, they were not acting as agents of the Congressional Black Caucus." See Clay, *Just Permanent Interests*, p. 204.

34. Imamu Amiri Baraka, "Black and Angry," *Newsweek*, July 10, 1972, pp. 35–36. The article also contains a photograph of a serious, stern-faced Baraka and another one of a group of excited delegates at the Gary convention.

35. Ibid., p. 35.

36. Ibid., pp. 36, 35.

37. Smith, *We Have No Leaders*, p. 54.

38. Among the few important black figures in attendance were Jesse Jackson, Atlanta Mayor Maynard Jackson, and Congressmen John Conyers, Ronald Dellums, and Parren Mitchell.

39. Smith, *We Have No Leaders*, p. 60.

40. Ibid., p. 61.

41. Smith, *We Have No Leaders*, p. 64.

42. Ibid., p. 70.

43. Ibid., pp. 63–64.

NOTES TO CHAPTER 14

1. Recall that in describing the excitement surrounding Baraka's forthcoming speech at the Sixth Pan-African Congress in Dar es Salaam, Hoyt Fuller mentioned that all concerned knew by then that Baraka had shifted his ideological allegiances to Marxism.

2. LeRoi Jones / Amiri Baraka, *The Autobiography of LeRoi Jones / Amiri Baraka* (New York: Freundlich Books, 1984), p. 305. This book is henceforth cited as *The Autobiography*.

3. Ibid., pp. 298, 305.

4. LeRoi Jones, *Raise Race Rays Raze* (New York: Random House, 1971), p. 130. In a 1970 interview, Baraka claimed that Marxism-Leninism was alien to black people: "Although we can learn from other people, the American blacks of 1970 are not going to be freed by nineteenth century Europeans. Our freedom won't be found in the teachings of Marx or Lenin. Neither Communism nor Capitalism nor Christianity has the energy, or the strength, necessary to orient black-colored people in a direction which will be beneficial to them." See Charles Reilly, ed., *Conversations with Amiri Baraka* (Jackson: University Press of Mississippi, 1994), p. 83.

5. In the first issue of *First World* (the short-lived successor to *Black World*), Addison Gayle lamented Baraka's "defection" to Marxism, concluding that it was an "aesthetic based upon economic and class determinism . . . which has minimal value to Black People." See Gayle's "Blueprint for Black Criticism," *First World* 1, no. 1 (January/February 1977).

6. Kalamu Ya Salaam, "Tell No Lies, Claim No Easy Victories: African Liberation Day: An Assessment," *Black World* 23, no. 4 (October 1974): 21.

7. *The Autobiography*, pp. 298, 312.

8. Gerald Early, "On LeRoi Jones / Amiri Baraka," *Salmagundi*, nos. 70–71 (Spring/Summer 1986): 345, 346.

9. This point was also raised in Josef Jarab, "Black Aesthetic: A Cultural or Political Concept," *Callaloo #25*, vol. 8, no. 3 (Fall 1985): 587–93.

10. When Madhubuti's understated criticism of Baraka's new leftism, "The Latest Purge," appeared in (September 1974), several black intellectuals came to Baraka's defense, and the editors of *The Black Scholar* published these rejoinder articles. Two were published in the October 1974 issue: Ronald Walters, pp. 47–49, and S. E. Anderson, pp. 50–51. The other two responses were published in the January/February issue: Kalumu Ya Salaam, pp. 40–43, and Mark Smith, pp. 44–52. The October 1974 issue of *Black Scholar* published an anti-Marxist response from Alonzo 4X (Cannady), the news editor of *Muhammad Speaks*. The opening sentence is "Now that the ideological bankruptcy of Imamu Amiri Baraka's black nationalist detour has become manifest and the old integration euphemism of Marxism-Leninism has become an integral part of his poetic vision, he is, alas—irrelevant" (p. 52).

11. LeRoi Jones / Amiri Baraka, *The Autobiography of LeRoi Jones* (Chicago:

Lawrence Hill Books, 1997), pp. 435–36. This later edition is henceforth cited as *The Autobiography II*.

12. This speech was subsequently issued as a CAP position paper. See Imamu Amiri Baraka, "National Liberation and Politics," March 1974, pp. 1–5.

13. Amiri Baraka, "Revolutionary Party: Revolutionary Ideology," CAP position paper, March 31, 1974, pp. 1, 3.

14. *The Autobiography II*, p. 435.

15. Amiri Baraka, "Toward Ideological Clarity," Congress of Afrikan Peoples ideological paper, May 24, 1974, p. 31.

16. Ibid., p. 24.

17. For a collection of Cabral's writings that appeared after Baraka left black nationalism, see Amilcar Cabral, *Unity and Struggle: Speeches and Writings of Amilcar Cabral*, trans. Michael Wolfers (New York: Monthly Review Press, 1979).

18. See Ronald H. Chilcote, *Amilcar Cabral's Revolutionary Theory and Practice: A Critical Guide* (Boulder, CO: Lynne Rienner, 1991), esp. pp. 26–27, 37–40, 51–52; and Michael S. Morgado, "Amilcar Cabral's Theory of Cultural Revolution," *Black Images* 3 (Summer 1974): 3–16.

19. Baraka, "Toward Ideological Clarity," p. 28.

20. Chilcote, *Amilcar Cabral's Revolutionary Theory and Practice*, pp. 26–38. Also see Jock McCulloch, "Amilcar Cabral: A Theory of Imperialism," *Journal of Modern African Studies* 19 (September 1981): 503–10, and *In The Twilight of Revolution* (Boston: Routledge & Kegan Paul, 1983), a study of Cabral.

21. See Amilcar Cabral, "Connecting the Struggles: An Informal Talk with Black Americans," in Amilcar Cabral, *Return to the Source: Selected Speeches of Amilcar Cabral*, ed. Africa Information Service (New York: Monthly Review Press, 1973), p. 78.

22. Baraka, "Toward Ideological Clarity," p. 31.

23. Amiri Baraka, "The Congress of Afrikan People: A Position Paper," *Black Scholar*, January/February 1975, p. 9.

24. Baraka, "Black Nationalism and Socialist Revolution: Why I Changed My Ideology," *Black World*, July 1975, p. 30.

25. Ibid., pp. 31–32.

26. Baraka was somewhat prophetic in this regard. Approximately a year after this essay was published, Andrew Young, the U.S. ambassador to the United Nations, played such a role in Africa during the Carter administration. Young traveled throughout the continent, meeting with African elites and selling capitalist development and alliances with the United States as the true hope for Africa.

27. Baraka, "Black Nationalism," p. 33.

28. Ibid., p. 38.

29. Amiri Baraka, *Daggers and Javelins: Essays* (New York: Morrow, 1984), p. 10. Needless to say, the M-L-M refers to Marxist-Leninist-Mao Zedong thought.

30. Leo Ou-fan Lee, *Voices from the Iron House: A Study of Lu Xun* (Bloomington: Indiana University Press, 1987), p. 124. Lu Xun was the pen name for Zhou

Shuren. For a contextual discussion of his writings, see Bonnie S. McDougall and Kam Louie, *The Literature of China in the Twentieth Century* (New York: Columbia University Press, 1997), pp. 22–27, 46–48, 93–99.

31. For the historical context of Lu Xun (Lu Hsun) see Jonathan D. Spence, *The Gate of Heavenly Peace: The Chinese and Their Revolution, 1895–1980* (New York: Viking Press, 1981); Chow Tse-tsung, *The May Fourth Movement: Intellectual Revolution in Modern China* (Stanford, CA: Stanford University Press, 1967); and Tsi-An Hsia, *The Gate of Darkness: Studies on the Leftist Literary Movement in China* (Seattle: University of Washington Press, 1968). For collections of Lu Xun's work, see Gladys Yang, ed. and trans., *Silent China: Selected Writings of Lu Xun* (Oxford: Oxford University Press, 1973), *Lu Hsun: Writing for the Revolution: Essays by Lu Hsun and Essays on Lu Hsun* (San Francisco: Red Sun Publishers, 1976), and *Selected Stories of Lu Hsun* (Peking: Foreign Language Press, 1972).

32. See Ou-fan Lee, *Voices from the Iron House*, p. 111.

33. Ibid., p. 125.

34. Ibid., p. 133.

35. Reilly, ed., *Conversations with Amiri Baraka*, p. 244. Since his adoption of Marxism, Baraka has made numerous claims concerning the censorship of his work, repeatedly stating that he has been unable to get some of his works published, even though his works have sold quite well. While I have no proof to substantiate this claim, it seems reasonable to accept Baraka's formulations at face value. As a prominent, prolific, frequently anthologized American writer, Baraka certainly would know when he is having difficulty finding a publisher.

36. Baraka, *Daggers and Javelins*, p. 23.

37. Ibid., pp. 91, 95, 96.

38. Harry Haywood, *Black Bolshevik: Autobiography of an Afro-American Communist* (Chicago: Liberator Press, 1978).

39. See Robin D. G. Kelley, *Hammer and Hoe: Alabama Communists during the Great Depression* (Chapel Hill: University of North Carolina Press, 1990). Contrary to Baraka's false historical depictions, Kelley shows that the black nation thesis made little impact on the communists' popularity among blacks.

40. Baraka, *Daggers and Javelins*, pp. 58–59

41. For an excellent discussion of socialist realism, see Luc Herman, *Concepts of Realism* (Columbia, SC: Camden House, 1996), esp. chaps. 5 and 8.

42. A sampling of various ideas about Marx and art can be found in Maynard Solomon, ed., *Marxism and Art: Essays Classic and Contemporary* (New York: Knopf, 1973).

43. Terry Eagleton, *Marxism and Literary Criticism* (Berkeley and Los Angeles: University of California Press, 1976), p. 37.

44. Jürgen Rühl, *Literature and Revolution: A Critical Study of the Writer and Communism in the Twentieth Century*, trans. and ed. Jean Steinberg (New York: Praeger, 1969), p. 136.

45. From the First All-Union Congress of Soviet Writers, 1934, p. 716; reprinted in Abram Tertz, *The Trial Begins and On Socialist Realism* (Berkeley and Los Angeles: University of California, Press, 1982), p. 148.

46. Eagleton, *Marxism and Literary Criticism*, p. 38.

47. See Anne Fremantle, ed., *Mao Tse-Tung: An Anthology of His Writings* (New York: New American Library, 1962), "Talks at the Yenan Forum on Art and Literature," May 23, 1942, pp. 242–63.

48. Reilly, ed., *Conversations with Amiri Baraka*, p. 137.

49. I use the word *supposedly*, since Baraka does respect the thought of Enver Hoxha, even though Hoxha had not been the leader of a major revolutionary movement. Baraka's celebration of Hoxha probably derives from the fact that Hoxha was favorably mentioned in the literature of the People's Republic of China. Albania, the only Communist east European nation that remained completely outside the Soviet orbit, developed strong ties to "Red China."

50. Perhaps the reductionist Baraka should be asked a reductionist question. What is it about the former LeRoi Jones that led him to believe that this was the best literary criticism he had ever read? Admittedly, this question is unfair and somewhat patronizing, but it seems appropriate given the enormity of Baraka's claim concerning Mao's views of literature. After all, why is it that Mao, a great political figure and revolutionary leader, also emerges as the best literary critic ever read by a well-read American writer?

51. Ibid., p. 140. One can only wonder whether Baraka viewed the Schomberg Collection of slave narratives as a counterhegemonic event.

52. I can only assume that Baraka did not include Johnson's *God's Trombones* in this same category.

53. Baraka, *Daggers and Javelins*, pp. 142–43.

54. Ibid., p. 145.

55. Ibid., pp. 146–47.

56. Baraka, *Daggers and Javelins*, pp. 310, 313.

57. Ibid., p. 314. Perhaps a better example of Wright's attraction to black nationalism can be found in *Twelve Million Black Voices*.

58. Ralph Ellison, "Richard Wright's Blues," in his *Shadow and Act* (New York: Vintage Books, 1972), pp. 77–94. The essay was originally published in the *Antioch Review* (Summer 1945).

59. Michelle Wallace, *Black Macho and the Myth of the Superwoman* (New York: Dial, 1978); Ntozake Shange, *For Colored Girls Who Have Considered Suicide When the Rainbow Is Enuf* (New York: Macmillan, 1977).

60. The insightful study of Baraka by William Harris, *The Poetry and Poetics of Amiri Baraka: The Jazz Aesthetic* (Columbia: University of Missouri Press, 1985), becomes flawed at precisely the moment that Harris treats Baraka's "Marxism" as if it were a serious intellectual engagement. Literary critics like Harris can be excused for being unfamiliar with Marxist political and economic thought. However, in 1985, there remained little justification for an American literary critic not to be familiar with

Walter Benjamin, Raymond Williams, Fred Jameson, Terry Eagleton, Jean-Paul Sartre, and Georg Lukacs, as well as other significant Marxist literary intellectuals. Baraka's Marxism and, in particular, his conception of a Marxist aesthetic are not part of this intellectual ball game!

NOTES TO CHAPTER 15

1. Amiri Baraka, *The Motion of History and Other Plays* (New York: Morrow, 1978), p. 7.

2. My mention of the manipulation of rhetoric placing God on the side of the black oppressed should not be confused with liberation theology, which also asserts that God is on the side of the oppressed *but does not assume that emancipation is inevitable.*

3. Baraka, *The Motion of History*, pp. 33, 34–35.

4. Ibid., p. 40.

5. In a footnote to this instruction, Baraka noted that after "the first few performances, the company suggested that discussion be after the production so the actors could participate, and this was done with good results, without plants" (ibid., p. 75).

6. Ibid.

7. In portraying Elijah Muhammad as displaying all of the profundity of a scratched record that replays the same lyrics endlessly, Baraka issued one of his few public condemnations of the leader of the Nation of Islam.

8. The play can be found in Baraka's *The Motion of History and Other Plays*, pp. 152–206. Baraka included a glossary of Marxist-Leninist terminology in the original program notes which was subsequently reprinted in this volume. In addition, Baraka included a short description of the provisions of the S-1 crime bill as it was debated in the U.S. Senate.

9. Here Baraka chides Elijah Muhammad and even an earlier version of himself for advocating essentialist views about the inherent "evil" nature of white people.

10. Baraka, *The Motion of History*, p. 173.

11. The play was published in Amiri Baraka, *Selected Plays and Prose of Amiri Baraka / LeRoi Jones* (New York: Morrow, 1979), pp. 252–76.

12. Ibid., p. 253.

13. E. San Juan Jr., a Marxist literary critic, was so impressed by this play that he called it "the most significant theatrical achievement of 1978 in the western hemisphere." Moreover, San Juan evidently believed that the only critics who would find serious fault with this play were bourgeois academics. While his views may reflect those of other economistic Marxists, I can only conclude that San Juan was as crude as Baraka in his understanding of Marxist aesthetics. See E. San Juan Jr., "Amiri Baraka, Revolutionary Playwright: Baraka Unmasks the Lone Ranger in the Long March toward a People's Theater," in *Amiri Baraka: The Kaleidoscopic Torch: A Literary Tribute.*

A special issue of *Steppingstones: A Literary Anthology toward Liberation*, ed. James B. Gwynne (New York: Steppingstones Press, 1985), p. 151.

14. C. W. E. Bigsby, *A Critical Introduction to Twentieth-Century American Drama*, vol. 3: *Beyond Broadway* (Cambridge: Cambridge University Press, 1985), p. 403.

15. Amiri Baraka, *Hard Facts* (Newark: Congress of Afrikan People, 1975), 1st page of introduction (unnumbered).

16. Ibid., 3d page of introduction.

17. Ibid., 3d and 4th pages of introduction.

18. Ibid., p. 3.

19. Baraka's understanding of Jesus stems from a rather orthodox materialist Marxist critique of religion. As such, it also suffers from the same limitations of any understanding of Christianity that ignores the centrality of the fear of death as a source of religious beliefs. See Merold Westphal, *God, Guilt, and Death: An Existential Phenomenology of Religion* (Bloomington: Indiana University Press, 1984).

20. Baraka, *Hard Facts*, p. 6.

21. Ibid., p. 7.

22. Ibid., p. 11. The term *ho* is slang for "whore."

23. Excerpts from *Poetry for the Advanced* can be found in Amiri Baraka, *Selected Poetry of Amiri Baraka / LeRoi Jones* (New York: Morrow, 1979), pp. 275–340.

24. Werner Sollors, *Amiri Baraka / LeRoi Jones: The Quest for a "Populist Modernism"* (New York: Columbia University Press, 1978), pp. 236–37.

25. Baraka takes "scientific" Marxism to mean that it is true and beyond "subjective" intellectual debate. As such, he misunderstands that "scientific Marxism" also has a contested intellectual tradition. Incidentally, in calling Mao a scientific Marxist, Baraka differs with Alvin Gouldner, who found more elements of "critical Marxism" than "scientific Marxism" in Maoism. See Alvin Gouldner, *The Two Marxisms: Contradictions and Anomalies in the Development of Theory* (New York: Seabury Press, 1980), chap. 2, esp. pp. 51–53.

26. Baraka admits that "Kawaida was and is, if it still exists, a *religion*." See LeRoi Jones / Amiri Baraka, *The Autobiography of LeRoi Jones / Amiri Baraka* (New York: Freundlich Books, 1984), p. 298. This book is henceforth cited as *The Autobiography*.

27. The interview with the literary critic Kimberly Benston was published in *Boundary 2: A Journal of Postmodern Literature* 6, no. 2 (Winter 1978): 309.

28. *The Autobiography*, p. 312.

29. Lloyd W. Brown, *Amiri Baraka* (Boston: Twayne, 1980), p. 168.

30. Interview with Baraka by Tish Dace, "LeRoi Jones / Amiri Baraka: From Muse to Malcolm to Mao," *Village Voice*, August 1, 1977, p. 13.

NOTES TO CONCLUSION

1. Paul Vangelisti, ed., *Transbluesency: The Selected Poems of Amiri Baraka / LeRoi Jones (1961–1995)* (New York: Marsilio Publishers, 1995).

2. Born Sondra Lee Jones, Kimako Baraka was forty-seven years old when she was murdered in early February 1984 in her own apartment in Manhattan. A suspect was immediately arrested. See Leonard Buder, "Baraka's Sister Slain in Manhattan Plaza; Suspect Arrested," *New York Times*, February 2, 1984, p. B3.

3. *W. E. B. Du Bois: A Biography in Four Voices* (San Francisco: California Newsreel 1995); St. Clair Bourne, *In motion: Amiri Baraka* (Chicago: Facets Video, 1988).

4. Phillip Rieff, *Fellow Teachers* (New York: Harper & Row, 1973), p. 103.

5. Robert Hanley, "Black Poet Says Faculty 'Nazis' Blocked Tenure," *New York Times*, March 15, 1990, p. B3.

6. In October 1990, Baraka wrote, "But still it was easier to be heard from with hate whitey than hate imperialism." See William J. Harris, ed., *The LeRoi Jones / Amiri Baraka Reader* (New York: Thunder's Mouth Press, 1991), p. xiii.

7. See Michael Paul Rogin, *Ronald Reagan the Movie and Other Episodes in Political Demonology* (Berkeley and Los Angeles: University of California Press, 1987).

8. How else would one describe James Foreman's interruption of the services at Riverside Church in New York in May 1969 to issue the "Black Manifesto" seeking reparations from white Americans for what they had done to black Americans? My point here is not that white Americans do not have a debt to pay to black Americans. However, asking one's "oppressor" to give one money in the hope of redressing past oppression is not confronting the power of the oppressor. Despite his rhetoric of black self-determination, Malcolm X was also locked in a complex victim-status relationship with white America. After all, the Nation of Islam included in its list of demands that white America not only cede the southern "black belt" states to black Americans but also subsidize this new nation financially until it could exist as a self-determined unit. The "white devil," in other words, was supposed to fund black emancipation. It is somewhat astounding to recall that this idea was at the very center of the vision of one of black America's most respected black nationalist organizations.

9. For a discussion of the war against black militants, see Cathy Perkins, ed., *COINTELPRO: The FBI's Secret War on Political Freedom* (New York: Monad Press, 1975). Also see Robert Justin Goldstein's *Political Repression in Modern America: 1870 to the Present* (Cambridge, MA: Schenkman, 1978).

10. Baraka, "'Black Nationalism': 1972," *Black Scholar*, September, 1972, p. 26. Baraka certainly could have been talking about himself. No one threatened whites with death more often than he did. But to what avail? I am not sad that Baraka's threats proved untrue, but I do wonder about the impact on one's character of having made so many unfulfilled threats. After all the vicious nonsense that Baraka shouted at white Americans, what does it do to him now to have to "eat crow"? Baraka is a testimony to individual and perhaps collective Afro-American weakness. For all his bold posturing, bad, loud-mouthed LeRoi Jones operated under the protection of the First Amendment. Perhaps this is why the idea of conversion is so important to my analysis, for it allows me to explain how Baraka rid himself of those past sins associated with the previous ideology. By adopting a new ideology, he became a new man, and in the process he saved face.

11. For a brilliant analysis of Nixon's assault on the black victim status, see Gary Wills, *Nixon Agonistes: The Crisis of the Self-Made Man* (New York: New American Library, 1970).

12. See Lyndon Johnson, *The Vantage Point: Perspectives of the Presidency, 1963–1969* (New York: Holt, Rinehart and Winston, 1971).

13. See Alvin W. Gouldner, *The Dialectic of Ideology and Technology* (New York: Seabury Press, 1976).

14. Frank Lentricchia, *Criticism and Social Change* (Chicago: University of Chicago Press, 1983), p. 11.

15. The most vociferous critic of Baraka in recent times has been the essay writer Stanley Crouch. See Stanley Crouch, "Comrade, Comrade, Where You Been," review of *What Was the Relationship of the Lone Ranger to the Means of Production*, by Amiri Baraka, *Village Voice*, June 11, 1979, p. 89; Also see Crouch, "The Lone Ranger's Revenge," *Village Voice*, June 18, 1979, and "The King of Constant Repudiation," *Village Voice*, September 9, 1979.

16. Lentricchia, *Criticism and Social Change*, pp. 9–10.

17. Ibid., p. 10.

18. Ibid.

19. Harold Cruse, *The Crisis of the Negro Intellectual* (New York: Morrow, 1967), p. 543.

20. Michael Walzer, *The Company of Critics: Social Criticism and Political Commitment in the Twentieth Century* (New York: Basic Books, 1988).

21. See Hannah Arendt, *The Jew as Pariah: Jewish Identity and Politics in the Modern Age*, ed. Ron H. Feldman (New York: Grove Press, 1978); Hannah Arendt, *The Origins of Totalitarianism*, 2d ed. (New York: Harcourt Brace Jovanovich, 1973), esp. "Between Pariah and Parvenu," pp. 56–68; and Michael Löwy, *Redemption and Utopia: Jewish Libertarian Thought in Central Europe, A Study in Elective Affinity*, trans. Hope Heaney (Stanford, CA: Stanford University Press, 1992), esp. chap.3, "Pariahs, Rebels and Romantics: A Sociological Analysis of the Central European Jewish Intelligentsia." Also see Walzer, *The Company of Critics*, esp. "Albert Camus's Algerian War," pp. 136–52. I find Edward Said's analysis of Camus's position far more persuasive and ethically sound than Walzer's. See Edward Said, *Culture and Imperialism* (New York: Knopf, 1993), esp. "Camus and the French Imperial Experience," pp. 169–85.

Bibliography

All works by LeRoi Jones / Amiri Baraka are listed under Amiri Baraka.

Abramson, Doris E. *Negro Playwrights in the American Theatre: 1925–1959.* New York: Columbia University Press, 1969.

Adam, Barry D. *The Survival of Domination: Inferiorization and Everyday Life.* New York: Elsevier, 1978.

Adamolekun, Ladipo. *Sekou Touré's Guinea: An Experiment in Nation Building.* London: Methuen, 1976.

Ahmed, Akbar Muhammad (Max Stanford). "The Roots of the Pan-African Revolution." *Black Scholar* 3 (1972): 48–55.

Allen, Donald M., ed. *New Amsterdam Poetry, 1945–1960.* New York: Grove Press, 1960.

Allen, Robert L. *Black Awakening in Capitalist America.* Garden City, NY: Doubleday, 1969.

Allen, Theodore W. *The Invention of the White Race.* Vol. 2, *The Origin of Racial Oppression in Anglo-America.* London: Verso, 1997.

Appiah, Kwame Anthony. *In My Father's House: Africa in the Philosophy of Culture.* New York: Oxford University Press, 1992.

"Art and Guns: Political Poetry at Home and Abroad." *Poetry East,* nos. 9 and 10 (Winter 1982 / Spring 1983).

Artaud, Antonin. *Selected Writings.* Ed. Susan Sontag. New York: Farrar, Straus & Giroux, 1976.

Asante, Molefi Kete. *The Afrocentric Idea.* Philadelphia: Temple University Press, 1987.

Baker, Houston A. *Afro-American Poetics: Revisions of Harlem and the Black Aesthetic.* Madison: University of Wisconsin Press, 1988.

———. *Blues, Ideology, and Afro-American Literature: A Vernacular Theory.* Chicago: University of Chicago Press, 1984.

———. *The Journey Back: Issues in Black Literature and Criticism.* Chicago: University of Chicago Press, 1980.

Banes, Sally. *Greenwich Village 1963: Avant-Garde Performance and the Effervescent Body.* Durham, NC: Duke University Press, 1993.

Baraka, Ameer. "The Black Aesthetic." *Negro Digest* 18 (September 1969): 5–6.

Baraka, Amiri (LeRoi Jones). *The Autobiography of LeRoi Jones / Amiri Baraka.* New York: Freundlich Books, 1984.

———. *The Autobiography of LeRoi Jones.* Chicago: Lawrence Hill Books, 1997.

Baraka, Amiri (LeRoi Jones). *The Baptism and the Toilet.* New York: Grove Press, 1967.

———. *Black Magic: Collected Poetry, 1961–1967.* Indianapolis: Bobbs-Merrill, 1969.

———. *Black Music.* New York: Morrow, 1967.

———. "Black Revolutionary Poets Should Also Be Playwrights." *Black World* 21, no. 6 (April 1972): 4–6.

———. *Blues People: Negro Music in White America.* New York: Morrow, 1963.

———. "Confessions of a Former Anti-Semite." *Village Voice,* December 17, 1980, pp. 1, 19–23.

———. *Daggers and Javelins: Essays, 1974–1979.* New York: Morrow, 1984.

———. *Dutchman* and *The Slave.* New York: Morrow, 1967.

———. *Eulogies.* New York: Marsilio Publishers, 1996.

———. *Four Black Revolutionary Plays.* Indianapolis: Bobbs-Merrill, 1969.

———. *Funk Lore: New Poems (1984–1995).* Ed. Paul Vangelisti. Los Angeles: Littoral Books, 1996.

———. *Hard Facts.* Newark, NJ: Congress of Afrikan People, 1975.

———. *Home: Social Essays.* New York: Morrow, 1966.

———. *Jello.* Chicago: Third World Press, 1970.

———. "Jesse 88." Forward to *Journal of Socialist Thought* 8 (Spring 1988): 1–23.

———. *The LeRoi Jones / Amiri Baraka Reader.* Ed. William J. Harris. New York: Thunder's Mouth Press, 1991.

———. *The Motion of History and Other Plays.* New York: Morrow, 1978.

———. "Nina Returns." *Forward: Journal of Socialist Thought* 7 (Summer 1987): 93–108.

———. *Preface to a Twenty Volume Suicide Note. . . .* New York: Corinth Books, 1961.

———. *Raise Race Rays Raze.* New York: Random House, 1971.

———. *Selected Plays and Prose of Amiri Baraka / LeRoi Jones.* New York: Morrow, 1979.

———. *The Sidney Poet Heroical: In 29 Scenes.* New York: I. Reed Books, 1979.

———. *Spirit Reach.* Newark, NJ: Jihad Productions, 1972.

———. *Tales.* New York: Grove Press, 1967.

———. *Three Books by Imamu Amiri Baraka: The System of Dante's Hell, The Dead Lecturer, Tales.* New York: Grove Press, 1975.

———. "Why I Changed My Ideology: Black Nationalism and Socialist Revolution." *Black World* 24 (July 1975): 30–42.

———. *Why's, Wise, Ys.* Chicago: Third World Press, 1995.

———, ed. *African Congress: A Documentary of the First Modern Pan-African Congress.* New York: Morrow, 1972.

———, ed. *The Moderns: An Anthology of New Writing in America.* New York: Corinth Books, 1963.

———, and Amina Baraka, eds. *The Music: Reflections on Jazz and Blues.* New York: Morrow, 1987.

———, eds. *Confirmation: An Anthology of African American Women.* New York: Morrow, 1983.

————, and Larry Neal, eds. *Black Fire: An Anthology of Afro-American Writing*. New York: Morrow, 1968.

Baraka, Imamu Ameer. "Black Nationalism: 1972." *Black Scholar* 4 (September 1972): 23–29.

Baraka, Imamu Amiri. (LeRoi Jones). "Black Woman." *Black World* 19 (July 1975): 7–11.

————. "The Coronation of the Black Queen." *Black Scholar* 19, no. 8 (June 1970): 46–48.

————. *It's Nation Time*. Chicago: Third World Press, 1970.

————. *Kawaida Studies: The New Nationalism*. Chicago: Third World Press, 1972.

————. "Needed: A Revolutionary Strategy." *Black Scholar* 7 (October 1975): 42–45.

————. "Toward Ideological Clarity." *Black World* 24 (November 1974): 24–33, 84–95.

————, and Fundi. *In Our Terribleness*. Indianapolis: Bobbs-Merrill, 1970.

Barbour, Floyd B., ed. *The Black Power Revolt: A Collection of Essays*. Boston: Porter Sargent, 1968.

Barnes, Hazel. *An Existentialist Ethics*. Chicago: University of Chicago Press, 1978.

Baxandall, Lee, ed. *Radical Perspectives in the Arts*. Baltimore: Penguin Books, 1972.

Becker, Howard S. *Art Worlds*. Berkeley and Los Angeles: University of California, 1982.

Bennett, Lerone Jr. "Pan-African at the Crossroads: Dreams and Realities Clash as Delegates Debate Class and Color at Historic Congress in Tanzania." *Ebony*, September 1974, pp. 148–52, 154–60.

Benston, Kimberly. *Baraka: The Renegade and the Mask*. New Haven, CT: Yale University Press, 1976.

Bentley, Eric. *The Theatre of Commitment*. New York: Atheneum, 1967.

Bernotas, Bob. *Amiri Baraka*. New York: Chelsea House, 1991.

Bernstein, Charles, ed. *Close Listening: Poetry and the Performed World*. New York: Oxford University Press, 1998.

Betts, Raymond, ed. *The Ideology of Blackness*. Lexington, MA: Heath, 1971.

Bien, Peter. *Kazantzakis: Politics of the Spirit*. Princeton, NJ: Princeton University Press, 1989.

Bigsby, C. W. E. *Confrontation and Commitment*. Columbia: University of Missouri Press, 1967.

————. *A Critical Introduction to Twentieth-Century American Drama*. Vol. 3, *Beyond Broadway*. Cambridge: Cambridge University Press, 1985.

————, ed. *The Black American Writer*. Vol. 1, *Fiction*. Baltimore: Penguin Books, 1971.

————, ed. *The Black American Writer*. Vol. 2, *Poetry and Drama*. Baltimore: Penguin Books, 1969.

Blair, Thomas L. *Retreat to the Ghetto: The End of a Dream?* New York: Hill & Wang, 1977.

Blauner, Robert. *Racial Oppression in America*. New York: Harper & Row, 1972.

Bloom, Alexander. *Prodigal Sons: The New York Intellectuals and Their World*. New York: Oxford University Press, 1986.

Boggs, James. *Racism and the Class Struggle: Further Pages from a Black Worker's Notebook*. New York: Monthly Review Press, 1970.

Brooks, Gwendolyn. *Report from Part One*. Detroit: Broadside Press, 1973.

Brown, Cecil M. "Black Literature and LeRoi Jones." *Black World* 19 (June 1970): 24–31.

Brown, Elaine. *A Taste of Power: A Black Woman's Story*. New York: Pantheon, 1992.

Brown, Lloyd W. *Amiri Baraka*. Boston: Twayne, 1980.

———, ed. *The Black Writer in Africa and the Americas*. Los Angeles: Hennesy and Ingalls, 1973.

———, ed. *New Black Voices: An Anthology of Contemporary Afro-American Literature*. New York: New American Library, 1972.

Brustein, Robert. *The Theatre of Revolt: Studies in Modern Drama from Ibsen to Genet*. Boston: Atlantic Monthly Press / Little Brown, 1964.

Bryant-Jackson, Paul, and Louis Moore Overbeck, eds. *Intersecting Boundaries: The Theatre of Adrienne Kennedy*. Minneapolis: University of Minnesota Press, 1992.

Bullins, Ed, ed. *New Plays from the Black Theatre*. New York: Bantam Books, 1969.

Burger, Peter. *Theory of the Avant-Garde*. Trans. Michael Shaw. Minneapolis: University of Minnesota Press, 1984.

Burkman, Katherine H., and Judith Roof, eds. *Staging the Rage: The Web of Misogyny in Modern Drama*. Madison, NJ: Fairleigh Dickinson University Press, 1998.

Cabral, Amilcar. *Return to the Source: Selected Speeches*. New York: Monthly Review Press, 1973.

———. *Revolution in Guinea: Selected Texts*. Trans. and ed. Richard Handyside. New York: Monthly Review Press, 1972.

———. *Unity and Struggle: Speeches and Writings*. Trans. Michael Wolfers. New York: Monthly Review Press, 1979.

Carbado, Devon W., ed. *Black Men on Race, Gender, and Sexuality: A Critical Reader*. New York: New York University Press, 1999.

Caws, Peter. *Sartre*. London: Routledge & Kegan Paul, 1979.

Cesaire, Aime. *The Collected Poetry*. Trans. Clayton Eshelman and Annette Smith. Berkeley and Los Angeles: University of California Press, 1983.

Chapman, Abraham, ed. *New Black Voices: An Anthology of Contemporary Afro-American Literature*. New York: New American Library, 1972.

Chilcote, Ronald H. *Amilcar Cabral's Revolutionary Theory and Practice: A Critical Guide*. Boulder, CO: Lynne Rienner, 1991.

Chisholm, Shirley. *The Good Fight*. New York: Harper & Row, 1973.

Churchill, Ward, and Jim Vander Wall. *Agents of Repression: The FBI's Secret Wars against the Black Panther Party and the American Indian Movement*. Boston: South End Press, 1988.

Clarke, John Henrik, ed. *Malcolm X: The Man and His Times*. New York: Macmillan, 1969.

Clay, William L. *Just Permanent Interests: Black Americans in Congress, 1870–1992*. New York: Amistad Press, 1993.

Cleaver, Eldridge. *Soul on Ice*. New York: Dell, 1968.

Clegg, Claude Andrew III. *An Original Man: The life and Times of Elijah Muhammed*. New York: St. Martin's Press, 1997.

Clurman, Harold. *The Naked Image: Observations on the Modern Theatre*. New York: Macmillan, 1966.

Cohen, Robert Carl. *Black Crusader: A Biography of Robert Franklin Williams*. Secaucus, NJ: Lyle Stuart, 1972.

Cone, James. *For My People: Black Theology and the Black Church*. Maryknoll, NY: Orbis, 1984.

Cook, Mercer, and Stephen E. Henderson. *The Militant Black Writer in Africa and the United States*. Madison: University of Wisconsin Press, 1969.

Coser, Lewis. *The Functions of Social Conflict*. New York: Free Press, 1966.

———. *Greedy Institutions: Patterns of Undivided Commitment*. New York: Free Press, 1974.

Craig, E. Quita. *Black Drama of the Federal Theatre Era: Beyond the Formal Horizons*. Amherst: University of Massachusetts Press, 1980.

Cross, William Jr. *Shades of Black: Diversity in African-American Identity*. Philadelphia: Temple University Press, 1991.

Crouch, Stanley. *Notes of a Hanging Judge: Essays and Reviews, 1979–1989*. New York: Oxford University Press, 1990.

Cruse, Harold. *The Crisis of the Negro Intellectual*. New York: Morrow, 1967.

———. "The Little Rock National Black Political Convention, Part I." *Black World* 23 (October 1974): 10–17,82–88.

———. "The National Black Political Convention, Part II." *Black World* 24 (November 1974): 4–21.

Damon, Maria. *The Dark End of the Street: Margins in American Vanguard Poetry*. Minneapolis: University of Minnesota Press, 1993.

Daniels, Ron. "The National Black Political Assembly: Building Independent Black Politics in the 1980s." *Black Scholar* 11 (March/April 1980): 32–42.

Davis, Angela. *An Autobiography: With My Mind on Freedom*. New York: Bantam Books, 1974.

Davis, Charles. *Black Is the Color of the Cosmos: Essays on Afro-American Literature and Culture, 1942–1981*. Washington, DC: Howard University Press, 1989.

DeCaro, Louis A. Jr. *On the Side: A Religious Life of Malcolm X*. New York: New York University Press, 1996.

Delaney, Samuel. *Motion of Light in Water*. New York: Arbor House, 1988.

DeVeaux, Scott. *The Birth of BeBop: A Social and Musical History*. Chicago: University of Chicago Press, 1997.

Dickstein, Morris. *Gates of Eden: American Culture in the Sixties*. New York: Basic Books, 1977.

Di Prima, Diane. *Memoirs of a Beatnik*. San Francisco: Last Gasp, 1988.

Dorrien, Gary. *The Neoconservative Mind: Politics, Culture, and the War of Ideology.* Philadelphia: Temple University Press, 1993.

Duberman, Martin. *Black Mountain: An Exploration in Community.* New York: Dutton, 1972.

———. *The Uncompleted Past.* New York: Random House, 1969.

Dubey, Madhu. *Black Women Novelists and the Nationalist Aesthetic.* Bloomington: Indiana University Press, 1994.

Duignan, Peter, and L. H. Gann. *The United States and Africa: A History.* Cambridge: Cambridge University Press, 1984.

Duval, Elaine I. "Reasserting and Raising Our History: An Interview with Amiri Baraka (August 27, 1987)." *Obsidian II* 3 (Spring 1988): 1–17.

Early, Gerald. *Tuxedo Junction: Essays on American Culture.* New York: Ecco Press, 1989.

———, ed. *Speech and Power.* Vol. 1. Hopewell, NJ: Ecco Press, 1992.

Eagleton, Terry. *Marxism and Literary Criticism.* Berkeley and Los Angeles: University of California Press, 1976.

Ebaugh, Helen Rose Fuchs. *Becoming an EX: The Process of Role Exit.* Chicago: University of Chicago Press, 1988.

Edwards, Harry. *The Struggle That Must Be: An Autobiography.* New York: Macmillan, 1980.

Ellison, Ralph. *Shadow and Act.* New York: Random House, 1964.

Fabio, Sarah Webster. "A Black Paper: An Essay on Literature." *Black World* 18 (July 1969).

Fabre, Genevieve. *Drumbeats, Masks, and Metaphor: Contemporary Afro-American Theatre.* Trans. Melvin Dixon. Cambridge, MA: Harvard University Press, 1983.

Fanon, Frantz. *Black Skin, White Masks.* Trans. Charles Lam Markmann. New York: Grove Press, 1967.

———. *A Dying Colonialism.* Trans. Haakon Chevalier. New York: Grove Press, 1967.

Farbre, Genevieve. *Drumbeats, Masks, and Metaphor: Contemporary Afro-American Theatre.* Trans. Melvin Dixon. Cambridge, MA: Harvard University Press, 1983.

Fiedler, Leslie A. *To the Gentiles.* New York: Stein & Day, 1972.

———. *Waiting for the End.* New York: Stein & Day, 1964.

———. *What Was Literature: Class, Culture and Mass Society.* New York: Simon & Schuster, 1982.

Finkenstaedt, Rose L. H. *Face to Face: Blacks in America: White Perceptions and Black Realities.* New York: Morrow, 1994.

Fishbein, Leslie. *Rebels in Bohemia: The Radicals of "the Masses," 1911–1917.* Chapel Hill: University of North Carolina Press, 1983.

Flowers, Sandra Hollin. *African American Nationalist Literature of the 1960s.* New York: Garland, 1996.

Forman, James. *The Making of Black Revolutionaries.* Washington, DC: Open Hand Publishing, 1985.

Fowler, Virginia, ed. *Conversations with Nikki Giovanni.* Jackson: University Press of Mississippi, 1992.

Fox, Robert Elliot. *Conscientious Sorcerers: The Black Postmodernist Fiction of LeRoi Jones / Amiri Baraka, Ishmael Reed, and Samuel R. Delany.* Westport, CT: Greenwood Press, 1987.

Fremantle, Anne, ed. *Mao Tse-Tung: An Anthology of His Writings.* New York: New American Library, 1962.

Fuller, Hoyt. *Journey to Africa.* Chicago: Third World Press, 1971.

Fullinwider, S. P. *The Mind and Mood of Black America.* Homewood, IL: Dorsey Press, 1969.

Gates, Henry Louis Jr. *Figures in Black: Words, Signs, and the "Racial" Self.* New York: Oxford University Press, 1987.

Gay, Peter. *Weimar Culture: The Outsider as Insider.* New York: Harper & Row, 1968.

Gayle, Addison. "Cultural Strangulation: Black Literature and the White Aesthetic." *Negro Digest* 18 (July 1969).

———. "An Open Letter to the Editor of the New York Times Book Review." *Black World* 21 (May 1972): 92–94.

———. *The Way of the World: The Black Novel in America.* Garden City, NY: Doubleday, 1976.

———. *Wayward Child: A Personal Odyssey.* Garden City, NY: Doubleday, 1977.

———, ed. *The Black Aesthetic.* Garden City: Doubleday, 1971.

Geiss, Imanuel. *The Pan-African Movement: A History of Pan-Africanism in America, Europe, and Africa.* Trans. Ann Keep. New York: Holmes and Meier, 1974.

George, Paul, and Jerold M. Starr. "Beat Politics: New Left and Hippie Beginnings in the Postwar Counterculture." In *Cultural Politics: Radical Movements in Modern History*, ed. Jerold Starr. New York: Praeger, 1985.

Gerard, Charley. *Jazz in Black and White: Race, Culture, and Identity in the Jazz Community.* Westport, CT: Praeger, 1998.

Gibson, Donald B. *Five Black Writers: Essays on Wright, Ellison, Baldwin, Hughes, and LeRoi Jones.* New York: New York University Press, 1970.

Gillette, Michael. *Launching the War on Poverty: An Oral History.* New York: Twayne, 1996.

Gilman, Richard. *The Confusion of Realms.* New York: Random House, 1969.

Giovanni, Nikki. *Sacred Cows . . . And Other Edibles.* New York: Morrow, 1988.

Goldberg, David Theo. *Racist Culture: Philosophy and the Politics of Meaning.* Oxford: Blackwell, 1993.

Golden, Thelma. *Bob Thompson.* New York: Whitney Museum of American Art, 1998.

Goldstein, Robert Justin. *Political Repression in Modern America: 1870 to the Present.* Cambridge, MA: Schenkman, 1978.

Gordon, Vivian Verdell, ed. *Lectures: Black Scholars on Black Issues.* Washington, DC: University Press of America, 1979.

Gosse, Van. *Where the Boys Are: Cuba, Cold War America and the Making of a New Left.* New York: Verso, 1993.

Gouldner, Alvin. *The Two Marxisms: Contradictions and Anomalies in the Development of Theory.* New York: Seabury Press, 1980.

Grana, Cesar, and Marigay Grana. *On Bohemia: The Code of the Self-Exiled.* New Brunswick, NJ: Transaction Publishers, 1990.

Gruen, John. *The New Bohemia: The Combine Generation.* New York: Grosset & Dunlap, 1966.

Guerrero, Ed. *Framing Blackness: The African-American Image in Film.* Philadelphia: Temple University Press, 1993.

Gussow, Mel. *Theatre on the Edge: New Visions, New Voices.* New York: Applause, 1998.

Gwynne, James B., ed. *Amiri Baraka: The Kaleidoscopic Torch: A Literary Tribute.* A special issue of *Steppingstones: A Literary Anthology towards Liberation.* New York: Steppingstones Press, 1985.

Haines, Herbert H. *Black Radicals and the Civil Rights Mainstream, 1954–1970.* Knoxville: University of Tennessee Press, 1988.

Halisi, Imamu Clyde. "Maulana Ron Karenga: Black Leader in Captivity." *Black Scholar* 3 (May 1972): 27–31.

Hampton, Henry, and Steve Fayer. *Voices of Freedom: An Oral History of the Civil Rights Movement from the 1950s through the 1980s.* New York: Bantam Books, 1990.

Harlem Youth Opportunities Unlimited (HARYOU). *Youth in the Ghetto: A Study of the Consequences of Powerlessness and a Blueprint for Change.* New York: Orans Press, 1964.

Harlow, Barbara. *Resistance Literature.* New York: Methuen, 1987.

Harper, Michael S., and Robert B. Stepto, eds. *Chant of Saints: A Gathering of Afro-American Literature, Art, and Scholarship.* Champaign-Urbana: University of Illinois Press, 1979.

Harper, Phillip Brian. *Are We Not Men? Masculine Anxiety and the Problem of African American Identity.* New York: Oxford University Press, 1996.

Harrington, Michael. *Fragments of the Century.* New York: Saturday Review Press, 1973.

Harrington, Oliver W. *Why I Left America and Other Essays.* Jackson: University Press of Mississippi, 1993.

Harris, William J. *The Poetry and Poetics of Amiri Baraka: The Jazz Aesthetic.* Columbia: University of Missouri Press, 1985.

Harrison, Paul Carter. *The Drama of Nommo.* New York: Grove Press, 1972.

Hatch, James V. *Sorrow Is the Only Faithful One: The Life of Owen Dodson.* Champaign-Urbana: University of Illinois Press, 1993.

Hauser, Arnold. *The Sociology of Art.* Trans. Kenneth Northcott. London: Routledge & Kegan Paul, 1982.

Hayden, Tom. *Rebellion in Newark, N.J.: Official Violence and Ghetto Response.* New York: Vintage Books, 1967.

Haywood, Harry. *Negro Liberation.* Chicago: Liberator Press, 1976.

Heard, Nathan. *Howard Street.* New York: Dial Press, 1968.

Henderson, Stephen E., ed. *Understanding the New Black Poetry: Black Speech and Black Music as Poetic References.* New York: Morrow, 1973.

Hill, Errol. *The Theater of Black Americans*. Vols. 1 and 2. Englewood Cliffs, NJ: Prentice-Hall, 1980.

Hill, Herbert, ed. *Anger, and Beyond: The Negro Writer in the United States*. New York: Harper & Row, 1966.

Hilliard, David, and Lewis Cole. *This Side of Glory: The Autobiography of David Hilliard and the Story of the Black Panther Party*. Boston: Little, Brown, 1993.

Hoffman, Daniel, ed. *Harvard Guide to Contemporary American Writing*. Cambridge, MA: Harvard University Press, 1979.

hooks, bell. *Ain't I a Woman: Black Women and Feminism*. Boston: South End Press, 1981.

Horne, Gerald. *Black Liberation / Red Scare: Ben Davis and the Communist Party*. Newark: University of Delaware Press, 1994.

———. *Fire This Time: The Watts Uprising and the 1960s*. Charlottesville: University Press of Virginia, 1995.

Howe, Irving. *Selected Writings: 1950–1990*. New York: Harcourt Brace Jovanovich, 1990.

Howe, Stephen. *Afrocentrism: Mythical Pasts and Imagined Homes*. London: Verso, 1998.

Hudson, Theodore R. *From LeRoi Jones to Amiri Baraka: The Literary Works*. Durham, NC: Duke University Press, 1973.

Ilie, Paul. *Literature and Inner Exile: Authoritarian Spain, 1939–1975*. Baltimore: Johns Hopkins University Press, 1980.

Innes, Christopher. *Avant Garde Theatre: 1892–1992*. London: Routledge, 1993.

"Intellectuals." A special issue. *Salmagundi*, nos. 70 and 71 (Spring/Summer 1986).

Jackson, Kathryn. "LeRoi Jones and the New Black Writers of the Sixties." *Freedomways* 9, no. 3 (Summer 1969): 232–46.

Jacoby, Russell. *The Last Intellectuals: American Culture in the Age of Academe*. New York: Noonday Press, 1987.

JanMohamed, Abdul R. *Manichean Aesthetics: The Politics of Literature in Colonial Africa*. Amherst: University of Massachusetts Press, 1983.

Jarab, Josef. "Black Aesthetic: A Cultural or Political Concept." *Callaloo* 8, no. 25 (Fall 1985): 587–93.

Johnson, Abby Arthur, and Ronald Maberry Johnson. *Propaganda and Aesthetics: The Literary Politics of Afro-American Magazines in the Twentieth Century*. Amherst: University of Massachusetts Press, 1991.

Johnson, Charles. *Being and Race: Black Writing since 1970*. Bloomington: Indiana University Press, 1988.

Johnson, John H., with Lerone Bennett Jr. *Succeeding against the Odds*. New York: Warner Books, 1989.

Johnson, Joyce. *Minor Characters*. Boston: Houghton Mifflin, 1983.

Jones, Gayle. *Liberating Voices: Oral Tradition in African-American Literature*. New York: Penguin Books, 1992.

Jones, Hettie. *How I Became Hettie Jones*. New York: Dutton, 1990.

Jordan, Glenn, and Chris Weedon. *Cultural Politics: Class, Gender, Race and the Postmodern World*. Oxford: Blackwell, 1995.

Karenga, Ron. "In Defense of Sis. Joanne: For Ourselves and History." *Black Scholar*, July/August 1975, pp. 37–42.

———. "In Love and Struggle: Toward a Greater Togetherness." *Black Scholar*, March 1975, pp. 16–28.

———. "A Strategy for Struggle." *Black Scholar*, November 1973, pp. 8–21.

Karnig, Albert K., and Susan Welch. *Black Representation and Urban Policy*. Chicago: University of Chicago Press, 1980.

Kazin, Alfred. *Contemporaries*. Boston: Little, Brown, 1962.

Keil, Charles. *Urban Blues*. Chicago: University of Chicago Press, 1966.

Kennedy, Adrienne. *People Who Led to My Plays*. New York: Knopf, 1987.

Kent, George. *Blackness and the Adventure of Western Culture*. Chicago: Third World Press, 1972.

Kesteloot, Lilyan. *Black Writers in French: A Literary History of Negritude*. Trans. Ellen Conroy Kennedy. Philadelphia: Temple University Press, 1974.

Kilson, Martin L. "Black Power: Anatomy of a Paradox." *Harvard Journal of Negro Affairs* 2, no. 1 (1968): 30–34.

———. "Politics and Identity among Black Intellectuals." *Dissent*, Summer 1981, 339–49.

King, Woodie, and Ron Milner, eds. *Black Drama Anthology*. New York: Columbia University Press, 1972.

Klein, Marcus. *After Alienation: American Novels in Mid-Century*. Chicago: University of Chicago Press, 1978.

Klugar, Richard. *Simple Justice*. New York: Knopf, 1976.

Knight, Etheridge. *Black Voices from Prison*. New York: Pathfinder Press, 1970.

Kofsky, Frank. *Black Nationalism and the Revolution in Music*. New York: Pathfinder Press, 1970.

Kolin, Philip C., ed. *Conversations with Edward Albee*. Jackson: University Press of Mississippi, 1988.

Kostelanetz, Richard. *The End of Intelligent Writing: Literary Politics in America*. New York: Sheed & Ward, 1974.

Krim, Seymour. *Views of a Nearsighted Cannoneer*. New York: Dutton, 1968.

Kukla, Barbara J. *Swing City: Newark Nightlife, 1925–1950*. Philadelphia: Temple University Press, 1991.

Lacey, Henry C. *To Raise, Destroy, and Create: The Poetry, Drama, and Fiction of Imamu Amiri Baraka*. Troy, NY: Whitston Publishing, 1981.

Lee, Don L. "Black Critics: Voices of the Seventies." *Black World* 19 (September 1970): 24–30.

———. "The Black Writer and the Black Community." *Black World* 21 (May 1972): 85–87.

———. *Don't Cry, Scream*. Detroit: Broadside Press, 1969.

Lee, Leo Ou-fan. *Voices from the Iron House: A Study of Lu Xun*. Bloomington: Indiana University Press, 1987.

Leeming, David. *Amazing Grace: A Life of Beauford Delaney*. New York: Oxford University Press, 1998.

Lemelle, Sidney, and Robin D. G. Kelley, eds. *Imagining Home: Class, Culture, and Nationalism in the African Diaspora*. London: Verso, 1994.

Lentriccia, Frank. *Criticism and Social Change*. Chicago: University of Chicago Press, 1983.

Lester, Julius. *All Is Well: An Autobiography*. New York: Morrow, 1976.

Levine, Lawrence. *Black Culture and Black Consciousness: Afro-American Folk Thought from Slavery to Freedom*. New York: Oxford University Press, 1977.

Leyland, Winston, ed. *Allen Ginsberg and Peter Orlovsky: Straight Hearts' Delight, Love Poems and Selected Letters*. San Francisco: Gay Sunshine Press, 1980.

Liebenow, J. Gus. *African Politics: Crises and Challenges*. Bloomington: Indiana University Press, 1986.

Littlejohn, David. *Black on White: A Critical Survey of Writing by American Negroes*. New York: Viking Press, 1966.

Lowry, Michael. *George Lukacs—From Romanticism to Bolshevism*. Trans. Patrick Camiller. London: New Left Books, 1979.

Lumumba, Patrice. *Lumumba Speaks: The Speeches and Writings of Patrice Lumumba, 1958–1961*. Ed. Jean Van Lierd. Boston: Little, Brown, 1972.

Lynch, Acklyn. *Nightime Overhanging Darkly: Essays on Black Culture and Resistance*. Chicago: Third World Press, 1992.

Mackey, Nathaniel. *Discrepant Engagement: Dissonance, Cross-Culturality, and Experimental Writing*. Cambridge: Cambridge University Press, 1993.

Madhubuti, Haki R. (Don L. Lee). *Claiming Earth: Race, Rage, Rape, Redemption*. Chicago: Third World Press, 1994.

———. *Enemies: The Clash of Races*. Chicago: Third World Press, 1978.

———. "Enemy: From the White Left, White Right and In-Between." *Black World* 23 (October 1974): 36–47.

———. *From Plan to Planet: Life Studies: The Need for Afrikan Minds and Institutions*. Detroit: Broadside Press, 1973.

Mailer, Norman. *The White Negro*. San Francisco: City Lights Books, 1957.

Major, Clarence. *The Dark and Feeling: Black American Writers and Their Work*. New York: Third World Press, 1974.

Manning, Kenneth. *Black Apollo of Science: The Life of Ernest Everett Just*. New York: Oxford University Press, 1983.

Mannoni, O. *Prospero and Caliban: The Psychology of Colonization*. Trans. Pamela Powesland. New York: Praeger, 1964.

Marable, Manning. *Black American Politics: From the Washington Marches to Jesse Jackson*. London: New Left Books, 1985.

———. *Blackwater: Historical Studies in Race, Class Consciousness and Revolution*. Dayton, OH: Black Praxis Press, 1981.

Marable, Manning. *Race, Reform and Rebellion: The Second Reconstruction in Black America, 1945–1990*. Rev. 2d ed. Jackson: University Press of Mississippi, 1991.

Marcuse, Herbert. *The Aesthetic Dimension: Toward a Critique of Marxist Aesthetics*. Boston: Beacon Press, 1978.

———. *Counterrevolution and Revolt*. Boston: Beacon Press, 1972.

Margolies, Edward. *Native Sons: A Critical Study of Twentieth-Century Negro American Authors*. Philadelphia: Lippincott, 1968.

McCartney, John T. *Black Power Ideologies: An Essay in African-American Political Thought*. Philadelphia: Temple University Press, 1992.

McEwan, P. J. M., ed. *Twentieth Century Africa*. Oxford: Oxford University Press, 1968.

Melhem, D. H. *Heroism in the New Black Poetry: Introductions and Interviews*. Lexington: University Press of Kentucky, 1990.

Memmi, Albert. *Dominated Man*. Boston: Beacon Press, 1968.

Merleau-Ponty, Maurice. *Sense and Non-sense*. Trans. Hubert L. Dreyfus and Patricia Dreyfus. Evanston, IL: Northwestern University Press, 1964.

Merquior, J. G. *The Veil and the Mask: Essays on Culture and Ideology*. London: Routledge & Kegan Paul, 1979.

Mesa-Lago, Carmelo, and June S. Belkin, eds. *Cuba in Africa*. Latin American Monograph and Document Series 3. Pittsburgh: Center for Latin American Studies, University of Pittsburgh, 1982.

Miles, Barry. *Jack Kerouac: King of the Beats, a Portrait*. New York: Henry Holt, 1998.

Miller, James A. "Amiri Baraka in the 1980's." *Callaloo* 9 (Winter 1986): 184–92.

Morgan, Edmund. *American Slavery, American Freedom: The Ordeal of Colonial Virginia*. New York: Norton, 1975.

Moynihan, Daniel Patrick. *Maximum Feasible Misunderstanding: Community Action in the War on Poverty*. New York: Free Press, 1970.

Muhammed, Elijah. *Message to the Blackman*. Chicago: Muhammad's Temple No. 2, 1965.

Naison, Mark. *Communist in Harlem during the Depression Years*. New York: Grove Press, 1983.

Neal, Larry. *Visions of a Liberated Future: Black Arts Movement Writings*. Ed. Michael Schwartz. New York: Thunder's Mouth Press, 1989.

Nichols, Charles H., ed. *Arna Bontemps–Langston Hughes Letters: 1925–1967*. New York: Dodd, Mead, 1980.

Nicosia, Gerald. *Memory Babe: A Critical Biography of Jack Kerouac*. New York: Grove Press, 1983.

———, ed. *Cranial Guitar: Selected Poems by Bob Kaufman*. Minneapolis: Coffee House Press, 1966.

Nielsen, Aldon Lynn. *Black Chant: Languages of African-American Postmodernism*. Cambridge: Cambridge University Press, 1997.

———. *Writing between the Lines: Race and Intertextuality*. Athens: University of Georgia Press, 1994.

Njeri, Itabari. *Every Good-bye Ain't Gone: Family Portraits and Personal Escapades.* New York: Random House, 1990.

North, Michael. *The Dialect of Modernism: Race, Language and Twentieth-Century Literature.* New York: Oxford University Press, 1994.

Novick, David. *That Noble Dream: The "Objectivity Question" in American History.* Cambridge: Cambridge University Press, 1988.

Obadele, Imari Abubakari. "National Black Elections Held by Republic of New Africa." *Black Scholar* 7 (October 1975): 27–30, 35–38.

O'Reilly, Kenneth. *Racial Matters: The FBI's File on Black America, 1960–1972.* New York: Free Press, 1989.

Ostendorf, Berndt. *Black Literature in White America.* Totowa, NJ: Barnes & Noble Books, 1982.

Oxaal, Ivar. *Black Intellectuals and the Dilemmas of Race and Class in Trinidad.* Cambridge, MA: Schenkman, 1982.

Parish, Jon. *The Color of Jazz: Race and Representation in Postwar American Culture.* Jackson: University Press of Mississippi, 1997.

Parks, Carole A. *Nommo: A Literary Legacy of Black Chicago (19667–1987).* Chicago: OBAhouse, 1987.

Pells, Richard H. *The Liberal Mind in a Conservative Age: American Intellectuals in the 1940s and 1950s.* New York: Harper & Row, 1985.

Perkins, Cathy, ed. *COINTELPRO: The FBI's Secret War on Political Freedom.* New York: Monad Press, 1975.

Perkins, Eugene. "The Changing Status of Black Writers." *Black World* 19 (June 1970): 18–23, 95–98.

Peter, John. *Vladimir's Carrot: Modern Drama and the Modern Imagination.* London: Andre Deutsch, 1987.

Pinkney, Alphonso. *Red, Black, and Green: Black Nationalism in the United States.* Cambridge: Cambridge University Press, 1976.

Podhoretz, Norman. *Doings and Undoings: The Fifties and after in American Writing.* London: Rupert Hart-Davis, 1965.

Poggioli, Renato. *The Theory of the Avant-Garde.* New York: Harper & Row, 1971.

Poinsett, Alex. "Unity without Uniformity: National Black Political Convention Blazes New Trails for 1972 and Beyond." In *Homage to Hoyt Fuller,* ed. Dudley Randall. Detroit: Broadside Press, 1984.

Redding, J. Saunders. *An American in India: A Personal Report on the Indian Dilemma and the Nature of Her Conflicts.* Indianapolis: Bobbs-Merrill, 1954.

———. *A Scholar's Conscience: Selected Writings.* Ed. Faith Berry. Lexington: University Press of Kentucky, 1992.

Redmond, Eugene. *Drumvoices: The Mission of Afro-American Poetry.* Garden City, NY: Doubleday, 1976.

Reed, Adolph. "Black Particularity Reconsidered." *Telos* 39 (Spring 1979): 71–93.

———, ed. *Race, Politics and Culture: Critical Essays on the Radicalism of the 1960s.* New York: Greenwood Press, 1986.

Reed, Ishmael. *Shrovetide in Old New Orleans*. Garden City, NY: Doubleday, 1978.

Reilly, Charlie, ed. *Conversations with Amiri Baraka*. Jackson: University Press of Mississippi, 1994.

Ricard, Alain. *Theatre and Nationalism: Wole Soyinka and LeRoi Jones*. Trans. Femi Osofisan. Ibadan, Nigeria: University of Ife Press, 1983.

Rieff, Philip. *Fellow Teachers*. New York: Harper & Row, 1973.

Rivers, Larry, with Arnold Weinstein. *What Did I Do? The Unauthorized Autobiography*. New York: HarperCollins, 1992.

Riviere, Claude. *Guinea: The Mobilization of a People*. Trans. Virginia Thompson and Richard Adloff. Ithaca, NY: Cornell University Press, 1977.

Robinson, Armstead, Craig Foster, and Donald Ogilvie. *Black Studies in the University: A Symposium*. New Haven, CT: Yale University Press, 1969.

Rodgers, Carolyn M. "Uh Nat' chal Thang—The WHOLE TRUTH—US." *Black World*, September 1971, pp. 4–14.

Rosenberg, Bernard, and Norris Fliegel. *The Vanguard Artist: Portrait and Self-Portrait*. Chicago: Quadrangle Books, 1965.

Rosenthal, David. *Hard Bop: Jazz and Black Music, 1955–1965*. New York: Oxford University Press, 1992.

Ross, Andrew. *No Respect: Intellectuals and Popular Culture*. New York: Routledge, 1989.

———, ed. *Universal Abandon? The Politics of Postmodernism*. Minneapolis: University of Minnesota Press, 1988.

Rühle, Jürgen. *Literature and Revolution: A Critical Study of the Writer and Communism in the Twentieth Century*, trans. and ed. Jean Steinberg. New York: Praeger, 1969.

Salaam, Kalamu ya. *What Is Life: Reclaiming the Black Blues Self*. Chicago: Third World Press, 1994.

Sammons, Jeffrey. *Literary Sociology and Practical Criticism: An Inquiry*. Bloomington: Indiana University Press, 1977.

Sanders, Leslie Catherine. *The Development of Black Theater in America: From Shadows to Selves*. Baton Rouge: Louisiana State University Press, 1988.

Sartre, Jean-Paul. *What Is Literature?* Trans. Bernard Frechtman. New York: Harper & Row, 1965.

Savran, David. *Taking It like a Man: White Masculinity, Masochism, and Contemporary American Culture*. Princeton, NJ: Princeton University Press, 1998.

Schalk, David L. *The Spectrum of Political Engagement: Mounier, Benda, Nizan, Brasillach, Sartre*. Princeton, NJ: Princeton University Press, 1979.

Scheler, Max. *Ressentiment*. Ed. Lewis Coser and trans. William W. Holdheim. New York: Schocken Books, 1961.

Semmes, Clovis E. *Cultural Hegemony and African American Development*. Westport, CT: Praeger, 1992.

Sidran, Ben. *Black Talk*. New York: Holt, Rinehart and Winston, 1971.

Skurnik, W. A. E., ed. *African Political Thought: Lumumba, Nkrumah, and Toure.* Monograph Series in World Affairs. Denver: University of Denver, 1968.

Slotkin, Richard. *Gunfighter Nation: The Myth of the Frontier in Twentieth Century America.* New York: HarperPerennial, 1993.

Smith, David Lionel. "The Black Arts Movement and Its Critics." *American Literary History* 3, no. 1 (Spring 1991): 93–110.

Smith, Robert. *We Have No Leaders: African Americans in the Post–Civil Rights Era.* Albany: State University of New York Press, 1996.

Smythe, Mabel, ed. *The Black American Reference Book.* Englewood Cliffs, NJ: Prentice-Hall, 1976.

Sollors, Werner. *Amiri Baraka / LeRoi Jones: The Quest for a "Populist Modernism."* New York: Columbia University Press, 1978.

Sollors, Werner, and Maria Diedrich, eds. *The Black Columbiad: Defining Moments in African-American Literature and Culture.* Harvard English Studies no. 19. Cambridge, MA: Harvard University Press, 1994.

Solomon, Barbara Probst. *Horse-Trading and Ecstasy: Essays.* San Francisco: North Point Press, 1989.

Sontag, Susan. *Against Interpretation.* New York: Dell, 1966.

Soyinka, Wole. *The Open Sore of a Continent: A Personal Narrative of the Nigerian Crisis.* New York: Oxford University Press, 1996.

Special supplement on Amiri Baraka. *Boundary* 2, no. 6 (Winter 1978): 303–442.

Standley, Fred, and Louis Pratt, eds. *Conversations with James Baldwin.* Jackson: University Press of Mississippi, 1989.

Staniland, Martin. *American Intellectuals and African Nationalists, 1955–1970.* New Haven, CT: Yale University Press, 1991.

Staples, Robert. *The Black Woman in America: Sex, Marriage and the Family.* Chicago: Nelson-Hall, 1973.

Steiner, George. *Language and Silence.* New York: Atheneum, 1967.

Stember, Charles Herbert. *Sexual Racism: The Emotional Barrier to an Integrated Society.* New York: Harper & Row, 1978.

Stone, Albert E. *The Return of Nat Turner: History, Literature, and Cultural Politics in Sixties America.* Athens: University of Georgia Press, 1992.

Storey, John. *An Introductory Guide to Cultural Theory and Popular Culture.* Athens: University of Georgia Press, 1993.

Strickland, William. "Whatever Happened to the Politics of Black Liberation?" *Black Scholar* 7, no. 2 (October 1975): 20–26.

Swearingen, M. Wesley. *FBI Secrets: An Agent's Exposé.* Boston: South End Press, 1995.

Tate, Claudia, ed. *Black Women Writers at Work.* New York: Continuum Press, 1985.

Tate, Greg. *Flyboy in the Buttermilk: Essays on Contemporary America.* New York: Simon & Schuster, 1992.

Tertz, Abram. *The Trial Begins* and *On Socialist Realism.* Berkeley and Los Angeles: University of California Press, 1982.

Thomas, Tony. "Black Nationalism and Confused Marxists." *Black Scholar* 4 (September 1972): 47–52.

Toure, Ahmed Sekou. *Africa on the Move*. Conakry, Guinea: Patrice Lumumba Press, 1972.

———. *The United States of Africa*. Conakry, Guinea: Press Office, 1977.

Troupe, Quincy, ed. *James Baldwin: The Legacy*. New York: Simon & Schuster, 1989.

Turner, Darwin T. 1970. "Afro-American Literary Critics." *Black World* 19 (July 1970): 54–67.

Turner, Sherry. "An Overview of the New Black Arts." *Freedomways* 9 (Spring 1969): 156–63.

Tyler, Bruce Michael. "Black Radicalism in Southern California, 1950–1982." Ph.D. diss., University of California at Los Angeles, 1983.

Ungar, Sanford J. *Africa: The People and Politics of an Emerging Continent*. 3d rev. ed. New York: Simon & Schuster, 1986.

Van Deburg, William L. *New Day in Babylon: The Black Power Movement and American Culture, 1965–75*. Chicago: University of Chicago Press, 1992.

Von Eschen, Penny. *Race against Empire: Black Americans and Anticolonialism, 1937–1957*. Ithaca, NY: Cornell University Press, 1997.

Wakefield, Dan. *New York in the Fifties*. Boston: Houghton Mifflin, 1992.

Wald, Alan M. *Writing from the Left: New Essays on Radical Culture and Politics*. New York: Verso, 1994.

Wallace, Michelle. *Black Macho and the Myth of the Superwoman*. New York: Dial Press, 1978.

———. *Invisibility Blues: From Pop to Theory*. London: Verso, 1990.

Walters, Ronald W. *Black Presidential Politics in America: A Strategic Approach*. Albany: State University of New York Press, 1988.

———. "Black Presidential Politics in 1980: Bargaining or Begging?" *Black Scholar* 11 (March/April 1980): 22–31.

———. *Pan-Africanism in the African Diaspora: An Analysis of Modern Afrocentric Political Movements*. Detroit: Wayne State University Press, 1993.

Walzer, Michael. *The Company of Critics: Social Criticism and Political Commitment in the Twentieth Century*. New York: Basic Books, 1988.

Warren, Earl. *The Memoirs of Earl Warren*. Garden City, NY: Doubleday, 1977.

Warren, Robert Penn. *Who Speaks for the Negro?* New York: Vintage Books, 1966.

Watson, Steven. *The Birth of the Beat Generation: Visionaries, Rebels, and Hipsters, 1944–1960*. New York: Pantheon Books, 1995.

Watts, Jerry. *Heroism and the Black Intellectual: Ralph Ellison, Politics, and Afro-American Intellectual Life*. Chapel Hill: University of North Carolina Press, 1994.

———. "The Political Sociology of Ethnically Marginal Black Intellectuals." Ph.D. diss., Yale University, 1985.

Weales, Gerald. "The Day LeRoi Jones Spoke on Penn's Campus: What Were the Blacks Doing in the Balcony?" *New York Times Magazine*, May 4, 1969, pp. 38–40.

————. *The Jumping-off Place: American Drama in the 1960s*. London: Macmillan, 1969.

Weisbrot, Robert. *Freedom Bound: A History of America's Civil Rights Movement*. New York: Plume, 1991.

Weiss, Nancy J. *Whitney M. Young, Jr. and the Struggle for Civil Rights*. Princeton, NJ: Princeton University Press, 1989.

Weixlmann, Joe, and Charles J. Fontenot, eds. *Studies in Black American Literature*. Vol. 2, *Belief vs. Theory in Black American Literary Criticism*. Greenwood, FL: Penkevill, 1986.

Werner, Craig Hansen. *Playing the Changes: From Afro-Modernism to the Jazz Impulse*. Champaign-Urbana: University of Illinois Press, 1994.

West, Cornel. *Keeping Faith: Philosophy and Race in America*. New York: Routledge, 1993.

Whittemore, L. H. *Together: A Reporter's Journey into the New Black Politics*. New York: Morrow, 1971.

Wiegman, Robyn. *American Anatomies: Theorizing Race and Gender*. Durham, NC: Duke University Press, 1995.

Wilentz, Elias, ed. *The Beat Scene*. New York: Corinth Books, 1960.

Williams, John A., and Charles F. Harris, eds. *Amistad 1: Writings on Black History and Culture*. New York: Vintage Books, 1970.

Williams, Mance. *Black Theatre in the 1960s and 1970s: A Historical-Critical Analysis of the Movement*. Westport, CT: Greenwood Press, 1985.

Williams, Sherley Anne. *Give Birth to Brightness: A Thematic Study in Neo-Black Literature*. New York: Dial Press, 1972.

Wills, Garry. *The Second Civil War: Arming for Armageddon*. New York: New American Library, 1968.

Wilmer, Valerie. *As Serious as Your Life: The Story of the New Jazz*. Westport, CT: Lawrence Hill, 1977.

Winston, Henry. *Class, Race and Black Liberation*. New York: International Publishers, 1977.

Wolf, Daniel, and Edwin Fancher, eds. *The Village Voice Reader*. Garden City, NY: Doubleday, 1962.

Wolfenstein, Eugene Victor. *Psychoanalytic-Marxism: Groundwork*. New York: Guilford Press, 1993.

————. *The Victims of Democracy: Malcolm X and the Black Revolution*. Berkeley and Los Angeles: University of California Press, 1981.

Wood, Joe, ed. *Malcolm X: In Our Image*. New York: St. Martin's Press, 1992.

Woodward, K. Komozi. "The Making of the New Ark: Imamu Amiri Baraka (LeRoi Jones), the Newark Congress of African People, and the Modern Black Convention Movement. A History of the Black Revolt and the New Nationalism, 1966–1976." Ph.D. diss., University of Pennsylvania, 1991.

————. *A Nation within a Nation: Amiri Baraka (Leroi Jones) and Black Power Politics*. Chapel Hill: University of North Carolina Press, 1999.

Wright, Nathan. *Black Power and Urban Unrest*. New York: Holt, Rinehart and Winston, 1967.

————. *Ready to Riot*. New York: Holt, Rinehart and Winston, 1968.

————. *What Black Politicians Are Saying*. New York: Hawthorn Books, 1972.

Wright, Richard. *White Man Listen*. New York: Doubleday, 1957.

Yang, Gladys, ed. and trans. *Silent China: Selected Writings of Lu Xun*. Oxford: Oxford University Press, 1973.

Young, Coleman, and Lonnie Wheeler. *Hard Stuff: The Autobiography of Mayor Coleman Young*. New York: Viking Press, 1994.

Index

Abernathy, Ralph, 382, 384
Abrahams, Peter, 59–60
Addonizio, Hugh, mayor of Newark, 23, 296, 304, 307, 353–362, 534n. 23. *See also* Newark Politics
African Free School, 340, 368–369
African Liberation Day/African Liberation Day Support Committee, 388–390, 540n. 39
Afro-American Studies Programs, 218–220
Agnew, Spiro T., 2, 469
Ali, Muhammad, 305
Alkalimat, Abdul (Gerald McWhorter), 386
All African Peoples Revolutionary Party, 389
Allen, Donald, 245
Allen, Robert, 304
Amin, Idi, 399
Amini, Johari (Jewel C. Lattimore), 191
Artaud, Antonin, 173–174, 271–272, 506nn. 5, 10
Atlanta Congress of African People, 340, 381–387. *See also* Pan-Africanism
Axelrod, Beverly, 254

Baker, Ella, 325
Baker, Houston, 482n. 11
Baldwin, James, 59–60, 64–65, 126–127, 163, 180, 440–441, 492n. 56
Bambara, Toni Cade, 191
Baraka, Amina (Sylvia Robinson), 292–295, 299, 340, 345–347, 356, 367–368
Baraka, Amiri (LeRoi Jones)
  PERSONAL: anti-Semitism of, 148–150, 229–231; bohemian life, 27–65, 85–87, 126–140; Bumi, 291–293; homophobia/homoeroticism, 177, 331–336, 507n. 15, 530n. 16, 531n. 26; at Howard University, 22–27, 484n. 8, 485n. 21; jazz critic, 112–126; marriage to Amina, 292–295; marriage to Hettie, 44, 141–152, 501nn. 2, 3, 503nn. 27, 28; mysogyny of, 330–334;

racism of, 180–181; sexism of, 325–330; Sunni Muslim, 310–311; Yoruba, 310–311
  WRITINGS: BOOKS–AUTHOR: *Black Music*, 47, 464; *Blues People*, 46, 117–126, 312, 497nn. 78, 84, 498nn. 88, 91, 92; *Daggers and Javelins*, 432–443; *Eulogies*, 464; *The Music*, 464; *Raise Race Rays Raze*, 241–258; *The System of Dante's Hell*, 87–96; *Tales*, 234; BOOKS–EDITOR: *Confirmation: An Anthology of African American Women*, 346; *The Moderns: An Anthology of New Writing in America*, 46–47, 63–64, 245; JOURNALS–EDITOR: *The Floating Bear*, 46; *Yugen*, 44–46; ESSAYS: "Africa, Superpower Contention and the Danger of World War," 434–435; "Afro-American Literature and Class Struggle," 441; "American Sexual Reference: Black Male," 143, 330–333, 507–508n. 25; "Black and Angry," 413–414; "'Black' Is a Country," 55–56; "Black Liberation / Socialist Revolution," 435–436; "Black Nationalism and Socialist Revolution: Why I Changed My Ideology," 430–432; "Black People and Imperialism," 426; "Black Woman," 338–339; "Black Writing," 60–62; "Brief Reflections on Two Hot Shots," 59–60, 127; "City of Harlem," 56–57; "Cold, Hurt, and Sorrow," 57; "The Congress of Afrikan People: A Position Paper," 430; "Cuba Libre," 52–54; "Jazz and the White Critic," 115–116; "Jazz Avant-Garde," 114–115; "The Last Days of the American Empire," 133–135; "LeRoi Jones Talking," 131–133; "Letter to Jules Feiffer," 54; "The Myth of Negro Literature," 57–59, 162–163; "National Liberation and Politics," 424–426; "Philistinism and the Negro Writer," 162–164; "The Revolutionary Theatre," 171–175; "Revolutionary Party: Revolutionary Ideology," 425–426; "Revolutionary Tradition in Afro-American Literature," 439–441; "Street Protest," 57; "Tokenism,"

571

About the Author

JERRY GAFIO WATTS is an associate professor of American studies and political science at Trinity College, Hartford, Connecticut. He is the author of *Heroism and the Black Intellectual: Ralph Ellison, Politics, and Afro-American Intellectual Life,* and his articles have appeared in *The Village Voice, The Nation, Dissent,* and *New Politics,* among many other journals.